Reference Library of

BLACK AMERICA

Reference Library of

BLACK AMERICA

VOLUME III

Edited by
Jessie Carney Smith
Joseph M. Palmisano

Distributed exclusively by:

African American Publications
Proteus Enterprises

Staff

Jessie Carney Smith and Joseph M. Palmisano, *Editors*
Patrick J. Politano, *Assistant Editor*
William Harmer, Ashyia N. Henderson, Brian J. Koski, Gloria Lam, Jeffrey Lehman, Allison McClintic Marion, Mark F. Mikula, David G. Oblender, Rebecca Parks, Shirelle Phelps, Kathleen Romig, *Contributing Staff*
Linda S. Hubbard, *Managing Editor, Multicultural Team*

Maria Franklin, *Permissions Manager*
Margaret Chamberlain, *Permissions Specialist*
Keasha Jack-Lyles and Shalice Shah-Caldwell, *Permissions Associates*

Justine H. Carson, *Manager, Vocabulary Development and Indexer*
Rebecca Abbott Forgette, *Indexing Specialist*

Mary Beth Trimper, *Production Director*
Wendy Blurton, *Senior Buyer*
Cynthia Baldwin, *Product Design Manager*
Gary Popiela, *Graphic Artist*
Barbara J. Yarrow, *Imaging/Multimedia Manager*
Randy Bassett, *Image Database Supervisor*
Pamela A. Reed, *Imaging Coordinator*
Robert Duncan, *Imaging Specialist*
Christine O'Bryan, *Desktop Publisher*

Victoria B. Cariappa, *Research Manager*
Barbara McNeil, *Research Specialists*
Patricia Tsune Ballard, *Research Associate*

ISBN 0-7876-4363-7 (set)
ISBN 0-7876-4364-5 (volume 1)
ISBN 0-7876-4365-3 (volume 2)
ISBN 0-7876-4366-1 (volume 3)
ISBN 0-7876-4367-X (volume 4)
ISBN 0-7876-4368-8 (volume 5)

Printed in the United States of America

10 9 8 7 6 5 4 3 2 1

Advisory Board

Contributors

Donald F. Amerman, Jr.
Editorial Consultant, A & M Editorial Services

Stephen W. Angell
Associate Professor of Religion, Florida A & M University

Calvert Bean
Associate Editor, *International Dictionary of Black Composers*

Lean'tin Laverne Bracks
Editorial Consultant

Rose M. Brewer
Morse Alumni Distinguished Teaching Professor of Afro-American and African Studies, University of Minnesota-Minneapolis

Christopher A. Brooks
Professor of African American Studies, Virginia Commonwealth University

Paulette Coleman
General Officer, African Methodist Episcopal Church

DeWitt S. Dykes, Jr.
Professor of History, Oakland University

James Gallert
Vice President, Jazz Alliance of Michigan

Joseph Guy
Jazz and Touring Coordinator, Southern Arts Federation

Tracey Desirnaí Hicks
Membership and Volunteer Services Coordinator,
Charles H. Wright Museum of African American History

Phyllis J. Jackson
Assistant Professor of Art and Art History, Pomona College

Kristine Krapp
Editor, *Notable Black American Scientists* and *Black Firsts in Science and Technology*

Kevin C. Kretschmer
Reference Librarian, Blazer Library, Kentucky State University

Bernadette Meier
Editorial Consultant

Hollis F. Price, Jr.
Professor of Economics, Tennessee State University

Guthrie P. Ramsey Jr.
Assistant Professor of Music, University of Pennsylvania

Houston B. Roberson
Assistant Professor of History, University of the South

Gil L. Robertson IV
Founder, The Robertson Treatment

Audrey Y. Williams
Professor of Management, Zicklin School of Business, Baruch College, City University of New York

Raymond A. Winbush
Director, Race Relations Institute, Fisk University
Benjamin Hooks Professor of Social Justice, Fisk University

Michael D. Woodard
President, Woodard & Associates

Linda T. Wynn
Assistant Director of State Programs, Tennessee Historical Commission
Adjunct Professor, Department of History, Fisk University

Contents

◆ VOLUME 3

Introduction

The *Reference Library of Black America* is based on the eighth edition of *The African American Alamanac*, first published in 1967 as *The Negro Almanac* and subsequently cited by *Library Journal*, in conjunction with the American Library Association, as "Outstanding Reference Source." It offers a comprehensive and accurate survey of black culture in the United States and around the world.

New Features in This Edition

All material was extensively reviewed by the editors and a board of prominent advisors and, where appropriate, updated and/or expanded; in many instances completely new topics were added to the existing essays. As a result, most chapters have been rewritten and focus on issues facing African Americans as we enter a new millenium.

African American women and their significant contributions have been given greater emphasis in the reference work than ever before. Examples of this expanded coverage include: speeches and writings of Sojourner Truth, Ida B. Wells-Barnett, Mary McLeod Bethune, and Barbara Jordan (Chapter 3); genetic evidence of a link between Sally Hemings and Thomas Jefferson (Chapter 6); biographical profiles of historic female activists of the black nationalist and civil rights movements (Chapters 8 and 9); female leadership in African American churches (Chapter 17); prominent women artists in the musical fields of gospel, blues, and jazz (Chapters 23, 24, and 25); and the increasing presence of female athletes in professional sports (Chapter 28).

The tremendous impact of the Internet is also reflected in the content of the *Reference Library of Black America*. Many entry listings in such sections as "National Organizations" (Chapter 9); "Historically and Predominantly African American Colleges and Universities" and "Research Institutions" (Chapter 16); "African American Media in Cyberspace" and "Magazines and Journals" (Chapter 19); "Museums and Galleries Exhibiting African American Art" (Chapter 26); and "Popular African American Internet Sites" (Chapter 27) now include website addresses. In addition, the promising effects of information technology on the African American community are discussed in "Entrepreneurship" (Chapter 14), "Media" (Chapter 19), and "Science and Technology" (Chapter 27).

Important African American towns and settlements are described for the first time in "African American Landmarks" (Chapter 4) and "Population" (Chapter 12). Included are listings of such historic sites as Nicodemus, Kansas; Boley, Oklahoma; the Sea Islands in South Carolina and Georgia; and Eatonville, Florida. In addition, expanded, up-to-date profiles of African and Western Hemisphere nations are offered in "Africa and the Black Diaspora" (Chapter 5).

Two new chapters have been added that significantly enhance the broad coverage of the *Reference Library of Black America:*

- "Film and Television" (Chapter 20) offers an overview of African Americans in the film and television industries, a selected filmography of more than two hundred films and documentaries depicting African American themes and issues, and biographical profiles of actors, filmmakers, and industry executives both current and historical.
- "Sacred Music Traditions" (Chapter 23) provides an essay that thoroughly describes the important periods

and styles of African American sacred music, as well as concise biographical profiles of notable sacred music composers, musicians, and singers.

Approximately thirty new statistical charts compiled by the Bureau of the Census for the *Statistical Abstract of the United States* appear in pertinent chapters. Finally, a completely revised name and keyword index provides improved access to the contents of the *Reference Library of Black America.*

Content and Arrangement

Information in this edition of the *Reference Library of Black America* appears in 29 subject chapters. Many chapters open with an essay focusing on historical developments or the contributions of African Americans to the subject area, followed by concise biographical profiles of selected individuals. Although the listees featured here represent only a small portion of the African American community, they embody excellence and diversity in their respective fields of endeavor. Where an individual has made a significant contribution in more than one area, his or her biographical profile appears in the subject area for which he or she is best known.

Nearly seven hundred photographs, illustrations, maps, and statistical charts aid the reader in understanding the topics and people covered in the reference work. An expanded appendix contains the names and contributions of African American recipients of selected awards and honors.

Politics

◆ Race, Politics, and Government
◆ Congressional Black Caucus Members (106th U.S. Congress) ◆ Government Officials
◆ Political Statistics

by Paulette Coleman

◆ RACE, POLITICS, AND GOVERNMENT

The history of African American participation in the political process is complex and includes multiple responses to the deliberate and systematic exclusion of African Americans from American life. In colonial times, most African Americans were slaves and thus denied the basic rights of citizenship. Legally, they were prohibited from voting and other means of political expression. Though they could not participate formally in the political process, slaves found other avenues for political expression including various forms of resistance.

A small number of free African Americans were occasionally allowed to vote in certain places. There is evidence that some free African Americans voted in South Carolina's 1701 gubernatorial election. In the early eighteenth century, African Americans petitioned the courts and political leaders for legal protection.

Prior to the Revolutionary War, political participation by African Americans was rare. Slave revolts were an exception. The revolutionary fervor of the times did not go unnoticed by the African Americans. The revolutionary rhetoric resonated with the slaves and served as a catalyst for the filing of petitions with the state legislature and even the U.S. Congress to protest slavery. During the Revolutionary War, some free African Americans saw military service as a way to be included as citizens in the new nation.

The American Colonization Society, founded by African Americans in 1816, promoted emigration to Africa that eventually led to the genesis of the west African nation of Liberia. Meanwhile, others emigrated to other parts of the black diaspora including Canada, Central and South America, and island nations such as Haiti.

In 1830, free African Americans in Philadelphia convened the National Negro Convention. For two decades the national convention movement continued its development as a mass self-help movement involving African American churches, fraternal organizations, and mutual aid societies. The more militant participants became dominant in the convention by the 1850s. As a result, there was a growing determination to build African American institutions while demanding rights as full citizens.

The abolitionist movement of the 1830s was part of a multiracial quest for African American emancipation and equality. In addition to campaigning for civil rights through traditional legal means, the abolitionists took a daring step by operating the Underground Railroad system, a covert network of safe havens that assisted fugitive slaves in their flight to freedom in the North. Approximately 50,000 slaves are believed to have escaped to the Northern United States and Canada through the Underground Railroad prior to the Civil War.

In the 1850s, new efforts were made to exclude African Americans from citizenship with the passage of the Fugitive Slave Act. Similarly, the Kansas-Nebraska Act attempted to extend slavery into new territories. The U.S. Supreme Court's decision in the *Dred Scott* case held that African Americans had no rights as U.S. citizens and that a state could not forbid slavery. These legal decisions convinced large numbers of African Americans that radical action was necessary. Among them were Martin Delany and Henry McNeal Turner who advocated separation from the white race, and

John Brown, who believed nothing short of a violent overthrow of the slave system would yield any meaningful results. Frederick Douglass, who opposed such a move, pushed for African Americans to seek rights through assimilation. The ultimate compromise between the two factions was proposed in 1853 when the Colored National Convention in Rochester, New York, advanced the idea of a separate African American society on American soil.

The Union victory in the Civil War and the abolition of slavery under President Abraham Lincoln consolidated African American political support in the Republican Party. This affiliation lasted throughout the end of the nineteenth century and into the early decades of the twentieth century—even after the Republicans began to loosen the reins on the Democratic South in 1876 after the last federal troops were removed.

During the Reconstruction era, from 1865 to 1877, African Americans made significant gains towards increased participation in the political process. Both the Civil Rights Act of 1866 and the Fourteenth Amendment to the Constitution were intended to provide full citizenship—with all its rights and privileges—to all African Americans. The Fifteenth Amendment, ratified in 1870, granted African American men the right to vote. But the voting rights amendment failed in its attempts to guarantee African Americans the absolute freedom to choose at the ballot box. Poll taxes, literacy tests, and grandfather clauses were established by some state and local governments to deny African Americans their right to vote. (The poll tax would not be declared unconstitutional until 1964, with the passage of the Twenty-fourth Amendment.)

These legalized forms of oppression and exclusion presented huge obstacles to African American advancement in the politics of the United States. During the Reconstruction era, twenty African American congressmen, two senators, a governor, six lieutenant governors, and numerous state and local officials were elected. In 1869, Ebenezer Don Carlos Bassett became the first African American diplomat when he was appointed consul general to Haiti. In 1870 Hiram R. Revels became the first African American senator when he finished former confederate president Jefferson Davis's last year of term. Blanche K. Bruce became the first African American elected to the Senate for a full term five years later. P. B. S. Pinchback had won a Senate seat in 1873, but a vote of the other senators rejected him in 1876. The same thing had happened one year earlier when, in 1875, Pinchback was ejected from a House seat to which he had been elected in 1872.

A flashy, colorful individual, Pinchback had made enemies because of a gambling habit and a strong stance in matters pertaining to equal rights for African Americans. Pinchback was the nation's first African American governor. Named lieutenant governor of Louisiana in 1871, Pinchback became governor after getting Governor Warmouth impeached on bribery charges. When the new election was held, Pinchback was defeated.

During the 1870s other forms of white supremacist sentiment came to the fore. The Jim Crow laws of segregation allowed for legal, systematic discrimination on the basis of race. Voting rights abuses persisted. Violence became another common tool of oppression between 1889 and 1922 as nearly 3,500 lynchings took place—mainly in the Southern states of Alabama, Georgia, Louisiana, and Mississippi, but also in some Northern cities.

During the nineteenth century most African Americans were supporters of the Republican Party, but as the century drew to a close, a backlash occurred. In the 1890s, a group of white Republicans calling themselves the "Lily Whites" were heavily opposed to rights for African Americans and thus resented the presence of the so-called "Black and Tan Republicans" in their party. African Americans would remain locked into a pattern of almost automatic support of Republicans until the late 1920s.

By the turn of the twentieth century, Booker T. Washington had gained prominence as the chief spokesperson on the state of African Americans. Recognized throughout the United States as the prominent African American leader and mediator, he advocated accommodationism as the preferred method of attaining African American rights. His leading opponents included journalist Thomas T. Fortune, an African American historian, and author W. E. B. Du Bois.

Fortune, who had founded the paper the*New York Freeman* in 1884, attempted to create a national political organization for African Americans. His short-lived, Chicago-based National Afro-American League was aimed at remedying the disenfranchisement of African Americans. Du Bois, on the other hand, felt it was necessary to take more aggressive measures in the fight for equality. In addition to participating in the first Pan-African Conference (London) in 1900, in 1905 he spearheaded the Niagara Movement, a radical African American intellectual forum. Members of the group merged with white progressives four years later to form the National Association for the Advancement of Colored People (NAACP). After Washington's death in 1915, the NAACP became a greater force in the struggle for racial reform.

Women played a significant role at the turn of the century as well, coming together as the National Association of Colored Women in 1896. The female activists met with success in their agitation for rights. Standouts

First African American Senator and Representatives, in the 41st and 42nd Congress of the United States (The Library of Congress).

included founder Mary Church Terrell and presidents Ida B. Wells-Barnett and Mary McLeod Bethune. Chief among their causes were speaking out against lynching and the promotion of women's rights.

A massive African American migration to the North in the 1920s showed that racial tension was no longer just a Southern issue. In 1928, Oscar DePriest became the first African American elected to Congress in the twentieth century. His career began in 1915, when he was elected to the Chicago city council.

Racist attitudes, combined with the desperate economic pressures of the Great Depression, exerted a profound effect on politics nationwide. Democrat Franklin Delano Roosevelt attracted African American voters with his "New Deal" relief and recovery programs in the 1930s. For seventy years African Americans had been faithful to the Republican Party, but their belief in Roosevelt led many to switch party allegiance. Housing and employment opportunities began opening up, and African Americans gained seats in various state legislatures in the 1930s and 1940s.

The Communist Party of the United States of America offered an alternative for African Americans alienated by the Republicans and the Democrats. White Communists actively solicited African Americans for their ranks, supporting civil rights through demonstrations and boycotts. They even selected an African American, James Ford, as their vice presidential candidate during the U.S. presidential campaigns of 1932, 1936, and 1940.

World War II ushered in an era of unswerving commitment to the fight for civil rights. As African Americans migrated to the North in search of jobs, several urban entities gained new concentrations of African American. In cities such as Detroit, New York, Philadelphia, and Cleveland, African Americans had such a presence that the course of local politics was often swayed by the influence of their vote. At times the African American vote affected the balance of power on the national front as well.

Adam Clayton Powell, Jr. was elected to the New York City Council in 1941. By 1944, Powell had gained a seat in the U.S. House of Representatives. As a House member, he challenged a white racist representative who refused to sit next to him. During his tenure he also initiated legislation against lynching, poll taxes, and discriminatory job hiring practices. The so-called "Pow-

Ebenezer Don Carlos Bassett, consul general to Haiti (Schomburg Center for Research in Black Culture).

ell Amendment" referred to his attempts to tack anti-discriminatory measures onto each and every measure that came before the House.

African Americans were advancing in all areas—national associations, political organizations, unions, the federal branch of the U.S. government, and the nation's court system. President Harry S. Truman contributed to African American advancement by desegregating the military, establishing fair employment practices in the federal service, and beginning the trend toward integration in public accommodations and housing. In 1949, Rep. William L. Dawson became the first African American to head a standing committee of Congress when he was elected chairman of House Expenditures. Meanwhile, the civil rights proposals of the late 1940s came to fruition a decade later during President Dwight D. Eisenhower's administration. Eisenhower's administrative aide, E. Frederic Morrow, was the first African American granted an executive position among White House staff.

The Civil Rights Act of 1957, also known as the Voting Rights Act of 1957, was the first major piece of civil rights legislation passed by Congress in more than eight decades. It expanded the role of the federal government in civil rights matters and established the U.S. Commission on Civil Rights to monitor the protection of African American rights. The commission determined that unfair voting practices persisted in the South with African Americans were still being denied the right to vote in certain Southern districts. Because of these abuses, a second act was passed in 1960 that offered more protection to African Americans at the polls. In 1965, the third Voting Rights Act was passed to eliminate literacy tests and safeguard African American rights during the voter registration process.

The post-war movement for African American rights had yielded slow but significant advances in school desegregation and suffrage despite bold opposition from some whites. By the mid to late-1950s, as the African American fight for progress gained ground, white resistance continued mounting. The Reverend Martin Luther King, Jr., took the helm of the fledgling Civil Rights movement and launched a multiracial effort to eliminate segregation and achieve equality for blacks through nonviolent resistance. The movement began with the boycott of city buses in Montgomery, Alabama, and by 1960, became a national crusade for black rights. During the course of the next decade, civil rights workers organized economic boycotts of racist businesses and attracted front-page news coverage with African American voter registration drives and anti-segregationist demonstrations, marches, and sit-ins. Bolstered by the new era of independence that was sweeping through sub-Saharan Africa, the movement for African American equality gained international attention.

Racial tensions in the South reached violent levels with the emergence of new white supremacist organizations and an increase in Ku Klux Klan activity. Racially motivated discrimination in all arenas—from housing to employment—rose as Southern resistance to the Civil Rights movement intensified. By the late 1950s, racist hatred had once again degenerated into brutality and bloodshed with African Americans being murdered for the cause, and their white killers were escaping punishment.

Democrat John F. Kennedy gained the African American vote in the 1960 presidential elections. His domestic agenda espoused an expansion of federal action in civil rights cases—especially through the empowerment of the U.S. Department of Justice on voting rights issues and the establishment of the Committee on Equal Employment Opportunity. Civil rights organizations continued their peaceful assaults against barriers to integration, but African American resistance to racial injustice was escalating. The protest movement heated up in 1961 when groups such as the Congress of Racial Equality

(CORE), the Student Non-Violent Coordinating Committee (SNCC), and the Southern Christian Leadership Conference (SCLC) organized "freedom rides" that defied segregationist policies on public transportation systems.

Major demonstrations were staged in Birmingham, Alabama, under the leadership of King. Cries for equality met with harsh police action against the African American crowds. In 1963, Mississippi's NAACP leader, Medgar Evers, was assassinated. Meanwhile, on August 28, 1963, more than 200,000 black and white demonstrators convened at the Lincoln Memorial to push for the passage of a new civil rights bill. This historic "March on Washington," highlighted by King's legendary "I Have a Dream" speech, brought the promise of stronger legislation from the president.

After Kennedy's assassination that November, President Johnson finally instigated an aggressive civil rights program. The passage of the Civil Rights Act of 1964 sparked violence throughout the country including turmoil in cities of New York, New Jersey, Pennsylvania, and Illinois. The Ku Klux Klan stepped up its practice of intimidation with venomous racial slurs, cross burnings, firebombings, and acts of murder.

The call for racial reform in the South became louder early in 1965. King, who had been honored with the Nobel Peace Prize for his commitment to race relations, commanded the spotlight for his key role in the 1965 Freedom March from Selma to Montgomery, Alabama. But African Americans were disheartened by the lack of true progress in securing African American rights. Despite the legislative gains made over two decades, economic prospects for African Americans were bleak.

African American discontent over economic, employment, and housing discrimination reached frightening proportions in the summer of 1965, with rioting in the Watts section of Los Angeles. This event marked a major change in the temper of the Civil Rights movement. Nearly one decade of nonviolent resistance had failed to remedy the racial crisis in the United States and a more militant reformist element began to emerge. "Black Power" became the rallying cry of the middle and late 1960s, and more and more civil rights groups adopted all-black leadership. Despite such gains as the election of Carl Stokes in 1967 and Richard Hatcher in 1972 as the first African American mayors of Cleveland, Ohio, and Gary, Indiana, King's assassination in 1968 only compounded the nation's explosive racial situation. The new generation of African American leaders seemed to champion independence and separatism for African Americans rather than integration into white American society.

Through the 1960s, some prominent African Americans served as members of Congress. Shirley Chisholm was elected to the U.S. House of Representatives in 1968, making her the first African American woman to serve in Congress. The next year, Charles Diggs, Jr., a member of the U.S. House of Representatives, founded the Democratic Select Committee, a group comprised of the eight other African American members of Congress. Two years later they renamed themselves the Congressional Black Caucus (CBC).

In 1970 the creation of the Joint Center for Political Studies, geared towards monitoring political developments in the African American community, became the CBC's most important political contribution. Data provided by the Joint Center for Political Studies assisted the Reverend Jesse Jackson during his 1984 presidential campaign. After its founding, the center expanded to include economic studies and currently operates as the Joint Center for Political and Economic Studies. The CBC also laid the groundwork for TransAfrica, a 40,000 person organization dedicated to African American foreign affairs. Founded by Randall Robinson in 1977, TransAfrica came about after the CBC protested against U.S. governmental policy towards minority white rule in such African nations as Rhodesia. Meeting with 130 leaders in September of 1976, the CBC helped Robinson's initiative gain credibility. In the 1990s, the CBC produced such leaders as Kweisi Mfume, who would later head the NAACP.

In the late 1970s, President Jimmy Carter moved stridently to help African Americans. During his tenure he appointed African Americans to key cabinet positions. For example, Andrew Young was named a United Nations ambassador and Patricia Roberts Harris was first the secretary of Housing and Urban Development and then of secretary of Health, Education, and Welfare. Fear of black advancement led many whites to shift their allegiance to the Republican Party in the late 1960s. With the exception of Carter's term in office from 1977 to 1981, Republicans remained in the White House for the rest of the 1970s and 1980s. The rise of conservatism gave birth to such important figures as African American conservatives Thomas Sowell, Anne Wortham, and Shelby Steele. A new era of African American liberal activity began with the institution of Reverend Jesse Jackson's Rainbow Coalition. Despite two unsuccessful campaigns for the presidency in the 1980s, Jackson helped swing the pendulum back in favor of liberalism. In 1992, a Democrat, Bill Clinton, was elected president.

After a dozen years of conservatism under Presidents Ronald Reagan and George Bush, Clinton projected a moderate image. Clinton espoused policies that would cut across the lines of gender, race, and economics and offered a vision of social reform, urban renewal, and domestic harmony for the United States. Once in office, Clinton appointed African Americans to key posts in his cabinet, and the African American population began wielding unprecedented influence in government.

In the 1990s, African American participation in government and politics was significant. In 1990, Gary Franks became the only black Republican in Congress when he earned a seat in the U.S. House where he was joined four years later by J. C. Watts, Jr. An ordained Baptist minister, Watts left the Democratic Party in 1989. Watts declined membership in the liberal CBC.

The year of 1992 saw the election of the first black woman, Carol Mosley Braun, to the U.S. Senate. She shocked political observers by scoring a stunning upset over incumbent Senator Alan Dixon in the Democratic primary on March 17, 1992. In the 1992 November election, she was elected senator. Her term was marred by scandal, however, and she was defeated in 1998 in her bid for reelection.

President Bill Clinton's cabinet included a record number of African Americans. Jesse Brown became the first African American to head the Veterans Affairs Department; Lee P. Brown was selected as head of the Office of National Drug Control Policy; Ron Brown was chosen as secretary of commerce; Dr. Jocelyn Elders was named U.S. surgeon general; Michael Espy was awarded the position of secretary of Agriculture; Hazel O'Leary was chosen as secretary of Energy; Rodney Slater was appointed secretary of Transportation; and Clifton Wharton, Jr. became the deputy secretary of state. Clinton also nominated a number of African Americans to major positions in federal government agencies including Jacqueline L. Williams-Bridgers to the State Department as inspector general and Shirley A. Jackson to the Nuclear Regulatory Commission as chairperson. As director of the White House Office of Public Liaison, African American Alexis Herman has been one of the president's most trusted advisors. And during Clinton's regime, the Justice Department's Civil Rights Division has been headed by Deval Patrick, an African American.

In 1996, Alan Keyes became the first African American Republican in modern times to seek the nomination of the party for the presidency. Keyes attracted little notice, however, and faded from the spotlight. After the reelection of President Clinton, the Supreme Court dealt African Americans a blow in a series of cases that invalidated "Black majority" congressional districts. These gerrymandered districts were created to ensure African Americans were elected to the U.S. House of Representatives. However, the Court ruled several times, including in 1999, that race could not be the only factor in creating a district.

Alan Keyes (AP/Wide World Photos, Inc.)

The Democratic Party has had to rely on African American voters to sustain Democratic candidates in tough elections. In the 1998 congressional elections, the Democrats, crippled by the personal, ethical and legal scandals around President Clinton, relied on the African American vote to prevent any loses in either chamber of Congress. Republican leaders acknowledged after the election that they needed to reach out to the African American community.

◆ CONGRESSIONAL BLACK CAUCUS MEMBERS (106TH U.S. CONGRESS)

Sandford D. Bishop, Jr.
Democrat: Georgia, 2nd District
1433 Longworth H.O.B.
Washington, DC 20515-1002
(202) 225-3631

Corinne Brown
Second Vice-Chairperson
Democrat: Florida, 3rd District
1610 Longworth H.O.B.
Washington, DC 20515-0903
(202) 225-0123

Julia Carson
Democrat: Indiana, 10th District
1541 Longworth H.O.B.
Washington, DC 20515-1410
(202) 225-4011

Donna Christian-Green
Democrat: Virgin Islands, Delegate
1711 Longworth H.O.B.
Washington, DC 20515-5501
(202) 225-1790

William Clay
Democrat: Missouri, 1st District
2306 Rayburn H.O.B.
Washington, DC 20515-2501
(202) 225-2406

Eva M. Clayton
Democrat: North Carolina, 1st District
2440 Rayburn H.O.B.
Washington, DC 20515-3301
(202) 225-3101

James E. Clyburn
Chairperson
Democrat: South Carolina, 6th District
319 Cannon H.O.B.
Washington, DC 20515-4006
(202) 225-3315

John Conyers, Jr.
Democrat: Michigan, 14th District
2426 Rayburn H.O.B.
Washington, DC 20515-2214
(202) 225-5126

Elijah E. Cummings
Secretary
Democrat: Maryland, 7th District
1632 Longworth H.O.B.
Washington, DC 20515-2007
(202) 225-4741

Danny Davis
Democrat: Illinois, 7th District
1218 Longworth H.O.B.
Washington, DC 20515-1307
(202) 225-5006

Julian Dixon
Democrat: California, 32th District
2252 Rayburn H.O.B.
Washington, DC 20515-0532
(202) 225-7084

Chaka Fattah
Democrat: Pennsylvania, 2nd District
1205 Longworth H.O.B.
Washington, DC 20515-3802
(202) 225-4001

Harold E. Ford, Jr.
Democrat: Tennessee, 9th District
1523 Longworth H.O.B.
Washington, DC 20515-4209
(202) 225-3265

Alcee L. Hastings
Democrat: Florida, 23rd District
1039 Longworth H.O.B.
Washington, DC 20515-0923
(202) 225-2976

Earl F. Hilliard
Democrat: Alabama, 7th District
1314 Longworth H.O.B.
Washington, DC 20515-0107
(202) 225-2665

Jesse Jackson, Jr.
Democrat: Illinois, 2nd District
313 Cannon H.O.B.
Washington, DC 20515-1302
(202) 225-0773

William J. Jefferson
Democrat: Louisiana, 2nd District
240 Cannon H.O.B.
Washington, DC 20515-1802
(202) 225-6636

Eddie Bernice Johnson
First Vice-Chairperson
Democrat: Texas, 30th District
1123 Longworth H.O.B.
Washington, DC 20515-4330
(202) 225-8885

Stephanie Tubbs Jones
Democrat: Ohio, 11th District
1516 Longworth H.O.B.
Washington, DC 20515-3511
(202) 225-7032

Carolyn Kilpatrick
Democrat: Michigan, 15th District
503 Cannon H.O.B.
Washington, DC 20515-2215
(202) 225-2261

Sheila Jackson Lee
Whip
Democrat: Texas, 18th District
410 Longworth H.O.B.
Washington, DC 20515-4318
(202) 225-3816

John Lewis
Democrat: Georgia, 5th District
229 Cannon H.O.B.
Washington, DC 20515-1005
(202) 225-3801

Cynthia A. McKinney
Democrat: Georgia, 11th Distict
124 Cannon H.O.B.
Washington, DC 20515-1004
(202) 225-1605

Carrie P. Meek
Democrat: Florida, 17th District
401 Cannon H.O.B.
Washington, DC 20515-0917
(202) 225-4506

Gregory W. Meeks
Democrat: New York, 6th District
1035 Longworth H.O.B.
Washington, DC 20515-3206
(202) 225-3461

Juanita Millender-McDonald
Democrat: California, 37th District
419 Cannon H.O.B.
Washington, DC 20515-0537
(202) 225-7924

Eleanor Holmes Norton
Democrat: District of Columbia, Delgate
1424 Longworth H.O.B.
Washington, DC 20515-5001
(202) 225-8050

Major R. Owens
Democrat: New York, 11th District
2305 Rayburn H.O.B.
Washington, DC 20515-3211
(202) 225-6231

Donald M. Payne
Democrat: New Jersey, 10th District
2244 Rayburn H.O.B.
Washington, DC 20515-3010
(202) 225-3436

Charles B. Rangel
Democrat: New York, 15th District
2354 Rayburn H.O.B.
Washington, DC 20515-3215
(202) 225-4365

Bobby L. Rush
Democrat: Illinois, 1st District
131 Cannon H.O.B.
Washington, DC 20515-9997
(202) 225-4372

Robert C. Scott
Democrat: Virginia, 3rd District
2464 Rayburn H.O.B.
Washington, DC 20515-4603
(202) 225-8351

Bennie G. Thompson
Democrat: Mississippi, 2nd District
1408 Longworth H.O.B.
Washington, DC 20515-2402
(202) 225-5876

Edolphus Towns
Democrat: New York, 10th District
2232 Rayburn H.O.B.
Washington, DC 20515-3210
(202) 225-5936

Maxine Waters
Democrat: California, 35th District
2344 Rayburn H.O.B.
Washington, DC 20515-0535
(202) 225-2201

Melvin L. Watt
Democrat: North Carolina, 12th District
1230 Longworth H.O.B.
Washington, DC 20515-3312
(202) 225-1510

Albert R. Wynn
Democrat: Maryland, 4th District
407 Cannon H.O.B.
Washington, DC 20515-2004
(202) 225-8699

◆ GOVERNMENT OFFICIALS

(To locate biographical profiles more readily, please consult the index at the back of the book.)

Dennis Archer (AP/Wide World Photos, Inc.)

Dennis Archer (1942–)
Municipal Government Official, Attorney

Former Michigan State Supreme Court justice Dennis Archer, became mayor of Detroit on January 3, 1994. During his campaign he promised better city services, a tougher stance on crime, and increased incentives for businesses choosing to locate in the city. Following Coleman Young's combative reign, Archer represented a distinct change.

Archer was born on January 1, 1942, in Detroit. The family moved to Cassopolis, Michigan, when he was an infant. After graduating from Cassopolis High School in 1959, Archer worked his way through college. Following studies at Wayne State University and the Detroit Institute of Technology, Archer received his B.S. from Western Michigan University in 1965.

For a time Archer worked with emotionally impaired children. While teaching he met Trudy DunCombe, who became his wife in 1967. Archer was able to earn a J.D. from the Detroit College of Law in 1970. He practiced law for several years as a partner with Hall, Stone, Allen, Archer & Glenn and then with Charfoos, Christensen & Archer, until he was appointed to the Michigan Supreme Court by then-Governor James Blanchard.

Archer had been active in Democratic politics in the late 1970s and early 1980s, directing campaigns for mayor Coleman Young and congressman George Crocket, Jr. His wife, who had also gone through law school and had become a district court judge, supported her husband's decision to run for mayor. Facing Coleman Young, a city fixture, was a daunting proposition, even for one with the impressive political ties Archer had garnered over the years. Archer's tough decision to face Young became a moot point when Young decided not run for a sixth term. Young did, however, back Archer's rival, Sharon McPhail.

The race became sullied when McPhail suggested that Archer, who many considered to be a mild-mannered, upper-class elitist, was the candidate of white businessmen. Archer balanced these assessments by recalling the hard times of his early life as well as by going on record in support of the city's disenfranchised, including children and the homeless. Archer went on to win the election with 57 percent of the vote compared to McPhail's 43 percent, although she had also won 52 percent of the African American vote.

One of Archer's first aims was to heal the racial breaches in the community by bringing his constituents together with common goals. Archer used his influence with the Clinton administration to capture a chunk of federal monies to be used for creating empowerment zones throughout the city. The high profile 1994 G-7 Jobs Conference was held in Detroit. Archer challenged Governor Engler's veto of a decision by Detroit voters to build a casino downtown. He also managed to hammer out a deal with the Major League Baseball's Detroit Tigers, who had threatened to leave the city if a compromise could not be reached in regard to building a new stadium in the city.

Archer's first term was characterized by a robust economy, a balanced budget, a low unemployment rate, and downtown revitalization. Plans began for a new stadium for the Detroit Lions and temporary casinos were built. Perhaps the most important legacy of Archer's first term in office was the restoration of civic pride and confidence in the city and its future. Following his successful first term in office, Archer handily won a second term in 1997 with over 83 percent of the vote.

After his reelection school reform became Archer's priority. His plan required new legislation at the state level that would wrest power and control of the schools from the locally elected school board. Under the reform scheme, the mayor would have the authority to appoint a new school board and the top administrators. Other aspects of the proposal for educational reform include reduced class size; the hiring of 1200 new certified teachers; legislative benchmarks for assessing the school system's success or failure; mandatory summer school in particular cases; a substantial array of after school programs; technical training for teachers; and site-based decision making.

In the spring of 1999, a group called "The Black Slate" spearheaded the effort to collect enough signatures to recall Archer. Backers of the recall cited factors such as the mayor's handling of a riverfront housing development project, problems with snow removal in January of 1999, damage done to Detroit's People Mover from the implosion of the J. L. Hudson building, and Archer's failure to grant one of Detroit's casino licenses to an African American. The recall effort failed.

Marion Barry (1936–)

Municipal Government Official

Marion Shepilov Barry was born in Itta Bena, Mississippi, on March 6, 1936, and grew up in Memphis, Tennessee. He earned a B.S. and M.S. in chemistry by 1960, and while a graduate student at Fisk University he became active in NAACP politics and the burgeoning Civil Rights movement. He eventually co-founded the famous Student Non-Violent Coordinating Committee, a civil rights protest group that made significant gains in erasing the last institutional vestiges of racism in the South. Barry was the SNCC's first national chairperson.

Marion Barry (AP/Wide World Photos, Inc.)

After he moved to Washington, DC, in the mid-1960s, Barry became active in local politics through efforts to move the capital city toward self-government free from congressional interference. Among other achievements, he was instrumental in obtaining federal funding for a citywide youth employment and community service program and was elected to the local school board in 1970. When the "Free D.C." political movement succeeded in loosening Congressional rule over the city, Barry ran for a seat on its first council, which he held for three years.

In 1977, Barry was wounded in an altercation involving the seizure of Washington's District Building by radical Muslims. Elected mayor in 1978, over the next few years his administration was marked by both controversy and achievement. His former wife was charged with embezzling federal funds, but Barry himself was never under any suspicion. As mayor, he initiated community-improvement programs to better employment opportunities and housing conditions for Washington's more disadvantaged neighborhoods. During Barry's administration, access increased for contracting opportunities with the city for women- and minority-owned businesses. One of the hallmarks of Barry's tenure as mayor was launching of large numbers of youth development and summer employment programs. He was reelected in 1982 and again in 1986. Near the end of his third term, Barry was indicted by a federal grand jury for drug possession. He was convicted of a misdemeanor for usage after being filmed snorting crack cocaine and served the maximum six months.

Despite the setback, Barry's support among his Washington, DC, constituency did not diminish. In 1992, he again won a city council seat, and he ran successfully for mayor in 1994. His fourth term was sullied when Congress established a financial control board in 1995 to oversee the district's financial recovery. The city faced a growing debt in excess of $722 million. In 1997, Congress and the president extended the control board's power to nearly every facet of the DC government, thus stripping Barry of most of his executive power. He did not seek reelection.

Sidney John Barthelemy (1942–)

Sociologist, Municipal Government Official, State Legislator

Sidney Barthelemy was born in New Orleans on March 17, 1942. He attended Epiphany Apostolic Junior College from 1960 to 1963 and received a B.A. from the St. Joseph Seminary in 1967. Two years later he earned a M.S.W. from Tulane University. After graduation,

Sidney Barthelemy campaigning for reelection in 1990 (AP/ Wide World Photos, Inc.).

Barthelemy worked in administrative and professional positions in various organizations including Total Community Action, the Parent-Child Development Center, Family Health Inc., and the Urban League of New Orleans. From 1972 to 1974, Barthelemy was the director of the Welfare Department of the City of New Orleans. In 1974, he was elected to the Louisiana State Senate. In 1978, Barthelemy left the state legislature after winning a seat on the New Orleans City Council, where he stayed until his 1986 election as mayor.

Barthelemy has taught at Xavier University as an associate professor of sociology from 1974 to 1986 at Tulane University and the University of New Orleans. He has been the vice-chairman for voter registration for the Democratic National Party, second vice president for the National League of Cities, and president of the Louisiana Conference of Mayors. Barthelemy belongs to the NAACP, National Association of Black Mayors, Democratic National Committee, National Institute of Education, National League of Cities, and the New Orleans Association of Black Social Workers. He has won numerous awards including Outstanding Alumnus of Tulane University, and the 1987 Louisiana Chapter of the National Association of Social Workers' Social Worker of the Year Award. He has also won the American Freedom Award presented by the Third Baptist Church of Chicago (1987), the 1989 American Spirit Award given by the U.S. Air Force Recruiting Service, and the NAACP's New Orleans Chapter Daniel E. Byrd Award (1990).

In 1993, Barthelemy decided not to seek another term as mayor of New Orleans. He went back to teaching at Tulane and the University of New Orleans.

Sharon Sayles Belton (1951–)
Municipal Government Official

Belton was born in St. Paul, Minnesota, and attended Macalester College. She did not graduate as she dropped out when she became pregnant. Belton worked in the Twin Cities areas as a volunteer, eventually establishing a series of rape shelters in the area.

Her community involvement led her to pursue a city council seat in Minneapolis. She was elected to the city council in 1984, and represented the 8th ward until her election as mayor. In 1993, Belton made the decision to run for mayor. She was endorsed by incumbent mayor Don Fraser and won nearly 60 percent of the vote, despite the fact that less than a quarter of the voters were African American.

As mayor, Belton continued to seek to build coalitions to solve the city's problems. This style was her hallmark as a member of city council. She appointed many women and minorities to positions of power within the city government, changing the political culture in Minneapolis. She was reelected as mayor and has remained a popular figure.

Mary Frances Berry (1938–)
Educator, Federal Government Official, Civil Rights Activist, Attorney

Mary Frances Berry was born in 1938. She received her B.A. degree from Howard University in 1961 and her M.A. in 1962. In 1966, she received a Ph.D. from the University of Michigan, and her J.D. in 1970. Berry worked for several years as a professor of history and law at several universities throughout the United States. She was appointed assistant secretary of education in the U.S. Department of Health, Education, and Welfare by President Jimmy Carter in 1977. Prior to her service at HEW, Berry was provost at the University of Maryland College Park and Chancellor at the University of Colorado at Boulder.

In 1980 Berry became commissioner and vice-chairman of the U.S. Commission on Civil Rights. She was fired from the commission by President Ronald Reagan in 1983 for criticizing his civil rights policies. She sued him and won reinstatement in federal court. In 1993, President Bill Clinton named her chairperson of the Civil Rights Commission. She currently is the Geraldine

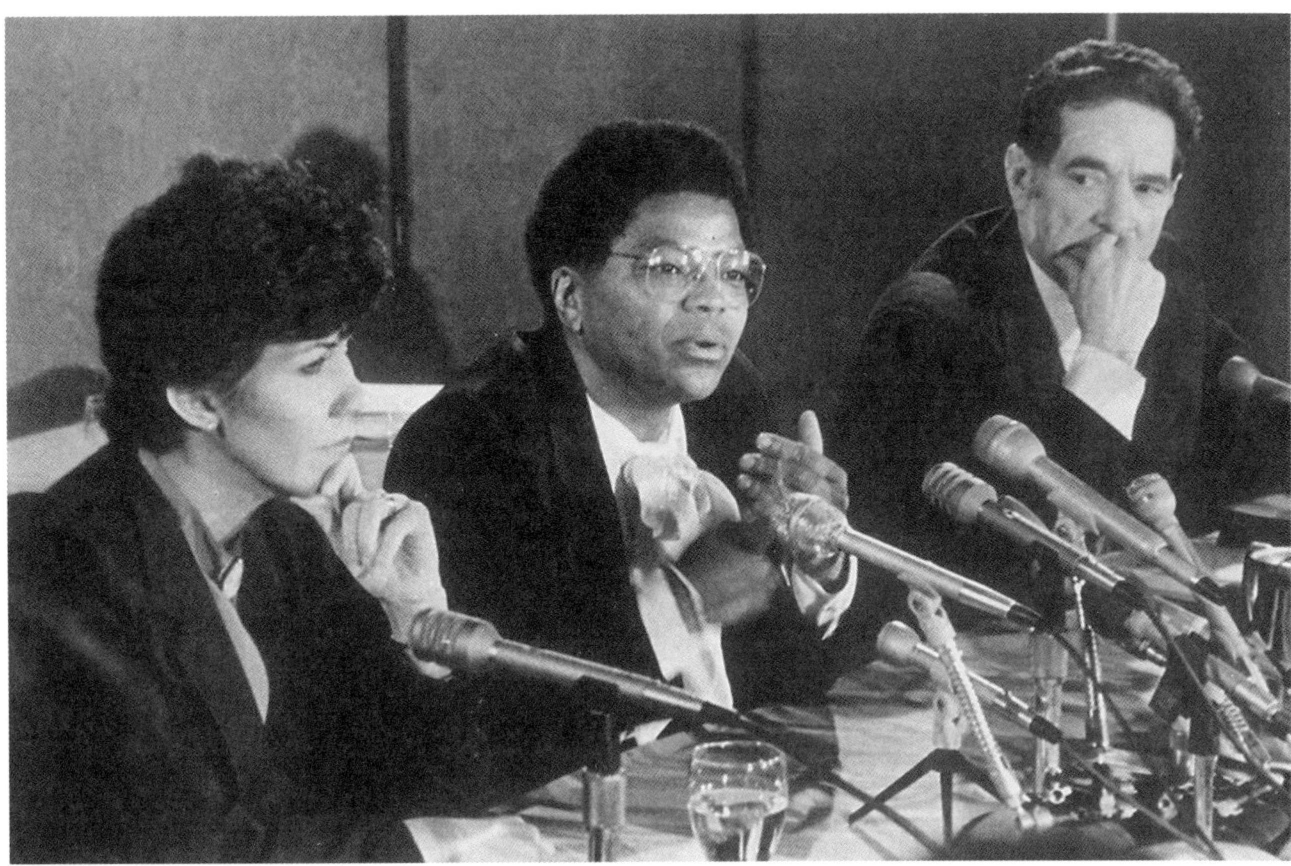

Mary Frances Berry (center) speaks at a news conference in 1984 (AP/Wide World Photos, Inc.).

R. Segal professor of American Social Thought at the University of Pennsylvania where she teaches law and history.

Julian Bond (1940–)

State Representative, Lecturer, Civil Rights Activist, Organization Executive, State Senator, Educator, Media Personality, Media Executive

Throughout his career Julian Bond has been labeled everything from a national hero to a national traitor. He has faced violent segregationists and his own political and personal failures and scandals. He has, however, remained an influential voice in politics, education, and the media.

Bond was born on January 14, 1940. His father, an eminent scholar and president of Lincoln University in Pennsylvania, wanted Julian to follow his footsteps into the world of academics. Although Julian attended fine private schools, he showed little desire for educational pursuits. In 1960, Bond attended Morehouse College in Atlanta where he was a mediocre student. While at Morehouse, however, Bond developed an interest in civil rights activism. He and several other students formed the Atlanta Committee on Appeal for Human Rights (COHAR). Along with other members, Bond participated in several sit-ins at segregated lunch counters in downtown Atlanta. The activities of Bond and his cohorts attracted the attention of Dr. Martin Luther King, Jr. and the Southern Christian Leadership Conference. King invited Bond and other COHAR members to Shaw University in North Carolina to help devise new civil rights strategies. At this conference, the Student Non-Violent Coordinating Committee was created. SNCC eventually absorbed COHAR and Bond accepted a position as the SNCC director of communications. By 1965, Bond had grown tired of the SNCC and decided to embark on a new career in politics.

In 1965, Bond campaigned for a seat in the Georgia House of Representatives. He won the election and prepared to take his seat in the Georgia legislature. However, Bond was soon embroiled in a controversy when he announced that he opposed U.S. involvement in Vietnam and supported students who burned their draft cards to protest against the war. These statements outraged many conservative members of the Georgia House of Representatives and on January 10, 1966, they voted to prevent Bond's admission to the legislature.

Julian Bond celebrating his primary election victory for the U.S. House of Representatives in 1986 (Corbis Corporation [Bellevue]).

Bond sought legal recourse to overturn this vote and the case eventually went to the U.S. Supreme Court. On December 5, 1966, the Court ruled that the Georgia vote was a violation of Bond's First Amendment right of free speech and ordered that he be admitted to the legislature. The members of the Georgia House of Representatives reluctantly allowed Bond to take his seat, but treated him as an outcast.

In 1968, Bond and several other members of the Georgia Democratic Party Forum protested Governor Lester Maddox's decision to send only six African American delegates out of 107 to the Democratic National Convention. Bond and his supporters arrived at the convention and set up a rival delegation. After several bitter arguments with Georgia's official delegation, Bond's delegation captured nearly half of Georgia's delegate votes. He became the Democratic Party's first African American candidate for the U.S. vice presidency, but he did not meet the minimum age requirement.

From 1974 to 1989, Bond was president of the Atlanta branch of the NAACP. He was elected to the Georgia Senate in 1975 and remained a member until 1987. In 1976, he declined an invitation to become a part of President Jimmy Carter administration. Bond ran for a seat in the U.S. Congress in 1986 but lost the election to John Lewis. In 1989, he divorced his wife after 28 years of marriage. During the bitter divorce, allegations of Bond's drug use surfaced. Shortly thereafter, he became embroiled in a paternity suit. He initially denied the allegations, but admitted in May of 1990 to fathering the child and was ordered to pay child support.

Bond has served as a visiting professor at Drexel and Harvard Universities. He is a lecturer and writer and is often called upon to comment on political and social issues. Bond has hosted a popular television program *America's Black Forum*, the oldest African American-owned show in television syndication; and narrated the highly acclaimed public television series *Eyes on the Prize*. He has written a nationally distributed newspaper column. In 1994 he became involved in a power struggle with NAACP Board Chairman William Gibson, which cost Bond his position on the board. In 1998, Bond was elected chair of the NAACP board of directors and chair of the board of the NAACP's magazine *The Crisis*. He is currently a distinguished scholar in residence at American University and a lecturer in history at the University of Virginia.

Thomas Bradley (1917–1998)

Civil Rights Activist, Municipal Government Official, Organization Executive, City Council Member, Attorney

Bradley was born December 29, 1917, in Calvert, Texas, the son of a sharecropper. In 1924 he moved with his family to Los Angeles. Bradley graduated from Polytechnic High School in 1937 and attended the University of California, Los Angeles, on an athletic scholarship. He excelled at track before quitting college in 1940 and joining the Los Angeles Police Department. While a member of the police force, Bradley worked as a detective, community relations officer, and in the departments juvenile division. In the early 1950s, Bradley began studying law at two Los Angeles colleges, Loyola University and later at Southwestern University. He was awarded an LL.B. from Southwestern University in 1956. Bradley stayed with the LAPD until 1961, when he entered private law practice.

In 1963, Bradley became the first African American elected to the Los Angeles City Council. He was reelected in 1967 and 1971. In the 1973 election Bradley became mayor of Los Angeles, winning 56 percent of the vote. During his time as mayor, Bradley compiled a record and was both lauded and criticized. Bradley's defenders credited him with opening city government to minorities and women, expanding social services to the urban poor, and spurring growth. During Bradley's tenure as mayor, Los Angeles overtook San Francisco as the West Coast's financial center and gained international prominence. Though Bradley is credited with turning Los Angeles into a modern metropolis, his detractors accused him of not keeping up with the city's problems.

One of the toughest situations Bradley faced was the occurrence of the 1992 riots that followed the announcement of not guilty verdicts for Los Angeles Police Department officers who were charged with beating African American motorist Rodney King. Bradley was vilified for what some considered to be his lack of response to the incident. Many demanded the firing of Police Chief Daryl Gates. Under the limits of the law, however, Bradley could do no more than ask Gates to resign. Though Gates eventually did leave his most, many considered the situation a serious challenge to Bradley's authority.

Bradley did attempt to heal the community in other ways. Even before the rioting had ended, he set up the nonprofit organization, Rebuild LA. That organization was criticized for creating unreal expectations, but Bradley's Neighbor to Neighbor group was viewed in a positive light. Comprised of nearly 800 volunteers, the outreach group regularly canvassed neighborhoods to

Tom Bradley (AP/Wide World Photos, Inc.)

give residents an outlet for discussing problems and to help citizens organize themselves in order to solve their own difficulties. In a second trial, two of four LAPD officers charged with violating King's civil rights were found guilty.

One of Bradley's final acts as a city official was to sign a bill that banned smoking in all restaurants. He was honored for his years of service by the U.S. Conference of Mayors in June of 1993. He officially left the mayoral post on July 1, 1993, effectively ending a thirty-year public career. After his last term, Bradley returned to the private practice of law. He was then ensnared in a political finance scandal that also caught other California lawmakers including Governor Pete Wilson and Senator Dianne Feinstein. Laundered campaign funds were traced to Evergreen America Corp., the world's largest container shipping company. Los Angeles's Ethics Commission ordered Bradley and others to repay a total of $15,000, but Bradley refused, claiming he did not know the money had been improperly donated.

Bradley served as president of the National League of Cities and the Southern California Association of Governments. He belonged to the Urban League of Los Angeles and was a founding member of the NAACP's

Black Achievers Committee. On the national level he served on President Gerald Ford's National Committee on Productivity & Work Quality and on the National Energy Advisory Council. Bradley won numerous awards and honors including the 1974 University of California's Alumnus of the Year, the 1974 Thurgood Marshall Award, the 1978 Award of Merit given by the National Council of Negro Women, and the NAACP's 1985 Springarn Medal.

Edward W. Brooke (1919–)

Attorney, Federal Legislator

Edward W. Brooke was born on October 26, 1919, in Washington, DC. He moved to Massachusetts, and in a state that was overwhelmingly Democratic and in which African Americans constituted only 3 percent of the population, became a popular Republican figure. He first achieved statewide office in 1962 when he defeated Elliot Richardson to become attorney general. His record in that post led to his 1966 election to the Senate over former Massachusetts governor Endicott Peabody.

Born into a middle-class environment, Brooke attended public schools and went on to graduate from Howard. Inducted into an all-African American infantry unit during World War II, Brooke rose to the rank of captain and was ultimately given a Bronze Star for his work in intelligence. Returning to Massachusetts after the war, Brooke attended the Boston University Law School, compiling a top academic record and editing the *Law Review*. After law school, he established himself as an attorney and also served as chairman of the Boston Finance Commission.

Brooke was later nominated for the attorney general's office, encountering stiff opposition within his own party. He eventually won both the Republican primary and the general election against his Democratic opponent. In the Senate, Brooke espoused the notion that the Great Society could not become a reality until it was preceded by the "Responsible Society." He called this a society in which "it's more profitable to work than not to work. You don't help a man by constantly giving him more handouts."

When first elected, Brooke strongly supported U.S. participation in the Vietnam War, though most African American leaders were increasingly opposing it. However, in 1971, Brooke supported the McGovern-Hatfield Amendment which called for withdrawal of the United States from Vietnam. Matters of race rather than foreign affairs were to become Brooke's area of expertise. Brooke was a cautious legislator. However, as pressure mounted from the established civil rights groups and African American militants he decided to attack President Nixon's policies. Brooke was roused into a more active role by the administration's vacillating school desegregation guidelines, its firing of HEW official Leon Panetta, and the nominations to the Supreme Court of judicial conservatives Clement Haynsworth and G. Harrold Carswell.

Edward W. Brooke (AP/Wide World Photos, Inc.)

In 1972, Brooke was reelected to the Senate overwhelmingly, even though Massachusetts was the only state not carried by his party in the presidential election. While Brooke seconded the nomination of President Richard M. Nixon at the 1972 Republican Convention, he became increasingly critical of the Nixon administration. He also began to appear publicly at meetings of the Congressional Black Caucus, a group he had tended to avoid in the past. Brooke was considered a member of the moderate wing of the Republican Party. In 1978, Brooke's bid for a third term in the Senate was denied by Democrat Paul Tsongas, and Brooke returned to his private law practice.

Ronald H. Brown (1941–1996)

Attorney, Federal Government Official, Organization Executive

Brown was born in Washington, DC, on August 1, 1941, and raised in Harlem. He attended White Plains High School and Rhodes and Walden Preparatory Schools in New York. He graduated from Middlebury College in Middlebury, Vermont, with a B.A. in political science in 1962. Upon graduating he enlisted in the U.S. Army where he achieved the rank of captain while serving in West Germany and Korea. In 1970, Brown graduated from New York City's St. John's University Law School.

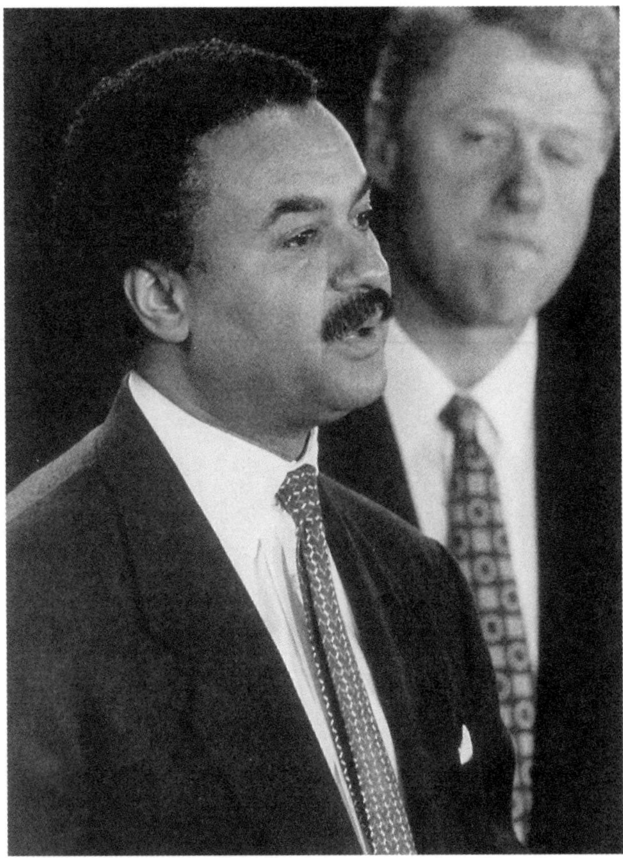

Former Commerce Secretary Ron Brown with President Bill Clinton (Corbis Corporation [Bellevue])

While attending law school, Brown began working in 1988, for the National Urban League's job training center in the Bronx, New York. He continued with them until 1979, working as general counsel, Washington spokesperson, deputy executive director, vice president of Washington operations, and lobbyist. In 1980 he resigned to become chief counsel of the U.S. Senate Judiciary Committee. Largely because of his effectiveness as chief counsel of the Judiciary Committee, he became the general counsel and staff coordinator for Senator Edward Kennedy. Brown also became chief counsel for the Democratic National Committee (DNC) and subsequently the deputy chairman of the DNC. After his term as deputy chairman expired, Brown joined the law firm of Patton, Boggs & Blow.

In 1989 Brown was appointed chairman of the DNC, making him the first African American to head a major American political party. As head of the DNC, Brown proved to be a successful fund-raiser and an effective team builder. During Brown's tenure, Democrats elected an African American governor in Virginia and an African American mayor in New York City. Brown was also considered one of the architects of President Bill Clinton's 1992 election victory. In 1993, President Clinton appointed Brown commerce secretary. He was subsequently confirmed by the U.S. Senate, thus becoming the first African American secretary of commerce.

As commerce secretary, Brown was a leader in developing trade and economic policies which were sometimes controversial. He opened doors which allowed women and minorities to be more involved and aware of business opportunities through the Commerce Department. Brown's service as a cabinet member was marred somewhat by charges of financial impropriety and influence-peddling. An independent counsel was appointed to investigate the allegations. Brown's last official act was leading a group of American businessmen and women to war-torn Croatia so that they might assist in rebuilding the country. Brown died in a plane crash on April 3, 1996, near the Croatian coast.

Blanche K. Bruce (1841–1898)

Federal Government Official, Civil Rights Activist, Federal Legislator

Blanche Kelso Bruce was born a slave in Farmville, Prince Edward County, Virginia. He received his early formal education in Missouri, where his parents had moved while he was young, and may have studied at Oberlin College in Ohio. In 1868, Bruce settled in Floreyville, Mississippi, where he was a successful educator. He later worked as a planter and eventually built up a considerable fortune in property.

In 1870, Bruce entered politics and was elected sergeant-at-arms of the Mississippi Senate. A year later he was named assessor of taxes in Bolivar County. In 1872 he served as sheriff of the county and as a member of the Board of Levee Commissioners of Mississippi. Bruce was nominated for the U.S. Senate from Mississippi in February of 1874. He was elected, becoming the first African American person to serve a full term in the Senate. Bruce became an outspoken defender of the rights of minority groups including the Chinese and Native Americans. In 1879, he became the first African American to preside over the Senate during a debate. He chaired the investigation into the failure of the Freedmen's Savings and Trust and worked for the improvement of navigation on the Mississippi in the hope of increasing interstate and foreign commerce. Bruce also supported legislation aimed at eliminating reprisals against those who had opposed African American emancipation.

After Bruce completed his term in the Senate in 1881, he failed to win a second term due to the loss of power and influence of the Radical Republicans in the South He. rejected an offer for a diplomatic post to Brazil, because slavery was still practiced there. In 1881, he was named register of the U.S. Treasury Department by

Blanche K. Bruce

Ralph J. Bunche (Courtesy of Carl Van Vechten)

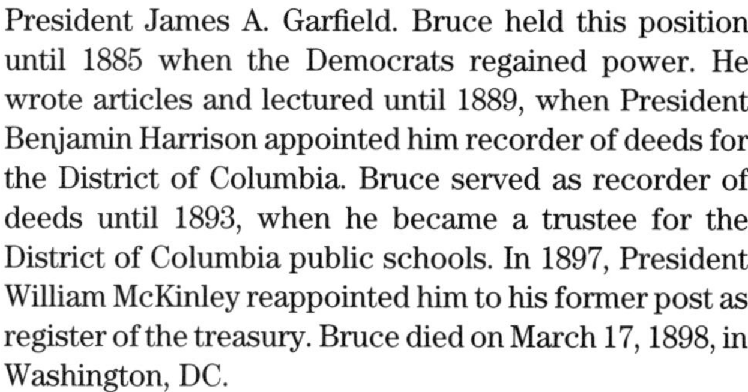

President James A. Garfield. Bruce held this position until 1885 when the Democrats regained power. He wrote articles and lectured until 1889, when President Benjamin Harrison appointed him recorder of deeds for the District of Columbia. Bruce served as recorder of deeds until 1893, when he became a trustee for the District of Columbia public schools. In 1897, President William McKinley reappointed him to his former post as register of the treasury. Bruce died on March 17, 1898, in Washington, DC.

Ralph J. Bunche (1904–1971)
Federal Government Official, Diplomat, Educator

The first African American to win the Nobel Peace Prize, Ralph Bunche was an internationally acclaimed statesman whose record of achievement places him among the most significant American diplomats of the twentieth century. Bunche received the Peace Prize in 1950 for his role in effecting a cease fire in the Arab-Israeli dispute.

Born in Detroit on August 7, 1904, Bunche graduated *summa cum laude* in 1927 with Phi Beta Kappa honors from UCLA. A year later he received his M.A. in government from Harvard. Soon thereafter he was named head of the Department of Political Science at Howard University until 1932 when he resumed his work toward his doctorate from Harvard. He later studied at Northwestern University, the London School of Economics, and Capetown University. Before World War II broke out in 1939, Bunche did field work with the Swedish sociologist Gunnar Myrdal, author of the widely acclaimed *An American Dilemma.* During the war, he served initially as senior social analyst for the Office of the Coordinator of Information in African and Far Eastern Affairs, and was then reassigned to the African section of the Office of Strategic Services. In 1942, he helped draw up the territories and trusteeship sections ultimately earmarked for inclusion in the United Nations charter.

The single event that brought the name of Ralph Bunche into the international spotlight occurred soon after his appointment in 1948 as chief assistant to Count Folke Bernadotte, U.N. mediator in the Palestine crisis. With the latter's assassination, Bunche continued cease-fire talks between Egypt and Israel. After six weeks of intensive negotiations, Bunche worked out the "Four Armistice Agreements," which brokered an immediate cessation of the hostilities between the two combatants.

Once the actual cease-fire was signed, Bunche received numerous congratulatory letters and telegrams from many heads of state and was given a hero's welcome upon his return to the United States.

Bunche served as undersecretary of Special Political Affairs from 1957 to 1967. By 1968, Bunche had attained the rank of undersecretary general, the highest position ever held by an American at the United Nations. Bunche retired in October of 1971 and died on December 9, 1971. The library of the Department of State was dedicated and renamed in his honor in May of 1997 in recognition of his political and humanitarian contributions.

Yvonne Braithwaite Burke (1932–)

Attorney, State Legislator

Attorney and former California State Assembly Woman Yvonne Braithwaite Burke became the first African American woman from California ever to be elected to the House of Representatives in November of 1972. More than twenty years later, she became the first woman and African American to chair the Los Angeles County Board of Supervisors. Prior to her governmental career, Burke was a practicing attorney, during which time she served as a deputy corporation commissioner, a hearing officer for the Los Angeles Police Commissioner, and an attorney for the McCone Commission which investigated the Watts riots.

Yvonne Braithwaite Burke speaking at a press conference in 1976 (AP/Wide World Photos, Inc.).

Born on October 5, 1932, in Los Angeles, Congresswoman Burke served in the State Assembly for six years prior to her election to Congress. During her final two years, she was chairperson of the Committee on Urban Development and Housing and a member of the Health, Finance and Insurance committees. As a state legislator, Burke was responsible for the enactment of bills that provided for needy children, relocation of tenants, owners of homes taken by governmental action, and which required major medical insurance programs to grant immediate coverage to newborn infants of the insured.

Burke's district, created in 1971 by the California legislature, was about fifty percent African American. In 1972, the district gave 64 percent of its vote to Burke. During Burke's first term in the House, she proved to be an ardent spokesperson for the downtrodden. She became a member of the Committee on Appropriations in December of 1974, and used her position on this committee to advocate an increase in funding for senior citizen services and community nutrition and food programs. Although her proposal for increased spending was defeated by the House of Representatives, Burke's efforts earned the respect of the African American community. In January of 1977, Burke worked diligently for the passage of the Displaced Homemakers Act, which proposed the creation of counseling programs and job training centers for women entering the work force for the first time.

In 1978, Burke resigned to run for attorney general in California. She lost the race but was appointed to the Los Angeles County Board of Supervisors. She resigned from the board in December 1980, and returned to her private law practice. Burke remained a prominent figure in California politics, taking on a number of civic responsibilities including serving as a member of the University of California Board of Regents. In 1992, Burke was elected as chairperson of her old stomping ground, the Los Angeles County Board of Supervisors.

Chuck Burris (1951–)

Municipal Government Official

Burris was born in New Orleans in 1951, and was raised in Atlanta. He attended Morehouse College, and in 1971 he received his B.A. In 1975, he received his LL.B. from John Marshall Law School. Burris worked on several of the campaigns of Maynard Jackson and Andrew Young. He worked for the city of Atlanta as a member of the Crime Analyst Team and as budget officer. He was also affiliated with the city's housing department.

While working for the state of Georgia, Burris first discovered the town of Stone Mountain. The city was the birthplace of the modern Ku Klux Klan and had a large monument to the Confederacy carved on Stone Mountain. Burris moved to the town and in 1991, won election to the city council. Burris was determined to change the town's image from intolerance to inclusiveness.

In 1997, Burris was elected as the mayor of Stone Mountain. The symbolic victory attracted national attention. In 1998, Burris sat next to Hillary Clinton at the State of the Union address.

Bill Campbell (1954–)
Municipal Government Official

Bill Campbell was born in 1954 in Raleigh, North Carolina. Campbell became mayor of Atlanta in 1992 at the age of forty, signaling a new generation of leadership for the people of Atlanta.

In 1974, Campbell graduated *cum laude* from Vanderbilt University, completing a triple major (history, political science, and sociology) in just three years. He received his J.D. from Duke University in 1977 and went to work for an Atlanta law firm. Campbell worked from 1980 to 1981, for the U.S. Justice Department in Atlanta.

Campbell began his political career in 1981 when he served on the Atlanta City Council. He served three consecutive terms through 1993, co-sponsoring more than three hundred pieces of legislation. By 1993, he had become a partner in an Atlanta law firm, along with serving as floor leader of the city council under Atlanta Mayor Maynard Jackson. When Jackson's health began to wane, Campbell was mentioned as a mayoral candidate. The importance of who would be the new mayor was heightened by the city's preparation for the 1996 Olympics.

The election for mayor included other city council members, former mayoral candidates, and 12 nonpartisan candidates. Campbell won 49 percent of the vote, shy of the 50 percent needed to win the office outright. He won the runoff election with 73 percent of the vote.

Campbell appointed the first female police chief of a major American city. He installed mini-police precincts in Atlanta's housing projects, planned alliances between the city and historically African American colleges, and encouraged young people to become active in community services. In 1996, Campbell hosted many dignitaries, including President Bill Clinton, in celebration of the tenth official holiday celebration of Martin Luther King, Jr. Day. Campbell proposed a $150 million plan to repair Atlanta's infrastructure before the Olympics. Since the Olympics, Campbell's major efforts have been in downtown redevelopment, privatization of the Water Department, and a transformation of the housing authority in Atlanta from one of the worst in the nation.

Shirley Chisholm (1924–)
Educator, Federal Legislator, Organization Executive, Civil Rights Activist

Shirley Chisholm was born November 30, 1924, in New York City. She graduated *cum laude* from Brooklyn College in 1946 with a B.A. in sociology and in 1952 from Columbia University with a M.A. in elementary education. She had an early career in child care and preschool education, culminating in her directorship of the Hamilton-Madison Child Care Center in New York. From 1959 to 1964 she was a consultant to the Day Care Division of New York City's Bureau of Child Welfare.

In 1964, Chisholm was elected New York State Assemblywoman representing the 55th district in New York City. In 1968 she became the first African American woman elected to the U.S. House of Representatives, where she served until her retirement in 1982. In 1972, Chisholm announced her candidacy for the Democratic presidential nomination. She campaigned and entered primaries in 12 states, winning 28 delegates and 152 first ballot votes. Chisholm served as a delegate to the Democratic National Mid-Term Conference in 1974 and as a Democratic National Committee-woman. After retiring from politics Chisholm taught political science at Mount Holyoke College. In 1984, Chisholm co-founded the National Political Congress of Black Women. She spent the next year as a visiting scholar at Spelman College. In 1993, U.S. president Bill Clinton hoped to appoint her as ambassador to Jamaica.

Chisholm is the author of *Unbossed & Unbought* (1970) and *The Good Fight* (1973). She is a member of the NAACP, the National Association of Colored Women, and the League of Women Voters. She has won numerous awards including the 1965 Woman of Achievement Award presented by Key Women Inc. and the 1969 Sojourner Truth Award given to her by the Association for the Study of Negro Life and History.

William Clay (1931–)
Civil Rights Activist, Federal Legislator

William Clay, the first African American to represent the state of Missouri in the U.S. Congress, was born on April 30, 1931, in the lower end of what is now St. Louis's 1st District. Clay received a degree in political science at St. Louis University, where he was one of four African

William Clay speaking at a press conference in 1989 (AP/ Wide World Photos, Inc.).

Americans in a class of 1,100. After serving in the U.S. Army until 1955, Clay became active in a host of civil rights organizations including the NAACP Youth Council and CORE. During this time he worked as a cardiographic aide, bus driver, and insurance agent.

In 1959 and 1963, Clay was elected alderman of the predominantly African American 26th Ward. During his first term, he served nearly four months of a nine-month jail sentence for demonstrations at a local bank. In 1964, Clay stepped down from his alderman's post to run for ward committeeman, he won and was reelected in 1968.

Clay's election platform in 1969 included a number of progressive, even radical, ideas. He advocated that all penal institutions make provisions for the creation of facilities in which married prisoners could set up house with their spouses for the duration of their sentences. He branded most testing procedures and diploma requirements, as well as references to arrest records and periods of unemployment, unnecessary obstacles complicating the path of a prospective employee. In his view, a demonstrated willingness to work and an acceptance of responsibility should be the criteria determining one's selection for a job.

Clay's last job before his election to Congress was as race relations coordinator for Steamfitters Union Local 562. Subjected to considerable criticism from other St. Louis African Americans who labeled the union racist, Clay pointed out that dramatic changes in the hiring practices of the union since he had joined it in 1966 were responsible for the employment of thirty African American steamfitters in St. Louis. Still, Clay conceded that the high-paying job had led him to reduce his active involvement with the civil rights struggle to some degree.

As a congressman, Clay sponsored many pieces of legislation including the Hatch Act Reform Bill, the City Earnings Tax Bill, the IRS Reform Bill, and the Family and Medical Leave Bill, which was the first bill that President Bill Clinton signed into law. In 1993 the Hatch Act, which Clay championed for two decades, was signed into law. Clay has served as chairman of the Subcommittee on Postal Operations and Civil Service, the House Education and Labor Committee, and the House Administration Committee. He has also been a member of the board of directors for Benedict College, Tougaloo College, and the Congressional Black Caucus Foundation. In 1990, Clay's first book, *To Kill or Not to Kill*, was published. In 1993, Clay published *Just Permanent Interests: Black Americans in Congress, 1870–1991.*

Eva Clayton (1934 –)
Federal Legislator

Eva M.Clayton was born in Savannah, Georgia. Clayton earned a B.S. in 1955 from Johnson C. Smith University in Charlotte, North Carolina. She earned a M.S. in 1963 from North Carolina Central University. She later attended the University of North Carolina Law School.

Clayton first ran for a congressional seat in 1968 without success. She later worked for the campaign of Jim Hunt who was elected governor. Clayton was rewarded with the post of Assistant Secretary for Community Development. Clayton later worked in the Warren County public offices.

In 1992, she was elected representative from the First District of North Carolina. However, her district and others came under fire as racially gerrymandered districts. The district is no longer an African American-majority district. Clayton has still held her seat, and has become a member of the Budget Committee in the House.

Cardiss Collins (1931–)
Accountant, Federal Legislator, Civil Rights Activist

Collins was born Cardiss Robertson on September 24, 1931. She moved to Detroit and graduated from

Cardiss Collins (AP/Wide World Photos, Inc.)

Commerce High School. Collins then moved to Chicago where she worked as a secretary for the state's Department of Revenue. She began studying accounting at Northwestern University and was promoted to accountant and then auditor.

In 1973, Collins was elected U.S. Representative from Illinois's 7th district. She was elected to fill the seat vacated by her husband George Collins, who was killed in an airplane crash. She became the first African American and the first woman to hold the position of Democratic whip-at-large. Collins served on congressional subcommittees dealing with consumer protection, national security, hazardous materials, narcotic abuse and control, and energy concerns. At various points, she also served as active secretary, vice chair, and chair of the Congressional Black Caucus. Collins has been a proponent of civil rights, busing, and anti-apartheid legislation.

In 1994, the CBC Foundation elected her the group's chair. Early in 1995, Collins became the top Democrat on the Government Reform and Oversight Committee. On November 8, 1995, Collins announced her decision to retire after 23 years in the House; her 12 terms made her the longest-serving African American female member of Congress. Collins belongs to the NAACP, Chicago Urban League, Northern Virginia Urban League, National Women's Political Caucus, Alpha Kappa Alpha, Congressional Women's Caucus, Alpha Kappa Psi, Black Women's Agenda, and the National Council of Negro Women. Besides the degree she obtained from Northwestern in 1967, she has honorary degrees from Barber-Scotia College, Winston-Salem State University, and Spelman College. The Black Coaches Association (BCA) named Collins Sportsperson of the Year in 1994, after she supported the group's contention that standardized college entrance examinations are racially and culturally biased and, therefore, should not be used by the National Collegiate Athletic Association to establish athletic eligibility.

John Conyers (1929–)

Attorney, Federal Legislator, Federal Government Official, Civil Rights Activist, Organization Executive

Conyers was born in Detroit on May 16, 1929. In 1950, three years after graduating from high school, he enlisted in the U.S. Army as a private and served in Korea before being honorably discharged in 1957 as a second lieutenant. He attended Wayne State University in Detroit, and, after studying in a dual program, he received a B.A. in 1957 and a J.D. in 1958.

Conyers served as a legislative assistant to Congressman John Dingell, Jr. from 1958 to 1961 and was a senior partner in the law firm of Conyers, Bell & Townsend from 1959 to 1961. In 1961 he took a referee position with the Michigan Workman's Compensation Department. In 1964 he won election as a Democrat to the U.S. House of Representatives. Conyers had long been active in the Democratic Party, belonging to the Young Democrats, University Democrats, and serving as a precinct delegate to the Democratic Party. After his election Conyers was assigned to the powerful House Judiciary Committee. From that position he worked on legislation dealing with civil rights, medicare, immigration reform, and truth-in-packaging laws. He was an early opponent of U.S. involvement in Vietnam and an early proponent on the Voting Rights Act of 1965.

In 1994, Conyers, the most senior African American member of Congress, supported a grass-roots movement comprised of nearly 1,000 individuals seeking reparations from the federal government on behalf of their slave ancestors. The participants held their fifth annual Conference on Reparations in Conyers's hometown, Detroit. Other prominent African Americans lending support included Reverend Jesse Jackson. In 1998 and 1999, Conyers served as the ranking Democrat on the House Committee of Impeachment.

Conyers has been vice-chairman of the National Board of Americans for Democratic Action and the American Civil Liberties Union. He is on the executive board of the Detroit Chapter of the NAACP and belongs to the Wolverine Bar Association. He is the recipient of the

John Conyers (AP/Wide World Photos, Inc.)

Ronald V. Dellums (AP/Wide World Photos, Inc.)

1967 Rosa Parks Award and in 1969 received an honorary law degree from Wilberforce University.

Ronald V. Dellums (1935–)
Social Worker, Federal Legislator, Organization Executive, Lecturer

Ronald Dellums was born in Oakland, California, on November 24, 1935. After attending McClymonds and Oakland Technical High Schools Dellums joined the U.S. Marine Corps in 1954 and was discharged after two years of service. He returned to school, receiving an associate of arts degree from Oakland City College in 1958, a B.A. from San Francisco State College in 1960, and a M.S.W. from the University of California at Berkeley in 1962.

For the next eight years, Dellums engaged in a variety of social work positions. He was a psychiatric social worker with the Berkeley Department of Mental Hygiene starting in 1962, and then two years later became the Bayview Community Center's program director. Dellums spent one year as director of the Hunters Point Youth Opportunity Center and one year as a consultant to the Bay Area Social Planning Council. In 1967, Dellums worked as a program director for the San Francisco Economic Opportunity Council. From 1968 to 1970, Dellums lectured at San Francisco State College and the University of California's School of Social Work. He also served as a consultant to Social Dynamics Inc.

Dellums was elected to the Berkeley City Council in 1967, and served until his election as a Democrat to the U.S. House of Representatives in 1971. As a representative he chaired the House Committee on the District of Columbia and served on the House Armed Services Subcommittee on Military Facilities and Installations as well as the Sub-committee on Military Research and Development. In 1983, Dellums wrote *Defense Sense: The Search for a Rational Military Policy.*

Dellums, who has chaired the Defense Policy Panel, became the first African American to head the House Armed Services Committee on January 27, 1993. Once a militant pacifist, he was recognized as one of the most highly regarded members of Congress to extensively work towards U.S. demilitarization. Dellums chastised U.S. president Bill Clinton for giving into fear and ignorance, when the president did not follow through on his promise to lift the ban on homosexuals in the military. Dellums retired in 1998 after 27 years in Congress.

Oscar Stanton DePriest (1871–1951)
County Commissioner, Federal Legislator

Oscar DePriest was the first African American to win a seat in the U.S. House of Representatives in the twentieth century. Born in Florence, Alabama, in 1871, De Priest moved to Kansas with his family at the age of six. His formal education consisted of business and bookkeeping classes which he completed before running away to Dayton, Ohio, with two white friends. By 1889, he had reached Chicago and become a painter and master decorator.

In Chicago, DePriest amassed a fortune in real estate and the stock market, and in 1904, he entered politics successfully when he was elected Cook County commissioner. In 1908, he was appointed an alternate delegate to the Republican National Convention and in 1915 became Chicago's first African American alderman. He served on the Chicago City Council from 1915 to 1917 and became Third Ward committeeman in 1924. In 1928, DePriest became the Republican nominee for the Congressional seat vacated by fellow Republican Martin Madden. DePriest won the November election over his Democratic rival and an independent candidate to become the first African American from outside of the South to be elected to Congress.

Following his election to Congress, DePriest became the unofficial spokesman for the 11 million African Americans in the United States during the 1920s and 1930s. He proposed that states that discriminated against African American Americans should receive fewer congressional seats. Also, he proposed that a monthly pension be given to ex-slaves over the age of 75. During the early 1930s, with the United States mired in the Depression, DePriest was faced with a difficult dilemma. Although he empathized with the plight of poor black and white Americans, he did not support the emergency federal relief programs proposed by President Franklin Roosevelt. Rather, DePriest and his fellow Republicans believed that aid programs should be created and implemented by individual states or local communities. DePriest's stance on the issue of federal relief programs dismayed many of his constituents. In 1934, he was defeated by Arthur Mitchell, the first African American Democrat elected to serve in Congress.

DePriest remained active in public life, serving from 1943 to 1947 as alderman of the Third Ward in Chicago. His final withdrawal from politics came about after a dispute with the Republican Party. DePriest returned to his real estate business, and he died on May 12, 1951.

David Dinkins (AP/Wide World Photos, Inc.)

David Dinkins (1927–)
Attorney, Municipal Government Official, State Legislator

In September of 1989, David Dinkins surprised political observers by defeating incumbent Mayor Edward I. Koch in New York City's Democratic mayoral primary. Two months later, in the November election, he defeated Republican contender Rudolph Giuliani. Dinkins's victory marked the first time an African American was elected as mayor of New York. Dinkins thus faced the difficult task of leading a racially polarized and financially troubled city. While many supporters cited Dinkins's calm, professional demeanor as having a soothing effect upon New York's festering racial problems, others chided him for not responding forcefully enough to the many fiscal and social challenges facing the city.

David Dinkins was born in Trenton, New Jersey, in 1927. His parents separated when he was quite young and he moved to Harlem with his mother and sister. He returned to Trenton to attend high school. Following a stint in the U.S. Marines during World War II, he attended Howard University in Washington, DC, and graduated in 1950 with a B.S.. In 1956, Dinkins graduated from the Brooklyn Law School. He became an attorney, and, eventually, a partner in the law firm of Dyett, Alexander, Dinkins, Patterson, Michael, Dinkins, and Jones.

Dinkins's first foray into the world of politics occurred in 1965, when he won an election to the New York State Assembly. He served until 1967, but did not seek reelection after his district was redrawn. In 1972, Dinkins was appointed as president of elections for the City of New York and served for one year. Two years later, in 1975, he was appointed as city clerk and served until 1985. Dinkins ran for the office of Manhattan borough president in 1977 and 1981. He lost both elections by a wide margin. Dinkins ran again in 1985 and was elected. As Manhattan borough president, he was viewed as a mediator who tried to address a myriad of community concerns such as school decentralization, AIDS treatment and prevention services, and pedestrian safety.

As mayor, Dinkins remained true to the issues he had addressed as Manhattan borough president. Other causes he championed included tolerance and acceptance of gays and lesbians, economic parity for women and minorities, and affirmative action. Dinkins set up a program to provide government contracts to businesses owned by women and minorities. Though the program was blemished by faulty bookkeeping and by the complexity of determining which companies were truly eligible, Dinkins's successor kept it in place.

In 1991, when riots erupted between African Americans and Jews in the Crown Heights neighborhood, Dinkins entreated both sides to think about their actions and possible consequences rather than react to the emotional volatility surrounding an incident in which a Jewish man's automobile accidentally struck and killed an African American youth. When riots seized Los Angeles in 1992, most of the nation feared that the violence would spread to other large urban areas with mixed or predominately African American populations. But Dinkins was able to assuage his constituents and prevent the terror and destruction that incapacitated Los Angeles.

In November of 1993, Dinkins's bid for reelection fell short when he was narrowly defeated by Rudolph W. Giuliani. Dinkins left office on December 31, 1993. Poor management had been an Achilles heel of the Dinkins administration. In 1994, the New York Court of Appeals fined the city more than $3.5 million to compensate 5,000 homeless families forced to live in inadequate shelters. In 1994, Dinkins also began hosting a radio talk show. Later in the year, he became a member of the AMREP Corp. board of directors and began teaching at Columbia University. Dinkins successfully underwent triple bypass heart surgery in 1995 and continues his professorship in the practice of public affairs in his role as senior fellow, Barnard-Columbia Center for Urban Policy.

Julian C. Dixon (1934–)

Attorney, Federal Legislator, Women's Rights Activist

Julian C. Dixon was born August 8, 1934, in Washington, DC. He received a B.S. in political science from California State University and an LL.B. from Southwestern University Law School in 1967. In 1972, Dixon was elected on the Democratic ticket to the California State Assembly. In 1978, he was elected to the U.S. House of Representatives.

While in the House of Representatives, Dixon has served on the House Committee on Standards of Official Conduct, West Point Board of Supervisors, and the Appropriations Sub-Committee on Foreign Operations. He also chaired the Appropriations Sub-Committee on the District of Columbia. This latter appointment made Dixon the first African American to chair an appropriations sub-committee. Dixon was an original co-sponsor of the Equal Rights Amendment and is active in the Congressional Black Caucus. Dixon also served in the U.S. Army from 1957 to 1960.

Michael Espy (1953–)

Federal Government Official, Attorney

Espy was born November 30, 1953. He received a B.A. from Howard University in 1975, and a J.D. from the Santa Clara School of Law in 1978. After graduating, Espy practiced law in Yazoo City, Mississippi, and managed the Central Mississippi Legal Services from 1978 to 1980. Espy worked for the State of Mississippi as assistant secretary of state for public lands, and from 1984 to 1985, as assistant attorney general for consumer protection.

Espy was elected to the U.S. House of Representatives in 1986, where he served on numerous committees including the House Budget Committee; House Agricultural Committee; Select Committee on Hunger; Sub-Committee on Cotton, Rice & Sugar; Sub-Committee on Conservation, Credit and Rural Development; Consumer Relations & Nutrition Committee. In addition, he chaired the Domestic Task Force on Hunger. In 1993, Espy was appointed secretary of agriculture by President Bill Clinton, the first African American to hold this post. However, Espy quickly became the subject of a federal ethics investigation into charges that he accepted gifts from companies that were regulated by the agency he headed. Although he denied any wrongdoing, Espy resigned his post on December 31, 1994. Nearly one year later, charges developed that Espy, while still a cabinet member, had improperly approached an agribusiness lobbyist for money, asking him to help pay

Julian Dixon (AP/Wide World Photos, Inc.)

off a debt incurred by his brother, who had unsuccessfully run for a House seat.

Espy was the object of a four-year investigation by an independent counsel who charged him with thirty counts of political corruption. The investigation was based on allegations of accepting $33,000 in free gifts, sports tickets, and expensive meals from companies that sought to benefit from good relations with Espy in their dealings with the Department of Agriculture. Espy was exonerated in December 1998 when the jury returned not guilty verdicts on all the counts.

Espy practices law in Mississippi. He is affiliated with the American Bar Association, Mississippi Trial Lawyers Association, and National Conference of Black Leaders, and is on the board of directors of the Jackson Urban League.

Chaka Fattah (1956–)

State Legislator, Civil Rights Activist

Born as Arthur Davenport in Philadelphia, Pennsylvania, on November 21, 1956, Fattah was renamed after the legendary Zulu warrior Chaka by his mother, who with her husband, took new Swahili root names to represent their African heritage. Fattah's mother, Falaka Fattah started the nationally known youth program House of Umoja as a means of combating and controlling gangs. At the age of 14 in an effort to assist his mother, Fattah received twenty abandoned houses in the neighborhood after giving a slide presentation and written proposal to the First Pennsylvania Bank. Falaka Fattah used the structures to expand the growing House of Umoja youth program.

Fattah continued to help with the youth program while in high school. With the help of Congressman Bill Gray, Fattah won a federal grant to renovate the houses. Meanwhile at Overbrook High School, Fattah organized the Youth Movement to Clean Up Politics. After attending the Community College of Philadelphia, the University of Pennsylvania, and Wharton Community Education Program, Fattah worked as a special assistant to the managing director of the Office of Housing and Community Development in Philadelphia for two years.

Then in 1982, Fattah decided to run for the Pennsylvania House of Representatives and became the youngest man ever elected to the Pennsylvania General Assembly at the age of 25. While serving as a representative, Fattah earned a master's degree in government administration from Fels School for State and Local Government at the University of Pennsylvania. In 1988, Fattah won an election for state senator in the Seventh District. As a state senator, Fattah raised money for the city of Philadelphia and pioneered programs to rebuild 100 of the country's deteriorating cities. In 1994, Fattah won a seat in the U.S. House of Representatives. He has won an "outstanding contribution award" from the Pennsylvania House of Representatives and the Simpson Fletcher Award for religion and race.

Walter E. Fauntroy (1933–)

Federal Legislator, Religious Leader, Civil Rights Activist

Born February 6, 1933, Walter E. Fauntroy represented the District of Columbia in the House of Representatives from 1971 until 1990. He was Washington, DC, coordinator for the March on Washington for Jobs and Freedom in 1963, coordinator for the Selma to Montgomery March in 1965, and national coordinator for the Poor People's Campaign in 1969. Fauntroy served as chairman of the caucus task force for the 1972 Democratic National Committee and of the platform committee of the National Black Political Convention. He was the chief architect of legislation in 1973 that permitted the District of Columbia to elect its own mayor and city council and engineered the passage by both the House and Senate of a constitutional amendment calling for full congressional representation for District of Columbia residents in the U.S. Congress.

Michael Espy (AP/Wide World Photos, Inc.)

During his tenure in the House of Representatives, Fauntroy built a record of achievement by playing key roles in the mobilization of African American political power from the National Black Political Convention in 1972 to the presidential elections of 1972 and 1976. For 15 years, Fauntroy chaired a bipartisan congressional task force on Haiti. In November of 1984, Fauntroy and two prominent national leaders launched the "Free South Africa Movement" with their arrest at the South African embassy. He served as co-chair of the steering committee of the FSAM. He was a member of the House Select Committee on Narcotics Abuse and Control and co-sponsored the 1988 $2.7 billion anti-drug bill.

In the 95th Congress Fauntroy was a member of the House Select Committee on Assassinations and chairman of its Subcommittee on the Assassination of Martin Luther King Jr. He was a ranking member of the House Banking, Finance, and Urban Affairs Committee and chairman of its Subcommittee on Government Affairs and Budget. He was also the first ranking member of the House District Committee.

Fauntroy was the recipient of several awards during his political career. In 1984, he was presented with the Hubert H. Humphrey Humanitarian Award by the National Urban Coalition. He also received honorary degrees from Georgetown University Law School, Yale University, and Virginia Union University. After leaving public service, Fauntroy founded Project We Care, a social service located in the Washington, DC, area. The project is comprised of teams of ministers and church members who canvass neighborhoods in order to serve as conduits between residents and the city. Fauntroy also began his own company.

Fauntroy contracted tuberculosis in the mid 1990s. Through a diligent regimen, however, he remained healthy and actually became an unofficial spokesperson for the disease, urging the public to get tested. Then a discovery was made that he had incorrectly listed a church donation on a disclosure form presented to the Congress. In 1995, Fauntroy was sentenced to a two-year probation, $1,000 fine, and 300 hours of community service after pleading guilty to a misdemeanor charge of falsifying a financial report to Congress.

Gary A. Franks (1953–)

Federal Legislator, Organization Executive

Gary Franks was born February 9, 1953, in Waterbury, Connecticut. He received a B.A. from Yale University in 1975. Before being elected to the U.S. House of Representatives, Franks was active in local politics and business. He was president of GAF Realty in Waterbury. Franks was also on the Board of Alderman, vice-chairman of the Zoning Board, a member of the Environmental Control Commission, director of the Naugatuck (Connecticut) chapter of the American Red Cross, president of the Greater Waterbury Chamber of Commerce, and a member of the Waterbury Foundation.

In 1991, Franks was elected to the U.S. House of Representatives, thus becoming the only African American Republican in the House until J. C. Watts was elected in 1995. Franks served on the Armed Services Committee, Small Business Committee, and the Select Committee on Aging. In 1993, he was appointed to the highly prized House Energy and Commerce Committee.

Franks has fulfilled a controversial role, that of an African American opposed to affirmative action and other programs based on preference for women and minorities. With such views, Franks had his share of congressional ruckuses. Formerly the only Republican member of the Congressional Black Caucus, he was actually voted out of the organization in 1993 by members who did not consider Franks a legitimate African American spokesperson. In 1994, Franks testified in support of a lawsuit to dismantle the African American-majority 11th Congressional District of Cynthia McKinney, an African American Democrat from Georgia. Franks and his political cohorts felt that the district had been improperly designed to increase African American voting strength in the area at the expense of the white electorate.

Franks was known as one of the Republican party's most prominent African American lawmakers. He entered the political landscape at a time when African American Republicans were nonexistent as members of the Senate and absent at municipal and state levels as mayors of major American cities or governors of any states. He was defeated in 1997 after serving three terms. Franks has been named the 1980 Outstanding Young Man by the Boy's Club and Man of the Year by the Negro Professional Women's Club.

Lenora Fulani (1950–)

Political Party Leader, Psychologist, Social Therapist

Born Lenora Branch on April 25, 1950, in Chester, Pennsylvania, she changed her name to Lenora Branch Fulani in 1973. She received a B.S. from Hofstra University. She furthered her education in social therapy with a M.S.T. from Columbia University Teachers College and a Ph.D. from the New York Institute for Social Therapy and Research. Affiliated with the Institute, Fulani opened her own therapy practice in Harlem in the 1970s, the Eastside Center for Short Term Psychotherapy. Concurrently, she founded the National Alliance Party (NAP), a political party for social change.

Fulani has made bids for election as lieutenant governor of New York in 1982 and governor in 1986 and 1990. She also campaigned for election as mayor of New York City in 1985. In 1988 and 1992, she campaigned for election as president of the United States. She made history in 1988 when she became the first woman and the first African American to be included on the presidential ballot in all 50 states. In 1992, she became the first woman to qualify for federal primary matching funds to run her campaign. In 1994, she made a run again for governor of New York, garnering 21 percent of the votes in the primary. Following her gubernatorial defeat, Fulani contributed to the formation of the Patriot Party. The Patriot Party planned to gain wide-range support by appealing to voters independent of the two main political parties in the 1996 elections. The formation of this party was followed by Fulani's creation of the Committee for a Unified Independent Party.

Fulani has written widely on the subject of politics. She wrote *Independent Black Leadership in America* in 1990, and *The Making of a Fringe Candidate.* in 1992. In the mid 1990s, her newspaper column, "This Way for Black Empowerment" was carried in more than 140 newspapers nationwide. She is the founder and executive producer of the "All-Stars Talent Show," the largest anti-violence program for inner city youth in the country. She hosted her own cable television show *Fulani!*, which aired in more twenty cities nationwide each week. Fulani remains a leading advocate for the Reform Party and chairs the Committee for a Unified Independent Party.

W. Wilson Goode (1938–)

Municipal Government Official

W. Wilson Goode was born on August 19, 1938, in Seaboard, North Carolina. He received a B.A. in 1961 from Morgan State University. Goode served in the U.S. Army from 1961 to 1963, where he earned a commendation medal for meritorious service and the rank of captain with the military police. In 1968, he earned a M.P.A. from the University of Pennsylvania's Wharton School.

Between 1966 and 1978 Goode held a wide variety of positions including probation officer, building maintenance supervisor, insurance claims adjuster, and president of the Philadelphia Council for Community Advancement. From 1978 until 1980, Goode was chairman of the Pennsylvania Public Utilities Commission and

W. Wilson Goode (AP/Wide World Photos, Inc.)

was managing director of the City of Philadelphia from 1980 to 1982. In 1983, Goode was elected the first African American mayor of Philadelphia.

Goode's tenure as mayor of Philadelphia was marred by charges that he was a weak and ineffective leader who was unable to handle the traditionally rough and tumble politics of Philadelphia city government. In May of 1985, during a violent confrontation between the city of Philadelphia and members of MOVE, a radical "back-to-nature" cult that took over a row house in West Philadelphia, Goode ordered police to drop a bomb on the roof of the house to evict MOVE members. A massive explosion and fire resulted that killed 11 people, destroyed 61 homes, and caused $8 million dollars in damage.

Goode barely won reelection in 1987 and was faced with mounting problems. Decades of corruption, racial tension, and urban decay had dampened Philadelphia's civic spirit and created a sense of apathy. Acute tensions between Goode and the city council resulted in a huge budget deficit. In September of 1990, Goode announced that the city was on the verge of bankruptcy. Although a consortium of banks helped to avert disaster, Philadelphia reported a massive $200 million deficit in June of 1991.

Barred by law from seeking a third term, Goode was succeeded as mayor by Edward Rendell in January of 1992. That same year, he wrote his autobiography *In Goode Faith*. After leaving office, Goode started his own company.

William Gray (AP/Wide World Photos, Inc.)

William H. Gray III (1941–)

Politician, United Negro College Fund President, Special Envoy to Haiti

Born to a minister and a high school teacher in Baton Rouge, Louisiana, on August 20, 1941, William H. Gray III earned a B.A. from Franklin and Marshall College in 1963, serving during his senior year as an intern for Pennsylvania congressman Robert N. C. Nix. He received a masters of divinity from Drew Theological School in 1966 and a masters of theology from Princeton Theological Seminary in 1970. He also attended the University of Pennsylvania, Temple University, and Oxford University.

Gray served as assistant pastor at Union Baptist Church in Montclair, New Jersey, from 1964 until 1966. He was promoted to senior pastor in 1966 and served in this capacity until 1972. Gray moved to Philadelphia in 1972 to become pastor of Bright Hope Baptist Church.

In 1976, Gray decided to become involved in politics, challenging Robert N. C. Nix for his congressional seat. His first attempt to unseat Nix was unsuccessful. However, in 1978, Gray defeated Nix and was elected to Congress. He became a vocal and influential member of the House, challenging the administration of Ronald

Reagan on such issues as social spending and U.S. support for the government of South Africa. He served on the House Budget Committee, becoming chair in 1985 and earned the admiration and respect of even his most implacable political foes. Gray was a member of the House Foreign Affairs Committee for twelve years. For ten of those twelve years, he served on the Appropriations Subcommittee on Foreign Operations. He was also vice-chair of the Congressional Black Caucus. Gray left the House of Representatives in 1991 to head the United Negro College Fund.

On May 8, 1994, President Bill Clinton appointed Gray as his special envoy to Haiti. In this capacity, Gray played an instrumental role in the eventual removal of Haiti's brutal military government in October of 1994.

Patricia Roberts Harris (1924–1985)

Organization Executive, Diplomat, Civil Rights Activist, Federal Government Official, Attorney, Educator

Born in Mattoon, Illinois, on May 31, 1924, Harris received her undergraduate degree in 1945 from Howard University. While at Howard, Harris also served as vice-chairman of a student branch of the NAACP and was involved in early nonviolent demonstrations against racial discrimination. Harris worked for the YWCA in Chicago and served as executive director of Delta Sigma Theta, an African American sorority, from 1953 to 1959. After completing post-graduate work at the University of Chicago and at American University, in 1960, she earned her Ph.D. in jurisprudence from George Washington University Law School in 1960.

An attorney and professor before she entered politics, Harris was appointed co-chairman of the National Women's Committee on Civil Rights by President John F. Kennedy and later was named to the Commission on the Status of Puerto Rico. In 1965, Harris was chosen by President Lyndon B. Johnson to become U.S. ambassador to Luxembourg, the first African American woman ever to be named an American envoy. In 1969 Harris was appointed dean of the Howard University Law School and served in that role until 1970 when she was selected to join a major Washington, DC, law firm.

Harris served as secretary of the Department of Health and Human Services and also secretary of Housing and Urban Development under President Jimmy Carter. Under President Ronald Reagan, she served as ambassador to Luxembourg, becoming the first African American woman to hold this diplomatic rank in U.S. history. Harris was also the first African American woman to serve in a cabinet post. In 1982, Harris ran an unsuccessful campaign for mayor of Washington, DC. She became a law professor at George Washington University in 1983 and remained there until her death from cancer on March 23, 1985.

Jesse L. Jackson, Jr. (1965–)

United States Congressman, Civil Rights Activist, Organization Executive, Author

U.S. Representative Jesse Louis Jackson, Jr. was born to the Reverend Jesse and Jacqueline (Davis) Jackson, Sr. on March 11, 1965, in Greenville, South Carolina. He attended Le Mans Academy and St. Albans Episcopal Prep School. After completing his secondary education, Jackson entered North Carolina Agricultural and Technical University in Greensboro, where he graduated magna cum laude in 1987 with a bachelor of science degree in business management. Three years later, he earned the master of arts degree in theology from Chicago Theological Seminary. Jackson continued his education and received the juris doctorate from the University of Illinois College of Law in 1993. Two years before completing his juris doctorate, Jackson married Sandra Lee Stevens.

In 1986, Jackson was arrested for taking part in a demonstration against apartheid at the South African embassy in Washington, DC. He also participated in protests held in front of the South African consulate in Chicago, Illinois. Jackson's long-time stance against South Africa's system of racial discrimination provided him the unique opportunity of being the only American to share the platform with Nelson Mandela, the major symbol of the struggle for human rights in the Republic of South Africa, following Mandela's February of 1990 release from prison.

During the Democratic National Convention in 1988, Jackson was the last of his siblings to introduce his father, the Reverend Jesse Jackson, Sr. The younger Jackson's introduction of his father catapulted him to a successful public speaking career. While pursuing his law degree, Jackson, Jr. frequently campaigned for Democratic candidates. After graduating from the University of Illinois College of Law, he became the national field director for the Rainbow Coalition, a political action band conceived by the Reverend Jackson, Sr. While serving in this position, Jackson established a nationwide non-aligned program that successfully registered a multitude of new voters. He also inaugurated a voter education program to educate citizens about the importance of participating in the political system including how to utilize technology to win at the polls and to more effectively participate in the political arena. Additionally, he established new local chapters of Operation Push (People United to Save Humanity).

Jackson, born during the African American struggle to obtain the ballot, resigned his position at the Rainbow Coalition in 1995. A Democrat, he entered the world of politics as a candidate for Chicago's Second Congressional District, a seat previously held by Mel Reynolds. After winning the primary and general elections, Representative Jesse L. Jackson, Jr. became a member of the 104th Congress in the U.S. House of Representatives on December 12, 1995. Jackson co-wrote the book, *Legal Lynching* with his father in 1996.

Self-described as "a public servant—not a politician—with a progressive agenda," Representative Jackson is part of a new generation of African American leaders who see their work as an extension of their parents' struggle to eradicate the remaining covert vestiges of discrimination.

Maynard Jackson (1938–)
Attorney, Municipal Government Official, Organization Executive

Jackson was born on March 23, 1938, in Dallas, Texas. At the age of 14 he was admitted to Morehouse College as a Ford Foundation Early Admissions Scholar. He graduated with a B.A. in 1956, with a concentration in history and political science. After graduation, he worked for the Ohio State Bureau of Unemployment Compensation as claims examiner from 1957 to 1958 and as a sales manager and associate district sales manager for P. F. Collier Inc. from 1958 to 1961.

In 1964, Jackson received a J.D. from the North Carolina Central University School of Law and then worked as a lawyer for the National Labor Relations Board. In 1968 and 1969 Jackson was named the managing attorney and director of community relations for the Emory Community Legal Service Center in Atlanta and was a senior partner in the law firm of Jackson, Patterson & Parks from 1970 to 1973.

Jackson had been active in Democratic politics and was the vice-mayor of Atlanta from 1970 to 1974. In 1974, he was elected mayor. At the time of his election to Atlanta's highest office, Jackson was the youngest mayor of a major U.S. city. He remained mayor of Atlanta until 1982. Jackson returned to private life and worked as a bond lawyer before being reelected mayor of Atlanta in 1989. The selection of Atlanta as host of the 1994 Super Bowl and the site of the 1996 Summer Olympic Games were two of the greatest achievements of Jackson's second term.

In 1993, Jackson vetoed domestic partnership legislation claiming that the City Council did not provide details on funding benefits for partners of city employees. The response of the gay and lesbian community was fervent, as leaders of forty Atlanta-based lesbian and gay organizations coordinated a barrage of protest actions during that year's Fourth of July holiday. Jackson was also deluged with complaints from angry city taxpayers who felt that Jackson's decision to order more than $45,000 worth of furniture for the mayor's office was government waste in action. Jackson admitted that city purchasing guidelines had not been followed.

Even after leaving office, Jackson has fallen into controversy. Accusations were levied against him that while he was in office, he improperly influenced the manner in which a $1.3 billion financial portfolio was invested as a city audit revealed that nearly 80 percent of the city's 1993 investments were turned over to a firm whose principal was Jackson's 1989 campaign treasurer. Jackson emphatically denied the allegations that he swayed any investment decisions.

Despite the alleged improprieties, Jackson earned a reputation as an aggressive and outspoken mayor. He had the difficult task of leading Atlanta through the difficult transition years from predominantly white leadership to a mixed power structure. Under Jackson's leadership Atlanta made serious gains as a financial center and distribution hub. Expanded international convention facilities turned Atlanta into a major convention center. In 1981, the prestigious *Almanac of Places Rated* named Atlanta the best major city in which to live and work. Jackson had taken advantage of affirmative action programs to improve city housing and social conditions. He also transformed the mass transit system into one of the most modern in the country.

Shortly after his last term, Jackson became chairman of the board and a majority stockholder in Jackson Securities Inc., a banking firm. He also holds interest in Jackmont Hospitality, a group of real estate company that hoped to stimulate the economy of some of Atlanta's depressed areas. In 1995, Jackson became the principal owner of a joint venture to operate a TGI Friday's restaurant at the city's Hartfield International Airport. Many complained that Jackson's use of Atlanta's affirmative action program to land the premier location was an abuse of a system designed to aid the disadvantaged.

Jackson has served as vice-chairman of the White House Committee on Balanced Growth & Economic Development and the White House Committee on the Windfall Profits Tax. He is also the founding chairman of the Atlanta Economic Development Corporation and the chairman of the Atlanta Urban Residential Finance Authority. Jackson belongs to the Georgia and New York Bar Associations, the National League of Cities, and the National Black Caucus of Local Elected Officials.

In 1975, Jackson was named to *Time* magazine's list of 200 young American leaders and *Ebony* magazine's list of 100 Most Influential Black Americans in 1976. In 1994, Jackson and six other Morehouse graduates were honored at the college's sixth annual Candle in the Dark awards dinner.

Sheila Jackson Lee (1950–)
Federal Legislator

Jackson Lee was born in Queens in 1950 and was raised in New York City. She graduated in 1972 from Yale University with a B.A. and then, in 1975, graduated from the University of Virginia Law School with a J.D. Her husband was an official at the University of Houston, and Jackson Lee began her practice in Texas.

Jackson Lee became an associate judge in the Houston court system in 1987, and three years later was elected to the city council. In 1994, she defeated an incumbent Democrat in the congressional primary and was then elected to the seat once held by Barbara Jordan.

Jackson Lee has been associated with Congresswoman Maxine Waters and is a member of the Congressional Black Caucus. In 1997, she was named the caucus's whip. Jackson Lee served on the House Judiciary Committee that impeached President Clinton and made a name for herself as one of the President's staunchest defenders.

Barbara Jordan (1936–1996)
Educator, Federal Legislator, Civil Rights Activist, State Legislator, Attorney

Barbara Jordan was born on February 21, 1936, in Houston, Texas. Afflicted with multiple sclerosis, she died of viral pneumonia, a complication of leukemia, on January 17, 1996.

Jordan attended Phillis Wheatley High School, and in 1952, graduated as a member of the Honor Society. In 1956, Jordan an received a B.A. from Texas Southern University in history and political science. She went on to Boston University, where she earned a J.D. in 1959. After teaching at Tuskegee Institute for one year, Jordan returned to Houston, where she practiced law and was appointed administrative assistant to a Harris County judge.

In 1966, Jordan was elected to the Texas Senate. She was the first African American to serve as president *pro tem* of that body and to chair the important Labor and Management Relations Committee.

In 1972, Jordan was elected to the U.S. House of Representatives, thus becoming the first African American woman from a southern state elected to Congress. As a member of Congress, she served on the Judiciary Committee which heard the impeachment proceedings of President Richard M. Nixon and was the first African American selected as the keynote speaker at the Democratic National Convention in 1976. While a representative, Jordan served on the House Judiciary and Government Operations committees. During her terms in both the Texas Senate and U.S. House, Jordan was known as a champion of civil rights for all and especially minorities and the poor.

Barbara Jordan speaking at the 1976 Democratic National Convention (AP/Wide World Photos, Inc.).

From 1979 to 1982, Jordan taught at the Lyndon Baines Johnson School of Public Affairs at the University of Texas. In 1982, she was made holder of the Lyndon Baines Johnson Centennial Chair of National Policy, a post she held until her death. After 15 years out of politics, Jordan was appointed as chair of the U.S. Commission on Immigration Reform by U.S. president Bill Clinton in 1993. Jordan was credited for her efforts to address the burgeoning U.S. hostility towards immigrants.

Jordan co-authored two books, *Barbara Jordan: A Self-Portrait* (1979) and *The Great Society: A Twenty Year Critique* (1986). She also served on the Democratic Caucus Steering and Policy Committee, and in 1976 and 1992, she was the keynote speaker at the Democratic National Convention.

Jordan belonged to the American Bar Association as well as the Texas, Massachusetts, and District of Columbia bars. She was a member of the Character Counts Coalition, a group whose aim is to address the values of

American society, particularly emphasizing youth. She had been on the board of directors of the Mead Corporation and the Henry J. Kaiser Family Foundation. Jordan is the recipient of a long list of awards and honors including the 1984 Eleanor Roosevelt Humanities Award, membership in the Texas Women's Hall of Fame (public service category 1984), listing in both the *Ladies Home Journal* "100 Most Influential Women in America" and *Time* magazine's 1976 "Ten Women of the Year" list. She was bestowed the nation's highest civilian honor in 1994 when President Clinton gave her the Presidential Medal of Freedom for her distinguished career in public service. Jordan had also received 27 honorary doctorate degrees. The LBJ School of Public Affairs has named an endowed chair in her honor and the Barbara Jordan Forum each year in February around the time of her birthday.

Sharon Pratt Kelly (1944–)

Attorney, Municipal Government Official, Media Executive, Educator

Kelly was born Sharon Pratt in Washington, DC, on January 30, 1944. For a time, she worked under the name Sharon Pratt Dixon, assuming the surname of her former husband. She graduated from Howard University with a B.A. in political science in 1965 and received a J.D. in 1968. In 1967, she edited the Howard University Law School Journal.

From 1970 through 1971, Kelly was the house counsel for the Joint Center for Political Studies in Washington, DC. Between 1971 and 1976 she was an associate in the law firm of Pratt and Queen. During this time she also taught at Antioch Law School. In 1976, Kelly began a 14 year association with the Potomac Electric Power Company. While there, she held increasingly responsible positions including associate general counsel, director of consumer affairs, and vice president of public policy.

In 1990, Kelly left the private sector to win the office of mayor of Washington, DC. In doing so she became the first African American woman elected mayor of a major American city. She was not able to deliver on campaign promises to reform city government and to fire 2,000 middle managers in the DC bureaucracy. Her relations with the Democratic Congress were strained and Kelly's administration was perceived as ineffective which helped pave the way for her defeat and the comeback of former Mayor Marion Barry.

In 1976 and 1977, Kelly was general counsel to the Washington, DC Democratic Committee. Between 1985 and 1989, she was treasurer of the Democratic Party and has also sat as a national committeewoman on the Washington DC Democratic State Committee.

Kelly belongs to the American Bar Association and the Washington, DC Women's Bar Association. She is affiliated with the Legal Aid Society, the American Civil Liberties Union, and the United Negro College Fund. Kelly was a Falk Fellow at Howard University and has received numerous awards including the 1983 NAACP Presidential Award, the 1985 United Negro College Fund's Distinguished Leadership Award, and the 1986 Distinguished Service Award presented by the Federation of Women's Clubs.

Alan L. Keyes (1950–)

Federal Government Official, Lecturer, Author

Alan Lee Keyes was born on August 7, 1950, in New York City. Keyes lived in the United States and Italy during his childhood. He began his political career by serving as president of his high school's student council and as the first African American president of the American Legion Boys Nation. Keyes earned a B.A. from Harvard in 1972. He received his Ph.D. in political science from Harvard in 1979.

Following his graduate work, Keyes took a position at the U.S. State Department in 1978. He won Jeane Kirkpatrick as a mentor by defending her from verbal attack while serving as U.S. vice-consul in India. At the State Department, Keyes served in the South African Affairs Division, on the Policy Planning Council, in UNESCO (the United Nations Educational, Scientific, and Cultural Organization), and as an assistant secretary of state for International Organizational Affairs. Keyes was the African American of highest station at the State Department in 1987, but he resigned over a dispute over allocation of U.S. funds to the United Nations.

In 1988 and 1992, Keyes lost senatorial elections in Maryland. In between, he served as president of the Washington, DC, organization Citizens Against Government Waste from 1989 to 1991. He also served as interim president in 1991 for Alabama A & M University. In 1992, following his second defeat, Keyes started his own talk radio show in Baltimore, *America's Wake-Up Call: The Alan Keyes Show*. Bolstered by the response to his radio show, Keyes announced his candidacy for the U.S. presidency on March 26, 1995. In so doing, he became the first Republican African American in the twentieth century to run for president. He attracted little support, however, and did not win a primary.

Ron Kirk (1954–)

Attorney, Municipal Government Official

Ron Kirk was born on June 27, 1954, in Austin, Texas. He received a B.A. in political science and sociology from Austin College in 1976, during which time he served in 1974 as a legislative aide to the Texas Constitutional Convention. This experience prompted an interest in politics and drove him to complete his law degree in 1979 at the University of Texas School of Law. After two years, Kirk was unsatisfied as a private practice attorney. He moved to Washington, DC, to work for U.S. Senator Lloyd Bentsen from 1981 to 1983. He returned to Dallas in 1983 to work for the Dallas City Attorney's Office and became the chief lobbyist of Dallas until 1989. He then worked for the firm of Johnson & Gibbs and volunteered for Big Brothers/Big Sisters of America, the Dallas Zoological Society, Dallas Helps, and the North Texas Food Bank among other organizations. In 1994, Kirk took over the Texas secretary of state position from John Hannah. Kirk was elected the mayor of Dallas in 1995 with 62 percent of the vote.

As mayor, Kirk maintains his role as a partner in the law firm of Gardere & Wynn. He was honored in 1992 with a Volunteer of the Year Award from Big Brothers/ Big Sisters and a Distinguished Alumni Award from the Austin College Alumni Association. He was named Citizen of the Year by Omega Psi Phi in 1994, the same year that he earned the C. B. Bunkley Community Service Award from the Turner Legal Association.

John Mercer Langston (1829–1897)

Educational Administrator, Federal Legislator, Diplomat, Attorney, Lecturer

Congressman John Mercer Langston was born in Virginia in 1829. Upon the death of his father, Langston was emancipated and sent to Ohio, where he was given over to the care of a friend of his father. Langston spent his childhood there, attending private school in Cincinnati before graduating in 1849 from Oberlin College. Four years later, after getting his degree from the theological department of Oberlin, he studied law and was admitted to the Ohio bar.

Langston began his practice in Brownhelm, Ohio. He was chosen in 1855 to serve as clerk of this township by the Liberty Party. During the Civil War, he was a recruiting agent for African American servicemen, helping to organize such regiments as the 54th and 55th Massachusetts, and the 5th Ohio. In 1867, Langston served as inspector-general of the Freedmen's Bureau and as dean and vice president of Howard University from 1868 to 1875. In 1877 he was named minister resident to Haiti and *charge d'affaires* to Santo Domingo, remaining in diplomatic service until 1885.

Soon after returning to his law practice in the United States, Langston was named president of the Virginia Normal and Collegiate Institute. In 1888, he was elected to Congress from Virginia, but was not seated for two years until vote-counting irregularities had been investigated. He was defeated in his bid for a second term. In 1894 Langston wrote an autobiography, *From the Virginia Plantation to the National Capital.* Langston died in 1897.

George Thomas "Mickey" Leland (1944–1989)

Civil Rights Activist, Federal Legislator, Educator

Leland was born on November 27, 1944, in Lubbock, Texas. He graduated from Texas Southern University in 1970 with a B.S. in pharmacy. Leland had been active in the Civil Rights movement during his student years, and he was elected to the Texas state legislature in 1973. In 1978 he was elected to the U.S. House of Representatives to fill Barbara Jordan's vacated seat. While a representative, Leland served on various committees including Interstate and Foreign Commerce, Post Office and Civil Service, and the committee on the District of Columbia.

In spite of serving on these committees, Leland was devoted to easing the hunger of starving persons in the United States and in other countries, especially African countries. He chaired the House Select Committee on World Hunger and visited starving peoples throughout Africa. In 1989, while traveling to a United Nations refugee camp in Ethiopia the plane on which Leland was traveling crashed near Gambela, Ethiopia, killing all on board.

John Robert Lewis (1940–)

Civil Rights Activist, Federal Legislator, Organization Executive

Committed to nonviolence and the advancement of African Americans, John Lewis was born in Troy, Alabama on February 21, 1940. He received a B.S. in 1961 from the American Baptist Theological Seminary and a B.A. from Fisk University in 1967. Before entering politics Lewis was associated with numerous social activist organizations including the Student Non-Violent Coordinating Committee. He served as associate director of the Field Foundation, project director of the Southern Regional Council, and executive director of the Voter Education Project Inc. beginning in 1970.

In 1982, Lewis was elected Atlanta City Councilman-at-Large, and voters sent him to the U.S. House of Representatives as a Democrat in 1986. While in the House, Lewis has served on the Public Works, Interior and Insular Affairs committees as well as the powerful House Ways and Means Committee. He has also been a member of the Select Committee on Aging. Lewis's pet

Mickey Leland (AP/Wide World Photos, Inc.)

John Lewis

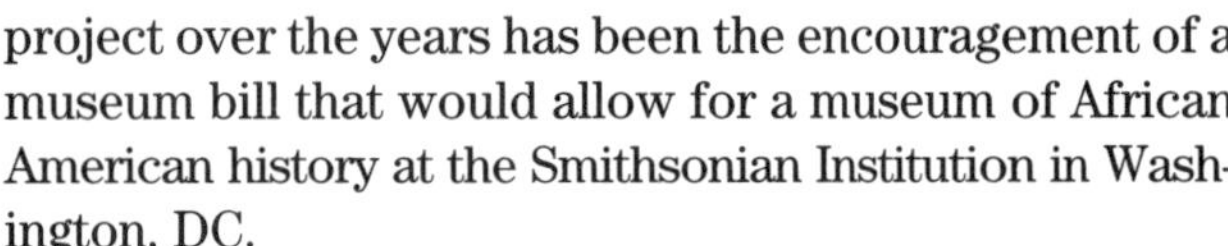

project over the years has been the encouragement of a museum bill that would allow for a museum of African American history at the Smithsonian Institution in Washington, DC.

Lewis denounced the rhetoric of his homophobic colleagues during a House debate that ultimately led to the adoption of legislation to discourage homosexual enlistment in the military. He considered the Republican "Contract With America" as the genesis of a wave of intolerance in American society in the early to mid-1990s. In 1995, Lewis headed a group of nearly 100 trade unionists who interrupted a speech on proposed Medicare changes by House Speaker Newt Gingrich during a conference sponsored by the Congressional Institute. Many of Lewis's critics suggested that the demonstration did little but gain media attention, but Lewis countered that saving Medicare benefits for the elderly was his priority, and he was willing to seize any opportunity to stir up a public debate.

In the 1960s, Lewis was known for his involvement with the U.S. Civil Rights movement. A strict follower of nonviolent social protest, Lewis was a organizer and participant in numerous sit-ins, freedom rides, and protest marches throughout the South. He abstained from the 1995 Million Man March because he felt that he could not participate in an effort led by Louis Farrakhan. Lewis worked steadfastly in the mid 1990s to help produce a spirit of racial harmony and team spirit in Atlanta as the city prepared for the 1996 Olympics.

Lewis is a recipient of the Martin Luther King Jr. Non-Violent Peace Prize and has been named to *Ebony*'s "One of the Nation's Most Influential Blacks" list (1991–92) and *Time* magazine's 1974 "One of America's Rising Leaders" list. He belongs to the Martin Luther King Jr. Center for Social Change, the National Democratic Institute for International Affairs, Friends of Vista, and the African-American Institute. He was elected president of Americans for Democratic Action.

Kweisi Mfume (1948–)
Federal Legislator, Educator, Civil Rights Activist, Organization Executive

Kweisi Mfume was born Fizzell Gray in Baltimore on October 24, 1948. Mfume once ran the streets and fathered five children out of wedlock. He turned to education and received a B.S. from Morgan State University in 1976, and an M.A. from Johns Hopkins University in 1984.

Kweisi Mfume (AP/Wide World Photos, Inc.)

In 1979, Mfume was elected to the Baltimore City Council by a margin of three votes. He worked hard to diversify city government, improve public safety, enhance minority business development, and divest city funds from South Africa. Active in Democratic politics, Mfume was a member of the Maryland Democratic State Central Committee and a delegate to the Democratic National Conventions in 1980, 1984, and 1988. Mfume was elected to the U.S. House of Representatives in 1987. During his tenure he served on the Banking, Finance and Urban Affairs Committee; the Small Business Committee; the Education and Labor Committee; and the Narcotics Abuse & Control subcommittee. The House speaker chose Mfume to serve on the Ethics Committee and on the Joint Economic Committee of the House and Senate. He also was vice-chair, and later chairperson, of the Congressional Black Caucus. In addition, Mfume was a member of the Caucus for Women's Issues, the Congressional Arts Caucus, and the Federal Government Service Task Force.

In February 1996, Mfume became president and CEO of the NAACP after the NAACP Board of Director unanimously elected him to that post. His priorities were to restore the confidence of members and supporters in this seminal organization, to ensure greater fiscal accountability, and to secure private sector funding. Within weeks of Mfume's appointment, Nissan Motor Corp USA donated $100,000 to the NAACP. Since assuming the chief executive position, Mfume has eliminated the association's debt; set new standards and expectations for NAACP branches nationwide, and diligently worked to engage seasoned local volunteers and a new generation of younger civil rights activists in the mission of the NAACP.

Mfume is a trustee of the Baltimore Museum of Art and the Morgan State University Board of Regents, where he previously taught political science and communications. He is also a member of the Senior Advisory Committee of Harvard's John F. Kennedy School of Government and the Board of Trustees for the Enterprise Foundation.

Arthur W. Mitchell (1883–1968)

Civil Rights Activist, Federal Legislator, Lecturer, Attorney, Organization Executive

Born to slave parents in 1883 in Chambers County, Alabama, Mitchell was educated at Tuskegee Institute and at Columbia and Harvard Universities. By 1929, he had founded Armstrong Agricultural School in West Butler, Alabama, and become a wealthy landowner and a lawyer with a thriving practice in Washington, DC. When he left the nation's capital that year, it was with the purpose of entering politics and becoming a representative from Illinois.

Mitchell won Democratic approval only after Harry Baker died suddenly. Aided by the overwhelming national sentiment for the Democratic Party during this period, he unseated Oscar De Priest by the slender margin of 3,000 votes. Mitchell's most significant victory on behalf of civil rights came, not in the legislative chamber, but in the courts. In 1937, Mitchell brought suit against the Chicago and Rock Island Railroad after having been forced to leave his first class accommodations en route to Hot Springs, Arkansas, and sit in a "Jim Crow" car. He argued his own case before the Supreme Court in 1941 and won a decision which declared Jim Crow practices illegal.

Mitchell proposed that states that discriminated against African Americans should receive fewer congressional seats and advocated strong sanctions against states that practiced lynching. Also, he worked for the elimination of poll taxes to make it easier for African Americans to vote. Following the end of World War II, Mitchell demonstrated that because African Americans fought bravely for the United States, they should be able to vote for their government representatives.

In 1942, Mitchell retired from Congress and continued to pursue his civil rights agenda as a private citizen. He also lectured occasionally and pursued farming on his estate near Petersburg, Virginia, where he died in 1968 at the age of 85.

Marc Morial (1958–)

Municipal Official

Morial was born in 1958 to a prominent, African American family in New Orleans. Morial received his B.A. in 1980 from the University of Pennsylvania and his J.D. three years later from the Georgetown University Law School.

Morial became a supporter of the Reverend Jesse L. Jackson, Sr. and worked for Jackson's 1988 campaign for president. In 1991, he was elected to the state Senate in Louisiana. Two years later he announced his candidacy for mayor of New Orleans. The election was marred by racial questions and a run-off was needed before Morial could be declared the winner.

Morial battled crime in his first term as mayor, introducing several innovative and controversial reforms within the police department. In 1998, he began his second term as mayor.

Carol Moseley-Braun (1947–)

Attorney, Federal Legislator

Born Carol Moseley in Chicago on August 16, 1947, Moseley-Braun received her B.A. from the University of Illinois in 1969 and her J.D. in 1972 from the University of Chicago Law School. While attending law school, Moseley-Braun worked as a legal intern and an associate attorney for a number of private law firms. After graduating from law school Moseley-Braun was an assistant U.S. attorney for the northern district of Illinois from 1973 until 1977. In 1979, Moseley-Braun was elected an Illinois state representative from the 25th district, where she became known as an ardent supporter of civil rights legislation. After a bid for the lieutenant governorship was thwarted, Moseley-Braun was elected in 1986 as the Cook County recorder of deeds.

In 1992 Moseley-Braun became the nation's first African American woman elected to the U.S. Senate, making her an icon of the "Year of the Woman." The following year, Moseley-Braun, along with Senator Dianne Feinstein, was selected for the formerly all-male Senate Judiciary Committee. Her first major legislative proposal—an amendment to an omnibus crime bill that would try young offenders implicated in serious crime from the age of 13 and up as adults—was overwhelmingly approved by the Senate.

A recipient of many honors, Moseley-Braun won the 1981 and 1982 Best Legislation Award presented by the Independent Voters of Illinois. She has also won the 1981 National Association of Negro Business & Professional Women's Clubs' Community Recognition Award, the 1981 Chicago Alliance of Black School Educators' Recognition of Excellence in Education Award, the 1982 Afro-American Voters Alliance Community Recognition Award, and a 1993 Essence Award for African American women of achievement. In 1993, she was chosen as the keynote speaker for the annual, prestigious National Urban League dinner. Moseley-Braun belongs to the League of Black Women; Operation PUSH; Federal, Illinois and Chicago Bar Association; and the Women's Political Caucus.

In spite of her national prominence, her celebrity status, and the numerous honors, Moseley-Braun's Senate career was dogged by ethical questions which often overshadowed her legislative record. Despite investigations which found no criminal wrongdoing on her part, Moseley-Braun was defeated. She is a consultant to the U.S. Department of Education.

Eleanor Holmes Norton (1938–)

Attorney, Federal Legislator, Civil Rights Activist, Organization Executive, Educator

Eleanor Norton was born Eleanor Holmes on April 8, 1938, in Washington, DC. She attended Antioch College in Ohio but transferred to Yale University and received an M.A. in American Studies in 1963 and a J.D. in 1964 from Yale's law school. After graduating from law school, Norton clerked for a federal judge in Philadelphia before joining the American Civil Liberties Union in 1965 as a litigator specializing in free speech issues. She stayed with the ACLU until 1970, reaching the position of assistant legal director and successfully arguing a First Amendment case before the U.S. Supreme Court. In 1970, she became chairwoman of the New York City Commission on Human Rights, a post she held until 1977, when she headed the Equal Employment Opportunity Commission. In 1981, she was a senior fellow at the Urban Institute. In 1982, she accepted the position of professor of law at Georgetown University. As a tenured professor, Norton still teaches at Georgetown. Norton had previously taught African American history at Pratt Institute in Brooklyn, New York, and law at New York City University Law School.

In 1990 Norton was elected congressional delegate to the U.S. House of Representatives for the District of Columbia. In 1993, the same year she sponsored legislation that would make Washington, DC, the 51st state, she was allowed to cast a vote in the full house, thus becoming the first resident of the district to vote on the floor of Congress. In 1995, however, the House voted to strip Washington, DC, of its floor-voting right. Norton protested that she was elected by federal tax-paying citizens who are entitled to full representation. A bipartisan alliance was formed among Norton, Republican House Speaker Newt Gingrich, and Democratic Washington, DC, Mayor Marion Barry in an effort to save home rule for the district.

Norton is the ranking minority member of the District of Columbia Subcommittee. She is also a member of the Transportation and Infrastructure Committee and the Government Reform and Oversight Committee.

Norton has been named to the *Ladies Home Journal* 1988 "One Hundred Most Important Women" list and the 1989 "One Hundred Most Powerful Women in Washington" list by *Washington* magazine. She is also a recipient of the 1985 Distinguished Public Service Award presented by the Center for National Policy.

Hazel O'Leary (1937–)

Attorney, Federal Government Official, Financial Planner

Hazel O'Leary was born Hazel Reid on May 17, 1937, in Newport News, Virginia. She graduated Phi Beta Kappa in 1959 from Fisk University with a B.A. She received her J.D. in 1966 from Rutgers University School of Law. O'Leary was a utilities regulator under Presidents Ford and Carter, an executive vice president of the Northern States Power Co., and a Washington lobbyist. A proponent of energy conservation and alternative energy sources, President Bill Clinton appointed her secretary of energy in 1993.

In addition to formulating energy policy, O'Leary worked to dismantle the nation's nuclear weaponry complex and to help energy producers finance nuclear-waste storage programs. Reorganizing the Department of Energy at the end of the Cold War was one of the first accountabilities assigned to O'Leary. O'Leary's campaigned to unveil the expansive network of secret atomic laboratories and weapons plants harbored in the nation. Results of Cold War nuclear tests, radiation releases, and experiments on civilians were also revealed. O'Leary also encouraged domestic resource development.

In the mid-1990s, O'Leary came under heavy scrutiny. First she was criticized for having spent thousands of government dollars on hiring a consultant firm to rank a number of reporters to find out which had given her the most favorable coverage. Then it was disclosed that she had spent much more than other cabinet members on overseas travel. Vice president Al Gore came to O'Leary's defense by noting that her trips had helped create new job opportunities in the United States. For example, O'Leary led a delegation of nearly one hundred aides, energy experts, and business leaders to South Africa to uncover possibilities in the newly democratic country.

O'Leary is a certified financial planner, a member of the New Jersey and Washington bars, and has been vice president and general counsel of O'Leary Associates in Washington, DC. In 1993, the Congressional Black Caucus honored O'Leary for her achievements. After completing her term as secretary of energy, O'Leary resigned and returned to the private sector.

Clarence McClane Pendleton, Jr. (1930–1988)

Federal Government Official, Organization Executive

Clarence Pendleton, Jr. was born in Louisville, Kentucky, on November 10, 1930. Raised in Washington, DC, he attended Dunbar High School and received a B.S. in 1954 from Howard University. Pendleton served three years in the U.S. Army and was assigned to a medical unit. After his discharge in 1957, Pendleton returned to Howard University where he received a masters degree in 1961 and coached swimming, football, rowing, and baseball.

In 1968, Pendleton became the recreation coordinator of the Baltimore Model Cities Program and became the director of the Urban Affairs Department of the National Recreation and Parks Association in 1970. Pendleton soon began attracting national attention and in 1972 he headed San Diego's Model Cities Program. In 1975 he became the director of the San Diego Urban League.

By 1980, a change took place in Pendleton's political philosophy. He began to feel that African Americans' reliance on government programs was trapping them in a cycle of dependence and welfare handouts. Pendleton believed that it was in the best interest of African Americans to build strong ties with a strong, expanding private sector and eschew the more traditional ties with liberal bureaucrats and liberal philosophies.

To this end he supported the election of Ronald Reagan to the presidency and was appointed chairman of the Civil Rights Commission by President Reagan in 1981. Pendleton's chairmanship was controversial mostly because of his opposition to affirmative action and forced busing as a means of desegregating schools. Pendleton retained a more liberal philosophy on other matters however by supporting the Equal Rights Amendment and the Voting Rights Act. Pendleton died unexpectedly of a heart attack on June 5, 1988, in San Diego.

Clarence M. Pendleton, Jr. speaking at a press conference in 1984.

Pinckney Benton Stewart Pinchback (1837–1921)

Attorney, Federal Legislator, State Government Official, Municipal Government Official

Pinchback was born in Macon, Georgia on May 10, 1837. Although his mother had been a slave, at Pinchback's birth she had been emancipated by Pinchback's father. Moving to Ohio with his mother, Pinchback attended high school in Cincinnati in 1847, and he began working on riverboats as a cabin boy and then as a steward in 1848.

At the outbreak of the Civil War, Pinchback went to Louisiana and in 1862 enlisted in the Union Army. He soon began recruiting soldiers for an African American unit known as the Louisiana Native Guards or the Corps d'Afrique. Racial problems soon arose with the military hierarchy and Pinchback resigned his commission in protest. After the war Pinchback became active in Louisiana politics. He organized a Republican Club in 1867, and was a delegate to a state constitutional convention in 1868. In that year he was also elected to the state senate and became president *pro-tempore* of that body in 1871. He became lieutenant governor of Louisiana through the line of political succession. In late 1872 and early 1873, Pinchback was governor of Louisiana while the elected official underwent impeachment proceedings. In 1872 and 1873 Pinchback was elected to the U.S. Senate and the U.S. House of Representatives. He was refused seating both times when the elections were contested and his Democratic opponent was named to Congress.

In 1877, Pinchback switched his allegiance to the Democratic Party and in 1882 was appointed surveyor of customs for New Orleans. In 1887, he began attending law school at Straight University in New Orleans and was later admitted to the bar. In 1890, Pinchback moved to Washington, DC, where he died December 21, 1921.

Adam Clayton Powell, Jr. (1908–1972)

Federal Legislator

Born on November 29, 1908, in New Haven, Connecticut, Powell was raised in New York City and graduated in 1930 from to Colgate University. In 1931, Powell graduated from Columbia University with a masters degree in religious education. Powell launched his career as a crusader for reform during the Depression. He forced several large corporations to drop their unofficial bans on employing African Americans and directed a kitchen and relief operation that fed, clothed, and provided fuel for thousands of Harlem's needy and destitute. He was instrumental in persuading officials of Harlem Hospital to integrate their medical and nursing staffs, helped many African Americans find employment along 125th Street, and campaigned against the city's bus lines, which were discriminating against Negro drivers and mechanics.

When Powell Sr. retired from Abyssinian Baptist Church in 1936, his son, who had already served as manager and assistant pastor there, was named his successor. In 1939, Powell served as chairman of the Coordinating Committee on Employment, which organized a picket line before the executive offices of the World's Fair in the Empire State Building and eventually succeeded in getting employment at the fair for hundreds of African Americans.

Powell won a seat on the New York City Council in 1941 with the third highest number of votes ever cast for a candidate in municipal elections. In 1942, he turned to journalism for a second time and published and edited the weekly *The People's Voice*, which he called "the largest Negro tabloid in the world." He became a member of the New York State Office of Price Administration in 1942 and served until 1944.

In 1944, Powell was elected to Congress and represented a constituency of 300,000, 89 percent of whom were African American. Identified at once as "Mr. Civil

Rights," he encountered a host of discriminatory procedures upon his arrival in the nation's capital. He could not rent a room or attend a movie in downtown Washington. Within Congress itself, he was not allowed to use such communal facilities as dining rooms, steam baths, showers, and barber shops. Powell met these rebuffs head on by making use of all such facilities and insisting that his entire staff follow his lead.

As a first-year legislator, Powell engaged in fiery debates with segregationists, fought for the abolition of discriminatory practices at U.S. military installations, and sought to deny federal funds to any project where discrimination existed. The latter effect was called the Powell amendment and eventually became part of the Flanagan School Lunch Bill, making Powell the first African American Congressman since Reconstruction to have legislation passed by both houses.

Powell also sponsored legislation advocating federal aid to education, a minimum-wage scale, and greater benefits for the chronically unemployed. He also drew attention to certain discriminatory practices on Capitol Hill and worked toward their elimination. It was Powell who first demanded that an African American journalist be allowed to sit in the Senate and House press galleries, introduced the first anti-Jim Crow transportation legislation, and the first bill to prohibit segregation in the armed forces. At one point in his career, the *Congressional Record* reported that the House Committee on Education and Labor had processed more important legislation than any other major committee. In 1960, Powell, as senior member of this committee, became its chairman. He had a hand in the development and passage of such significant legislation as the Minimum Wage Bill of 1961, the Manpower Development and Training Act, the Anti-Poverty Bill, the Juvenile Delinquency Act, the Vocational Educational Act, and the National Defense Education Act. The Powell committee helped pass 48 laws involving a total outlay of 14 billion dollars. Powell, however, was accused of putting an excessive number of friends on the congressional payroll, of a high rate of absenteeism from congressional votes, and of living a permissive lifestyle.

In 1967, the controversies and irregularities surrounding him led to censure in the House and a vote to exclude him from his seat in the 90th Congress. The House based its decision on the allegation that he had misused public funds and was in contempt of the New York courts due to a lengthy and involved defamation case which had resulted in a trial for civil and criminal contempt. Despite his exclusion, Powell was readmitted to the 91st Congress in 1968. In mid-1969, the Supreme Court ruled that the House had violated the Constitution by excluding him from membership.

However, rather than return to Congress, Powell spent most of his time on the West Indian island of Bimini, where process servers could not reach him. But photographers did and the ensuing photos of Powell vacationing on his boat while crucial votes were taken in Congress affected Powell in his home district. In 1970, he lost the Democratic Congressional primary to Charles Rangel by 150 votes. Powell retired from public office and worked as a minister at the Abyssinian Baptist Church. On April 4, 1972, Powell died in Miami.

Joseph H. Rainey (1832–1887)

Civil Rights Activist, Federal Legislator, Federal Government Official

Joseph H. Rainey, the first African American member of the House of Representatives, was born on June 21, 1832, in Georgetown, South Carolina. Rainey's father purchased his family's freedom and moved them to Charleston. During the Civil War, Rainey was drafted to work on Confederate fortifications in Charleston harbor and serve passengers on a Confederate ship. However, Rainey escaped with his wife to the West Indies and remained there until the end of the Civil War in 1865.

Rainey and his wife returned to South Carolina in 1866. In 1868, Rainey was elected as a delegate to the state constitutional convention and was elected to the State Senate in 1870. A year later, he was elected to the House of Representatives. As a member of Congress, Rainey presented some ten petitions for a civil rights bill which would have guaranteed African Americans full constitutional rights and equal access to public accommodations. On one occasion, Rainey dramatized the latter issue by refusing to leave the dining room of a hotel in Suffolk, Virginia. He was forcibly ejected from the premises. Rainey was a staunch supporter of legislation that prevented racial discrimination in schools, on public transportation, and in the composition of juries. He supported legislation that protected the civil rights of the Chinese minority in California and advocated the use of federal troops to protect African American voters from intimidation by the Ku Klux Klan. Rainey was reelected in 1872 and, during a debate on Indian rights in 1874, became the first African American representative to preside over a session of Congress. Rainey gained reelection to Congress in 1874 and 1876.

Rainey retired from Congress in 1879. He was appointed as a special agent for the U.S. Treasury Department in Washington, DC. He served there until 1881, after which he worked for a banking and brokerage firm. After the firm failed, Rainey took a job at a wood and coal factory. In 1886, he returned to Georgetown, where he died on August 2, 1887.

Charles Rangel (1930–)
Federal Legislator

Harlem-born Charles Rangel entered the national spotlight in 1970, when he defeated Adam Clayton Powell, Jr. for the Democratic nomination in New York's 18th Congressional District.

Born June 11, 1930, Rangel attended Harlem elementary and secondary schools before volunteering to serve in the U.S. Army during the Korean War. While stationed in Korea with the 2nd Infantry, he saw heavy combat and received the Purple Heart and the Bronze Star Medal for Valor, as well as U.S. and Korean Presidential citations. Discharged honorably as a staff sergeant, Rangel returned to finish high school and to study at New York University's School of Commerce, from which he graduated in 1957. In 1960, Rangel received his J.D. while on scholarship at St. John's University.

After being admitted to the bar, Rangel was appointed in 1961 as assistant U.S. attorney in the Southern District of New York. For the next five years, he worked as legal counsel to the New York City Housing and Redevelopment Board, as legal assistant to Judge James L. Watson, as associate counsel to the speaker of the New York State Assembly, and as general counsel to the National Advisory Commission on Selective Service. In 1966, Rangel was chosen to represent the 72nd District, Central Harlem, in the State Assembly. He has served as a member of, and secretary to, the New York State Commission on Revision of the Penal Law and Criminal Code.

In 1972, Rangel easily defeated Livingston Wingate in the Democratic primary and went on to an overwhelming victory in November. In 1974, he was elected chairperson of the Congressional Black Caucus. In his first term, he was appointed to the Select Committee on Crime and was influential in passing the 1971 amendment to the drug laws that authorized the president to cut off all military and economic aid to any country that refused to cooperate with the United States in stopping the international traffic in drugs. In 1976, Rangel, a leading congressional expert on the subject, was appointed to the Select Committee on Narcotics Abuse and Control.

Rangel served as chairperson of the Congressional Black Caucus from 1974 to 1975 and was a member of the Judiciary Committee when it voted to impeach U.S. President Richard M. Nixon. In 1975, he moved to the Ways and Means Committee, becoming the first African American to serve on the committee. Two years later, his colleagues in the New York Congressional delegation voted him the majority whip for New York State. Rangel, who has served as deputy whip for the House Democratic Leadership, was a speaker at the 1995 Million Man March.

Kenneth Reeves (1951–)
Municipal Government Official, Attorney

The first openly gay mayor in the state of Massachusetts, Reeves was popular enough to be elected to a second term in 1994, running on the promise to break down the barriers between city government and local political groups.

Born to Jamaican parents, Reeves grew up in a middle-class Detroit neighborhood. After high school, he attended Harvard. In college, he was active in community service, working at a housing development in Dorchester, Massachusetts. After graduation, Reeves traveled to the African nation of Benin, studying there for one year before returning to the United States. In 1976, he graduated from the University of Michigan Law School. Seeking a position in Cambridge, he was hired by the National Consumer Law Center. He ran for public office in a grass-root effort but lost. He opted to run for city council a second time and was elected in 1989. During that time he also founded the W. E. B. Du Bois Academy, a mentor program pairing established African American professional men with young African American males for intense tutoring sessions.

Hiram Rhodes Revels (1822–1901)
Federal Legislator

Hiram Rhodes Revels, a native of North Carolina, was the first African American to serve in the U.S. Senate. Revels was elected from his adopted state of Mississippi, and served for approximately one year, from February of 1870 to March of 1871.

Born in 1827, in Fayetteville, North Carolina, Revels was educated in Indiana and attended Knox College in Illinois. Ordained a minister in the African Methodist Church, he worked among African American settlers in Kansas, Maryland, Illinois, Indiana, Tennessee, Kentucky, and Missouri before settling in 1860 in Baltimore. There he served as a church pastor and school principal.

During the Civil War, Revels helped organize a pair of Negro regiments in Maryland, and went to St. Louis in 1863 to establish a freedmen school and to carry on his work as a recruiter. For a year he served as chaplain of a Mississippi regiment before becoming provost marshal of Vicksburg. Revels settled in Natchez, Mississippi, in 1866 and was appointed alderman by the Union military governor of the state. In 1870, Revels was elected to the U.S. Senate to replace Jefferson Davis, the former president of the Confederacy. Revels's appointment caused a

Hiram Rhodes Revels

storm of protest from white Southerners. However, Revels was allowed to take his seat in the Senate.

As a U.S. Senator, Revels quickly won the respect of many of his constituents for his alert grasp of state issues and for his courageous support of legislation which would have restored voting and office-holding privileges to disenfranchised Southerners. He believed that the best way for African Americans to gain their rightful place in American society was not through violent means, but by obtaining an education and leading an exemplary life of courage and moral fortitude. He spoke out against the segregation of Washington, DC's public school system and defended the rights of African Americans who were denied work at the Washington Navy Yard because of their race.

In 1871, Revels left the Senate. He was named president of Alcorn University near Lorman, Mississippi. He left Alcorn in 1873 to serve as Mississippi's secretary of state on an interim basis. In 1876, he returned to Alcorn. That year, he became editor of the *South-Western Christian Advocate*, a religious journal. In 1882, he retired from Alcorn University. Revels lived in Holly Springs, Mississippi, during his later years and taught theology at Shaw University. He died on January 16, 1901.

Norm Rice (1943–)
Municipal Government Official

Rice was born on May 4, 1943, in Denver, Colorado, and attended the University of Colorado. He was disappointed by the segregated housing and labor practices, and dropped out in his second year. Moving to Seattle in 1969, Rice went back to college in the Economic Opportunity Program at the University of Washington, earning a B.A. in communications and an M.P.A. in 1974.

At the age of 35, he ran for City Council in 1978 and beat the incumbent. In 1983, Rice was named president of the council, and was encouraged to run for mayor. He was defeated in 1985 but regrouped and ran again in 1989. He became the first African American to become mayor of Seattle. He began his first term by convening an education summit to include all those interested in discussing ways to improve Seattle's public schools. An outgrowth of that summit was the Families and Education Levy, which raised $69 million for student health services, drug and alcohol counseling, and after-school activities.

Because African Americans comprised only 10 percent of Seattle's population, Rice forged a broad based coalition to win an overwhelming victory in 1993 for reelection. Along with his many duties as mayor of Seattle, Rice is also president of the Conference of Mayors.

In March of 1996, Rice announced his candidacy for governor of Washington, but he lost the election. Had Rice been elected, he would be the first African American to be governor of Washington and the second elected African American governor in the United States. Rice did not seek a third term as mayor in 1997 and took a job in the banking sector.

Edith Sampson (1901–1979)
Attorney, Diplomat, Judge, Lecturer

Sampson was born on October 13, 1901, in Pittsburgh, Pennsylvania. The first African American woman to be named an official representative to the United Nations, Sampson served in the United Nations from 1950 until 1953, first as an appointee of President Harry S. Truman and later during a portion of the Eisenhower administration. A native of Pittsburgh, Sampson acquired a LL.B. from the John Marshall Law School in Chicago in 1925 and two years later became the first woman to receive a LL.M. from Loyola University.

A member of the Illinois bar since 1927, she argued in front of the Supreme Court in 1934. During the 1930s, she maintained her own private practice, specializing particularly in domestic relations and in criminal law. After her U.N. appointment, Sampson traveled around the world as a lecturer. She was elected associate judge

Edith Sampson (United Nations)

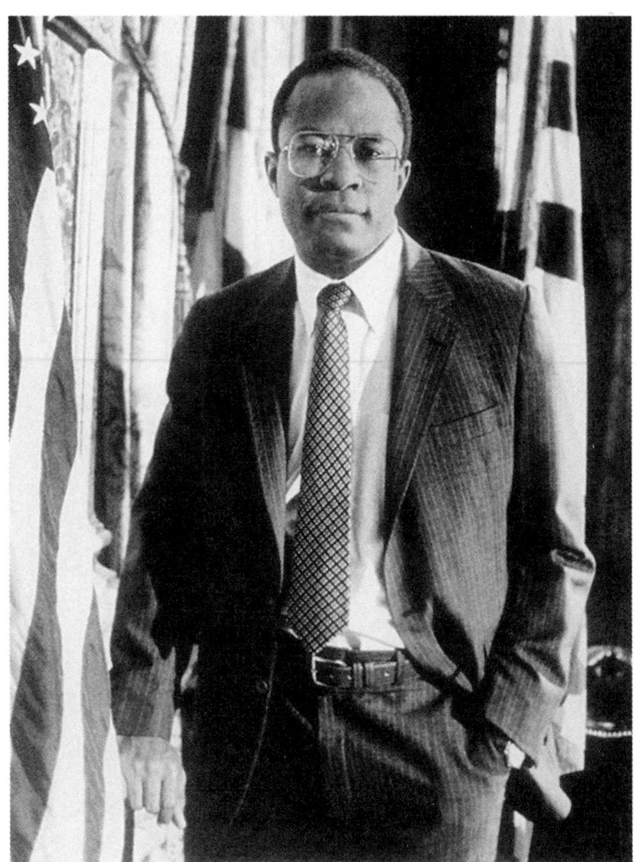

Kurt L. Schmoke (AP/Wide World Photos, Inc.)

of the Municipal Court of Chicago in 1962, becoming the first African American woman ever to sit as a circuit court judge. Sampson presided over divorce courts, traffic courts, and landlord-tenant relations courts. In 1978, she retired from Cook County Circuit Court. Sampson died on October 7, 1979, at Northwestern Hospital in Chicago, Illinois.

Kurt L. Schmoke (1949–)

Attorney, Municipal Government Official, Federal Government Official

Born on December 1, 1949, Kurt L. Schmoke was inaugurated as the first elected African American mayor of Baltimore on December 8, 1987. Schmoke graduated with honors from Baltimore City College High School. In 1967, he won the award as the top scholar-athlete in the city. Schmoke went on to receive his Bachelor of Arts degree from Yale University in 1971, studied at Oxford University as a Rhodes Scholar, and earned his law degree from Harvard University in 1976.

After graduating from Harvard, Schmoke began his law practice with the prestigious Baltimore firm of Piper & Marbury, and shortly thereafter was appointed by President Jimmy Carter as a member of the White House Domestic Policy staff. Schmoke returned to Baltimore as an assistant U.S. attorney, where he prosecuted narcotics and white collar crime cases. He then returned to private practice and was involved in assorted civic activities.

In November of 1982, Schmoke was elected state's attorney for Baltimore, the chief prosecuting office of the city. He created a full time Narcotics Unit to prosecute all drug cases and underscored the criminal nature of domestic violence and child abuse by setting up separate units to handle those cases. Also, Schmoke hired a community liaison officer to make sure that his office was being responsive to neighborhood questions and concerns.

In his inaugural address, Schmoke set the tone and future direction for his administration when he said that he wanted Baltimore to reduce its large high school dropout and teenage pregnancy rates and combat illiteracy. He has overseen the passage of the largest ever increase in the city's education budget, and, in partnership with Baltimore businesses and community based organizations, Schmoke developed the Commonwealth Agreement and the College Bound Foundation with the goal of guaranteeing opportunities for jobs or college-entrance to qualifying high school graduates. Since taking office, Schmoke has also begun major initiatives in housing, economic development, and public health. Schmoke proposed educational programs to prepare Baltimore's citizens for high-tech jobs and he has also pushed growth at Baltimore's Inner Harbor. The mayor came under fire in the early 1990s because of Baltimore's persistent crime problems and his failed attempt to privatize nine Baltimore public schools.

Despite being considered the leading contender for the role of Maryland governor, Schmoke decided to run for a third term as Baltimore mayor. Interested in drug reform, Schmoke ran on the platform of decriminalizing drugs to stop related crime. An unexpectedly high turnout of close to 52 percent of registered Democrats gave Schmoke a racially polarized election win in 1995. In December 1998, Schmoke announced he would not seek a fourth term as mayor.

Throughout his career, Schmoke has been active in the civic and cultural life of the Baltimore community by serving as a member of numerous boards of trustees. In recognition of his commitment to excellence in education and his service to the community, Schmoke has received honorary degrees from several colleges and universities.

Robert Smalls (The Library of Congress)

Robert Smalls (1839–1916)
Federal Legislator

Robert Smalls served a longer period in Congress than any other African American Reconstruction congressman. Born a slave in Beaufort, South Carolina, in 1839, Smalls received a limited education before moving to Charleston with the family of his owner. While in Charleston, Smalls worked at a number of odd jobs and eventually became adept at piloting boats along the Georgia and South Carolina coasts.

At the outbreak of the Civil War, Smalls was forced to become a crew member on the Confederate ship *Planter*. On the morning of May 13, 1862, Smalls smuggled his wife and three children on board, assumed command of the vessel, and sailed it into the hands of the Union squadron blockading Charleston harbor. His daring exploit led President Abraham Lincoln to name him a pilot in the Union Navy. He was also awarded a large sum of money for what constituted the delivery of war booty. In December of 1863, during the siege of Charleston, Smalls again took command of the *Planter* and was promoted to captain, the only African American to hold such a rank during the Civil War.

After the war, Smalls was elected to the South Carolina House of Representatives and served from 1868 to 1870. In 1870, Smalls became a member of South Carolina's State Senate and served until 1874. Smalls campaigned for a U.S. Congressional seat in 1874 against an independent candidate and won the election. He took his seat in Congress on March 4, 1875. During his tenure in Congress, Smalls supported a wide variety of progressive legislation including a bill to provide equal accommodations for African Americans in interstate travel and an amendment designed to safeguard the rights of children born to interracial couples. He also sought to protect the rights of African Americans serving in the armed forces.

Smalls won reelection in 1876, an election that was bitterly contested by Smalls's Democratic challenger, George Tillman. Tillman tried unsuccessfully to have Smalls's election to Congress overturned. However, Tillman's supporters were undeterred. In 1877, Smalls was accused of taking a $5,000 bribe while serving as a senator. Although Smalls was exonerated by Governor William D. Simpson, his popularity plummeted. Smalls lost his reelection bid in 1878. In 1880, Smalls ran again for Congress. He lost the election, but maintained that the results were invalid due to vote-counting irregularities. Smalls's charges were substantiated and he was allowed to take his seat in Congress in July 1882. Two months later, another congressional election was held and Smalls lost his seat to fellow Republican Edward W. M. Mackey. However, Mackey died in January of 1884 and Smalls was allowed to serve the remainder of Mackey's term. In 1886, Smalls lost an election to Democratic challenger William Elliott. Though Smalls was no longer a congressman, he remained involved in political activities. From 1889 to 1913, Smalls served as collector of the port of Beaufort. He died on February 22, 1916.

Louis Stokes (1925–)

Civil Rights Activist, Federal Legislator, Attorney

Stokes was born in Cleveland, Ohio, on February 23, 1925. He was in the U.S. Army from 1943 until 1946. After leaving the service he attended Case Western Reserve University from 1946 to 1948 and was awarded a J.D. in 1953 from Cleveland Marshall Law School. After 14 years in private practice with the law firm of Stokes, Character, Terry and Perry, he was elected as a democrat to the U.S. House of Representatives in 1969.

As Ohio's first African American representative, Stokes has served on a number of committees including the Committee on Education and Labor, the House Internal Security Committee, and the Appropriations Committee. He has also chaired the House Ethics Committee. As part of the House Assassination Committee, Stokes has investigated the deaths of Martin Luther King, Jr. and President John F. Kennedy. In 1972 and 1973 Stokes chaired the Congressional Black Caucus, and he was a delegate to the Democratic National Convention in 1972, 1976, and 1980. Stokes was the first African American to chair the Intelligence Committee of the House and the only African American that served on the Iran Contra Committee. After almost two decades in Congress, Stokes retired in July 1998.

Stokes belongs to the Urban League, the American Civil Liberties Union, the American Legion, and the African American Institute. He is on the board of trustees of the Martin Luther King Jr. Center for Social Change and was vice president of the Cleveland chapter of the NAACP in 1965 and 1966. He is a recipient of the Distinguished Service Award, the William C. Dawson Award, and a Certificate of Appreciation from the U.S. Commission on Civil Rights, of which he was vice-chairman of the Cleveland subcommittee in 1966.

Louis W. Sullivan (1933–)

Educational Administrator, Federal Government Official

Louis W. Sullivan was born on November 3, 1933, in Atlanta, Georgia. On March 1, 1989, the U.S. Senate confirmed Dr. Sullivan as secretary of health and human services by a vote of 98 to 1, making him the first African American appointed to a cabinet position during the administration of U.S. President George Bush.

Instrumental in the development of the Morehouse School of Medicine, which he founded in 1975 as a separate entity from Morehouse College, Sullivan served as professor of biology and medicine and as director and founder of the medical education program at Morehouse College. In 1981, he became Morehouse School of Medicine's first dean and president.

Sullivan graduated from Morehouse College *magna cum laude* with a B.S. in 1954, and received his M.D. in 1958, graduating *cum laude*from Boston University. He completed his internship at New York Hospital Cornell Medical Center and his medical and general pathology residencies at Cornell Medical Center and Massachusetts General Hospital. He then fulfilled two fellowships and served in a variety of positions with Harvard Medical School, Boston City Hospital, New Jersey College of Medicine, Boston University Medical Center, the Boston Sickle Cell Center, and others.

Sullivan has been involved in numerous educational, medical, scientific, professional, and civic organizations; has earned advisory, consulting, research and academic positions; and has received many professional and public service awards. Sullivan's research and activities focus on hematology, a branch of biology that deals with the formation of blood and blood-forming organs, and he has authored and coauthored more than sixty publications on this and other subjects. He is also the founding president of the Association of Minority Health Professions.

On January 20, 1989, Sullivan was nominated by President George Bush for the position of secretary of health and human services. He was sworn in on March 10, 1989. In his position, Sullivan was responsible for ensuring the safety of food, drugs, and medical research, and promoting health education. Upon the expiration of his term in January of 1993, he returned to Atlanta to resume his presidency of the Morehouse School of Medicine.

Harold Washington (1922–1987)

Federal Legislator, Municipal Government Official, Attorney

Washington was born in Chicago on April 15, 1922. After serving with the Army Air Corps in the Pacific theater during World War II, he received a B.A. from Roosevelt University in 1949. Washington then received a J.D. in 1952 from Northwestern University Law School. After graduation, Washington worked as an assistant city prosecutor in Chicago from 1954 to 1958 and while establishing a private law practice, was an arbitrator with the Illinois Industrial Commission from 1960 to 1964.

Running on the Democratic ticket, Washington was elected to the Illinois House of Representatives in 1965

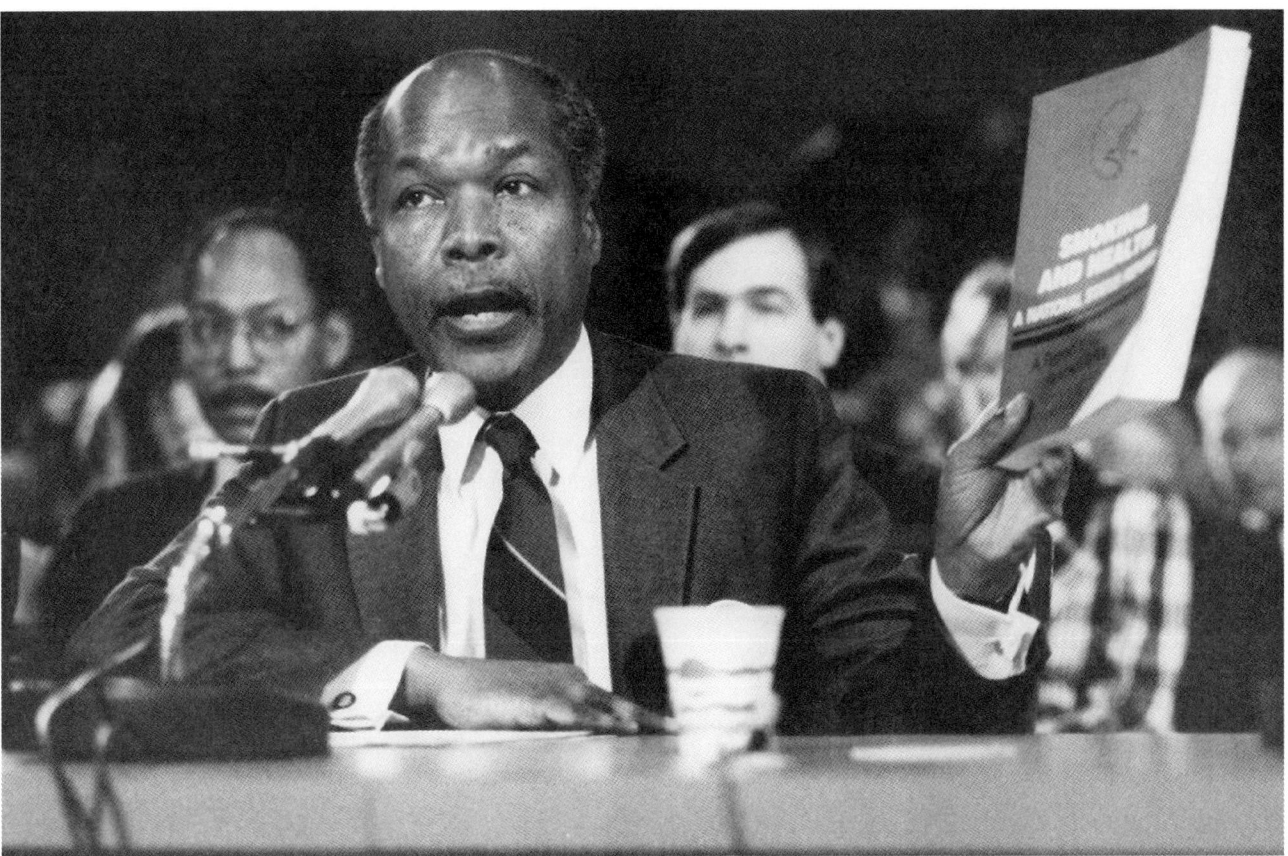

Louis Sullivan speaking before the U.S. Senate Labor and Human Resources Committee (AP/Wide World Photos, Inc.).

and served until 1976 when he was elected to the Illinois Senate. He served in the State Senate from1977 to 1980. While a state legislator, Washington helped establish Illinois's Fair Employment Practices Commission, secured passage of consumer protection legislation, and worked to designate Martin Luther King, Jr's birthday as a state holiday. After the death of longtime Chicago Mayor Richard J. Daly in 1977, Washington finished third in a the four-man contest for the Democratic nomination for mayor of Chicago. In 1980, Washington was elected to the U.S. House of Representatives and became a member of the 97th Congress. Washington served on the Education and Labor, Government Operations, and Judiciary Committees. Shortly after his reelection to the House, Washington won the Democratic nomination for mayor. In 1983 he won the election to become Chicago's first African American mayor.

Although Washington's mayoralty was marked by political infighting he did manage to institute some reforms including increased city hiring of minorities, deficit reduction, the appointment of an African American police commissioner, and reduction of patronage influence. Washington died while in office on November 25, 1987.

Maxine Waters (1938–)
Federal Legislator, Diplomat, State Representative

Waters was born in St. Louis on August 15, 1938. After graduating from high school she moved to Los Angeles where she worked at a garment factory and for a telephone company. She eventually attended college and received a B.A. in sociology from California State University. She became interested in politics after teaching in a Head Start program and serving as a delegate to the Democratic National Convention in 1972.

In 1976, Waters was elected to the California State Assembly, where she served on numerous committees including the Ways and Means Subcommittee on State Administration, the Joint Committee of Public Pension Fund Investments, the Joint Legislative Budget Committee, the Judiciary Committee, the Joint Committee on Legislative Ethics, the Select Committee on Assistance to Victims of Sexual Assault, the California Committee on the Status of Women, the Natural Resources Committee, and the Elections, Reapportionment and Constitutional Amendment Committee. As a member of the California Assembly, she created the nation's first statewide child abuse prevention training program, gained passage of a law prohibiting strip searches for nonvio-

Harold Washington (right) addressing an audience after his victory in the 1983 Chicago mayoral race (AP/Wide World Photos, Inc.).

lent misdemeanors, and promoted legislation to prevent toxic chemical catastrophes.

In 1990, Waters was elected to the U.S. House of Representatives where she has become an outspoken figure. She has served there on the Banking, Finance and Urban Affairs Committee and the Veterans Affairs Committee. She has fought for legislation promoting aid to poor and minority neighborhoods in American cities and combating apartheid in South Africa. Waters is on the board of directors of *Essence* magazine and is involved with the National Woman's Political Caucus, the National Steering Committee on Education of Black Youth, and the National Steering Committee of the Center for Study of Youth Policy.

J. C. Watts, Jr. (1957–)

Federal Legislator, Religious Leader

Julius Caesar Watts was born on November 18, 1957, in Eufaula, Oklahoma. His father is a minister and Eufaula City councilman, and his uncle once headed Oklahoma's NAACP chapter. Educated at the University of Oklahoma, Watts was a star quarterback and was named Most Valuable Player of the 1980 and 1981 Orange Bowls. He graduated with a journalism degree but chose to continue in athletics, joining the Canadian Football League's Ottawa Rough Riders. He played five years with the Rough Riders and one with the Toronto Argonauts. An ordained minster and motivational speaker for youth and church groups, Watts served as youth director at the Sunnylane Baptist Church at Del City, Oklahoma, and presided over the Watts Energy Corp.

Though he had long considered himself a Democrat, Watts became disenchanted with the direction the party was taking and decided to in 1989, become a Republican. The following year he was elected chairperson of Oklahoma's Corporation Commission. The win made him the first African American Oklahoman to win a statewide election. Strongly in favor of welfare reform, defense spending cuts, and a balanced budget, the charismatic Watts built a rapport with his home state that led to his 1994 election victory over the Democratic incumbent to the U.S. House of Representatives. In doing so, Watts became the first African American Republican from a southern state to win a seat in Congress since the Reconstruction, and only the second

Maxine Waters (AP/Wide World Photos, Inc.)

African American Republican to win a seat in the House in sixty years.

Robert C. Weaver (1907–1997)

Lecturer, Federal Government Official, Educator

Robert Weaver became the first African American appointed to a presidential cabinet post when President Lyndon B. Johnson named him head of the newly created Department of Housing and Urban Development (HUD) on January 13, 1966. Previously, Weaver had served as head of the Housing and Home Finance Agency (HHFA) from 1961 to 1966.

Robert Weaver was born on December 29, 1907, in Washington, DC, where he attended Dunbar High School and worked during his teens as an electrician. Encountering discrimination when he attempted to join a union, Weaver decided to go to college instead and concentrated on economics. Weaver attended Harvard University where he majored in economics receiving a B.S., an M.S., and a Ph.D. Weaver's grandfather, Dr. Robert Tanner Freeman, was the first African American to earn a D.O. in dentistry at Harvard.

Weaver was one of the academics brought to Washington during the New Deal. From 1934 to 1938, he served in the Department of the Interior in various roles. He was also a part of President Roosevelt's "Black Cabinet." After leaving the Interior Department, Weaver served as a special assistant to the head of the National Housing Authority from 1938 to 1940. From 1940 to 1944, Weaver continued his work with the federal government through the War Production Board and the Negro Manpower Commission.

Weaver left the federal government because he felt implementation of anti-discriminatory measures was moving too slow. He moved in 1944 to Chicago, where he directed the Mayor's Committee on Race Relations. From Chicago he divided his time between teaching and government service.

During the late 1940s and 1950s, Weaver concentrated his energies on the field of education. He became a professor of economics at the Agricultural and Technical College of North Carolina in Greensboro from 1931 to 1932. In 1947, he became a lecturer at Northwestern University and then became a visiting professor at Teachers College (Columbia University) and at the New York University School of Education. During this period, he was also a professor of economics at the New School for Social Research. From 1949 to 1955 he was director of the Opportunity Fellowships Program of the John Hay Whitney Foundation. Weaver also served as a member of the National Selection Committee for Fulbright Fellowships from 1952 to 1954, chairman of the Fellowship Committee of the Julius Rosenwald Fund, and a consultant to the Ford Foundation from 1959 to 1960.

In 1955, Weaver was named deputy state rent commissioner by New York's Governor Averell Harriman. By the end of the year, he had become state rent commissioner and the first African American to hold state cabinet rank in New York. From 1960 to 1961, he served as vice chairman of the New York City Housing and Redevelopment Board, a three-man body which supervised New York's urban renewal and middle-income housing programs. Weaver headed the Department of Housing and Urban Development until 1968. From 1969 to 1970, he served as president of Baruch College. Weaver accepted a teaching position at the Department of Urban Affairs at Hunter College in New York in 1971. After he retired from Hunter College in 1978, Weaver continued to serve on the boards of corporations, educational and public institutions. Weaver wrote four books and 185 articles. In 1985, he was elected into the American Academy of Arts and Sciences. Weaver died in his New York City home on July 17, 1997.

Wellington Webb (1941–)
Municipal Government Official

Born February 17, 1941, Webb had to leave his South Side Chicago home to live with his grandmother in Denver, Colorado, due to asthma. After graduating from Colorado State College in 1964 with a B.A. in education, Webb worked in various public service-sector jobs, including welfare caseworker and special education teacher, while obtaining a master's degree.

In 1972, Webb was elected to the Colorado state legislature as a representative from the northeast section of Denver. There he served four years, and rose to prominence within the Democratic Party during the time when, in 1976, Democratic presidential hopeful Jimmy Carter chose Webb to head the state's national election committee. Upon Carter's election, Webb was named a regional director of the U.S. Department of Health, Education, and Welfare. After leaving federal government service in 1981, Colorado's governor appointed Webb executive director of the Colorado Department of Regulatory Agencies. During his tenure in the early 1980s, Webb was the only African American in the state cabinet.

Webb ran for mayor of Denver first in 1983, but lost. In 1987, he ran successfully for the city auditor post. As city auditor, he was credited with restoring professionalism to the office. In 1991, he faced his city hall colleague, a popular African American district attorney, in another mayoral race. Webb won with 58 percent of the vote, despite being outspent by his well-financed opponent. He was reelected for a second term in 1995 and counts among his accomplishments a lower crime rate, a strong economic base, low unemployment, creation of 50,000 jobs, and the completion of a new airport. On February 10, 1999, Webb announced his plans to run for a third term by introducing an ambitious plan to revitalize Denver's poor neighborhoods, create more affordable housing, and manage traffic congestion and growth.

Michael R. White (1951–)
Municipal Government Official

Born and raised on the east side of Cleveland, Ohio, Michael White was elected mayor of Cleveland in 1989. At the time, 40 percent of the city's population was at or below the poverty line.

An alumnus of the Ohio State University, White received a B.A. in education and an M.P.A. His political career started in 1974 when he became a special assistant for the mayor's office in Columbus, Ohio. In 1978, White began six years on Cleveland's city council, followed by four years in Columbus as a state senator. In 1989, White entered Cleveland's mayoral race, running against three white candidates and City Council's President George Forbes. Forbes was supported by the African American community, but had alienated the white community. Cleveland's population was evenly balanced between African Americans and whites. West won the election with a combination of voter support for him and voter animosity towards Forbes.

The central issue for White's administration was the future of Cleveland's young people. Two focal points White worked toward was an upgrade of public education and the development of new jobs programs. White supported the development of the Lake Erie waterfront and the completion of the Rock and Roll Hall of Fame.

When Bill Clinton became president in 1992, White was invigorated by the potential changes with government's relationship to the cities. He was an outspoken supporter of Clinton's plans to get rid of the old welfare system. In 1995, White met with the National Football League Commissioner Paul Tagliabue to try and keep the Browns from moving to Baltimore. White secured a new team to begin play in 1999, the same year a new football stadium will open. A federal court order recently placed control of Cleveland's beleaguered school district with the mayor, an appointed nine-member school board, and a superintendent chosen by the mayor.

Lawrence Douglas Wilder (1931–)
Attorney, State Government Official

Wilder was born on January 17, 1931, in Richmond, Virginia. He graduated from Virginia Union University in 1951 with a B.S. in chemistry. After graduation he was drafted into the U.S. Army and assigned to a combat infantry unit in Korea. During the Korean War he was awarded a Bronze Star for bravery and valor in combat. After being discharged from the army in 1953 Wilder worked as a chemist in the Virginia State Medical Examiner's Office. In 1959 Wilder graduated with a J.D. from Howard University Law School.

Wilder practiced law in Richmond until he became the first African American elected to the Virginia State Senate since Reconstruction. Wilder chaired the important Privileges and Elections Committee and worked on legislation supporting fair-housing, union rights for public employees, and minority hiring. He also voted against capital punishment (a position he has since rescinded.) In 1985 Wilder was elected lieutenant-governor and in 1989 he became Virginia's first African American governor, winning the election by a 1/3 of 1 percent of the vote.

As governor, Wilder streamlined the state's budget, eliminated the state's $2.2 billion deficit, and worked to get civil rights legislation passed. Virginia law does not allow its governor to serve consecutive terms. After his term as governor, Wilder remained active in Virginia politics. Since 1995, Wilder has hosted a popular weekly radio program, *The Doug Wilder Show*. In 1998 he was selected as president of his alma mater, Virginia Union University, but rescinded his acceptance of the position shortly before he was to be inaugurated as president.

In 1979, Wilder won the Distinguished Alumni Award presented by Virginia Union University. In succeeding years he received the 1982 President's Citation from Norfolk State University, was named the 1993 Alumnus of the Year from the Howard Law School Alumni Association, and earned the1985 Distinguished Postgraduate Achievement in Law and Politics Award. Wilder belongs to the Richmond Urban League, Richmond Bar Association, American Judicature Society, American Trial Lawyers Association, Virginia Trial Lawyers Association, National Association of Criminal Defense Lawyers, NAACP, and is vice president of the Virginia Human Relations Council.

Andrew Young (1932–)

Diplomat, Municipal Government Official/Executive, Federal Legislator, Civil Rights Activist

Andrew Young was born in New Orleans, on March 12, 1932, and received a B.S. degree from Howard University and a B.Div. in 1955 from the Hartford Theological Seminary. He was ordained a minister in the United Church of Christ and then served in churches in Alabama and Georgia before joining the National Council of Churches in 1957.

The turning point of Young's life came in 1961, when he joined Reverend Martin Luther King, Jr. and became a trusted aide and close confidante. He became executive vice president of the Southern Christian Leadership Conference (SCLC) in 1967, and remained with King until King's 1968 assassination. During his years with SCLC, Young also developed several programs including antiwar protests, voter registration projects, and other major civil rights drives.

In 1970 Young lost a bid for the U.S. House of Representatives. In the aftermath of the election, Young was appointed chair of the Community Relations Committee (CRC). Though the CRC was an advisory group with no enforcement powers, Young took an activist role, pressing the city government on many issues, from sanitation and open housing to mass transit, consumer affairs, and Atlanta's drug problem. Young's leadership in the CRC led to a higher public profile and answered critic's charges that he was inexperienced in government.

Young launched another bid for a congressional seat in 1972. African Americans comprised only 44 percent of the voters in Young's congressional district. However, Young captured 23 percent of the white vote and 54 percent of the total vote to win by a margin of 8,000 votes. Young was the first African American representative to be elected from Georgia since Jefferson Long in 1870.

Andrew Young (AP/Wide World Photos, Inc.)

Young was one of the most vocal supporters of his fellow Georgian Jimmy Carter's campaign for the U.S. presidency in 1976. Following President Carter's inauguration, Young left Congress in 1977 to become America's ambassador to the United Nations. Young's tenure there was marked by controversy—his outspoken manner sometimes ruffled diplomatic feathers—as well as achievement, represented primarily in the tremendous improvement he fostered in relations between the United States and lesser developed countries.

Young's career as a diplomat came to an end in 1979 when he met secretly with a representative of the Palestine Liberation Organization (PLO) to discuss an upcoming vote in the UN. America had a policy that none of its representatives would meet with the PLO as long as it refused to recognize the right of Israel to exist as a state. When the news of Young's meeting leaked out, an uproar followed. Young tendered his resignation, which President Carter accepted. The incident badly strained African American-Jewish relations as

African Americans felt Jewish leaders were instrumental in Young's removal.

When Maynard Jackson was prevented by law from running for his third term of office as mayor of Atlanta in 1981, Young entered the race. Race entered the campaign when Jackson charged that African Americans who supported the white candidate, State Legislator Sidney Marcus, with "selling out" the Civil Rights movement. Jackson's remarks were widely criticized, and it was feared that they would create a backlash against Young too. However, Young ended up with 55 percent of the total vote. He'd won 10.6 percent of the white vote, compared to the 12 percent he had won in the primary, and 88.4 percent of the black vote, up from 61 percent earlier.

Young took office at a time when Atlanta was going through several economic and social problems including a shrinking population and a stagnating tax base. In addition, almost a quarter of the city's residents were below the poverty line, and the city was still shaken by the recent murders of 28 African American youths and the disappearance of another. Some critics doubted Young's ability to deal with Atlanta's problems. He was seen as anti-business and a weak administrator. But by 1984, the city had become so successful at attracting new businesses that it was experiencing a major growth spurt. In addition, the crime rate dropped sharply and racial harmony seemed an established fact. Young was decisively reelected

Limited by law to two terms as mayor, Young ran unsuccessfully for governor of Georgia in 1990. His wife died of cancer four years later. In 1994,Young wrote his autobiography *A Way Out of No Way: The Spiritual Memoirs of Andrew Young.* He was co-chair of the Atlanta Committee for the 1996 Olympic Games and a member of various boards of directors including those of Delta Airlines and Host Marriott Corp. He also remained very active as president of Young Ideas, a consulting firm he founded. In 1995, Young headed up the Southern Africa Enterprise Development Fund, which, in 1996, began offering low-interest loans to small businesses in South Africa and other countries in the same region.

Coleman A. Young (1918–1997)
Municipal Government Official

Long-time Detroit icon Coleman Young announced on June 22, 1993, that he would not seek reelection for the mayoralty of the city that fall. Young had won each of his mayoral elections by a wide margin. The only mayor in the history of Detroit to serve five consecutive terms led the media to dub him "mayor for life." Once recognized as an urban savior, Detroit's highly publicized problems—crime, declining population, and poor economic standing—had finally instilled doubts in the voters regarding Young's abilities.

Coleman A. Young (AP/Wide World Photos, Inc.)

Young was born in Tuscaloosa, Alabama, on May 24, 1918. His family moved to Detroit in 1926, after the Ku Klux Klan ransacked a neighborhood in Huntsville, where his father was learning to be a tailor. In Detroit, Young attended Catholic Central and then Eastern High School, graduating from the latter with honors. He had to reject a scholarship to the University of Michigan when the Eastern High School Alumni Association, in contrast to policies followed with poor white students, declined to assist him with costs other than tuition.

Young entered an electrician's apprentice school at the Ford Motor Company. He finished first in the program but was passed over for the only available electrician job in favor of a white candidate. Working on the assembly line, he soon became engaged in underground union activities. Attacked by a company man one day, Young defended himself by hitting his assailant on the head with a steel bar leading to Young's dismissal.

During World War II, Young was a navigator in the U.S. Army Air Force and was commissioned a second lieutenant. Stationed at Freeman Field, Indiana, he demonstrated against the exclusion of African Americans from segregated officers' clubs and was arrested along with one hundred other African American airmen including Thurgood Marshall and Percy Sutton, former president of New York's Borough of Manhattan. Young spent three days in jail. Shortly thereafter, the clubs were opened to African American officers.

After the war, Young returned to his union organizing activities and was named director of organization for the Wayne County AFL-CIO in 1947. However, the union fired him in 1948 when he supported Henry Wallace, candidate of the Progressive Party, in the presidential election. The union regarded Wallace as an agent of the Communist Party and supported Harry Truman. Young managed a dry cleaning plant for a few years, then founded and directed the National Negro Labor Council in 1951. The council successfully prevailed on Sears Roebuck & Co. and the San Francisco Transit System to hire African Americans. However, they also aroused the interest of the House Un-American Activities Committee, which was in the midst of hunting for alleged communists. When brought before the committee, Young, who denied he was ever a communist, refused to name anyone. Though he emerged from the hearing with his self-respect intact, his council was placed on the attorney general's subversive list. In 1956, the council was disbanded, and charges of Young's communist involvement were used against him, albeit unsuccessfully, during his first mayoral campaign.

After working at a variety of jobs, Young won a seat on the Michigan Constitutional Convention in 1961. The following year he lost a race for state representative but became director of campaign organization for the Democratic gubernatorial candidate in Wayne County (Detroit). He sold life insurance until 1964, when, with union support, he was elected to the state senate. In the senate, he was a leader of the civil rights forces fighting for low-income housing for people dislocated by urban renewal and for bars to discrimination in the hiring practices of the Detroit police force.

Young declared his candidacy for mayor of Detroit in 1973, and mounted a vigorous campaign for the office. He won the office after a racially divisive campaign. Among his early successes in office were the integration of the Detroit police department and promotion of African American officers into administrative positions. The new mayor also created a coalition of business and labor to preserve the industries remaining in Detroit and attract new ones. Young's outspoken and opinionated nature and his fondness for using expletives, earned him both passionate supporters and bitter enemies. A Democrat and one of the first big-city mayors to support Jimmy Carter's presidential campaign in 1976, Young had a very close relationship with the Carter administration. He turned down a federal cabinet position offered to him by Carter, but his relationship with the president proved helpful in securing funds for Detroit.

In the 1980s, Young was intensely critical of the administrations of President Ronald Reagan and President George Bush, with their cutbacks in federal aid to urban areas. The federal government seized serval opportunities to scrutinize Young as well. Over the years, Young's administration was investigated on more than six different charges including improprieties in the awarding of city contracts and illegal personal use of city funds by the police department; however, Young himself was never personally implicated in the scandals.

Young's popularity was bolstered by a number of citywide improvements credited to him such as the expansion of riverfront attractions, which brought increased convention and tourist traffic to the city and favorable tax abatements that attracted new businesses including two major automobile plants. Middle-class and white flight to the suburbs, that had begun at the end of the 1960s, continued to rob the city's coffers of essential tax revenue. Some critics argued that Young's attitude toward suburbanites contributed to the phenomenon. Near the end of his tenure, Young endured a barrage of disapproval for autocratic style and his emphasis on cosmetic improvements rather than focusing on true remedies for the decay of the city.

In 1989, Coleman Young won his fifth term as Motor City mayor. Despite a high unemployment rate, a shortage of cash, and a high crime rate, the voters returned the popular Young to office. During 1990, both Detroit and its mayor were targets of highly critical feature stories in the *New York Times* and on CBS. Commentary revolved around Detroit's sagging economy, brutal crime statistics, racial stratification, and a supposed general air of despair. Young countered that under his administration, the city managed to balance its budget despite a dramatic cutback in federal and state aid. He also noted that many neighborhoods had undergone extensive renovation and a new automobile manufacturing plant had opened within the city limits.

In 1993, when Young felt that he no longer had the necessary vitality to run a big city, a major chapter in Detroit politics came to a close. Young turned his attentions towards writing, with Lonnie Wheeler, *Hard Stuff: The Autobiography of Coleman Young.* After he left politics, Young was a professor of urban affairs at Detroit's Wayne State University, where he continued to raise dialogue about race and class issues. Young was in poor health during his last years and suffered from heart trouble, chronic emphysema, and other respiratory problems. He died on November 29, 1997.

◆ POLITICAL STATISTICS

Political Party Identification of the Adult Population, by Degree of Attachment, 1972 to 1994, and by Selected Characteristics, 1994

[In percent. Covers citizens of voting-age living in private housing units in the contiguous United States. Data are from the National Election Studies and are based on a sample and subject to sampling variability; for details, see source]

YEAR AND SELECTED CHARACTERISTIC	Total	Strong Democrat	Weak Democrat	Independent Democrat	Independent	Independent Republican	Weak Republican	Strong Republican	Apolitical
1972	100	15	26	11	13	11	13	10	1
1980	100	18	23	11	13	10	14	9	2
1984	100	17	20	11	11	12	15	12	2
1986	100	18	22	10	12	11	15	11	2
1988	100	18	18	12	11	13	14	14	2
1990	100	20	19	12	11	12	15	10	2
1992	100	18	18	14	12	12	14	11	1
1994, total [1]	**100**	**15**	**19**	**13**	**10**	**12**	**15**	**16**	**1**
Age:									
17 to 24 years old	100	9	20	22	10	8	19	10	1
25 to 34 years old	100	11	19	14	12	11	16	16	1
35 to 44 years old	100	13	18	14	12	11	14	18	-
45 to 54 years old	100	15	16	15	7	16	12	17	1
55 to 64 years old	100	18	22	8	8	16	12	15	-
65 to 74 years old	100	28	17	6	8	13	14	15	-
75 to 99 years old	100	19	26	9	9	5	17	13	2
Sex:									
Male	100	13	17	12	11	14	14	18	1
Female	100	18	21	13	10	9	15	13	1
Race:									
White	100	12	19	12	10	13	16	17	1
Black	100	38	23	20	8	4	2	3	1
Education:									
Grade school	100	26	26	7	13	7	11	6	4
High school	100	15	22	14	13	10	13	11	1
College	100	14	16	13	7	13	16	21	-

- Represents zero. [1] Includes other characteristics, not shown separately.

Source: Center for Political Studies, University of Michigan, Ann Arbor, MI, unpublished data. Data prior to 1988 published in Warren E. Miller and Santa A. Traugott, *American National Election Studies Data Sourcebook, 1952-1986*, Harvard University Press, Cambridge, MA, 1989 (copyright).

Black Elected Officials, by Office, 1970 to 1993, and by Region and State, 1993

[As of January 1993, no Black elected officials had been identified in Hawaii, Idaho, Montana, North Dakota, or Utah]

STATE	Total	U.S. and State legislatures [1]	City and county offices [2]	Law enforcement [3]	Education [4]
1970 (Feb.)	1,469	179	715	213	362
1980 (July)	4,890	326	2,832	526	1,206
1985 (Jan.)	6,016	407	3,517	661	1,431
1990 (Jan.)	7,335	436	4,485	769	1,645
1991 (Jan.)	7,445	473	4,496	847	1,629
1992 (Jan.)	7,517	499	4,557	847	1,614
1993 (Jan.)	**7,984**	**561**	**4,819**	**922**	**1,682**
AL	699	23	529	58	89
AK	3	1	2	-	-
AZ	15	4	3	3	5
AR	380	13	214	51	102
CA	273	13	72	82	106
CO	20	4	4	10	2
CT	62	14	38	2	8
DE	23	3	14	-	6
DC	198	[5]4	185	-	9
FL	200	22	133	28	17
GA	545	43	371	32	99
IL	465	25	282	37	121
IN	72	12	50	4	6
IA	11	1	6	1	3
KS	21	6	7	3	5
KY	63	4	47	5	7
LA	636	33	346	104	153
ME	1	-	1	-	-
MD	140	32	79	23	6

STATE	Total	U.S. and State legislatures [1]	City and county offices [2]	Law enforcement [3]	Education [4]
MA	30	8	18	2	2
MI	333	17	133	68	115
MN	16	1	2	10	3
MS	751	42	495	88	126
MO	185	18	134	14	19
NE	6	1	2	-	3
NV	10	3	4	1	2
NH	2	2	-	-	-
NJ	211	13	113	-	85
NM	3	-	-	2	1
NY	299	30	63	70	136
NC	468	28	328	31	81
OH	219	16	124	30	49
OK	123	6	95	1	21
OR	10	4	2	4	-
PA	158	18	55	52	33
RI	12	9	3	-	-
SC	450	26	269	15	140
SD	3	1	2	-	-
TN	168	16	104	24	24
TX	472	18	323	40	91
VT	2	2	-	-	-
VA	155	14	126	15	-
WA	19	2	9	5	3
WV	21	1	17	3	-
WI	30	8	15	4	3
WY	1	-	-	-	1

- Represents zero. [1] Includes elected State administrators. [2] County commissioners and councilmen, mayors, vice mayors, aldermen, regional officials, and other. [3] Judges, magistrates, constables, marshals, sheriffs, justices of the peace, and other. [4] Members of state education agencies, college boards, school boards, and other. [5] Includes two shadow senators and one shadow representative.

Source: Joint Center for Political and Economic Studies, Washington, DC, *Black Elected Officials: A National Roster*, annual, (copyright).

Population

◆ The Size of the African American Population ◆ Regional Distribution ◆ African American Towns and Settlements ◆ Contemporary Demographic Characteristics ◆ Population Projections for the Twentieth–first Century ◆ Population Statistics

by Audrey Y. Williams

In 1997, according to the United States Bureau of the Census, the African American population of 32.3 million constituted 12.0 percent of the nation's total resident population. Approximately 194.5 million people, roughly 73.0 percent of the population considered themselves non-Hispanic white. Approximately 29.3 million people, or 11.0 percent of the population, were of Hispanic heritage. Asians and Pacific Islanders numbered 9.4 million or 4.0 percent of the population.

◆ THE SIZE OF THE AFRICAN AMERICAN POPULATION

1619 to 1790

The beginning of America's black population is usually dated to the year 1619, when a small number of British colonists and European and African indentured servants landed in Jamestown, Virginia. Historians are uncertain as to the exact number, but between fourteen and twenty black indentured servants were evidently part of this first settlement; within a short time, the practice of enslaving newly arrived Africans developed and spread throughout the colonies. By 1630, there were some sixty slaves in the American colonies; by 1660, the number of enslaved Africans had increased to 2,920.

Within two decades, the colonies were beginning to flourish. The emerging agrarian society demanded a larger labor force, and the system of slavery became the economic venture that provided it. By 1690, seventy years after the first importation of Africans, the total slave population in the American colonies had grown to 16,729. By 1740, the slave population reached 150,000; it increased to 575,000 by 1780. Although a free black population did exist, it grew at a slower rate than the slave population; in 1780, there was only one free black for every nine slaves.

1790 to 1865

In the first official census of the United States, taken in 1790, some 757,000 blacks were counted. At that time, blacks constituted 19.3 percent of the nation's population, of which 9 percent, or some 59,527, were free blacks. (By 1790, Pennsylvania, Massachusetts, Connecticut, Rhode Island, New York, New Jersey, and the Northwest Territory had enacted legislation providing for the gradual emancipation of slaves.) By 1860, there were almost four million blacks in the United States, over ninety percent of them in the South; the freed population, most of whom were in the North, numbered under half a million.

Population Growth Since 1865

During the late nineteenth and early twentieth centuries, the white population grew faster than the black population. The primary reasons were the increased European immigration into the United States and the decline and eventual cessation of the slave trade. In 1900, there were 8.8 million African Americans in the United States, representing 11.6 percent of the total population. Between 1910 and 1930, the percentage of African American population declined, reaching a low point in 1930, when African Americans constituted only 9.7 percent of the total United States population. Since 1930, however, the African American population has grown at a rate faster than the national average. According to the 1990 census, the African American population constituted 12.1 percent of the population, up from 11.7 percent in 1980. By 1997, the African American population in the United States had grown to 32.3 million or 12.0 percent of the nation's total resident population.

The growth of the African American population since the 1980 census is largely due to natural increase and net immigration. Natural increase has been the major source of growth. This increase in the number of births over deaths was due mainly to two factors: (1) a young age structure, placing a large percentage of African Americans in the childbearing ages and a smaller percentage in the ages of high mortality risk; and (2) a high age-specific fertility rate for African American women under twenty-five years of age.

The African American population has also grown through immigration—legal as well as illegal. While streams of Asian and Hispanic migrants to the United States have been more highly publicized, black immigration has also increased. The Caribbean basin is one source of black immigration, with immigrants primarily from Jamaica and Haiti entering the United States to look for work. The Mariel boatlift in 1980 also brought some blacks from Cuba. Political and economic conditions in Africa, in addition, have provided many people with incentive to emigrate to the United States. African students overstaying their student visas and working in the United States have contributed to immigration rates. Estimations of the size and effects of some of these sources of new population growth are speculative. But according to the U.S. Census Bureau, legal immigration in 1996 from several Caribbean countries (ex., Jamaica, Haiti, Dominican Republic, Trinidad and Tobago, and Cuba) and African nations amounted to approximately 170,000.

The increase in the African American population can also be attributed to higher than average fertility rates. As a result, the black population is somewhat younger than the white population and contains a slightly larger proportion of persons in the prime reproductive ages. A second reason is that blacks have higher age-adjusted fertility rates than whites (i.e., higher fertility even when differences in age composition are taken into account).

Census Bureau reports from 1997 show that the African American population is roughly 32,298,000, or approximately 12.0 percent of the U.S. population. This figure is higher than the total populations for many nations. The African American population in the United States, for example, is slightly larger than the entire population of Canada. The only African nations with populations larger than the African American population are Nigeria (110.5 million), Egypt (66.1 million), Ethiopia (58.4 million), Democratic Republic of the Congo (49.0 million), South Africa (42.8 million), and Sudan (33.6 million). (Population figures for these African countries are taken from 1998 U.S. Census Bureau statistics.)

Between 1991–1996, more than 114,000 Haitian refugees fled the political and economic strife in their homeland for the United States (AP/Wide World Photos, Inc.).

◆ REGIONAL DISTRIBUTION

1790 to 1900

From 1790 until 1900, approximately ninety percent of the African American population resided in the South, mostly in rural areas. Even the abolition of slavery following the Civil War had only a minimal short-term impact on the Southern, rural character of the African American population. Once the Reconstruction Period ended, however, some African American leaders urged others to migrate from the South.

Early Migration

One early exodus occurred in the period 1879 to 1881, when some fifty thousand African Americans moved into Kansas from southern Louisiana. The impetus behind this initial migration was the need for social, political, and economic freedom. The immigration to Kansas strained the resources of the state, and several

Even after the end of slavery, many African Americans remained in the South and continued to cultivate the white-owned lands as sharecroppers (Schomburg Center for Research in Black Culture).

cities became African American refugee camps. One of the towns created by this exodus was Nicodemus, Kansas, which still exists as a small, all-African American community. Later in 1891, several thousand African Americans migrated to Kansas from South Carolina. Eventually, they were joined by thousands more from Alabama.

Although other migrations by African Americans to the Midwest or Northeast have been chronicled, the effect on the regional distribution of the total African American population was minor: when the Emancipation Proclamation was signed, under eight percent of all African Americans lived in the Northeast or Midwest. After the Civil War, the percentage of the nation's African American population living in the Northeast fell slightly, while the percentage rose in the Midwest. By 1900, only ten percent of all African Americans lived in these two Northern regions.

1900 to 1970

In 1900, almost ninety percent of African Americans still lived in the South. Between 1910 and 1920, however, the percentage of African Americans living in the South began to fall. By 1930, more than 21.2 percent of African Americans resided outside of the South. For the next four decades, the percentage of African Americans living in the South steadily fell. In 1970, about 39 percent of African Americans were Northerners, 53 percent were Southerners, and about 7.5 percent lived in the West.

The Great Migration

Historians and social scientists have long debated why African Americans failed to leave the South in larger numbers at the end of the Civil War. Virtually every migration stream is the product of both push and pull factors—prejudice, discrimination, and a poor economic opportunities in the South obviously provided the strong push factors needed to generate out-migration, while a somewhat more open society and the presence of jobs in the industrializing North should have provided the pull to establish a strong South-to-North migration stream. Some African Americans did leave the South during the last decades of the nineteenth century, typically following transportation routes directly northward. However, the number of African Americans moving North has always seemed smaller than what might be expected given the combined push and pull forces.

European immigration may be one explanation for the relatively slow start of the Southern exodus by African Americans. As the North industrialized in the late nineteenth and early twentieth centuries, it generated a huge demand for labor, which was met in large part by massive immigration of Europeans. Many of the urban factory jobs were filled first by Irish and German laborers and later by immigrants from Southern and Eastern Europe, particularly Italy. If Northern industries had not been able to meet their labor needs through immigration, they might have relied more on domestic sources including African Americans from the South.

As immigration to the United States was curtailed by World War I and restrictive legislation passed in the 1920s, African Americans began to leave the South in larger numbers. As a consequence, the proportion of the nation's African American population living in the South fell more rapidly between 1910 and 1920 than during the entire period since Emancipation.

Although African American migration from the South was reduced somewhat during the Great Depression of the 1930s, the proportion of African Americans living in the South continued to decrease. The greatest volume of migration of African Americans in the South occurred in the decade between 1940 and 1950. This migration was precipitated partly by mobilization for World War II. Therefore, both World War I and World War II provided a powerful impetus for African Americans to leave the South.

During the 1940s, 1950s, and 1960s, the net migration of African Americans from the South totaled about 4.3 million persons. Mechanization of Southern agriculture after World War II decreased the demand for low-wage labor and gave African Americans further incentive to leave agricultural areas. The continued exodus of rural African Americans decreased the supply of farm labor and encouraged Southern farmers to adopt labor-saving methods.

The exodus of African Americans from the South during the thirty years between 1940 and 1970 is one of the major migrations in U.S. history. In volume, it equals the total Italian immigration to the United States during its peak, the thirty-year period from the mid-1890s to the mid-1920s. For most African Americans, this journey out of the South meant exchanging a rural, agricultural existence for an urban life based on factory jobs.

Migration During the 1970s and 1980s

By the 1970s, the African American migration from the South had slowed dramatically. Although African Americans continued to leave the South, many returned; a few Northern-born African Americans, the children of earlier migrants, moved to the South in response to the availability of jobs and a change in the political and social climate. In the early 1970s, as many African Americans were moving to the region as were leaving it. By the mid-1980s, due to reduced economic growth in some areas of the South, particularly in those areas where economies had been built around the oil and gas industries, African American migration to the South had leveled off. The percentage of African Americans living in the western United States has increased from 0.5 percent in 1910 to 9.4 percent in 1990.

Migration During the 1990s and Beyond

The 1990s marked the start of a new migration, whereby more African Americans were returning to the South. During the early 1990s, 368,800 African Americans—primarily business professionals, blue-collar workers, and retirees—returned to various Southern states. This had a sizeable effect on the rest of the United States population: In the Northeastern states, the African American population decreased by 233,600; in the Midwestern states, the African American population decreased by 106,500; and the Western states incurred a loss of 28,700 African Americans. Consequently, from 1990 to 1996, the overall Southern population grew faster than any other region of the United States. In the year 2000, about 37 percent of African Americans are projected to live in the North, 53 percent in the South, and 10 percent in the West.

◆ AFRICAN AMERICAN TOWNS AND SETTLEMENTS

Between 1830 and 1840, the Five Civilized Nations (i.e., Cherokee, Choctaws, Creeks, Chickasaws, and Seminoles) were forced to migrate from the South to the Indian Territory, which is now present-day Oklahoma. With them, they brought their African American slaves to resume their primarily agricultural way of life. After the Civil War—a conflict in which both Native and African Americans participated—most of these tribes freed their slaves. (One exception being the Chickasaws, who refused to recognize the Treaty of 1866, which mandated that the Five Civilized Nations adopt their freedmen.)

Along with approximately ten thousand African American settlers that migrated westward to Kansas and to Oklahoma during the Land Rush of 1889, these freedmen established approximately 27 towns and settlements in the Indian and Oklahoma Territories. Today, no traces exist of many of these places. Listed below in chronological order, however, are some Oklahoma towns and settlements, as well as several African American towns of the South, that are still in existence.

Nicodemus, Kansas

Founded in 1877, Nicodemus, Kansas, is one of the first all-African American settlements on record. This early westward migration was chiefly due to the efforts of lecturer Benjamin Singleton, who urged African Americans throughout the South to move to Kansas and Oklahoma in order to gain greater, social, political, and economic freedom. Though many other settlements disappeared because of crop failures and the lure of growing urban areas, Nicodemus has remained. In 1974, it was declared a national historic landmark.

Langston, Oklahoma

Langston, Oklahoma was founded in 1889 by Edwin P. McCabe, the first African American to serve as state auditor in Kansas. After purchasing 320 acres of land in Oklahoma, he named the settlement after John Mercer Langston, a Virginian who had recently been elected to Congress. By 1897, Langston grew to a population of more than two thousand residents, and the Oklahoma territorial legislature granted the settlement enough land to establish the Colored Agricultural and Normal University, the first African American agricultural and mechanical college. (Today, it is known as Langston University, the most westward institution of the historical African American colleges and universities.) Shortly afterwards, McCabe initiated an unsuccessful campaign to make Oklahoma an all-African American state.

During the nineteenth century, some African Americans married and raised families within Native American communities (The Denver Public Library).

Boley, Oklahoma

In 1903, the historical black town of Boley was founded in the seized land of the Creek Nation of the Indian Territory. In 1905, the prominent leader Booker T. Washington praised this developing town as a social experiment in self-government and recommended that other African Americans migrate there. By 1910, Boley had four thousand residents and was comprised of eighty acres of land. For a time, it seemed that such burgeoning Oklahoma towns as Boley would finally offer African Americans the opportunity for greater political, economic, and social freedom.

As Oklahoma pushed toward statehood, however, it became evident that these dreams would not be realized. Though African American leaders asked President Theodore Roosevelt and Congress for assurances that Jim Crow laws would not be enacted in Oklahoma, the territory was granted statehood in 1907 without such guarantees. By 1910, grandfather clauses prohibiting African and Native Americans from voting or holding elected office and racial violence made Oklahoma yet another nightmare for minorities. Today, Boley is a much smaller town with a total population of approximately 750 residents. Each Memorial Day weekend, the town hosts the Boley Black Rodeo, in which horseriders from throughout the region participate in various skills events.

The Sea Islands, South Carolina and Georgia

The Gullah or Geechee people are an African American fishing community located on the sea islands along the coasts of Georgia and South Carolina. Captured from the west coast of Africa and sold into slavery in Charleston, South Carolina, in the 1800s, the Gullah, unlike other African slaves, were kept together, due to their rice farming skills, tolerance of the semitropical climate of the sea islands, and resistance to malaria. Since the Gullah people remained on islands, there was no imminent danger of the slaves escaping from their masters. Thus, a laissez-faire policy was adopted towards the slaves, allowing the Gullah people to retain their traditional ways of life.

Today, the Gullah still share many similarities with the people of the west coast of Africa, specifically Sierra Leone. Besides music, art, religion, food, and labor skills, the best example is their language. A Creole blend of Elizabethan English and African languages spoken by the Wolof and Fula peoples, it developed in the slave communities of the isolated plantations of the coastal South. Even after the sea islands were freed in 1861, the Gullah speech flourished, since access to the islands was limited through the 1950s. Each May, the Gullah Festival is held to celebrate the heritage of these unique African Americans.

Eatonville, Florida

The town of Eatonville, Florida, incorporated in 1888, is considered the oldest African American municipality in the United States. The hometown of African American author, folklorist, and anthropologist Zora Neale Hurston, Eatonville is located approximately ten miles northeast of downtown Orlando. In late 1987, the Association to Preserve the Eatonville Community, Inc. was formed to preserve this unique town and its cultural traditions. The association achieves its aim by, among other things, annually holding the Zora Neale Hurston Festival of the Arts and Humanities.

American Beach, Florida

In 1935, African American insurance millionaire Abraham Lincoln Lewis purchased twenty acres of land on Florida's Amelia Island and renamed it American Beach. His goal was to encourage other prominent African

American business professionals to do the same and, eventually, to offer African Americans a resort for rest and relaxation.(Segregation laws at that time prohibited African Americans from using public beaches, reserving them for whites only.)

In 1999, there were 150 permanent residents on American Beach spanning an area of 78 acres. Thus far, the local residents have kept its historical identity intact. However, with upscale developers building expensive, trendy resorts around the residents and speculators coveting their property, they feel that their community maybe soon threatened.

Virgina Key, Florida

Throughout the early twentieth century, Jim Crow laws banned African Americans from visiting the scenic beaches of southern Florida. However in 1945, the local Dade County government made a deserted barrier island called Virginia Key the county's only beach for African Americans. It became an important recreational and cultural center for the community, drawing families, church groups, fraternities, sororities, entertainers, athletes, and others. This tradition continued until the mid-1960s, when the county government was mandated by desegregation laws to open other beaches to African Americans. During that same decade, a hurricane destroyed much of what remained of the permanent buildings.

In 1999, the city of Miami, its legal owner, began to consider leasing the property to developers of resort hotels and upscale campgrounds. However, an alliance of environmentalists, historians, and African American activists are fighting that plan. They would prefer that the key remain undeveloped, with the exception of a civil rights park that would honor African American residents who fought against segregation.

◆ CONTEMPORARY DEMOGRAPHIC CHARACTERISTICS

The African American Population By State

African Americans are most populous in the South, which contains 53 percent of the nation's total African American population. In 1997, of the ten states with the largest African American populations (New York, California, Texas, Florida, Georgia, Illinois, North Carolina, Maryland, Louisiana, and Michigan), six were in the South. Fifty-nine percent of the African American population resided in these states. Six other states had African American populations of one million or more in 1997: Virginia (1,344,000), Ohio (1,278,000), New Jersey (1,170,000), Pennsylvania (1,164,000), South Carolina (1,130,000), and Alabama (1,120,000).

The African American Urban Population

In 1960, 64.7 percent of the African American population resided in metropolitan areas in the United States, 51.4 percent of whom resided in central cities, as opposed to suburban areas and rural areas outside the city. In 1970, 74.3 percent of the African American population resided in metropolitan areas, with 58.2 percent living in central cities. By 1990, 83.8 percent of the African American population resided in metropolitan areas, while the proportion residing in central cities declined slightly to 57.3 percent.

In 1960, African Americans constituted 16.7 percent of all central city residents; by 1970, African Americans constituted 20.6 percent. One reason for this increase has been the continued growth, although at a slower rate than in earlier decades, of the African American population. A second reason for this change has been the migration of whites out of the central cities to suburban and rural areas.

As a consequence of migration and population shifts, African Americans increasingly became concentrated in urban areas called ghettos. As in the South, the land and buildings of the ghettos were frequently owned by whites who controlled the community from afar. These urban areas not only supported segregation between racial groups, but also created intragroup boundaries among African Americans of differing socioeconomic status.

Ghettos offered lower-income African Americans two harsh choices: either dilapidated, privately-owned housing or large public housing projects that posed significant problems, such as poorly maintained facilities, unsafe conditions, and incentives for crime. Later in the century, as African Americans migrated outside large metropolitan areas, many of these problematic housing projects were demolished.

In 1980, African Americans made up 22.5 percent of the total central city population. However, by 1990 this number fell to 22.1 percent. Similar to the white population, though in smaller numbers, the African American population was migrating out of central cities to suburban and rural areas.

Among the fifteen cities with the largest African American concentrations, Washington, DC and Atlanta had African American majorities by 1970. By 1990, four additional cities (i.e., Detroit, Baltimore, Memphis, and New Orleans) had African American majorities, and five of the eleven largest cities in the nation were more than fifty percent African American.

In 1996, the city of New York, the most populous city in the United States, also has the largest African American population in the nation; over 3.8 million African

Americans resided in Greater New York City. Washington, DC, Chicago, Los Angeles, Philadelphia, Detroit, Atlanta, and Houston follow, in that order, as cities with the largest African American populations.

The African American Suburban and Nonmetropolitan Populations

The 1970s marked a turning point in the percentage of African Americans outside of central cities. Between 1980 and 1990, the black population living in suburbs grew faster than did the white suburban population. The white suburban population grew by 9.1 percent, whereas the black suburban population increased by 9.9 percent. In 1980, African Americans constituted 6.1 percent of the suburban population; by 1990, African Americans constituted 6.9 percent. In 1960, only 13.3 percent of African Americans residing in metropolitan areas lived in suburban areas. By 1970 this number increased to 16.1 percent; by 1980 it had increased to 23.3 percent. In 1990, 26.6 percent of the African American metropolitan population resided in suburban areas.

This is an important development since it signifies that, for the first time, the number of African Americans moving to suburban areas has become large enough to significantly affect the overall distribution of the African American population. The access by African Americans to suburban residences is important for many reasons. One reason is that African American suburbanization may further such ideals as an open housing market, freedom of movement, and the ability to choose a neighborhood that balances a family's income and its preferences and needs, such as the availability of quality public schools for children.

African American suburbanization may be beneficial in other ways as well. Since many jobs have moved from cities to the suburbs, a greater share of African Americans living in suburbs might have long-term consequences for improving employment opportunities and occupational mobility. Finally, for many Americans, a move to the suburbs has meant owning a home, a major form of wealth accumulation for middle-class families. African Americans have been less likely to own their own home than whites, even when income and other socioeconomic characteristics are taken into account. A trend toward suburbanization might offer more African Americans the opportunity to build equity in a home and thus help to secure middle-class status and the transmission of that status across generations.

The reasons for the increased movement of African Americans to suburbs are doubtlessly heterogeneous. On the one hand, open housing legislation and changing attitudes have contributed to breaking down the barriers to African American access to the suburbs. On the other hand, there has been an increase in the number of middle-income African American families. Many of these African American families rely on dual incomes, allowing them to afford the safety, good schools, acreage, and other amenities often cited by those who have chosen to move from the city to the suburbs.

Although the number of African Americans residing in suburban areas has increased, the numbers are still far below those of the white population. According to the Bureau of the Census, in 1991 only 26.7 percent of the African American population resided in suburbs, compared to 50.7 percent of the white population.

Median Age

Although both the black and white populations have aged, the African American population has remained younger than the white population throughout most of the twentieth century. In 1980, the black population had a median age of 24.8 years, the white population a median age of 30.8 years. In 1997, the black population's median age rose to 29.8 years, while the median age for the white population rose to 36.0 years.

The aging of the "baby boomers" (i.e., persons born between the years 1946 and 1964) was the primary reason for the rise in median ages for both the black and white populations. One reason for the difference between the black and white median ages is the differing age structures of the two populations. Compared with the white population, a greater percentage of the African American population is under 18 years of age, while a smaller percentage of the population is over 65 years. In 1997, 32 percent of the African American population was under the age of 18 and 8 percent over the age of 65 years. Only 23 percent of the white population was under the age of 18 in this same year, while 14 percent of the population was over the age of 65.

◆ POPULATION PROJECTIONS FOR THE TWENTIETH-FIRST CENTURY

The African American population is projected to grow significantly during the next fifty years. Based on 1997 U.S. Bureau of Census figures, the African American population is projected to increase by nearly 3.3.million by 2000, over 5.2 million by 2010, and almost 13.2 million by 2030. Overall, during the next fifty years, the African American population is projected to grow by 60 percent to 53.5 million. The African American share of the total national population is expected to increase to 12.2 percent in 2000, 12.6 percent in 2010, and 13.6 percent in 2050.(These figures reflect middle series projections cited in the *Statistical Abstract of the United States: 1998.*)

However, Hispanic and Asian American populations are projected to increase at an even greater rate, while the white population will decrease. Hispanic Americans, considered the fastest growing ethnic group, made up 11.0 percent of the U.S. population in 1997. By 2050, they will comprise almost 25.0 percent of the overall population. Asian Americans comprised 4.0 percent of the national population in 1997. By 2050, they will more than double to nearly 8.2 percent. On the other hand, whites comprised approximately 73.0 percent of the national population in 1997. By 2050, they are projected to decrease to about 53.0 percent. These population shifts will most likely precipitate racial tension, as these various groups compete for increased political representation, government funding, and affirmative action policies.

In addition, as the population continues to diversify, the issue of how to enumerate people of mixed racial backgrounds on the U.S. Census and other federal forms will need to be addressed in the twenty-first century. This, too, will have an impact on population figures and, consequently, political representation of all groups at the local, state, and federal levels.

◆ POPULATION STATISTICS

Resident Population, by Race, Hispanic Origin, and Single Years of Age: 1997

[**In thousands, except as indicated.** As of **July 1**. Resident population.]

AGE	Total	RACE				Hispanic origin [1]	NOT OF HISPANIC ORIGIN			
		White	Black	American Indian, Eskimo, Aleut	Asian, Pacific Islander		White	Black	American Indian, Eskimo, Aleut	Asian, Pacific Islander
Total	**267,636**	**221,334**	**33,947**	**2,322**	**10,033**	**29,348**	**194,571**	**32,298**	**1,976**	**9,443**
Under 5 yrs. old . .	19,150	15,184	2,892	202	872	3,347	12,128	2,703	166	806
Under 1 yr. old .	3,797	3,021	555	41	180	690	2,390	517	33	166
1 yr. old	3,773	3,009	550	39	175	674	2,392	513	32	162
2 yrs. old	3,795	3,016	567	39	172	666	2,408	530	32	159
3 yrs. old	3,838	3,034	591	41	173	658	2,432	554	34	160
4 yrs. old	3,947	3,105	628	42	172	658	2,505	590	35	159
5-9 yrs. old.	19,738	15,560	3,147	226	805	2,928	12,900	2,976	190	745
5 yrs. old	4,022	3,168	634	43	176	657	2,568	597	36	164
6 yrs. old	4,043	3,196	633	42	172	625	2,625	598	36	160
7 yrs. old	4,029	3,185	640	47	157	584	2,656	606	40	145
8 yrs. old	3,732	2,934	607	46	146	521	2,464	575	38	134
9 yrs. old	3,912	3,076	633	48	154	542	2,587	599	40	143
10-14 yrs. old	19,040	15,093	2,937	239	770	2,515	12,819	2,790	202	714
10 yrs. old	3,873	3,065	612	47	150	521	2,594	580	40	138
11 yrs. old	3,813	3,031	585	47	149	509	2,571	556	39	138
12 yrs. old	3,799	3,011	587	48	154	494	2,564	558	40	143
13 yrs. old	3,725	2,954	566	48	157	488	2,512	539	41	145
14 yrs. old	3,829	3,033	586	49	161	502	2,578	558	42	149
15-19 yrs. old	19,068	15,151	2,963	219	735	2,580	12,802	2,819	184	683
15 yrs. old	3,870	3,061	604	48	157	503	2,606	575	40	146
16 yrs. old	3,815	3,031	585	46	152	513	2,565	557	39	142
17 yrs. old	3,915	3,106	614	46	150	522	2,630	585	38	139
18 yrs. old	3,679	2,928	576	40	134	503	2,469	548	33	125
19 yrs. old	3,789	3,024	583	40	141	538	2,532	554	34	131
20-24 yrs. old	17,512	13,970	2,598	186	758	2,571	11,609	2,466	155	711
20 yrs. old	3,738	2,985	572	38	143	537	2,493	543	32	134
21 yrs. old	3,510	2,799	525	37	149	522	2,321	498	31	139
22 yrs. old	3,450	2,764	501	36	149	507	2,297	476	30	139
23 yrs. old	3,337	2,659	490	36	152	492	2,208	465	30	143
24 yrs. old	3,476	2,762	510	38	166	513	2,291	484	32	156
25-29 yrs. old	18,869	15,163	2,615	191	900	2,567	12,821	2,477	157	847
25 yrs. old	3,637	2,896	526	39	177	504	2,434	500	33	166
26 yrs. old	3,876	3,104	545	40	186	521	2,629	517	33	175
27 yrs. old	3,890	3,139	526	39	186	518	2,666	498	32	174
28 yrs. old	3,578	2,906	471	34	167	489	2,460	445	28	157
29 yrs. old	3,888	3,118	547	38	185	535	2,632	517	31	174
30-34 yrs. old	20,741	16,903	2,762	184	892	2,664	14,476	2,610	152	839
30 yrs. old	3,882	3,147	527	36	173	531	2,662	497	29	162
31 yrs. old	3,901	3,154	535	36	176	528	2,673	505	29	165
32 yrs. old	4,146	3,378	554	37	178	533	2,892	523	30	168
33 yrs. old	4,288	3,519	557	37	176	528	3,037	527	30	166
34 yrs. old	4,524	3,706	590	39	189	544	3,212	558	32	178
35-39 yrs. old	22,625	18,710	2,858	183	874	2,415	16,513	2,716	155	825
35 yrs. old	4,573	3,770	586	38	179	513	3,303	557	32	168
36 yrs. old	4,492	3,722	559	36	175	508	3,259	530	31	165
37 yrs. old	4,572	3,772	584	37	178	488	3,329	555	32	168
38 yrs. old	4,249	3,525	529	34	161	435	3,129	504	29	153
39 yrs. old	4,739	3,921	599	38	181	472	3,493	570	32	171
40-44 yrs. old	21,373	17,806	2,582	165	820	1,976	16,013	2,464	142	778
40 yrs. old	4,583	3,803	571	36	173	437	3,407	544	31	164
41 yrs. old	4,308	3,576	527	34	171	416	3,198	502	29	162
42 yrs. old	4,257	3,546	515	33	163	396	3,187	492	28	154
43 yrs. old	4,098	3,412	490	33	163	363	3,083	468	29	155
44 yrs. old	4,128	3,468	480	30	150	364	3,137	459	26	142

See footnotes at end of table.

Resident Population, by Race, Hispanic Origin, and Single Years of Age: 1997—Continued

AGE	Total	RACE				Hispanic origin [1]	NOT OF HISPANIC ORIGIN			
		White	Black	American Indian, Eskimo, Aleut	Asian, Pacific Islander		White	Black	American Indian, Eskimo, Aleut	Asian, Pacific Islander
45-49 yrs. old	18,470	15,564	2,077	134	694	1,494	14,205	1,990	118	662
45 yrs. old	3,951	3,325	454	29	143	331	3,024	434	25	136
46 yrs. old	3,674	3,087	419	27	141	316	2,800	401	24	134
47 yrs. old	3,681	3,072	434	28	147	300	2,801	416	24	140
48 yrs. old	3,420	2,906	364	24	126	268	2,661	349	21	120
49 yrs. old	3,744	3,174	406	27	138	280	2,919	389	24	132
50-54 yrs. old	15,163	13,049	1,500	103	510	1,116	12,030	1,438	92	487
50 yrs. old	3,898	3,382	367	25	124	270	3,135	352	22	118
51 yrs. old	2,724	2,319	280	21	105	225	2,113	267	18	100
52 yrs. old	2,770	2,368	285	19	98	214	2,172	273	17	94
53 yrs. old	2,790	2,400	281	19	91	203	2,214	270	17	87
54 yrs. old	2,981	2,582	288	19	92	204	2,395	276	17	88
55-59 yrs. old	11,757	10,091	1,208	77	380	836	9,327	1,161	70	364
55 yrs. old	2,532	2,156	275	17	84	178	1,995	264	16	81
56 yrs. old	2,440	2,100	246	16	78	177	1,937	236	14	75
57 yrs. old	2,356	2,015	249	16	77	170	1,859	239	14	74
58 yrs. old	2,168	1,879	210	14	66	154	1,737	202	12	64
59 yrs. old	2,260	1,942	229	15	74	156	1,799	220	13	70
60-64 yrs. old	10,056	8,683	1,004	61	308	677	8,062	967	55	295
60 yrs. old	2,087	1,797	210	13	67	144	1,665	202	12	64
61 yrs. old	2,030	1,754	201	12	62	141	1,625	193	11	60
62 yrs. old	2,048	1,771	203	12	61	139	1,643	195	11	59
63 yrs. old	1,923	1,668	187	11	57	127	1,551	180	10	55
64 yrs. old	1,968	1,693	204	11	60	126	1,578	197	10	57
65-69 yrs. old	9,762	8,525	935	48	254	579	7,993	903	44	244
65 yrs. old	1,947	1,679	203	11	55	120	1,570	196	10	53
66 yrs. old	1,996	1,736	197	10	53	123	1,623	190	9	51
67 yrs. old	1,985	1,734	191	10	51	119	1,625	184	9	49
68 yrs. old	1,889	1,659	173	9	48	110	1,558	167	8	46
69 yrs. old	1,946	1,717	172	9	48	108	1,618	166	8	46
70-74 yrs. old	8,736	7,785	713	39	199	442	7,376	691	35	192
70 yrs. old	1,854	1,636	165	9	45	98	1,545	160	8	43
71 yrs. old	1,787	1,585	152	8	42	94	1,499	148	7	40
72 yrs. old	1,788	1,600	139	8	41	90	1,516	135	7	40
73 yrs. old	1,683	1,512	128	7	36	82	1,436	124	7	35
74 yrs. old	1,623	1,452	129	7	35	77	1,380	125	6	34
75-79 yrs. old	7,063	6,366	538	28	131	299	6,088	524	26	127
75 yrs. old	1,619	1,456	125	7	32	72	1,389	121	6	31
76 yrs. old	1,529	1,383	112	6	29	67	1,320	109	6	28
77 yrs. old	1,383	1,244	107	5	27	59	1,189	104	5	26
78 yrs. old	1,316	1,188	100	5	23	53	1,139	97	5	22
79 yrs. old	1,216	1,095	95	5	21	47	1,051	93	4	20
80-84 yrs. old	4,642	4,226	325	18	74	182	4,056	317	17	71
80 yrs. old	1,090	991	77	4	18	42	953	75	4	17
81 yrs. old	1,008	920	68	4	16	39	884	66	3	15
82 yrs. old	930	849	63	3	15	37	815	62	3	14
83 yrs. old	848	773	58	3	13	34	742	57	3	13
84 yrs. old	766	692	59	3	12	31	663	57	3	12
85-89 yrs. old	2,456	2,238	172	10	35	100	2,145	168	9	34
90-94 yrs. old	1,058	952	85	5	15	45	910	84	5	14
95-99 yrs. old	298	263	27	2	5	13	251	27	2	5
100 yrs. old and over	60	50	8	1	1	3	48	8	1	1
Median age (yr.)	34.9	36.0	29.7	27.2	31.0	26.4	37.4	29.8	27.8	31.3

[1] Persons of Hispanic origin may be of any race.

Source: U.S. Bureau of the Census, Population Paper Listing 91.

Resident Population, by Hispanic Origin Status, 1980 to 1997, and Projections, 1998 to 2050

[In thousands, except as indicated. As of July, except as indicated. These data are consistent with the 1980 and 1990 decennial enumerations and have been modified from the official census counts; see text, Section 1, for explanation. See headnote, Table 3. Minus sign (-) indicates decrease]

YEAR	Total	Hispanic origin [1]	NOT OF HISPANIC ORIGIN			
			White	Black	American Indian, Eskimo, Aleut	Asian, Pacific Islander
1980 (April) [2]	226,546	14,609	180,906	26,142	1,326	3,563
1981	229,466	15,560	181,974	26,532	1,377	4,022
1982	231,664	16,240	182,782	26,856	1,420	4,367
1983	233,792	16,935	183,561	27,159	1,466	4,671
1984	235,825	17,640	184,243	27,444	1,512	4,986
1985	237,924	18,368	184,945	27,738	1,558	5,315
1986	240,133	19,154	185,678	28,040	1,606	5,655
1987	242,289	19,946	186,353	28,351	1,654	5,985
1988	244,499	20,786	187,012	28,669	1,703	6,329
1989	246,819	21,648	187,713	29,005	1,755	6,698
1990 (April) [3]	248,765	22,372	188,307	29,299	1,796	6,992
1991	252,124	23,432	189,590	29,849	1,829	7,425
1992	255,002	24,361	190,657	30,333	1,856	7,794
1993	257,753	25,334	191,606	30,778	1,882	8,153
1994	260,292	26,302	192,426	31,189	1,906	8,469
1995	262,761	27,274	193,198	31,566	1,929	8,794
1996	265,179	28,305	193,875	31,927	1,952	9,120
1997	267,636	29,348	194,571	32,298	1,976	9,443
PROJECTIONS						
Lowest series:						
1998	268,396	29,115	195,037	32,647	1,999	9,598
1999	269,861	29,757	195,307	32,962	2,020	9,815
2000	271,237	30,393	195,505	33,267	2,041	10,030
2005	276,990	33,527	195,589	34,652	2,145	11,077
2010	281,468	36,652	194,628	35,856	2,243	12,088
2015	285,472	39,927	193,150	36,956	2,337	13,102
2020	288,807	43,287	191,047	37,913	2,424	14,136
2030	291,070	49,834	183,295	39,202	2,573	16,166
2040	287,685	56,104	171,054	39,841	2,695	17,991
2050	282,524	62,230	157,701	40,118	2,793	19,683
Middle series:						
1998	270,002	29,566	195,786	32,789	2,005	9,856
1999	272,330	30,461	196,441	33,180	2,029	10,219
2000	274,634	31,366	197,061	33,568	2,054	10,584
2005	285,981	36,057	199,802	35,485	2,183	12,454
2010	297,716	41,139	202,390	37,466	2,320	14,402
2015	310,134	46,705	205,019	39,512	2,461	16,437
2020	322,742	52,652	207,393	41,538	2,601	18,557
2030	346,899	65,570	209,998	45,448	2,891	22,993
2040	369,980	80,164	209,621	49,379	3,203	27,614
2050	393,931	96,508	207,901	53,555	3,534	32,432
Highest series:						
1998	271,647	30,019	196,521	32,971	2,010	10,127
1999	274,865	31,172	197,556	33,457	2,038	10,642
2000	278,129	32,350	198,594	33,952	2,066	11,166
2005	295,318	38,648	203,949	36,589	2,218	13,914
2010	314,571	45,760	209,963	39,572	2,391	16,885
2015	335,597	53,686	216,482	42,800	2,575	20,055
2020	357,702	62,279	223,082	46,183	2,765	23,392
2030	405,089	81,803	235,898	53,604	3,192	30,593
2040	458,444	105,274	248,715	62,132	3,703	38,620
2050	518,903	133,106	262,140	71,863	4,295	47,498
PERCENT DISTRIBUTION						
Middle series:						
2000	100.0	11.4	71.8	12.2	0.7	3.9
2010	100.0	13.8	68.0	12.6	0.8	4.8
2020	100.0	16.3	64.3	12.9	0.8	5.7
2030	100.0	18.9	60.5	13.1	0.8	6.6
2040	100.0	21.7	56.7	13.3	0.9	7.5
2050	100.0	24.5	52.8	13.6	0.9	8.2
PERCENT CHANGE (middle series)						
2000-2010	8.4	31.2	2.7	11.6	12.9	36.1
2010-2020	8.4	28.0	2.5	10.9	12.1	28.9
2020-2030	7.5	24.5	1.3	9.4	11.1	23.9
2030-2040	6.7	22.3	-0.2	8.6	10.8	20.1
2040-2050	6.5	20.4	-0.8	8.5	10.3	17.4

[1] Persons of Hispanic origin may be of any race. [2] See footnote 4, Table 1. [3] The April 1, 1990, census count (248,765,170) includes count resolution corrections processed through August 1997, and does not include adjustments for census coverage errors except for adjustments estimated for the 1995 Census Test in Oakland, California; Patterson, New Jersey; and six Louisiana parishes. These adjustments amounted to a total of 55,297 persons.

Source: U.S. Bureau of the Census, *Current Population Reports*, P25-1095 and P25-1130; and Population Paper Listing PPL-91.

Metropolitan Areas With Large Numbers of Selected Racial Groups and of Hispanic Origin Population: 1996

[As of **July 1**. For Black, Hispanic origin, and Asian and Pacific Islander populations, areas selected had 100,000 or more of specified group; for American Indian, Eskimo, and Aleut population, areas selected are ten areas with largest number of that group.]

METROPOLITAN AREA	Number of specified group (1,000)	Percent of total metro. area	METROPOLITAN AREA	Number of specified group (1,000)	Percent of total metro. area
BLACK			**HISPANIC ORIGIN [1]**		
New York-Northern New Jersey-Long Island, NY-NJ-CT-PA CMSA/NECMA [2]	3,839	19.3	Los Angeles-Riverside-Orange County, CA CMSA	5,850	37.8
Washington-Baltimore, DC-MD-VA-WV CMSA	1,840	25.7	New York-Northern New Jersey-Long Island, NY- NJ-CT-PA CMSA/NECMA [2]	3,325	16.8
Chicago-Gary-Kenosha, IL-IN-WI CMSA	1,656	19.3	Miami-Fort Lauderdale, FL CMSA	1,286	36.6
Los Angeles-Riverside-Orange County, CA CMSA	1,306	8.4	San Francisco-Oakland-San Jose, CA CMSA	1,228	18.6
Philadelphia-Wilmington-Atlantic City, PA-NJ-DE-MD CMSA	1,160	19.4	Chicago-Gary-Kenosha, IL-IN-WI CMSA	1,125	13.1
Detroit-Ann Arbor-Flint, MI CMSA	1,108	21.0	Houston-Galveston-Brazoria, TX CMSA	1,005	23.6
Atlanta, GA MSA	914	25.8	San Antonio, TX MSA	777	52.1
Houston-Galveston-Brazoria, TX CMSA	778	18.3	Dallas-Fort Worth, TX CMSA	690	15.1
Miami-Fort Lauderdale, FL CMSA	688	19.6	San Diego, CA MSA	666	25.1
Dallas-Fort Worth, TX CMSA	651	14.2	Phoenix-Mesa, AZ MSA	536	19.5
San Francisco-Oakland-San Jose, CA CMSA	573	8.7	El Paso, TX MSA	503	73.5
Cleveland-Akron, OH CMSA	481	16.5	McAllen-Edinburg-Mission, TX MSA	433	87.3
New Orleans, LA MSA	459	35.0	Fresno, CA MSA	355	41.2
Norfolk-Virginia Beach-Newport News, VA-NC MSA	458	29.7	Washington-Baltimore, DC-MD-VA-WV CMSA	351	4.9
Memphis, TN-AR-MS MSA	452	41.9	Denver-Boulder-Greeley, CO CMSA	320	14.0
St. Louis, MO-IL MSA	449	17.6	Boston-Worcester-Lawrence-Lowell-Brockton, MA-NH NECMA	297	5.1
Boston-Worcester-Lawrence-Lowell-Brockton, MA-NH NECMA	331	5.7	Philadelphia-Wilmington-Atlantic City, PA-NJ-DE-MD CMSA	278	4.7
Richmond-Petersburg, VA MSA	280	29.9	Brownsville-Harlingen-San Benito, TX MSA	266	84.4
Charlotte-Gastonia-Rock Hill, NC-SC MSA	270	20.4	Albuquerque, NM MSA	257	38.4
Birmingham, AL MSA	259	28.9	Austin-San Marcos, TX MSA	253	24.3
Raleigh-Durham-Chapel Hill, NC MSA	248	24.2	Sacramento-Yolo, CA CMSA	235	14.4
Milwaukee-Racine, WI CMSA	243	14.8	Corpus Christi, TX MSA	217	56.5
Kansas City, MO-KS MSA	225	13.3	Tucson, AZ MSA	214	27.9
Tampa-St. Petersburg-Clearwater, FL MSA	224	10.2	Bakersfield, CA MSA	211	33.8
Greensboro—Winston-Salem—High Point, NC MSA	224	19.6	Tampa-St. Petersburg-Clearwater, FL MSA	189	8.6
Jacksonville, FL MSA	223	22.1	Las Vegas, NV-AZ MSA	169	14.1
Cincinnati-Hamilton, OH-KY-IN CMSA	222	11.5	Laredo, TX MSA	168	94.9
Indianapolis, IN MSA	203	13.6	Visalia-Tulare-Porterville, CA MSA	157	44.9
Pittsburgh, PA MSA	197	8.3	Orlando, FL MSA	149	10.5
Orlando, FL MSA	195	13.8	Stockton-Lodi, CA MSA	148	27.7
Columbus, OH MSA	189	13.1	Salinas, CA MSA	135	39.9
Jackson, MS MSA	182	43.3	Seattle-Tacoma-Bremerton, WA CMSA	133	4.0
Baton Rouge, LA MSA	176	31.1	Detroit-Ann Arbor-Flint, MI CMSA	124	2.3
Nashville, TN MSA	176	15.7	Santa Barbara-Santa Maria-Lompoc, CA MSA	124	32.1
San Diego, CA MSA	169	6.4	Portland-Salem, OR-WA CMSA	115	5.6
Seattle-Tacoma-Bremerton, WA CMSA	165	5.0	Modesto, CA MSA	111	26.7
Greenville-Spartanburg-Anderson, SC MSA	161	17.9	Atlanta, GA MSA	105	3.0
			ASIAN AND PACIFIC ISLANDER		
Charleston-North Charleston, SC MSA	154	31.1	Los Angeles-Riverside-Orange County, CA CMSA	1,713	11.1
Augusta-Aiken, GA-SC MSA	149	32.9	New York-Northern New Jersey-Long Island, NY- NJ-CT-PA CMSA/NECMA [2]	1,222	6.2
Columbia, SC MSA	147	30.2	San Francisco-Oakland-San Jose, CA CMSA	1,198	18.1
Mobile, AL MSA	145	28.0	Honolulu, HI MSA	561	64.3
West Palm Beach-Boca Raton, FL MSA	143	14.4	Washington-Baltimore, DC-MD-VA-WV CMSA	342	4.8
Shreveport-Bossier City, LA MSA	138	36.3	Chicago-Gary-Kenosha, IL-IN-WI CMSA	340	3.9
Dayton-Springfield, OH MSA	136	14.3	San Diego, CA MSA	272	10.2
Buffalo-Niagara Falls, NY MSA	134	11.4	Seattle-Tacoma-Bremerton, WA CMSA	254	7.7
Louisville, KY-IN MSA	129	13.0	Houston-Galveston-Brazoria, TX CMSA	206	4.8
Minneapolis-St. Paul, MN-WI MSA	122	4.4	Boston-Worcester-Lawrence-Lowell-Brockton, MA-NH NECMA	195	3.4
Denver-Boulder-Greeley, CO CMSA	119	5.2	Philadelphia-Wilmington-Atlantic City, PA-NJ-DE-MD CMSA	164	2.7
Macon, GA MSA	119	38.0	Sacramento-Yolo, CA CMSA	159	9.7
Montgomery, AL MSA	116	36.7	Dallas-Fort Worth, TX CMSA	154	3.4
Sacramento-Yolo, CA CMSA	115	7.0	**AMERICAN INDIAN, ESKIMO, ALEUT**		
Little Rock-North Little Rock, AR MSA	114	20.8	Los Angeles-Riverside-Orange County, CA CMSA	113	0.7
Oklahoma City, OK MSA	111	10.8	Phoenix-Mesa, AZ MSA	65	2.4
Phoenix-Mesa, AZ MSA	110	4.0	New York-Northern New Jersey-Long Island, NY- NJ-CT-PA CMSA/NECMA [2]	61	0.3
Las Vegas, NV-AZ MSA	109	9.1	Tulsa, OK MSA	50	6.6
Rochester, NY MSA	108	9.9	San Francisco-Oakland-San Jose, CA CMSA	49	0.7
Columbus, GA-AL MSA	108	39.6	Oklahoma City, OK MSA	48	4.7
Lafayette, LA MSA	107	29.1	Seattle-Tacoma-Bremerton, WA CMSA	45	1.3
Austin-San Marcos, TX MSA	104	10.0	Albuquerque, NM MSA	38	5.7
Hartford, CT NECMA	104	9.4	Flagstaff, AZ-UT MSA	34	28.4
Savannah, GA MSA	104	36.6	Minneapolis-St. Paul, MN-WI MSA	28	1.0

[1] Persons of Hispanic origin may be of any race. [2] Includes data for New Haven-Bridgeport-Stamford-Waterbury-Danbury, CT NECMA.

Source: U.S. Bureau of the Census, *State and Metropolitan Area Data Book, 1997-98*, 1998.

Population Projections, by Hispanic-Origin Status—States: 2000 to 2010

[**In thousands.** As of **July 1**. The projections shown here are based on certain internal migration assumptions: Series A, is the preferred series model and uses State-to-State migration observed from 1975-76 through 1993-94. Persons of Hispanic origin may be of any race]

STATE	HISPANIC ORIGIN			NOT OF HISPANIC ORIGIN								
	2000	2005	2010	WHITE			BLACK		AMERICAN INDIAN, ESKIMO, ALEUT		ASIAN, PACIFIC ISLANDER	
				2000	2005	2010	2000	2010	2000	2010	2000	2010
U.S.	**31,366**	**36,057**	**41,138**	**197,062**	**199,802**	**202,390**	**33,569**	**37,466**	**2,055**	**2,321**	**10,585**	**14,402**
AL	37	42	47	3,231	3,355	3,468	1,133	1,223	18	20	32	42
AK	31	37	41	461	476	487	27	31	91	91	44	94
AZ	1,071	1,269	1,450	3,254	3,441	3,518	150	179	232	256	91	119
AR	33	40	46	2,155	2,249	2,320	407	432	15	18	19	23
CA	10,647	12,268	14,214	15,562	15,123	15,394	2,138	2,268	170	165	4,006	5,603
CO	594	682	770	3,268	3,434	3,505	178	216	30	37	98	132
CT	288	332	386	2,622	2,574	2,561	293	338	6	6	76	109
DE	25	29	33	582	596	597	143	165	2	2	15	19
DC	40	46	55	152	156	163	315	322	-	-	13	19
FL	2,390	2,845	3,319	10,405	10,764	11,145	2,159	2,536	39	44	239	319
GA	189	226	252	5,270	5,515	5,671	2,262	2,702	15	16	138	181
HI	107	119	132	363	372	383	27	29	4	5	755	891
ID	96	121	140	1,211	1,314	1,368	6	8	18	23	15	19
IL	1,267	1,450	1,637	8,553	8,487	8,445	1,813	1,900	18	19	399	512
IN	140	162	179	5,338	5,453	5,509	494	540	14	15	58	74
IA	54	61	71	2,737	2,755	2,762	60	72	8	10	41	56
KS	138	166	191	2,293	2,337	2,377	167	193	23	26	48	60
KY	32	38	42	3,643	3,727	3,781	285	306	6	8	27	35
LA	119	138	156	2,792	2,803	2,841	1,438	1,588	18	20	58	79
ME	8	10	14	1,230	1,251	1,284	5	5	6	6	9	13
MD	214	258	300	3,371	3,368	3,372	1,462	1,687	14	14	213	284
MA	437	524	619	5,182	5,123	5,063	332	391	10	10	239	350
MI	261	289	319	7,790	7,767	7,732	1,417	1,517	55	59	157	208
MN	95	114	132	4,387	4,480	4,546	152	202	61	76	135	192
MS	21	24	27	1,755	1,804	1,836	1,010	1,076	8	8	19	25
MO	90	105	121	4,745	4,863	4,953	622	689	22	26	61	76
MT	20	26	28	861	904	926	3	4	59	72	7	9
NE	61	72	80	1,540	1,572	1,596	70	84	14	18	21	29
NV	277	350	403	1,366	1,456	1,445	128	156	25	26	77	101
NH	17	20	22	1,184	1,233	1,273	7	8	2	2	14	21
NJ	1,044	1,196	1,348	5,558	5,462	5,387	1,104	1,232	14	15	456	656
NM	736	821	912	912	958	984	34	37	157	195	22	28
NY	2,805	3,071	3,357	11,640	11,271	11,023	2,668	2,790	53	56	981	1,304
NC	121	139	154	5,748	6,040	6,233	1,726	1,943	92	99	92	124
ND	6	8	10	611	620	625	5	5	32	43	6	7
OH	183	206	230	9,672	9,669	9,638	1,306	1,433	20	22	136	181
OK	124	143	167	2,653	2,700	2,769	276	332	273	309	47	61
OR	195	237	278	2,990	3,133	3,253	59	71	45	53	110	147
PA	334	391	448	10,460	10,398	10,325	1,181	1,276	16	18	210	285
RI	76	92	112	851	838	834	40	48	4	6	26	39
SC	42	50	58	2,624	2,738	2,848	1,152	1,249	8	9	31	40
SD	8	9	10	698	721	729	5	6	60	72	5	7
TN	57	67	75	4,607	4,828	4,969	925	1,051	12	14	55	70
TX	5,875	6,624	7,421	11,273	11,587	11,866	2,406	2,833	60	66	506	671
UT	138	164	185	1,961	2,117	2,219	18	23	33	43	58	81
VT	6	6	8	600	619	630	2	4	2	2	6	8
VA	269	322	376	5,061	5,175	5,270	1,394	1,606	16	17	257	358
WA	360	437	519	4,881	5,115	5,346	179	203	95	112	342	477
WV	11	15	17	1,758	1,761	1,757	58	58	2	2	11	15
WI	136	156	173	4,732	4,799	4,833	318	390	45	51	97	143
WY	35	42	48	469	501	529	4	6	12	17	4	7

Source: U.S. Bureau of the Census, Population Paper Listings PPL-47.

Native and Foreign-Born Population, by Selected Characteristics: 1997

[**In thousands**. The foreign-born population includes some undocumented immigrants, refugees, and temporary residents such as students and temporary workers as well as legally-admitted immigrants. Based on Current Population Survey; see text, Section 1 and Appendix III]

CHARACTERISTIC	Native population	FOREIGN-BORN POPULATION				
		Total	Year of entry			
			Before 1970	1970 to 1979	1980 to 1989	1990 to 1997
Total	**241,014**	**25,779**	**4,749**	**4,936**	**8,555**	**7,539**
Under 5 years old	19,482	299	(X)	(X)	(X)	299
5 to 17 years old	49,124	2,319	(X)	13	810	1,498
18 to 24 years old	22,047	2,940	(X)	395	990	1,555
25 to 29 years old	16,489	2,770	25	408	1,149	1,190
30 to 34 years old	17,843	3,154	146	514	1,499	995
35 to 44 years old	38,664	5,296	526	1,477	2,209	1,084
45 to 64 years old	48,276	6,211	2,226	1,778	1,490	716
65 years old and over	29,088	2,789	1,827	350	408	203
Male	117,690	12,946	2,081	2,453	4,476	3,937
Female	123,324	12,832	2,669	2,482	4,080	3,601
White	202,566	17,504	4,060	3,195	5,362	4,887
Black	32,190	2,028	233	413	833	550
American Indian/Eskimo/Aleut	2,291	142	13	17	43	69
Asian or Pacific Islander	3,967	6,105	444	1,310	2,318	2,032
Hispanic origin [1]	18,311	11,393	1,550	2,276	4,236	3,331
EDUCATIONAL ATTAINMENT						
Persons 25 years old and over	150,361	20,220	4,749	4,528	6,755	4,188
Not high school graduate	23,515	7,009	1,499	1,548	2,526	1,436
High school grad/some college	91,098	8,261	2,299	1,823	2,612	1,526
Bachelor's degree	24,185	3,172	571	747	1,079	776
Graduate or professional degree	11,563	1,778	380	410	538	450
LABOR FORCE STATUS						
Persons 16 years old and over [2]	179,733	23,649	4,749	4,935	7,991	5,971
In the civilian labor force	119,635	15,593	2,299	3,717	5,769	3,806
Employed	113,156	14,524	2,197	3,496	5,383	3,447
Unemployed	6,479	1,069	102	221	386	359
Not in the labor force	59,275	8,013	2,447	1,195	2,209	2,162
INCOME IN 1996						
Persons 16 years old and over	179,733	23,649	4,749	4,935	7,991	5,971
Without income	11,310	3,376	313	434	1,171	1,455
With income	168,423	20,273	4,436	4,501	6,820	4,516
$1 to $9,999 or loss	50,469	7,036	1,494	1,257	2,317	1,970
$10,000 to $19,999	39,068	5,565	1,072	1,135	2,009	1,349
$20,000 to $34,999	39,380	4,023	857	1,051	1,456	658
$35,000 to $49,999	19,773	1,728	474	495	500	259
$50,000 or more	19,733	1,921	539	563	538	280
POVERTY STATUS [3]						
In poverty	31,117	5,412	497	651	1,943	2,320
Not in poverty	209,342	20,347	4,252	4,284	6,611	5,201
HOMEOWNERSHIP						
In owner-occupied unit	169,581	12,442	3,602	3,109	3,756	1,975
In renter-occupied unit	71,433	13,336	1,147	1,826	4,799	5,564

X Not applicable. [1] Persons of Hispanic origin may be of any race. [2] Includes persons in Armed Forces, not shown separately. [3] Persons for whom poverty status is determined.

Source: U.S. Bureau of the Census, *Current Population Reports*, P20-507 and Population Paper Listing PPL-92.

13

Employment and Income

◆ Employment Trends ◆ Factors in Employment and Unemployment Levels
◆ Federal Government Response to Employment Discrimination ◆ Income and Poverty Trends
◆ Federal and State Programs that Address Poverty ◆ Status of African Americans
◆ Employment and Income Statistics

The changing social and economic status of African Americans continues to be a major issue in contemporary America. Some of these changes are internal as African Americans with different levels of education and experience are differentially able to take advantage of once-denied opportunities of employment and income growth. Many analysts, in fact, point to the increasing number of African Americans in high-status occupations as proof that discrimination in the workplace is a less dominant force in the lives of African Americans. On the other hand, some of these changes are external, as the competition for existing jobs increases at a time when government and industry are downsizing their respective labor forces.

◆ EMPLOYMENT TRENDS

At one time relegated to service-oriented jobs and positions with little power, African Americans are now participating in all areas of employment. In the U.S. government, African Americans are well-represented in the Clinton administration, as well as the House of Representatives and the Senate. In the past, African Americans in the entertainment world were underrepresented and their contributions were largely unrecognized. Today, many of the prominent stars in the music, television, and film industries are African American. In addition, African Americans are increasingly making strides in production roles, as well as executive positions. African Americans continue to thrive in professional sports, too. To say that the conditions have not improved in the United States for African Americans is certainly inconsistent with the facts.

Yet, despite the increase in opportunities for the black upper- and middle-class, blacks as a group trail whites in every measure of socioeconomic standing. African Americans continue to be disproportionately employed in lower-paying, blue-collar jobs. The rate of unemployment for blacks has consistently been twice that for whites for at least two decades. Black single and family income continues to be a fraction of that for whites. The poverty rate for blacks has been three times as high as that for whites for over thirty years. Perhaps the most troubling aspect of these trends is the lack of indication that these measures will improve in the foreseeable future.

In a sense, the story of African Americans has two very different chapters. The first is one of the growing African American middle class that is experiencing a greater range of occupational and economic opportunities than ever before. The second part of the story is more somber, and concerns an increasing number of African Americans who are disadvantaged and, for all intents and purposes, locked out of the mainstream of American life. This growing schism in the social and economic conditions among African Americans has serious implications for the future of the African American community.

◆ FACTORS IN EMPLOYMENT AND UNEMPLOYMENT LEVELS

Unemployment is a major problem in the African American community as high levels of unemployment among African Americans have persisted for several decades. Recent data from the U.S. Bureau of the Census shows that this pattern continues into the 1990s. For example, in 1990 the unemployment rate for African Americans was 11.4 percent. The rate among whites for that year was 4.8 percent. In other words, the rate for blacks was 42 percent higher as that for whites. During the early 1990s, the unemployment rate fluctuated for both blacks and whites. However, it was not until 1995 that the unemployment rate for African Americans dropped below 11.0 percent. In 1997, the unemployment rate was 10.0 percent for blacks and 4.2 percent for whites, a continual decrease given the overall health of the economy.

The Effects of Occupational Discrimination

Much of the variance in unemployment rates between blacks and whites is a direct result of discrimination, past and present, in the job market and other spheres of economic opportunity. In fact, until relatively recently, there were many occupations that African Americans could not enter—irrespective of their levels of education. This has resulted in an occupational structure for blacks that is substantially different from that for whites and which remains in place despite advances of civil rights legislation. Data from the U.S. Census reveal that, in 1997, 7.3 percent of all employed African Americans held managerial and professional specialty positions; 15.1 percent were employed in the operators, fabricators, and laborers category; and 17.6 percent were involved in service occupations.

This data becomes more revealing when the occupational categories are more closely scrutinized for both groups. African American males are more likely than any other group to be in the most vulnerable occupational category—operators, fabricators, and laborers. In 1997, 30.0 percent of all employed black males held these types of jobs compared to 17.7 percent of all white males. In addition, 16.0 percent of employed black males maintained jobs in the lower-paying service sector; comparatively, 7.4 percent of white males held service occupations. However, only 18.4 percent of employed black males held managerial and professional jobs. For white males, this figure was 31.6 percent, representing the largest single category for this group.

Nonracial Economic Changes Affect Employment and Income

Undoubtedly, racial discrimination continues to be a significant factor that exacerbates African American employment problems. However, the strong focus on racial bias in the workplace tends to discount the nonracial economic changes in the global economy that have heightened joblessness and lowered real wages among many African Americans in the past several decades. These economic changes include: 1) the shift from mass production to a highly computerized economy; 2) the lowering of both variety and quality of blue-collar employment; and 3) shifting patterns of occupational staffing with businesses and industries.

In 1997, African Americans comprised 3.6 percent of all health diagnosing occupations (Index Stock Imagery).

These shifts in labor demand continue to have an adverse effect on the African American community. Coupled with the cumulative experiences of racial restrictions, the high number of unskilled African American workers have suffered the most. This situation is further compounded for inner-city minorities that are geographically isolated from the growing number of jobs in the suburbs and socially isolated from informal job networks that have become a major source of job placement.

However, the more educated and highly trained African Americans, similar to their counterparts in other ethnic groups, have benefitted from these changes in labor demand. This point is corroborated by sociologi-

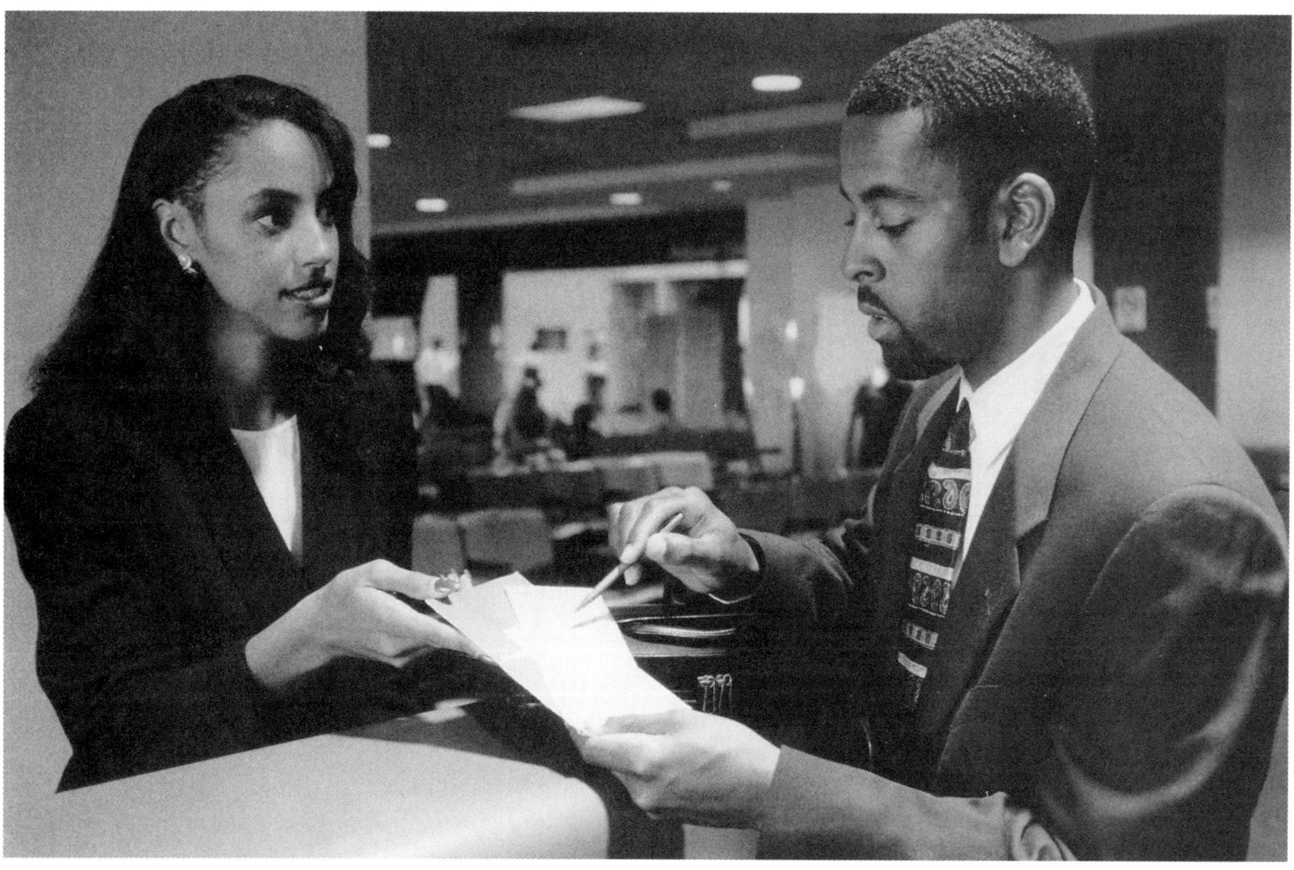

In 1997, African Americans comprised 17.6 percent of all service industry occupations (Index Stock Imagery).

cal studies that find a strong positive relationship between the attainment of higher education, computer skills, and income.

◆ FEDERAL GOVERNMENT RESPONSE TO EMPLOYMENT DISCRIMINATION

Public Policy on Bias in Employment

The Civil Rights Act of 1964 prohibits discrimination on the basis of race, color, gender, or national origin. This law formed part of an array of public programs that comprised the "Great Society" legislation of the Kennedy-Johnson administrations. Among these measures was the Economic Recovery Act of 1964, which included the Job Corps, the Manpower Training Programs, and many other social interventions. It is generally acknowledged that these programs were important to improving the employment prospects of African Americans.

However, according to many policy experts, the Reagan administrations of the 1980s "turned back the clock" to a time of overt and blatant discrimination toward African Americans. They argue that President Ronald Reagan attacked many of the social programs that protected the rights of minorities and used the U.S. Civil Rights Commission to advance his conservative agenda. Indirect support to their claim is the fact that only 4.1 percent of Reagan's political appointments were African American, as compared to 21 percent for Jimmy Carter, the previous president. Moreover, experts claim that Reagan's record of recruitment and hiring of African Americans was worse than those of the Johnson, Nixon, and Ford administrations as well. In the estimation of many analysts, the Bush administration extended the damaging trends of the Reagan policies into the early 1990s.

Even the Clinton administration, which enjoyed the widespread support of African Americans, received allegations of wrongdoing in the area of racial concerns. In 1997, employees of the Department of Energy leveled accusations against the heads of the department that they skewed data in order to make it appear that they had awarded more minority contracts than they did in reality. While the department had made an impressive 42 percent increase in the number of contracts awarded to minorities, this figure did not approach the 59 percent figure presented to President Clinton. Other information was deliberately misleading in order to boost the image of the department as being committed to minority business advancement.

Discrimination Lawsuits Decided by the Courts

Although job discrimination does still exist, African Americans found recourse in the court system in the late 1990s as several high-profile lawsuits forced companies to treat their employees equally, regardless of race. In 1996, African American workers won a case against Circuit City after charging that the nation's largest retailer of brand-name consumer electronics and major appliances systematically discriminated against them in promotions at the company's headquarters. That same year Texaco agreed to pay $176 million in the largest race discrimination settlement ever after 1,350 African American employees filed a suit to protest the oil company's discriminatory working environment. In addition to the settlement, the company set up diversity workshops for all 20,000 of its employees and boosted its minority hiring from 23 percent to 26 percent.

The federal government has not been exempt from discrimination lawsuits. In 1999, Secretary of Agriculture Dan Glickman settled a class-action lawsuit against his department filed by African American farmers in 1997. The settlement—which could balloon to as much as $600 million, depending on how many farmers file claims—attempted to make amends to the thousands of minority farmers who were denied government loans over the years because of race. According to the terms of the settlement, each farmer would receive $50,000, and any government loans would be forgiven. But many farmers pointed out that their commercial loans—which would not be forgiven and carry a higher interest rate than government loans—generally far exceeded the amount of money being granted, leaving them with significant loans they may not have accrued had they been granted government loans in the first place. In addition, none of the agents who applied discriminatory practices were punished for their past actions.

◆ INCOME AND POVERTY

Despite gains in occupational status over the last two decades, black households have yet to gain equality in income with whites. Recent sociological studies have found that blacks of comparable levels of education, occupation, and experience tend to earn less than their white counterparts. Data on household income from the U.S. Census Bureau confirm those findings. In 1996, the median income for black families was $23,482, compared to $37,161 for whites. In other words, black families had a median income that was approximately 63 percent less than that of white families.

The Impact of Family Structure on the Income of African American Families

Family structure has a bearing on the incomes of black families and how they compare to white families. For instance, African American married-couple households had a median income in 1996 of $42,069. This represents 84 percent of the $50,302 median income reported for white married-couple families that year.

Similarly, black families with a male householder, wife absent earned $30,995 or 84 percent of the $36,938 median income of white families of the same structure. Among racial comparisons based on family structure types, however, black single female householders, husband absent fared the worst, making only 67 percent ($16,256) as much as single white female householders, husband absent ($24,375) in 1996.

The Distribution of African American Family Income

Another perspective on African American economic life can be gained by examining the income distribution of this group. In 1996, 29.6 percent of all black households had income of less than $15,000, while only 11.3 percent of whites were in this category. Some 47.2 percent of all African American households had income of less than $25,000, while in comparison only 24.3 percent of whites were in this category. Slightly more than 61 percent of blacks, compared to 37.8 percent of whites, had less than $35,000 in income in 1996. Nearly 80 percent (76.6 percent) of all black households had less than $50,000 in income, compared to 56.1 percent of white households. In short, black and white income distributions continue to be disparate in contemporary America, with blacks still more likely than whites to have households at the lower ends of the income distribution. This trend is consistent with the gap persisting over the years in overall family income for blacks and whites.

Household Size and African American Family Income

Factoring in household size is another way of assessing the degree of economic progress that African Americans have made in recent years. Data from the Department of Commerce show that in 1996 these income differences remain consistent across household size categories. For four-person households, the black median income is $25,683, whereas for white four-person households, the figure is $43,363. In no household size category does the black median income equal that of whites. Black median income across household sizes ranges from 55 to 66 percent of white median income. A similar pattern is observed when comparing mean incomes across household sizes for blacks and whites.

African American female laundry workers staging a strike for improved benefits and wages (The Library of Congress).

Regional Differences in Black Family Income

Income for African American families is likely to vary among different regions of the country. Data from 1990 show that the median family income for African Americans was highest in the West, at $27,947, and lowest in the Midwest, at $20,512. These two regions also reported the highest and lowest percentages of black-to-white median family income. These differences reflect the variations in regional economies and occupational opportunities for blacks and whites.

Age of Householder and African American Family Income

Age is one of the most important factors to consider when assessing income within the African American community as it is a reasonably accurate measure of work experience. One fact that is often overlooked when considering black-white income differences is the significant variation in the age distributions of the two groups—variation in itself reflecting sociological factors. In other words, it is necessary to compare blacks and whites in the same age categories to obtain a complete picture of the African American income situation. Family income data for 1990 from the U.S. Department of Commerce confirm the relationship between income and age. Generally speaking, family income increases for African Americans as the age of the householder increases. African American householders in the 15 to 24 age category had a median family income of $7,218. For those in the 25 to 34 age category, the median family income was $17,130. Family income gradually rises for African Americans until it peaks in the 45 to 54 age category at $30,847. Beyond that age, there is a gradual and expected decline in income as householders withdraw from the labor force. Nonetheless, in no age category do blacks equal whites in median family income. The figures range from forty percent in the 15 to 24 age group to 72 percent in the 65 to 74 age group. Overall, black householders under age 65 earn only 59 percent as much as their white counterparts.

Poverty and the African American Community

Employment, unemployment, and income all have an impact on the level of poverty that exists in the African American community. Government statistics on poverty show that, in total numbers, there were nearly as many African Americans in poverty in 1996 as there were forty years before. In 1959, there were 9.9 million blacks living below the poverty line. In 1996 that figure was 9.7 million. The major difference is between the poverty rates in the two periods. In 1959 the poverty rate was 55.2 percent compared to the 1996 rate of 13.7 percent.

There were 2.6 million African American families living in poverty in 1996. This represented a poverty rate of 26.1 percent. However, there were important differences in rates of poverty across family types. For instance, African American married-couple families without children had the lowest poverty rate at 12.6 percent; those with children had a poverty rate of 14.3 percent. The highest rates were those for female-headed householders. Female-headed householders without children had a poverty rate of 48.1 percent. For those with children, the poverty rate was 56.1 percent. Comparing the poverty rates racially shows that, in every category, black family poverty exceeded that for whites. Black families overall had a poverty rate that was nearly four times the rate for whites. Even black married-couple families without children had a rate of poverty two and one-half times that for white families of this type.

Poverty and African American Teenage Pregnancy

One problem associated with poverty in the African American community is that of teenage pregnancy. However, African American teenage pregnancy is part of a larger problem of nonmarital births. Rates of pregnancy and nonmarital childbirth are higher for black teenagers than whites, though the gap is closing. Studies indicate that the differences between the two groups can be explained by differences in (1) sexual activity; (2) rates of abortion; (3) the use of contraceptives; and (4) rates of marriage before the child's birth.

Irrespective of the causes of African American teenage pregnancy, the consequences are dramatic for the African American community. Generally speaking, teenage mothers are more likely to be poor and are less likely to finish high school. In more cases than not, the fathers are absent or non-supportive. Thus, it is not unusual for teenage mothers to be dependent on public assistance as a means of support. Teenage mothers tend to be unprepared for the adult responsibilities of parenting. Their children are more likely to be the victims of child abuse and to suffer physical, emotional, and educational problems later on in life.

African American community organizations have attempted to tackle the problem of teenage pregnancy. Groups such as the Children's Defense Fund, the National Urban League, Delta Sigma Theta, and a host of others have developed teenage pregnancy prevention programs. Often these efforts focus on teenage males as well as females.

◆ FEDERAL AND STATE PROGRAMS THAT ADDRESS POVERTY

The issue of African American teenage pregnancy is only one dimension of the overall problem of poverty within the African American community. Many of the programs that address the needs of the poor were developed during the Great Society era of the 1960s. Headstart, Medicaid and Medicare, the Food Stamp Program and several other forms of assistance were part of a comprehensive effort referred to as the "War on Poverty." Critics of the Great Society programs argue that these programs were expensive, wasteful, and ineffective. Supporters claim that the programs have not failed, but America's determination to secure a Great Society has done so.

The Results of 1990s Welfare Reform

The most abrupt shift in public policy regarding poverty occurred in 1996 when President Bill Clinton signed sweeping welfare reform legislation into law. Designed to end what critics had called an expensive and ineffective bureaucratic system, the legislation called for a mandatory five-year limit for all welfare recipients, in addition to stricter rules, such as work requirements which forced many recipients off the welfare rolls. Within a year, the welfare caseloads in each state had dropped at a startling pace, falling 27 percent nationally from 1994, when the number of recipients was highest. Among the nation's poor, the impact of this legislation was swift, especially in the African American community where poverty is endemic. In early 1997, African Americans accounted for 37 percent of the nation's welfare caseload, even though they only comprised 13 percent of the general population. While the reform caused the welfare load to decline, whites left welfare at a greater rate than blacks—25 percent versus 17 percent decline for blacks—which left some African American activists to worry that such numbers will reinforce the welfare stereotype of unemployed African Americans.

Three years after the legislation passed, most observers claimed that it was too early to determine whether the reform had a positive or negative impact on the poor. Most studies demonstrated that around fifty percent of those who left welfare had jobs, many of whom worked for minimum wage. Blacks had greater obstacles to overcome in becoming financially independent than whites due to a variety of factors including a larger minority concentration in inner-cities where jobs are scarce, larger families, and less education.

Affirmative Action Programs Receive Criticism

Certainly, the sentiment toward programs that address poverty and employment discrimination has changed. The most controversial program to date is affirmative action. Affirmative action was initiated during the late 1960s by the Nixon administration rather than during the Great Society era of Kennedy and Johnson. Affirmative action programs call for guidelines and goals in the hiring of underutilized groups: racial/ethnic minorities, the handicapped, and women. They also require documentation of a good faith effort to hire persons from these groups. Affirmative action programs have been effective in promoting change in hiring practices because they have the weight of the federal government behind them. As a direct result, a broader range of opportunities have become available for African Americans in government, the corporate world, and colleges and universities.

Affirmative action programs have their critics and have been under particularly heavy attack in the mid-1990s, with several programs being restricted or dismantled altogether. One major criticism is that affirmative action programs do not promote occupational opportunities in general. Studies have documented that while whites support the general principle of equality for all, most do not support the idea of programs and social intervention specifically designed to improve the conditions of blacks and other minorities. Also, an increasing number of white Americans are of the opinion that social and economic differences between blacks and whites are due to individual factors. This backlash is a direct result of the large-scale restructuring of America's economy and the resulting unemployment and underemployment for many white Americans—both working- and middle-class.

However, affirmative action programs have their share of African American critics as well. Many African American conservatives argue that affirmative action programs do not help the African American disadvantaged. They claim that these programs primarily benefit the African American middle class—a group that needs no assistance in achieving its economic goals. In addition, critics of affirmative action argue that it unfairly stigmatizes all African Americans, whereby the success of African Americans in any field is often dismissed as being due to affirmative action. Whites can also perceive the need for affirmative action as confirming their belief in the inferiority of blacks.

◆ STATUS OF AFRICAN AMERICANS

The issue of the social and economic status of African Americans is complex. It is clear that major changes have occurred within the African American community as a result of the Civil Rights movement, civil rights legislation, and affirmative action policies. Many African Americans are holding more high-status jobs and earning higher incomes than ever before. Yet, the number of African Americans who are impoverished remains extremely high. In other words, when one speaks of the conditions or the future of the African American community, one has to be clear that it is a community that consists of many segments. The lifestyles and opportunities for African Americans in one segment may be vastly different than the conditions experienced by African Americans in another segment.

Despite the dramatic changes that have occurred within the African American community as a whole, one thing has remained the same: blacks have yet to achieve equality with whites on any measure of social and economic standing. Blacks have consistently had rates of unemployment that were at least twice as high as those for whites. Blacks who are employed are more likely than whites to hold blue-collar jobs—the type of jobs that are most likely to be eliminated during the restructuring of the American economy. In addition, the future will continue to be filled with obstacles for African American workers and families. However, as history has demonstrated, African Americans are equal to the challenge.

Economic Gap Between Racial Groups Persists

The gap between blacks and whites persists in family income as well. Black families still have only a fraction of the income of white families. Neither family size, family structure, age of householder, presence of children, marital status, nor regional location fully explains the black-white difference in family income. The gap that remains demonstrates that racial discrimination is still pervasive within American society. This persisting inequality explains many of the problems that are associated with poverty, such as teenage pregnancy and financially unstable female-headed households.

In spite of the grim numbers, statistics in the late 1990s cautiously indicated that the economic gap between blacks and whites had narrowed between 1993 and 1996. A critical drop in overall poverty rates in the United States in 1997 was largely due to the economic improvement of the African American community. The poverty rate among African Americans dropped from 33.1 percent in 1993 to 26.5 percent in 1997—the lowest since the collection of such data began in 1959. In the same time period, the poverty rate for whites remained relatively unchanged at 8.6 percent. Between 1996 and 1997, the number of families in poverty dropped from 7.7 million to 7.3 million, with African American families accounting for more than half of the decrease. Even black female-headed households—a group chronically plagued by poverty—had income growth of eight percent in 1997, compared with only three percent for whites. An increase in minimum wage and the availabili-

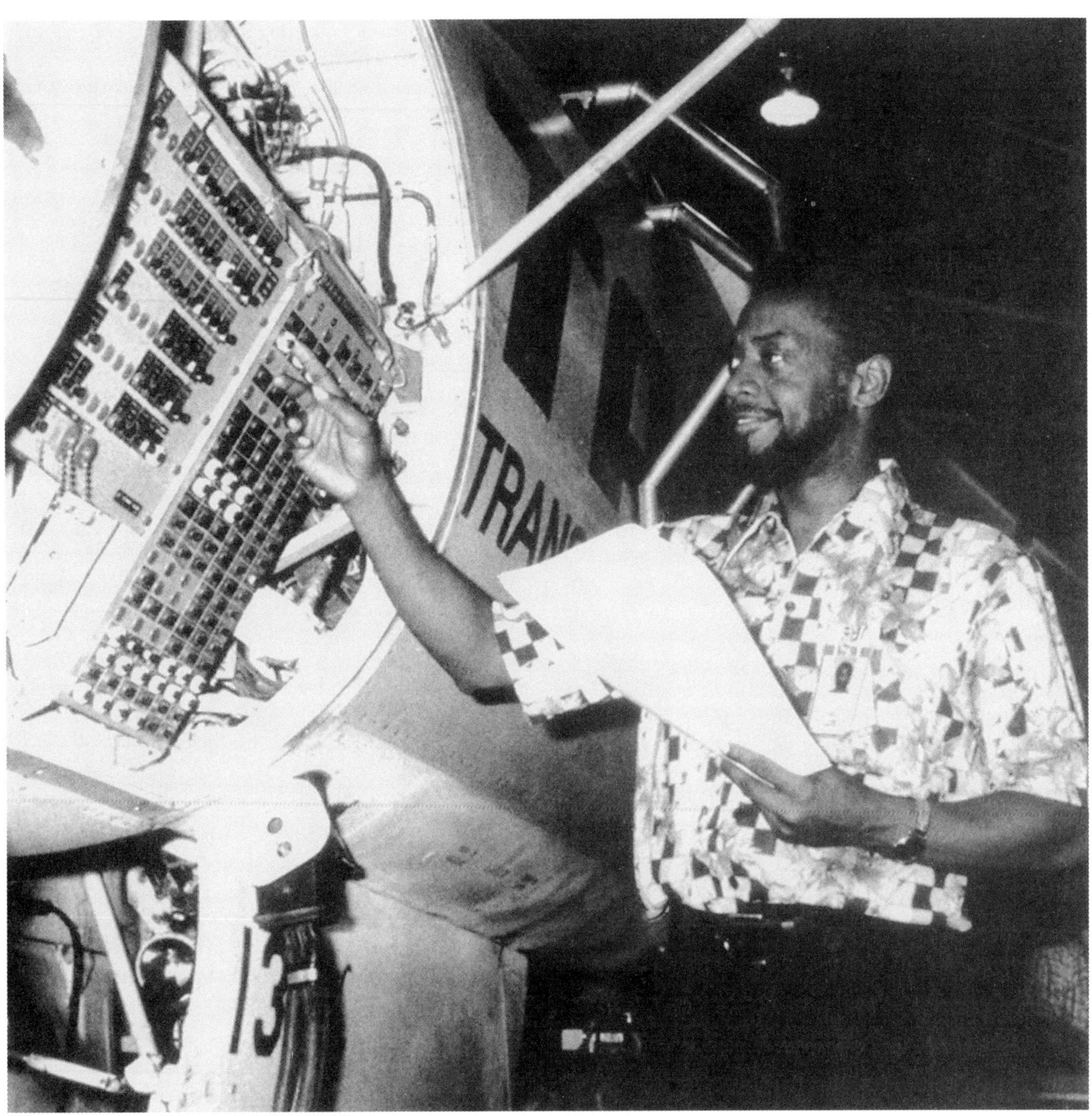

African Americans are holding more well-paying, technical jobs than ever.

ty of earned income tax credit to low-income workers were at least partly responsible.

U.S. Census Bureau officials were cautiously optimistic about the impact of this economic growth on the gap between black and white incomes. While some officials cheered the fact that overall income inequality had not changed negatively in four consecutive years, other officials decried the lack of greater improvement in black-white economic disparity in the midst of one of the healthiest economies in thirty years. Even though African American households enjoyed a 15 percent gain in median income in four years, some analysts predicted that this upward trend would reverse when the American economy as a whole took a downturn.

Social Welfare Programs and the Trend towards Greater Self-sufficiency

Many of the programs developed to address poverty and racial discrimination in employment were initiated during the 1960s. Generally speaking, these programs have been instrumental in providing opportunities to African Americans that had been denied long after the end of slavery. However, in recent years, whites have increasingly come to resist and resent programs that secure such opportunities for blacks and other racial/ethnic minorities. As opportunities decline for whites, the competition for good jobs is expected to increase. Blacks and other minority populations are growing at rates that far exceed that of whites. As these populations become better educated, the struggle for desirable jobs will intensify.

Major social programs are not likely to be initiated by the federal government within the near future. Because of the changing social and political climate in the United States, many African Americans are advocating a greater emphasis on self-help and internal community development. One sociological model of African American community development is the Black Organizational Autonomy (BOA) Model. This model maintains that viable African American communities are those that possess community-based organizations with five basic components: (1) economic autonomy; (2) internally developed and controlled data sources; (3) programs to develop and promote African American female leadership; (4) programs that emphasize African American history and culture; and (5) programs that are socially inclusive in leadership. The model proved successful in a case study in Little Rock, Arkansas of a church-based African American community organization, and has considerable potential for meeting the present and future needs of the African American community.

However, community action may be hampered by a growing schism within the African American community itself, a phenomenon referred to by Dr. Henry Louis Gates, Jr., as "the two nations of Black America." Gates, the Du Bois Professor of the Humanities at Harvard University, commented on what he sees as a troubling divide between African American professionals and the African American underclass in the inner-cities. According to Gates, the African American middle- and upper-class now have more in common with their white colleagues than with the poor of their own race. This disassociation could hinder the upward mobility of the underclass and stagnate community efforts to improve the conditions of the poor if those African Americans with the resources to help feel less inclined to invest in a community of which they are not a part.

African Americans and the Financial Stock Market

African Americans have traditionally steered clear of the investment arena—both in terms of employment and participation in the buying and selling of stocks. Growing up without an understanding of the benefits of long-term investing, most African American children become adults who are leery of putting money into a system they do not understand. A 1998 survey showed that 64 percent of black noninvestors attribute their lack of participation to a "lack of knowledge," compared with 55 percent of whites. When African Americans did choose to invest, they typically selected avenues with low-yield returns such as insurance funds, savings accounts, or real estate—the result being that their money grew at a much slower rate than whites with a substantially greater number of stock portfolios.

The effect of this cautious investment strategy is a gross economic disparity between blacks and whites, particularly in the retirement years. A study of wealth distribution by the Rand Corporation revealed that, among people over seventy years of age, blacks have less than one-tenth of the average financial assets available to whites. Many elderly African Americans become overly-dependent on Social Security and fall into poverty. The African American community is already financially handicapped by lower wages and over-representation in blue-collar jobs with few benefits programs such as 401(k) plans; the reluctance to become involved in the stock market has a further crippling effect on African American economic growth.

Towards the end of the 1990s, however, African American distrust of the stock market began to dissolve. Buoyed by a strong market, many African Americans sought out information on how to invest wisely, and investment companies started active minority recruitment programs to entice these new investors. Investment seminars specifically geared towards African American women have been particularly effective in recruiting a group that has typically been too burdened with family concerns to set aside money for investing. In addition, African American groups such as the Coalition of Black Investors (COBI) have formed to promote financial literacy among African Americans and to connect black investors and investment clubs in order to exchange ideas and investment strategies.

But even as blacks close the investment gap, they continue to be far outnumbered by whites in investment jobs. Of the country's 90,000 brokers, only 600 were African American in 1998, and the percentage of African American employees in the securities industry actually fell from 10.6 percent in 1990 to 8.4 percent in 1996. In 1998, the Reverend Jesse Jackson held a three-day conference with some of the top names on Wall Street to discuss ways to improve minority participation in the financial arena.

Racial Discrimination Encountered in Mortgage Lending

African Americans have also experienced racism in the mortgage market. A study conducted by the Federal Bank of Boston, published in 1992, posited that lending bias against minorities was rampant. In their much-debated findings, the researchers concluded that Boston-area banks rejected 11 percent of mortgage applications by whites and 29 percent of applications by minorities. Such numbers, they argued, proved that discrimination in lending still existed. However, other analysts claim that the study was flawed in its interpretation of the data, and that discrepancies which appear to point to discrimination actually clear up under careful analysis.

Apart from the debate, it is undisputed that there is a far greater rate of white homeowners than black. In spite of the fact that the rate of home ownership reached a record 65.7 percent in 1997, a study found that, while 71.3 percent of whites were homeowners, only 43.6 percent of blacks could boast the same. According to a report by the Federal Reserve Board and the Joint Center for Housing Studies at Harvard University, the main reason for the disparity is known as "redlining" in the banking industry, when banks refuse mortgage loans to low-income buyers—usually minorities. Unable to buy homes, African Americans have frequently been forced to rent in city neighborhoods which are often destabilized by the lack of homeowners.

There are some recent examples of court decisions and corporate initiatives that have been enacted to address incidents of lending bias. In 1998, three Texas mortgage lenders agreed to make nearly $1.4 billion available to low-income and minority home buyers over the next three years after they were found to have applied discriminatory practices against minority applicants. These civil rights violations were discovered when white federal government housing officials who posed as applicants received better treatment and larger loans than minority applicants of similar financial standing.

◆ EMPLOYMENT AND INCOME STATISTICS

Employed Civilians, by Occupation, Sex, Race, and Hispanic Origin: 1983 and 1997

[**For civilian noninstitutional population 16 years old and over.** Annual average of monthly figures. Persons of Hispanic origin may be of any race.]

OCCUPATION	1983				1997 [1]			
	Total employed (1,000)	Percent of total			Total employed (1,000)	Percent of total		
		Female	Black	Hispanic		Female	Black	Hispanic
Total	**100,834**	**43.7**	**9.3**	**5.3**	**129,558**	**46.2**	**10.8**	**9.8**
Managerial and professional specialty	**23,592**	**40.9**	**5.6**	**2.6**	**37,686**	**48.9**	**7.3**	**5.0**
Executive, administrative, and managerial [2]	10,772	32.4	4.7	2.8	18,440	44.3	6.9	5.4
Officials and administrators, public	417	38.5	8.3	3.8	606	49.5	11.9	5.6
Financial managers	357	38.6	3.5	3.1	688	49.3	5.6	5.1
Personnel and labor relations managers	106	43.9	4.9	2.6	108	63.4	7.5	2.9
Purchasing managers	82	23.6	5.1	1.4	114	40.9	6.4	4.6
Managers, marketing, advertising and public relations	396	21.8	2.7	1.7	711	34.6	3.7	4.8
Administrators, education and related fields	415	41.4	11.3	2.4	733	61.3	10.7	5.8
Managers, medicine and health	91	57.0	5.0	2.0	701	76.8	7.4	4.3
Managers, properties and real estate	305	42.8	5.5	5.2	535	49.4	7.1	10.3
Management-related occupations [2]	2,966	40.3	5.8	3.5	4,604	57.7	8.4	5.1
Accountants and auditors	1,105	38.7	5.5	3.3	1,625	56.6	7.9	5.0
Professional specialty [2]	12,820	48.1	6.4	2.5	19,245	53.3	7.8	4.5
Architects	103	12.7	1.6	1.5	169	17.9	1.7	5.1
Engineers [2]	1,572	5.8	2.7	2.2	2,036	9.6	3.9	3.8
Aerospace engineers	80	6.9	1.5	2.1	87	4.7	1.3	2.2
Chemical engineers	67	6.1	3.0	1.4	92	17.3	7.4	1.1
Civil engineers	211	4.0	1.9	3.2	248	7.7	2.2	4.2
Electrical and electronic	450	6.1	3.4	3.1	652	9.2	5.5	3.8
Industrial engineers	210	11.0	3.3	2.4	258	16.4	4.1	5.6
Mechanical	259	2.8	3.2	1.1	352	5.9	2.5	3.2
Mathematical and computer scientists [2]	463	29.6	5.4	2.6	1,494	30.4	7.5	3.1
Computer systems analysts, scientists	276	27.8	6.2	2.7	1,236	28.6	7.7	3.1
Operations and systems researchers and analysts	142	31.3	4.9	2.2	201	40.5	7.0	3.3
Natural scientists [2]	357	20.5	2.6	2.1	529	31.0	5.1	2.2
Chemists, except biochemists	98	23.3	4.3	1.2	144	25.5	5.5	4.2
Biological and life scientists	55	40.8	2.4	1.8	106	44.7	5.7	0.9
Medical scientistis	(3)	(3)	(3)	(3)	77	46.9	9.6	1.1
Health diagnosing occupations [2]	735	13.3	2.7	3.3	1,027	25.2	3.6	4.0
Physicians	519	15.8	3.2	4.5	724	26.2	4.2	4.8
Dentists	126	6.7	2.4	1.0	138	17.3	2.6	1.1
Health assessment and treating occupations	1,900	85.8	7.1	2.2	2,886	86.5	8.4	3.3
Registered nurses	1,372	95.8	6.7	1.8	2,065	93.5	8.3	2.9
Pharmacists	158	26.7	3.8	2.6	200	45.9	4.1	2.6
Dietitians	71	90.8	21.0	3.7	101	88.7	28.5	6.0
Therapists [2]	247	76.3	7.6	2.7	455	75.4	6.6	4.0
Respiratory therapists	69	69.4	6.5	3.7	85	59.4	7.7	2.0
Physical therapists	55	77.0	9.7	1.5	110	64.0	5.0	4.1
Speech therapists	51	90.5	1.5	-	102	95.0	3.6	3.7
Physicians' assistants	51	36.3	7.7	4.4	65	63.2	5.5	8.7
Teachers, college and university	606	36.3	4.4	1.8	869	42.7	6.5	3.4
Teachers, except college and university [2]	3,365	70.9	9.1	2.7	4,798	75.7	10.2	5.4
Prekindergarten and kindergarten	299	98.2	11.8	3.4	574	97.8	13.2	9.7
Elementary school	1,350	83.3	11.1	3.1	1,872	83.9	10.9	5.4
Secondary school	1,209	51.8	7.2	2.3	1,173	58.4	8.3	4.0
Special education	81	82.2	10.2	2.3	384	82.9	10.8	3.2
Counselors, educational and vocational	184	53.1	13.9	3.2	248	66.2	12.4	4.1
Librarians, archivists, and curators	213	84.4	7.8	1.6	217	77.1	6.3	4.7
Librarians	193	87.3	7.9	1.8	188	80.5	6.5	5.4
Social scientists and urban planners [2]	261	46.8	7.1	2.1	441	54.9	8.1	4.5
Economists	98	37.9	6.3	2.7	135	52.2	6.6	3.7
Psychologists	135	57.1	8.6	1.1	256	59.3	9.2	4.5
Social, recreation, and religious workers [2]	831	43.1	12.1	3.8	1,357	54.8	17.2	6.9
Social workers	407	64.3	18.2	6.3	781	69.3	21.7	8.7
Recreation workers	65	71.9	15.7	2.0	126	70.8	13.4	4.9
Clergy	293	5.6	4.9	1.4	350	13.6	12.4	5.0
Lawyers and judges	651	15.8	2.7	1.0	925	26.7	2.8	3.8
Lawyers	612	15.3	2.6	0.9	885	26.6	2.7	3.8
Writers, artists, entertainers, and athletes [2]	1,544	42.7	4.8	2.9	2,234	49.3	5.0	5.8
Authors	62	46.7	2.1	0.9	137	53.6	1.7	2.1
Technical writers	(3)	(3)	(3)	(3)	61	51.1	3.9	3.7
Designers	393	52.7	3.1	2.7	658	58.5	2.9	6.6
Musicians and composers	155	28.0	7.9	4.4	155	36.6	10.5	9.3
Actors and directors	60	30.8	6.6	3.4	136	38.2	7.3	5.1
Painters, sculptors, craft-artists, and artist printmakers	186	47.4	2.1	2.3	251	45.8	3.0	5.6
Photographers	113	20.7	4.0	3.4	132	29.2	6.6	5.3
Editors and reporters	204	48.4	2.9	2.1	257	51.2	4.8	1.7
Public relations specialists	157	50.1	6.2	1.9	148	65.7	7.4	6.7
Announcers	(3)	(3)	(3)	(3)	61	14.2	9.2	9.9
Athletes	58	17.6	9.4	1.7	92	27.0	7.1	5.5

See footnotes at end of table.

Employed Civilians, by Occupation, Sex, Race, and Hispanic Origin: 1983 and 1997—Continued

OCCUPATION	1983				1997 [1]			
	Total employed (1,000)	Percent of total			Total employed (1,000)	Percent of total		
		Female	Black	Hispanic		Female	Black	Hispanic
Technical, sales, and administrative support	**31,265**	**64.6**	**7.6**	**4.3**	**38,309**	**64.1**	**10.5**	**7.9**
Technicians and related support	3,053	48.2	8.2	3.1	4,214	51.9	9.7	6.1
Health technologists and technicians [2]	1,111	84.3	12.7	3.1	1,693	80.2	13.0	6.3
Clinical laboratory technologists and technicians	255	76.2	10.5	2.9	388	75.9	16.1	7.4
Dental hygienists	66	98.6	1.6	-	107	98.2	1.5	2.3
Radiologic technicians	101	71.7	8.6	4.5	148	69.5	7.5	1.6
Licensed practical nurses	443	97.0	17.7	3.1	408	94.1	15.4	5.6
Engineering and related technologists and technicians [2]	822	18.4	6.1	3.5	960	18.6	7.4	6.7
Electrical and electronic technicians	260	12.5	8.2	4.6	391	14.2	7.4	6.8
Drafting occupations	273	17.5	5.5	2.3	222	16.7	3.9	4.6
Surveying and mapping technicians	(3)	(3)	(3)	(3)	76	10.2	5.1	5.3
Science technicians [2]	202	29.1	6.6	2.8	287	39.5	9.4	8.3
Biological technicians	52	37.7	2.9	2.0	106	57.2	11.2	6.0
Chemical technicians	82	26.9	9.5	3.5	85	22.8	10.4	3.7
Technicians, except health, engineering, and science [2]	917	35.3	5.0	2.7	1,275	42.2	7.1	4.8
Airplane pilots and navigators	69	2.1	-	1.6	120	1.2	1.8	2.4
Computer programmers	443	32.5	4.4	2.1	626	30.0	5.9	4.5
Legal assistants	128	74.0	4.3	3.6	346	83.9	9.8	5.8
Sales occupations	11,818	47.5	4.7	3.7	15,734	50.2	8.1	7.6
Supervisors and proprietors	2,958	28.4	3.6	3.4	4,635	38.4	4.8	6.8
Sales representatives, finance and business services [2]	1,853	37.2	2.7	2.2	2,613	44.0	6.9	4.5
Insurance sales	551	25.1	3.8	2.5	594	42.8	7.7	4.7
Real estate sales	570	48.9	1.3	1.5	781	50.0	4.6	5.1
Securities and financial services sales	212	23.6	3.1	1.1	429	31.2	5.5	2.6
Advertising and related sales	124	47.9	4.5	3.3	173	56.6	10.0	4.2
Sales representatives, commodities, except retail	1,442	15.1	2.1	2.2	1,507	24.9	3.0	5.0
Sales workers, retail and personal services	5,511	69.7	6.7	4.8	6,887	65.7	11.9	10.0
Cashiers	2,009	84.4	10.1	5.4	3,007	78.4	15.6	12.1
Sales-related occupations	54	58.7	2.8	1.3	91	73.5	5.0	4.6
Administrative support, including clerical	16,395	79.9	9.6	5.0	18,361	78.8	12.8	8.6
Supervisors	676	53.4	9.3	5.0	685	59.8	14.4	6.1
Computer equipment operators	605	63.9	12.5	6.0	392	58.5	15.4	7.0
Computer operators	597	63.7	12.1	6.0	385	58.4	15.0	7.1
Secretaries, stenographers, and typists [2]	4,861	98.2	7.3	4.5	3,692	97.9	9.8	6.9
Secretaries	3,891	99.0	5.8	4.0	3,033	98.6	8.7	6.4
Typists	906	95.6	13.8	6.4	555	94.4	17.0	9.7
Information clerks	1,174	88.9	8.5	5.5	1,993	88.4	11.3	9.5
Receptionists	602	96.8	7.5	6.6	1,005	96.5	8.8	9.7
Records processing occupations, except financial [2]	866	82.4	13.9	4.8	935	80.5	15.3	9.5
Order clerks	188	78.1	10.6	4.4	231	74.1	15.9	11.0
Personnel clerks, except payroll and time keeping	64	91.1	14.9	4.6	89	85.0	18.5	13.2
Library clerks	147	81.9	15.4	2.5	155	76.3	13.2	6.6
File clerks	287	83.5	16.7	6.1	295	84.7	15.5	11.7
Records clerks	157	82.8	11.6	5.6	175	82.6	15.0	5.1
Financial records processing [2]	2,457	89.4	4.6	3.7	2,196	92.2	7.1	6.4
Bookkeepers, accounting, and auditing clerks	1,970	91.0	4.3	3.3	1,735	92.3	6.3	5.9
Payroll and time keeping clerks	192	82.2	5.9	5.0	155	92.7	10.2	10.4
Billing clerks	146	88.4	6.2	3.9	161	93.8	12.2	6.0
Cost and rate clerks	96	75.6	5.9	5.3	(3)	(3)	(3)	(3)
Billing, posting, and calculating machine operators	(3)	(3)	(3)	(3)	98	91.6	8.2	10.1
Duplicating, mail and other office machine operators	68	62.6	16.0	6.1	77	59.4	18.4	12.3
Communications equipment operators	256	89.1	17.0	4.4	185	81.5	21.6	9.7
Telephone operators	244	90.4	17.0	4.3	173	83.5	21.5	8.4
Mail and message distributing occupations	799	31.6	18.1	4.5	977	38.0	20.8	9.5
Postal clerks, except mail carriers	248	36.7	26.2	5.2	320	45.1	27.9	7.0
Mail carrier, postal service	259	17.1	12.5	2.7	314	30.7	15.8	9.3
Mail clerks, except postal service	170	50.0	15.8	5.9	181	51.7	24.2	12.7
Messengers	122	26.2	16.7	5.2	161	22.7	12.4	11.3
Material recording, scheduling, and distributing [2,4]	1,562	37.5	10.9	6.6	1,953	44.2	14.8	11.4
Dispatchers	157	45.7	11.4	4.3	233	51.3	14.7	9.0
Production coordinators	182	44.0	6.1	2.2	263	54.1	5.3	4.3
Traffic, shipping, and receiving clerks	421	22.6	9.1	11.1	638	30.5	17.2	15.2
Stock and inventory clerks	532	38.7	13.3	5.5	454	41.1	16.9	12.8
Weighers, measurers, and checkers	79	47.2	16.9	5.8	53	56.2	11.9	10.9
Expediters	112	57.5	8.4	4.3	245	69.4	14.0	10.1
Adjusters and investigators	675	69.9	11.1	5.1	1,701	74.4	14.0	8.9
Insurance adjusters, examiners, and investigators	199	65.0	11.5	3.3	434	72.5	11.1	8.5
Investigators and adjusters, except insurance	301	70.1	11.3	4.8	983	74.8	14.4	8.6
Eligibility clerks, social welfare	69	88.7	12.9	9.4	112	86.9	15.1	13.6
Bill and account collectors	106	66.4	8.5	6.5	172	68.6	18.3	8.4
Miscellaneous administrative support [2]	2,397	85.2	12.5	5.9	3,576	83.4	14.6	9.4
General office clerks	648	80.6	12.7	5.2	818	80.6	12.7	9.8
Bank tellers	480	91.0	7.5	4.3	446	90.1	9.8	9.0
Data entry keyers	311	93.6	18.6	5.6	664	81.9	18.3	9.8
Statistical clerks	96	75.7	7.5	3.4	89	89.0	22.9	3.2
Teachers' aides	348	93.7	17.8	12.6	623	93.1	15.2	12.6

See footnotes at end of table.

Employed Civilians, by Occupation, Sex, Race, and Hispanic Origin: 1983 and 1997—Continued

OCCUPATION	1983				1997 [1]			
	Total employed (1,000)	Percent of total			Total employed (1,000)	Percent of total		
		Female	Black	Hispanic		Female	Black	Hispanic
Service occupations	**13,857**	**60.1**	**16.6**	**6.8**	**17,537**	**59.4**	**17.6**	**14.6**
Private household [2]	980	96.1	27.8	8.5	795	95.4	16.2	26.6
Child care workers	408	96.9	7.9	3.6	260	96.8	11.8	17.4
Cleaners and servants	512	95.8	42.4	11.8	512	94.9	17.8	31.3
Protective service	1,672	12.8	13.6	4.6	2,300	17.9	18.7	8.8
Supervisors, protective service	127	4.7	7.7	3.1	181	12.5	16.5	8.5
Supervisors, police and detectives	58	4.2	9.3	1.2	108	17.4	14.8	6.0
Firefighting and fire prevention	189	1.0	6.7	4.1	233	3.4	11.9	5.7
Firefighting occupations	170	1.0	7.3	3.8	218	3.1	12.4	4.6
Police and detectives	645	9.4	13.1	4.0	1,005	16.4	18.1	7.6
Police and detectives, public service	412	5.7	9.5	4.4	579	11.8	13.4	9.1
Sheriffs, bailiffs, and other law enforcement officers	87	13.2	11.5	4.0	142	22.2	18.6	7.2
Correctional institution officers	146	17.8	24.0	2.8	284	22.9	27.4	4.9
Guards	711	20.6	17.0	5.6	881	24.4	21.6	11.0
Guards and police, except public service	602	13.0	18.9	6.2	738	18.2	23.7	11.6
Service except private household and protective	11,205	64.0	16.0	6.9	14,442	64.0	17.5	14.9
Food preparation and service occupations [2]	4,860	63.3	10.5	6.8	5,999	56.8	11.6	16.4
Bartenders	338	48.4	2.7	4.4	310	57.2	2.0	6.3
Waiters and waitresses	1,357	87.8	4.1	3.6	1,375	77.8	4.7	10.2
Cooks	1,452	50.0	15.8	6.5	2,126	41.8	16.7	20.4
Food counter, fountain, and related occupations	326	76.0	9.1	6.7	322	69.4	12.4	8.5
Kitchen workers, food preparation	138	77.0	13.7	8.1	278	72.6	9.8	14.2
Waiters' and waitresses' assistants	364	38.8	12.6	14.2	536	48.5	9.9	18.4
Health service occupations	1,739	89.2	23.5	4.8	2,447	88.2	30.8	9.2
Dental assistants	154	98.1	6.1	5.7	231	96.7	6.1	11.5
Health aides, except nursing	316	86.8	16.5	4.8	341	76.0	27.6	6.2
Nursing aides, orderlies, and attendants	1,269	88.7	27.3	4.7	1,875	89.4	34.5	9.5
Cleaning and building service occupations [2]	2,736	38.8	24.4	9.2	3,108	43.2	21.5	21.3
Maids and housemen	531	81.2	32.3	10.1	643	80.1	27.1	24.8
Janitors and cleaners	2,031	28.6	22.6	8.9	2,226	34.0	19.9	21.0
Personal service occupations [2]	1,870	79.2	11.1	6.0	2,888	80.9	14.3	9.6
Barbers	92	12.9	8.4	12.1	79	22.8	36.6	7.8
Hairdressers and cosmetologists	622	88.7	7.0	5.7	748	90.3	10.2	8.7
Attendants, amusement and recreation facilities	131	40.2	7.1	4.3	206	34.8	13.8	7.8
Public transportation attendants	63	74.3	11.3	5.9	115	82.7	10.5	6.2
Welfare service aides	77	92.5	24.2	10.5	95	86.2	25.8	11.3
Family child care providers	(NA)	(NA)	(NA)	(NA)	513	98.2	11.0	11.2
Early childhood teachers' assistants	(NA)	(NA)	(NA)	(NA)	432	95.6	17.2	10.8
Precision production, craft, and repair	**12,328**	**8.1**	**6.8**	**6.2**	**14,124**	**8.9**	**8.1**	**12.1**
Mechanics and repairers	4,158	3.0	6.8	5.3	4,675	3.9	7.9	10.2
Mechanics and repairers, except supervisors [2]	3,906	2.8	7.0	5.5	4,428	3.7	8.0	10.6
Vehicle and mobile equipment mechanics/repairers [2]	1,683	0.8	6.9	6.0	1,698	1.3	7.0	12.0
Automobile mechanics	800	0.5	7.8	6.0	905	1.5	7.8	13.2
Aircraft engine mechanics	95	2.5	4.0	7.6	135	2.9	8.4	10.2
Electrical and electronic equipment repairers [2]	674	7.4	7.3	4.5	726	9.5	10.7	9.8
Data processing equipment repairers	98	9.3	6.1	4.5	190	13.3	7.1	8.5
Telephone installers and repairers	247	9.9	7.8	3.7	197	13.1	12.2	6.4
Construction trades	4,289	1.8	6.6	6.0	5,378	2.4	7.1	13.7
Construction trades, except supervisors	3,784	1.9	7.1	6.1	4,685	2.4	7.4	14.6
Carpenters	1,160	1.4	5.0	5.0	1,335	1.6	6.6	12.9
Extractive occupations	196	2.3	3.3	6.0	145	1.3	8.6	14.2
Precision production occupations	3,685	21.5	7.3	7.4	3,926	24.1	9.7	12.2
Operators, fabricators, and laborers	**16,091**	**26.6**	**14.0**	**8.3**	**18,399**	**24.7**	**15.1**	**15.4**
Machine operators, assemblers, and inspectors [2]	7,744	42.1	14.0	9.4	7,962	37.7	14.8	17.9
Textile, apparel, and furnishings machine operators [2]	1,414	82.1	18.7	12.5	1,083	72.1	18.8	28.0
Textile sewing machine operators	806	94.0	15.5	14.5	607	82.0	16.0	33.8
Pressing machine operators	141	66.4	27.1	14.2	102	70.6	22.4	44.1
Fabricators, assemblers, and hand working occupations	1,715	33.7	11.3	8.7	2,113	34.3	14.1	14.1
Production inspectors, testers, samplers, and weighers	794	53.8	13.0	7.7	787	47.6	12.9	16.9
Transportation and material moving occupations	4,201	7.8	13.0	5.9	5,389	9.6	15.2	11.0
Motor vehicle operators	2,978	9.2	13.5	6.0	4,089	11.3	15.3	10.9
Trucks drivers	2,195	3.1	12.3	5.7	3,075	5.7	13.4	11.1
Transportation occupations, except motor vehicles	212	2.4	6.7	3.0	174	3.3	11.3	2.6
Material moving equipment operators	1,011	4.8	12.9	6.3	1,125	4.5	15.4	12.7
Industrial truck and tractor operators	369	5.6	19.6	8.2	526	7.2	19.4	17.9
Handlers, equipment cleaners, helpers, and laborers [2]	4,147	16.8	15.1	8.6	5,048	20.3	15.5	16.3
Freight, stock, and material handlers	1,488	15.4	15.3	7.1	1,930	24.5	16.0	12.9
Laborers, except construction	1,024	19.4	16.0	8.6	1,323	21.3	16.1	15.6
Farm operators and managers	1,450	12.1	1.3	0.7	1,317	23.1	1.2	2.4
Other agricultural and related occupations	2,072	19.9	11.7	14.0	2,030	17.9	6.6	33.6
Farm workers	1,149	24.8	11.6	15.9	796	19.0	4.8	41.3
Forestry and logging occupations	126	1.4	12.8	2.1	108	5.1	6.7	6.8

- Represents or rounds to zero. NA Not available. [1] See footnote 2, Table 644. [2] Includes other occupations, not shown separately. [3] Level of total employment below 50,000. [4] Includes clerks.

Source: U.S. Bureau of Labor Statistics, *Employment and Earnings,* monthly, January issues; and unpublished data.

Unemployed and Unemployment Rates, by Educational Attainment, Sex, Race, and Hispanic Origin: 1992 to 1997

[As of **March.** For the civilian noninstitutional population 25 to 64 years old.]

YEAR, SEX, AND RACE	UNEMPLOYED (1,000)					UNEMPLOYMENT RATE [1]				
	Total	Less than high school diploma	High school gradu-ates, no degree	Less than a bach-elor's degree	College graduate	Total	Less than high school diploma	High school gradu-ate, no degree	Less than a bach-elor's degree	College graduate
Total: [2]										
1992	6,846	1,693	2,851	1,521	782	6.7	13.5	7.7	5.9	2.9
1995	5,065	1,150	1,833	1,329	753	4.8	10.0	5.2	4.5	2.5
1996	5,147	1,285	1,947	1,239	675	4.8	10.9	5.5	4.1	2.2
1997 [3]	4,902	1,253	1,853	1,157	640	4.4	10.4	5.1	3.8	2.0
Male:										
1992	4,207	1,151	1,709	854	493	7.5	14.8	8.8	6.4	3.2
1995	2,925	765	1,064	656	440	5.1	10.9	5.7	4.4	2.6
1996	3,088	815	1,205	682	385	5.3	11.0	6.4	4.5	2.3
1997 [3]	2,797	752	1,069	616	359	4.7	9.9	5.6	4.0	2.1
Female:										
1992	2,639	542	1,142	666	289	5.7	11.4	6.5	5.3	2.5
1995	2,140	385	770	673	313	4.4	8.6	4.6	4.5	2.4
1996	2,059	471	742	556	289	4.1	10.7	4.4	3.8	2.1
1997 [3]	2,105	500	783	541	281	4.1	11.3	4.5	3.6	2.0
White:										
1992	5,247	1,285	2,146	1,176	641	6.0	12.9	6.8	5.3	2.7
1993	5,129	1,175	2,025	1,166	763	5.8	12.4	6.5	5.0	3.1
1995	3,858	831	1,362	1,054	612	4.3	9.2	4.6	4.2	2.3
1996	3,865	969	1,386	934	575	4.2	10.2	4.6	3.7	2.1
1997 [3]	3,674	910	1,395	867	502	3.9	9.4	4.6	3.4	1.8
Black:										
1992	1,353	361	619	291	81	12.4	17.2	14.1	10.7	4.8
1995	905	225	377	218	86	7.7	13.7	8.4	6.3	4.1
1996	1,061	258	479	255	69	8.9	15.3	10.8	6.9	3.3
1997 [3]	997	291	381	235	89	8.1	16.6	8.2	6.1	4.4
Hispanic: [4]										
1992	757	408	224	88	36	9.8	13.6	9.6	5.9	4.2
1995	746	393	211	102	40	8.0	10.9	8.1	5.2	3.7
1996	826	462	202	118	44	8.5	12.3	7.3	5.7	4.0
1997 [3]	768	379	221	128	39	7.3	9.6	7.5	5.5	3.0

[1] Percent unemployed of the civilian labor force. [2] Includes other races, not shown separately. [3] See footnote 2, Table 644. [4] Persons of Hispanic origin may be of any race.

Source: U.S. Bureau of Labor Statistics, unpublished data.

Persons Below Poverty Level, by Selected Characteristics: 1996

[Persons as of **March 1996.**]

AGE AND REGION	NUMBER BELOW POVERTY LEVEL (1,000)				PERCENT BELOW POVERTY LEVEL			
	All races [1]	White	Black	Hispanic [2]	All races [1]	White	Black	Hispanic [2]
Total	**36,529**	**24,650**	**9,694**	**8,697**	**13.7**	**11.2**	**28.4**	**29.4**
Under 18 years old	14,463	9,044	4,519	4,237	20.5	16.3	39.9	40.3
18 to 24 years old	4,466	3,123	1,095	1,051	17.9	15.6	29.6	29.0
25 to 34 years old	5,093	3,487	1,276	1,259	12.7	10.7	23.8	22.9
35 to 44 years old	4,343	2,976	1,053	1,032	9.9	8.2	19.4	23.5
45 to 54 years old	2,516	1,764	584	416	7.6	6.3	16.6	16.9
55 to 59 years old	1,086	770	257	180	9.4	7.7	21.7	19.2
60 to 64 years old	1,134	820	250	151	11.5	9.6	25.4	22.2
65 years old and over	3,428	2,667	661	370	10.8	9.4	25.3	24.4
65 to 74 years old	1,580	1,170	357	231	8.8	7.3	22.8	23.3
75 years old and over	1,848	1,497	303	140	13.3	12.0	29.0	26.6
Northeast	6,558	4,279	1,987	1,563	12.7	9.9	30.6	33.4
Midwest	6,654	4,794	1,668	596	10.7	8.8	27.8	27.6
South	14,098	8,200	5,378	2,568	15.1	11.4	28.8	26.9
West	9,219	7,377	662	3,969	15.4	14.7	22.6	30.1

[1] Includes other races not shown separately. [2] Persons of Hispanic origin may be of any race.

Source: U.S. Bureau of the Census, *Current Population Reports*, P60-198;

No. 765. Families Below Poverty Level, by Selected Characteristics: 1996

[Families as of **March 1997.**]

CHARACTERISTIC	NUMBER BELOW POVERTY LEVEL (1,000)				PERCENT BELOW POVERTY LEVEL			
	All races [1]	White	Black	Hispanic [2]	All races [1]	White	Black	Hispanic [2]
Total	**7,708**	**5,059**	**2,206**	**1,748**	**11.0**	**8.6**	**26.1**	**26.4**
Age of householder:								
15 to 24 years old	970	600	338	227	33.7	27.8	55.7	43.6
25 to 34 years old	2,293	1,467	701	543	16.7	13.2	35.4	28.5
35 to 44 years old	2,080	1,381	572	549	10.9	8.8	23.5	28.5
45 to 54 years old	974	653	245	203	6.8	5.3	15.5	18.9
55 to 64 years old	690	463	179	126	7.7	6.0	20.0	19.0
65 years old and over	664	474	158	87	6.0	4.8	17.2	16.7
Northeast	1,393	879	441	348	10.4	7.7	28.3	32.0
Midwest	1,382	976	378	124	8.4	6.7	25.1	25.1
South	3,136	1,765	1,264	533	12.3	8.7	26.9	23.6
West	1,797	1,440	123	744	12.0	11.3	17.9	26.6
Education of householder: [3]								
No high school diploma	2,819	1,902	762	1,024	24.4	20.7	39.9	37.5
High school diploma, no college	2,231	1,422	700	291	10.2	7.7	25.1	18.4
Some college, less than bachelor's degree	1,246	821	348	154	7.3	5.7	16.2	13.4
Bachelor's degree or more	404	294	45	39	2.4	2.0	4.6	6.2
Work experience of householder:								
Total [4]	7,037	4,580	2,046	1,657	11.9	9.4	27.2	27.1
Worked during year	3,886	2,671	1,026	943	7.6	6.2	17.2	19.2
Year-round, full time	1,202	875	275	398	3.1	2.6	6.6	11.4
Not year-round, full time	2,684	1,796	751	545	22.1	18.4	41.2	38.3
Did not work	3,151	1,909	1,020	714	39.6	32.0	65.5	59.8

[1] Includes other races not shown separately. [2] Hispanic persons may be of any race. [3] Householder 25 years old and over. [4] Persons 16 years old and over.

Source: U.S. Bureau of the Census, *Current Population Reports,* P60-198; and unpublished data.

Money Income of Households—Percent Distribution, by Income Level, Race, and Hispanic Origin, in Constant (1996) Dollars: 1970 to 1996

[Constant dollars based on CPI-U-X1 deflator. Households as of March of following year.]

YEAR	Number of house-holds (1,000)	PERCENT DISTRIBUTION							Median income (dollars)
		Under $10,000	$10,000-$14,999	$15,000-$24,999	$25,000-$34,999	$35,000-$49,999	$50,000-$74,999	$75,000 and over	
ALL HOUSEHOLDS [1]									
1970	64,778	13.7	7.7	15.6	16.4	21.3	16.8	8.5	33,181
1975	72,867	13.0	8.8	16.2	15.6	19.4	17.8	9.2	32,943
1980	82,368	12.9	8.2	16.4	14.3	19.1	17.9	11.2	33,763
1985	88,458	12.7	8.3	15.6	14.2	17.8	17.8	13.5	34,439
1990	94,312	12.0	7.9	15.0	14.1	17.8	17.9	15.2	35,945
1994	98,990	12.6	8.7	15.8	14.1	16.3	16.9	15.5	34,158
1995	99,627	11.8	8.5	15.6	13.9	16.9	17.4	15.7	35,082
1996	101,018	11.8	8.6	15.4	13.7	16.3	18.0	16.4	35,492
WHITE									
1970	57,575	12.5	7.2	14.9	16.5	22.0	17.7	9.0	34,560
1975	64,392	11.6	8.4	15.9	15.5	20.0	18.8	9.9	34,451
1980	71,872	11.3	7.7	16.0	14.5	19.7	18.9	12.1	35,620
1985	76,576	11.1	7.8	15.2	14.3	18.4	18.6	14.5	36,320
1990	80,968	10.2	7.6	14.8	14.3	18.3	18.8	16.2	37,492
1994	83,737	10.8	8.4	15.5	14.2	16.8	17.7	16.5	36,026
1995	84,511	10.2	8.2	15.4	14.0	17.3	18.1	16.8	36,822
1996	85,059	10.0	8.2	15.1	13.7	16.7	18.8	17.4	37,161
BLACK									
1970	6,180	25.0	12.1	21.5	15.2	14.5	8.7	2.8	21,035
1975	7,489	25.4	13.3	19.0	16.0	14.1	9.4	2.8	20,682
1980	8,847	25.9	12.9	19.8	13.2	14.4	10.0	3.8	20,521
1985	9,797	25.8	11.9	19.1	13.1	13.9	11.0	5.2	21,609
1990	10,671	26.3	11.1	17.0	13.3	14.5	11.2	6.5	22,420
1994	11,655	25.2	11.1	18.3	13.4	13.1	11.7	7.2	22,261
1995	11,577	23.5	11.3	18.5	13.7	14.7	11.5	6.7	23,054
1996	12,109	23.1	11.6	17.7	13.9	14.0	12.4	7.4	23,482
HISPANIC [2]									
1975	2,948	16.8	11.7	22.1	17.5	18.1	10.3	3.5	24,749
1980	3,906	16.7	10.7	21.2	16.2	16.9	12.8	5.5	26,025
1985	5,213	17.9	12.0	19.5	15.2	16.4	12.3	6.6	25,467
1990	6,220	16.7	11.6	18.6	15.8	17.0	12.8	7.5	26,806
1994	7,735	19.2	12.1	19.1	15.2	15.0	11.8	7.6	24,796
1995	7,939	19.2	12.3	21.0	15.2	14.0	11.8	6.5	23,535
1996	8,225	17.2	11.9	21.0	15.0	15.0	12.3	7.7	24,906

[1] Includes other races not shown separately. [2] Persons of Hispanic origin may be of any race. Income data for Hispanic origin households are not available prior to 1972. Source of Table: U.S. Bureau of the Census, *Current Population Reports*, P60-197; and Internet site <http://www.census.gov/hhes/income/histinc/inchhdet.html> (accessed 25 March 1998).

Money Income of Households—Distribution, by Income Level and Selected Characteristics: 1996

CHARACTERISTIC	Number of house-holds (1,000)	NUMBER (1,000)							Median income (dollars)
		Under $10,000	$10,000-$14,999	$15,000-$24,999	$25,000-$34,999	$35,000-$49,999	$50,000-$74,999	$75,000 and over	
Total [1]	**101,018**	**11,879**	**8,659**	**15,509**	**13,808**	**16,466**	**18,170**	**16,527**	**35,492**
Age of householder:									
15 to 24 years	5,160	1,124	636	1,220	864	702	439	176	21,438
25 to 34 years	19,314	1,790	1,345	2,940	3,322	3,756	3,966	2,195	35,888
35 to 44 years	23,823	1,711	1,239	2,789	3,173	4,474	5,545	4,893	44,420
45 to 54 years	18,843	1,354	850	1,895	2,014	3,209	4,211	5,310	50,472
55 to 64 years	12,469	1,422	975	1,649	1,484	1,991	2,395	2,553	39,815
65 years and over	21,408	4,479	3,614	5,016	2,952	2,334	1,614	1,400	19,448
White	85,059	8,575	6,980	12,853	11,658	14,184	15,998	14,809	37,161
Black	12,109	2,794	1,399	2,144	1,679	1,691	1,502	900	23,482
Hispanic [2]	8,225	1,415	980	1,731	1,230	1,231	1,009	628	24,906
Northeast	19,724	2,473	1,611	2,689	2,492	3,096	3,670	3,692	37,406
Midwest	23,972	2,471	1,973	3,700	3,335	4,037	4,696	3,761	36,579
South	35,693	4,604	3,288	5,873	5,166	5,763	5,877	5,123	32,422
West	21,629	2,332	1,787	3,246	2,815	3,569	3,927	3,951	37,125
Size of household:									
One person	25,402	6,728	4,172	5,321	3,516	2,891	1,717	1,057	17,897
Two persons	32,736	2,406	2,420	5,541	4,945	5,823	6,261	5,339	37,283
Three persons	17,065	1,336	905	1,969	2,195	3,133	3,804	3,723	44,813
Four persons	15,396	836	606	1,423	1,841	2,660	3,938	4,092	51,405
Five persons	6,774	361	322	780	790	1,278	1,646	1,598	47,841
Six persons	2,311	138	122	288	346	425	509	483	42,439
Seven or more persons	1,334	74	111	187	174	265	295	236	40,337
Type of household:									
Family households	70,241	4,870	4,154	9,407	9,448	12,593	15,225	14,542	43,082
Married-couple	53,604	1,635	2,250	6,079	6,821	10,096	13,222	13,499	49,858
Male householder, wife absent	3,847	296	288	666	640	786	735	436	35,658
Female householder, husband	12,790	2,939	1,616	2,663	1,987	1,710	1,268	606	21,564
Nonfamily households	30,777	7,009	4,504	6,102	4,360	3,872	2,945	1,986	20,973
Male householder	13,707	2,066	1,534	2,592	2,315	2,218	1,750	1,231	27,266
Female householder	17,070	4,942	2,971	3,509	2,045	1,654	1,195	754	16,398
Educational attainment of householder: [3]									
Total	**95,857**	**10,756**	**8,023**	**14,288**	**12,944**	**15,764**	**17,731**	**16,351**	**36,516**
Less than 9th grade	7,628	2,300	1,427	1,675	945	648	435	197	15,376
9th to 12th grade (no diploma)	9,933	2,377	1,538	2,164	1,369	1,234	875	377	19,652
High school graduate	30,293	3,408	2,811	5,384	4,551	5,609	5,499	3,031	32,295
Some college, no degree	17,078	1,410	1,195	2,439	2,664	3,189	3,582	2,599	38,398
Associate degree	6,855	430	371	885	952	1,252	1,662	1,303	44,509
Bachelor's degree or more	24,070	831	682	1,741	2,462	3,832	5,678	8,845	59,978
Bachelor's degree	15,501	556	513	1,272	1,789	2,688	3,791	4,892	55,137
Master's degree	5,705	189	139	332	505	827	1,395	2,318	63,887
Professional degree	1,631	51	14	68	122	184	255	937	90,344
Doctorate degree	1,233	34	16	69	46	133	236	697	81,159
Tenure:									
Owner occupied	66,356	4,795	4,344	8,530	8,568	11,355	14,365	14,400	43,793
Renter occupied	32,968	6,722	4,089	6,606	4,994	4,871	3,651	2,035	23,436
Occupier paid no cash rent	1,693	363	225	373	246	240	155	92	21,479
Work experience of householder:									
Total	**101,018**	**11,879**	**8,659**	**15,509**	**13,808**	**16,466**	**18,170**	**16,527**	**35,492**
Worked	72,377	3,509	3,987	9,529	10,416	13,686	16,216	15,034	43,975
Worked at full-time jobs	62,729	1,881	2,732	7,846	9,089	12,401	14,904	13,876	46,316
50 weeks or more	52,699	660	1,695	6,000	7,495	10,763	13,343	12,744	49,530
27 to 49 weeks	6,649	444	628	1,202	1,097	1,189	1,210	880	34,365
26 weeks or less	3,381	779	410	644	497	449	351	252	22,355
Worked at part-time jobs	9,648	1,627	1,255	1,684	1,327	1,284	1,312	1,159	26,742
50 weeks or more	4,744	545	596	880	677	693	671	682	29,719
27 to 49 weeks	2,240	387	278	362	291	311	336	275	27,589
26 weeks or less	2,664	695	381	442	359	281	305	201	20,662
Did not work	28,641	8,370	4,671	5,979	3,392	2,780	1,954	1,493	16,730

[1] Includes other races not shown separately. [2] Persons of Hispanic origin may be of any race. [3] 25 years old and over.

Source: U.S. Bureau of the Census, *Current Population Reports,* P60-197.

14

Entrepreneurship

◆ Colonial Entrepreneurial Efforts by African Americans
◆ Pre–Civil War Entrepreneurship in the African American Community
◆ Post–Civil War Entrepreneurship in the African American Community
◆ African American Entrepreneurship in the Early Twentieth Century
◆ Post–Civil Rights Era Assistance to African American Businesses ◆ Recent Economic Trends
◆ Entrepreneurs and Business Executives

by Michael D. Woodard and Hollis F. Price, Jr.

African Americans have a long and rich history of entrepreneurship in the United States. Indeed, African Americans have been in business since before the Civil War and continue their entrepreneurial tradition today. Segments of the African American population have exhibited the same entrepreneurial spirit as segments of other ethnic groups who have migrated to this country. Very often, however, the history of African American entrepreneurship has been either overlooked or misconstrued. This essay, which draws heavily from Michael D. Woodard's important book *Black Entrepreneurs in America: Stories of Struggle and Success* (1997), presents an outline of the African American entrepreneurial tradition over time.

◆ COLONIAL ENTREPRENEURIAL EFFORTS BY AFRICAN AMERICANS

As America began to take shape, a number of people of African origin were successful in carving out an economic stake for themselves. Anthony Johnson is believed to be the first person of African descent to have become an entrepreneur in America. Once a slave, Johnson became free around 1622, accumulated substantial property from the Jamestown colonial government, and amassed enough wealth to import five servants of his own by 1651. Other free American Americans soon joined Johnson in an attempt to launch an independent African American community. At its height, the settlement had 12 homesteads with sizeable holdings.

In the early 1770s, entrepreneur Jean Baptist Du Sable established the first settlement in the area later called Chicago. Having impressed the British as a well-educated man and capable frontiersman, he was sent to the St. Clair region to manage trade and act as a liaison between Native Americans and the British. Later returning to his original settlement, DuSable built a bakery, dairy, smoke house, horse mill and stable, workshop, and a poultry house. He also traded, trapped, and served as the local cooper and miller. Through Du Sable's efforts, Chicago became a major center for frontier commerce.

◆ PRE-CIVIL WAR ENTREPRENEURSHIP IN THE AFRICAN AMERICAN COMMUNITY

While slavery defined the existence of most African Americans prior to the Civil War, two categories of business persons were able to develop and sustain business enterprises. The first group was composed of free African Americans who could accumulate the capital to generate business activity. Numbering about sixty thousand, free African Americans developed enterprises in almost every area of the business community including merchandising, real estate, manufacturing, construction, transportation, and extractive industries.

The second group consisted of slaves who—as a result of thrift, ingenuity, industry, and/or the liberal paternalism of their masters—were able to engage in business activity. Although the constraints of slavery were such that even highly skilled slaves could not become entrepreneurs in the true sense of the word, some slaves did, during their limited free time, sell their labor and create products to sell.

The fact that African American entrepreneurship existed at all during the era of slavery is testimony to an entrepreneurial spirit and the determination of a people to achieve economic freedom even under the harshest conditions.

If it was all but impossible for slaves to engage in private enterprise, it was also hazardous for "free" African Americans to do so, since they were effectively only half free. Free African Americans lived under constant fear of being labeled as "runaway slaves" and being sold into slavery. In addition, in areas where free African Americans lived, laws were passed to restrict their movement and thus their economic freedom. This was one intention, for example, of laws that Virginia, Maryland, and North Carolina passed by 1835 forbidding free African Americans to carry arms without a license. The right of assembly was also denied African Americans throughout the South—making it illegal for African American civic, business, or benevolent organizations to convene. In addition to reflecting white slaveowners's fears of an African American uprising, such legal restriction had the purpose and effect of making it difficult for free African Americans to earn a living.

Despite the economic exploitation of African Americans in the South, the development of business enterprises by African Americans in the North flourished. In 1838, for example the *Register of Trades of Colored People* in the city of Philadelphia listed 8 bakers, 25 blacksmiths, 3 brass founders, 15 cabinet makers and carpenters, 5 confectioners, 2 caulkers, 2 chair bottomers, 15 tailoring enterprises, 31 tanners, 5 weavers, and 6 wheelwrights. The Philadelphia business register also listed businesses run by African American women. Among these were 81 dressmakers and tailors, 4 dyers and scourers, 2 fullers, and 2 glass and paper makers. The 98 hairdressers registered, comprising the largest trade group, operated some of the most lucrative enterprises.

Another profitable business controlled by African Americans in Philadelphia during the 1820s and 1830s was sailmaking. In 1838, 19 sailmakers were recorded in the business register for that year. Janee Forster, who lived between 1766 and 1841, ran a major manufacturing firm that made sails. In 1829, Forster employed forty workers, black and white.

Although several individuals succeeded in the manufacturing trades, the business enterprise that brought prosperity to the largest number of African Americans in Philadelphia was catering. Robert Boyle, an African American waiter, is believed to have developed the idea of contracting to provide formal dinners to serve in domestic entertaining. Catering quickly spread across the developing country, but it was in Philadelphia, the city of its birth, that catering was king.

Significantly, most of the businesses discussed thus far involved the craft or service trades. These were small enterprises that required only a modest capital investment and allowed African Americans to develop an economic niche without threatening larger white-owned businesses.

◆ POST-CIVIL WAR ENTREPRENEURSHIP IN THE AFRICAN AMERICAN COMMUNITY

The promise of freedom and political enfranchisement held out by Lincoln's Emancipation Proclamation of 1863 was soon undermined by racist judicial rulings. In 1878, in *Hall v. DeCuir*, the U.S. Supreme Court ruled that a state could not prohibit segregation on a common carrier. In 1896, with the *Plessy v. Ferguson* ruling, "separate but equal" became the law of the land. Following these decisions, a pattern of rigid segregation of the races was established that remained the norm in the North and South until the advent of the Civil Rights movement in the 1960s.

Nevertheless, even within the context of disenfranchisement and segregation, Booker T. Washington saw the possibility of securing African American economic stability through business development. In 1900, Washington spearheaded the development of the National Negro Business League to encourage African American enterprise. During the organization's first meeting, the delegates concluded that: "a useless class is a menace and a danger to any community, and. . . when an individual produces what the world wants, whether it is a product of the hand, heart, or head, the world does not long stop to inquire what is the color of the skin of the producer. . . .[I]f every member of the race should strive to make himself the most indispensable man in his community, and to be successful in business, however humble that business might be, he would contribute much toward soothing the pathway of his own and future generations."

◆ AFRICAN AMERICAN ENTREPRENEURSHIP IN THE EARLY TWENTIETH CENTURY

During the early 1900s, although services continued to be the cornerstone of the African American business community, some African Americans found it easier to

African American slaves were oftentimes hired out to craftsmen, allowing them to acquire impressive manufacturing skills (Ploski-Negro).

Free African American shoe cobbler (Schomburg Center for Research in Black Culture).

Madame C.J. Walker (The Library of Congress)

raise capital and venture into other entrepreneurial endeavors. One of the finest examples was Madame C. J. Walker.

Working as a domestic, Walker developed a hair care system in 1905 that softened and straightened hair. She also developed the Wonderful Hair Grower product for women who had experienced hair loss. As an indication of her business acumen, Madame Walker was the first woman to sell products by mail order, and she also formed a national membership of door-to-door agents known as The Madame C.J. Walker Hair Culturists Union of America. To train young women in hair care, Madame Walker opened her own beauty school, the Walker College of Hair Culture. Millions of women, both black and white, throughout the United States, the Caribbean, and South America, became customers of Walker's beauty parlors and products. Before her death in 1919, Madame C.J. Walker had become the first African American female millionaire.

Durham, North Carolina: A Special Case

Turn of the century Durham, North Carolina, represented a special case of enterprise and economic resilience. In publications of the time, Durham was referred to as "The Wall Street of Negro America." By the late 1940s, more than 150 businesses owned by African Americans flourished in Durham. Among these businesses were traditional service providers such as cafes, movie theaters, barber shops, boarding houses, pressing shops, grocery stores, and funeral parlors. What distinguished Durham, however, was the presence of large African American businesses.

One of the largest and most successful African American businesses in the nation was the North Carolina Mutual Life Insurance Company. Surrounding the North Carolina Mutual Life Insurance Company were the Banker's Fire Insurance Company, the Mutual Building and Loan Association, the Union Insurance and Realty Company, the Durham Realty and Insurance Company, the People's Building and Loan Association, the Royal Knights Savings and Loan Association, T. P. Parham and Associates (a brokerage corporation), and the Mortgage Company of Durham. Such businesses established Durham as a "city of enterprise" for African Americans.

Although Durham was a success, external economic pressure and racial hostility made it difficult for African Americans to develop businesses that could compete in the larger economy. Jim Crow laws and segregation forced most African American-owned businesses to limit their market to their own community. Somewhat of an exception, however, was the Durham textile mill, the only hosiery mill in the world owned and operated by African Americans at the time. The Durham textile mill operated 18 knitting machines and did business in the open market. Their salesmen, who were white, traveled mostly in North Carolina, Indiana, Georgia, South Carolina and Alabama to market products. The Durham textile manufacturing firm was exceptional in the sense that it was perhaps the first large-scale African American-owned enterprise to compete in the larger economy.

Nevertheless, race relations in Durham during this time were such that the most successful retail and service businesses tended to generate a white clientele. For example, in 1940 Smith's Fish Market, established by the former postal clerk Freeman M. Smith, supplied Durham's largest white-operated hotel, the Washington Duke. Smith was also the major supplier for smaller white and black-owned businesses. In 1940, Smith grossed more than $90,000 and opened four other outlets throughout the city. Similarly, Rowland and Mitchell established a tailor shop in 1930 where they did work for "exclusive whites and department stores." It was estimated that eighty percent of their customers were white. Among other successful businesses was Thomas Baily & Sons, a meat and grocery store that opened in 1919 and grossed $80,000 a year by 1940. The Home Modernization and Supply Company, founded in 1938 by the brothers U. M. and R. S. George, grossed more than $100,000 in constructing five hundred homes in the Durham area and employed 35 people by 1948.

African American businesses were so stable and the outlook for the future was so promising that, in 1924, Durham was chosen as the location for the headquarters of the National Negro Finance Corporation. Capitalized with $1 million, the organization was started to provide working capital to individuals, firms, and corporations in all parts of the country. Durham, from the turn of the century until the 1950s, remained unrivaled as the African American business capital of America.

Present-Day Durham

Today, 150 or so African American businesses and professionals are still held together by the Durham Business and Professional Chain, founded more than fifty years ago. It would be difficult, however, to replicate the entrepreneurial excitement that existed in Durham between 1900 and 1950. Indeed, scholars have noted that grassroots entrepreneurship tends to develop quickly by groups who newly enter the economy of a country, as did African Americans after the abolition of slavery. However, from generation to generation, there is typically a decrease in the number or rate of entrepreneurs as subsequent generations tend to choose the professions over entrepreneurship. In the case of African Americans, a full blown civil rights movement was required to create another surge in the entrepreneurial spirit.

◆ POST-CIVIL RIGHTS ERA ASSISTANCE TO AFRICAN AMERICAN BUSINESSES

The Civil Rights movement prompted the development of legislation and a number of government agencies to ensure the social, political, and economic rights of African Americans. Perhaps the greatest boost to African American entrepreneurship came in 1967 with the establishment of the Small Business Administration 8 (a) program.

Under Section 8 (a) of the Small Business Act Amendments (Pub.L. 90–104), the SBA is authorized to enter into contract with federal agencies on behalf of small and disadvantaged businesses. Participation in the 8 (a) program for small and disadvantaged businesses is contingent upon SBA approval of the business plan prepared by the prospective firms. The total dollar value of contracts processed through Section 8 (a) had grown from $8.9 million in 1969 to $2.7 billion in 1985. Through the program, many small and African American-owned businesses have been able to stabilize and grow. During the early 1980s, however, the Section 8 (a) program was criticized because less than five percent of the firms have achieved open market competitiveness, which implies that the program is assisting the marginal entrepreneur more so than the promising self-employed minority businessperson.

Another product of the Civil Rights movement has been the 1977 Public Works Employment Act (Pub.L. 95–28). Supplementing the Section 8 (a) Program, the Public Works Act requires that all general contractors bidding for public works projects allocate at least ten percent of their contracts to minority subcontractors. The SBA 8(a) Program and the 1977 Public Works Employment Act constituted the first attempt at "set-asides" to provide access to contracts for small, disadvantaged, and minority businesses.

Impact of the *City of Richmond v. Croson* Case

The fundamental concept of set-aside minority assistance programs was later called into question during the height of the Reagan-Bush era. In 1989, the landmark U.S. Supreme Court ruling in *City of Richmond v. Croson* struck down as unconstitutional under the Fourteenth Amendment a city ordinance of Richmond, Virginia, requiring that thirty percent of each public construction contract to be set aside for minority businesses. In striking down the Richmond ordinance, the Supreme Court made the distinction between local/state and federally enacted business development programs, holding that the U.S. Congress has far more authority than the states in formulating remedial legislation.

The *Croson* decision has had a devastating impact upon minority businesses. In Richmond, during the month of July 1987 when a lower court first ruled against the city's set-aside program, 40 percent of the city's total construction dollars were allocated for products and services provided by minority-owned construction firms. Immediately following the court's decision, the minority businesses's share of contracts fell to 15 percent, later dropping to less than 3 percent. In Tampa, Florida, the number of contracts awarded to African American-owned companies decreased 99 percent, and contracts with Latino-owned firms fell 50 percent after *Croson*. Such dramatic decreases in contracts awarded to minority businesses occurred throughout the country. More than 33 states and political subdivisions have taken steps to dismantle their racial/ethnic set-aside programs; more than seventy jurisdictions are conducting studies and/or holding hearings to review and evaluate their programs in light of *Croson*.

◆ RECENT ECONOMIC TRENDS

The geographic concentration of African American firms has roughly coincided with the African American population concentration over time. New York City had the greatest number of African American-owned firms in 1992 with 39,404. New York firms's gross receipts were $1.7 billion. Washington, DC, was second with 37,988 firms and $1.7 billion in gross receipts. These cities were followed by Los Angeles (32,645 and receipts of $3.6 billion), Chicago (24,644 and receipts of $1.6 billion), and Atlanta (23,488 and receipts of $1 billion).

The location of corporate headquarters in urban areas has provided increased business opportunities for African American business service enterprises. Large cities have become areas where administrative and service functions are the dominant economic activities. The growth in corporate and government administration in central city business districts has created a need for complementary advertising, accounting, computer, legal, temporary secretarial, and maintenance business services.

African American-Owned Businesses in the 1980s and 1990s

In certain respects, the opportunities and constraints that have affected the progress and potential for development of African American-owned businesses in the 1980s and 1990s are a reflection of the historical African American experience. There are periods of growth followed by periods of contraction. Over this time period, African American-owned businesses experienced a dramatic increase in both numbers and income in the face of considerable individual and institutionalized adversity. Moreover, as we enter the new millennium, a number of African American entrepreneurs are focusing on the unique challenges posed by the Information Age. Success stories are numerous, and the conventional wisdom still holds that the continued educational advances, especially technological education, of the African American community will translate into an increasing number of business successes.

African American business experiences, however, have always been paradoxical because progress does not typically translate into relative gains vis-á-vis the majority community, and parity is not even a remote possibility. While the size of the economic pie has indeed increased, the portion accorded to the African American businesspersons has remained virtually unchanged. In the business community, African Americans must run extremely hard just to keep pace. And, while a multiplicity of factors account for this "running in place," the evidence unequivocally confirms that the market is not "race neutral" or "color blind." As stated in *Black Entrepreneurs in America: Stories of Struggles and Success*, "Put differently, the kind of economic detour that negatively impacted the growth of black entrepreneurship in the pre-Civil Rights era has transformed itself but, nevertheless, continues to negatively impact the entrepreneurial experience of African Americans in the post-Civil Rights era."

Effects on the African American Worker

According to the *1992 Survey of Minority-Owned Business Enterprises: Black* (U.S. Bureau of the Census), the number of African American-owned businesses between 1987 and 1992 increased by 68 percent, from approximately 425,000 to almost 621,000, and revenues accruing to these businesses increased by 63 percent, from slightly less than $20 billion to more than $32 billion. In addition, African American-owned businesses were distributed throughout the major sectors of the economy, such as various service industries, retail, finance, insurance, real estate, wholesale trade, and construction.

However, the number of African American-owned businesses and their total revenues, in the context of the national economy, continued to be marginal. This could seriously undermine the long-term developmental potential of African Americans in the business sector. For example, African American workers comprise the overwhelming majority of employees of African American-

From 1987 to 1992, the total number of African American-owned businesses increased by 68 percent (AP/Wide World Photos, Inc.).

owned businesses including the top executives. African American-owned businesses, therefore, provide careers, skills development, and greater earnings opportunities for African Americans that otherwise may not be accessible to them in the majority corporations. To the extent that these businesses continue to be underrepresented in the marketplace, opportunities for African Americans to circumvent the "glass ceiling" will be similarly circumscribed. As T. A. Clark stated in "Minority Businesses in Urban Economies." in *Urban Studies*, "Low minority business ownership enhances the vulnerability of minorities to discrimination in the labor force because it limits the capacity to hire minority workers who are unfairly denied opportunity in the economy."

Dual Barriers to Greater Entrepreneurial Growth

In answer to the question of why have African American-owned businesses not achieved even more in the post-Civil Rights era, two levels of responsibility need be recognized. First, it is the responsibility of African American community to eliminate what is described as "internal barriers." First is socialization. The "successful entrepreneur" must be seen as an honored career path as having a good job as a teacher, lawyer, physician, social worker, or minister. Fortunately, entrepreneurship is now a part of the curriculum or extracurricular activities of some high schools. Parents, however, must explicitly include entrepreneurship in the mix of career options presented to their children. Second is commitment. . . .[W]e frequently fail to understand the level of sacrifice necessary in order to accomplish a goal, especially in business. In addition, entrepreneurs frequently suffer from fears and self-doubt concerning their chances of success. Commitment to and success in entrepreneurship is enhanced by acquiring the necessary educational background, acquiring work experience to be technically competent in the chosen field of enterprise, and saving sufficient start-up capital. In the post-Civil Rights era, African Americans must take full responsibility for eliminating internal barriers to entrepreneurship."

In terms of external barriers, the majority business community and government sector must assume the responsibility for mitigating the artificial hindrances to the credit markets that have impeded the investment possibilities and profit potential of African American-owned businesses. A recent analysis conducted by National Bureau of Economic Research economists to determine the extent to which minority-owned businesses encounter prejudice in applying for loans concluded that African American-owned businesses faced significant and persistent constraints in the credit market. Furthermore, the study revealed that these constraints extended beyond the availability of credit to also include the cost of credit—African American-owned businesses paid higher interest rates on the loans than did their majority counterparts.

The Promise of Information Technology

Economic growth in the twenty-first century will be realized in the area of information technology. Technological changes will continue to enable businesses to more efficiently generate, use, and manage information, as well as compete with larger companies. Evidence suggests that African American entrepreneurs have already been participants and beneficiaries of this Information Revolution. In fact, Tariq K. Muhammad, an acknowledged expert in this area, chronicled the emergence of a class of African American technocrats whom he labeled the "Black Digerati." He states in his *Black Enterprise* article of the same title, "In an industry seemingly dominated by white males, there are numerous African Americans making their presence felt. And, they aren't just in the Valley. Blacks in the information industry can be found in roles which include inventors,

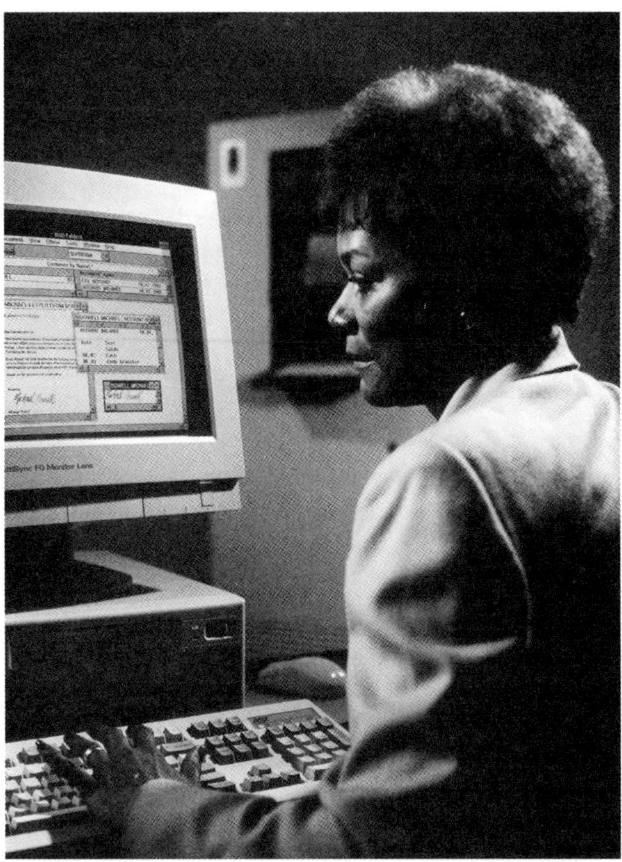

The information technology sector offers promising business opportunities for African American entrepreneurs (Index Stock Imagery).

Wally Amos (AP/Wide World Photos, Inc.)

engineers, entrepreneurs, executives, consultants, venture capitalists, lawyers, and headhunters. There are brothers and sisters all over the country who are masters and creators of the Digital Revolution."

Specifically, the Internet is expected to continue to provide opportunities for small business success for African Americans in the twenty-first century. Two characteristics of web-based businesses operations will continue to be especially relevant for African American entrepreneurs: anonymity and relatively low startup costs. The former allows African American business owners to minimize the possibility that ethnic biases can negatively affect sales, while the latter reduces the capital requirements for launching and operating a business enterprise.

Thus, there is a good basis for optimism that the information technology sector will afford African American entrepreneurs greater opportunities in obtaining a share of the economic market more commensurate with their population percentage. The accomplishments of African American entrepreneurs in the information technology sector also provides current evidence that the entrepreneurial spirit among African Americans burns bright as we move into the new millennium.

◆ ENTREPRENEURS AND BUSINESS EXECUTIVES

(To locate biographical profiles more readily, please consult the index at the back of the book.)

Wally Amos, Jr. (1937–)
Entrepreneur

Wallace Amos, Jr. was born in Tallahassee, Florida, on July 1, 1937, and grew up there until his parents divorced when he was 12 years old. Following his parents's divorce, he went to New York City to live with his Aunt Della. She loved to cook and often made Amos her special chocolate chip cookies. After spending several years in New York City, he dropped out of high school to join the U.S. Air Force, where he earned his high school equivalency degree.

Upon discharge from the Air Force, Amos achieved success as the first African American talent agent for the William Morris Agency. Starting there as a mail clerk, he

James Beckwourth (The Granger Collection Ltd.)

quickly worked his way up to executive vice president. While there he "discovered" Simon & Garfunkel for the agency and served as agent for such well known acts and entertainers as the Supremes, the Temptations, Marvin Gaye, Dionne Warwick, and Patti Labelle.

In 1975 Amos founded Famous Amos Chocolate Chip Cookies. Based on his Aunt Della's recipe, the cookies became a nationwide success as they spread across the country from his original store on Sunset Boulevard in Los Angeles. By 1980 Amos was selling five million dollars worth of cookies each year and his operation had expanded to include a large production facility in Nutley, New Jersey. Amos's success and expansion was enhanced by the backing of such well known entertainers as Bill Cosby and Helen Reddy. In 1985 Amos became vice chairman of the company and served in that capacity until 1989. Amos left the Famous Amos Cookie Corporation in 1989 following a dispute with a group of investors and financial difficulties. He began a new business, Wally Amos Presents . . . Chip & Cookie, in 1990. In 1993, Amos started yet another company, Uncle Noname Cookie Company, and serves as its president. Uncle Noname Cookie Company, based in Honolulu, Hawaii, specializes in five varieties of gourmet cookies. Proceeds from the sale of Uncle Noname cookies are donated to the support of Cities in Schools, a national dropout prevention program of which he is a member of the board of directors.

Amos has donated personal items to the Business Americana Collection at the Smithsonian's Collection of Advertising History and received the Presidential Award for Entrepreneurial Excellence Award from President Ronald Reagan in 1986. In 1987, he received a citation from the Horatio Alger Association. Amos also served as a national spokesperson for Literacy Volunteers of America.

James Pierson Beckwourth (1798–1866)

Author, Trapper, Entrepreneur

Jim Beckwourth was born on April 26, 1798, near Fredericksburg, Virginia. His father was a landowner and member of a prominent Virginia family; his mother was an African American woman, possibly a slave. The family moved to a farm near St. Charles, Missouri, in 1806 and Jim attended school in St. Louis from 1810 to 1814. He was apprenticed to a St. Louis blacksmith but soon found himself heading west. Similar to many other events in Beckwourth's life, there are conflicting stories concerning the dissolution of the apprenticeship. Evidently at this time, Beckwourth also changed the spelling of his last name.

In 1824, Beckwourth joined a westward bound fur trapping and trading expedition under the leadership of William Henry Ashley. Beckwourth soon became known as a man of many adventures and exploits. Although the basis of these stories are factual many, with Beckwourth's approval, have been greatly exaggerated. Nevertheless he undoubtedly embodied the spirit of the legendary mountain men of the American west. In 1827, while still engaged in the fur trade he married a Blackfoot Indian woman. In 1829, he took refuge from a debt collector by hiding with the Crow Indians where he married again. It must be remembered that marriage on the frontier was a much less formal arrangement than it is today. Beckwourth claims he was made a Crow chief in recognition of his fighting prowess against the Blackfeet.

By 1837, Beckwourth was with the U.S. Army in Florida serving as a scout during the Seminole wars. He soon returned to the Rocky Mountains, married a woman in New Mexico, and, in 1842, opened a trading post near what is now Pueblo, Colorado. Between 1844 and 1850, he fought in the California uprising against Mexico and the Mexican-American War. In 1850, Beckwourth joined the California gold rush and while in the Sierra Nevadas discovered a mountain pass that bears his name today. He made the gap more passable, opened an inn, and, by 1851, was guiding wagon trains through the pass.

Dave Bing

Beckwourth's memoirs, entitled *Life and Adventures of James P. Beckwourth, Mountaineer, Scout and Pioneer*, were in part ghost written by T.D. Bonner and published in 1856. Beckwourth traveled to St. Louis and Kansas City where the popularity of his book enhanced his reputation and he was regarded as somewhat of a celebrity. Beckwourth returned to Denver, married again, opened a trading post, and was acquitted on a charge of manslaughter. Tiring of city life he signed on with the Army as a scout and fought the Cheyenne Indians. Beckwourth probably died of food poisoning on or around September 25, 1866 while riding to a Crow encampment. Accounts of his purposely being poisoned by Crows are largely discounted today.

Dave Bing (1943–)

Business Executive, Former Professional Basketball Player

Bing was born November 29, 1943, in Washington, DC, where he played basketball at Springarn High School. He was named to play on a national All-Star team and was voted most valuable player on the tour. Bing attended Syracuse University on a basketball scholarship graduating in 1966 with a B.A. in economics. He was the second overall pick in the 1966 National Basketball Association draft and was chosen by the Detroit Pistons.

During his first season he was the league's top rookie and the league's high scorer his second year. In the 1974–1975 season Bing played for the Washington, DC, Bullets and in the 1977–1978 season he was with the Boston Celtics. Bing was voted the league's Most Valuable Player in 1976 and played in seven NBA All-Star games. The Professional Basketball Writer's Association of America gave him their Citizenship Award in 1977. Bing was named National Minority Small Businessperson of the Year in 1984. In 1989 he was elected to the Naismith Memorial Basketball Hall of Fame.

After being associated with management programs at the National Bank of Detroit, Chrysler Corporation, and Paragon Steel, Bing formed Bing Steel Inc. in Detroit, a very successful steel supplier to the automobile industry.

Bing has served on the board of directors of Children's Hospital of Detroit, Michigan Association of Retarded Children and Adults, Black United Fund, Detroit Urban League, and the March of Dimes.

Marie Dutton Brown (1940–)

Entrepreneur

Marie Brown's career is a picture book example of the kind of tenacious nature entrepreneurs need to have, and how to expand on opportunities when they present themselves. She received a degree in psychology in 1962, from Penn State University, where she was part of the one percent of the student body's African American population. She went to work as a social studies teacher in the Philadelphia public school system. Two years later, when a salesperson from a publishing firm in New York came to sell her some of his company's titles for the school, the meeting turned into a job offer to work for Doubleday.

Brown stayed at Doubleday for two years, then moved to Los Angeles with her new husband. She moved back to New York in 1972 and returned to Doubleday as an associate editor. During the 1970s, as an interest in African American literary titles grew, so grew Brown's position, as she brought many ethnic titles to print.

In 1980, Brown quit Doubleday to become founding editor of *Elan* magazine, which focused on the cultural life of the international black community. After only three issues were launched, Brown's financial backers pulled out, leaving Brown jobless. She went to work at a bookstore, giving her firsthand retail experience.

In the fall of 1984, Brown started her own business, Marie Brown Associates, a literary agency that was run from Brown's Harlem apartment. Although, similar to any new business venture, times were lean for several years, things started to turn around as Brown began signing more and more writers through her agency. As the 1990s began, the larger publishing houses began courting African American writers, but Brown was far ahead of them, as one of only five African American literary agents in the country. Brown still contributes her time to the community, sitting on several boards including the Studio Museum of Harlem.

Malcolm CasSelle (1970–)

Computer Entrepreneur

Born on March 22, 1970, in Allentown, Pennsylvania, CasSelle has accomplished a great deal at a young age. Growing up in Allentown, Pennsylvania, CasSelle developed a passion for writing computer programs in high school. CasSelle attended and graduated from Massachusetts Institute of Technology (MIT).

CasSelle left for Japan three days after finishing his undergraduate work in order to enter MIT's Japan program. While overseas, he worked for Shroders Securities and NTT Software Labs. Upon his return to the United States he took a job with Apple Computers. After earning his master's at Stanford, he occupied the position of director of digital publishing and marketing for Blast Publishing. CasSelle would later introduce E. David Ellington, his partner, to the wonders of cyberspace.

Malcolm CasSelle (NetNoir)

Along with Ellington, CasSelle co-founded NetNoir Inc., an African American-oriented online site. Based in San Francisco and available through America Online, NetNoir explores a wide range of news and information. *Vibe* magazine, along with Motown Records and the clothing company Blue Marlin, channel their through services or goods through CasSelle's cybersite.

Emma Chappell (1941–)

Banking Executive

Emma Chappell was born in Philadelphia, Pennsylvania, in 1941 and was a member of the Zion Baptist Church. Through her church connections, she began to work for the Continental Bank. She took classes at both Temple and Rutgers University and slowly moved up the bank's hierarchy. By 1977, she was the first African American female vice president at the bank.

She was active in the community during her assent to the top of Continental. She worked for a variety of community action groups that were concerned with redeveloping the inner-city. In 1984, she took time off from Continental to be the treasurer for the presidential campaign of the Reverend Jesse Jackson.

In 1987, Chappell and a group of community business leaders founded the Union Bank of Philadelphia, the only African American owned bank in the city. The bank struggled to find funding in the late 1980s; however, by 1992 it had found appropriate funding and opened for business. United struggled upon its opening and, in 1995 and 1996, neared insolvency. However, the bank became successful by the end of the decade. Chappell is currently the chief executive officer of the United Bank.

Comer Cottrell (1931–)

Entrepreneur

Cottrell was born in Mobile, Alabama, on December 7, 1931. He began his sales career at the age of eight, joining his father for visits to clients selling insurance. Cottrell continued his sales career at Sears Roebuck after graduating from the University of Detroit in 1952. Years later, while managing a post exchange at a military base, Cottrell observed that there were no hair products for African Americans. Cottrell decided to form a company that would sell products specifically for hair styles worn by African Americans.

In 1970, Cottrell began his company with an empty Los Angeles warehouse, $600, and a typewriter. He started out marketing hair spray to African American beauticians and barbers. With the moderate success of this product, the Proline company was born. Five years later, Proline opened a distribution center in Birmingham, Alabama. By 1980, Proline had outgrown Los Angeles and moved to Dallas, coinciding with the release of the Curly Kit Home Permanent product. Soon Proline enjoyed sales figures in excess of $11 million dollars and began to expand into overseas markets. By 1989, Proline was ranked nineteenth on *Black Enterprise*'s list of top 100 African American businesses with sales of $36 million annually.

In 1989, Cottrell became—as a member of a 14-owner consortium of investors that purchased the Texas Rangers—the first African American to own a Major League Baseball franchise. Cottrell used his position to speak out about affirmative action in professional sports. In 1990, he continued his philanthropy by purchasing the bankrupt Bishop College, a Dallas school founded by free slaves and Baptist missionaries, and he convinced Paul Quinn College to relocate from Waco, Texas, to the Bishop College grounds. In 1994, Cottrell visited South Africa as part of an envoy of African American businessmen sponsored by Langston University's National Institute for the Study of Minority Enterprise to establish links with black-owned businesses there.

Jean Baptiste Pointe Du Sable (1750?–1818)
Entrepreneur, City Founder

Jean Baptiste Du Sable was reportedly born in Sante-Dominque around 1750 to a French mariner and an African-born slave. It is believed that he may have been educated in Paris and worked as a sailor during his young adult years. Du Sable entered North America through either Louisiana or French Canada.

In the early 1770s, entrepreneur Jean Baptist Du Sable established the first settlement in the area later called Chicago. Having impressed the British as a well-educated man and capable frontiersman, he was sent to the St. Clair region to manage trade and act as a liaison between Native Americans and the British. Later returning to his original settlement, Du Sable built a bakery, dairy, smoke house, horse mill and stable, workshop, and a poultry house. He also traded, trapped, and served as the local cooper and miller. Through Du Sable's efforts, Chicago became a major center for frontier commerce.

In 1788 Du Sable wedded a Potawatomi woman named Kittihawa, or Catherine, with whom he raised two children. Once married, Du Sable became increasingly involved in the Kittihawa community. His bid in 1800, however, for tribal chieftaincy failed, and soon after he sold his holdings and moved from the Chicago area. Real estate records suggest that he moved to St. Charles, Missouri, and that he probably died there in poverty in 1818.

E. David Ellington (1960–)
Computer Entrepreneur

Ellington was born in New York, New York, on July 10, 1960. Growing up in Harlem, he was raised primarily by his mother. While earning his undergraduate degree at Adelphi University, which he received in 1981, Ellington worked in the office of a U.S. congressman. In 1983, he received his master's from Howard University, then spent a great deal of his time travelling in such places as Europe, Japan, China, and India. Later, he earned his law degree from Georgetown University. He founded the Law Offices of E. David Ellington and chaired for the International Law Section of the Beverly Hills Bar Association.

In 1995, Ellington and computer entrepreneur, Malcolm CasSelle, cofounded NetNoir Online, an African American-oriented site on the Internet. Billing itself as "The Cybergateway to Afrocentric Culture," NetNoir explores a wide range of news and information. Participants include journalist Charlayne Hunter-Gault and athlete Carl Lewis. Extremely innovative, NetNoir was named one of the "25 Cool Companies of the Year" by *Fortune* magazine. With minority investors, NetNoir News Media Services planned to venture into CD-ROMs and the designing of web sites in 1996.

Ann Marie Fudge (1951–)
Corporate Executive

Ann Marie Fudge was born in Washington, DC, in 1951. She received a bachelor's of arts with honors from Simmons College in 1973 and an Master's of Business Administration from Harvard Business School in 1977. She began her business career at General Electric in 1973 as a manpower specialist, where she worked until 1975, when she received a job at General Mills in Minneapolis. There she began as a marketing assistant until she was promoted to assistant product manager in 1977, product manager in 1980, and marketing director in 1983. She remained in that position until she joined Kraft General Foods in 1986.

At Kraft, Fudge started out as the associate director of strategic planning, but by 1989, her worth to the company earned her a vice presidency in charge of marketing and development of the Dinners and Enhancers Division working on products, such as Log Cabin Syrup, Minute Rice, and Stove Top Stuffing. She managed to reposition the products in the overburdened food market and increased sales. She moved up to general manager of that division in 1991, and executive vice president in 1994. That year Fudge took over as president of Kraft's struggling Maxwell House Coffee division.

Fudge has served as president and vice president of the Executive Leadership Council and holds memberships with the National Black MBA Association and the Junior League. She serves on the board of directors for Allied Signal Inc., Liz Clairborne Inc., Simmons College, Harvard Business School, and the Catalyst Advisory Board. She was a COGME Fellow in 1975 and won a Leadership Award from the Young Women's Christian Association in 1979.

S.B. Fuller (1905–1988)

Entrepreneur

S.B. Fuller was born in Louisiana in 1905 and moved with his family to Memphis. He dropped out of school after the sixth grade and worked at various jobs. In 1928, he moved to Chicago and began selling products door-to-door. By the mid 1930s he had established a successful business on the South side of Chicago.

In 1947, he acquired Boyer International Laboratories, a white-owned cosmetics company, and greatly expanded his business. His company grew in size and he became famous for his motivational techniques. However, when whites in the South learned that Boyer was owned by an African American, they boycotted Boyer's products. In 1969, Fuller Products was forced to declare bankruptcy.

Fuller reorganized the company, and it reemerged from bankruptcy in the early 1970s. The company reestablished its sales techniques and grew into a large company again. Fuller died in 1988 after receiving numerous honors.

Arthur G. Gaston (1892–1996)

Entrepreneur

Arthur G. Gaston was the living embodiment of what makes up an entrepreneur. He had stated many times in interviews, that one of his primary rules for business success is "Find a need and fill it." Gaston's business accomplishments are a testimony to the man's lifelong adherence to this rule. He started his business career in 1923 by founding the Booker T. Washington Burial Society, guaranteeing African Americans a decent burial. In 1932 it had grown large enough to be incorporated. In 1930, Smith and Gaston Funeral Directors was formed to complement the services of the burial society. The "Smith" was A. L. Smith, Gaston's father-in-law, who helped him financially get started in business.

Finding it hard to staff his growing company with skilled clerical employees, Gaston started the Booker T. Washington Business College in 1939. The college provided a place where African American students could learn proficiency in working on business machines. (The school continues to this day.)

In 1946, Gaston started the Brown Belle Bottling Company, offering Joe Louis Punch. Next came a cemetery in 1947, a motel in 1954, an investment firm in 1955, a savings and loan association in 1957, a senior citizens home in 1963, two radio stations in 1975. In 1986, at the hearty age of 94, Gaston opened the A. G. Gaston Construction Company. From the original burial society in 1923 to his sprawling empire seven decades later, bringing in more than $24 million in revenues in 1991, Arthur Gaston was the quintessential self-made man.

Archibald H. Grimké (1849–1930)

Lawyer, Writer, Activist, Diplomat

Archibald Grimké was born on a plantation near Charleston, South Carolina, in 1849. His father was a successful lawyer who had given up his profession to become a planter. His mother had been a family slave and served as the nurse for Henry Grimké's first wife, Selena. Archibald was considered a slave due to South Carolina law at the time. He, along with his mother and siblings, were passed on to relatives after his father's death. Grimké attended a special school during his youth. He later fled his home. Grimké enrolled in a school directed by Frances Pillsbury and impressed the instructors there with his superior academic abilities. He completed undergraduate studies in only three years and obtained his master's degree from Lincoln University two years following that, in 1872.

Grimké moved to Boston and practiced law there from 1875 to 1883. Beginning in 1885, he presided over the Women's Suffrage Association of Massachusetts. In the early 1890's, Grimké wrote for Boston-area publications, before being appointed the American consul for Santo Domingo (now the Dominican Republic) for four years. He then assumed the presidential role for the Washington chapter of the NAACP while writing, lecturing, and presiding over the American Negro Academy. Grimk write several books, including biographies of William Lloyd Garrison in 1891 and Charles Sumner in 1892, and numerous essays and speeches.

Le-Van Hawkins (1960–)

Fast Food Restaurant Entrepreneur

Hawkins was born and raised in Chicago, Illinois. He suffered as a youth through drug addiction and gang membership. However, after starting to work at McDonald's in downtown Chicago, he turned his life around. He quickly rose through the ranks at McDonald's, becoming director of operations before leaving the company to work for Kentucky Fried Chicken.

He managed inner-city projects for KFC and became a district manager. In 1986, he joined T. Boone Pickens in various investment schemes that earned him large amounts of money. In 1990, he began franchising Check-

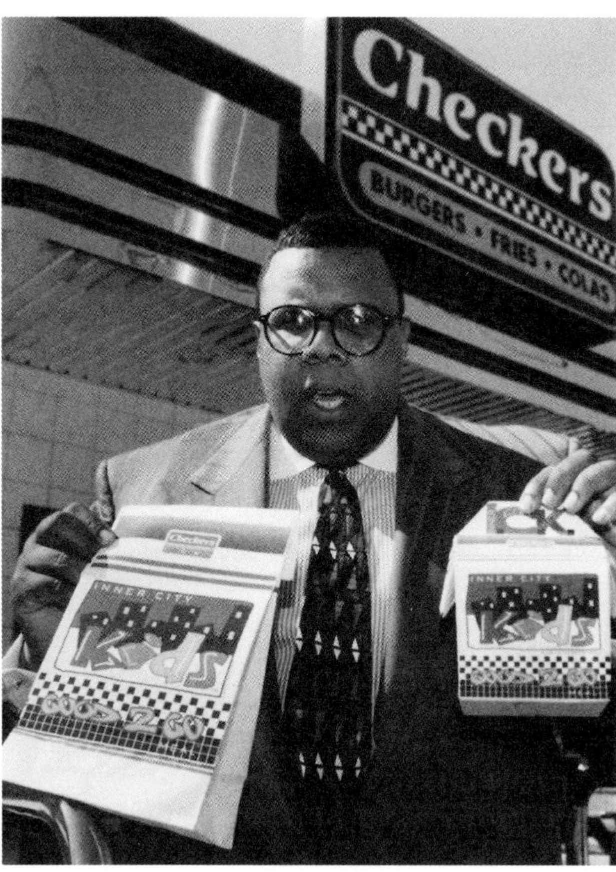

Le-Van Hawkins (AP/Wide World Photos, Inc.)

George E. Johnson (AP/Wide World Photos, Inc.)

ers restaurants. By 1995, the success of this chain had made him a multi-millionaire.

In 1995, officials for Burger King approached Hawkins about fronting several of their restaurants in urban areas. Hawkins accepted the offer and now owns Burger Kings in various cities and several federal empowerment zones. Hawkins continues to add restaurants each year and has more than a dozen Burger Kings in Detroit.

Robert Holland, Jr. (1940–)
Business Executive

Robert Holland, Jr. was born in April of 1940, in Albion, Michigan. Holland earned a bachelor's of science in mechanical engineering from Union College in Schenectady, New York in 1962, and in 1969, he completed a master's of business administration in international marketing at Bernard Baruch Graduate School of Manhattan. In 1968, Holland moved from his job at the Mobil Oil Co. as an engineer and sales manager to join the McKinsey & Co. consulting firm, where he worked as an associate and eventually a partner until 1981. During that time, he worked abroad in the Netherlands, England, Mexico, and Brazil. He returned to Michigan in 1981 as CEO of City Marketing, a beverage distributor. In 1987, he switched companies again, accepting the chair position for Gilreath Manufacturing, Inc. in Howell, Michigan, a manufacturer of plastic injection molds.

In 1991, Holland started Rohker-J Inc. in White Plains, New York, a company of his own that bought struggling companies, turning them around and selling them. In 1994, Holland's business savvy and his whimsy with poetic verse won him a position as president and CEO of Ben & Jerry's Homemade Ice Cream, Inc. After accomplishing his goals of stabilizing Ben & Jerry's manufacturing operations and bringing more professional management to the company, he resigned in October 1996. In 1997 he founded WorkPlace Integrators, a leading dealer of Steelcase office furniture, in Bingham Farms, Michigan. In addition to his business, Holland sits on the board of directors for the Harlem Junior Tennis Program, UNC Ventures, and Atlanta University Center. He is chairman of the board at Spelman College.

George E. Johnson (1927–)
Business Executive

Johnson was born in Richton, Mississippi, on June 16, 1927. He attended Wendell Phillips High School in

Chicago then went to work as a production chemist for a firm that produced cosmetic products for African Americans. While there, he developed a hair straightener for men and began marketing it himself in 1954. By 1957 he had formed Johnson Products and was selling products under the Ultra-Sheen label. The company prospered and, by 1971, its stock was being traded on the American Stock Exchange. Johnson Products was the first African American-owned company to trade on a major stock exchange. In June 1993 Joan B. Johnson, chair and CEO of Johnson Products, announced the sale of the company to Ivax Corp., a white-owned pharmaceutical firm. Johnson Products was officially sold to Ivax in August 1993.

Johnson has served as a director of the Independence Bank of Chicago, the U.S. Postal Service, and the Commonwealth Edison Co. Johnson also is responsible for the George E. Johnson Foundation ,which funds charitable and educational programs for African Americans.

Johnson has received the Abraham Lincoln Center's Humanitarian Service Award (1972), *Ebony* magazine's Black Achievement Award (1978), and the public service award presented by the Harvard Club of Chicago. He has also been awarded the Horatio Alger Award (1980) and the Babson Medal (1983).

Johnson has received honorary degrees from many institutions of learning including Chicago State University (1977), Fisk University (1977), and the Tuskegee Institute (1978).

Dennis Kimbro (1950–)
Author, Educator, Motivational Speaker

Dennis Paul Kimbro was born on December 29, 1950, in Jersey City, New Jersey. He graduated from Oklahoma University with a bachelor's in 1972 and later from Northwestern University with a Ph.D. in political economy in 1984, while working as a salesperson at Smithkline Beckman pharmaceutical corporation. In 1987, he left Smithkline to work at ABC Management Consultants Inc. until 1991. Meanwhile, Kimbro worked at revising a manuscript left to publisher W. Clement Stone written by the late Napoleon Hill, the author of *Think and Grow Rich.* Hill had been working on a version for an African American audience when he died. Stone gave the manuscript to Kimbro. Kimbro interviewed many successful African Americans to chart how they managed to maximize potential and channel positive thinking to build their success.

In 1991, Kimbro's book—co-authored originally by Hill—*Think and Grow Rich: A Black's Choice* was published by Ballantine Books and became the first ever major released African American self-help book. In the next two years, the book sold more than 250,000 copies and was a best seller among African American audiences, earning Kimbro an Award of Excellence from the Texas Association of Black Personnel in Higher Education in 1992. Kimbro already held a Dale Carnegie Personal Achievement award from 1988. In 1992, Kimbro accepted a post as associate professor and director of the Center for Entrepreneurship at Clark Atlanta University School of Business and Administration. *Daily Motivations for African-American Success*, Kimbro's second book, was published by Ballantine in 1993.

Reginald F. Lewis (1942–1993)
Business Executive

Lewis was born December 7, 1942, in Baltimore, Maryland. He received an A.B. from Virginia State College in 1965 and a law degree from Harvard Law School in 1968. He first worked with the firm of Paul, Weiss, Rifkind, Wharton & Garrison until 1970. He was a partner in Murphy, Thorpe & Lewis, the first African American law firm on Wall Street until 1973. Between 1973 and 1989 Lewis was in private practice as a corporate lawyer. In 1989 he became president and CEO of TLC Beatrice International Holdings Inc. With TLC's leveraged acquisition of the Beatrice International Food Co. Lewis became the head of the largest African American owned business in the United States. TLC Beatrice had revenues of $1.54 billion in 1992.

Lewis was a member of the American and National Bar Associations and the National Conference of Black Lawyers. He was on the board of directors of the New York City Off-Track Betting Corp., the Central Park Conservance, the NAACP Legal Defense Fund, and WNET-Channel 13, the public television station in New York. He was the recipient of the Distinguished Service Award presented by the American Association of MESBIC (1974) and the Black Enterprise Achievement Award for the Professions. Lewis died unexpectedly January 19, 1993, in New York.

James B. Llewellyn (1927–)
Business Executive

James Llewellyn was born July 16, 1927, in New York City and earned a B.S. from City College of New York. He attended Columbia University's Graduate School of Business and New York University's School of Public Administration before receiving a degree from New York Law School.

Before attending law school, Llewellyn was the proprietor of a retail liquor store. While attending law school he was a student assistant in the District Attorney's Office for New York County from 1958 to 1960.

After graduating he practiced law as part of Evans, Berger and Llewellyn. Between 1964 and 1969 he worked in a variety of professional positions for various governmental agencies including the Housing Division of the Housing and Re-Development Board (1964–1965), Small Business Development Corporation (1965), and the Small Business Administration (1965–1969).

In 1969, as part of a syndicate buyout, he became president of Fedco Food Stores of New York. By 1975, the company had grown from 11 to 14 stores and had annual revenues of $30 million and 450 employees.

Llewellyn has served on the boards of the City College of New York and its Graduate Center, American Can Co., American Capital Management Research, and the Freedom National Bank. He has belonged to the Harlem Lawyers Association, the New York Interracial Council for Business Opportunity, and the New York Urban Coalition and its Venture Capital Corporation.

Llewellyn has honorary doctorates from Wagner College, City University of New York, and Atlanta University. He spent four years in the U.S. Army Corps of Engineers from 1944 to 1948. He is currently CEO of Queen City Broadcasting Inc. and chairman of the Coca-Cola bottlers of Philadelphia.

Samuel Metters
Entrepreneur

Dr. Samuel Metters received his B.S. in architectural engineering from Prairie View A&M University, a B.A. in architecture and urban planning from the University of California at Berkeley, a M.S. in systems management and in public administration from the University of Southern California, and a Ph.D. in public administration from USC.

Metters founded Metters Industries, Inc. in 1981 after a career that included a stint in the Army. The firm, which has over 350 employees, is a strategic planning and analysis company that works in conjunction with various governmental entities. His customers include the IRS and the U.S. Patent and Trade Office, as well as Northwest Airlines, Howard University, Federal Express, and Fox Studios. Metters has also worked in Saudi Arabia building new cities and handling the logistical problems that go along with any new development. Not surprisingly, Metters Industries ranks among the *Black Enterprise* 100 leading African American-owned businesses with 1998 revenues of $40 million dollars.

In 1987 Metters was selected as a member of the board of directors of the U.S. Black Engineers Publications, Inc. He is also active in the USC Alumni Association, Washington ,DC, area Boy Scouts and with Prairie View University.

Rose Meta Morgan (1912?–)
Entrepreneur

Rose Meta Morgan was born c. 1912 in Shelby, Mississippi, but spent most of her growing years in Chicago. She started her own business at the early age of ten, making and selling artificial flowers door-to-door with the assistance of other neighborhood children. By the age of 14, she was earning money styling hair. Morgan claims she was a high school drop out even though she may have actually finished. Either way, she attended Morris School of Beauty, and after graduating, she rented space in a salon and began styling, grooming, and cutting hair full time. It was during this time that Morgan met Ethel Waters, a famous actress/singer, during a run of performances in Chicago in 1938. Waters invited Morgan to New York because of the stylist's prowess in hair design.

Within six months of moving to New York, Morgan opened her own beauty shop. Later, running out of room, she signed a ten-year lease for an old dilapidated mansion and began to renovate it. Three years later, Morgan's salon—the Rose Meta Morgan House of Beauty—was the most prestigious, most successful African American beauty salon in the world. By 1946, she drew one thousand customers a week and increased her staff to 29 people including a nurse and masseurs. Morgan began producing and selling a line of cosmetics and hosting fashion shows that matured into major social events at the Renaissance Casino and Rockford Plaza in Harlem. Soon she was considered one of the richest businesswomen in New York. Customers came from all over the country to visit the House of Beauty, and Morgan travelled abroad with her cosmetics, fashion designs, and ideas about beauty and women of color.

In the mid-1950s, Morgan bought and refurbished a new building for the House of Beauty. Thousands of people attended the grand opening and the building was dedicated by the New York City Mayor's wife. The new salon offered more features, such as a dressmaking department, a charm school, and a fitness department and later a wig salon to cash in on the renewed popularity in hair pieces. In 1965, Morgan created the Freedom National Bank, New York's only commercial bank run by and for African Americans. In 1972, Morgan created the Trim-Away Figure Contouring business, and shortly thereafter, in the 1980s, she retired with a salon and a set of businesses as a legacy that are the only ones of their kind in the world.

Morgan's marriages were less successful than her businesses. In 1955, she married Joe Louis, the heavyweight boxing champion of the world. But in 1957, they separated and their marriage was annulled in 1958. Later, Morgan married lawyer Louis Saunders, and though

Freedom National Bank, Harlem's first black commercial bank, was founded in 1965 (Courtesy of Andy Roy).

they separated in the early 1960s, Saunders died before they were divorced.

Henry G. Parks (1916–)
Entrepreneur, Business Executive

Parks was born September 20, 1916, in Atlanta, Georgia. He received a B.S. from Ohio State University and did graduate work there in marketing.

After graduating Parks worked at the Resident War Production Training Center in Wilberforce, Ohio, where he was associated with Dr. Mary McLeod Bethune. In 1939 he was a national sales representative for the Pabst Brewing Co. In addition he has been involved in a variety of enterprises including theatrical bookings in New York City, a failed attempt at marketing a beverage with Joe Louis, the former heavyweight boxing champion (now deceased), real estate, drug store operations and cement block production, mostly in Baltimore, Maryland.

Parks ultimately bought into Crayton's Southern Sausage Company of Cleveland, Ohio. After becoming familiar with the meat packing industry, he sold his interest in the company for a profit. In 1951 he started H. G. Parks Inc., a sausage packer and distributor with the aid of a group of investors. By 1971 the company had annual revenues of $10.4 million dollars and was distributing its products to over12,000 east coast stores.

Parks has also been vice president of the Chamber of Commerce of Metropolitan Baltimore, served on the board of directors of Magnavox, held a seat on the Baltimore City Council and has an interest in Tuesday Publications.

Richard Dean Parsons (1948–)
Corporate Executive

Born in the Bedford-Stuyvesant neighborhood of Brooklyn, New York, on April 4, 1948, Richard Dean Parsons grew up in the borough of Queens, New York. He graduated from high school at the age of 16 and attended the University of Hawaii, where he played varsity basketball. He earned a bachelor's from the university in 1968, and continued his education at the Union University of the University of Albany Law School. He graduated at the top of his class and received the highest score on the state bar exam in 1971.

Parsons started his career as a member of New York governor Nelson Rockefeller's legal staff, where he served when Rockefeller became vice president of the

United States under Gerald Ford in 1974. He continued in this capacity, also providing legal counsel for President Ford as deputy counsel and then as associate director of the domestic council. He left government service in 1977, to join the New York City law firm, Patterson, Belknap, Webb & Tyler, where he became a partner in 1979. He defended clients, such as Happy Rockefeller and Estee Lauder.

Parsons was appointed chief operating officer of the Dime Savings Bank of New York in 1988, becoming the first African American male to manage a financial institution of Dime's size. Parsons lead the bank to a comeback from severe debt. In 1993, because of Parsons's remarkable leadership skills, newly elected Mayor Rudolph Giuliani chose Parsons to head his transition council and later to be the Deputy Mayor for Economic Development. Parsons instead chose to act as chairman of the Economic Development Corporation for the city. Parsons, no stranger to sitting on boards of directors, has served on boards for Time Warner Inc., Philip Morris, Tristar Pictures, Howard University, and the Metropolitan Museum of Art. Due to these ties, Parsons took an offered position as president of Time Warner Inc. in January of 1995. Parsons has also served as a member of the presidential Drug Task Force, as chairperson of Wildcat Service Organization, and as a member of the board of the New York Zoological Society.

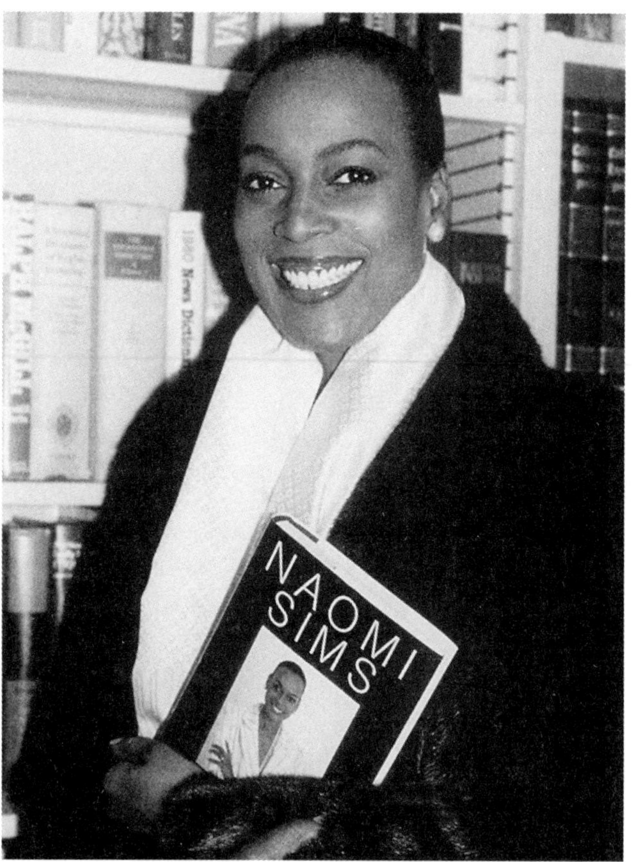

Naomi Sims (Corbis Corporation [Bellevue])

Herman J. Russell (1931–)
Housing Construction Entrepreneur

Russell was born in Atlanta and first went into business with his father. At the age of 16, they bought a small piece of land and built a duplex on it. Russell used the money he accrued from rent to pay for his education at the Tuskegee Institute. In 1953, he went to work for his father and, upon his father's death in 1957, took over the family home improvement business.

Russell built a reputation for high quality work that allowed him to break down many racial barriers to success. He began to bid on large construction jobs and has worked on many of the biggest projects built in Atlanta since the 1960s. He continued to built afforded housing despite the high-profile success of the company.

In 1997, Russell retired from the management of the company, passing it down to his children. He is well known in the Atlanta area for his philanthropy and for his work in the inner-city.

Naomi R. Sims (1949–)
Business Executive, Model

Sims was born March 30, 1949, in Oxford, Mississippi. She attended New York University, where she studied psychology, and the Fashion Institute of Technology, where she graduated in 1967

Sims was a fashion model with the Ford Agency in New York from 1970 to 1973. She was the first African American woman to be a high fashion model and the first to appear in a television commercial. She also appeared on the cover of *Life* Magazine.

In 1970 Sims also started lecturing and writing fashion and beauty articles on a freelance basis. In 1973 she co-developed a new fiber for her line of wigs and founded the Naomi Sims Collection which by 1977 had annual revenues of $4 million. Sims has also written a number of books including *All About Health and Beauty for the Black Woman* (1975), *How to Be a Top Model* (1979), *All About Hair Care for the Black Woman* (1982), and *All About Success for the Black Woman.*

In 1969 and 1970 Sims was voted Model of the Year by International Mannequins and won the *Ladies Home Journal* Women of Achievement Award. For her work with underprivileged children in Bedford-Stuyvesant, she also won an award from the New York City Board of Education. In 1977 Sims was voted into the Modeling Hall of Fame by International Mannequins and made the International Best Dressed List 1971–1973, 1976–1977.

Sims has also received recognition for her fund raising efforts for sickle cell anemia and cancer research. She belongs to the NAACP and works closely with drug rehabilitation programs.

She is currently with Naomi Sims Beauty Products Limited in New York City.

Percy E. Sutton (1920–)
Business Executive, Attorney

Sutton was born November 24, 1920, in San Antonio, Texas. He graduated from the Phillis Wheatley High School and attended a number of colleges including Prairie View College, Tuskegee Institute, and the Hampton Institute. His education was interrupted by World War II when Sutton enlisted in the U.S. Army Air Corps. He was promoted to captain and served as a combat intelligence officer in the Italian and Mediterranean theaters. He was decorated with Combat Stars for his service.

After his discharge, Sutton attended law school on the G.I. Bill, first at Columbia University in New York and then Brooklyn Law School where he received an LL.B. in 1950. During the Korean conflict, Sutton reenlisted in the USAF and served as an intelligence officer and a trial judge advocate.

Returning to civilian life, he opened a law office in Harlem with his brother and another attorney. In 1964, he was elected to the New York State Assembly, where he served until 1966. In 1966, he was appointed and later elected to the office of president of the Borough of Manhattan, a post he held until 1977.

Sutton then founded the Inner-City Broadcasting Corporation, from which he retired in 1990.

Sutton has been a civil rights advocate both as an attorney and a politician. He was a national director of the Urban League and a past president of the New York branch of the NAACP. He was voted Assemblyman of the Year by the Intercollegiate Legislative Assembly in 1966. Sutton has also served as a director of the Museum of the City of New York and the American Museum of Natural History.

Madame C. J. Walker (1867–1919)
Entrepreneur

Walker was born Sarah Breedlove near Delta, Louisiana, in 1867. She was orphaned as a child, raised by a sister in Vicksburg, Mississippi, married at the age of 14, and widowed in 1887 at the age of 20.

Walker moved with her daughter to St. Louis where she earned a living by taking in laundry and sewing. By 1905 she had become interested in hair care products for women and began working on a hot comb and her "Wonderful Hair Grower." In 1906 she moved to Denver and, with $1.50 in her pocket, started a hair preparations company. She soon married C. J. Walker, a newspaperman who taught her the fundamentals of advertising and mail order promotion. In 1908 she moved with her daughter to Pittsburgh where she founded a beauty school, the Walker College of Hair Culture, which trained cosmetologists in the use of her products.

In 1910, with a more central location in mind, she moved to Indianapolis, Indiana, where she established a laboratory and factory and developed a nationwide network of five thousand sales agents, mostly African American women, known as The Madame C.J. Walker Hair Culturists Union of America.

Her business prospered, and Walker became the first African American female millionaire. She had a townhouse in Harlem and a custom built mansion on the Hudson River near Irvington, New York. She died in New York on May 25, 1919.

Walker was a strong believer in self-reliance and education. She was proud of her accomplishments, especially of providing employment for thousands of African Americans who might otherwise have had less meaningful jobs. Walker was also a genius at marketing, promotion, and mail order sales. Beneficiaries of her estate included Mary McLeod Bethune's school in Daytona, Florida, and other African American schools, the NAACP and the Frederick Douglass home restoration project in Florida.

Maggie Lena Walker (1867–1934)
Banker

Walker was born on or around July 15, 1867, in Richmond, Virginia. She was the daughter of Elizabeth Draper, a former slave, and Eccles Cuthbert, a New York journalist of Irish extraction.

Walker attended Richmond public schools including Armstrong Normal School which functioned as a high school. After graduating in 1883 she taught in the Richmond schools for three years before marrying building contractor Armstead Walker in 1886.

While she had been in school, Walker joined the Grand United Order of Saint Luke, a mutual aid society that served as an insurance underwriter for African Americans. Walker became active in the organization and held a number of lesser positions before becoming the Right Worthy Grand Secretary in 1899. She soon changed the name of the organization to the Independent Order of Saint Luke and moved its headquarters to Richmond.

In 1903, she became the head of the Saint Luke Penny Bank and the first woman in the United States to hold such a position. Although legally separate, the bank had a close financial association with the Independent Order of Saint Luke. The bank later became the Saint Luke Bank and Trust Company and, finally, the Consolidated Bank and Trust Company.

By 1924 under Walker's guidance, the Order had a membership of 100,000, a new headquarters building, over two hundred employees and its own newspaper—the *Saint Luke Herald.*

Walker was active in many other organizations including the National Association of Colored Women, the Virginia Federation of Colored Women's Clubs, and its Industrial School for Colored Girls. In 1912 she founded the Richmond Council of Colored Women and was a founding member of the Negro Organization Society, a blanket association for African American clubs and organizations.

She was a board member of the NAACP from 1923 to 1934 and the recipient of an honorary degree from Virginia Union University. In 1927 she received the Harmon Award for Distinguished Achievement. Walker died on December 15, 1934.

The Family

◆ Family Structure and Stability ◆ Marriage ◆ Homosexuality/Bisexuality ◆ Fertility and Births ◆ Children ◆ Health ◆ Life Expectancy ◆ Assessment ◆ Social Activists ◆ Family Statistics

by Rose M. Brewer

The family, as defined by the U.S. Bureau of the Census, is a group of two or more persons (one of whom is the householder) who are related by birth, marriage, or adoption, and who reside together. In everyday social usage, this definition is usually refined to include diverse family pattern variations; however, the American value system has traditionally embraced the concept of lifetime monogamous marriage and prized the "nuclear" family pattern of husband and wife living with their own children in the same household. Yet, with divorce rates currently hovering at about fifty percent, the prevalence of this idealized pattern has diminished. Remarriages have created increasing numbers of "blended" families comprised of various configurations of stepparents and stepchildren. Formal adoptions of stepchildren and increasing adoptions of children from other countries are also more common today than in the past. The growth in the numbers of single-parent families headed by women has been called "one of the most startling social developments of the past quarter century."

◆ FAMILY STRUCTURE AND STABILITY

African American families, historically, have been more diverse in family structure than the idealized norm of the nuclear family. Black families have been crafted in the context of the remembered cultures of Africa, cultural creativity within the United States, enslavement, racism, and persistent institutionalized inequality. Family life was central to African cultures and social organization, and enslaved Africans brought this value with them to America. However, the conditions of slavery often prohibited the existence of a stable African American family. Harshness and cruelty, rape and the severing of family bonds were all too common during enslavement, and slave marriages were not recognized by law. Even so, strong bonds could be formed among enslaved men and women. Herbert Gutman's work *The Black Family in Slavery and Freedom* indicates that some unions lasted 10, 15, and as many as 25 years depending on the region and the time period. Nonetheless, kin relations rather than marriage were the linchpin of African American families under enslavement. This kin principle remains strong to the present.

Thus, one family pattern that has historically been common among African Americans is that of the "extended" family. This family grouping includes other relatives such as grandparents, aunts, uncles, cousins, nieces, nephews, or other relatives, formally or informally adopted, who share the household temporarily or for a longer time period with a nuclear family. Extended families have long been a strong support system within the African American community. Today, members of extended families may not all live in the same household because of the migratory patterns of family members, but they nonetheless function as a supportive intergenerational kinship unit.

Andrew Billingsley, in his classic work *Black Families in White America* (1968), identifies an additional category of families called "augmented" families, which include unrelated persons. In a more recent publication "Understanding African American Family Diversity," Billingsley describes these supportive, dependable, family—such as networks of relationships. Another classification, "fictive kin," as defined by Carol Stack in *All Our Kin*, includes "play" mothers, brothers, sisters, and so on, who usually do not live together. In some communities, these friendship networks resemble and substitute for extended family networks that may no longer exist. Foster families are also a growing phenomenon in the

Extended families have long been a strong support system within the African American community (Index Stock Imagery).

African American community and have been the source of considerable debate. It is usually argued that not enough African American families are sought out to foster African American children. As poverty has increased for many African American families, the issue of bureaucratized foster care will remain a contentious one, and so will the issue of the large number of single female-headed households. This family form is more characteristic of the African American population than of any other American racial or ethnic grouping today.

As Billingsley contends, diversity is and always has been characteristic of African American family life. African American households presently fall into the following categories: (1) married couples with children; (2) married couples without children; (3) extended families (usually those including grandparents); (4) blended families; (5) single-parent families (usually but not always headed by women); (6) cohabitating adults (with or without children); and (7) single-person households (predominantly female).

Number and Size of Families

According to U.S. Census reports, there were 8.5 million African American family households (in the United States in 1997, up from 6.2 million in 1980. This increase was most evident in the number of married-couple families and female-headed families with no husband present. In 1997, married-couple families comprised only 46 percent of all African American families, contrasted with 1980 when they comprised 56 percent. Forty-seven percent of African American families in 1997 were headed by a female householder with no husband present, quite an increase from the 1980 proportion of 40 percent. For the first time in U.S. history, this proportion is more than the percentage of married-couple families. The increase in African American female-headed families can be attributed to a multiplicity of factors: racism, the shortage of eligible African American males, the economic vulnerability of African Americans, the shorter life expectancy of African American males, increasing separation and divorce rates among African Americans, the rising rate of out-of-wedlock parenthood, increasing societal permissiveness regarding sexuality, and changing gender roles stressing female autonomy. This emerging American pattern of female autonomy coincides with the existing African American cultural norm of more egalitarian relationships between women and men than typically found in European American families. Male-headed households with no spouse present represented a mere seven percent of African American families in 1997.

The African American family's structure and status have changed dramatically over the last forty years, and its configuration, while following the majority population's general post-World War II trends, reflects historical inequities between the races that make the African American family's security especially tenuous as the nation enters the twenty-first century. The same forces that have molded the United States into what it is today have been at work on all facets of African American family life and culture. In that sense, the fortunes of African Americans ebb and flow with the tide of the general economic and social conditions of the nation, especially racial, class, and gender inequities. The African American family also faces dilemmas that emanate from its unique position and identity within American society. African Americans experience problems related to their general minority group status as well as to their unique historical experiences of slavery, oppression, second-class citizenship, and the continuing stigma related thereto.

Furthermore, the political struggles of the Civil Rights movement culminated in increased opportunities for a segment of the African American population, but a significant number of African American families remain locked in poverty. Deindustrialization and globalization of the economy represent a notable structural shift with devastating consequences for many urban and rural African American families. As old city industries close down to settle in white suburbs or out of the country, many African Americans face increasing joblessness.

In fact, the U.S. Census data reveal that since the late 1960s the African American unemployment rate has been twice as high as the white unemployment rate, regardless of the economic condition of the country. The 1970s and 1980s, however, were periods of severe economic instability and recession in the United States. African American males were particularly hard-hit by joblessness and underemployment during these decades due to the decline of the manufacturing industries in which many African American males were employed (the automobile and steel industries, for example). This combination of double-digit inflation and high levels unemployment during the 1970s and 1980s disproportionately eroded the purchasing power of African American families. Yet even in the 1990s, during a period of economic expansion and prosperity, many African Americans were still marginalized from the economy.

Income is not the only area in which blacks lag behind whites. According to figures published in *Dollars & Sense* magazine in February of 1996, four of every ten black households have less than one thousand dollars in net worth and nearly 41 percent of black households are worth less than $11,612 versus 16 percent of white households. Most whites fall into the $25,000 to $49,999 net worth range. The discrepancy is partially attributed to the fact that African Americans tend not to have accumulated assets to pass onto the next generation through inheritance—one of the most significant ways in which people amass wealth.

While disproportionate segments of African American families are poor, significant growth in the number of middle-class and affluent African American families at the upper end of the family spectrum has occurred, particularly of younger, college-educated, dual-income, married-couple families. This growth has occurred since the opening of the opportunity structure in the mid-1960s with the passage of the Civil Rights Act of 1964 and the Voting Rights Act of 1965. Less research has been focused on these upper-strata families than on low-income African American families; as a result, less is known about African American families that are prospering in the current economic climate, though they are one of the largest and fastest-growing segments of the nation's consumer population.

In February of 1996, Stephen Garnett of *Dollars & Sense* noted that "blacks represent less than 13 percent of the American population but exercise a purchasing power that equals the gross national product of the ninth largest country in the world." In 1994, African Americans spent $304 billion—much of it on leisure-oriented goods and services, reflecting a more sophisticated consumer. In the recent past, African Americans tended to spend more on cars, furniture, and home appliances and to devoutly express brand loyalty. In the 1990s, African Americans began to seek superior quality and value rather than blindly purchasing products based on established shopping habits. Support of African American-owned businesses remains an issue, however.

African American families in the lower economic strata are earmarked by the growth in the numbers of households headed by poor, never-married African American females. The Center for the Study of Social Policy (1994) found that this growth in female-led families correlated almost perfectly with the growth of African American male joblessness. Other issues for these families include: high levels of teenage pregnancies (although overall rates have been falling over the past half decade, absolute numbers remain high); the shortage of marriageable, employed African American males; disparities between black and white earning power; inadequate housing and social services; and chronic unemployment and underemployment. Some of the social and psychological costs of these phenomena are the crime, violence, drug abuse, and despair that are frequently endemic in many low-income communities, along

Recreational and leisure time outlets must be made available to African American children, especially in urban areas (Index Stock Imagery).

with the disproportionate numbers of imprisoned African American males from those communities.

With drug trafficking pervasive in a significant number of inner-city areas, drug-related homicides among African Americans have reached record levels. Young people turn to the illegal economy as the broader economy remains closed to them. Moreover, a disproportionate amount of drugs and guns are brought in from the outside and dumped into these communities. These activities continue to have very negative impacts on African American families and communities.

Some analysts place the primary blame for the deterioration of inner-city African American families on public policies that are inimical to these families, or on the absence of public policies that provide corrective measures that could empower them to help themselves. Representative of those analysts is Robert B. Hill, who in his article "Economic Forces, Structural Discrimination, and Black Family Instability" (1990), contended that "the key economic policies that undermined black family stability have been anti-inflation fiscal and monetary policies, trade policies, plant closings, social welfare, block grants, and federal per capita formulas for allocating funds to states and local areas that have not been corrected for the census undercount."

Particularly crippling in Hill's view is the absence of policy to provide affordable housing for moderate and low-income families, an absence that has a greater impact on African American families because of their unique employment and income problems. One consequence of this shortage is a return to traditional African American extended or augmented family arrangements as dispossessed family members seek temporary housing with relatives and as friends share their abodes with the less fortunate. Another consequence is that increasing numbers of African American families are homeless. Hill estimated the number of homeless individuals and families in 1989 at two to three million. Many of these families, but not all, were single-parent families headed by women.

Other progressive analysts have placed the deterioration of inner-city families squarely on the structural inequality of increasing privatization and the deteriorating employment, income, and wage levels for these families. These analysts also argue that the dismantling of the social welfare state and mandatory work to welfare expectations now in effect will not lift single-parent, female-headed families out of poverty. This dismantling of the U.S. social welfare state through welfare reform is embedded in a fundamental shift in the social contract: increased pursuit of global private profit with little commitment to domestic social programs.

Other analysts, many of them neoconservative or conservative in their sociopolitical orientation, continue to attribute the marked erosion in the social and economic stability of African American families to internal factors within the families themselves, to the welfare system, and to the "Great Society" programs. For example, Irving Kristol notes that, while illegitimate births have increased startlingly since World War II, among African Americans the rate had risen to 66 percent in 1992 (By 1995, this rate had reached an alarming 70 percent.). Kristol decries the decline in "family values" among these "single moms" who, after having one illegitimate child, opt for and remain on public welfare support as they continue to produce additional children. Daniel Patrick Moynihan alleges that "Great Society" programs destroyed the inner-city black family structure, largely through welfare policies, and argues that social scientists still do not know what public policies will reverse the downward spiral of life conditions of inner-city African American families. Central to Moynihan's analysis and that of his neoconservative successors who have sought to understand changes in African American community and family relations are the relationships between African American family stability and male employment, unemployment, and labor force nonparticipation rates. In 1965, Moynihan and his staff reported strong indicators of change in behaviors of the African American urban poor including a rise in Aid to Families with Dependent Children (AFDC), even as the African American unemployment rate declined, and an increase in the percentage of non-white married women separated from their husbands. As a result of these factors, Moynihan argued, the African American community had become immersed in "a tangle of pathology" that included family breakdown. Many prominent African Americans disputed Moynihan's conclusions and accused him of "blaming the victims" of social conditions rather than looking at the causes of their problems (i.e., racism, segregation, economic inequities).

K. Sue Jewell continues this line of argument by maintaining that "policies, procedures, and assumptions underlying social and economic programs in the 1960s and 1970s, the "Great Society" years, contributed to the disintegration of black two-parent and extended families and to an increase in black families headed by women." Jewel asserts that "social and economic programs and civil rights legislation could not effectively remove social barriers, which prevent black families from participating fully in mainstream American society." In her view, the liberal social policy of the Great Society era resulted in modest, but not substantial, gains for middle-class African American families. Since Jewell's analysis, welfare reform legislation passed in 1996 which, in effect, ended AFDC. There is a five-year limit on how long families can receive AFDC aid with this legislation (sometimes less, depending on the state) and women are expected to work. This welfare to work feature is known as "workfare." It is too early to determine the long-term impact of these policy changes on African American families, but there is little evidence that the strategy will move a significant number of poor, female-led families out of poverty.

Families in the African American Community

By the mid-1990s, a growing economic differentiation among African American families was increasingly evident; approximately one-third are prospering. Indeed, some African American families—primarily married-couple families headed by highly educated spouses with two or more fully employed earners—are becoming more affluent. These families, who tend to live in suburban areas, are primarily nuclear families, though some are blended units. They may also be part of supportive friendship networks.

Affluent African American families have benefitted from the abolition of segregation and other legal barriers to social, educational, occupational, and residential access and equity. Many of them are headed by persons who are second-, third-, and even fourth-generation college graduates, the beneficiaries of a heritage of education, motivation, and hard work. Nonetheless, such affluent African Americans continue to face "glass ceilings" and attitude-related barriers in many jobs as they seek to move upward in corporate or government hierarchies.

Another third of African American families, the working (middle) class, is comprised of families that are struggling to maintain themselves and provide support systems for their young in the face of reductions in force (RIFs), layoffs, or terminations as the corporations upon which they depend for their livelihood have downsized, moved to different regions of the country, gone out of business, or exported jobs to other countries. The extended or augmented family structure is visible in many of these homes. "Fictive kin" often are part of these family relationships.

The final third includes the nation's poorer African American families. This grouping includes (1) former working-class families who have fallen on hard times; (2) the "working poor," who are employed daily but at minimum wages that do not permit secure or dependable livelihoods; and (3) families of the "underclass," poorest of the poor, most of which are headed by females alone. Many of this latter group have been supported by the welfare system for one or more generations.

Families in Poverty

The debate on cause continues as proportionally greater numbers of black than white families were in poverty in 1997—26.1 percent, compared with 8.6 percent of white families. Black families were more than three times more likely to be poor than were white families, a situation which has not changed measurably since 1967. Of 8,455,000 black families in 1997, 2,206,000 were below poverty level, whereas only 5,059,000 of 58,934,000 white families were in similar circumstances. In absolute numbers, more white families than black ones were poor, but the proportions of poor families was racially lopsided.

More than forty-nine percent of all African American families with related children under 18 years of age were poor in 1996. This was a decrease from the 1994 level of 52.9 percent and the 1990 level of 53.4 percent. Nearly 36 percent of the African American families in poverty in 1996 were maintained by women alone, 27.6 percent were maintained by married couples, and the remainder by men alone. For the past 23 years, the poverty rate for female-headed African American families has been consistently higher than the rate for other African American family types. The impact of gender inequality, race, and class converge in the lives of these women. Sex segregation in the labor market crowds a disproportionate number of women into the secondary labor market with low wages, few if any job benefits, and poor working conditions. African American women, especially, have faced race and gender inequality in the labor force. Jobs specifically segmented by race/gender have characterized a good deal of the workplace history of these women.

In 1996, 25.3 percent of elderly African American individuals (65 years old and over) were poor. While this marks an improvement over the 1967 figure of 53 percent, proportionally more elderly blacks than whites were poor in both comparison years—9.4 percent of elderly whites were poor in 1996 and 28 percent in 1967. Despite the presence of policies such as Social Security, Medicare, and Supplemental Security Income (SSI), designed to help all elderly Americans, elderly blacks were twice as likely as elderly whites to be poor in 1967, and, in 1996, they were more than two-and-a-half times more likely to be poor.

The Rural Underclass

The findings of O'Hare and Curry-White's 1992 study of rural, inner-city, and suburban underclass populations reveals that approximately three million underclass adults were in these areas in 1990. Using 1990 Current Population Survey (CPS) data on adults aged 19 to 64, they reported that underclass characteristics were much more prevalent in central cities and rural areas than in the suburbs, noting that 2.4 percent of the underclass lived in rural areas and 3.4 percent lived in central cities, yet only 1.1 percent lived in suburban areas. Approximately 32 percent of the rural underclass was African American in 1990, compared to 49 percent of the inner-city underclass. The rate of African American underclass membership was also higher in rural areas—9.1 percent—compared to 7.5 percent in central cities. A sizable body of impoverished rural African Americans live in the South and have higher underclass rates (about one in ten) than do African Americans in large northern cities.

In 1997, 9.7 million or 42.4 percent of African American adults (18 years old and over) were married (Index Stock Imagery).

◆ MARRIAGE

In 1997, married-couple families constituted only 46 percent of all African American families. Nearly 47 percent of African American families were headed by a female householder with no husband present. Over-

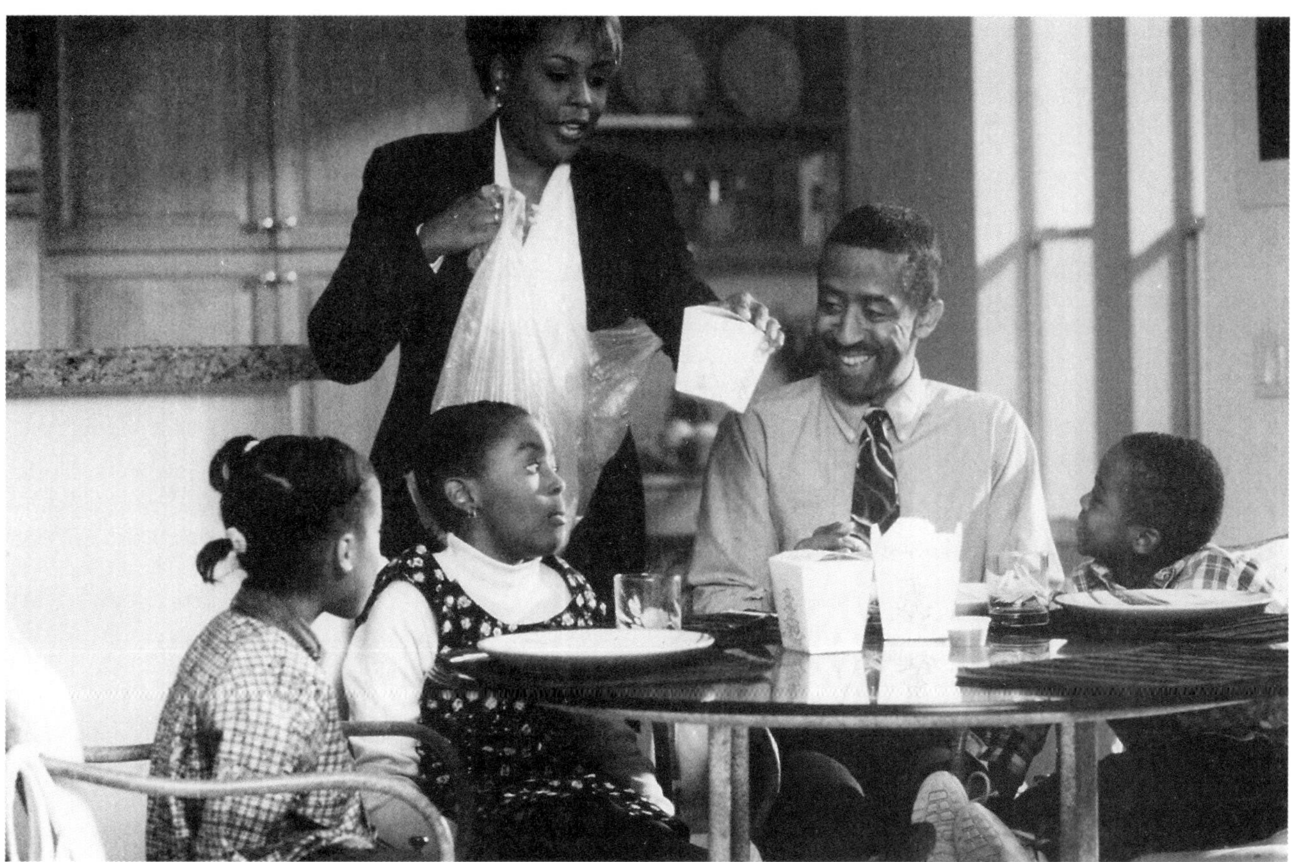

In 1997, married couple families comprised only 46 percent of all African American families (Index Stock Imagery).

whelmingly, the nation's poor black families fell into this latter category. In 1997, only 40 percent of African American women 18 years of age and over were married, compared to 60.3 percent in 1960. The corresponding percentages for African American men were 45.3 percent in 1990 and 63.3 percent in 1960. Clearly issues around sex ratios, redefinition of gender expectations in intimate relations, and alternative life styles such as increasing levels of co-habitation figure into the changes.

The Unavailability of African American Men

The population of African American males aged 15 years old and over in 1997 stood at 11,565,000 compared to 13,406,000 African American females in the same age grouping. The resulting ratio of approximately 86 males to every 100 females makes the matching of every African American female with a same-race male for the traditionally valued lifetime monogamous marriage a numerical impossibility—there simply are not enough African American men alive. When one also removes from consideration those males who are gay, the proportion of eligible African American men for African American women dwindles even more. Further, when one counts the number of African American males who are poorly educated and therefore educationally mismatched for marriage to their relatively more highly educated African American female counterparts, the pool of eligible men shrinks even smaller. High African American male unemployment rates further compound the problem. These factors help to explain the increasing numbers of never-married African American females.

Incarcerated single African American men are unavailable as marriage partners, and African American men in prison who are married are unavailable to be at home with their families and/or provide for them. According to *Statistical Abstracts*, there were 221,000 African American male prison inmates in 1996 (not including those in federal and state prisons or juvenile institutions).

Reportedly, many of today's young African American men delay marriage or never marry because of their unemployment or underemployment status, the rationale being that lack of a job or small earnings will not enable them to support families. However, well-educated black men who are employed at good salaries are also less likely to be married than their white counterparts. Marriage outside the race further reduces the number of African American men available for marriage to African American women. In 1997, there were 201,000 marriages of black men to white women, compared to 110,000 marriages of white men to black women. This represented the "loss" of another 91,000 marriageable black men.

Although not often explored in African American family studies, shifting norms around gender expectations are impacting African American marriage expectations. Validating self through marriage has been challenged. The marriage rate for upper income, highly-educated African American women has traditionally been low and continues to be so. Issues of sexism, male violence, and domestic abuse also figure into the equation in African American women's decisions of whether to marry or not.

Interracial Marriage

In the three decades between 1960 and 1990, interracial marriages more than quadrupled in the United States, but the number remains small. By 1997 less than one percent of all marriages united African Americans with people of another racial heritage. As late as 1967, anti-miscegenation laws prohibiting the marriage of whites to members of another race were still on the books in 17 states; that year, the U.S. Supreme Court finally declared such laws unconstitutional. Surveys indicate that young Americans approaching adulthood at the dawn of the twenty-first century are much more open to the idea of interracial unions than earlier generations. A decline in social bias has led experts to predict an increase in cross-cultural marriages throughout the 1990s.

Still, according to the 1994 National Health and Social Life Survey, 97 percent of African American women are likely to choose a partner of the same race. Conflict in the United States over black-white relationships stems from the nation's brutal history of slavery, when white men held all the power in society. More than a century after the abolition of slavery, America's shameful legacy of racism remains. According to some observers, high rates of abortion, drug abuse, illness, and poverty among African Americans sparked a movement of African American solidarity in the early 1990s. Many black women—"the culture bearers"—oppose the idea of interracial marriage, opting instead for racial strength and unity through the stabilization of the African American family.

◆ GAY/LESBIAN/BISEXUALITY/ TRANSGENDER ISSUES

African American gays, lesbians, and bisexuals have made some strides in the 1990s in terms of increasing visibility and activism. However, while there appears to be greater awareness of gay and lesbian concerns, there are continuing hate crimes and homophobia. Certainly most would agree that true equality and acceptance have hardly been achieved, but a course has been set for those looking to break the same chains of oppression with which all African Americans—gay or straight—are familiar.

Historically, from Bruce Nugent, "The Bohemian of the Harlem Renaissance" and the first African American writer to deal openly with homosexuality, to James Baldwin and Audre Lorde, African American literature has had its share of gay/lesbian/bisexual representation. In the 1980s and 1990s, the mantle has been passed to Samuel R. Delany, E. Lynn Harris, and Alice Walker's *The Color Purple.* In music and fashion, supermodel/house music maven/actor RuPaul had an impact on the American psyche as has bassist and songwriter Me'Shell NdegeOcello. In Hollywood, Wesley Snipes was unafraid to play a drag queen in the film *To Woo Fong, Thanks For Everything! Julie Newmar*, while Denzel Washington played an extremely homophobic lawyer who has a change of heart after working with a gay client dying of AIDS in *Philadelphia.* The poignant documentary *Paris Is Burning*, a depiction of several cross-dressers and drag queens in New York City, was well-received by audiences and critics alike. Another penetrating documentary, gay African American filmmaker Marlon Riggs's *Black Is . . . Black Ain't*, attempted to peel away the levels of meaning attached to black skin and the impact of those meanings on gay and straight members of the African American community. African American actresses, meanwhile, had prominent roles in the lesbian-focused commercial releases *Go Fish, The Incredibly True Adventures of Two Girls in Love*, and *Bar Girls.*

Outside of the mainstream, the black gay/lesbian/bisexual community is replete with heroes and heroines unknown to the rest of society. Rights activists include: Gregory Adams; Bayard Rustin, Alliance founder and executive director; Derek Charles Livingston, North Carolina Pride Political Action Committee executive director; Gilberto Gerald, African American Gay and Lesbian Studies Center founder and director; Cary Allen Johnson, International Lesbian and Gay Human Rights Commission board member; Ron Simmons, Us Helping Us, People Into Living, Inc. executive director; Paul Davis, Minority AIDS Project of Los Angeles director of education; Nadine Smith, Human Rights Task Force of Florida executive director; Cornelius Baker, National Association of People With AIDS president; Charles W. B. Tarver, IV, the first African American male lobbyist for the Human Rights Campaign Fund (HRCF); and Keith Boykin, National Black Gay and Lesbian Leadership Forum executive director.

Examples of African American individuals contributing to the visible image of gays in society include: Peter Gomes, Harvard University chaplain; Willa Taylor, the education program coordinator for the Lincoln Center Theater; Sabrina Sojourner, legislative aide to California Congresswoman Maxine Waters; Wynn P. Thomas, production and set designer for director Spike Lee's film production company; H. Alexander Robinson, legal representative for both the American Civil Liberties Union AIDS Project and the Lesbian and Gay Civil Rights Project; Darlene Garner, the first African American elder in the Metropolitan Community Church, a universal fellowship created in 1968 by and for gay Christians; Sherry Harris, Seattle City Council member; Evelyn C. White, *San Francisco Chronicle* reporter and editor of *Black Women's Health Book: Speaking for Ourselves;* Bill E. Jones, president of New York City's Health and Hospitals Corporation, the largest public health network in the United States; Pat Norman, San Francisco Institute for Community Health Outreach executive director and Stonewall 25 Organizing Committee member, Suzanne Shende, director of the Center for Constitutional Rights' Anti-Bias Violence Project; Sandra Robinson, president and CEO of Samaritan College, the international school of ministry for the Universal Fellowship of Metropolitan Community Churches; and Keith St. John, the first African American, openly gay elected official in the United States (Second Ward Alderman, Albany, New York). They are joined in every field and industry and in every region of the country by a host of peers who face challenges because of their sexual orientation, but who do not allow intolerance to hold them back.

◆ FERTILITY AND BIRTHS

Fertility Rates

The year 1995 saw 70.6 live births per 1,000 black women aged 15 to 44 years of age, and 59.2 such live births to comparable white women. The 603,139 live births by African American females that year accounted for approximately 15.5 percent of all births nationwide. Black women have had higher fertility rates than white women for the past two centuries; however, birth rates are similar for black and white women with the same level of educational attainment.

The Thompson Sextuplets

On May 8, 1997, in Washington, DC, Linden and Jacqueline Thompson gave birth to the first set of African American sextuplets in the United States. The naturally-conceived pregnancy, which lasted 29 weeks and six days, was the longest gestational period for sextuplets born in the United States. In spite of the remarkable nature of this event, the surviving five babies—four girls and one boy—received little attention from the media until the birth of septuplets to a white Iowa couple a month later. In the wake of the attention and financial support that family received, certain African American groups protested that the Thompsons had not received similar treatment. The National Political Congress of Black Women, Inc. "adopted" the Thompsons, and many companies such as Toys 'R' Us came forward to pledge needed items for the financially-strapped family. For many in the African American community, the neglect of the Thompson family further demonstrated the inherent racism of American society, arguing that if the Thompsons had been white and middle-class, the media would have rushed to publish their story.

Teenage Pregnancy

For a number of years Marian Wright Edelman of the Children's Defense Fund has stressed that teenage pregnancy is a special problem among poor and minority groups who usually have limited opportunities to offer their offspring. Joyce Ladner has explained that the causes of teenage pregnancy range from attempts to find emotional fulfillment and the desire to achieve "womanhood" to ignorance of contraceptives. Political conservatives and neoconservatives maintain that poor teenagers view welfare programs such as Aid to Families with Dependent Children (AFDC) as a viable source of economic support and consequently perceive pregnancy as a means of tapping into the welfare system at an early age. This belief helped shape welfare reform legislation in the 1990s that required adolescent mothers to stay within the households of their families of origin if they are to continue to receive benefits.

Teenage pregnancy is both a national problem and an African American problem. Data from the National Center for Health Statistics reveal that in 1996 the birth rate for all teenagers aged 15 to 19 years old was 54.7 live births per 1,000. Black girls in that age group were almost two times more likely than white girls to give birth (91.7 compared with 48.4 per 1,000). For girls between 15 to 17 years old, the birth rate was well over two times higher among blacks than whites. Furthermore, black girls in the 18 to 19 year old age group had a birthrate of 133.0 live births per 1,000 as compared to 86.5 live births for white girls. This state of affairs and its social, economic, and political ramifications cause great consternation in the African American community as well as in the larger society. Teenage childbearing exacerbates such social problems as high infant mortality, poor physical and mental health, educational insufficiencies, long-term welfare dependency, and poverty. Many teenage mothers do not complete high school, the basic educational expectation in this country; as a result, they are often seriously undereducated and lack marketable skills. Others do not know how to care adequately for their children. By and large, their children will not have the same opportunities as their more advantaged counterparts in any race or ethnic group. Some research, however, suggests that the prospects of these very young mothers are not entirely bleak. For example, research indicates that grandmothers play a significant role in the care and raising of these children.

Even still, various efforts have been aimed at stemming the tide of teenage pregnancy. At the bureaucratic level, some states have decreed punitive measures such as sterilization and/or reduced welfare payments for girls and women on public assistance who have more than one out-of-wedlock birth. African American sororities, fraternities, churches, and civil groups have initiated programs to work directly with African American teenagers. The Children's Defense Fund continues to enlighten the public through a multimedia campaign that urges African American males as well as females to be more responsible for their sexual behavior.

Births of Mixed Racial Parentage

According to the Population Reference Bureau's December of 1992 report, the proportion of mixed-race births for which the race of both parents was known increased from one percent to 3.4 percent between 1968 and 1989; births of children with a black and a white parent increased from 8,700 in 1968 to 45,000 in 1989. This increase was described as "a striking sign of social change" with respect to attitudes about interracial relationships.

Attitudes towards persons with multi-racial identities have remained volatile in the 1990s, but those with mixed heritages who refuse to be reduced to "black" or "white" have become more vocal. A key issue concerns the manner in which the federal government categorizes people. In 1977, guidelines for creating race and ethnicity on all federal forms were established with four major groups identified: American Indian/Alaskan Native, Asian/Pacific Islander, black, and white. Specification of a less broad ethnicity would have to fall into one of the "big four." In 1995, however, the Office of Management and Budget was considering making changes to the existing policy in response to a deluge of complaints from people of all walks of life including European Americans who want to be recognized as more than just white. To address such issues, the government proposed a "multi-racial" category. Opponents felt that such a seemingly superficial change could lead to significant cultural difficulties including a hidden caste system like the one already in existence between light- and dark-skinned African Americans. Interestingly, *Newsweek* reported that 49 percent of blacks favored the new category versus 36 percent of whites.

◆ CHILDREN

Living Arrangements of Children

In 1997, only 35 percent of African American children lived with both parents, compared to 67 percent in 1960 and 58.5 percent in 1970. This dramatic decline roughly parallels the changes in living arrangements of African American adults resulting from increased divorce and separation rates as well as increases in births to never-married females. By contrast, 75 percent of white children were living with both their parents in 1997, down from 90.9 percent in 1960 and 89.5 percent in 1970. In 1990, 12 percent of black children lived with their grandparents, compared to four percent of whites and six percent of Hispanics. Black grandparents, particularly grandmothers, are more likely to care for their grandchildren than are whites or Hispanics. Also in 1990, 6.5 percent of African American children lived with other relatives, and one percent lived with non-relatives.

In 1997, 66 percent of African American female-headed families had one or more children under 18 years of age present in the household; 37 percent had two or more. These families were more likely to be poor than were married-couple families. They were also more likely to live in inner cities; about thirty percent lived in public housing. Many economic analysts maintain that there is a very strong probability that children from such households will grow up poor and on welfare, be environmentally disadvantaged compared to their middle-class counterparts, drop out of school, have one or more out-of-wedlock births themselves, and be unemployed or unemployable in their adult lives.

Child Support

In years past, when parents have been unable to support their children, extended family members were expected to assist in the process. In today's dismal economic climate, many more mothers than in the past are working in the paid labor force and contributing a larger share of their earned income to their families. Grandparents continue to do and provide what they can, including providing child care while the parent or parents work. Poor families are supported by the welfare system, but with fixed terms of support; this source of income will be phased out for recipients after five years. Many families have been forced to accept unemployment compensation as their support base when one or more member loses a job.

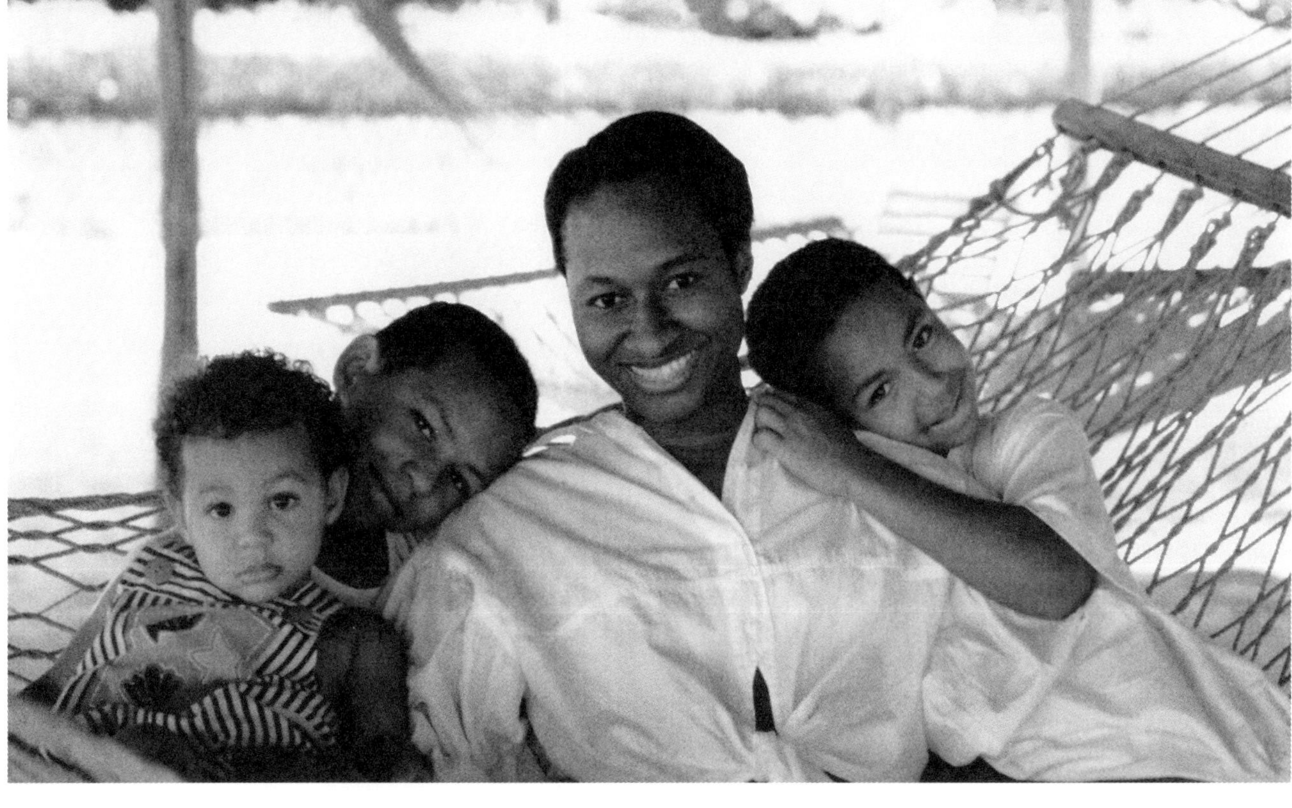

In 1995, 31 percent of black children under six years old were regularly left in a relative's care, compared to 18 percent of white children of the same age range (Index Stock Imagery).

When African American parents divorce, child support becomes a critical issue. In 1989 there were 2,770,000 divorced or separated African American women. Child support payments were court-awarded to only 955,000 (35 percent) of these women. Of those who were supposed to receive child support, only seventy percent actually received payment. The mean child support amount received was $2,263, or 16 percent of total household income. As these figures reveal, in the event of divorce or separation, African American women were primarily responsible for the support of their children. In terms of dollars received, African American women with incomes below the poverty level fared worse than the average in 1989. Of 325,000 such women who were supposed to receive child support, seventy percent actually received payment. Their mean child support sum, a mere $1,674, nevertheless amounted to 32 percent of their total household income.

◆ HEALTH

For African Americans, the incidence of heart disease, high blood pressure, diabetes, obesity, cancer, asthma, and several other conditions is higher than the national average. Another area in which African Americans lag is organ donorship. In 1995, nearly 20,000 minorities were in need of an organ transplant according to statistics from the Center for Organ Recovery and Education. That year *CQ Researcher* projected that by 2010, one out of every twenty people will need an organ, tissue, or corneal transplant at some point in their lives. While medical advances have improved survival rates, the best chances for a successful transplant—particularly with bone marrow transplants and skin grafts—are when an organ comes from someone of the same race. Unfortunately, not nearly enough African Americans choose to donate. The lack of available organ donors ultimately means long waits for a compatible organ, death for those who do not receive one, higher costs due to low supply and high demand, and lack of coverage by insurance carriers because of the expense.

The Tuskegee Syphilis Study

At least part of the reason behind the higher rates of disease in African Americans stems from a reluctance to get regular check-ups because of a general distrust of doctors by the African American community. In 1997, a national poll survey conducted for Emory University's

Institute of Minority Health Research revealed that 36 percent of African Americans believed it was "very likely" they would unwittingly be used as guinea pigs for medical research. This belief is grounded in an actual instance of the government's exploitation of African American men for the purposes of medical research in the mid-twentieth century. Now known as "The Tuskegee Syphilis Study," the experiment, conducted by government doctors from the Public Health Service, studied the effects of untreated syphilis on four hundred African American men in Macon County, Alabama. The doctors never informed the men as to the nature of the study and even withheld medical treatment when it became available in 1942. As a result, over one hundred men had died by the time the details of the study were revealed in 1972, and others suffered from serious syphilis-related conditions that could have been relieved by penicillin had it been given to them. Civil rights lawyer Fred Gray brought a class-action lawsuit against the institutions and doctors involved in the experiment in 1973, and the government agreed to a ten million dollar out-of-court settlement. In 1997, President Bill Clinton formally apologized to the survivors of the experiment.

Medicaid

Many American families receive health care through the federally-funded Medicaid program. Disproportionately high percentages of these families are African American. The total number of Medicaid recipients in the United States increased from 25.3 million in 1990 to 36.1 million in 1996. In 1996, 66.1 percent of the recipients were children in AFDC families. That same year, 8.5 million African Americans were covered by Medicaid; 5.5 million of these had incomes below the poverty line and 3.0 million had incomes above it.

Child Health

Many African American children suffer from the lack of quality health care. In 1990, only about half of inner-city children had been immunized against measles, mumps, and rubella. Measles outbreaks have erupted in many American cities in the 1990s; most were among poor, inner-city children. Nearly 100 deaths from measles were reported in 1990.

A new and growing population of children are born of mothers who used drugs (including alcohol) during their pregnancies. Many of these children experience after-birth withdrawal problems from drugs that affected them *in utero;* they are later more prone to physical and mental disabilities, behavioral problems, and learning impairments when they arrive in the nation's schools. Infants whose mothers drink alcoholic beverages during pregnancy are at risk of Fetal Alcohol Syndrome. Each year, Acquired Immune Deficiency Syndrome (AIDS) afflicts a growing number of children, who usually contract the disease from their mothers before or at birth. Urban children who live in old and/or poor housing also remain at risk of being exposed to high levels of lead. It has been estimated that 12 million American children, primarily those who are poor, are at risk of lead poisoning and potentially will have their intellectual growth stunted because of exposure to lead. Similar to African American adults and, perhaps due to their affiliation with them, African American children are also at greater risk of accidents, physical abuse, and other violence that may result in disability or death.

AIDS

African Americans suffer disproportionately from AIDS, the final stage of a disease caused by the Human Immunodeficiency Virus (HIV). The HIV virus severely weakens the body's immune system, leaving HIV-infected people vulnerable to other infections. At this writing, there is no cure for AIDS; although the life expectancy of its victims varies, it is one hundred percent fatal. Though African Americans represent only 12.1 percent of the U.S. population, 46 percent of all new AIDS cases in 1997 were African American. This figure was up from 32 percent in 1990. A report "The Challenge of HIV/AIDS in Communities of Color" stated that blacks and Hispanics, representing 21 percent of the population, accounted for 46 percent of all AIDS cases as of September of 1992.

The U.S. Centers for Disease Control have kept updated statistics concerning reported cases of AIDS, deaths caused by the disease with breakdowns for various age groups, and various data on the occurrence of AIDS across ethnicities. Data from those organizations show that in 1996 the age-adjusted AIDS death rate for blacks was higher than that for whites (42.6 percent to 37.5 percent). Data also reveal that, between 1991 and 1996, the number of Africans American AIDS-related deaths increased nearly 8 percent compared to a 13.2 percent decrease in its incidence among gay or bisexual men.

AIDS is spread by viral passage during unprotected sexual intercourse, intravenous drug use, or blood transfusions; it can also be transmitted from mother to child *in utero* or during birth. It is estimated that a clear majority of the AIDS cases among African Americans result from intravenous drug use. While AIDS is fatal, it is preventable if sexually active adults and teenagers engage in "safe sex" practices such as using condoms and avoid behaviors that put them at risk of AIDS infection such as promiscuity, having multiple sex partners, using drugs, and exchanging drug paraphernalia. The African American community and the larger society are saturating the public with information about AIDS in

Herman Shaw, a victim of the Tuskegee Syphilis Study, attends a 1997 press conference in which President Clinton and Vice President Gore apologized for the shameful experiment (AP/Wide World Photos, Inc.).

the hope that education will cause people to behave differently and thereby slow the progress of the disease.

Lupus

Lupus is a chronic, autoimmune disorder in which the body's immune system loses the ability to differentiate between itself and foreign substances and forms antibodies that attack healthy tissues and organs. Inflammation of the skin, joints, and kidneys are the most common result, although other areas of the body are subject to swelling as well. The medical community has not yet discovered why the disease overwhelmingly tends to affect women more than men. In fact, nine of every ten sufferers are women. Lupus seemingly targets women of childbearing age, i.e. between the ages of 15 and 40 and is three times more common in black women than white women.

An incurable, excruciating, and often debilitating condition, lupus can present itself in many different forms, making the initial diagnosis difficult. A range of mild to severe symptoms gradually develop including hair and/or weight loss, fatigue, photosensitivity, loss of appetite, fever, nausea, abdominal pain, and pain in any inflamed areas. With improvements in early diagnosis and better treatments, lupus is no longer considered fatal. Most patients are able to continue with their lives and lifestyles. The American Lupus Society (1-800-331-1802) and the Lupus Foundation of America (1-800-558-0121) can both offer more information.

Diabetes

Persons with diabetes are unable to convert food sugar, or glucose, into energy that is used by the body's cells or stored for later use. The hormone insulin, produced by the pancreas, plays a crucial role in the conversion. Diabetics either do not produce enough insulin, or any at all, or may produce ineffective insulin. Regardless, the unused glucose collects in the blood and urine and can damage organs such as the kidneys and eyes. The onset of insulin-dependent, or type I diabetes, which usually affects children and young adults, can be very rapid. Symptoms can include frequent urination, excessive thirst, extreme hunger, weight loss, irritability, weakness and fatigue, nausea, and vomiting. Ninety percent of diabetes is noninsulin-dependent. Known as Type II diabetes, the illness most often occurs in adults over the age of forty and particularly in obese individuals. Symptoms are similar to those associated with the Type I form, however, Type II is also characterized by the chronic presence of wounds that will not heal, stubborn infections, blurred vision, tingling or numbness in the extremities, and burning or itching sensations.

Similar to lupus, diabetes is noncontagious, incurable, potentially debilitating, and disproportionately strikes African Americans. Figures from the American Diabetes Association estimate that blacks are 1.6 times more likely than whites to contract the condition and, in the mid-1990s, it afflicted nearly two million African Americans. African Americans also experience higher rates of serious complications from the disease including blindness, kidney failure, and the need for amputations of the legs or feet. Unfortunately, nearly half of those African Americans affected are unaware of their illness, a dangerous statistic because immediate, appropriate medical attention is crucial.

Once informed of their condition, diabetics can maintain relative good health by eating low fat, high carbohydrate meals with a moderate amount of protein; engaging in physical activity that stimulates the body's cells into utilizing glucose; and by tracking their glucose levels. Low blood sugar, or hypoglycemia, is just as much a danger as is the presence of a high glucose level. Overweight individuals are very much encouraged to lose excess weight in order to increase the body's ability to use insulin. Physicians can prescribe medication including insulin shots to help a patient maintain a normal glucose level.

In an effort to reach the African American community, the American Diabetes Association launched the African American Program in 1994. They educate the public through media campaigns and community-based forums such as local churches. For more information contact the American Diabetes Association, 1680 Duke St., Alexandria, VA 22314 or call 1-800-DIABETES.

Cigarette, Alcohol, and Drug Use

The use and abuse of cigarettes, alcohol, marijuana, and cocaine (including addiction thereto) is a serious social problem in contemporary American society. The National Center for Health Statistics reports that, in a given month in 1991, four percent of black youth 12 to 17 years old smoked cigarettes, compared with 13 percent of whites and nine percent of Hispanics of the same age. Cigarette smoking has been identified as a major risk factor in lung cancer, cardiovascular disease, and chronic obstructive lung disease. Twenty percent of blacks, 20 percent of whites, and 23 percent of Hispanics in this same age group had used alcohol; 5 percent of blacks and Hispanics and 4 percent of whites had used marijuana; and 0.5 percent of blacks, 0.3 percent of whites, and 1.3 percent of Hispanic youths had used cocaine. In the 18 to 25 year old group in the given month, 22 percent of blacks had smoked cigarettes compared to 36 percent of whites and 25 percent of Hispanics; and 56 percent of blacks had used alcohol compared to 67 percent of whites and 53 percent of Hispanics. Fifteen percent of blacks compared to 14 percent of whites and nine percent of Hispanics, had used marijuana; and 3.1 percent of blacks had used cocaine compared to 1.7 percent of whites and 2.7 percent of Hispanics. It is clear that youth are using these substances as early as age twelve and that usage increases through the young adult period. These percentages represent large numbers of young people. In regard to all age groups, a higher percentage of whites—sixty percent—reported alcohol use compared to 42 percent of blacks.

Sickle Cell Anemia

Sickle Cell Anemia (SCA) is a chronic inherited affliction caused by a defect in the hemoglobin component of the blood. It occurs as a result of the mating of two people, each of whom carries the gene for the defective trait, which is passed on to their children. The presence of this abnormal hemoglobin trait can cause distortion (sickling) of the red blood cells and a decrease in their number. The source of SCA seems to be malarious countries; people with sickle cell disease are almost always immune to malaria, so it appears that the sickle cell is a defense mechanism against malaria.

Sickled red blood cells have been found in 1of every 12 African Americans; but the active disease occurs about once in every 600 American blacks and once in every 1,200 American whites. It is estimated that about 50,000 persons in the United States suffer from the disease. Persons of other races and nationalities are affected by the trait and the anemia including people from Southern India, Greece, Italy, Syria, Caribbean Islands, South and Central America, Turkey, and other countries.

The disease is diagnosed through microscopic and electrophoretic analysis of the blood. The first symptoms of SCA usually appear in children with the disease at about six months of age. Because SCA is a chronic disease, medical management is directed toward both the quiescent and active periods (called "crises") of the malady. Good medical and home care may make it possible for persons with SCA to lead reasonably normal lives. When crises occur, they experience fever, pain, loss of appetite, paleness of the skin, generalized weakness, and sometimes a striking decrease in the number of red blood corpuscles. Complications and infections from these crises can be controlled with antibiotic drugs. A drug, hydroxyurea, has been developed to stimulate fetal hemoglobin to produce more red blood cells and thereby ameliorate SCA crises. However, hydroxyurea is very toxic, and thus far has only been tested on adults with SCA. In other efforts, a female SCA sufferer, also stricken with leukemia, recently received a radical bone marrow transplant from her brother. Since the transplant, she has been free of symptoms from both diseases. This case, the first of its kind, is being closely monitored to determine the mechanisms by which the patient's remission occurred and to see if the results of this procedure can be duplicated with other persons with SCA.

African American people who intend to have children are advised to undergo blood tests to determine whether they are carriers of the sickle cell gene. Two such carriers should agree not to produce children, since half the children will have the trait and one in four the anemia. There is only one chance in four that their child will be free of the disease. Some jurisdictions (Washington, DC, for example) have enacted laws mandating that newborns be screened for sickle cell anemia, along with other diseases. As a result of such legislation, newborns found to be afflicted with SCA can be cared for from birth.

Breast Cancer

In 1993, the National Cancer Institute estimated that one in eight women in the United States will develop breast cancer during her life, the risk increasing with age. Breast cancer is the leading cause of cancer death among African American women. Although black women develop breast cancer at slightly lower rates than white women, blacks are twice as likely to die from the disease and at a younger age. Though more research needs to be done, some reasons for the discrepancy include the facts that black women are often in poorer general health than whites; are often less likely to seek out preventive medical care and when they do are less likely to receive adequate medical care; are more likely to have worse prognoses for tumors that do not respond to treatment; and are often pessimistic about their own outlooks. (Studies have shown that maintaining a positive attitude can have an impact on just about any illness.)

African American women must focus on early detection. Approximately ninety percent of breast cancers are discovered via self-examination. Besides self-examinations—which should be conducted monthly, one week after one's menstrual period—the importance of mammograms should not be overlooked. In a recent study, the U.S. Department of Health and Human Services determined that nearly three out of four African American women over the age of forty had never had a mammogram, though all women regularly should after reaching that age. Many women do not follow early detection guidelines because they can not afford health care, because they have had no prior incidence in their family history, or because they do not display any symptoms, failing to acknowledge that treatment prior to symptoms is more effective. Once discovered, breast lumps may be diagnosed as premenstrual lumpiness or fluid retention caused by hormonal changes; cysts; benign tumors; or cancers.

Treatment programs are determined on a case-by-case basis. In the mid-1990s, the experimental drug tamoxifen was being introduced to breast cancer patients. The Cancer Information Service Center can provide more information at 1-800-4-CANCER as can the Breast Cancer Resource Committee (1765 N St., NW, Ste. 100; Washington, DC 20036-2802; telephone: 1-202-463-8040), founded by Zora Brown, an African American.

Prostate Cancer

As the most common cancer in men, prostate cancer afflicts black men more often than whites; in fact, blacks are more than twice as likely to get the disease and are three times as likely to die of the disease. Particularly at risk are those living in rural areas, because they are less likely to regularly visit a physician. As with other forms of cancer, early detection plays a role in treatment and in deterring the likelihood of dying from the disease. Diet is a factor as well; high-fat, low-fiber diets increase the risk of developing cancer. Genetics and personal history are a third factor. In 1996, a new type of radiation treatment option which was twenty percent more effective than conventional radiation was being used on patients with early cancer. Called neutron therapy, Seattle's University of Washington and Detroit's Karmanos Cancer Institute were the first two facilities to make the innovative technique available.

◆ LIFE EXPECTANCY

Life expectancy at birth increased substantially during the first ninety years of this century, from 33 years for African Americans of both sexes in 1900 to 70.3 years in 1996. Corresponding figures for both sexes of all races are 47.3 years in 1900 and 76.1 years in 1996. Provisional data of the National Vital Statistics System project a life expectancy of 65.2 years for African American males born in 1995 and 73.9 years for African American females born that year. Corresponding life expectancy projections for white males and females born in 1995 are 73.4 and 79.6 years, respectively, averaged at 76.8 years. That black babies born should have a lower life expectancy at birth than their white counterparts is an ignominious social problem. At the other end of the age continuum, African American males aged 65 years old in 1996 are projected to live 13.9 more years, and African American females 17.2 additional years.

This compares with 15.8 more years for white males, and 19 additional years for white females. Thus the same pattern holds: white people in the United States continue to have longer life expectancy than African Americans.

These black/white differences can be attributed to a number of factors. African Americans have higher death rates due to the following major causes: accidents, homicides, suicides, heart disease, strokes, liver disease, cancer, diabetes, and AIDS. It is also true that whites, more than blacks, have health insurance coverage of some kind and sufficient personal income to partake of higher-quality health care, both preventive and curative. Whites' higher education and income levels also assure them the greater likelihood of eating nutritionally balanced, healthy meals. Dietary patterns and food choices of low-income African Americans include too many fats and sweets, factors that contribute to obesity and high blood pressure, which carry their own sets of health risks.

Homicide and Death by Accident

Homicide among African American men is a primary cause for the drop in their life expectancy. In 1995, 56.3 percent of all African American male deaths; data for African American female deaths from accidents and violence due to homicide was not made available. Some social theorists claim that the increasing numbers of African Americans who are poor and hopeless, added to those who are involved in drugs or other substance abuse, account for the homicide rates among African Americans. In 1995, motor vehicle deaths and other accidents also accounted for many deaths among African American males and females, 24.6 and 9.0, respectively.

Suicide

Suicide rates are significantly lower among blacks than whites, but black suicide rates are on the rise, a most undesirable form of parity. In 1985, the suicide rate for white males exceeded that for black males by seventy percent; by 1989, the difference had narrowed to forty percent. Data from the National Center for Health Statistics show that more than 30,000 lives are lost through suicide annually. Among all Americans, the age-adjusted death rate by suicide in 1989 was 11.3 deaths per 100,000. For African American males, the rate was 12.5 per 100,000, and for African American females, it was 2.4 per 100,000. Among African American adolescents and young adults aged 15 to 24 years old, the suicide rate for males was 16.7 per 100,000, and 2.8 per 100,000 for African American females, increases of 49 percent (from 1984 to 1989) and forty percent (from 1986 to 1989), respectively.

Infant Mortality

Infant mortality rates for African Americans remain more than double that of whites. In 1995, 15.1 deaths per 1,000 live births were reported for black infants, compared to 7.1 deaths per 1,000 live births for whites. The black/white infant death ratios have changed appreciably since 1950, however, when the black infant mortality rate was 43.9 deaths per 1,000 live births and the white rate was 26.8 deaths per 1,000. Progress has been made since 1950, as the infant mortality statistics have improved for both races.

African American women are more likely than whites to give birth to low-weight babies, many of whom fall victim to serious health problems or die during their first year. These babies are particularly susceptible to Sudden Infant Death Syndrome (SIDS), respiratory distress syndrome, infections, and injuries. This phenomenon occurs because disproportionate numbers of African American babies are born to low-income, less-educated teenage mothers who have inadequate prenatal care and poor nutrition, and who smoke, use drugs, or otherwise fail to take care of themselves properly during their pregnancies.

Social Change Possibilities and African American Families

Within the African American community itself, certain attitudinal and behavioral changes are essential. Most significant is economic fairness across racial lines since many problems confronting the African American community stem from poverty. There is also the need for gender justice in the labor market. Salary equity and occupational opportunities which pay a living wage for African American women would make a tremendous difference in poor African American families. Marriage as something other than an fading option could make a difference for many families. Family planning information, including sex education and intervention programs, must be disseminated among teenagers, so that the out-of-wedlock birth rate can be reduced. Substance abuse must be curtailed; people who have hope for the future and who feel that they have some power and control over their lives are less likely to "escape" through drugs or alcohol. At the same time, drug dealers should be severely prosecuted. Children and youth need more adult interaction and supervision in their lives, whether it comes from family members or "significant others" such as mentors provided by such organizations as Concerned Black Men, Inc. or other community service-minded groups.

So many of the problems faced by African American and other low-to-moderate-income families are systemic and interlocking. Action on only one problem will not solve the network of family woes that our society has allowed to accumulate. Once again, the National Urban League has called for a "Marshall Plan for the Cities" to address the totality of current problems. If our society wants to save its cities and a significant portion of its human capital—of which these families comprise a significant part—it must give serious consideration to the formation and implementation of such a plan in both the cities and the rural areas. By so doing, the nation can help all its citizens become productive workers, consistent taxpayers, meritorious parents, and contributing members of stable families.

The Million Man March

On October 16, 1995, The Million Man March, a rally masterminded by Nation of Islam Minister Louis Farrakhan, was held 21 blocks from the steps of the U.S. Capitol Building in Washington, DC. Intended as "a national day of atonement," the thousands of attendees pledged their commitments to family and community. The gathering had spiritual, economic, and political implications for non-marchers as well, including women and children; they were asked to stay home from work/school and spend the day praying and fasting.

The march was organized by the Nation of Islam and promoted by the National African American Leadership Summit. Women, excluded from the actual demonstration, were welcome in the nearly 120 local organizing committees scattered about the country. A grass-roots affair, expenses were covered mostly by donations. Linda Green, appointed as national director of fundraising, also found financial support for the march. However, a number of African American women such as Angela Davis spoke out publically about the exclusionary nature of the march.

Other forms of support came from a wide range of camps—political, religious, and business-oriented—including civil rights heroine Rosa Parks; former NAACP head Rev. Ben Chavis; Rainbow Coalition leader Rev. Jesse Jackson; Georgia Congresswoman Cynthia McKinney; Southern Christian Leadership Conference (SCLC) executive director E. Randel Osburn; and Melvin Foote and Ambassador Andrew Young, constituency for Africa's executive director and chairperson, respectively. African American colleges scheduled bus trips to the march and the NAACP Youth Councils also encouraged participation from the younger generation. Nonetheless, many African Americans who upheld the tenets of the march distanced themselves from the socio-political action because of Farrakhan's inflammatory views which are often perceived as misogynistic, anti-gay, and anti-Catholic.

Still, the march was deemed a success on many levels given the sheer number of men it reached and the changed representation of African American men it offered, helping to shake the myth of all African American men as convicts, hustlers, and pimps, and replacing it with one of responsible, self-confident, culturally aware men. A number of men registered to vote and a national database of African American male voters was established. The march also spawned a number of spin-off demonstrations including the cross-theological gathering "The New Revival in America: The Emerging Black Male as Man, Husband, Father, and Leader," which took place November 16–18, 1995.

The Million Woman March

The Million Man March was followed by the Million Woman March in Philadelphia, Pennsylvania, on October 25, 1997. Organizers cited their desire to strengthen the cohesiveness of African American women of all walks of life as the primary reason for the march, and key speakers included Winnie Mandela, former wife of South African activist Nelson Mandela, and Congresswoman Maxine Waters. Thousands of women came to Pennsylvania from across the United States to participate in the show of solidarity and to address such issues as the growing number of African American women in prisons, the start of independent African American schools and the hiring of African American women, and the importance of getting more African American women into business and politics.

◆ SOCIAL ACTIVISTS

(To locate biographical profiles more readily, please consult the index at the back of the book.)

Paula Giddings (1947–)
Editor, Educator, Journalist, Social Historian

Paula Giddings has followed a definite focus in her life's work, that of giving a voice to generations of African American women. Through her writings, many issues previously not discussed such as race, gender, and discrimination, came to the forefront of discussion. Beginning at a young age, Giddings knew she wanted to write. She attended Howard University in Washington, DC, became editor of the literary magazine *Afro-American Review*, and began moving away from creative writing toward journalism and social history. Giddings received an undergraduate degree in English in 1969.

After graduating, Giddings worked as a Random House copy editor during a very exciting time; some of the authors there included the political activists Stokely Carmichael and Angela Davis. A fellow editor was the now-famous author Toni Morrison. In 1984, after five years of extensive research and with the help of a Ford Foundation Grant, Giddings's first book was published,

When and Where I Enter: The Impact of Black Women on Race and Sex in America. Some of the themes covered in the book include the relationship between sexism and racism, the effect of "double discrimination" on the basis of gender and race on African American women, and the relevance of historical issues to contemporary life.

In 1988, Giddings came out with a second book called *In Search of Sisterhood: Delta Sigma Theta and the Challenge of the Black Sorority Movement.* Giddings has been lauded for her accomplishments by many groups, such as the New York Urban League and the National Coalition of 100 Black Women; Bennett College in North Carolina awarded her an honorary doctorate in humane letters in 1990. In 1992, she was a visiting professor at Princeton University. She earned several fellowships during the next few years and served as a visiting scholar with Phi Beta Kappa in 1995 and 1996.

Lorraine Hale (1926?–)
Humanitarian, Educator, Hale House Co-founder

Hale was born in Philadelphia in the mid-1920s, but moved with her family to New York City shortly afterwards. Her father owned his own business, but died when Hale was six years old; their mother took both day and evening work as a cleaning person to support the family, but was dismayed about leaving her daughter and two sons in childcare facilities. Eventually the elder Hale began taking in children in her own home, and by 1940 she was a foster parent whose modest Harlem apartment often included her own three offspring and seven or eight foster children as well.

Growing up in such an atmosphere, Hale became determined to make a difference in her community, earning a B.A. from Long Island University in 1960 and then becoming a public school teacher in New York City. She also pursued her master's degree in special education, and worked variously as a guidance counselor, school psychologist, and special education teacher until 1969.

One spring night that year, Hale was driving home from a visit with her mother who had recently retired as a foster parent; she saw a young woman in obvious distress on a street corner and felt sympathy for both the woman and the baby she had with her. She gave the woman her mother's address and, within a few months, the elder Hale's apartment was again home to several children—this time babies born addicted to drugs. For the next year and a half, Hale and her two brothers worked overtime to financially support what would come to be known as Hale House, a pioneering facility in the treatment of babies born to drug-addicted mothers. Their organization received a city grant in 1971 and a federal grant four years later that helped it move into its own five-story Harlem facilities. Hale served as its executive director from 1969 to 1989, and then she assumed the post of chief executive officer and president.

Hale House has become renowned for its innovative treatment and research into mother-infant addictions and boasts a tremendous success rate in helping the women overcome their abuse patterns to reunite with their children. Hale chronicled this work in her 1992 book *Hale House: Alive With Love.* The elder Hale—known affectionately as "Mother" Clara Hale—passed away in 1987, but her daughter has continued the work her mother began, expanding the foundation's services to assist mothers and children afflicted with AIDS; she is also working toward establishing a hospice retreat for such needs in a rural setting. In 1994 Hale traveled to Zaire under the auspices of the relief organization AmeriCares to provide aid for children in refugee camps.

Charleszetta (Mother) Waddles (1912–)
Community Activist, Spiritual Leader

Charleszetta Waddles was born in St. Louis in 1912, the oldest of seven children of a successful barber. When her father, an upstanding member of his local church, was ostracized when his business failed, his daughter vowed to repudiate the hypocrisy she witnessed in organized religion by instead promoting truly Christian principles. As a young girl, Waddles worked as a domestic and married at the age of 14. Widowed before she was 20 years of age, she married again and eventually had ten children. She left her second husband, due to his lack of ambition, after they had relocated to Detroit. In 1946, Waddles learned that her neighbor, a single mother of two, was about to be evicted; Waddles collected food from neighboring businesses to enable the woman to feed her children while making immediate payments to keep her home. Soon afterward, Waddles entered a Bible study course and eventually became an ordained Pentecostal minister. Her religious work soon turned into charitable work, however, and in 1950 she opened her Helping Hand restaurant in a rough area of Detroit, where the indigent could get a sit-down, home-cooked meal for 35 cents. Her third husband, Payton Waddles, provided much support for his wife's work during these years.

In 1956, Waddles expanded the aims of restaurant when she founded the Perpetual Mission for Saving Souls of All Nations, which later became simply the Mother Waddles Perpetual Mission. The center is home to numerous community outreach programs including a medical clinic, a job placement service, and a tutoring program. Staffed entirely by volunteers—sometimes numbering up to two hundred—and financed solely through the donations Waddles extracts from a supportive local business community, the Mission is famous in

Detroit for its decades of service. Still actively involved even though well into her eighties, Waddles sees her work as evidence of Christian principles in action. She has won numerous awards including several presidential commendations and the National Urban League's 1988 Humanitarian Award.

Phill Wilson (1956–)
Activist, Educator

Phill Wilson was born into a close-knit Chicago family in 1956, and during his formative years, he became an active participant in local African American issues-raising organizations such as Operation PUSH. He graduated from Illinois Wesleyan University with a dual degree in Spanish and theater, but forsook law school for marriage and a career with AT&T. Both choices left Wilson with a troubling feeling that there was something lacking, and he ventured into Chicago's gay community in the late 1970s. He met his partner, Chris Brownlie, in 1979, and two years later they relocated to the Los Angeles area where they began an African American-centered giftware company.

The specter of AIDS changed Wilson's life in several ways. He and Brownlie first became politically active in 1986 when they campaigned to win voter rejection of Proposition 64, a ballot referendum that called for the quarantine of all AIDS patients in California. It was also during this time that Brownlie was diagnosed with AIDS himself and, before he died in 1989, he and Wilson founded the AIDS Health Care Foundation and the National Black Gay and Lesbian Conference and Leadership Forum. Wilson has also been involved as Stop AIDS Los Angeles's director of community outreach and has served as the national director of training for the National Task Force on AIDS Prevention. Of especial import to the activist is the building of recognition and support between the African American community and the gay community, and he was a significant force behind the 1990 "Summit on Homosexuality in the Black Community" symposium at Atlanta's Martin Luther King, Jr. Center. Since 1992 Wilson has been the director of public policy for AIDS Project Los Angeles, and, as a spokesperson for gay issues, met with Bill Clinton shortly after his election in 1992.

Phill Wilson (Office of Public Policy)

◆ FAMILY STATISTICS

Family Groups with Children Under 18 Years Old, by Race and Hispanic Origin: 1980 to 1997

[As of **March**. Family groups comprise family households, related subfamilies, and unrelated subfamilies. Excludes members of Armed Forces except those living off post or with their families on post.]

RACE AND HISPANIC ORIGIN OF HOUSEHOLDER OR REFERENCE PERSON	NUMBER (1,000)				PERCENT DISTRIBUTION			
	1980	1990	1995	1997	1980	1990	1995	1997
All races, total [1]	**32,150**	**34,670**	**37,168**	**37,619**	100	100	100	100
Two-parent family groups	25,231	24,921	25,640	25,577	79	72	69	68
One-parent family groups	6,920	9,749	11,528	12,042	22	28	31	32
Maintained by mother	6,230	8,398	9,834	10,012	19	24	26	27
Maintained by father	690	1,351	1,694	2,030	2	4	5	5
White, total	**27,294**	**28,294**	**29,846**	**30,242**	100	100	100	100
Two-parent family groups	22,628	21,905	22,320	22,294	83	77	75	74
One-parent family groups	4,664	6,389	7,525	7,948	17	23	25	26
Maintained by mother	4,122	5,310	6,239	6,396	15	19	21	21
Maintained by father	542	1,079	1,286	1,552	2	4	4	5
Black, total	**4,074**	**5,087**	**5,491**	**5,679**	100	100	100	100
Two-parent family groups	1,961	2,006	1,962	2,020	48	39	36	36
One-parent family groups	2,114	3,081	3,529	3,659	52	61	64	64
Maintained by mother	1,984	2,860	3,197	3,268	49	56	58	58
Maintained by father	129	221	332	391	3	4	6	7
Hispanic, total [2]	**2,194**	**3,429**	**4,527**	**4,870**	100	100	100	100
Two-parent family groups	1,626	2,289	2,879	3,115	74	67	64	64
One-parent family groups	568	1,140	1,647	1,756	26	33	36	36
Maintained by mother	526	1,003	1,404	1,500	24	29	31	31
Maintained by father	42	138	243	256	2	4	5	5

[1] Includes other races, not shown separately. [2] Hispanic persons may be of any race.
Source: U.S. Bureau of the Census, *Current Population Reports*, P20-509, and earlier reports; and unpublished data.

Married Couples of Same or Mixed Races and Origins: 1980 to 1997

[**In thousands**. As of **March**. **Persons 15 years old and over**. Persons of Hispanic origin may be of any race.]

RACE AND ORIGIN OF SPOUSES	1980	1990	1995	1997
Married couples, total	**49,714**	**53,256**	**54,937**	**54,666**
RACE				
Same race couples	48,264	50,889	51,733	51,489
White/White	44,910	47,202	48,030	47,791
Black/Black	3,354	3,687	3,703	3,698
Interracial couples	651	964	1,392	1,264
Black/White	167	211	328	311
Black husband/White wife	122	150	206	201
White husband/Black wife	45	61	122	110
White/other race [1]	450	720	988	896
Black/other race [1]	34	33	76	57
All other couples [1]	799	1,401	1,811	1,912
HISPANIC ORIGIN				
Hispanic/Hispanic	1,906	3,085	3,857	4,034
Hispanic/other origin (not Hispanic)	891	1,193	1,434	1,662
All other couples (not of Hispanic origin)	46,917	48,979	49,646	48,970

[1] Excluding White and Black.

Source: U.S. Bureau of the Census, *Current Population Reports*, P20-509, and earlier reports; and unpublished data.

Marital Status of the Population, by Sex, Race, and Hispanic Origin: 1980 to 1997

[**In millions, except percent.** As of **March. Persons 18 years old and over.** Excludes members of Armed Forces except those living off post or with their families on post.]

MARITAL STATUS, RACE, AND HISPANIC ORIGIN	TOTAL				MALE				FEMALE			
	1980	**1990**	**1995**	**1997**	**1980**	**1990**	**1995**	**1997**	**1980**	**1990**	**1995**	**1997**
Total [1]	**159.5**	**181.8**	**191.6**	**195.6**	**75.7**	**86.9**	**92.0**	**94.2**	**83.8**	**95.0**	**99.6**	**101.4**
Never married	32.3	40.4	43.9	45.9	18.0	22.4	24.6	25.4	14.3	17.9	19.3	20.5
Married	104.6	112.6	116.7	116.6	51.8	55.8	57.7	57.9	52.8	56.7	58.9	58.7
Widowed	12.7	13.8	13.4	13.7	2.0	2.3	2.3	2.7	10.8	11.5	11.1	11.1
Divorced	9.9	15.1	17.6	19.3	3.9	6.3	7.4	8.2	6.0	8.8	10.3	11.1
Percent of total	100.0	100.0	100.0	100.0	100.0	100.0	100.0	100.0	100.0	100.0	100.0	100.0
Never married	20.3	22.2	22.9	23.5	23.8	25.8	26.8	27.0	17.1	18.9	19.4	20.2
Married	65.5	61.9	60.9	59.7	68.4	64.3	62.7	61.5	63.0	59.7	59.2	57.9
Widowed	8.0	7.6	7.0	7.0	2.6	2.7	2.5	2.9	12.8	12.1	11.1	10.9
Divorced	6.2	8.3	9.2	9.9	5.2	7.2	8.0	8.7	7.1	9.3	10.3	11.0
White, total	**139.5**	**155.5**	**161.3**	**164.1**	**66.7**	**74.8**	**78.1**	**79.8**	**72.8**	**80.6**	**83.2**	**84.3**
Never married	26.4	31.6	33.2	34.5	15.0	18.0	19.2	19.7	11.4	13.6	14.0	14.7
Married	93.8	99.5	102.0	101.8	46.7	49.5	50.6	50.8	47.1	49.9	51.3	50.9
Widowed	10.9	11.7	11.3	11.7	1.6	1.9	1.9	2.3	9.3	9.8	9.4	9.4
Divorced	8.3	12.6	14.8	16.1	3.4	5.4	6.3	6.9	5.0	7.3	8.4	9.2
Percent of total	100.0	100.0	100.0	100.0	100.0	100.0	100.0	100.0	100.0	100.0	100.0	100.0
Never married	18.9	20.3	20.6	21.0	22.5	24.1	24.6	24.7	15.7	16.9	16.9	17.5
Married	67.2	64.0	63.2	62.1	70.0	66.2	64.9	63.8	64.7	61.9	61.7	60.4
Widowed	7.8	7.5	7.0	7.1	2.5	2.6	2.5	2.8	12.8	12.2	11.3	11.2
Divorced	6.0	8.1	9.1	9.8	5.0	7.2	8.1	8.7	6.8	9.0	10.1	10.9
Black, total	**16.6**	**20.3**	**22.1**	**22.8**	**7.4**	**9.1**	**9.9**	**10.2**	**9.2**	**11.2**	**12.2**	**12.6**
Never married	5.1	7.1	8.5	8.9	2.5	3.5	4.1	4.2	2.5	3.6	4.4	4.7
Married	8.5	9.3	9.6	9.7	4.1	4.5	4.6	4.6	4.5	4.8	4.9	5.0
Widowed	1.6	1.7	1.7	1.6	0.3	0.3	0.3	0.3	1.3	1.4	1.4	1.3
Divorced	1.4	2.1	2.4	2.6	0.5	0.8	0.8	1.0	0.9	1.3	1.5	1.6
Percent of total	100.0	100.0	100.0	100.0	100.0	100.0	100.0	100.0	100.0	100.0	100.0	100.0
Never married	30.5	35.1	38.4	39.1	34.3	38.4	41.7	41.5	27.4	32.5	35.8	37.2
Married	51.4	45.8	43.2	42.4	54.6	49.2	46.7	45.3	48.7	43.0	40.4	40.0
Widowed	9.8	8.5	7.6	7.2	4.2	3.7	3.1	3.3	14.3	12.4	11.3	10.4
Divorced	8.4	10.6	10.7	11.3	7.0	8.8	8.5	9.9	9.5	12.0	12.5	12.4
Hispanic, [2] **total**	**7.9**	**13.6**	**17.6**	**19.1**	**3.8**	**6.7**	**8.8**	**9.7**	**4.1**	**6.8**	**8.8**	**9.4**
Never married	1.9	3.7	5.0	5.8	1.0	2.2	3.0	3.5	0.9	1.5	2.1	2.3
Married	5.2	8.4	10.4	11.1	2.5	4.1	5.1	5.5	2.6	4.3	5.3	5.6
Widowed	0.4	0.5	0.7	0.7	0.1	0.1	0.2	0.1	0.3	0.4	0.6	0.6
Divorced	0.5	1.0	1.4	1.4	0.2	0.4	0.6	0.6	0.3	0.6	0.8	0.9
Percent of total	100.0	100.0	100.0	100.0	100.0	100.0	100.0	100.0	100.0	100.0	100.0	100.0
Never married	24.1	27.2	28.6	30.6	27.3	32.1	33.8	35.7	21.1	22.5	23.5	25.2
Married	65.6	61.7	59.3	58.1	67.1	60.9	57.9	56.9	64.3	62.4	60.7	59.3
Widowed	4.4	4.0	4.2	3.8	1.6	1.5	1.8	1.5	7.1	6.5	6.6	6.1
Divorced	5.8	7.0	7.9	7.6	4.0	5.5	6.6	5.8	7.6	8.5	9.2	9.3

[1] Includes persons of other races and not of Hispanic origin, not shown separately. [2] Hispanic persons may be of any race.

Source of tables 60 and 61: U.S. Bureau of the Census, *Current Population Reports*, P20-506, and earlier reports; and unpublished data.

Births to Teens, Unmarried Mothers, and Prenatal Care: 1985 to 1995

[In percent. Represents registered births.]

CHARACTERISTIC	1985	1990	1991	1992	1993	1994	1995
Percent of births to teenage mothers	12.7	12.8	12.9	12.7	12.8	13.1	13.1
White	10.8	10.9	11.0	10.9	11.0	11.3	11.5
Black	23.0	23.1	23.1	22.7	22.7	23.2	23.1
American Indian, Eskimo, Aleut	19.1	19.5	20.3	20.0	20.3	21.0	21.4
Asian and Pacific Islander [1]	5.5	5.7	5.8	5.6	5.7	5.7	5.6
Filipino	5.8	6.1	6.1	5.6	5.8	6.0	6.2
Chinese	1.1	1.2	1.1	1.0	1.0	1.0	0.9
Japanese	2.9	2.9	2.7	2.6	2.7	2.8	2.5
Hawaiian	15.9	18.4	18.1	18.4	18.5	19.6	19.1
Other	(NA)	(NA)	(NA)	(NA)	6.5	6.4	6.3
Hispanic origin [2]	16.5	16.8	17.2	17.1	17.4	17.8	17.9
Mexican	17.5	17.7	18.1	18.0	18.2	18.6	18.8
Puerto Rican	20.9	21.7	21.7	21.4	22.3	23.2	23.5
Cuban	7.1	7.7	7.1	7.1	6.8	7.3	7.7
Central and South American	8.2	9.0	9.4	9.6	9.9	10.4	10.6
Other and unknown Hispanic	(NA)	(NA)	(NA)	(NA)	21.0	20.8	20.1
Percent births to unmarried mothers	22.0	26.6	28.0	30.1	31.0	32.6	32.2
White	14.5	16.9	18.0	22.6	23.6	25.4	25.3
Black	60.1	66.7	68.2	68.1	68.7	70.4	69.9
American Indian, Eskimo, Aleut	40.7	53.6	55.3	55.3	55.8	57.0	57.2
Asian and Pacific Islander [1]	10.1	(NA)	(NA)	14.7	15.7	16.2	16.3
Filipino	12.1	15.9	16.8	16.8	17.7	18.5	19.5
Chinese	3.7	5.0	5.5	6.1	6.7	7.2	7.9
Japanese	7.9	9.6	9.8	9.8	10.0	11.2	10.8
Hawaiian	(NA)	45.0	45.0	45.7	47.8	48.6	49.0
Hispanic origin [2]	29.5	36.7	38.5	39.1	40.0	43.1	40.8
Mexican	25.7	33.3	35.3	36.3	37.0	40.8	38.1
Puerto Rican	51.1	55.9	57.5	57.5	59.4	60.2	60.0
Cuban	16.1	18.2	19.5	20.2	21.0	22.9	23.8
Central and South American	34.9	41.2	43.1	43.9	45.2	45.9	44.1
Percent of mothers beginning prenatal care 1st trimester	76.2	74.2	76.2	77.7	78.9	80.2	81.3
White	79.4	77.7	79.5	80.8	81.8	82.8	83.6
Black	61.8	60.7	61.9	63.9	66.0	68.3	70.4
American Indian, Eskimo, Aleut	60.3	57.9	59.9	62.1	63.4	65.2	66.7
Asian and Pacific Islander [1]	75.0	(NA)	(NA)	76.6	77.6	79.7	79.9
Filipino	77.2	77.1	77.1	78.7	79.3	81.3	80.9
Chinese	82.4	81.3	82.3	83.8	84.6	86.2	85.7
Japanese	85.8	87.0	87.7	88.2	87.2	89.2	89.7
Hawaiian	(NA)	65.8	68.1	69.9	70.6	77.0	75.9
Hispanic origin [2]	61.2	60.2	61.0	64.2	66.6	68.9	70.8
Mexican	59.9	57.8	58.7	62.1	64.8	67.3	69.1
Puerto Rican	58.3	63.5	65.0	67.8	70.0	71.7	74.0
Cuban	82.5	84.8	85.4	86.8	88.9	90.1	89.2
Central and South American	60.6	61.5	63.4	66.8	68.7	71.2	73.2
Percent of mothers beginning prenatal care 3d trimester or no care	5.7	6.0	5.8	5.2	4.8	4.4	4.2
White	4.7	4.9	4.7	4.2	3.9	3.6	3.5
Black	10.0	10.9	10.7	9.9	9.0	8.2	7.6
American Indian, Eskimo, Aleut	11.5	12.9	12.2	11.0	10.3	9.8	9.5
Asian and Pacific Islander [1]	6.1	(NA)	(NA)	4.9	4.6	4.1	4.3
Filipino	4.6	4.5	5.0	4.3	4.0	3.6	4.1
Chinese	4.2	3.4	3.4	2.9	2.9	2.7	3.0
Japanese	2.6	2.9	2.5	2.4	2.8	1.9	2.3
Hawaiian	(NA)	8.7	7.5	7.0	6.7	4.7	5.1
Hispanic origin [2]	12.5	12.0	11.0	9.5	8.8	7.6	7.4
Mexican	12.9	13.2	12.2	10.5	9.7	8.3	8.1
Puerto Rican	15.5	10.6	9.1	8.0	7.1	6.5	5.5
Cuban	3.7	2.8	2.4	2.1	1.8	1.6	2.1
Central and South American	12.5	10.9	9.5	7.9	7.3	6.5	6.1
Percent of births with low birth weight [3]	6.8	7.0	7.1	7.1	7.2	7.3	7.3
White	5.6	5.7	5.8	5.8	6.0	6.1	6.2
Black	12.4	13.3	13.6	13.3	13.3	13.2	13.1
American Indian, Eskimo, Aleut	5.9	6.1	6.2	6.2	6.4	6.4	6.6
Asian and Pacific Islander [1]	6.1	(NA)	(NA)	6.6	6.6	6.8	6.9
Filipino	6.9	7.3	7.3	7.4	7.0	7.8	7.8
Chinese	5.0	4.7	5.1	5.0	4.9	4.8	5.3
Japanese	5.9	6.2	5.9	7.0	6.5	6.9	7.3
Hawaiian	6.4	7.2	6.7	6.9	6.8	7.2	6.8
Hispanic origin [2]	6.2	6.1	6.1	6.1	6.2	6.2	6.3
Mexican	5.8	5.5	5.6	5.6	5.8	5.8	5.8
Puerto Rican	8.7	9.0	9.4	9.2	9.2	9.1	9.4
Cuban	6.0	5.7	5.6	6.1	6.2	6.3	6.5
Central and South American	5.7	5.8	5.9	5.8	5.9	6.0	6.2

NA Not available. [1] Includes other races not shown separately. [2] Hispanic persons may be of any race. Includes other types, not shown separately. [3] Births less than 2,500 grams (5 lb.-8 oz.).

Source: U.S. National Center for Health Statistics, *Vital Statistics of the United States*, annual; and *Monthly Vital Statistics Reports*.

Regular Child Care Arrangements for Children Under 6 Years Old, by Type of Arrangement: 1995

[**In percent, except as indicated.** Estimates are based on children under 6 years old who have yet to enter kindergarten. Based on 14,064 interviews from a sample survey of the civilian, noninstitutional population in households with telephones; see source for details]

CHARACTERISTIC	CHILDREN		TYPE OF NONPARENTAL ARRANGEMENT				No nonparental arrangement
	Number (1,000)	Percent distribution	Total [1]	In relative care	In nonrelative care	In center-based program [2]	
Total	**21,421**	**100**	**60**	**21**	**18**	**31**	**40**
Race-ethnicity:							
White, non-Hispanic	13,996	65	62	18	21	33	38
Black, non-Hispanic	3,344	16	66	31	12	33	34
Hispanic	2,838	13	46	23	12	17	54
Other	1,243	6	58	25	13	28	42
Mother's employment status: [3]							
35 or more hours per week	7,101	34	88	33	32	39	12
Less than 35 hours per week	4,034	19	75	30	26	35	25
Looking for work	1,635	8	42	16	4	25	58
Not in labor force	8,354	40	32	7	6	22	68
Household income:							
Less than $10,001	4,502	21	50	22	10	25	50
$10,001 to $20,000	2,909	14	54	27	12	24	46
$20,001 to $30,000	3,385	16	53	22	14	25	47
$30,001 to $40,000	3,047	14	60	23	20	27	40
$40,001 to $50,000	2,304	11	63	19	22	32	37
$50,001 to $75,000	3,063	14	74	20	26	40	26
$75,001 or more	2,211	10	77	14	30	49	23

[1] Columns do not add to total because some children participated in more than one type of nonparental arrangement. [2] Center-based programs include day care centers, head start programs, preschool, prekindergartens, and other early childhood programs. [3] Children without mothers are not included.

Source: U.S. National Center for Education Statistics, *Statistics in Brief*, October 1995 (NCES 95-824).

Expectation of Life at Birth, 1970 to 1996, and Projections, 1995 to 2010

[**In years.** Excludes deaths of nonresidents of the United States]

YEAR	TOTAL			WHITE			BLACK AND OTHER			BLACK		
	Total	Male	Female	Total	Male	Female	Total	Male	Female	Total	Male	Female
1970	70.8	67.1	74.7	71.7	68.0	75.6	65.3	61.3	69.4	64.1	60.0	68.3
1975	72.6	68.8	76.6	73.4	69.5	77.3	68.0	63.7	72.4	66.8	62.4	71.3
1980	73.7	70.0	77.4	74.4	70.7	78.1	69.5	65.3	73.6	68.1	63.8	72.5
1982	74.5	70.8	78.1	75.1	71.5	78.7	70.9	66.8	74.9	69.4	65.1	73.6
1983	74.6	71.0	78.1	75.2	71.6	78.7	70.9	67.0	74.7	69.4	65.2	73.5
1984	74.7	71.1	78.2	75.3	71.8	78.7	71.1	67.2	74.9	69.5	65.3	73.6
1985	74.7	71.1	78.2	75.3	71.8	78.7	71.0	67.0	74.8	69.3	65.0	73.4
1986	74.7	71.2	78.2	75.4	71.9	78.8	70.9	66.8	74.9	69.1	64.8	73.4
1987	74.9	71.4	78.3	75.6	72.1	78.9	71.0	66.9	75.0	69.1	64.7	73.4
1988	74.9	71.4	78.3	75.6	72.2	78.9	70.8	66.7	74.8	68.9	64.4	73.2
1989	75.1	71.7	78.5	75.9	72.5	79.2	70.9	66.7	74.9	68.8	64.3	73.3
1990	75.4	71.8	78.8	76.1	72.7	79.4	71.2	67.0	75.2	69.1	64.5	73.6
1991	75.5	72.0	78.9	76.3	72.9	79.6	71.5	67.3	75.5	69.3	64.6	73.8
1992	75.8	72.3	79.1	76.5	73.2	79.8	71.8	67.7	75.7	69.6	65.0	73.9
1993	75.5	72.2	78.8	76.3	73.1	79.5	71.5	67.3	75.5	69.2	64.6	73.7
1994	75.7	72.3	79.0	76.4	73.2	79.6	71.7	67.5	75.8	69.6	64.9	74.1
1995	75.8	72.5	78.9	76.5	73.4	79.6	71.9	67.9	75.7	69.6	65.2	73.9
1996	76.1	73.0	79.0	76.8	73.8	79.6	(NA)	(NA)	(NA)	70.3	66.1	74.2
Projections: [1] 1995	75.9	72.5	79.3	76.9	73.6	80.1	(NA)	(NA)	(NA)	69.7	64.8	74.5
2000	76.4	73.0	79.7	77.4	74.2	80.5	(NA)	(NA)	(NA)	69.7	64.6	74.7
2005	76.9	73.5	80.2	77.9	74.7	81.0	(NA)	(NA)	(NA)	69.9	64.5	75.0
2010	77.4	74.1	80.6	78.6	75.5	81.6	(NA)	(NA)	(NA)	70.4	65.1	75.5

NA Not available. [1] Based on middle mortality assumptions; for details, see source. Source: U.S. Bureau of the Census, *Current Population Reports*, P25-1130.

Source: Except as noted, U.S. National Center for Health Statistics, *Vital Statistics of the United States*, annual, and *Monthly Vital Statistics Reports*.

Death Rates, by Leading Causes and Age: 1980 to 1995

[Deaths per 100,000 population in specified group. Except as noted, excludes deaths of nonresidents of the United States.]

YEAR, RACE, AND AGE	Heart disease	Malignant neoplasms	Accidents and adverse effects	Cerebrovascular diseases	Chronic obstructive pulmonary diseases [1]	Pneumonia, flu	Suicide	Chronic liver disease, cirrhosis	Diabetes mellitus	Homicide and legal intervention
All races, both sexes: [2]										
1980	336.0	183.9	46.7	75.1	24.7	24.1	11.9	13.5	15.4	10.7
1990	289.5	203.2	37.0	57.9	34.9	32.0	12.4	10.4	19.2	10.0
1994	281.3	205.2	35.1	58.9	39.0	31.3	12.0	9.8	21.8	(NA)
1995	280.7	204.9	35.5	60.1	39.2	31.6	11.9	9.6	22.6	(NA)
1 to 4 years old	1.8	3.3	15.9	(NA)	(NA)	1.1	(NA)	(NA)	(NA)	3.0
5 to 14 years old	0.9	2.8	9.3	(NA)	0.3	0.3	0.9	(NA)	(NA)	1.5
15 to 24 years old	2.8	4.8	38.7	0.5	0.6	0.6	13.8	(NA)	(NA)	22.6
25 to 44 years old	20.2	26.4	32.5	4.2	(NA)	2.6	15.3	5.3	3.0	13.8
45 to 64 years old	202.3	261.0	29.9	29.3	25.6	10.8	14.0	20.8	22.5	(NA)
65 years old and over	1,840.7	1,134.5	85.4	405.2	262.5	219.4	(NA)	(NA)	128.5	(NA)
All races, males: 1995	282.7	219.5	47.9	48.0	42.0	29.4	19.8	(NA)	20.4	13.8
1 to 4 years old	1.8	3.5	18.7	(NA)	(NA)	1.2	(NA)	(NA)	(NA)	3.3
5 to 14 years old	0.9	3.1	12.0	(NA)	0.4	0.3	1.2	(NA)	(NA)	1.9
15 to 24 years old	3.4	5.8	56.8	0.5	0.8	0.6	23.4	(NA)	(NA)	38.3
25 to 44 years old	28.8	24.4	50.2	4.5	(NA)	3.2	24.8	7.7	3.6	21.7
45 to 64 years old	295.5	289.6	43.9	33.3	28.2	13.7	22.1	30.5	24.4	(NA)
65 years old and over	2,043.6	1,463.6	105.0	370.4	341.0	237.6	(NA)	(NA)	127.6	(NA)
All races, females: 1995	278.8	191.0	23.7	71.7	36.4	33.6	(NA)	(NA)	24.6	(NA)
1 to 4 years old	1.8	3.0	12.9	(NA)	(NA)	1.0	(NA)	(NA)	(NA)	2.7
5 to 14 years old	0.8	2.4	6.6	(NA)	0.2	0.2	0.5	(NA)	(NA)	1.2
15 to 24 years old	2.1	3.9	19.8	(NA)	0.5	0.6	3.7	(NA)	(NA)	6.2
25 to 44 years old	11.7	28.3	15.1	4.0	(NA)	2.0	5.9	3.0	2.4	5.8
45 to 64 years old	115.3	234.4	16.7	25.7	23.1	8.1	6.4	11.7	20.8	(NA)
65 years old and over	1,701.7	909.2	72.0	429.0	208.8	207.0	(NA)	(NA)	129.1	(NA)
White, both sexes: 1995	297.6	215.0	35.7	62.6	43.6	33.8	12.9	9.8	21.8	(NA)
1 to 4 years old	1.4	3.3	13.9	(NA)	(NA)	0.9	(NA)	(NA)	(NA)	2.1
5 to 14 years old	0.8	2.8	8.5	(NA)	0.2	0.2	0.9	(NA)	(NA)	1.0
15 to 24 years old	2.2	4.9	40.1	0.5	0.5	0.6	14.2	(NA)	(NA)	10.9
25 to 44 years old	17.2	25.1	31.7	3.2	(NA)	2.0	16.3	5.0	2.6	8.1
45 to 64 years old	188.7	252.8	27.9	24.1	26.0	9.6	15.2	19.7	19.2	(NA)
65 years old and over	1,848.9	6,126.3	85.4	401.3	274.7	223.0	(NA)	(NA)	118.8	(NA)
White males: 1995	297.9	228.1	47.4	48.6	46.1	30.8	21.4	13.2	20.0	(NA)
1 to 4 years old	1.4	3.7	16.5	0.4	(NA)	1.0	(NA)	(NA)	(NA)	2.3
5 to 14 years old	0.8	3.1	10.9	(NA)	0.3	0.2	1.3	(NA)	(NA)	1.1
15 to 24 years old	2.8	5.9	58.3	0.5	0.5	0.6	24.1	(NA)	(NA)	17.4
25 to 44 years old	25.4	23.2	48.8	3.4	(NA)	2.5	26.1	7.4	3.2	12.3
45 to 64 years old	280.8	[illegible]	40.4	27.1	28.3	11.9	23.8	28.8	21.4	(NA)
65 years old and over	2,051.4	[illegible]	103.4	361.4	351.8	237.9	(NA)	(NA)	120.9	(NA)
White females: 1995	297.4	202.4	24.4	76.0	41.2	36.6	(NA)	(NA)	23.5	(NA)
1 to 4 years old	1.4	2.9	11.2	(NA)	(NA)	0.9	(NA)	(NA)	(NA)	1.9
5 to 14 years old	0.8	2.5	6.0	0.2	(NA)	0.2	0.5	(NA)	(NA)	0.8
15 to 24 years old	1.6	3.9	21.0	0.4	(NA)	0.5	3.8	(NA)	(NA)	3.9
25 to 44 years old	8.9	27.0	14.3	2.9	(NA)	1.5	6.5	2.6	2.0	3.7
45 to 64 years old	100.9	231.0	15.9	21.4	23.9	7.4	7.0	10.9	17.1	(NA)
65 years old and over	1,709.5	911.9	73.1	428.7	221.6	212.7	(NA)	(NA)	117.4	(NA)
Black, both sexes: 1995	237.3	182.9	38.5	55.9	20.1	23.5	(NA)	(NA)	31.4	32.5
1 to 4 years old	4.2	3.3	26.3	(NA)	(NA)	1.9	(NA)	(NA)	(NA)	7.4
5 to 14 years old	1.3	2.9	13.8	(NA)	1.1	0.4	0.7	(NA)	(NA)	4.3
15 to 24 years old	5.7	4.8	23.4	(NA)	1.7	(NA)	11.6	(NA)	(NA)	88.1
25 to 44 years old	43.5	37.6	41.3	11.6	(NA)	6.8	10.5	7.8	6.0	53.0
45 to 64 years old	353.4	373.2	47.9	74.5	27.8	22.7	(NA)	31.8	52.8	18.5
65 years old and over	1,988.3	1,349.2	89.0	478.4	167.3	196.7	(NA)	(NA)	240.1	(NA)
Black males: 1995	244.2	209.1	56.2	51.0	24.9	25.6	(NA)	(NA)	26.1	56.3
1 to 4 years old	3.9	3.2	30.8	(NA)	(NA)	2.1	(NA)	(NA)	(NA)	8.4
5 to 14 years old	1.5	3.3	18.0	(NA)	1.3	(S)	1.1	(NA)	(NA)	5.6
15 to 24 years old	6.8	5.4	52.6	(NA)	2.1	(NA)	20.6	(NA)	1.0	157.6
25 to 44 years old	57.6	35.4	65.3	12.3	(NA)	8.5	18.9	10.7	7.1	90.9
45 to 64 years old	484.7	468.2	78.4	92.1	34.1	32.9	(NA)	49.0	54.9	33.4
65 years old and over	2,203.6	1,933.5	126.4	485.2	264.5	244.6	(NA)	(NA)	211.1	(NA)
Black females: 1995	231.3	159.1	22.5	60.4	15.8	21.7	(NA)	(NA)	36.1	(NA)
1 to 4 years old	4.4	3.4	21.7	(NA)	(NA)	1.8	(NA)	(NA)	(NA)	6.4
5 to 14 years old	1.2	2.5	9.5	(NA)	0.8	(NA)	(S)	(NA)	(NA)	3.0
15 to 24 years old	4.7	4.2	15.0	(NA)	1.2	(NA)	2.7	(NA)	(NA)	18.7
25 to 44 years old	31.0	39.6	9.7	11.0	3.5	5.3	(NA)	5.3	5.0	19.5
45 to 64 years old	247.8	296.8	23.3	60.3	22.7	14.5	(NA)	18.0	51.2	(NA)
65 years old and over	1,852.6	981.0	65.5	474.1	106.0	166.5	(NA)	(NA)	258.4	(NA)

NA Not available. S Figure does not meet publication standards. [1] Includes allied conditions. [2] Includes other races not shown separately.

Source: U.S. National Center for Health Statistics, *Vital Statistics of the United States*, annual; and *Monthly Vital Statistics Report.*

Participation in Various Leisure Activities: 1997

[**In percent, except as indicated.** Covers activities engaged in at least once in the prior 12 months.]

ITEM	Adult population (mil.)	ATTENDANCE AT—			PARTICIPATION IN—				
		Movies	Sports events	Amusement park	Exercise program	Playing sports	Charity work	Home improvement/repair	Computer hobbies
Total	**195.6**	**66**	**41**	**57**	**76**	**45**	**43**	**66**	**40**
Sex: Male	94.2	66	49	58	75	56	40	71	44
Female	101.4	65	34	57	77	35	46	61	37
Race: Hispanic	19.1	59	35	66	69	35	31	61	25
White	146.1	68	44	56	78	48	45	70	43
African American	22.1	60	35	55	74	34	44	51	37
American Indian	3.0	65	34	59	83	49	34	58	37
Asian	5.3	76	29	58	70	48	41	58	62
Age: 18 to 24 years old	23.7	88	51	76	85	67	35	57	68
25 to 34 years old	40.1	79	51	70	82	63	41	63	51
35 to 44 years old	45.3	73	46	68	79	52	50	76	47
45 to 54 years old	33.7	65	42	53	77	40	46	75	40
55 to 64 years old	20.9	46	33	40	69	19	44	71	23
65 to 74 years old	19.6	38	21	29	65	23	40	55	11
75 years old and over	12.3	28	16	18	56	13	40	44	7
Education: Grade school	13.7	14	13	34	46	13	20	40	1
Some high school	26.9	52	25	54	66	30	31	59	19
High school graduate	62.0	62	38	58	74	41	36	65	35
Some college	50.3	78	48	64	81	54	50	71	52
College graduate	25.2	82	59	61	87	61	55	76	63
Graduate school	17.4	81	55	53	88	57	67	73	59
Income: $10,000 or less	15.0	37	15	39	55	19	32	42	19
$10,001 to $20,000	26.5	46	26	51	69	27	34	53	22
$20,001 to $30,000	29.4	56	28	55	72	40	37	61	30
$30,001 to $40,000	32.1	71	42	64	77	46	47	68	40
$40,001 to $50,000	25.9	73	51	67	80	51	42	75	47
$50,001 to $75,000	35.0	82	54	65	86	60	50	80	54
$75,001 to $100,000	16.2	81	66	64	86	61	51	79	64
Over $100,000	15.5	87	65	56	90	66	59	81	69

Source: U.S. National Endowment for the Arts, *1997 Survey of Public Participation in the Arts* Research Division Note #70, July 1998.

16

Education

◆ Educational Opportunities in Colonial America
◆ African American Educational Institutions in the Nineteenth Century
◆ Philanthropy and Education ◆ African American Education in the Twentieth Century
◆ Current Educational Trends ◆ Administrators, Educators, and Scholars
◆ Historically and Predominantly African American Colleges and Universities
◆ Research Institutions
◆ African Americans Holding Endowed University Chairs, Chairs of Excellence, or Chaired Professorships (1999) ◆ Education Statistics

by Jessie Carney Smith

◆ EDUCATIONAL OPPORTUNITIES IN COLONIAL AMERICA

Historically, the attainment of education for African Americans has been a struggle. As far back as the late 1600s to the mid-1700s, there is some evidence of sporadic, systematic instruction of Africans in colonial America. Prior to 1830, some were even taught to read, write, and, in some instances, perform simple arithmetic. However, between 1830 and 1835, stringent laws were passed prohibiting whites from teaching African Americans to read and write. In spite of these laws though, many individuals struggled to provide informal and formal education to African Americans. In addition, churches and charitable organizations also played an important role in the creation of educational institutions for African Americans in the United States.

Early Christian Missionary Endeavors

Early attempts to educate African Americans can be traced back to the missionary efforts of Christian churches in the early 1600s. French Catholics in Louisiana were probably the earliest group to provide instruction to African American laborers. Although the primary goal was to convert them to Christianity, the process often involved general education. In addition, the French *code noir*, a system of laws, made it incumbent upon masters to educate slaves.

Pennsylvania Quakers, who were opposed to the institution of slavery, organized monthly educational meetings for African Americans during the early 1700s, so that they might have the opportunity for improvement. One such Quaker, Anthony Benezet, established an evening school in his home in 1750 that was successful until 1760. In 1774 Quakers in Philadelphia joined together to open a school for African Americans.

The Society for the Propagation of the Gospel in Foreign Parts, organized by the Church of England in 1701 for the purpose of converting African slaves to Christianity, was another organization that provided educational opportunities to African Americans. In 1751 the Society sent Joseph Ottolenghi to convert and educate African Americans in Georgia. Ottolenghi "promised to spare no pains to improve the young children."

◆ AFRICAN AMERICAN EDUCATIONAL INSTITUTIONS IN THE NINETEENTH CENTURY

African Free Schools in New York and Philadelphia

Similar to the churches, the anti-slavery movement played an important part in the creation of schools. In 1787 the Manumission Society founded the New York

The first New York African Free School opened its doors in 1787. School No. 2 is shown here (Schomburg Center for Research in Black Culture).

African Free School; by 1820 more than five hundred African American children were enrolled. Support increased as other African Free Schools were established in New York until 1834 when the New York Common Council took over control of the schools.

In the North, there were opportunities for elementary education for African Americans in mostly segregated schools or in schools run in conjunction with African American churches. For example, in 1804 African Episcopalians in Philadelphia organized a school for African American children. In 1848 an African American industrial training school opened in Philadelphia at the House of Industry. Other schools in operation in Philadelphia included the Corn Street Unclassified School (1849), the Holmesburg Unclassified School (1854), and the Home for Colored Children (1859). By the mid-1860s, there were 1,031 pupils in the African American public schools of Philadelphia: 748 in the charity schools; 211 in the benevolent schools, and 331 in private schools. Howev-

An American history class at Tuskegee Institute in 1902 (The Library of Congress).

er, high schools in the North were almost inaccessible to African Americans in much of the nineteenth century.

Freedmen's Organizations and Agencies

At the close of the Civil War, hundreds of thousands of newly-freed African Americans were left without homes and adequate resources. As a means for providing temporary assistance to the former slaves, numerous organizations were formed. The American Missionary Association (AMA), established on September 3, 1846, had maintained an interest in African American education before and after the war. The AMA opened its first school for newly-freed slaves on September 17, 1861, at Fortress Monroe, Virginia. Mary S. Peake became the first teacher in an AMA school. The AMA also established a network of elementary schools, normal schools, and colleges throughout the South. In time, however, most of these schools were absorbed into local and state systems of education. Following the AMA's early efforts, other voluntary and denominational groups responded to the need for freedmen's aid and sent teachers into the Southern and border states, established elementary schools on plantations, in small towns, and in larger cities in the South. Although most of the schools were to be racially integrated, few whites attended.

The New England Freedmen's Aid Society, organized in Boston on February 7, 1862, was founded to promote education among free African Americans. Supporters of the organization included Edward Everett Hale, Samuel Cabot, Charles Bernard, William Lloyd Garrison, and William Cullen Bryant. In New York, a similar organization was founded on February 20, 1862, the National Freedmens Relief Association. The Port Royal Relief Committee, later known as the Pennsylvania Freedmens Relief Association, founded in Philadelphia on March 3, 1862, followed this trend. In 1863 several of these organizations merged to form the United States Commission for the Relief of the National Freedmen, which, in 1865, became the American Freedman's Aid Union.

The federal government responded to the needs of African Americans in the South. During the 1860s, Congress passed several Freedman's Bureau Acts, creating and financing an agency designed to provide temporary assistance to newly freed slaves. Under the acts, the bureau's chief functions were to provide food, clothing, and medical supplies. Working in conjunction with various benevolent organizations, Bureau Commissioner

General Oliver Otis Howard established and maintained schools and managed to provide for teachers. By 1870 the Freedman's Bureau operated over 2,600 schools in the South with 3,300 teachers educating 150,000 students; almost 4,000 schools were in operation prior to the abolition of the agency.

Independent Schools in the Late Nineteenth Century

The education of African Americans has been largely a function of independent schools, private institutions founded to meet the educational and employment needs of African Americans. In the second half of the century, these schools filled the gap until African American land grant colleges were founded in 1890. They also supplied many of the African American teachers in the South.

One of the earliest surviving African American independent schools, Tuskegee Normal and Industrial Institute (now Tuskegee University), was established in 1881 by an act of the Alabama general assembly. Booker T. Washington, the school's organizer and first principal, established a curriculum that provided African American students with the means to become economically self-supporting.

Similarly, other independent schools developed around the country. In a lecture room at the Christ Presbyterian Church, Lucy C. Laney opened what would become the Haines Normal and Industrial Institute in Savannah, Georgia in 1883. In 1901 Nannie Helen Burroughs founded the National Training School for Women and Girls in Washington, DC. By the end of the first year the school had enrolled 31 students; 25 years later more than 2,000 women had trained at the school. In Sedalia, North Carolina, Charlotte Hawkins Brown founded the Palmer Memorial Institute in 1901.

With only $1.50 and five students, Mary McLeod Bethune founded Daytona Normal and Industrial Institute for Girls (now Bethune-Cookman College) in 1904 in Daytona Beach, Florida. Nineteen years later, the institute merged with the Cookman Institute of Jacksonville, Florida, founded in 1872 by D.S.B. Darnell. Over 2,000 students now study at Bethune-Cookman College.

Early African American Institutions of Higher Education

Lincoln University in Pennsylvania (founded in 1854 as Ashmun Institute) and Wilberforce University (founded in 1856) are often regarded as the oldest of the historically African American institutions of higher education. Wilberforce College, as the latter school was first known, was founded in 1856 by the African Methodist Episcopal Church and named for the English abolitionist William Wilberforce. The school awarded its first degree in 1857. Wilberforce and Lincoln were the first African American colleges to remain in their original location and to develop into degree-granting institutions. The oldest institution in operation today, however, is Cheyney University of Pennsylvania (earlier known as the Institute for Colored Youth and, eventually, Cheyney State College), which was founded in 1837. The primary purpose of these institutions was to train African American youth for service as teachers and ministers.

Between 1865 and 1871, several predominantly African American institutions of higher learning were founded, including Atlanta University (now Clark-Atlanta University), Shaw University and Virginia Union University (1865), Fisk University and Lincoln Institute in Missouri (now Lincoln University) (1866), Talladega College, Augusta Institute (now Morehouse College), Biddle University (now Johnson C. Smith University), Howard University and Scotia Seminary (now Barber-Scotia College) (1867), Hampton Institute (now Hampton University) (1868), Tougaloo College (1869), Alcorn College (now Alcorn State University), and Benedict College (1871). Religious organizations were instrumental in the founding and supporting of these early African American institutions. The Freedmen's Bureau either founded or aided in the development of Howard University, St. Augustine's College, Lincoln Institute in Missouri, and Storer College (now merged with Virginia Union University). The American Missionary Association founded seven African American colleges; the first of these was Hampton. Other AMA-founded institutions were Atlanta, Fisk, LeMoyne (now LeMoyne-Owen College), Straight (now merged with New Orleans University to become Dillard University), Talladega, Tillotson College (now Huston-Tillotson), and Tougaloo. Benedict College, Shaw University, and Virginia Union were founded and supported by the American Baptist Home Mission Society.

Alcorn College (now Alcorn State University), founded in 1871, was the first African American land grant college. This was made possible under the Morrill Act of 1862, which provided federal land grant funds for higher education. In 1890 Congress passed the second Morrill Act, also known as the Land Grant Act of 1890. The second act stipulated that no federal aid was to be provided for the creation or maintenance of any white agricultural and mechanical school unless that state also provided for a similar school for African Americans. As a result, a system of separate, African American land grant institutions developed and became the basis of publicly-supported higher education of African Americans in the South.

African American colleges offered diversity in history, purpose, and curriculums. For example, early in their history, some African American colleges prepared their

African American female college graduate in the late 1800s (Schomburg Center for Research in Black Culture).

students for careers in medicine and medical-related fields. Those that prepared students for degrees in dentistry and medicine included Howard University, Meharry Medical College, Shaw University, and New Orleans Medical School. The nation's only degree program in veterinary medicine among historically African American colleges and universities is still offered at Tuskegee University. Bennett College (founded 1873) and Spelman College (founded 1881) are the only two African American women's colleges. At first coeducational, Bennett became a women's two-year college in 1926. Xavier (founded in 1925) is the nation's only Catholic-supported college for African Americans.

By 1900 there were some 34 African American institutions in the United States for higher education and more than 2,000 African Americans with earned degrees.

◆ PHILANTHROPY AND EDUCATION

Pre-Civil War efforts did not fully address the educational needs and desires of African Americans, especially concerning the freed slaves. Northern philanthropy took up some of the burden of improving African American education. Agencies of the antebellum period aided in educating African Americans through their support of private and sectarian schools before and after the Civil War. By the end of the war, however, the South—the region where African Americans were concentrated—still had not addressed the educational needs of African Americans. Neither the newly-freed slaves nor their children had access to free public education. In 1867, a new type of support for education began when Massachusetts merchant George Peabody established the first educational philanthropy in the country. In his concern for the desolate South, he created the Peabody Education Fund to benefit "elementary education to children of the common people." The fund later was credited with stimulating states to develop systems of free schools for the races, "creating favorable public opinion to levy tax to support the schools, and stimulating the development of state teachers associations and normal schools."

So successful was the Peabody effort that in 1882 Connecticut manufacturer John F. Slater, impressed with the developments, created the Slater Fund to uplift the "lately emancipated" people of the South, thus becoming the first philanthropy devoted to the education of African Americans. Through the fund's efforts, private African American colleges and four-year high schools for African American were developed. The Fund stimulated vocational and industrial training and established the idea of county training schools. The Daniel Hand Fund, established in 1888, provided for the education of "needy and indigent" African Americans in the South; it was entrusted to the American Missionary Association. By 1914 the Peabody and Slater funds worked in similar areas; Peabody then transferred its assets to Slater.

Anna T. Jeanes further advanced the education of African Americans by giving $1 million to Booker T. Washington of the Tuskegee Institute and Hollis B. Frissell of the Hampton Institute to strengthen rural schools for African Americans in the South in 1907. The gift established the Fund for Rudimentary Schools for Southern Negroes, known as the Jeanes Fund. Initially the Fund supported "industrial teachers" who moved from school to school in the South teaching industrial and utilitarian subjects. The concept was expanded to provide master teachers, known as "Jeanes teachers," to supervise the African American schools. Later the program added new teaching methods, organized in-service training for teachers, and generally improved instruction. The program lasted from 1908 until 1968, when counties took over the Jeanes teachers' work and paid their salaries. Much of the credit for the program was due to Virginia E. Randolph, the first Jeanes teacher. In recognition of her work, the Jeanes teachers established the Virginia Randolph Fund to supplement the Jeanes Fund in 1936.

The Jeanes Fund and the Slater Fund, then working in similar areas, merged in 1937 to form the Southern Education Foundation (SEF). Later that year the Virginia Randolph Fund was incorporated into the SEF. The SEF extended the work of the predecessor funds and ensured that innovative approaches to the education of African Americans continued. From 1937 to 1950, the SEF concentrated on supporting the Jeanes teachers. It also worked with such agencies as the General Education Board (GEB), the Julius Rosenwald Fund, the Carnegie Corporation, and State Agents for Negro Schools. The GEB was a source of support for African American colleges, library collections, and, sometimes, library buildings. It also supported African American teachers and other aspects of education and welfare for African Americans. In its 31-year history, the Julius Rosenwald Fund, established in 1917, helped to build more than 5,000 rural schools for African Americans as a part of regular school systems in 15 Southern states. In various villages and counties, blacks and whites raised additional funds to support these schools. The fund also strengthened African American higher education. Early on, the Carnegie Corporation had provided grants to the Slater and Jeanes programs. Later, the corporation built African American branches of public libraries in various cities in the South. During the first quarter of the twentieth century, several African American colleges received funds from the Carnegie Corporation and Andrew Carnegie himself to support the erection of library buildings. They included the institutions of Atlanta, Cheyney, Fisk, Howard, Tuskegee, and Wilberforce.

In addition, the SEF worked to prepare the South to resolve racial problems. When the *Brown v. Board of Education of Topeka, Kansas* decision was rendered in 1954, bringing about desegregation of public education, the SEF contributed to the decision by conducting studies of African American education in the South largely through support of the Ford Foundation. Its efforts to desegregate public education continued: those Southern states that failed to desegregate higher education were challenged by the lawsuit originally known as *Adams v. Richardson.* The SEF supported the Legal Defense Fund in litigation and helped dismantle the dual system of public education. It also supported conferences, studies, and publications dealing with desegregation of higher education. Its report *Miles to Go*, published in 1998, is an example of the SEF's efforts. The study found that over two decades of efforts to desegregate higher education has left blacks in the South and elsewhere out of pace with whites in undergraduate and graduate school enrollment, rates of graduation, faculty diversity, among other areas.

Located in Atlanta since 1948, the SEF is now a public charity that has several interests including programs to increase the supply of minority teachers in the South and to strengthen African American colleges. The SEF, its predecessor agencies, and other private and public agencies, figure prominently in the history and progress of African American education.

◆ AFRICAN AMERICAN EDUCATION IN THE TWENTIETH CENTURY

Early Promoters of African American Studies

From its beginnings, the purpose of African American studies has been to disseminate knowledge about the social, cultural, political, and historical experiences of Africans.

One of the forerunners in the field of African American studies, theologian and educator Reverend Alexander Crummell, along with a group of African American intellectuals, founded the American Negro Academy in Washington, DC, in 1897. The purpose of the organization was to foster scholarship and promote literature, science, and art, among African Americans. The organization's members hoped that through the academy, an educated African American elite would shape and direct society. Crummell first conceived the idea of an American Negro Academy while a student at Cambridge University in England. The organization's founding members included Paul Laurence Dunbar, William Sanders Scarborough, and W.E.B. Du Bois, among other noted educators. Following Crummell's death in 1908, Du Bois was elected president of the academy.

In September of 1915, Carter G. Woodson, a Harvard Ph.D. graduate, organized the Association for the Study of Negro Life and History (now the Association for the Study of Afro-American Life and History). The association's primary purpose was to promote research, encourage the study of African American history, and to publish material on African American history. In 1916, the organization began publishing the *Journal of Negro History*, for which Woodson served as editor until his death in 1950.

Other early scholars of African American studies include: sociologist E. Franklin Frazier (1894–1963); John Edward Bruce (1856–1924); and Arthur Schomburg, founder of the Negro Society for Historical Research (1911); and Alain Locke, founder of the Associates in Negro Folk Education (1934).

The End of Legal Segregation in Public Education

In the years that followed the United States Supreme Court's 1896 ruling in *Plessy v. Ferguson*, segregation in public education became the general practice. Prior to the Court's decision in *Brown v. Board of Education of*

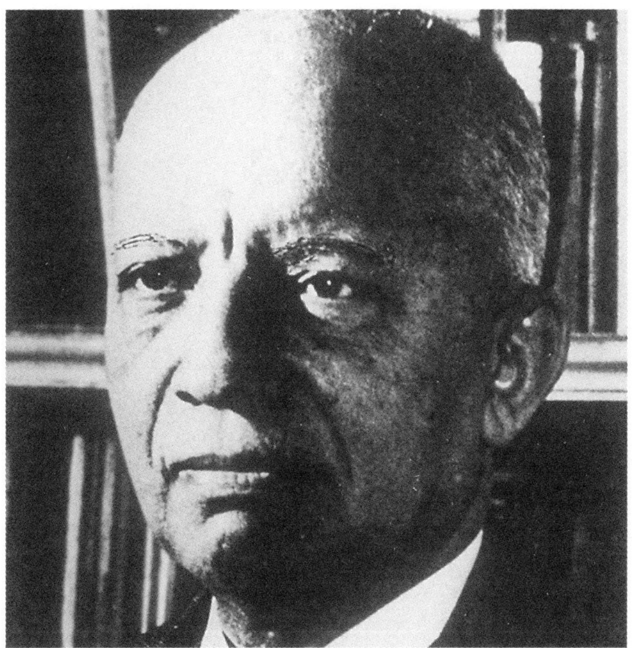

Carter G. Woodson (AP/Wide World Photos, Inc.)

Topeka, Kansas African American children were often subjected to inferior educational facilities. However, by the 1930s, a string of school desegregation cases reached the Court.

When Lloyd Lionel Gaines, an African American, had been refused admission to the law school of the State University of Missouri, he applied to state courts for an order to compel admission on the grounds that refusal constituted a denial of his rights under the Fourteenth Amendment of the U.S. Constitution. At that time, the state of Missouri maintained a practice of providing funds for African Americans to attend graduate and professional schools outside of the state, rather than provide facilities itself. The university defended its action by maintaining that Lincoln University, a predominantly African American institution, would eventually establish its own law school, which Gaines could then attend. Until then the state would allow him to exercise the option of pursuing his studies outside the state on a scholarship. Ruling in the case Missouri ex rel. *Gaines v. Canada* in 1938, the United States Supreme Court ruled that states were required to provide equal educational facilities for African Americans within its borders.

Taking an even greater step, in 1950 the United States Supreme Court ruled that a separate law school for African Americans provided by the state of Texas violated the equal protection clause of the Fourteenth Amendment. According to the Court, Herman Marion Sweat's rights were violated when he was refused admission to the law school of the University of Texas on the grounds that substantially equivalent facilities were already available to African Americans at another Texas school. Ruling in the case *Sweatt v. Painter*, the Court ruled that the petitioner be admitted to the University of Texas Law School since "in terms of number of the faculty, variety of courses and opportunity for specialization, size of the student body, scope of the library, availability of law review and similar activities, the University of Texas Law School is superior."

In 1952, five different cases, all dealing with segregation in public schools, reached the United States Supreme Court. Four of the cases *Brown v. Board of Education* (out of Kansas), *Briggs v. Elliott* (out of South Carolina), *Davis v. Prince Edward County School Board* (out of Virginia), and *Gebhart v. Belton* (out of Delaware) were considered together; the fifth case *Bolling v. Sharpe*, coming out of the District of Columbia, was considered separately since the District is not a state.

After hearing initial arguments, the Court found itself unable to reach a decision. In 1953, the Court heard reargument. Thurgood Marshall, legal consul for the NAACP Legal Defense and Education Fund, presented arguments on behalf of the African American students. On May 17, 1954, the Court unanimously ruled that segregation in all public education deprived minority children of equal protection under the Fourteenth Amendment. (In the *Bolling* case, the Court determined that segregation violated provisions of the Fifth Amendment, since the Fourteenth Amendment is expressly directed to the states.)

African American Colleges and Universities

Predominantly African American colleges and universities continue to account for the majority of African American graduates, especially in the areas of science, mathematics, and engineering. In 1964, over 51 percent of all African Americans in college were still enrolled in historically African American colleges and universities. By 1970 the proportion was 28 percent, and by the fall of 1978, 16.5 percent. As recently as 1977, 38 percent of all African Americans receiving baccalaureate degrees earned their degrees at African American institutions. In 1980 some 190,989 African Americans were enrolled at historically African American institutions. By 1994 the total African American enrollment at these institutions reached 280,071. In 1997, Florida A & M University was the leading producer of African Americans earning a baccalaureate degree in all disciplines and had the largest number of graduates go on to earn doctorates. Between 1991 and 1995, Fisk was grouped with such large institutions as the University of Michigan, Berkeley, Harvard, and Michigan State in the number of African American undergraduates who went on to achieve

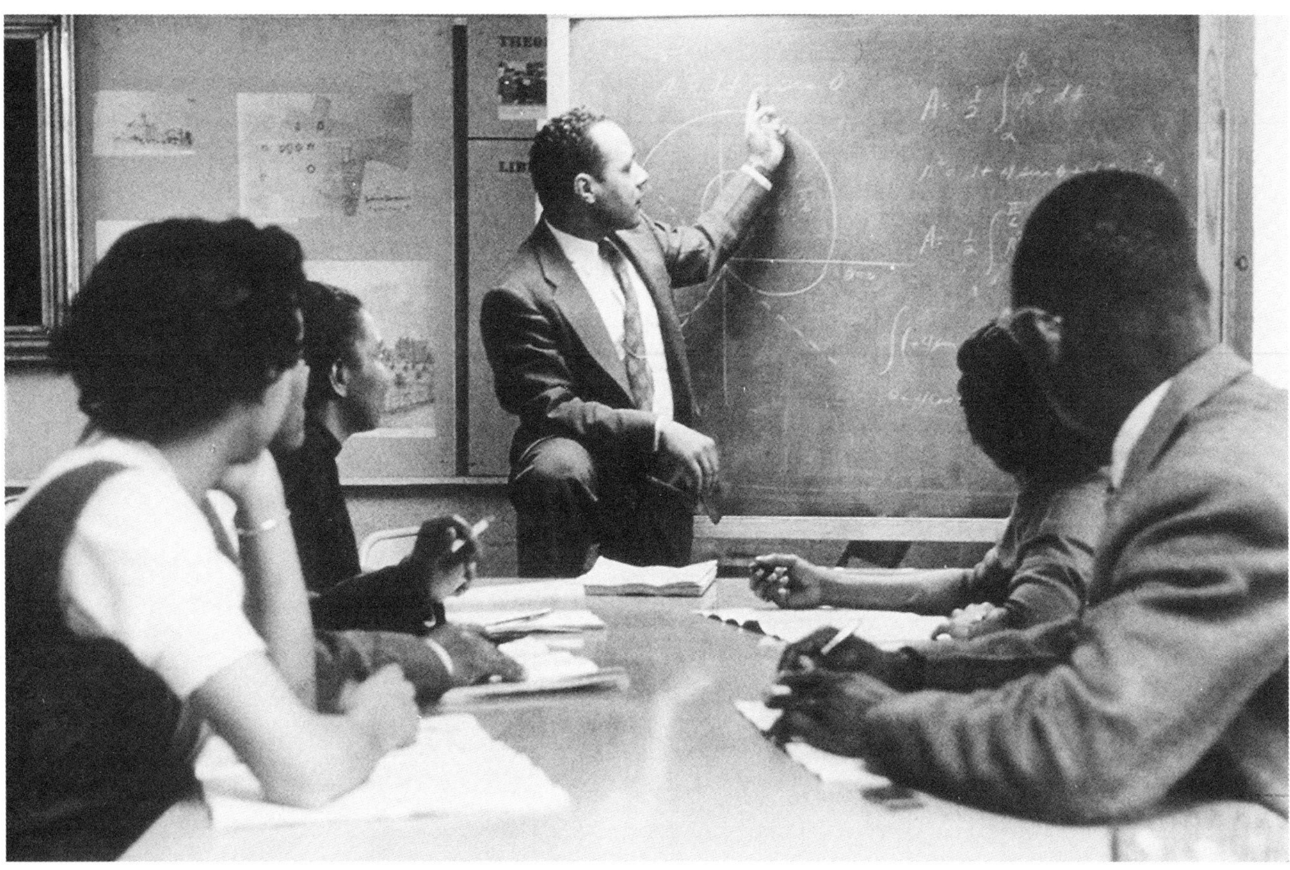

A teacher leads his math class at a historical African American university.

doctorates from the 13 most productive schools. In the natural sciences, Fisk ranked first of all colleges and universities who continued their studies in such institutions, while Xavier led the nation in the percent of African American students accepted into medical school in 1998.

The racial composition of some African American colleges has changed dramatically; some of these colleges now have a predominantly white student body. Mandated by court order to raise its white population to fifty percent, the enrollment at Tennessee State University in 1998 was about thirty percent white. Those historically African American institutions with predominantly white enrollments by 1998 are Lincoln University in Missouri (72 percent white), Bluefield State College in West Virginia (89 percent white), and West Virginia State University (85 percent white).

Independent Schools

For years independent schools have been founded in order to exert greater control, ensure quality in education, and to meet the needs of African American children.

In 1932, in order to promote religious growth in the African American Muslim community, the Nation of Islam founded the University of Islam, an elementary and secondary school to educate African American Muslim children in Detroit. Clara Muhammad, wife of Elijah Muhammad, served as the school's first instructor. In 1934 a second school was opened in Chicago; by 1965 schools were operating in Atlanta and Washington, DC. The current system of African American Muslim schools, named for Clara Muhammad, is an outgrowth of the earlier University of Islam. There are currently 38 Sister Clara Muhammad schools in the United States.

Gertrude Wilks and other African American community leaders in East Palo Alto, California, organized the Nairobi Day School, a Saturday school in 1966. In 1969 the school became a full-time school. It closed in 1984.

Also founded as a Saturday school program in 1972, the New Concept Development Center in Chicago set out to create an educational institution which promoted self-respect, cooperation, and an awareness of African American history and culture. In 1975 public school teacher and nurse, Marva Collins founded the Westside Preparatory School in Chicago.

In recent years, the educational and social needs of urban youth, particularly African American males, have

Marva Collins with her class at the Westside Preparatory School in Chicago in 1982 (AP/Wide World Photos, Inc.).

been given increased attention. Studies show that nearly forty percent of adult African American males are functionally illiterate, and that the number of African American males incarcerated far outnumbers the number of African American males in college. Addressing these issues, large urban school systems, including Baltimore, Detroit, and Milwaukee, have attempted to create programs that focus on the needs of African American males.

Although African American students have shown improved performance on achievement tests, gaps between black and white students still exist. Progress has been made in the quality of education for African American children, yet inadequacies remain in the provision of resources for the education of African Americans. In recent years, efforts at creating alternative schools designed to meet the needs of African American children and to reflect the culture and social experiences of African Americans have received increased attention. In 1991 the Institute for Independent Education, an organization providing technical assistance to independent neighborhood schools, reported an estimated three hundred such schools serving children of color in the United States.

◆ CURRENT EDUCATIONAL TRENDS

Afrocentrism

An educational methodology that has sparked both widespread praise and criticism is Afrocentrism. Afrocentrism is based, in part, on the belief that the ancient Greeks stole most of their great philosophical and mathematical thought from the Egyptians, an African people, that the Greek philosopher Aristotle gleaned much of his philosophy from books plundered from the Egyptian city of Alexandria, and that the notable Greek philosopher Socrates was black. Afrocentrists claim that the current educational system in America is deeply flawed and promotes white supremacy. It teaches history, arts, science, and other disciplines from a purely traditional European point of view, while African contributions to these fields of endeavor are ignored entirely or given inadequate consideration. Proponents of Afrocentrism theorize that teaching African American children from an African-centered perspective through the championing of black culture, history, and achievement will increase their feelings of self-worth and give them a greater sense of identity and ethnic pride.

A principal with his students of the Malcolm X Academy, an Afrocentric school in Detroit, Michigan (Courtesy of Bruce Giffin).

The doctrine of Afrocentrism is not a new phenomenon. Such notable early twentieth century African Americans as activist Marcus Garvey and scholar Carter G. Woodson were among its most ardent supporters. Today, Afrocentrism is championed by African American scholars including, most prominently, Molefi K. Asante. Others include Leonard Jeffries, Asa Hillard, and, until his death, John Henrik Clark. Some public school systems with predominantly African American enrollment, such as Atlanta, New Orleans, Cleveland, Indianapolis, New York, Oakland, and Philadelphia have introduced African-centered principles to their curriculums.

Afrocentrism is not without its critics, however. Among them is Mary Lefkowitz, a professor of humanities at Wellesley College. In her book *Not Out of Africa: How Afrocentrism Became an Excuse to Teach Myth as History*, Lefkowitz disagrees with the assertions of Afrocentrists that the Greeks stole their philosophical and mathematical thought from the Egyptians or that Socrates was black. She argues that Afrocentrist beliefs are based on myth and conjecture, not historical fact and are designed to promote a political agenda. This criticism is echoed by Arthur Schlesinger, author of *The Disuniting of America*. Schlesinger remarks that African-centered education is divisive, un-American, and promotes the teaching of inaccuracy and distorted history.

Whether one is a supporter or critic, it is clear that Afrocentrism will continue to inspire heated debate for many years to come.

Ebonics

Black English, considered by some as a form of English and not a separate language, came to the forefront of discussion in 1996. While Black English has been explored as early as three decades ago, in 1996 some scholars renamed it Ebonics—a combination of the words ebony and phonics. Its roots are in the African languages that slaves brought to the United States. Some scholars further claim that Ebonics is "characterized by distinct grammar and syntax patterns such as the absence of forms of the verb 'to be.'" When the Oakland, California, school board passed a resolution in 1996 to make Ebonics a second language and declared that all of the teachers in the system should be trained to respect Ebonics—a form of speech spoken by many African American students a storm of criticism followed nationally. Opponents contended that Black English, or

Ebonics, was substandard grammar and, if regarded as a legitimate language, would be detrimental to African American students. The school board and the superintendent eventually rescinded the decision.

Abandoning Affirmative Action

National debate and actions in some states regarding affirmative action have impacted the education of African American students. The debate reached new heights in July 1995, when the California Board of Regents voted to remove race, gender, and ethnicity as criteria for admission to the system of higher education and to awarding contracts throughout the system. The *Hopwood v. Texas* ruling also had an impact on graduate school applications and admissions in California. This case held that race could not be used in deciding which applicants to accept for college and university admissions. Although the case is only binding as precedent in the 5th Circuit, it has had a national impact. Ultimately, California officials want academically diverse student bodies in the system, but challenge institutions to find another way to reach that goal.

During this period, affirmative action programs in other institutions, including medical schools, were challenged—a fact that alarmed educators and civil rights leaders. As a result, minority enrollment in medical schools across the nation declined. By January of 1998, however, California saw a small increase in applications from African Americans, Hispanic Americans, and other groups, partially reversing a sharp, two-year decline in such admissions.

Advocates of race-conscious admission policies, Derek Bok and William G. Bowen, completed a major study that challenges much of the conservative thinking about affirmative action. In their study *The Shape of the River: Long-Term Consequences of Considering Race in College and University Admissions*, the two scholars studied race-conscious admissions in elite higher education and confirmed that such practices "create the backbone of the black middle class."

Voucher Systems and Charter Schools

Some educators regard voucher programs and charter schools as "logical parts of a broad educational mix." The voucher idea originated forty years ago; it aimed to permit students to transfer from failing public schools to successful private schools. Critics feared, however, that the brightest students, both black and white, would be drawn away, leaving the inner-city schools, in terms of characteristics, African American and poor. Voucher systems have been initiated in a handful of cities, including Cleveland, Milwaukee, and Detroit, and are being considered in about half of the fifty states. The voucher programs that are operational serve low-income, largely African American and Hispanic American children.

Charter schools, or independent public schools, may be established by parents, community groups, local or state school boards, colleges and universities, or other individuals or groups. Some charter schools were once private schools, others were converted from existing public schools, and still others are newly established educational institutions. Generally, the schools report directly to the state and bypass local unions or other traditional bureaucracy. They are schools of choice for students and teachers; therefore, they must operate with the highest regard for equity and academic excellence. Supporters have little faith in traditional education systems and look to the charter schools as a viable solution to the problems of public school education. They see charter schools as a means of providing inner-city children the kind of education that students receive in the affluent suburbs. Some educators and parents see the charter school movement as another threat to public school education. By July of 1998, however, 33 states and the District of Columbia had passed charter school laws.

Single-Sex Schools

The nation has seen a number of incidences of single-sex schools opened in recent years. One such school opened in the fall of 1996, when the Young Women's Leadership School, an experimental public school for girls, opened in East Harlem. It emphasizes mathematics and science, subjects in which girls often lag behind boys in performance. The school provided for 56 seventh-grade girls and is expected to expand to grades ten through twelve by the fall of the year 2000. Advocates of the school based the need on studies that showed that girls, particularly from poor communities, performed better when boys were not present. Some groups, such as the New York Civil Liberties Union, challenged the school, however, arguing that it would violate the U.S. Constitution as well as the Federal statutory law. The group has challenged plans for other single-sex, single-race schools for young African American men in New York, Detroit, and Milwaukee.

Racial Isolation and Integration in Schools

Nearly a half-century after *Brown v. Board of Education of Topeka, Kansas* segregated public schools continue. Evidence of racial isolation in urban schools, as seen in Hartfort, Connecticut, in 1997, led the state's highest court to issue a mandate to desegregate the schools. Under the order, racially-isolated students in urban schools are able to enroll in predominantly white suburban schools on a space-available plan. The Connecticut decision seems to be running counter to the current trend to abandon racial "quotas" in schools, where predominance of one race is not necessarily grounds for legal relief unless the cause lies in segregation patterns of the past. The concern over affirmative action, however, is shifting from colleges and universities to public school districts. Districts that adopted voluntary desegregation plans, such as those in Montgomery County, Maryland, and Arlington, Virginia, wonder if they can continue race-conscious policies.

Desegregation orders imposed by the courts decades earlier are being lifted. In such cities as Nashville, Tennessee; Oklahoma City; Denver; Wilmington, Delaware; and Cleveland, courts have declared that past segregation practices have been remedied and judicial monitoring is no longer needed.

◆ ADMINISTRATORS, EDUCATORS, AND SCHOLARS

(To locate biographical profiles more readily, please consult the index at the back of the book.)

Molefi K. Asante (1942–)

Scholar

Molefi Kete Asante was born Arthur Lee Smith, Jr. on August 14, 1942, in Valdosta, Georgia. His name was legally changed to Molefi Kete Asante in 1973. In 1962, Asante graduated with an associate's degree from Southwestern Christian College. He graduated cum laude with a B.A. from Oklahoma Christian College in 1964, received an M.A. from Pepperdine University in 1965, and a Ph.D. from UCLA in 1968.

Asante has taught speech and communications at many universities in the United States. He was an instructor at California State Polytechnic University at Pomona (1966–1967) and California State University at Northridge (1967). In 1968 he accepted an assistant professorship at Purdue University in Lafayette, Indiana, where he remained until 1969 when he began teaching at UCLA. There he advanced from assistant to associate professor of speech and also served as the director of the Center for Afro-American Studies (1970–1973). In 1973 he accepted the position of professor of communications at the State University of New York. He soon became department chairman, a position he held until 1979 when he became a visiting professor at Howard University in Washington, DC (1979–1980). In 1981 and 1982, he was a Fulbright professor at the Zimbabwe Institute of Mass Communications. Since 1980, he has been a professor at Temple University in Philadelphia in the Department of African American Studies.

Asante is a prolific author with over 33 books dealing with both communication theory and the African American experience. Some of his most recent titles include: *Afrocentricity: The Theory of Social Change* (1980); *African Culture: The Rhythms of Unity* (1985); *The Afrocentric Idea* (1987); *Afrocentricity* (1987); *Kemet, Afrocentricity and Knowledge* (1990); *The Historical and Cultural Atlas of African-Americans* (1991); and *Fury in the Wilderness* (1993).

Molefi Kete Asante (Courtesy of Molefi Kete Asante)

Asante is also a founding editor of the *Journal of Black Studies* and has been a member of the advisory board of the *Black Law Journal* (1971–1973) and *Race Relations Abstract* (1973–1977). Asante has also served as the vice president for the National Council of Black Studies and the African Heritage Studies Association.

Maria Louise Baldwin (1856–1922)

Educator

Born on September 13, 1856 in Cambridge, Massachusetts, Maria Louise Baldwin was one of the most distinguished educators in the United States at the turn of the twentieth century. She was the principal of the Agassiz school in Cambridge, where children of affluent and established white families attended—a rarity for a woman and an African American.

Educated in Cambridge, Baldwin taught first in Chestertown, Maryland, and then was appointed teacher in Agassiz Grammar School. Eventually she taught all grades in the school—from first to the seventh—and in 1889 was promoted to school principal. In 1916, a new school was erected with more grades added and Baldwin's position was changed to master. She strengthened her credentials by enrolling in courses at nearby Harvard University. She remained at Agassiz until 1922.

Baldwin lectured throughout the country on such luminaries as Paul Lawrence Dunbar, Abraham Lincoln, and Thomas Jefferson and on women's suffrage, poetry, and history. During one of her lectures, she collapsed at Boston's Copley Plaza Hotel on January 9, 1922, and died suddenly. The entire nation mourned her death. About a year later, Aggasiz school recognized her by unveiling a tablet created in her memory. Other memorials followed, including the naming in her honor of the Aggasiz school auditorium and a women's residence center at Howard University in Washington, DC.

Lerone Bennett, Jr. (1928–)

Scholar

Born on October 17, 1928, in Clarksdale, Mississippi, Lerone Bennett, Jr. was educated at Morehouse College, receiving an A.B. in 1949. Bennett worked for the *Atlanta Daily World*, and *Jet* magazine before joining *Ebony* magazine in 1954. He was named executive editor in 1987. Beyond these positions though, Bennett has achieved fame for his essays and other writings.

His 1962 book *Before the Mayflower: A History of the Negro in America* made him one of the best-known and most influential African American historians of the twentieth century. *Before the Mayflower* was revised in 1982 and has been reprinted several times. Bennett's 1964 biography of Morehouse College classmate Martin Luther King, Jr., *What Manner of Man*, was welcomed as an evenhanded analysis of the African American leader's life and his role in fundamentally changing the nature of racial dynamics in the United States. Also in 1964, Bennett published *The Negro Mood and Other Essays*, a collection of essays that demonstrated a sharper editorial bite than his previous works. Probing such issues as the failed integration of African Americans into American life and the ways in which African Americans are denied the fruits of society, Bennett takes aim at the white liberal establishment for ignoring the accomplishments of African Americans and for just mouthing the words of racial justice rather acting on that creed. Bennett has also produced a number of other works including *Pioneers in Protest* (1968), *The Shaping of Black America* (1974), and *Wade in the Water: Great Moments in Black History* (1979).

Mary McLeod Bethune (Courtesy of Carl Van Vechten)

Bennett served as a visiting professor at Northwestern University in 1968–1969. In addition, he was a senior fellow of the Institute of the Black World in 1969.

Mary McLeod Bethune (1875–1955)

Founder, Educator

Born on July 10, 1875, near Mayesville, South Carolina, Mary McLeod received a sporadic education in local schools. She eventually received a scholarship and studied for seven years at the Scotia Seminary in Concord, North Carolina. In 1893 she went on to study at the Moody Bible Institute in Chicago in lieu of a missionary position in Africa. In 1895 she began teaching at the Haines Institute in Augusta, Georgia. Between 1900 and 1904, she taught in Sumter, Georgia, and Palatka, Florida.

In 1904 she founded her own school in Daytona Beach, Florida—the Daytona Educational and Industrial School for Negro Girls. John D. Rockefeller became an early admirer and supporter of the school after hearing a performance by its choir. Bethune went on to found the Tomoka Missions and, in 1911, the McLeod Hospital. In 1922 her school merged with the Cookman Institute to become Bethune-Cookman College.

Bethune's work received national attention, and she served on two conferences under President Herbert Hoover. In 1936 President Franklin Roosevelt appointed her director of the Division of Negro Affairs of the National Youth Administration. During World War II, she served as special assistant to the Secretary of War, responsible for selecting WAC officer candidates of African American descent.

Bethune also served on the executive board of the National Urban League and was a vice president of the NAACP. She received the Spingarn Award in 1935, the Frances A. Drexel Award in 1936, and the Thomas Jefferson Medal in 1942. Bethune was also instrumental in the founding of the National Council of Negro Women. She retired from public life in 1950 on her seventy-fifth birthday and died five years later on May 18, 1955.

Much of Bethune's philosophy concerned ennobling labor and empowering African Americans to achieve economic independence. Although a tireless fighter for equality, she eschewed rhetorical militancy in favor of a doctrine of universal love.

Charlotte Hawkins Brown (1883–1961)
Founder, Educator, Civic Leader

Charlotte Hawkins Brown was a pioneer in quality preparatory education for African American youth. She set her ideas and experiments in place at the Palmer Memorial Institute, which she founded in Sedalia, North Carolina, and headed for more than half a century.

Born Lottie Hawkins on June 11, 1883, in Henderson, North Carolina, Hawkins was the granddaughter of slaves. She and 18 members of her family moved to Cambridge, Massachusetts, in 1888 in search of better social and educational opportunities. By the time of her graduation from Cambridge English School, she had changed her name to Charlotte Eugenia Hawkins. In 1900 she enrolled in State Normal School in Salem, Massachusetts, and left in October 1901, to teach at the American Missionary Association's Bethany Institute near McLeansville, North Carolina. The school closed at the end of the year. Hawkins returned to Cambridge in 1902 and discussed with benefactor Alice Freeman Palmer, whom she met at the end of her high school studies, her plan to start a school in Sedalia, North Carolina. Palmer and other Northern philanthropists provided Hawkins funds for the school and on October 10, 1902, Hawkins founded a school, the Alice Freeman Palmer Institute, which she named in honor of her friend. After Palmer died that fall, the school was renamed Palmer Memorial Institute and was incorporated on November 23, 1907. By then Hawkins had a diploma from Salem Normal School, had studied at Harvard University and Wellesley and Simmons colleges, and married Edward Sumner Brown.

By 1916, the school was housed in four buildings. Fires in 1917 and 1922 destroyed two buildings; one of these, Memorial Hall, was replaced in 1922 with the Alice Freeman Palmer Building. By 1922 the school had built a fine reputation as one of the country's leading preparatory schools for African Americans. The junior college academic program that focused on agricultural and vocational training that Brown introduced in the mid-1920s gave way to secondary and post-secondary education. Later on the school also emphasized good manners and social graces as it prepared youth to assume positions in society. The school's presence, already felt strongly in the South, was now known across the country and students responded by enrolling in the institute in greater numbers. In 1922, Palmer graduated its first high school class.

Brown emerged as a national leader and was recognized for her work in directing the institute as well as her strong resolve in advancing the life of African Americans and African American women in particular. She was a staunch public opponent of lynching. She was an organizer of the North Carolina State Federation of Negro Women's Clubs and was also active in the National African American Women's Club Movement. She persuaded the state to establish homes for African American young women who were in legal difficulty, such as the Efland Home for Wayward Girls. As president of the North Carolina Teachers Association from 1935 to 1937, she helped effect change in the education of the state's African American residents. She was a key figure in the Southern interracial women's movement and also was the first African American member in the Twentieth Century Club of Boston.

Brown became known for her writings as well. Her works included *Mammy: An Appeal to the Heart of the South* and *The Correct Thing to Do, to Say, and to Wear*. The latter work, originally used as a guide for Palmer's students, attracted the attention of young people across the country and was reprinted five times.

After fifty years of service, Brown retired as president of Palmer on October 5, 1952, but remained on campus until 1955 as vice-chairman of the board of trustees and director of finances. Wilhelmina Marguerite Crosson replaced Brown as president. By the end of the decade, the school enrolled annually about two hundred junior and senior students who came from across the country, the Caribbean, and Africa.

Brown died in Greensboro on January 11, 1961, and was buried at the front of the Palmer campus. Although Brown's spirit and ideals continued for a while, the school began to suffer from declining enrollment, rising cost of maintenance, and reduced support from benefactors. Another fire in 1971 destroyed the Alice Freeman Palmer Building. In November of that year, Bennett

College in nearby Greensboro assumed the institute's debts and took over the site. The home that Brown had built on campus, Canary Cottage, has been preserved and, in 1983, was declared a state historic site. It was declared a national historic landmark in 1988. The institute's campus was designated a state historic site in the previous year.

Nannie Helen Burroughs (1879–1961)
Educator

Born in Orange Springs, Virginia, on May 2, 1879, Nannie Helen Burroughs was one of the most significant Baptist lay leaders of the twentieth century, a lifelong booster of women's education, and a tireless civic organizer. She addressed the National Baptist Convention in Virginia in 1900 on the subject "How the Sisters are Hindered from Helping" and, from that time until her death more than sixty years later, she exercised pivotal leadership. She was elected corresponding secretary for the Woman's Convention, Auxiliary to the National Baptist Convention, U.S.A., Inc., and in 1948 she became president of the Women's Convention.

In 1901 Burroughs founded and presided over the National Training School for Women and Girls, which emphasized industrial arts and proficiency in African American history. After only one year, she had recruited 31 students. In honor of her efforts, the school's curriculum was changed to accommodate elementary education, and its name was changed to the Nannie Helen Burroughs School.

Nannie Helen Burroughs (Schomburg Center for Research in Black Culture)

Burroughs was active in the anti-lynching campaign and a life member of the Association for the Study of Negro Life and History. She helped organize the Women's Industrial Club of Louisville and was responsible for organizing Washington, DC's first African American self-help program. She also edited such periodicals as the *Christian Banner* and was the author of *Roll Call of Bible Women*. She died on May 20, 1961.

Joe Clark (1939–)
Former Educator Lecturer Executive Director

Best known as the feisty, dedicated, baseball bat-wielding school principal portrayed by actor Morgan Freeman in the film *Lean on Me*, Clark has served as an exemplar of school discipline and boasts a distinguished record of achievements and laurels. A 14-year member of the New Jersey Board of Education and an elementary and secondary school principal until 1989, he has been honored by the White House, the NAACP, his alma mater Seton Hall University, and various newspapers and magazines.

Born in Rochelle, Georgia, in 1939, Clark served in the United States Army Reserve from 1958 to 1966. He received a B.A. from New Jersey's William Paterson College in 1960 and his master's degree from Seton Hall in 1974. From 1960 to 1974, Clark served on the board of education in Paterson, New Jersey. He was a coordinator of language arts from 1976 until 1979. Clark became a school principal for the first time in 1979 and quickly earned the admiration and respect of educators for his somewhat controversial, no-nonsense managerial style. In 1983, Clark received the NAACP Community Service Award and was named New Jerseyan of the Year by the *Newark Star Ledger*. The following year, *New Jersey Monthly* honored Clark as outstanding educator. In 1985, Clark appeared in Washington, DC, to receive honors at a presidential conference on academic and disciplinary excellence and also gained awards from Seton Hall and Farleigh Dickinson University. The National School Safety Center gave Clark the Principal of Leadership award in 1986, and the National Black Policemen's Association bestowed their Humanitarian Award upon him in 1988.

In 1989, Clark ended his tenure as principal of Eastside High School in Paterson, New Jersey, and traveled the country as a lecturer. He accepted a job as the director

Joe Clark (AP/Wide World Photos, Inc.)

of the Essex County, New Jersey, Youth House, a juvenile detention center in Newark, in August of 1995.

Kenneth Clark (1914–)
Psychologist, Educator, Writer

Born on July 24, 1914, in the Panama Canal Zone, Clark was brought to the United States as a youth by his mother so that he could be educated. He was educated in Harlem and then attended Howard University. He was awarded a B.A. in 1935 and an M.S. in 1936 in psychology. In 1940 he became the first African American awarded a Ph.D. in psychology from Columbia University. He then taught at the Hampton Institute, but left due to its conservative views, moving to City College of New York in 1942, an institution he was to remain at for the rest of his academic career.

Clark was deeply troubled by school segregation and studied its effects with his wife, the former Mamie Phipps. Clark came to the attention of the NAACP during its post-war campaign to overturn legalized segregation. Clark was intimately involved in the long legal struggle which culminated in *Brown v. Board of Education of Topeka, Kansas.* He testified as an expert witness at three of the four cases leading up to the Supreme Court's review of *Brown v. Board of Education* and his report on the psychology of segregation was read carefully by the justices. *Brown v. Board of Education* was not only a milestone in the modern Civil Rights movement, it also made Kenneth Clark into something of an academic superstar. Clark went on to become the most influential African American social scientist of his generation.

In the 1960s Clark was involved with the Great Society's unsuccessful HARYOU program in New York and the MARC Corp.'s program in Washington, DC. Both were efforts to improve integration of public schools and to set test score-based standards for schools and teachers. Both projects, however, were terminated by politics.

In 1975 Clark retired from CCNY and formed his own advisory company to counsel companies on integrating their workforces. Clark has continued to write vehemently on the subject of integration.

Septima Clark (1898–1987)
Educator, Civil Rights Activist

In her unassuming, workmanlike way, Septima Clark made a major impact on the voting rights of thousands of African American Southerners, though many Americans have never heard of her. Clark dedicated her life to education and drove home through her actions a simple concept in which she believed, namely, that before one could get people to register and vote, one had to teach them to read and write. Born on May 3, 1898, in Charleston, South Carolina, Clark was a schoolteacher for most of her life. She dedicated her entire career to educating her community.

In 1937 Clark studied under W. E. B. Du Bois at Atlanta University. She later went on to receive her B.A. at Benedict College in 1942, and her M.A. from Hampton Institute four years later. After teaching for nearly ten years in the Charleston school system, Clark began the "citizenship schools" program, through her position at Tennessee's Highlander Folk School, a center for civil organizing and dialogue in 1956. These citizenship schools taught people to write their names, balance check books, fill out a voting ballot, and understand their rights and duties as U.S. citizens. The schools were a success, and by 1961, had grown too big for Highlander to handle. The Southern Christian Leadership Conference (SCLC) expressed an interest in taking over, so Clark went to work for the SCLC as director of education.

After retiring from the SCLC in 1970, Clark stayed active in civil rights struggles. In 1974, at the age of 76,

Clark was elected to serve on the Charleston school board—the same school board that had fired her twenty years earlier for her active involvement with the NAACP. She died in Charleston on December 15, 1987.

Johnnetta B. Cole (1936–)
Spelman College President

A distinguished scholar, Johnnetta Cole has served on the faculties of Washington State University, University of Massachusetts-Amherst, Hunter College, and Spelman College, the historically African American women's institution in Atlanta. Born in Jacksonville, Florida, on October 19, 1936, Cole attended Oberlin College, which awarded her a B.A. in 1957. She went on to earn her master's and doctorate degrees at Northwestern in 1959 and 1967, respectively.

In 1967, Cole began her first teaching assignment at Washington State University, where she taught anthropology and served as director of black studies. The university honored her as Outstanding Faculty Member of the Year for 1969–1970. From 1970 until 1983, Cole was professor of anthropology and African American studies at the University of Massachusetts-Amherst. She left the University of Massachusetts-Amherst in 1983 for a position as professor of anthropology at Hunter College of the City of New York. Cole also served as director of Latin American and Caribbean studies at Hunter College from 1984 until 1987. In 1987, Cole was named president of Spelman College. She retired in 1997 and currently holds a professorship at Emory University in Atlanta.

As an anthropologist, Cole has done field work in Liberia, Cuba, and in the African American community. A prolific writer, she has published in many mainstream periodicals as well as scholarly journals. Since 1979 she has been a contributor and advising editor to *The Black Scholar*. Her most recent book *Conversations: Straight Talk with America's Sister President*, was published in 1993. She is a member of the National Council of Negro Women and a fellow of the American Anthropological Association.

Cole has received numerous awards and honorary degrees. She was presented with the Elizabeth Boyer Award in 1988 and the Essence Award in Education in 1989. In 1990, Cole won the American Women Award, the Jessie Bernard Wise Woman Award, and was inducted into the Working Woman Hall of Fame. In 1994, she received the Jewish National Fund's highest honor, the Tree of Life Award, which is named for the efforts of the Jewish National Fund to reclaim and develop barren land in Israel.

Marva Delores Nettles Collins (1936–)
Educator

Marva Delores Nettles Collins was born in Monroeville, Alabama, on August 31, 1936. She received a bachelor's degree from Clark College in 1957 and pursued graduate studies at Chicago Teachers College and Columbia University from 1965 until 1967.

Collins' teaching career began at the Monroe County Training School in her hometown in 1958. She taught at Chicago's Delano Elementary School from 1960 until 1975. In 1975, Collins founded the Westside Preparatory School in Chicago and currently serves as its director.

Collins has conducted educational workshops throughout the United States and Europe, and has appeared on several television programs including "60 Minutes," "Good Morning America," and "The Phil Donahue Show." She has served as director of the Right to Read Foundation and has been a member of the President's Commission on White House Fellowships since 1981. Collins has also been a consultant to the National Department of Children, Youth, and Family Services and a council member of the National Institute of Health.

A number of organizations have honored Collins for her distinguished career including the NAACP, the Reading Reform Foundation, the Fred Hampton Foundation, the Chicago Urban League, the United Negro College Fund, Phi Delta Kappa, and the American Institute for Public Service. Among the institutions that have given her honorary degrees are Washington University, Amherst College, Dartmouth University, Chicago State University, Howard University, and Central State University.

Anna Julia Cooper (1858/59–1964)
Educator, Writer, Activist

Anna Julia Cooper was a strong proponent of justice, equality for women, and racial uplift. She was born on August 10, 1858 or 1859, in Raleigh, North Carolina, to a slave mother; her father was possibly the slave owner. Cooper attended Saint Augustine's Normal School and Collegiate Institute (now Saint Augustine's College) in Raleigh and became a teacher at the school when she graduated. She was married briefly to George A. C. Cooper, who died in 1879.

Cooper graduated from Oberlin College in Ohio in 1884, then taught modern languages at Wilberforce University in 1884–1985. The next year she returned to Saint Augustine's and taught mathematics, Latin, and German. In 1888 she received an M.A. degree in mathematics from Oberlin and moved to Washington, DC, where she taught at the Preparatory High School for Colored Youth and was school principal from 1902 to

1906. The school later became the M Street High School, then the Paul Laurence Dunbar High School. She protested the board of education's plan to dilute the school's curriculum and was removed from the principalship. She chaired the languages department at Lincoln University in Missouri from 1906 to 1910, then returned to the M Street School as Latin teacher. On March 23, 1925, at age 66, she successfully defended her doctoral dissertation at the Sorbonne and became the fourth African American woman to earn a doctorate and the first woman to do so in France.

Cooper also became established as a lecturer and writer. As early as 1890, while teaching full-time, she lectured to groups of educators and African American women's groups. In 1900 she lectured on "The Negro Problem in America" at the first Pan-African Conference, then toured Europe. As a writer, she is best known for *A Voice from the South* (1892); the work marked her as a dedicated feminist and advocate for the African American race. Anna Cooper died on February 27, 1964, when she was 105 years old.

Fanny Coppin (1837–1913)
Educator

Fanny Coppin was born into slavery in 1837 and rose to prominence in the field of education. After her aunt purchased her freedom, Coppin went on to become the second African American woman to receive a degree from Oberlin College.

In 1865, Coppin was appointed principal of the women's department of the Institute for Colored Youth, a high school established by Quakers in 1837, and later principal of the entire school. In 1894 Coppin founded the Women's Exchange and Girls' Home. She served as president of the local Women's Mite Missionary Society and the Women's Home and Foreign Missionary Society and as a vice president of the National Association of Colored Women.

Coppin, an active member of the African Methodist Episcopal Church, served as president of the AME Home Missionary Society and accompanied her husband, Levi J. Coppin, on a missionary venture to South Africa.

Before her death at her Philadelphia home on January 21, 1913, Coppin began writing an autobiography *Reminiscences of School Life, and Hints on Teaching.*

Delores E. Cross (1938–)
Educational Administrator

Born on August 29, 1938, in Newark, New Jersey, Delores Cross grew up to become the first African American female president of a Illinois state university, when she was appointed the position at Chicago State University. In 1999 she became president of Morris Brown College in Atlanta, Georgia. A veteran educator with more than twenty years of experience, Cross pursued her own education at three prestigious institutions: Seton Hall University, from which she received a B.A. in elementary education in 1963; Hofstra University, from which she earned a master's degree in 1968; and the University of Michigan, from which she garnered a doctorate in 1971. Contact with a fourth well-reputed institution came in 1970, when she began a four-year stint as an assistant professor at Northwestern University.

In 1974, Cross joined the Claremont Graduate School as director of teacher education. After three years, she moved to New York City, where she served as vice chancellor for student affairs and special programs at City University of New York, then spent most of the 1980s as president of the New York State Higher Education Service Corporation. From 1988 to 1990, she was associate provost and associate vice president for academic affairs at the University of Minnesota. Then, in 1990, she was called to the predominantly African American Chicago State University, (CSU) with a dropout rate of 81 percent among enrolled freshman students.

Faced with such a daunting statistic—particularly since nearly one-third of all African American students in Illinois' public institutions attend CSU—Cross embarked on an ambitious program to turn the situation around. She created a model for success for the students, with one of the main tenets being the maintenance of pre-college initiatives going all the way back to elementary school-level children. Meanwhile, improvements to the actual facilities included first-time plans for residence halls and the addition of a $30 million science center. The latter is of grave importance since, in 1993, CSU boasted a nearly one hundred percent pass rate for nursing school graduates and the same percentage acceptance rate amongst graduate entrants to medical schools. Meanwhile, enrollment increased 58 percent during Cross's tenure, making CSU the only public university in the state to have significant growth.

Cross left Chicago State in 1997; later she was granted the GE Fund Distinguished Professorship in Leadership and Diversity at the City University of New York Graduate School and University Center. She took over the helm at Morris Brown College in 1999.

Throughout her career, Cross has been the recipient of several awards including honorary doctorates from Marymount Manhattan (1984) and Skidmore College (1988), the NAACP's Muriel Siverberg Award (1987), and the New York State Commission of Independent Colleges and Universities' John Jay Award (1989).

Howard Dodson, Jr. (1939–)
Historian, Educator, Curator

Born in Chester, Pennsylvania, on June 1, 1939, Howard Dodson, Jr. was always at or near the top of his class throughout junior high and high school. Out of 89 students at Chester High School, Dodson was one of nine who graduated from college. In 1961, he received a bachelor's of science from West Chester State College and, in 1964, he received a master's degree in history and political science from Villanova University. In 1964, driven by an interest in African people transplanted in the Western Hemisphere, Dodson worked in Ecuador as a member of the U.S. Peace Corps.

In 1969, Dodson entered the doctoral program in Black History and Race Relations at the University of California at Berkeley after spending one year in Puerto Rico. During that time, Dodson studied the socio-political factors behind the Civil Rights and Black Power movements of the time. As part of his doctoral studies, Dodson earned a position at the Institute of the Black World, a research branch of the Martin Luther King, Jr. Center for Nonviolent Social Change in Atlanta. Dodson served as director of the Institute from 1974 to 1979.

Dodson's doctoral dissertation "The Political Economy in South Carolina: 1780–1830" demonstrates that African American slave workers were not victims of their circumstances but rather contributors to a complex socio-economic system. In addition to his dissertation, Dodson has written widely on the subject of African American history. He served as editor-in-chief of *Black World View* magazine in 1977, and he has published books including *Thinking and Rethinking U.S. History* (1988), a book for children written with Madelon Bedell, and *Black Photographers Bear Witness: 100 Years of Social Protest* (1989), a book published by Williams College Museum of Art on which he collaborated with Deborah Willis.

In 1984, Dodson took a post as the head of the Schomburg Center for Research in Black Culture at the New York Public Library. In 1991, due to his ministrations and fund-raising, the Schomburg Center opened an expanded complex. Dodson has served as consultant to the National Endowment for the Humanities, the African American Museums Association, the Library of Congress, the U.S. Department of Education, the Congressional Black Caucus, and the National Council of Churches. He won the Association for the Study of Afro-American Life and History Service Award in 1976 and a Governor's Award for African Americans of Distinction in 1982.

Sarah Mapps Douglass (1806–1882)
Educator

The free-born Sarah Mapps Douglass was an outspoken anti-slavery activist and accomplished educator. She attended the Ladies Institute of the Pennsylvania Medical University. In the 1820s she organized a school for African American children in Philadelphia.

Douglass was an active member of the Philadelphia Female Anti-Slavery Society, which also provided support to Douglass's school. Moreover, she served as vice chairman of the Freedman's Aid Society and was a member of the New York Anti-Slavery Women.

In 1853 Douglass was appointed head of the girls' department at the Institute of Colored Youth (forerunner of Cheney State College). She remained there until her retirement in 1877. Douglass died in Philadelphia on September 8, 1882.

Michael Eric Dyson (1958–)
Eduoator and Writor

Michael Eric Dyson was born into a middle-class family in Detroit, Michigan, in 1958. He was ordained as a Baptist minister and attended divinity school at Tennessee's Knoxville College, ultimately earning a bachelor's degree in 1982 from Carson-Newman College. Three years later, he accepted a graduate fellowship at Princeton University, obtaining his master's and doctorate degrees by 1993. Dyson went on to become an assistant professor at Brown University. A non-traditional scholar, he chose to target his interests to a larger audience. Dyson reviewed books and films for newspapers, contributed record reviews to *Rolling Stone*, and became a columnist for *Christian Century* and *The Nation*. *Reflecting Black: African- American Cultural Criticism*, Dyson's first book-length collection of essays, addressed African American pop culture icons.

In 1994 Dyson published *Making Malcolm: The Myth and Meaning of Malcolm X*. The book was written in response to a confrontation with some of Dyson's African American male students at Brown University who objected to the presence of whites in his course on the radical Muslim leader. True to his goal of reaching beyond the scholarly community, Dyson's book was deliberately marketed to a wide, youthful readership. In his third book *Between God and Gangsta Rap*, Dyson attempted to put gangsta rap in its cultural and social perspective and established himself as an authority. As a result, he was asked to testify on the genre before a congressional subcommittee, gained popularity as a lecturer, and became a sought-after guest on talk shows. Dyson has been considered one of a group of "new intellectuals." In 1996, he headed the Institute of African American Research at the University of North Carolina in Chapel Hill and continued to address issues of race and culture in both scholarly and popular publications.

John Hope Franklin (1915–)

Scholar

Franklin's long and distinguished career includes the publication of numerous books of history and biography, several awards and honorary degrees, and a position of great stature in the scholarly community, and as a leader of a national dialogue about race.

Franklin was born in Rentiesville, Oklahoma, in 1915. He received his bachelor's degree from Fisk University in 1935 and then began graduate work at Harvard, which awarded him a master's in 1936 and a Ph.D. in 1941. He taught history at Fisk and St. Augustine's College while working on his doctorate, later moving on to North Carolina College at Durham, Howard University, Brooklyn College (where he chaired the history department), Cambridge University, the University of Chicago, and Duke University.

Among his many publications are such books as *From Slavery to Freedom, A History of Negro Americans, Militant South, Reconstruction After the Civil War, The Emancipation Proclamation, A Southern Odyssey, Race and History: Selected Essays*, and *The Color Line: Legacy for the Twenty-First Century.*

Twice a Guggenheim Fellow, Franklin received honors from the Fellowship of Southern Writers, Encyclopedia Britannica and many other organizations, was made professor emeritus of history at Duke, and earned the Publications Prize of the American Studies Association established in his name in 1986. Franklin has received of over ninety honorary degrees. In 1995, President Clinton awarded Franklin the Presidential Medal of Freedom, America's highest civilian honor.

In 1997 President Clinton named Franklin as chair of the White House Initiative on Race and Reconciliation, a position that enabled him to lead a year-long dialogue on race held in cities across the nation.

E. Franklin Frazier (1894–1962)

Educator, Sociologist, Activist

E. Franklin Frazier left a thirty-year legacy of research and writings on the African American family, youth, the church, and middle class. He combined theory with practice, and his work remains an authoritative source for later generations of scholars.

Born on September 24, 1894, in Baltimore, Maryland, Frazier attended the segregated schools of Baltimore and graduated from the Colored High School. On scholarship, he entered Howard University in Washington, DC, and used income from odd jobs to support his college career. He graduated cum laude in 1915 and a few months later began teaching mathematics at Tuskegee Institute (now Tuskegee University) in Alabama. He left two years later and taught at various African American schools and colleges. After spending some time in military service, he enrolled in Clark University in Worcester, Massachusetts, and graduated in 1920 with a master's degree in sociology.

Frazier was an American Scandinavian Foundation fellow from 1921 to 1922. In the fall of 1922, he moved to Atlanta and held a dual position as director of the School of Social Work and professor of sociology at Morehouse College. He remained productive in research and writing during his Atlanta years. He moved to Chicago and studied full-time for his doctorate at the University of Chicago. In 1929 he moved to Fisk University in Nashville, Tennessee, and in 1931 completed his Ph.D. dissertation "The Negro Family in Chicago," which was regarded as a landmark study. Frazier left Fisk in 1934 and moved to Howard University in Washington, DC, where he remained for 28 years as head of the Department of Sociology. While at Fisk and Howard, he also added to his body of research and writing. Prominent among his publications were *The Negro in the United States* (1949) and his most controversial book *Black Bourgeoise* (1955 and 1957).

Frazier later headed UNESCO's Division of Applied Sciences for two years and traveled and lectured abroad as well. He retired from Howard University as professor emeritus in 1959, but continued to teach there and at Johns Hopkins School of Advanced International Studies. Frazier died on May 17, 1962; his book *The Negro Church in America* was published posthumously that year.

Henry Louis Gates, Jr. (1950–)

Literary Scholar, Educator, Critic

Henry Louis Gates, Jr. was born on September 16, 1950, in Keyser, West Virginia. He was summa cum laude in 1973 at Yale University, where he earned a bachelor's in history. He went on to receive a master's in 1974 and a Ph.D. in 1979, from Clare College, Cambridge University. He served as a staff correspondent for *Time* magazine in London until 1975. There he studied with Nobel laureate playwright Wole Soyinka of Nigeria. His post-graduate studies examined African American literature as it has derived from the traditions of Africa and the Caribbean. He returned to the U.S. as a guest lecturer for Yale periodically from 1976 to 1979.

In 1979, Gates accepted an assistant professorship in the English department at Yale, where he served as director of the undergraduate Afro-American studies department until 1985. In 1981, the MacArthur Foundation awarded him $150,000 for his critical essays about African American literature. When he republished Harriet E. Wilson's *Our Nig*in 1983, he vaulted to the top of the world of African American scholarship. He has also been a Rockefeller Foundation fellow and has enjoyed grants from the National Endowment for the Humanities. During this time, he created the PBS television series *The Image of the Black in the Western Imagination*, which aired in 1982. From 1985 to 1990, he served as a professor of English and African Studies at Cornell University and as a W. E. B. Du Bois Professor of Literature at Duke University from 1988 to 1990. He moved to Harvard in 1990, where he was named W. E. B. Du Bois Professor in the Humanities, and in 1991 became chair of the Department of African American Studies.

In 1989, Gates won the American Book Award for *The Signifying Monkey* and an Ainsfield-Wolfe Book Award the same year for *Towards a Theory of Afro-American Literary Criticism.* In 1994, Gates's memoir *Colored People* was published; the work encompasses his experiences growing up in rural West Virginia. In 1996, Gates earned prestige for his African American studies department by attracting some of the country's leading scholars to Harvard. In addition, Gates and Kwame Appiah edited *Encarta Africana*, a multimedia encyclopedia on compact disc released in January 1999.

William L. Hansberry (1894–1965)

Historian, Educator

William Leo Hansberry was born on February 25, 1894, in Gloster, Mississippi. He earned a bachelor's in anthropology in 1921. Determined to eliminate American ethnocentrism regarding Africa, he issued a manifesto to African American schools and colleges titled "Announcing an Effort to Promote the Study and Facilitate the Teaching of the Fundamentals of Negro Life and History." The flier brought Hansberry three job offers from schools, and he accepted a post at Howard University in Washington, DC. Beginning in 1922, he began designing courses on African and African American history.

Despite Hansberry's ability to prove the material taught in his courses, the board of Howard University pulled his financial backing after spurious accusations by colleagues but agreed to keep the African studies program in place. Still, the scuffle cost him much in funds and promotions. Nevertheless, in 1932, Hansberry returned to Harvard to complete his master's in anthropology and history, continuing his studies in the mid-1930s at the University of Chicago's Oriental Institute. His studies won him a Rockefeller Foundation grant that allowed him to study at Oxford University in England from 1937 to 1938, when Howard University finally recognized his achievements with an assistant professorship. But entrenched racial prejudice kept Hansberry from earning more grants and fellowships to continue his work.

Howard University made little effort to compensate him and after over twenty years of service, he remained only an associate professor in 1945. But then the university climate changed and Hansberry was appointed advisor to African students in 1946; in 1950, he was made Emergency Aid to the African Students' Committee at Howard University in addition to his teaching load. Due to increased interest in African studies, Hansberry won a Fulbright scholarship to lecture at Cairo University and to study in Egypt, Ethiopia, and the Sudan in 1953. He also visited Kenya, Uganda, and Zimbabwe. Hansberry died in Chicago on November 3, 1965.

bell hooks (1952–)

Social Activist, Educator, Writer

Feminist educator bell hooks has done her most important work as a teacher in programs that allow a critique of racism that was absent during her own undergraduate years. She contributes essays to a variety of scholarly journals and also publishes fiction and poetry. hooks has gained notoriety as a writer of critical essays on systems of domination, making herself a prominent name in feminist debate. Her titles include: *Talking Back: Thinking Feminist, Thinking Black* (1989); *Black Looks: Race and Representation* (1992); *Killing Rage: Ending Racism* (1995); and *Black Is a Woman's Color* (1996).

Born Gloria Jean Watkins in 1952, hooks grew up with five siblings in Hopkinsville, a small town in rural Kentucky. Despite her family's poverty and hardship, hooks reveled in lessons of diligence and community. She attended segregated public schools, where her role models were single African American female teachers. Verbally and through poetry, hooks began defiantly resisting the sexism she perceived within her neighborhood. Rejecting her expected role as an obedient Southern girl, the writer eventually adopted a pseudonym to represent a new sense of self—a woman who spoke her mind and was not afraid to talk back.

When she won a scholarship to Stanford University, hooks sought out intellectual and political affirmation from the campus feminist movement. Disillusioned and alienated by the absence of material by or discussion about African American women, hooks began criticizing the persistent racism within feminism. Having gained her bachelor's degree in 1973, hooks faced obstacles at the University of Wisconsin and the University of California at Santa Cruz, where male faculty members were determined to prevent her from becoming a university professor. In 1981, hooks published *Ain't I a Woman: Black Women and Feminism*, which was sharply criticized for its defiance of academic convention. Nonetheless, the work became central to discussions of racism and sexism. hooks persisted with her studies, earned a Ph.D. in 1983, and went on to teach African American and women's studies at Yale University, Oberlin College, and City College of New York.

John Hope (1868–1936)
Educator, Activist

The progress made in higher education for African American students has been strongly helped by the efforts of John Hope. His life was committed to improving the school system of his time to afford more minority access. Hope was one of the most influential leaders of his time in the field of higher education.

In 1894, Hope graduated from Brown University in Worcester, Massachusetts, and was elected class orator for the commencement service. In later years, Hope would receive an honorary master of arts and law degree from Brown, along with being admitted into the Phi Beta Kappa Society. Upon graduating, Hope accepted a teaching job at Roger Williams University in Nashville, Tennessee. Four years later he accepted a teaching position at Atlanta Baptist College, located in Georgia, the state of his birth. At the college, Hope began a longtime friendship with the educator W. E. B. Du Bois. They both attended the 1895 Macon Convention which turned into the Georgia Equal Rights Convention.

In 1906, John Hope became acting president of Atlanta Baptist College, and the next year he was named president. He was the first African American to be appointed president at a Baptist school. As president, Hope expanded the college with funds donated by John T. Rockefeller and Andrew Carnegie. In 1913, the school was renamed Morehouse College and was very progressive in its stressing of the dignity of its African American students. During the 1920s, the college continued to expand as Hope developed the Atlanta School of Social Work.

In 1929, Hope fulfilled his lifelong ambition to establish a formal relationship among Atlanta's African American schools by having the Atlanta University Affiliation signed by the presidents of Atlanta University, Spelman, and Morehouse College. Hope was appointed president of Atlanta University while continuing as president of Morehouse College. Hope received the Harmon Award in 1930 for distinguished achievement in education. He died in Atlanta on February 20, 1936.

Charles S. Johnson (1893–1956)
Scholar

Charles Spurgeon Johnson was born in Bristol, Virginia, in 1893. He earned a B.A. from Virginia Union University and worked on a Ph.D. at the University of Chicago.

Johnson occupied a number of diverse positions, from editor to administrator. He served as the assistant executive secretary of the Chicago Commission on Race Relations and as research director of the National Urban League, where he founded the organization's journal *Opportunity*.

In 1928 Johnson was made chairman of Fisk University's Department of Social Sciences. While at Fisk he established the Fisk Institute of Race Relations. In 1933 he was appointed director of Swarthmore College's Institute of Race Relations. In 1946 Johnson was appointed president of Fisk University—the first African American to hold the position.

Johnson wrote several books before his death on October 27, 1956, including *The Negro in American Civilization* (1930), *The Economic Status of the Negro* (1933), *The Negro College Graduate* (1936), and *Educational and Cultural Crisis* (1951).

Mordecai W. Johnson (1890–1976)
Former College President, Minister

As president of Howard University in Washington, DC, for 34 years, Mordecai W. Johnson became a highly respected minister, educator, and orator of international note. He built the university into a highly visible academic institution that became known as the "Capstone of Negro Education."

Johnson was the son of former slaves. He was born in Paris, Tennessee, on December 12, 1890, and attended Roger Williams University in Nashville and the Howe Institute in Memphis, both of which are now defunct. He transferred to Atlanta Baptist College, now known as Morehouse College, where he completed the secondary and undergraduate programs. He taught at the college for a year, then continued his studies at the University of Chicago where he received a second undergraduate degree. Johnson earned his bachelor of divinity degree from Rochester Theological Seminary in Rochester, New York.

He was pastor of the First Baptist Church in Charleston, West Virginia, for nine years. In 1912 he took a leave of absence to study at Harvard University Divinity School graduating in June of 1922. In 1926, when he was 36-years old, Johnson was elected 11th president and the first African American president of Howard University. Johnson first concentrated on providing financial stability for the school. Starting with the medical school, he received solid support from the Julius Rosenwald Fund and the General Education Board. Then he moved to strengthen the law school and appointed Charles Hamilton Houston as dean of the school; he approached the country's top law schools for recommendations for Howard's law school faculty. One of its most notable graduates was Thurgood Marshall. The law school also engaged in research and analysis involving important civil rights issues that went before the court. Johnson was awarded the Spingarn Medal in 1928, the NAACP's highest award.

During the first half of his tenure, Johnson faced sharp criticism because he lacked a terminal academic degree and because some faculty and staff opposed his administrative style. He survived the controversy, maintained the support of the board of trustees, and continued fruitful contacts with foundations for financial support. He attracted outstanding scholars to the Howard faculty including philosopher Alain Locke, cell biologist Ernest E. Just, chemist Percy Julian, political scientist Ralph Bunche, historian Rayford Logan, and Charles Drew, who became known for his work with blood plasma. Johnson also erected new buildings and founded several honor societies on campus including a chapter of Phi Beta Kappa.

Johnson traveled widely; his lectures, given without notes, often lasted 45 minutes and held audiences spellbound. His themes often focused on racism, segregation, and discrimination. He retired from the presidency of Howard in 1960 and died on September 10, 1976, when he was 86 years old.

Laurence Clifton Jones (1884–1975)
School Founder, School Administrator

Laurence Clifton Jones founded a school in the deep woods of Mississippi's Black Belt and made it possible for thousands of African American youths to receive elementary and high school education. He uplifted the community as well by helping uneducated men and women to enhance their lives. He became known as "The Little Professor of Piney Woods."

Jones was born on November 21, 1884, in St. Joseph, Missouri, and worked his way to a degree from Iowa State University. Booker T. Washington inspired Jones first though his writings and later when he offered Jones a position at his school, Tuskegee Institute (now Tuskegee University). Jones declined and, instead, in 1910 founded what he called a "country life school" in Piney Woods, Mississippi. Officially, the school was established on May 17, 1913. He garnered the moral support of the community, and when the students lacked money for school expenses, he accepted payments in produce.

On June 29, 1912, Jones married Grace M. Allen, whom he had met while he was in college. Together the Joneses enabled the school to grow and engaged in fund-raising activities. Grace taught useful skills to community residents and also became a member of the school's faculty. With the help of the Cotton Blossom Singers—the school's ambassadors of music—the Joneses traveled the United States performing fundraising concerts. Laurence Jones organized the International Sweethearts of Rhythms in the late 1930s and engaged that group in fundraising concerts until the group, which became known worldwide, severed its relationship with the school in April of 1941.

The school then expanded, adding a department for blind children. Jones later became known through the television program "This is Your Life" aired in December of 1954. An appeal for support made during the program resulted in substantial funding for Piney Woods. Jones retired from the presidency in 1974, but continued to travel on official school business until he died in 1975.

E. J. Josey (1924–)
Librarian, Activist, Author

Elonnie Junius Josey was born in Norfolk, Virginia on January 20, 1924. He studied music and played the church organ until 1943, when he was drafted into the U.S. Army, serving for three years. Josey, known simply as E. J., went on to complete his education at Howard University's School of Music, later moving on to Columbia University's master's program in history and the State University of New York's Library School. In 1953, Josey began his career in libraries and rapidly became a leader in confronting segregation within them.

After his initial struggle against the Georgia Library Association when they denied him membership in 1960, Josey persevered in a diverse public and academic library career and gained a reputation as a wise, impassioned speaker on social issues. His publication *The Black Librarian in America* was a pioneering look into conditions for African Americans within librarianship. Its 1994 sequel *The Black Librarian in America Revisited* was an appraisal of changes that had been made in intervening years. Josey helped organize the Black Caucus of the American Library Association, which combated institutional racism and widespread discrimination both within the profession and in conjunction with library services.

As president of the American Library Association from 1984 to 1985, Josey fostered awareness of the value of libraries as an integral part of the nation's infrastructure. Fighting against severe budget cuts imposed by the Reagan administration, Josey rallied library advocates in Washington, DC, to march with him in protest. Josey has, in addition to his professional achievements, led community advocacy for civil and human rights as a leading member of the NAACP, was a contributor to intellectual development in emerging African countries, and was awarded four honorary doctorates. From the late 1980s until his retirement in 1995, Josey joined the faculty of the School of Library and Information Science at the University of Pittsburgh and devoted himself to achieving a racial balance in library education.

Maulana Karenga (1941–)

Activist-scholar, Educator, Ethicist

Dr. Maulana Karenga is professor and chair of the Department of Black Studies at California State University, Long Beach, where he also chairs the President's Task Force on Multicultural Education and Campus Diversity. He holds Ph.D. degrees in political science from United States International University and in social ethics with a focus on the classical African ethics of ancient Egypt from the University of Southern California. He has also been awarded an honorary doctorate from the University of Durban-Westville, South Africa for his "intellectual and practical work on behalf of African people."

Karenga came to prominence in the 1960s as founder of The Organization Us, a cultural and social change group whose name he explains, "simply means us Black people and stresses the communitarian focus of the organization and its philosophy *Kawaida*, which is an ongoing synthesis of the best of African thought and practice in constant exchange with the world." Karenga and Us have greatly influenced the development of the discipline of black studies, the black arts and black student movements, Afrocentricity, and ancient Egyptian studies. They have also advanced the independent school and rites of passage movements through the *Nguzo Saba* (The Seven Principles of Kawaida).

Moreover, Karenga and Us played important roles in the founding of the initial Black Power conferences in the 1960s and the National Black United Front in the 1980s. More recently they were in the forefront of organizing the National African American Leadership Summit and the Million Man March/Day of Absence. Karenga was a member of the executive council for the landmark 1995 gathering in Washington and authored its mission statement, co-editing the subsequent volume *The Million Man March/Day of Absence: A Commemorative Anthology*. Having celebrated its thirty-third anniversary in 1998, The Organization Us continues its declared commitment to "[s]truggle, service and institution-building."

An internationally recognized activist-scholar, Karenga has published numerous scholarly articles and books, among them the widely used *Introduction to Black Studies;* his retranslation and commentary on ancient Egyptian texts; *Selections from the Husia: Sacred Wisdom of Ancient Egypt;* and the influential *Kwanzaa: A Celebration of Family, Community and Culture*. In fact, he created the Kwanzaa celebration now observed throughout the world African community. He has lectured throughout the United States and the world and earned numerous scholarship, leadership, and community service awards.

Elizabeth Duncan Koontz (1919–1989)

Educator, Organizational Official

As teacher, assistant state school superintendent, leader in state and national teachers' associations, and the first African American president of the National Education Association (NEA), Elizabeth Duncan Koontz served the education needs of her constituents. Born on June 3, 1919, in Salisbury, North Carolina, she was the youngest of seven children. She graduated from Livingstone College with honors in 1938 and received a master's degree from Atlanta University in 1941. Beyond this, she studied at the graduate level in several colleges and universities.

Koontz moved from being an elementary school teacher in Dunn, North Carolina, to Aggrey Memorial School in Landis, then to Fourteenth Street School in Winston-Salem, and finally taught special education classes at Price High School in Salisbury. Her participating in the NEA began in 1952, when she was a member of the North Carolina Negro Teachers Association. That group was later admitted to the state chapter of the NEA. She served two terms as secretary, one as vice president, and one as president-elect of the NEA's Department of Classroom Teachers. In 1965, she became the department's first African American president. On July 6, 1968, Koontz was installed as the first African American president of the NEA. During her tenure, she brought a shift in the association from traditionally conservative to liberal. She supported agitation and, if necessary, strikes to bring about necessary change. She endorsed militant teachers and strongly supported teacher commitment and responsibility.

In January of 1969, President Richard Nixon appointed Koontz as director of the U.S. Department of Labor, Women's Bureau, making her the first African American director. Later she became deputy assistant secretary for Labor Employment Standards. In the latter capacity, she became the U.S. delegate to the United Nation's Commission on the Status of Women. She was active in numerous civic, religious, and educational organizations, and received approximately three dozen honorary degrees from various colleges and universities. Koontz held other positions until she retired in April of 1982. She suffered a heart attack at home in Salisbury and died on January 6, 1989.

Lucy C. Laney (1854–1933)
Educator, School Founder

Lucy Craft Laney spent her life assuring African Americans, particularly women, that they would be educated and had the freedom to educate others. She was born to former slaves on April 11, 1854, in Macon, Georgia. At age 15, Laney entered Atlanta University and graduated in 1873 in the school's first class. She then did graduate study at the University of Chicago during the summer months.

Although virtually penniless, in 1883 Laney opened a school for Augusta, Georgia's African American youth, held in Christ Presbyterian Church. The school was chartered in 1886 under Georgia law as a normal and industrial school. Haines Normal and Industrial Institute established the city's first kindergarten and nurse education department in the early 1890s. Later the nurse education department became the school of nursing at Augusta's University Hospital. By the 1930s, Haines dropped elementary education and offered a four-year high school program and some college-level courses. The Presbyterian Board of Missions, the schools' primary source of funds, withdrew support during the Great Depression. Haines school declined, then closed its doors in 1949. Later, a new public structure, the Lucy C. Laney High School, was built on the site. Laney died on October 23, 1933, in Augusta, and later was recognized as a leading African American educator in the South.

Sara Lawrence-Lightfoot (1944–)
Educator, Sociologist, Writer

Sara Lawrence-Lightfoot's sociological writing has been an attempts to create a clearer picture of the reality of African Americans lives. She has felt much of what has been previously written is a distorted view of who African Americans really are.

Lawrence-Lightfoot's 1994 book *I've Known Rivers: Lives of Loss and Liberation* details life in the African American middle class through interviews with six African American professionals. It was chosen as a Book-of-the-Month Club main choice. In 1978, her book *Worlds Apart* promoted cooperation between parents and teachers for the education of children. Her third book *The Good High School: Portraits of Character and Culture* chronicles the positive methods of six schools in the United States, offering the book as a catalyst for institutional change.

Lawrence-Lightfoot departed from her sociological writings to write a personal account of her mother's life in her 1988 book *Balm in Gilead: Journey of a Healer*. She received a MacArthur Award to fund the writing of the book. Along with writing her books, teaching at Harvard University as a professor of education, and conducting her research, Lawrence-Lightfoot gives lectures and serves on numerous committees and national boards, among them the National Academy of Education, the *Boston Globe*, and the John D. and Catherine T. MacArthur Foundation.

David Levering Lewis (1936–)
Educator, Writer

David Levering Lewis was born May 25, 1936, in Little Rock, Arkansas. He earned a bachelor's in history from Fisk University in 1956 and continued his studies at Columbia University, where he earned a master's degree in 1958. He received his Ph.D. from the London School of Economics and Political Science in 1962. He published his first paper as an undergraduate, titled "History of the Negro Upper Class in Atlanta, Georgia 1890–1958."

Lewis eventually began studying African American history after years as a scholar of French history, teaching at the University of Ghana, Notre Dame University, and Howard University. In 1971, he published a scholarly biography of Martin Luther King, Jr. titled *Martin Luther King: A Critical Biography*. Lewis followed this work with one on anti-Semitism called *Prisoners of Honor: The Dreyfus Affair* in 1973 at which time he accepted a teaching post at Federal City College in Washington, DC. In 1974, he became a full professor of history at the University of the District of Columbia.

Throughout the 1970s, he studied the Harlem Renaissance of the 1920s and 1930s, writing a work of definitive scholarship on the subject, published in 1981, as *When Harlem Was In Vogue: The Politics of the Arts in the Twenties and Thirties*. Next, Lewis tackled W. E. B. Du Bois, the great scholar and writer, in his biography *W. E. B. Du Bois: Biography of a Race, 1868–1919*, which won a Pulitzer Prize for biography in 1994 and a National Book Award the same year. By the time his Du Bois biography was published in 1993, Lewis had taken a position as the chair of the history department of Rutgers University, to which he commuted by train from his home on Capitol Hill in Washington, DC. Lewis contributes regularly to scholarly journals and the *Washington Post*.

Alain Locke (1886–1954)
Scholar

Born on September 3, 1886, in Philadelphia, Locke graduated Phi Beta Kappa with a B.A. degree from

Harvard University in 1907. He was then awarded a Rhodes scholarship for two years of study at Oxford University in England and did further graduate study at the University of Berlin (1910–1911). Upon returning to the United States, Locke took an assistant professorship in English and philosophy at Howard University in Washington, DC. He received his Ph.D. from Harvard in 1918 and the same year was made chairman of the philosophy department at Howard where he stayed until his retirement in 1953.

In 1934 Locke founded the Associates in Negro Folk Education. In 1942 he was named to the Honor Role of Race Relations. A prolific author, Locke's first book was entitled *Race Contacts and Inter-Racial Relations* (1916). His best known works include *The New Negro: An Interpretation* (1925), a book that introduced America to the Harlem Renaissance, and *The Negro in Art: A Pictorial Record of the Negro Artist and of the Negro Theme in Art* (1940). Locke died in New York City on June 9, 1954.

Benjamin E. Mays (1894–1984)

Former Morehouse College President

In addition to occupying the president's office at Morehouse, Benjamin Mays wrote, taught mathematics, worked for the Office of Education, served as chairman of the Atlanta Board of Education, preached in a Baptist church, acted as an advisor to the Southern Christian Leadership Council, and was a church historian.

Born in Epworth, South Carolina, in 1894, Mays attended Bates College and later received his master's and Ph.D. from the University of Chicago. He served as a pastor at Georgia's Shiloh Baptist Church from 1921 to 1924, and later taught at Morehouse College and South Carolina's State College at Orangeburg. After a stint at the Tampa Urban League, he worked for the YMCA as national student secretary and then directed a study of African American churches for the Institute of Social and Religious Research. From 1934 to 1940, he acted as dean of Howard University's School of Religion, before taking up the presidency of Morehouse from 1940 to 1967. He served in several other distinguished posts including the Atlanta Board of Education chairmanship and positions at HEW and the Ford Foundation. Awards earned by Mays include 43 honorary degrees, the Dorie Miller Medal of Honor, and the 1971 Outstanding Older Citizen Award. He died at his Atlanta home on March 21, 1984.

Jesse Edward Moorland (1863–1940)

Archivist, Clergyman

Jesse Moorland was born on September 10, 1863, in Coldwater, Ohio. Following the untimely death of his parents, Moorland was reared by his grandparents. His early education consisted of sporadic attendance at a small rural schoolhouse and being read to by his grandfather. Moorland eventually attended Normal University in Ada, Ohio, married, and taught school in Urbana, Ohio. He went on to attend Howard University in Washington and graduated with a degree in theology in 1891.

Moorland was ordained a congregational minister and, between 1891 and 1896, he served at churches in South Boston, Virginia, Nashville, and Cleveland. In 1891 he also became active in the YMCA, an association he would maintain for much of his life.

In 1909 Moorland's well known essay "Demand and the Supply of Increased Efficiency in the Negro Ministry" was published by the American Negro Academy. In it, Moorland called for a more pragmatic ministry, both in terms of the education of its members and its approach to social issues.

By 1910 Moorland had become quite active in the YMCA and was appointed secretary of the Colored Men's Department. In this position, Moorland raised millions of dollars for the YMCA's construction and building fund.

Having reached the mandatory retirement age in 1923, Moorland resigned from the YMCA and began devoting his time and considerable energy to other pursuits. Moorland was active with the Association for the Study of Negro Life and History, the National Health Circle for Colored People, and the Frederick Douglass Home Association.

From 1907 and onward, Moorland served as a trustee of Howard University. In 1914 he donated his private library of African American history to the university. Out of this gift grew the Moorland Foundation. The collection was renamed the Moorland-Spingarn Collection and later renamed the Moorland-Spingarn Research Center. This collection of documents on African American history and culture was the first African American research collection at a major American university. Moorland died in New York on April 30, 1940.

Frederick Douglass Patterson (1901–1988)

Former College President, Former United Negro College Fund President

Frederick Douglass Patterson was born in Washington, DC, on October 10, 1901. He received a D.V.M. degree in 1923 and a M.S. degree in 1927 from Iowa State University. In 1932 he received a Ph.D. from Cornell University.

Patterson joined the faculty of Tuskegee Institute in 1928, first as an instructor of veterinary science, later as

Benjamin Mays and other education leaders meet with President John F. Kennedy in 1962.

director of the school of agriculture, and finally as president. He also chaired the R. R. Moton Memorial Institute and served as director of education for the Phelps-Stokes Fund.

In 1944 Patterson organized the United Negro College Fund, a cooperative fund-raising organization designed to provide financial assistance to predominantly African American colleges and universities.

Benjamin F. Payton (1932–)

Former college president

Born in Orangeburg, South Carolina, in 1932, Benjamin Franklin Payton took a bachelor's degree with honors from South Carolina State College in 1955. He earned a B.D. from Howard University in 1958, a master's degree from Columbia University in 1960, and a Ph.D. from Yale University in 1963. He took a position as assistant professor at Howard University before working for the National Council of Churches as the Commission on Religion and Race's executive director of social justice—a position which he retained even as he took over the presidency of Benedict College in 1967. He left Benedict in 1972 for a position at the Ford Foundation, where he remained until he became the president of Tuskegee University in 1981.

Payton holds honorary degrees from Eastern Michigan University, Morris Brown, Benedict, and Morgan State. A recipient of the Napoleon Hill Foundation Gold Medal Award and the Benjamin E. Mays Award, he served as educational advisor to Vice President George Bush on Bush's seven-nation tour of Africa in 1982. Payton has also served as a member of several organizations including the National Association for Equal Opportunity in Higher Education, the Alabama Industrial Relations Council, the National Association of Independent Colleges and Universities, and the Executive Board of the National Consortium for Educational Access.

Arthur A. Schomburg (1874–1938)

Archivist, American Negro Academy President

Born in Puerto Rico in 1874, Arturo Schomburg led a richly varied public life. He worked as a law clerk and was a businessman, journalist, editor, lecturer, New York Public Library curator, and teacher of Spanish.

In 1911 Schomburg co-founded the Negro Society for Historical Research. He was also a lecturer for the

Arthur Schomburg (standing, second from right) with the staff of the Negro Society for Historical Research (AP/Wide World Photos, Inc.).

United Negro Improvement Association. Schomburg was a member of the New York Puerto Rico Revolutionary Party and served as secretary of the Cuban Revolutionary Party. In 1922 he headed the American Negro Academy, an organization founded by Alexander Crummell in 1879 to promote African American art, literature, and science.

Schomburg, who died on June 10, 1938, collected thousands of works on African American culture over his lifetime. In 1926 Schomburg's personal collection was purchased by the Carnegie Corporation and given to the New York Public Library. In 1973 the collection became known as the Schomburg Collection of Negro Literature and History; the name was later changed to the Schomburg Center for Research in Black Culture.

Shelby Steele (1946–)
Scholar

Steele was born January 1, 1946, in Chicago but grew up in Phoenix, Illinois, a blue-collar suburb of Chicago. He attended high school in Harvey, Illinois, where he was student council president his senior year prior to graduating in 1964. Steele then attended Coe College in Cedar Rapids, Iowa, where he was active in SCOPE—an organization associated with Martin Luther King, Jr.'s Southern Christian Leadership Conference. He graduated in 1968 and, in 1971, received an M.S. in sociology from Southern Illinois University. He went on to receive a Ph.D. in English literature from the University of Utah in 1974. While at Southern Illinois University, he taught African American literature to impoverished children in East St. Louis. Steele is currently a professor of English literature at San Jose State University.

In 1990 Steele published *The Content of Our Character: A New Vision of Race in America*, which won the National Book Critics Circle Award. In this controversial book, Steele argued that African-American self-doubt and its exploitation by the white and black liberal establishment is as great a cause of problems for African Americans as more traditional forms of racism. Steele has also written articles on this theme for such respected publications as *Harper's*, *New Republic*, *American Scholar*, and *Commentary*.

Because of his beliefs, Steele has been identified as part of an emerging African American neo-conservative movement, but in an interview with *Time* magazine

Shelby Steele (Time Life Syndication)

(August 12, 1991), he categorized himself as a classical liberal focusing on the freedom and sacredness of the individual.

H. Patrick Swygert (1943–)
University President, Lawyer

Since taking office as the 15th president of Howard University in Washington, DC, H. Patrick Swygert has worked to craft a strategy to move the institution into the twenty-first century. He aims to place the university on a firmer financial footing and sees Howard's role as one of shaping and implementing an academic and research agenda for African Americans.

Born on March 11, 1943, in Philadelphia, Swygert graduated from Howard University in 1965 with an A.B. degree and received his J.D. from the Howard University School of Law in 1968. After graduation, Swygert was law clerk to Chief Justice William H. Hastie of the U.S. Court of Appeals, Third Circuit in Philadelphia, and later served as administrative assistant to Congressman Charles B. Rangel. He held various positions at Temple University, first as vice president for university administration, then special counsel to the president, and later acting dean of the law school. He was also a full professor on the law school faculty. After serving as visiting professor at the University of Ghana and Tel Aviv University, he was a visiting lecturer in Cairo, Egypt; Rome, Italy; and Athens, Greece.

Swygert has also held several positions with the U.S. government including general counsel to the U.S. Service Commission. He was president of the State University of New York at Albany for five years, until he became president of Howard University on August 1, 1995. He is committed to sustaining Howard's stature among higher education institutions that serve African Americans.

Ivan Van Sertima (1935–)
Scholar

Born in British Guyana in 1935, anthropologist, linguist, and literary critic Ivan Van Sertima is currently professor of African studies at Rutgers University.

In 1977 Van Sertima published *They Came Before Columbus: The African Presence in Ancient America.* Drawing from various disciplines, Van Sertima presents evidence of pre-Columbian contact with the New World by Africans.

In 1979 Van Sertima founded *The Journal of African Civilizations*, which presents a revisionist approach to world history. He is also the author of *Caribbean Writers*, a collection of essays.

Clifton R. Wharton, Jr. (1926–)
Former University President

Clifton R. Wharton, born on September 13, 1926, was the first African American to head the largest university system in the United States—the State University of New York. He was also president of Michigan State University and served as chairman and CEO of the Teachers Insurance and Annuity Association and College Retirement Equities Fund.

A native Bostonian, Wharton took a bachelor's degree cum laude from Harvard in 1947. He received a master's at Johns Hopkins the following year, as the first African American admitted into the university's School for Advanced International Studies. In 1956 he took a second M.A. from the University of Chicago, which awarded him a Ph.D. in 1958. Between master's degrees he worked as a research associate for the University of Chicago. He then proceeded to the Agricultural Development Council, Inc., where he worked for 12 years. He also held a post as visiting professor at the University of Malaya and served as director and eventually vice president of the American Universities Research Program. Wharton took over the presidency of Michigan State in 1970 and stayed there for eight years; he moved on to the SUNY system from 1978 to 1987. He then worked for the

Clifton Wharton (AP/Wide World Photos, Inc.)

Teachers Insurance and Annuity Association and has since become the first African American to chair the Rockefeller Foundation.

Wharton won the President's Award on World Hunger in 1983 and has earned honorary degrees from more than 45 colleges and universities.

Carter Godwin Woodson (1875–1950)
Scholar

Carter Godwin Woodson was born December 9, 1875, in New Canton, Virginia. He received a B.Litt. degree from Berea College in 1903, a B.A. and an M.A. in 1907 and 1908 from the University of Chicago, and a Ph.D. from Harvard University in 1912.

Known as the "Father of Modern Black History," Woodson was a passionate proponent of African American economic self-sufficiency. In 1915 Woodson founded the Association for the Study of Negro Life and History (now the Association for the Study of Afro-American Life and History). One year later, the organization began publishing the *Journal of Negro History.* In 1920 he founded Associated Publishers Inc. and, in 1921 he founded the *Negro History Bulletin.* In 1926 Woodson launched Negro History Week (now Black History Month) to promote the study of African American history.

An historian, author, editor, and teacher, Woodson served as dean of the Howard University School of Liberal Arts and of the West Virginia Institute and was a Spingarn Medalist. His works include: *The Education of the Negro Prior to 1861* (1915); *A Century of Negro Migration* (1918); *The Negro in Our History* (1922); and *The Miseducation of the Negro* (1933). Woodson died on April 3, 1950, in Washington, DC.

◆ HISTORICALLY AND PREDOMINANTLY AFRICAN AMERICAN COLLEGES AND UNIVERSITIES

Alabama A and M University
PO Box 1357
Normal, AL 35762-1357
(256) 851-5000
www.aamu.edu
Established 1875.

Alabama State University
915 S. Jackson St.
Montgomery, AL 36101-0271
(334) 229-4100
www.alasu.edu
Established 1867.

Albany State University
504 College Dr.
Albany, GA 31705-2796
(912) 430-4600
www.alsnet.peachnut.edu
Established 1903.

Alcorn State University
PO Box 300
Lorman, MS 39096-9402
(601) 877-6100
www.alcorn.edu
Established 1871.

Allen University
1530 Harden St.
Columbia, SC 29204-1085
(803) 254-4165
Established 1870.

Arkansas Baptist College
1600 Bishop St.
Little Rock, AR 72202-6099
(501) 374-7856
Established 1884.

Atlanta Metropolitan College
Metropolitan Pkwy., SW
Atlanta, GA 30310-4448
(404) 756-4000
www.atlm.peachnet.edu
Established 1974.

Barber-Scotia College
145 Cabarrus Ave.
Concord, NC 28025-5187
(704) 789-2900
Established 1867.

Benedict College
Harden and Blanding Sts.
Columbia, SC 29204-1086
(803) 253-5000
www.benedict.edu
Established 1870.

Bennett College
900 E. Washington St.
Greensboro, NC 27401-3239
(336) 273-4431
www.bennett.edu
Established 1873.

Bethune-Cookman College
640 Dr. Mary McLeod Bethune Blvd.
Daytona Beach, FL 32114-3099
(904) 255-1401
www.bethune.cookman.edu
Established 1904.

Bishop State Community College
351 N. Broad St.
Mobile, AL 36603-5898
(334) 690-6801
www.bscc.cc.al.us
Established 1965.

Bluefield State College
219 Rock St.
Bluefield, WV 24701-2198
(304) 327-4000
www.bluefield.wvnet.edu
Established 1895.

Bowie State University
14000 Jericho Park Rd.
Bowie, MD 20715-3318
(301) 464-3000
www.bsu.umd.edu
Established 1865.

Central State University
1400 Brush Row Rd.
Wilberforce, OH 45384-9999
(937) 376-6011
www.ces.edu
Established 1887.

Charles R. Drew University of Medicine and Science
1621 E. 120th St.
Los Angeles, CA 90059-3025
(323) 563-4800
www.cdrew.edu
Established 1966.

Cheyney University of Pennsylvania
Cheyney and Creek Rds.
Cheyney, PA 19319-0200
(610) 399-2000
www.cheyney.edu
Established 1837.

Chicago State University
9501 S. King Dr.
Chicago, IL 60628-1598
(773) 995-2000
www.csu.edu
Established 1867.

Claflin College
700 College Ave., NE
Orangeburg, SC 29115-4477
(803) 535-5268
www.icusc.org/cchome.htm
Established 1869.

Clark Atlanta University
James P. Brawley Dr. at Fair St., SW
Atlanta, GA 30314-4385
(404) 880-8000
www.cau.edu
Established 1988.

Clinton Junior College
PO Box 968
Rock Hill, SC 29731
(803) 327-5587
Established 1894.

Coahoma Community College
3240 Friars Point Rd.
Clarksdale, MS 38614-9700
(601) 627-2571
Established 1949.

Compton Community College
1111 E. Artesia Blvd.
Compton, CA 90221-5393
(310) 900-1600
gopher://compton.cc.ca.us
Established 1927.

Concordia College
1804 Green St.
Selma, AL 36703-3323
(334) 874-5700
www.cuis.edu/www/cus/cual.html
Established 1922.

Coppin State College
2500 W. North Ave.
Baltimore, MD 21216-3698
(410) 383-5400
www.coppin.umd.edu
Established 1900.

Cuyahoga Community College
Metropolitan College Campus
2900 Community College Ave.
Cleveland, OH 44115
(216) 987-4200
www.tri-c.cc.oh.us
Established 1963.

Delaware State University
1200 N. DuPont Hwy.
Dover, DE 19901-2275
(302) 739-4924
www.dsc.edu
Established 1891.

Denmark Technical College
Solomon Blatt Blvd.
PO Box 327
Denmark, SC 29042-0327
(803) 793-5176
dtc401.den.tec.sc.us:8000
Established 1948.

Dillard University
2601 Gentilly Blvd.
New Orleans, LA 70122-3097
(504) 283-8822
www.dillard.edu
Established 1869.

Edward Waters College
1658 Kings Rd.
Jacksonville, FL 32209-6199
(904) 355-3030
Established 1866.

Elizabeth City State University
1704 Weeks Rd.
Elizabeth City, NC 27909-7806
(919) 335-3400
www.ecsu.edu
Established 1891.

Fayetteville State University
1200 Murchison Rd.
Newbold Station
Fayetteville, NC 28301-4298
(910) 486-1111
www.uncfsu.edu
Established 1867.

Fisk University
1000 17th Ave., N.
Nashville, TN 37208-3051
(615) 329-8500
www.fisk.edu
Established 1866.

Florida A and M University
1500 Wahnish Way
Tallahassee, FL 32307
(850) 599-3000
www.famu.edu
Established 1887.

Florida Memorial College
15800 NW 42nd Ave.
Miami, FL 33054-6199
(305) 626-3600
www.fmc.edu
Established 1879.

Fort Valley State University
1005 State University Dr.
Fort Valley, GA 31030-4313
(912) 825-6211
www.fcsc.edu
Established 1895.

Grambling State University
PO Box 864
Grambling, LA 71245-3091
(318) 274-3811
www.gram.edu
Established 1901.

Hampton University
Hampton, VA 23668-0199
(757) 727-5000
www.cs.hamptonu.edu
Established 1868.

Harris-Stowe State College
3026 Laclede Ave.
St. Louis, MO 63103-2199
(314) 340-3366
Established 1857.

Hinds Community College
Raymond, MS 39154-0999
(601) 857-5261
www.hinds.cc.ms.us
Established 1917.

Howard University
2400 6th St., NW
Washington, DC 20059-0001
(202) 806-6100
www.howard.edu
Established 1867.

Howard University School of Law
2900 Van Ness St., NW
Washington, DC 20008
(202) 806-8000
www.law.howard.edu
Established 1869.

Huston-Tillotson College
900 Chicon St.
Austin, TX 78702-2795
(512) 505-3000
www.htc.edu
Established 1876.

Interdenominational Theological Center
700 Martin Luther King Jr. Dr., SW
Atlanta, GA 30314-4112
(404) 527-7700
www.itc.edu
Established 1958.

J.F. Drake State Technical College
3421 Meridian St., N.
Huntsville, AL 35811-1584
(256) 539-8161
www.dstc.cc.al.us
Established 1961.

Jackson State University
1400 John R. Lynch St.
Jackson, MS 39217-0001
(601) 968-2121
www.jsums.edu
Established 1877.

Jarvis Christian College
PO Box 1470
Highway 80 W.
Hawkins, TX 75765-1470
(903) 769-5400
www.jarvis.edu
Established 1912.

Johnson C. Smith University
100-300 Beatties Ford Rd.
Charlotte, NC 28216-5398
(704) 378-1000
www.jcsu.edu
Established 1867.

Kennedy-King College
6800 S. Wentworth Ave.
Chicago, IL 60621-3798
(773) 602-5000
www.ccc.edu/KennedyKing/home.htm
Established 1976.

Kentucky State University
400 E. Main St.
Box PG-92
Frankfort, KY 40601-2355
(502) 227-6000
www.kysu.edu.
Established 1886.

Knoxville College
901 College St., NW
Knoxville, TN 36921
(423) 524-6511
falcon.nest.kxcol.edu
Established 1875.

LaGuardia Community College
31-10 Thompson Ave.
Long Island City, NY 11101
(718) 482-7206
www.lagcc.cuny.edu
Established 1971.

Lane College
545 Lane Ave.
Jackson, TN 38301-4598
(901) 426-7500
www.lc.lane-college.edu
Established 1882.

Langston University
PO Box 907
Langston, OK 73050-0907
(405) 466-2231
www.lunet.edu
Established 1897.

Lawson State Community College
3060 Wilson Rd., SW
Birmingham, AL 35221-1798
(205) 925-2515
Established 1965.

LeMoyne-Owen College
807 Walker Ave.
Memphis, TN 38126-6595
(901) 774-9090
www.lemoyne-owen.edu/lemoyne.html
Established 1862.

Lewis College of Business
17370 Meyers Rd.
Detroit, MI 48235-1498
(313) 862-6300
www.lewiscollege.edu
Established 1906.

Lincoln University (Missouri)
820 Chestnut St.
Jefferson City, MO 65102-0029
(573) 681-5000
Established 1866.

Lincoln University of Pennsylvania
PO Box 179
Lincoln University, PA 19352-0999
(610) 932-8300
www.lincoln.ed.
Established 1854.

Livingstone College
701 W. Monroe St.
Salisbury, NC 28144-5298
(704) 797-1000
www.lsc.edu
Established 1879.

Lomax-Hannon Junior College
PO Box 779
Greenville, AL 36037
(334) 382-2115
Established 1893.

Mary Holmes College
Hwy. 50 W
PO Drawer 1257
West Point, MS 39773-1257
(601) 494-6820
www.maryholmes.edu
Established 1892.

Medgar Evers College of City University of New York
1650 Bedford Ave.
Brooklyn, NY 11225
(718) 270-4900
www.greatcollegetown.com/medgar.html
Established 1969.

Meharry Medical College
1005 D.B. Todd Blvd.
Nashville, TN 37208-3051
(615) 327-6111
www.mmc.edu
Established 1876.

Miles College
PO Box 3800
Birmingham, AL 35208
(205) 929-1415
www.miles.edu
Established 1905.

Mississippi Valley State University
Hwy. 82 W.
Itta Bena, MS 38941-1400
(601) 254-9041
www.mcsu.edu
Established 1946.

Morehouse College
830 Westview Dr., SW
Atlanta, GA 30314-3773
(404) 681-2800
www.morehouse.edu
Established 1867.

Morehouse School of Medicine
720 Westview Dr., SW
Atlanta, GA 30310-1495
(404) 752-1500
www.msm.edu
Established 1984.

Morgan State University
1700 Cold Spring Ln.
Baltimore, MD 21251
(443) 885-3333
www.morgan.edu
Established 1867.

Morris Brown College
643 Martin Luther King Jr. Dr., NW
Atlanta, GA 30314-4140
(404) 220-0270
www.morrisbrown.edu
Established 1881.

Morris College
100 W. College St.
Sumter, SC 29150-3599
(803) 775-9371
www.icusc.org/morris/mchome.htm
Established 1908.

New York City Technical College
300 Jay St.
Brooklyn, NY 11201
(718) 260-5520
www.nyctc.suny.edu
Established 1946.

Norfolk State University
2401 Corprew Ave.
Norfolk, VA 23504-3989
(757) 683-8600
www.nsu.ed
Established 1935.

North Carolina A and T State University
1601 E. Market St.
Greensboro, NC 27411-0001
(336) 334-7500
www.ncat.edu
Established1891.

North Carolina Central University
PO Box 19717
Durham, NC 27707
(919) 560-6100
www.nccu.edu
Established 1910.

Oakwood College
Oakwood Rd., NW
Huntsville, AL 35896-0001
(256) 726-7000
www.oakwood.edu
Established 1896.

Paine College
1235 15th St.
Augusta, GA 30910-3182
(706) 821-8200
www.paine.edu
Established 1882.

Paul Quinn College
3837 Simpson Stuart Rd.
Dallas, TX 75241-4398
(214) 376-1000
www.pqc.edu
Established 1872.

Philander-Smith College
812 W. 13th St.
Little Rock, AR 72202-3799
(501) 375-9845
www.philander.edu
Established 1877.

Prairie View A and M University
PO Box 188
Prairie View, TX 77446-2610
(409) 857-3311
www.pvamu.edu
Established 1876.

Roxbury Community College
1234 Columbus Ave.
Roxbury Crossing, MA 02120-3400
(617) 427-0060
www.rcc.mass.edu
Established 1973.

Rust College
150 Rust Ave.
Holly Spring, MS 38635-2328
(601) 252-8000
www.rustcollege.edu
Established 1866.

Saint Augustine's College
1315 Oakwood Ave.
Raleigh, NC 27610-2298
(919) 516-4000
www.peterson.com/college
Established 1867.

Saint Paul's College
406 Windsor Ave.
Lawrenceville, VA 23868-1299
(804) 848-3111
www.saintpauls.edu
Established 1888.

Savannah State University
State College Branch
Savannah, GA 31404-5255
(912) 356-2187
www.savstate.edu
Established 1890.

Selma University
1501 Lapsley St.
Selma, AL 36701
(334) 872-2533
Established 1878.

Shaw University
118 E. South St.
Raleigh, NC 27611-2399
(919) 546-8300
Established 1865.

Shorter College
604 Locust St.
North Little Rock, AR 72114
(501) 374-6305
Established 1888.

Simmons University Bible College
1811 Dumesnil St..
Louisville, KY 40210.
(502) 776-1443.
www.klassy.com/simmonsbiblecollege.
Established 1879.

Sojourner-Douglass College
500 N. Caroline St.
Baltimore, MD 21205
(410)276-0306
host.sdc.edu
Established 1972.

South Carolina State University
300 College St., NE
Orangeburg, SC 29117-0001
(803) 536-7000
www.scsu.edu
Established 1896.

Southern University and A&M College-Baton Rouge
PO Box 9901
Baton Rouge, LA 70813-0001
(504) 771-4500
www.subr.edu
Established 1880.

Southern University at New Orleans
6400 Press Dr.
New Orleans, LA 70126-0002
(504) 286-5000
www.suno.edu
Established 1956.

Southern University at Shreveport-Bossier City
3050 Martin Luther King Jr. Dr.
Shreveport, LA 71107-4795
(318) 674-3300
www.susbo.edu
Established 1964.

Southwestern Christian College
PO Box 10
Terrell, TX 75160-9002
(972) 524-3341
swcc@juno.com
Established 1949.

Spelman College
350 Spelman Ln., SW
Atlanta, GA 30314-4399
(404) 681-3643
www.auc.edu
Established 1881.

Stillman College
PO Box 1430
3600 Stillman Blvd.
Tuscaloosa, AL 35403-1430
(205) 349-4240
www.stillman.edu
Established 1876.

Talladega College
627 W. Battle St.
Talladega, AL 35160-2354
(256) 362-0206
www.talladega.edu
Established 1867.

Tennessee State University
3500 John A. Merritt Blvd.
Nashville, TN 37209-1561
(615) 963-5000
www.tnstate.edu
Established 1912.

Texas College
2404 N. Grand Ave.
Tyler, TX 75702-1999
(903) 593-8311
www.texascollege.edu
Established 1894.

Texas Southern University
3100 Cleburne Ave.
Houston, TX 77004-4584
(713) 313-7011
www.tsu.edu
Established 1947.

Tougaloo College
300 E. County Line Rd.
Tougaloo, MS 39174-9999
(601) 977-7700
www.tougaloo.edu
Established 1869.

Trenholm State Technical College
1225 Air Base Blvd.
Montgomery, AL 36108-3199
(334) 832-9000
tstc.cc.al.us
Established 1963.

Tuskegee University
Tuskegee, AL 36088
(334) 727-8011
www.tusk.edu
Established 1881.

University of Arkansas at Pine Bluff
1200 University Dr.
Pine Bluff, AR 71601-2799
(501) 569-3000
www.uapb.edu
Established 1873.

University of Maryland, Eastern Shore
Princess Anne, MD 21853-1299
(410) 651-2200
www.umes.umd.edu
Established 1886.

University of the District of Columbia
4200 Connecticut Ave., NW
Washington, DC 20008-1174
(202) 274-5000
www.udc.edu
Established 1976.

University of the Virgin Islands
#2 John Brewer's Bay
Charlotte Amalie, VI 00802-9990
(340) 776-9200
www.uvi.edu
Established 1962.

Virginia Seminary and College
2058 Garfield Ave.
Lynchburg, VA 24501
(804) 524-5070
www.vsu.edu
Established 1888.

Virginia State University
PO Box 18
Petersburg, VA 23803-0001
(804) 524-5000
www.vsu.edu
Established 1882.

Virginia Union University
1500 N. Lombardy St.
Richmond, VA 23220-1784
(804) 257-5600
www.vuu.edu
Established 1865.

Voorhees College
1411 Voorhees Rd.
Denmark, SC 29042
(803) 793-3351
www.voorhees.edu
Established 1897.

Wayne County Community College
801 W. Fort Ave.
Detroit, MI 48226
(313)496-2500
www.wccc.edu
Established 1967.

West Virginia State College
P.O. Box 1000
Institute, WV 25112-1000
(800) 987-2112
www.wvsc.edu
Established 1891.

Wilberforce University
1055 N. Bickett Rd.
Wilberforce, OH 45384-1091
(937) 376-2911
www.wilberforce.edu
Established 1856.

Wiley College
711 Wiley Ave.
Marshall, TX 75670-5199
(903) 927-3300
www.wiley.edu
Established 1873.

Winston-Salem State University
601 Martin Luther King, Jr. Dr.
Winston-Salem, NC 27110-0001
(336) 750-2000
www.wssu.edu
Established 1892.

Xavier University of Louisiana
7325 Palmetto St.
New Orleans, LA 70125-1098
(504) 486-7411
www.xula.edu
Established 1915.

◆ RESEARCH INSTITUTIONS

African American Cultural Center
Indiana University Bloomington
Ashton Center-Coulter Hall
Bloomington, IN 47406-1363
(812) 855-9271
Fax: (812) 855-5168
www.indiana.edu

African American Studies Center
Boston University
138 Mountfort St.
Brookline, MA 02146
(617) 353-2795
Fax: (617)353-0455

African American Studies Program
College of Humanities, Fine Arts, and Communication
University of Houston
Agnes Arnold Hall
Houston, TX 77204-3783
(713) 743-2811
Fax: (713) 743-2818
www.uh.edu/academics/hfac/aas

African Heritage Studies Association
Africana Studies and Research Institute
Flushing, NY 11367
(718) 997-2845

African Studies Program
University of Wisconsin, Madison
205 Ingraham Hall
Madison, WI 53706
(608) 262-2380
Fax: (608) 265-5851
polyglot.lss.wisc.edu/afrst/asphome.html

African Studies and Research Institute
Queens College of City University of New York
65-30 Kissena Blvd.
Flushing, NY 11367
(718) 997-5000
Fax: (718) 520-7241

African-American Studies and Research Center
Purdue University
1367 LAEB
West Lafayette, IN 47907
(765) 494-5680
Fax: (765) 496-1581
www.sla.purdue.edu/academic/idis/african-american/

African-New World Studies Program
Florida International University
University Park
1120 SW 8th St.
Miami, FL 33199-0001
(305) 348-2000
www.fiu.edu/~africana/index.htm

Africana Research Center
Brooklyn College of City University of New York
2900 Bedford Ave.
Brooklyn, NY 11210
(718) 951-5350
Fax: (718) 951-4707

Africana Studies and Research Center
Cornell University
310 Triphammer Rd.
Ithaca, NY 14850
(607) 255-5218
Fax: (607) 255-0784

Afro-American Arts Institute
Indiana University-Bloomington
109 N. Jordan Ave.
Bloomington, IN 47405
(812) 855-9501

Afro-American Studies Program
Brown University
Box 1904
Providence, RI 02912
(401) 863-3137
Fax: (401) 863-3559

Afro-American Studies and Research Program
University of Illinois at Urbana-Champaign
1201 W. Nevada
Urbana, IL 61801
(217) 333-7781
Fax: (217) 244-4809
www.aasrp.uiuc.edu

Amistad Research Center
Tulane University
6823 St. Charles Ave.
New Orleans, LA 70118
(504) 865-5535
Fax: (401) 863-5580
www.tulane.edu/~amistad/mmenu.html

Archives of African American Music and Culture
Indiana University-Bloomington
Bloomington, IN 47405
(812) 855-8547
Fax: (812) 855-8545
www.indiana.edu/~aamc?

Association for Study of Afro-American Life and History, Inc.
1407 14th St., NW
Washington, DC 20005
(202) 667-2822
Fax: (202) 387-9802
www.artnoir.com/asalb.html

Avery Research Center for African American History and Culture
University of Charleston
125 Bull St.
Charleston, SC 29424
(843) 953-7609
Fax: (843) 953-7606

Black Abolitionist Papers Project
Florida State University
Department of History
Tallahassee, FL 32306
(850) 644-4527

Black Americana Studies
Western Michigan University
330 Moore Hall
Kalamazoo, MI 49008
(616) 387-2665
Fax: (616) 387-2507

Black Arts Research Center
30 Marion St.
Nyack, NY 10960
www.vrlab.fa.pitt.edu/admin/jgray/main.htm

Black Periodical Literature Project, 1827-1940
Harvard University
77 Dunster St.
Cambridge, MA 02138
(617) 496-7404
Fax: (617) 496-8547

Bureau of Educational Research
School of Education
Howard University
2441 14th St. NW
Washington, DC 20059
(202) 806-8120
Fax: (202) 806-8130

Carter G. Woodson Institute for Afro-American and African Studies
University of Virginia
108 Minor Hall
Charlottesville, VA 22903
(804) 924-3109
Fax: (804) 924-8820
www.virginia.edu/~woodson

Center for African and African-American Studies Center
University of Texas at Austin
Jester Center, Rm. A232A
Austin, TX 78705
(512) 471-1784
Fax: (512) 471-1798
www.utexas.edu/depts/caaas/

Center for African-American History and Culture
Temple University
Weiss Hall, Ste. B18
Philadelphia, PA 19122
(215) 204-4851
Fax: (215) 204-3794
www.temple.edu/caahc

Center for African/American Studies
University of California, Los Angeles
2308 Murphy Hall
Los Angeles, CA 90095-1545
(310) 825-7403
Fax: (310) 825-5019
www.sscnet.ucla.edu/caas

Center for African American Studies
Wesleyan University
343 High St.
Middletown, CT 06459
(860) 685-3568
Fax: (860) 685-2041
www.wesleyan.edu

Center for Afro American Studies
Ohio University
300 Lindley Hall
Athens, OH 45701
(614) 593-4546
Fax: (614) 593-0671

Center for Afro-American and African Studies
University of Michigan
200 West Hall Bldg.
Ann Arbor, MI 48109-1092
(734) 764-5513
Fax: (734) 764-0543
www.umich.edu/iinet/caas/

Center for Black Music Research
Columbia College
600 S. Michigan Ave.
Chicago, IL 60605-1996
(312) 663-1600
Fax: (312) 663-9019
www.cbmr.org/index.html

Center for Black Studies
Northern Illinois University
DeKalb, IL 60115
(815) 753-1709
Fax: (815) 753-9291

Center for Black Studies
University of California, Santa Barbara
South Hall 4603
Santa Barbara, CA 93106-3140
(805) 893-3914
Fax: (805) 893-7243
www.research.ucsb.edu.cbs

Center for Multi-Cultural Leadership
Institute for Life Studies
University of Kansas
Lawrence, KS 66045-0048
(913) 864-3990
Fax: (913) 864-3994

Center for Research on Multi-Ethnic Education
University of Oklahoma
455 Lindsey St., Rm. 804
Norman, OK 73019-0535
(405) 325-4529
Fax: (405) 325-4991

Center for Southern History and Culture
University of Alabama
PO Box 870342
Tuscaloosa, AL 35487-0342
(205) 348-7467

Center for Studies of Ethnicity and Race in America
University of Colorado at Boulder
Ketchum 30
Boulder, CO 80309-0339
(303) 492-8852
Fax: (303) 492-7799

Center for the Study and Stabilization of the Black Family
Niagara University
PO Box 367
Niagara University, NY 14109
(716) 285-1212

Center for the Study of Black Literature and Culture
University of Pennsylvania
3808 Walnut St.
Philadelphia, PA 19104-6136
(215) 898-5141
Fax: (215) 898-0765
www.ccat.sas.upenn.edu/csblac

Center for the Study of Civil Rights
University of Virginia
1512 Jefferson Park Ave.
Charlottesville, VA 22903
(804) 924-3109

Center for the Study of Race and Ethnicity in America
Brown University
Box 1886
Providence, RI 02912
(401) 863-3080
Fax: (401) 863-7589
www.brown.edu/department/race_ethnicity/

Center for the Study of Southern Culture
University of Mississippi
Barnard Observatory
University, MS 38677
(601) 232-5993
Fax: (601) 232-5814

Civil Rights Project
Harvard University
444 Gutman Library
Cambridge, MA 02136
(617) 496-6367
Fax: (617) 496-3095
www.law.harvard.edu/groups/civilrights/index.html

Committee on African and African-American Studies
University of Chicago
5828 S. University Ave.
Chicago, IL 60637
(773) 702-0902
Fax: (773) 702-2587

David C. Driskell Center for the Study of the African Diaspora
University of Maryland College Park
College Park, MD 20742-0001
(301) 405-1000

Frederick D. Patterson Research Institute
8260 Willow Oaks Corporate Dr.
PO Box 10444
Fairfax, VA 22031-4511
(703) 205-3570
FAX: (703) 205-2012
www.patterson-uncf.org/rbooks.htm

Frederick Douglass Institute for African and African-American Studies
University of Rochester
302 Morey Hall
Rochester, NY 14627-0440
(716) 275-7235
Fax: (716) 256-2594

Gilder Lehrman Center for the Study of Slavery, Resistance, and Abolition
Yale University
PO Box 208206
New Haven, CT 06520-8206
(203) 432-3339
Fax: (203) 432-6943
www.library.yale.edu/training/gilderle.htm

Houston Center for the Study of the Black Experience Affecting Higher Education
Clemson University
213 Martin St.
Clemson, SC 29634-5185
(864) 656-0313
Fax: (864) 656-0314
www.houston.clemson.edu

Institute for African American Affairs
Department of African Studies
Kent State University
18 Ritchie Hall
Kent, OH 44242
(330) 672-2300
Fax: (330) 672-4837

Institute for African American Studies
College of Staten Island of City University of New York
2800 Victory Blvd.
Staten Island
New York, NY 10314
(718) 982-2880
Fax: (718) 982-2864

Institute for African-American Studies
University of Connecticut
241 Glenbrook Rd., U-162
Storrs, CT 06269-2162
(860) 486-3630
Fax: (860) 486-3083
www.ucc.uconn.edu/~aasadm03/

Institute for African-American Studies
University of Georgia
164 Psychology Bldg.
Athens, GA 30602
(706) 542-5197
Fax: (706) 542-3071
www.uga.edu/~iaas

Institute for Race and Social Division
704 Commonwealth Ave.
Boston University
Boston, MA 02215-1700
(617) 353-5850
www.webdev.bu.edu/IRSD/contact.html

Institute for the Preservation and Study of African-American Writing
PO Box 50172
Washington, DC 20004
(202) 727-4047

Institute of Afro-American Affairs
New York University
269 Mercer St., Ste. 601
New York, NY 10003
(212) 998-2130
Fax: (212) 995-4109
www.nyu.edu

Institute of Jazz Studies
Rutgers University
Dana Library, 4th Fl.
Newark, NJ 07102
(973) 648-5595
Fax: (973) 648-5944

Joint Center for Political and Economic Studies
1090 Vermont Ave. NW, Ste. 1100
Washington, DC 20005-4961
(202) 789-3500
Fax: (202) 789-6390
www.jointctr.org

Martin Luther King, Jr. Center for Nonviolent Social Change, Inc.
449 Auburn Ave. NE
Atlanta, GA 30312
(404) 524-1956
Fax: (404) 526-8901

Melvin B. Tolson Black Heritage Center
Langston University
Langston, OK 73050
(405) 466-3346
Fax: (405) 466-2979

Moorland-Spingarn Research Center
Howard University
500 Howard Pl. NW
Washington, DC 20059
(202) 806-7239
Fax: (202) 806-6405

Morehouse Research Institute
Morehouse College
830 Westview Dr.
Atlanta, GA 30314
(404) 215-2676
Fax: (404) 222-0422
www.morehouse.edu/mri.htm

National Afro-American Museum and Cultural Center
1350 Brush Row Rd.
Wilberforce, OH 45384
(937) 376-4944
Fax: (937) 376-2007

National Black Child Development Institute
1023 15th St. NW, Ste. 600
Washington, DC 20005
(202) 387-1281
Fax: (202) 234-1738
www.nbedi.org

National Caucus and Center on Black Aged, Inc.
1424 K. St. NW, Ste. 500
Washington, DC 20005
(202) 637-8400
Fax: (202) 347-0895
www.ncba@aol.com

National Council for Black Studies
California State Univ., Dominguez Hills
Carson, CA 90747
(310) 243-2169
Fax: (310) 516-3987
www.wiu.edu/~ncbs

National Study of Black College Students
Department of Sociology
University of California, Los Angeles
Los Angeles, CA 90095-1551
(310) 825-7766
Fax: (310) 206-9838

New York African American Research Foundation
State University of New York
State University Plaza
Central Administration Bldg.
Albany, NY 12246
(518) 443-5798
Fax: (518) 443-5803

Nyumburu Cultural Center
Office of the Vice President for Academic Affairs
University of Maryland at College Park
College Park, MD 20742
(301) 314-7758
Fax: (301) 314-9505

Program for Research on Black Americans
University of Michigan
5062 Institute for Social Research
Ann Arbor, MI 48106-1248
(734) 763-0045
Fax: (734) 763-0044
www.isr.umich.edu/rcgd/prba

Program in African-American Studies Program
Princeton University
112 Dickinson Hall
Princeton, NJ 08544-1017
(609) 258-4270
Fax: (609) 258-5095

Race Relations Institute
Fisk University
1000 17th Ave., N.
Nashville, TN 37208-3051
(615) 329-8575
Fax: (615) 329-8806
www.fiskrri.org/

Race Relations Institute
College of Urban, Labor and Metropolitan Affairs
Wayne State University
656 W. Kirby, Rm. 3198 FAB
Detroit, MI 48202
(313) 577-5071
Fax: (313) 577-8800

Research Department
National Urban League
1111 14th St., NW, 6th Fl.
Washington, DC 20005
(202) 898-1604
Fax: (202) 408-1965

Rites and Reason
Brown University
Box 1148
Providence, RI 02912
(401) 863-3558
Fax: (401) 863-3559

Schomburg Center for Research in Black Culture
515 Malcolm X Blvd.
New York, NY 10037-1801
(212) 491-2200
(212) 491-6760
www.nypl.org/research/sc/sc.html

W. E. B. Du Bois Institute for Afro-American Research
Harvard University
Barker Center
Cambridge, MA 02138
(617) 495-4113
Fax: (617) 496-2871
www.web-dubois.fas.harvard.edu/

William Monroe Trotter Institute
University of Massachusetts at Boston
100 Morrissey Blvd.
Boston, MA 02125-3393
(617) 287-5880
Fax: (617) 287-5865
www.trotterinst.org

Women's Leadership Institute
Bennett College
900 E. Washington St., Box C
Greensboro, NC 27401-3239
(336) 370-0436
Fax: (336)370-4326

Women's Research and Resource Center
Spelman College
PO Box 115
Atlanta, GA 30314
(404) 223-7528
Fax: (404) 223-7665

◆ AFRICAN AMERICANS HOLDING ENDOWED UNIVERSITY CHAIRS, CHAIRS OF EXCELLENCE, OR CHAIRED PROFESSORSHIPS (1999)

Endowed university chairs are an honor—both for the person for whom the chair is named as well as for the person who is named to the chair. Endowments are bestowed upon academians of great talent who have distinguished themselves in their careers. Usually an organization separate from a collegiate institution will approach a university in hopes of setting up a chair and endowment fund. Seventeen such chairs have been identified as endowed and named for African Americans including Hannah Diggs Atkins, Sterling A. Brown, Constance E. Clayton, Bill and Camille Cosby, Charles R. Drew, W. E. B. Du Bois, Benjamin L. Hooks, Ernest

Everett Just, Martin Luther King, Jr. (three), LaSalle D. Leffall, Jr., Wade H. McCree, Jr., Willa B. Player, Paul Robeson, and Roy Wilkins.

In 1999, 131 African American professors held endowed chairs including eight of those named for African Americans. Others have either retired from endowed chairs, are professors emeriti, or are deceased, including T. J. Anderson (Tufts University); David C. Driskell (University of Maryland); Edgar G. Epps (University of Chicago); John Hope Franklin (three: Cambridge University, Duke University, and University of Chicago); James Lowell Gibbs, Jr. (Stanford University); Edmund Gordon (Columbia Teachers College); Harry E. Groves (University of North Carolina, Chapel Hill); James E. Jones, Jr. (University of Wisconsin); Barbara C. Jordan (the University of Texas at Austin); C. Eric Lincoln (Duke University and Clark University); Bertha Maxwell-Roddy (University of North Carolina, Charlotte); Samuel DeWitt Proctor (Rutgers University); William H. Peterson (Campbell University); Charlotte H. Scott (University of Virginia); Nathan A. Scott (University of Virginia); John B. Turner (University of North Carolina, Chapel Hill); and Marilyn V. Yarborough (University of North Carolina, Chapel Hill).

William A. M. Aikin, Jr., Regents' Chair in Junior and Community College Educational Leadership, College of Education, the University of Texas at Austin.

Emmanuel K. Akyeampong, Hugh K. Foster Associate Professor of African Studies, Harvard University.

Delores P. Aldridge, Grace Towns Hamilton Professor of Sociology and African-American Studies, Emory University.

Elijah Anderson, The Charles and William L. Day Professor, University of Pennsylvania.

Gloria Long Anderson, Fuller E. Callaway Professor of Chemistry, Morris Brown College.

Maya Angelou, Reynolds Professor of American Studies, Wake Forest University.

Regina Austin, William A. Schnader Professor of Law, University of Pennsylvania.

Mario J. Azevedo, Frank Porter Graham Professor, University of North Carolina, Charlotte.

Houston A. Baker, Jr., Albert M. Greenfield Professor of Human Relations, University of Pennsylvania.

William C. Banfield, Endowed Chair in Humanities and Fine Arts, University of St. Thomas, St. Paul, Minnesota.

Lucius Barker, Professor of Political Science, William Bennett Monroe Professor in Political Science, Stanford University.

Mary Frances Berry, Geraldine R. Segal Professor of American Social Thought and professor of history, University of Pennsylvania.

Joanne Braxton, Francis L. and Edwin L. Cummings Professor of American Studies and professor of English, College of William and Mary.

Frank Brown, Cary C. Boshamer Professor, School of Education, University of North Carolina.

Linda Beatrice Brown, Willa B. Player Endowed Chair in the Humanities, Bennett College.

Herrington J. Bryce, Life of Virginia Professor of Business Administration, College of William and Mary.

Roy S. Bryce-Laporte, MacArthur Professor of Sociology and director, Africana and Latin American Studies Program, Colgate University.

John S. Butler, Dallas TACA Centennial Professor in the Liberal Arts and Arthur James Douglass Centennial Professor in Entrepreneurship and Small Business, the University of Texas at Austin.

Clive O. Callender, LaSalle D. Leffall, Jr. Professor, Department of Surgery, Howard University College of Medicine.

Stephen L. Carter, William Nelson Cromwell Professor of Law, Yale University Law School.

Alan K. Colon, NEH Eminent Scholar's Endowed Chair in African Diasporan Studies, Dillard University.

James P. Comer, Maurice K. Falk Professor of Child Psychiatry, Yale Child Study Center, Yale University.

William W. Cook, Israel Evans Professor of Oratory and Belles Lettres and chair, Department of English, Dartmouth College.

Dolores Cross, General Electric Distinguished Professor in Leadership and Diversity, City University of New York.

Charles Curry, John B. Johnson Professor, Department of Medicine, Howard University College of Medicine

William Darity, Jr., Cary C. Boshamer Professor, Department of Economics, University of North Carolina at Chapel Hill.

Larry Davis, Desmond Lee Professor of Racial and Ethnic Diversity, Washington University, St. Louis, Missouri.

Charles Edward Daye, Henry P. Brandis Professor of Law, School of Law, University of North Carolina at Chapel Hill.

Dennis C. Dickerson, Stanfield Professor of History and chair, Department of History, Williams College.

Rita Dove, Commonwealth Professor of English, University of Virginia.

Michael Eric Dyson, Ida Wells-Barnett University Professor, DePaul University, Chicago, Illinois.

Harry J. Elam, Jr., Christensen Professor in the Humanities, Stanford University

Slayton A. Evans, Jr., Kenan Professor, Department of Chemistry, University of North Carolina at Chapel Hill.

Etta Falconer, Calloway Professor of Mathematics and interim provost, Spelman College.

Kenneth Forde, José Ferrer Professor of Surgery, College of Physicians and Surgeons, Columbia University.

Frances Smith Foster, Charles Howard Candler Professor of English and Women's Studies, Department of English, Emory University.

Oscar H. Gandy, Jr., Information Society Chair, Annenberg School for Communication, University of Pennsylvania.

Lisbeth Gant-Britton, Marlene Crandell Francis Trustee Professorship in the Humanities, Kalamazoo College.

Lawrence E. Gary, Samuel S. Wurtzel Chair for Eminent Scholars, School of Social Work, Virginia Commonwealth University.

Fannie Gaston-Johansson, Elsie M. Lawler Chair, School of Nursing, and director, International and Extramural Affairs, Johns Hopkins University.

Henry Louis Gates, Jr., W. E. B. Du Bois Professor of the Humanities, Harvard University.

Jewelle Taylor Gibbs, The Zellerbach Family Fund Chair in Social Policy, Community Change and Practice, University of California, Berkeley.

Cheryl Townsend Gilkes, MacArthur Associate Professor of African-American Studies and Sociology and director, African American Studies, Colby College.

Richard A. Goldsby, John Woodruff Simpson Lecturer and professor of biology, Amherst College.

Peter J. Gomes, Plummer Professor of Christian Morals and chaplain, Harvard University.

William B. Gould IV, Charles A. Beardsley Professor of Law, Stanford University.

J. Lee Greene, Bowman and Gordon Gray Professor of English, University of North Carolina at Chapel Hill.

Pamela Gunter-Smith, Porter Professor of Physiology, Spelman College.

Beverly Guy-Sheftall, Anna Julia Cooper Professor of English and Women's Studies and director of women's studies, Spelman College.

Raymond L. Hall, Orvil Dryfoos Professor of Public Affairs, Department of Sociology, Dartmouth College.

Charles V. Hamilton, Wallace S. Sayre Professor of Government, Columbia University.

Michael S. Harper, University Professor, I. J. Kapstein Professor of English, Brown University.

Trudier Harris, J. Carlyle Sitterson Professor of English, University of North Carolina at Chapel Hill.

J. K. Haynes, David Packard Professor of Biology, Morehouse College.

Asa Grant Hilliard, III, Fuller E. Callaway Professor of Urban Education, Georgia State University.

Darlene Clark Hine, John A. Hannah Professor of History, Michigan State University.

Matthew Holden, Jr., The Henry L. and Grace M. Doherty Professor of Government and Foreign Affairs, University of Virginia.

Thomas Holt, James Westphall Thompson Professor, Department of History, University of Chicago.

Alton Hornsby, Jr., Fuller E. Callaway Professor of History, Morehouse College.

Caroline M. Hoxby, Morris Kahn Associate Professor of Economics, Harvard University.

Jacqueline Irvine, Charles Howard Candler Professor of Urban Education, Division of Educational Studies, Emory University.

Alex M. Johnson, Jr., Mary & Daniel Loughran Professor of Law and vice provost for faculty recruitment and retention, University of Virginia.

Bernett L. Johnson, Jr., Herman Beerman Professor of Dermatology, School of Medicine, University of Pennsylvania.

Richard A. Joseph, Asa G. Candler Professor of Politics, Department of Political Science, Emory University.

George M. Langford, Ernest Everett Just 1907 Professorship, professor of biological sciences, Dartmouth College.

Risa L. Lavizzo-Mourey, The Sylvan Eisman Associate Professor of Medicine, University of Pennsylvania.

LaSalle D. Leffall, Jr., Charles R. Drew Professor of Surgery and chairperson, Department of Surgery, Howard University College of Medicine.

David Levering Lewis, Martin Luther King, Jr., University Professor, Department of History, Rutgers University.

Sara Lawrence Lightfoot, Emily Hargroves Fisher Professor of Education, Harvard University.

Richard A. Long, Atticus Haygood Professor of Interdisciplinary Studies, Graduate Institute of Liberal Arts, Emory University.

Kenneth R. Manning, Thomas Meloy Professor of Rhetoric and of the History of Science, Massachusetts Institute of Technology.

James L. Matory, Hugh K. Foster Associate Professor of Afro-American Studies and Anthropology, Harvard University

Ali Mazuri, Albert Schweitzer Professor of Political Science, SUNY, Binghamton.

Reuben R. McDaniel, Jr., Charles and Elizabeth Prothro Regents Chair in Health Care Management, the University of Texas at Austin.

Donald E. McHenry, Distinguished Professor of Diplomacy and Foreign Affairs, Georgetown University.

John S. McNeil, Louis and Ann Wolens Centennial Chair in Gerontology, School of Social Work, the University of Texas at Austin.

Ruth G. McRoy, Ruby Lee Piester Centennial Professor in Services to Children and Families, School of Social Work, the University of Texas at Austin.

Ronald E. Mickens, Fuller E. Calloway Distinguished Professorship-Physics, Clark Atlanta University

William Moore, Jr., A. M. Aikin Regents Chair in Junior and Community College Education Leadership, the University of Texas at Austin.

Toni Morrison, Robert F. Goheen Professor, Council of the Humanities, Princeton University.

John Howard Morrow, Jr., Franklin Professor of History, University of Georgia.

Lydie E. Mouldileno, M. Mark and Esther L. Watkins Assistant Professor in the Humanities, University of Pennsylvania.

Valentin Mudimbe, William R. Kenan, Jr. Professor of French, Comparative Literature, and Classics, Stanford University.

Clive Muir, Statler Foundation Visiting Professor, School of Hotel Administration, Cornell University.

Samuel L. Myers, Jr., Roy Wilkins Professor of Human Relations and Social Justice, Hubert H. Humphrey Institute of Public Affairs, University of Minnesota.

Dolores G. Norton, Samuel Deutsch Professor, School of Social Service Administration, University of Chicago.

Charles J. Ogletree, Jr., Jesse Climenko Professor of Law, Harvard University Law School.

Robert G. O'Meally, Zora Neale Hurston Professor of English, Columbia University.

Lucius Outlaw, T. Wistar Brown Professor of Philosophy, Haverford College.

Nell I. Painter, Edwards Professor of American History, Princeton University.

Orlando H. L. Patterson, John Cowles Professor of Sociology, Harvard University.

Gayle Pemberton, William Rand Kenan Professor of the Humanities, Wesleyan University.

Albert Jordy Raboteau, Henry W. Putnam Professor of Religion, Princeton University.

Arnold Rampersad, Sara Hart Kimball Professor in the Humanities, Stanford University.

William Raspberry, Knight Professor of Communications and Journalism, Duke University.

Robert L. Reddick, Frank M. Townsend, M.D. Professor and chair, Department of Pathology, University of Texas Health Science Center at San Antonio.

Ruthie G. Reynolds, Frist Professorship of Entrepreneurship, Tennessee State University

John R. Rickford, Martin Luther King, Jr., Centennial Professor of Linguistics and director, African and Afro-American Studies, Stanford University.

Joe Ritchie, Knight Professor of Journalism, School of Journalism, Media and Graphic Arts, Florida A&M University.

Sonia B. Sanchez, Laura H. Carnell Professor of English, Temple University.

Hereket H. Selassie, William E. Leuchtenburg Professor of African Studies, University of North Carolina at Chapel Hill.

Lemma W. Senbet, William E. Mayer Professor of Finance, University of Maryland at College Park.

Willis B. Sheftall, Jr., Merrill Professor of Economics and Business, Morehouse College.

George Shirley, Joseph Edgar Maddy Distinguished University Professor of Music, School of Music, University of Michigan.

Ronald R. Sims, Floyd Dewey Gottwald Senior Professor, College of William and Mary.

Elliot P. Skinner, Franz Boas Professor of Anthropology, Columbia University.

Diana T. Slaughter-Defoe, Constance E. Clayton Professor of Urban Education, University of Pennsylvania.

David L. Smith, Francis Christopher Oakley Professor of English and dean of the faculty, Williams College.

Jessie Carney Smith, William and Camille Cosby Professor of the Humanities and University Librarian, Fisk University.

Jon Michael Spencer, Tyler and Alice Haynes Professor of American Studies, University of Richmond.

Margaret Beale Spencer, Graduate School of Education Overseers Professor, University of Pennsylvania.

Claude M. Steele, Lucy Sterns Professor in the Social Sciences, Stanford University.

Chuck Stone, Walter Spearman Professor of Journalism and Mass Communication, School of Journalism and Mass Communication, University of North Carolina at Chapel Hill.

Dorothy S. Strickland, State of New Jersey Professor of Education, Rutgers University.

Gerald E. Thomson, Samuel Lambert Professor of Medicine and Robert Sunneburn Professor of Medicine, College of Physicians and Surgeons, Columbia University.

Lonnie H. Wagstaff, M. K. Hage Centennial Professor in Education, College of Education, the University of Texas at Austin.

Gloria Wade-Gayles, RosaMary Eminent Scholar's Chair in Humanities/Fine Arts, Dillard Universities

Sheila S. Walker, Annabel Irion Worsham Centennial Professor and director, Center for African and Afro-American Studies, Department of Anthropology, the University of Texas at Austin.

Jerry W. Ward, Jr., Lawrence Durgin Professor of English, Tougaloo College.

Isiah M. Warner, Philip W. West Professor of Analytical and Environmental Chemistry, Department of Chemistry, Louisiana State University.

Mary McKelvey Welch, Albert Werthan Professor of Biology, Fisk University.

Cornel West, Alphonse Fletcher, Jr., University Professor, Department of Afro-American Studies, Harvard University

Roger W. Wilkins, Clarence J. Robinson Professor of History and American Culture, George Mason University.

Dolores W. Williams, Tillich Professor of Theology and Culture, Union Theological Seminary.

James H. Williams, Jr., School Engineering Professor of Teaching Excellence, Charles F. Hopewell Faculty Fellow, and professor of applied mathematics, Massachusetts Institute of Technology.

Preston Noah Williams, Houghton Professor of Theology and Contemporary Change, Harvard University.

Walter A. Williams, John M. Olin Professor of Economics, George Mason University.

Charles V. Willie, Charles William Eliot Professor of Education, Harvard University.

Jan Willis, Walter A. Crowell University Professor of Social Sciences, Religion Department, Wesleyan University.

William Julius Wilson, Lewis P. and Linda L. Gayser University Professor, John F. Kennedy School of Government, Harvard University.

Raymond Winbush, Benjamin Hooks Professor of Social Justice, Fisk University

Herbert Graves Winful, The Arthur F. Turneau Professor of Electrical Engineering and Computer Science, University of Michigan.

May L. Wykle, Florence Cellar Professor of Gerontological Nursing, Frances Payne Bolton School of Nursing at Case Western Reserve University.

◆ EDUCATION STATISTICS

Educational Attainment, by Race, Hispanic Origin, and Sex: 1960 to 1997

YEAR	ALL RACES [1]		WHITE		BLACK		ASIAN AND PACIFIC ISLANDER		HISPANIC [2]	
	Male	Female	Male	Female	Male	Female	Male	Female	Male	Female
COMPLETED 4 YEARS OF HIGH SCHOOL OR MORE										
1960	39.5	42.5	41.6	44.7	18.2	21.8	(NA)	(NA)	(NA)	(NA)
1965	48.0	49.9	50.2	52.2	25.8	28.4	(NA)	(NA)	(NA)	(NA)
1970	51.9	52.8	54.0	55.0	30.1	32.5	(NA)	(NA)	37.9	34.2
1975	63.1	62.1	65.0	64.1	41.6	43.3	(NA)	(NA)	39.5	36.7
1980	67.3	65.8	69.6	68.1	50.8	51.5	(NA)	(NA)	67.3	65.8
1985	74.4	73.5	76.0	75.1	58.4	60.8	(NA)	(NA)	48.5	47.4
1990	77.7	77.5	79.1	79.0	65.8	66.5	84.0	77.2	50.3	51.3
1994 [3]	81.0	80.7	82.1	81.9	71.7	73.8	88.6	81.5	53.4	53.2
1995 [3]	81.7	81.6	83.0	83.0	73.4	74.1	(NA)	(NA)	52.9	53.8
1996 [3]	81.9	81.6	82.7	82.8	74.3	74.2	86.0	80.7	53.0	53.3
1997 [3]	82.0	82.2	82.9	83.2	73.5	76.0	(NA)	(NA)	54.9	54.6
COMPLETED 4 YEARS OF COLLEGE OR MORE										
1960	9.7	5.8	10.3	6.0	2.8	3.3	(NA)	(NA)	(NA)	(NA)
1965	12.0	7.1	12.7	7.3	4.9	4.5	(NA)	(NA)	(NA)	(NA)
1970	13.5	8.1	14.4	8.4	4.2	4.6	(NA)	(NA)	7.8	4.3
1975	17.6	10.6	18.4	11.0	6.7	6.2	(NA)	(NA)	8.3	4.6
1980	20.1	12.8	21.3	13.3	8.4	8.3	(NA)	(NA)	9.4	6.0
1985	23.1	16.0	24.0	16.3	11.2	11.0	(NA)	(NA)	9.7	7.3
1990	24.4	18.4	25.3	19.0	11.9	10.8	44.9	35.4	9.8	8.7
1994 [3]	25.1	19.6	26.1	20.0	12.8	13.0	45.8	37.2	9.6	8.6
1995 [3]	26.0	20.2	27.2	21.0	13.6	12.9	(NA)	(NA)	10.1	8.4
1996 [3]	26.0	21.4	26.9	21.8	12.4	14.6	46.4	37.3	10.3	8.3
1997 [3]	26.2	21.7	27.0	22.3	12.5	13.9	(NA)	(NA)	10.6	10.1

NA Not available. [1] Includes other races, not shown separately. [2] Persons of Hispanic origin may be of any race. [3] Beginning 1994, persons high school graduates and those with a BA degree or higher.

Source: U.S. Bureau of the Census, *U.S. Census of Population, 1960, 1970, and 1980, Vol.1;* and *Current Population Reports* P20-459, P20-489, P20-493, P20-505; and unpublished data.

High School Dropouts by Age, Race, and Hispanic Origin: 1970 to 1996

[As of **October. For persons 14 to 24 years old.**]

AGE AND RACE	NUMBER OF DROPOUTS (1,000)					PERCENT OF POPULATION				
	1970	1980	1990	1995	1996	1970	1980	1990	1995	1996
Total dropouts [1]	**4,670**	**5,212**	**3,854**	**3,963**	**3,763**	**12.2**	**12.0**	**10.1**	**9.9**	**9.4**
16 to 17 years	617	709	418	406	464	8.0	8.8	6.3	5.4	6.0
18 to 21 years	2,138	2,578	1,921	1,980	1,841	16.4	15.8	13.4	14.2	13.0
22 to 24 years	1,770	1,798	1,458	1,491	1,306	18.7	15.2	13.8	13.6	12.4
White [2]	3,577	4,169	3,127	3,098	2,951	10.8	11.3	10.1	9.7	9.2
16 to 17 years	485	619	334	314	369	7.3	9.2	6.4	5.4	6.0
18 to 21 years	1,618	2,032	1,516	1,530	1,411	14.3	14.7	13.1	13.8	12.6
22 to 24 years	1,356	1,416	1,235	1,181	1,047	16.3	14.0	14.0	13.4	12.4
Black [2]	1,047	934	611	605	672	22.2	16.0	10.9	10.0	11.0
16 to 17 years	125	80	73	70	77	12.8	6.9	6.9	5.8	6.1
18 to 21 years	500	486	345	328	368	30.5	23.0	16.0	15.8	16.6
22 to 24 years	397	346	185	194	213	37.8	24.0	13.5	12.5	14.9
Hispanic [2 3]	(NA)	919	1,122	1,355	1,350	(NA)	29.5	26.8	24.7	24.6
16 to 17 years	(NA)	92	89	94	105	(NA)	16.6	12.9	10.7	10.8
18 to 21 years	(NA)	470	502	652	665	(NA)	40.3	32.9	29.9	33.8
22 to 24 years	(NA)	323	523	598	545	(NA)	40.6	42.8	37.4	35.3

NA Not available. [1] Includes other groups not shown separately. [2] Includes persons 14 to 15 years, not shown separately. [3] Persons of Hispanic origin may be of any race.

Source: U.S. Bureau of the Census, *Current Population Reports*, P20-500; and earlier reports.

Proficiency Test Scores for Selected Subjects, by Characteristic: 1977 to 1996

[Based on The National Assessment of Educational Progress Tests which are administered to a representative sample of students in public and private schools. Test scores can range from 0 to 500. For details, see source]

TEST AND YEAR	Total	SEX		RACE		Hispanic origin	PARENTAL EDUCATION				
							Less than high school	High school	More than high school		
		Male	Female	White [1]	Black [1]				Total	Some college	College graduate
READING											
9 year olds:											
1979-80	215	210	220	221	189	190	194	213	226	(NA)	(NA)
1987-88	212	208	216	218	189	194	193	211	220	(NA)	(NA)
1993-94	211	207	215	218	185	186	189	207	221	(NA)	(NA)
1995-96	212	207	218	220	190	194	197	207	220	(NA)	(NA)
13 year olds:											
1979-80	259	254	263	264	233	237	239	254	271	(NA)	(NA)
1987-88	258	252	263	261	243	240	247	253	265	(NA)	(NA)
1993-94	258	251	266	265	234	235	237	251	269	(NA)	(NA)
1995-96	259	253	265	267	236	240	241	252	270	(NA)	(NA)
17 year olds:											
1979-80	286	282	289	293	243	261	262	278	299	(NA)	(NA)
1987-88	290	286	294	295	274	271	267	282	300	(NA)	(NA)
1993-94	288	282	295	296	266	263	268	276	299	(NA)	(NA)
1995-96	287	280	294	294	265	265	267	273	297	(NA)	(NA)
WRITING [2]											
4th graders:											
1983-84	204	201	208	211	182	189	179	192	217	208	218
1987-88	206	199	213	215	173	190	194	199	212	211	212
1993-94	205	196	214	214	173	189	188	202	(NA)	212	212
1995-96	207	200	214	216	182	191	190	203	(NA)	205	214
8th graders:											
1983-84	267	258	276	272	247	247	258	261	276	271	278
1987-88	264	254	274	269	246	250	254	258	271	275	271
1993-94	265	254	278	272	245	252	250	259	(NA)	270	275
1995-96	264	251	276	271	242	246	245	258	(NA)	270	274
11th graders:											
1983-84	290	281	299	297	270	259	274	284	299	298	300
1987-88	291	282	299	296	275	274	276	285	298	296	299
1993-94	285	276	293	291	267	271	269	279	(NA)	286	293
1995-96	283	275	292	289	267	269	260	275	(NA)	287	291
MATHEMATICS											
9 year olds:											
1977-78	219	217	220	224	192	203	200	219	231	230	231
1985-86	222	222	222	227	202	205	201	218	231	229	231
1993-94	231	232	230	237	212	210	210	225	(NA)	239	238
1995-96	231	233	229	237	212	215	220	221	(NA)	238	240
13 year olds:											
1977-78	264	264	265	272	230	238	245	263	280	273	284
1985-86	269	270	268	274	249	254	252	263	278	274	280
1993-94	274	276	273	281	252	256	255	266	(NA)	277	285
1995-96	274	276	272	281	252	256	254	267	(NA)	278	283
17 year olds:											
1977-78	300	304	297	306	268	276	280	294	313	305	317
1985-86	302	305	299	308	279	283	279	293	310	305	314
1993-94	306	309	304	312	286	291	284	295	(NA)	305	318
1995-96	307	310	305	313	286	292	281	297	(NA)	307	317
SCIENCE											
9 year olds:											
1976-77	220	222	218	230	175	192	199	223	233	237	232
1985-86	224	227	221	232	196	199	204	220	235	236	235
1993-94	231	232	230	240	201	201	211	225	(NA)	239	239
1995-96	230	232	228	239	201	207	215	222	(NA)	242	240
13 year olds:											
1976-77	247	251	244	256	208	213	224	245	264	260	266
1985-86	251	256	247	259	222	226	229	245	262	258	264
1993-94	257	259	254	267	224	232	234	247	(NA)	260	269
1995-96	256	261	252	266	226	232	232	248	(NA)	260	266
17 year olds:											
1976-77	290	297	282	298	240	262	265	284	304	296	309
1985-86	289	295	282	298	253	259	258	277	300	295	304
1993-94	294	300	289	306	257	261	256	279	(NA)	295	311
1995-96	296	300	292	307	260	269	261	282	(NA)	297	308
HISTORY, 1993-94											
4th graders	205	203	206	215	177	180	177	197	(NA)	214	216
8th graders:	259	259	259	267	239	243	241	251	(NA)	264	270
12th graders	286	288	285	292	265	267	263	276	(NA)	287	296
GEOGRAPHY, 1993-94											
4th graders	206	208	203	218	168	183	186	197	(NA)	216	216
8th graders	260	262	258	270	229	239	238	250	(NA)	265	272
12th graders	285	288	281	291	258	268	263	274	(NA)	286	294

NA Not available. [1] Non-Hispanic. [2] Writing scores revised from previous years; previous writing scores were recorded on a 0 to 400 rather than 0 to 500 scale.

Source: U.S. National Center for Education Statistics, *Digest of Education Statistics*, annual.

Religion

◆ Origins and History of African American Religious Traditions
◆ African American Female Religious Leadership
◆ African American Churches during Reconstruction
◆ African American Churches in the Twentieth Century
◆ Evolving Trends among African American Churches ◆ African American Denominations
◆ Religious Leaders ◆ Religious Statistics

by Stephen W. Angell

The first Africans who arrived on North American shores brought their own religious world views with them. While a minority had been Muslims or Christians prior to their kidnapping by slave traders, most adhered to their native African religions. Hundreds of these religions developed, but in general, the Africans believed that the world had been created by a high god who removed himself from direct intervention in worldly affairs after the act of creation.

◆ ORIGINS AND HISTORY OF AFRICAN AMERICAN RELIGIOUS TRADITIONS

Early African American Belief Systems

In Africa, worshipers directed their prayers to intermediary spirits, chief among whom were their ancestors or the "living dead." If proper offering was made to an ancestor, the individual would be blessed with great prosperity, but if the ancestor was slighted, misfortune would result. In addition, the Yorubas worshiped a variety of nature spirits or *orishas*. These spirits often possessed their devotees, who then became mediums of their gods. This kind of spirit-possession is a prominent feature of some modern African American religions, such as *santeria*, which recently has spread across large urban areas including Miami and New York. Also a part of the African worldview, especially among the Bakongo, was the practice of magic, variously known in the New World as *obeah, vaudou (voodoo)*, or *conjure*. This magic, designed to help friends (myalism) or to hurt enemies (obeah), at one time was widely practiced by Africans throughout the Western Hemisphere.

The type of African spirituality that took root in North America merged elements from many African cultures. Since slave masters intentionally mixed Africans from many tribal backgrounds, no "pure" African religion preserving one tradition emerged. Nevertheless, the longstanding scholarly controversy over the extent to which African traditions have been retained in African-based religions is gradually being resolved in favor of those who see extensive survivals. In addition to singing, church music, and preaching style, aspects where an African influence has generally been conceded, scholars have made persuasive arguments for African survivals in family structure, funeral practices, church organization, and many other areas.

Missionary Efforts by Christians

The first sustained effort at converting African Americans to Christianity was made by the Anglican Society for the Propagation of the Gospel in Foreign Parts, which sent missionaries to North America in 1701. These missionaries had little success among the Africans; many mocked those who imitated the whites too closely and, thus, resisted the missionaries. In addition, white slave masters often resented losing slaves's time to church services and feared that slaves would lay a claim to freedom through conversion. The numerous colonial laws, starting with Virginia in 1669, proclaiming that conversion failed to entitle slaves to freedom did not comfort some slave masters, who suspected that Christianity would undermine slave discipline—indeed, some remained unconvinced of the advisability of missionary efforts until emancipation occurred. On the other hand, some slave masters believed the Christianization of Africans to be justification for enslaving them.

Subsequent efforts to convert African Americans to Christianity were more successful. In his seven missionary tours throughout North America between 1742 and 1770, the spellbinding orator George Whitefield effected the conversions of large numbers of both black and white Americans. The ministry of Methodist circuit riders, such as Francis Asbury, was also well received by African Americans at the end of the eighteenth century. Baptist and Methodist churches were the most successful in attracting African American members. Since these churches did not require their ministers to be well educated, doors were opened for aspiring African American ministers, many of whom lived in states where teaching African Americans to read and write was forbidden by law. Furthermore, the Baptists and Methodists were not as hostile to the emotionalism of African American preachers and congregations as were more staid denominations, such as the Episcopalians. Finally, the anti-slavery stance of notable Methodist and Baptist leaders, such as John Wesley, Francis Asbury, and John Leland, and the greater degree of equality nurtured within many Baptist and Methodist congregations were attractive to African Americans.

Early Christian Congregations

Probably the first organizing effort by African Americans to bear fruit in an independent African American congregation was the Silver Bluff Baptist Church in South Carolina, which came into existence between 1773 and 1775. David George, an African American, and seven other men and women formed its organizing nucleus. George Liele, one of George's associates, often preached at the Silver Bluff Church before emigrating to Jamaica in 1782. Andrew Bryan, one of Liele's converts, founded the First African Baptist Church in Savannah, Georgia, in 1788.

Bryan's life well represented the complex predicament faced by African American religious leaders in the antebellum South. In the early years of his ministry, Bryan was whipped and twice imprisoned by whites who feared him. But he bought his freedom, prospered, and eventually came to own much property including eight slaves; his death in 1812 was mourned by blacks and whites alike. While many African American churches continued to be served by white ministers until 1865, African American pastors, licensed ministers, and exhorters ministering to African American Baptist and Methodist congregations were not at all unusual at this time, either in the South or the North.

Black Catholics

Before the Civil War, African American Catholics were confined largely to Maryland and Louisiana. However, Catholics made greater efforts to convert African Americans after the Civil War. By the end of the nineteenth century, nearly 200,000 African American Catholics were worshiping in the United States, but more Protestant African American ministers existed than did African American priests in the Catholic churches.

Discrimination in White Churches

While white preachers urged African Americans to convert, and many predominantly white congregations welcomed them into membership, racial prejudice was never absent from the religious scene. Although the level of discrimination varied from region to region and congregation to congregation, some factors were relatively constant.

One such factor was the relative paucity of ordained African American clergy. To take the Methodists as an example, some African American ministers were ordained as deacons within the Methodist Episcopal Church prior to 1820, but none in the thereafter four decades. No African American Methodist minister was ordained by the Methodist Episcopal Church to the higher office of elder or consecrated as a bishop prior to the Civil War, unless he was willing to emigrate to Liberia.

Other discriminatory practices also formed part of the religious landscape. The Methodists and many other denominations tried to reserve the administration of sacraments as the exclusive province of white clergy. Segregated seating in churches was pervasive in both the North and the South. Church discipline was often unevenly applied. Of course, racial discrimination in the churches was only a small part of the much larger political and moral controversy over slavery.

Resistance to discrimination took many forms. In the North, Peter Spencer in Wilmington, Delaware, Richard Allen in Philadelphia, and James Varick in New York, led their African American followers out of white Methodist churches and set up independent African American congregations. In Allen's case, his departure was preceded by a dramatic confrontation over segregated seating in Philadelphia's white Methodist church. Each of these men then used his congregation as the nucleus of a new African American Methodist denomination—Spencer formed the African Union Church in 1807; Allen, the African Methodist Episcopal Church (AME) in 1816; and Varick, a denomination eventually called

Congregation standing in front of the First African Baptist Church in Savannah, Georgia.

the African Methodist Episcopal Zion Church (AME Zion) in 1821.

Meanwhile, in Charleston, South Carolina, a more explosive situation was taking shape. Morris Brown, an African American Methodist minister from Charleston, who had helped Richard Allen organize the African Methodist Episcopal Church, organized an independent African American Methodist church in his home city. The authorities harassed Brown's church and sometimes arrested its leaders. Nevertheless, within a year, more than three-quarters of Charleston's African American Methodists had united with him. The oppression of African Americans in Charleston was so severe that many members of Brown's congregation, including prominent lay leaders, joined the insurrection planned by Denmark Vesey to take over the Charleston armory and, eventually, the whole environs of Charleston. The conspirators, apprehended before they could carry out their plans, testified that Brown had not known of their scheme, and the minister was allowed to move to Philadelphia, where Richard Allen made him the second bishop of the African Methodist Episcopal Church.

A few African Americans became acquiescent as a result of Christianity. One such example was Pierre Toussaint, a black Haitian slave who fled in 1787 to New York with his white owners, the Berards, just prior to the Haitian Revolution. In 1811, Mrs. Berard manumitted Toussaint on her death bed. Over the next forty years, Toussaint became a notable philanthropist, contributing funds to the building of St. Patrick's Cathedral. However, when the cathedral opened, Toussaint did not protest when a white usher refused to seat him for services. Some American Catholics recently revived the controversy over Toussaint, by campaigning for his canonization. Many African American Catholics have strongly objected, seeing Toussaint as passive and servile and thus a poor candidate for sainthood.

Emancipation Efforts of African American Church Leaders

The mid-nineteenth century saw increased anti-slavery activity among many African American church leaders and members. Some gave qualified support to the gradual emancipation program sponsored by the American Colonization Society, which sought to encourage free African Americans to emigrate to Africa in order to Westernize and Christianize the Africans. Virginia Baptist pastor Lott Cary and Maryland Methodist minister

Daniel Coker were the two most prominent African American religious leaders to emigrate to Africa in the 1820s. By the 1850s, enough African American Methodists were in Liberia for the Methodist Episcopal Church to consecrate an African American bishop, Francis Burns, to serve the Liberian churches. While some black Americans were emigrating to Africa, others emigrated to the West Indies—Episcopalian Bishop James T. Holly, for example, settled in Haiti to undertake missionary work.

Because of the extreme repression in the slave states, African Americans were unable to openly express their views on political issues. They were, however, often able to make their views clear; for example, a white minister who dwelled too long on the Biblical text that servants should obey their masters was apt to find his African American listeners deserting him. In addition, African American Christians often held secret meetings in "brush arbors," rude structures made of pine boughs, or in the middle of the woods. There they could sing spirituals and pray openly for the quick advent of freedom. Slave revolts, on the other hand, provided a violent outbreak of dissent much feared by whites. The 1831 revolt of Nat Turner, a Baptist preacher, in Northampton County, Virginia, was suppressed only after tremendous bloodshed had been visited upon both African Americans and whites. Frightened whites in the South intensified their surveillance of African American churches in the aftermath of the Turner revolt. Even conservative African American preachers, such as Presbyterian John Chavis in North Carolina and the Baptist "Uncle Jack" in Virginia, were prohibited from preaching.

African American leaders in the North could afford to be more open and forthright in their political stance. Most rejected outright the views of the American Colonization Society in favor of the immediate abolition of slavery. Presbyterian minister Henry Highland Garnet was a prominent abolitionist, urging African American slaves in 1843 to "let your motto be RESISTANCE! RESISTANCE! RESISTANCE!" African Methodist Episcopal Bishop Daniel Payne and African Methodist Episcopal Zion Bishop Christopher Rush, both emigrants from the Carolinas to the North, were outspoken abolitionists who, after the mid-1840s, became the most prominent leaders in their respective churches. Frederick Douglass was one of the few leading African American abolitionists who did not pursue a ministerial career, and even he had briefly served as an African Methodist Episcopal Zion preacher in New Bedford, Massachusetts. African American clergy were extraordinarily active in recruiting African American men to join the Union armies during the Civil War, after the Emancipation Proclamation opened up the possibility of military service to them. During the Civil War, nearly a dozen African American ministers, including the African Methodist Episcopal Church's Henry McNeal Turner, served as chaplains to African American army regiments.

◆ AFRICAN AMERICAN FEMALE RELIGIOUS LEADERSHIP

Early African American women ministers sometimes served as travelling evangelists, especially within African American denominations. While Sojourner Truth's oratory has become appropriately famous, Maria Stewart, Jarena Lee, Zilpha Elaw, and other early nineteenth century women also spoke eloquently and, in Lee's and Elaw's cases, travelled widely and labored diligently. None of these women were ordained, but Elizabeth (no last name known), a former slave from Maryland whose ministry began in 1796, spoke for many female preachers when she was accused of preaching without a license: "If the Lord has ordained me, I need nothing better." Rebecca Cox Jackson left the African Methodist Episcopal Church in the 1830s when she felt that men denied her the chance to exercise her ministry, and she eventually became head eldress of a predominantly African American Shaker community in Philadelphia.

During the postbellum years, some African American women sought and obtained formal ordination from their denominations. Sarah Ann Hughes, a successful North Carolina evangelist and pastor in the African Methodist Episcopal Church, was ordained by Bishop Henry McNeal Turner in 1885, but complaints from male pastors caused her ordination to be revoked two years later. The A.M.E. Church would not ordain another woman until 1948, when Rebecca Glover was ordained. Two women were ordained, however, by African Methodist Episcopal Zion bishops not long after the Hughes controversy—Mary J. Smalls in 1895 as a deacon and in 1898 as an elder, and also Julia A. J. Foote in 1894 and 1900, respectively. Pauli Murray, a distinguished lawyer and educator, in 1977 became the first African American woman to be ordained a priest in the predominantly white Episcopal Church. In 1989, Barbara Harris became the first woman bishop in the history of the Episcopal Church.

Throughout American history, many African American women exercised their ministry through para-ecclesiastical structures, such as women's temperance and missionary societies, while others, such as Anna Cooper and the African Methodist Episcopal Church's Frances Jackson Coppin, became renowned educators.

◆ AFRICAN AMERICAN CHURCHES DURING RECONSTRUCTION

African American church membership grew explosively after the Civil War, especially in the South, where

Although women were not allowed to become A.M.E. church leaders in the early years, they were permitted to teach and preach (The Library of Congress).

the African American clergy played a prominent part in the Reconstruction governments. African Methodist Episcopal minister Hiram Revels became the first African American to serve as a U. S. senator, when the Mississippi legislature sent him to Washington, DC, in 1870. However, Revels was only the ground breaker; many African American ministers went on to serve in the Congress or in their state governments. African American participation in Reconstruction politics was effective in large part because ministers in the AME and AME Zion Churches, and many African American Baptist ministers, carefully and patiently educated their congregation members on every civic and political issue. (Although the newly established African American denomination, the Colored Methodist Episcopal Church, largely stayed away from politics during Reconstruction.)

Even though African Americans were largely expelled from Southern state governments after the end of political Reconstruction in the 1870s, many African American ministers and laity continued to play an active political role on such issues as temperance, often campaigning on behalf of prohibition referenda. The Southern white campaign of terror, lynching, and disfranchisement steadily reduced African American political power and participation, however, until the onset of mid-twentieth century civil rights movements.

African American Churches's Response to Segregation

As the system of racial segregation imposed in the 1880s and 1890s took hold, African American ministers coordinated a manifold response. First, they forthrightly challenged new segregation laws, engaging in civil disobedience and boycotts. For example, when the city of Nashville, Tennessee, segregated its street cars in 1906, influential Baptist minister R. H. Boyd led an African American boycott of the streetcars, even operating his own streetcar line for a time. No defeat was ever seen as final.

Second, African American ministers helped to nurture a separate set of African American institutions to serve African Americans excluded from white establishments. The Congregationalists, Baptists, and Northern Methodists established schools in the South for African Americans during Reconstruction, but the African Methodist Episcopal, African Methodist Episcopal Zion, and Christian Methodist Episcopal bishops forged ahead with the establishment of their own network of schools. The African American denominations also built up their publishing houses, and the books and periodicals that they published were vital to the black community. Virtually every institution with ties to African American communities received some support from African American churches.

Third, some African American ministers believed that the civil rights retreats of the late nineteenth century should spur African Americans to leave the United States for a destination where their full civil rights would be respected. A "Back to Africa" movement grew to enable African Americans to find a home where they could run governments, banks, and businesses without interference from whites. Thus, Bishop Turner helped to organize a steamship line to carry African Americans back to Africa, and two shiploads of African American emigrants sailed to Liberia in 1895 and 1896 as a result of his efforts. Some African American church leaders, such as Christian Methodist Episcopal Bishop Lucius Holsey and AME Bishop Richard Cain, held views similar to those advocated by Turner, but many more church leaders opposed Turner's emigrationism vigorously. Simultaneously, African American missionary work continued to occupy the attention of African Americans at the end of the nineteenth century. Under the guidance of

Bishops Payne and Turner, for example, the African Methodist Episcopal Church had a vigorous missionary presence in Sierra Leone, Liberia, and South Africa.

◆ AFRICAN AMERICAN CHURCHES IN THE TWENTIETH CENTURY

In the twentieth century, African American religious life has become characterized by a far greater degree of diversity and pluralism. At the same time, traditional African American concerns, including the continuing quest for freedom and justice, have been not only maintained but strengthened. Pentecostalism, which burst on the American scene in 1906, has become a major religious force within the African American community. William Joseph Seymour, a preacher and son of ex-slaves from Louisiana, led an extraordinary interracial revival in Los Angeles from 1906 to 1909 that enabled Pentecostalism to spread worldwide. The claim that all heavenly gifts that were available to early Christians, including faith healing and speaking in tongues, were available to modern Christians, gave great impetus to the movement. The Pentecostal-oriented Church of God in Christ, founded by Charles H. Mason, who attended Seymour's revival, has become the second largest African American denomination in the United States. In the latter part of the century, the charismatic or Neo-Pentecostal movement has revitalized many congregations within mainline African American denominations.

The liturgy of the African American churches was transformed with the introduction of gospel music in the early part of the twentieth century. Influenced by the work of such composers as Charles Tindley, Charles Price Jones, Lucie Campbell Williams and Thomas Dorsey, the new music enabled worshipers to praise God with rhythms and harmonies imported from more secular musical genres, such as blues and jazz. This new fusion sparked the creation of compositions that perhaps expressed the deep religious feelings of ordinary worshipers in the pews more appropriately than any previous music. New instruments were brought into the churches for the performance of these new musical compositions including guitars, drums, and, eventually, synthesizers and electronic instruments. This music initially encountered strong resistance in many African American congregations, but the popularity of such performers as Mahalia Jackson and the passage of time have enabled it to win a very wide acceptability. Church choirs and ensembles, such as the Dixie Hummingbirds, helped to gain for gospel music an ever- increasing audience. While both Methodists and Baptists played a part in the spread of gospel music, the Holiness-Pentecostalist churches stemming from the 1906 revivals in Los Angeles played an especially important role in its increasing popularity.

The black nationalism of Bishop Turner came to full flower in the work of such men as Marcus Garvey (and his chaplain general, George A. McGuire), Elijah Muhammad, and Malcolm X. This black nationalism aided the growth on non-Christian religions, such as Islam and Black Judaism, within the African American community. Black nationalists often rejected Christianity as too complicit with slaveholding and racial oppression. A spectacular rise of storefront churches occurred, some of which were led by flamboyant showmen, such as Father Divine and "Sweet Daddy" Grace. Each of these trends has been significantly aided by the African American migrations after 1915 from southern states to the North, which greatly strengthened African American communities. A somewhat later migration from the Caribbean provided support for the growth of a diverse range of religions within the African American community including the Episcopal Church, Seventh-Day Adventism, Roman Catholicism, Rastafarianism, santeria, and voodoo. An early Caribbean migrant was Sarah Mae Manning, who brought up her son, Louis Eugene Wolcott, in Boston within the Episcopal Church. He later achieved fame as a Muslim under the name of Louis Farrakhan.

Many black ministers became advocates of a Social Gospel movement. One of the most famous was Rev. Ransom of the African Methodist Episcopal Church, who came into prominence between 1901 and 1904 as pastor of an Institutional Church in Chicago. ("Institutional churches" provided a whole panoply of social services to needy members and neighbors, in addition to regular worship.) Social Gospellers highlighted the reality of collective, societal sin, such as the starvation of children and the denial of human rights, and maintained that Christian repentance of these sins must be followed by concrete actions to rectify injustice and to assist the poor. The Reverend Dr. Martin Luther King, Jr. was profoundly influenced by this Social Gospel movement.

Many ministers and congregations maintained a kind of political involvement that built on a long tradition within the African American community and often with Social Gospel concerns in mind. Chicago AME minister Archibald Carey was a behind-the-scenes political organizer early in the twentieth century who effectively represented the interests of the African American community. New York's Adam Clayton Powell, Jr. and Floyd Flake and Atlanta's Andrew Young and John Lewis were ministers who achieved election to the U.S. House of

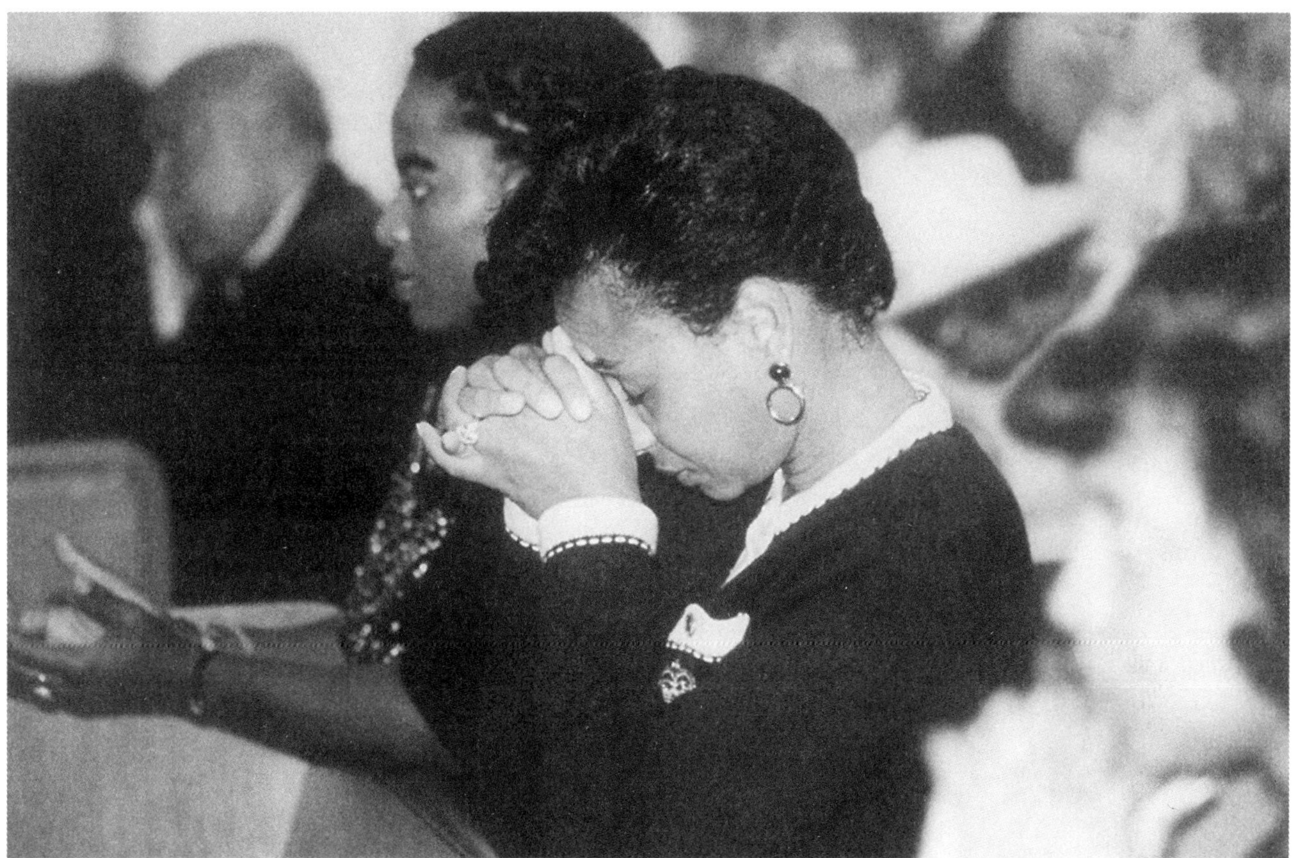

African American parishioners attend a service at the Church of the Transfiguration in Los Angeles (AP/Wide World Photos, Inc.).

Representatives, with Powell rising to the chairmanship of the influential Education and Labor Committee during the 1960s. Other African American ministers, including Malcolm X, Al Sharpton, and Calvin Butts, have played important roles as community organizers, although never serving in elective office. Jesse Jackson's attempts to gain the Democratic nomination for president in 1984 and 1988 brought the electoral clout of the African American church into the spotlight. The African American church's strong involvement in political, economic, and social affairs helps to point out its continuing and central relevance—even indispensability—within the national context.

The Civil Rights movement of the 1960s was deeply influenced by the African American church context from which its most prominent organizer, Martin Luther King, Jr., sprang. Its demonstrations, speeches, and movement songs were suffused with biblical images drawn from the Book of Exodus and other parts of the Bible. It was their deep religious faith that made it possible for the movement to keep progressing along a nonviolent path, even when King's home in Montgomery was firebombed or the Ninth Street Baptist Church in Birmingham in 1963 also was bombed, with four young girls the casualties of that violence. In a significant sense, King inherited his activism from his father, Martin Luther King, Sr., also a Baptist pastor, who had led rallies and economic boycotts against racial discrimination as far back as the 1930s. But it is also worth recalling that many African American religious leaders in the 1960s thought that King's brand of social activism was too radical. One of King's most determined critics during the 1960s was the theologically conservative president of the National Baptist Convention of the U.S.A., Inc., Joseph H. Jackson. The attempt by King's ministerial allies to unseat Jackson as president of the convention in 1960 and 1961 led to a schism, with King and his supporters forming a new denomination, the Progressive National Baptist Convention. King came under further criticism when, in 1967 and 1968, he made it clear that his advocacy of pacifism extended to opposition to U.S. military involvement in Vietnam.

The Black Theology movement, which grew rapidly after King's assassination, attempted to fashion a critique of the prevalent Christian theology out of the materials that Malcolm X and the Black Power movement provided. African American theologians were skeptical of the integrationist and non-violent thrusts of the

Dr. Joseph Jackson (AP/Wide World Photos, Inc.)

Civil Rights movement, calling the African American community toward greater pride in and reliance upon the community's own cultural resources. One such theologian, Albert Cleage, pastor of the Shrine of the Black Madonna in Detroit, argued that Jesus was a black messiah and that his congregation should follow the teachings of Jehovah, a black god. "Almost everything you have heard about Christianity is essentially a lie," he stated. Cleage was representative of many black theologians in arguing that black liberation should be seen as situated at the core of the Christian gospels. In the 1980s, African American women such as Jacquellyn Grant, Delores Williams, and Katie Cannon have formulated "womanist" theologies, which seek to combat the triple oppression of race, class, and gender suffered by most African American women.

Folk Art of Preaching

In most African American congregations, sermonizing is an interpersonal skill that African Americans have elevated to the level of art with such notable elements as call and response and repetition of phrases. The exuberance of all participants is highly dependent upon the tradition within which one worships. For example, in the more highly liturgical traditions such as Roman Catholicism and Eastern Orthodoxy sermons only tend to be instructional. By contrast, non-liturgical Protestant denominations, including Baptist and Pentecostal churches, tend to view sermons as verbal sacraments. In the 1990s, nondenominational churches have reached a new high in popularity, usually centered upon a solitary, charismatic figure. As the medium is the message, performance is as important as the words themselves. Among the most highly regarded "artists" are Gardner C. Taylor, pastor emeritus of Brooklyn, New York's Concord Baptist Church of Christ; Barbara King, founder and minister of Atlanta's nondenominational Hillside Chapel and Truth Center, Inc.; and James Forbes, senior minister of New York City's Riverside Church. They are just a few of those who have been earmarked as the great preachers of the late twentieth century. In 1996, both Forbes and Taylor were deemed two of the twelve most effective preachers by a Baylor University survey, and Taylor was named as one of President Bill Clinton's favorite evangelists.

◆ EVOLVING TRENDS AMONG AFRICAN AMERICAN CHURCHES

As the twenty-first century approaches, African American religions are undergoing substantial changes. The religious searches of prosperous middle-class African Americans has brought about surging enrollment at African American megachurches in many of the nation's metropolitan areas, such as Atlanta, Washington, DC, and Dallas. A growing interest in do-it-yourself spirituality has greatly enlarged the readership of inspirational writers, such as Iyanla Vanzant and T. D. Jakes. There has been an unprecedented interest in racial reconciliation among conservative Christian churches, joining liberal Christians who have pioneered in this area since the 1960s, even while an upsurge in African American church burnings, especially in the rural South demonstrated that the nation still has much work to do in addressing racism. Muslim leader Louis Farrakhan achieved spectacular success with his Million Man March in October 1995, stressing such spiritual themes as atonement, but he has not fashioned an effective follow-up to this headline-grabbing event. Meanwhile, the urban poor, especially young African American men, seem to be staying away from the churches in ever-increasing numbers.

Large African American churches, such as the Ebenezer African Methodist Episcopal Church in Mary-

Reverend Gardner Taylor, pastor of Concord Baptist Church in Brooklyn, addressing a protest rally in 1963 (AP/Wide World Photos, Inc.)

land with 12,000 members, have attracted the African American middle-class worshippers in unprecedented numbers. They have done so with very diverse offerings. For example, Ebenezer offers marriage counseling, workshops on financial planning, a ministry to lawyers and a socially involved, intellectually informed ministry. Many of the megachurch minsters, such as Ebenezer's pastor and assistant pastor, have doctoral degrees. African American megachurch members reach out to young African American men who are still in poverty, even though their churches are often in the suburbs, miles away from inner city problems. Some African American churches have traditionally had large memberships, but the new megachurches feature younger pastors who have earned doctorates and are often still in their thirties or forties. Unlike their white counterparts, African American megachurches often seek out social involvement and uplift with the poor. Other African American megachurches can be found in such metropolitan areas as Atlanta, Chicago, Dallas, and Memphis.

Increasingly, African American ministerial leadership is passing from those who were on the front lines of civil rights struggles in the 1960s to their children's generation. Perhaps this reality is best symbolized by recent events in Atlanta. In July 1997, 75-year-old Joseph Lowery, who had helped to found the Southern Christian Leadership Conference with his colleagues Martin Luther King, Jr. and Ralph Abernathy, stepped down from the presidency of that organization. Meanwhile, Bernice King, who was five years old when her father was assassinated, has established a successful ministry at the Greater Rising Star Baptist Church in Atlanta. Similar to her father, she preaches a message of forgiveness and reconciliation, and she calls upon churches to commune and fellowship more across racial and ethnic lines. Meanwhile, Atlanta's Ebenezer Baptist Church, where M. L. King, Jr., previously preached, opened a new sanctuary seating 1,600 worshipers in March 1999. The old church building, only half as large, will be taken over and maintained by the National Park Service.

African American Churches Address Social Issues

On the whole, African American churches continue to address a wide variety of social problems affecting the African American community. Perhaps most urgently, many churches have strong anti-drug programs. Some congregations have undertaken vigorous action against "crack" houses. Parochial schools, feeding centers, and housing for senior citizens are also part of the African American church's outreach to the community. Many African American ministers have noted, however, the growing division of the African American community along lines of social class and have exhorted middle-class African Americans to give more generously to programs that aid the poor. James Cone, a leading African American theologian, has stated that African American churches need to devote less time and attention to institutional survival and more to finding ways to deal with such pressing issues as poverty, gang violence, and AIDS. In 1997, five historically African American denominations formed Revelation Corporation of America, a partnership between corporations, charities, and churches; the income from the corporation will be used to help to subsidize home ownership among moderate-income residents of big cities, such as Philadelphia and Memphis.

African American churches have been involved in a wide variety of ecumenical efforts, both with white churches and other African American churches. While mainline Christian organizations, such as the National Council of Churches of Christ, have been involved in efforts for human rights for all and interracial reconciliation since the 1960s, it has only been in the 1990s that evangelical Christian organizations have joined in similar movements. In 1994, predominantly African American and predominantly white Pentecostalist churches formed an interracial umbrella organization for the first time. The Promise Keepers, a Christian men's movement designed to motivate men to become better husbands and fathers, fully included African Americans in the staff and leadership of the organization. In June 1995, the Southern Baptist Convention adopted a resolution apologizing for its previous defense of slavery and "unwaveringly" denouncing "racism, in all its forms, as deplorable sin." The predominantly white National Association of Evangelicals and the National Black Evangelical Association agreed to hold their future meetings jointly. Still, some racial discontent continued to surface among evangelical Christians. The National Baptist Convention, U.S.A., Inc. withheld its support from one of the Reverend Billy Graham's crusades because of Graham's refusal to support affirmative action. In addition, E. Edward Jones, president of the National Baptist Convention of America, Inc., refused to accept the Southern Baptist Convention's apology for slavery and racism, charging that the resolution was simply a cover for aggressive evangelism in the African American community that would draw members away from historically African American churches.

Dialogues between individual denominations continue to nurture the spirit of cooperation between them, with the result of establishing closer working relationships on the national and community levels. In June 1997, leaders of eight historically African American denominations met in Hampton, Virginia in a week-long conference. The church leaders evinced a remarkable spirit of unity, but agreed to disagree on such issues as whether it could be the church's responsibility to help redeem society by pursuing social and economic change, or the church was only responsible for the salvation of individual souls. African American men from four Methodist denominations met in Atlanta in October 1998, addressing issues relating to families, male mentoring, and reconciliation between their various traditions. Bishops from these four denominations—the predominantly white United Methodist Church and three African American Methodist denominations, the African Methodist Episcopal, the African Methodist Episcopal Zion, and the Christian Methodist Episcopal Churches—continue to explore the possibility of a merger early in the twenty-first century.

African American churches also have found themselves compelled to address issues related to the multiethnic tensions of the 1990s. In the aftermath of the devastating arson attacks on black churches in 1996, white churches and African American churches joined together in some cities to offer workshops against

An African Methodist Episcopal (AME) Church reunion.

racism. Leading African American pastors in Los Angeles have deplored both the violence of police revealed in the Rodney King incident and the violence of inner city rioters, while advocating urgent attention to the problems of inner-city residents. For example, James Lawson of the Holman United Methodist Church stated that those who burned buildings during the 1992 Los Angeles riots were "responding to a society of violence, not simply a society of racism," and issued "a call to repent." In Queens, New York, an African American Baptist congregation in 1991 warmly welcomed the opportunity to perform an ordination service for a Korean American minister, Chong S. Lee.

Black ministers and congregations have been increasingly opening themselves to frank discussions of human sexuality, impelled in part by the public health threat posed by the AIDS crisis, which has hit African American communities especially hard. In 1999, 5,000 churches participated in the Black Church Week of Prayer for the Healing of AIDS, a hundredfold increase in only ten years. Franklyn Richardson, senior pastor of Grace Baptist Church in Mount Vernon, New York, is one minister who has openly discussed AIDS with his congregation; Richardson's brother died of AIDS in 1993. Some African American congregations are still uncomfortable, however, about augmenting their traditional advocacy of monogamy and pre-marital abstinence with encouragement for sexually active individuals to use condoms to protect themselves from sexually transmitted diseases. Often African American ministers from conservative religious traditions (e.g., many Roman Catholics, Muslims, and Pentecostalists) are able to discuss this matter with their congregations only in an informal manner, if at all.

The cause of gender equality continues to make progress in African American churches. While two predominantly white denominations, the United Methodist and Protestant Episcopal Churches, have elevated African American women to the episcopacy in the past two decades, none of the largest historically African American denominations have done so. Nevertheless, women in some African American churches are achieving more prestigious ministerial assignments. Vashti McKenzie, a former model, disc jockey, and radio program director, has served as pastor of the Payne Memorial AME Church, an "old-line" church in Baltimore, since the early 1990s. Her innovative ministry, she says, is designed to "provide a message of hope for a hurting community." More than six hundred female pastors are ensconced in the African Methodist Episcopal Church.

Preaching the gospel in a faithful but relevant fashion remains the most important objective of black churches. In a recent survey, 22 percent of African American clergy considered the most important problem of the African American church to be "lack of evangelism in fulfilling its religious role." That was more than twice the figure for any other problem identified. Ministerial training and financial support is another area needing improvement in many African American churches. African American churches are not in danger of losing sight of their many, vital and extremely significant functions, within both the black community and American society as a whole. It is safe to predict that the African American churches will continue to sustain and develop their important and prophetic witness.

Membership Growth Within African American Churches

While many African American Methodist and Baptist denominations have shown only limited membership growth, other African American denominations are showing marked membership increases. Foremost among these are the Pentecostalist churches, whose lively worship and extensive social ministries are attracting members from all classes within the African American community. The largest of these denominations, the Church of God in Christ, is now estimated to have over three million members. Charismatic congregations, also known as neo-Pentecostalist, within such mainline African American churches as the African Methodist Episcopal Church, are also thriving and for similar reasons.

Other groups that have made substantial membership gains among African Americans include the Roman Catholic and Episcopal Churches and Islam. While estimates differ, apparently more than 1.5 million African Americans now belong to the Roman Catholic Church, which has worked hard in recent years to be sensitive to their needs. In many inner cities, it has maintained churches and schools in predominantly African American neighborhoods, although closings, mostly for financial reasons, are increasing in such dioceses as Detroit. Moreover, the Roman Catholic Church has been receptive to some liturgical variation, allowing gospel choirs and African vestments for priests in African American churches. Nevertheless, Roman Catholics confront some serious problems in serving African American parishioners. Fewer than 300 of the 54,000 priests in the United States are African American, meaning that some African American congregations must be served by white priests. In 1989, George A. Stallings, Jr., a priest in Washington, DC, broke away from Catholicism, arguing that the Catholic Church was still racist and did not do enough for its African American members.

In such large cities as New York, Afro-Caribbean immigrants are swelling the ranks of the Episcopal Church. For example, a substantial majority of the 1,300 members of St. Paul's Episcopal Church in Brooklyn are Caribbean immigrants. At least three Episcopal churches in New York City have escaped closing by church authorities because of the influx of members from the Caribbean. The Episcopal Church is not the only predominantly white denomination to seek to attract new immigrants of African descent to its pews. Presbyterian Church (USA) officials plan to increase their denominations ethnic minority membership to about 300,000, or about ten percent of total membership, within the next seven years, in part by targeting their outreach to new immigrants of African descent.

Mainstream Islam, despite raising its own complexities, has also made large gains in the United States. Of the six million Muslims in this country, one million are believed to be African American. Most African American Muslims do not distinguish between people of different races and worship cordially side by side with recent Muslim immigrants from Asia and Africa. Louis Farrakhan's Nation of Islam, however, which retains Elijah Muhammad's black separatist teachings, continues to maintain a devoted following. Due to its conservative stance on gender issues, Islam has proven to be more popular among African American men than among African American women. Following Farrakhan's successful Million Man March in 1995, he is quite able to fill the house, even in smaller cities such as Tallahassee, Florida, and hold his audiences spellbound for hours with a mixture of religious prophecy, candid social commentary, and moral exhortation for youth, but surprisingly the march has not achieved for him a sustained national presence. The chief organizer of the Million Man March, Benjamin Chavis Muhammad, converted to the Nation of Islam in April 1997, and then suffered the termination of his ministerial standing in his former denomination, the United Church of Christ.

African and Afro-Caribbean religions, such as the Yoruba worship of the spirits (orisha), Cuban santeria, and Haitian voodoo, have also been gaining ground in African American communities and on some African American college campuses. Caribbean immigrants to the United States have helped to stimulate the growth of these African-derived traditions. A typical Haitian American voodoo congregation in Brooklyn, New York, was the subject of Karen McCarthy Brown's groundbreaking work *Mama Lola: A Vodou Priestess in Brooklyn.* Some African Americans in the United States are also attracted by the honor shown to ancestors in these African traditions. Iyanla Vanzant, brought up as a Christian but

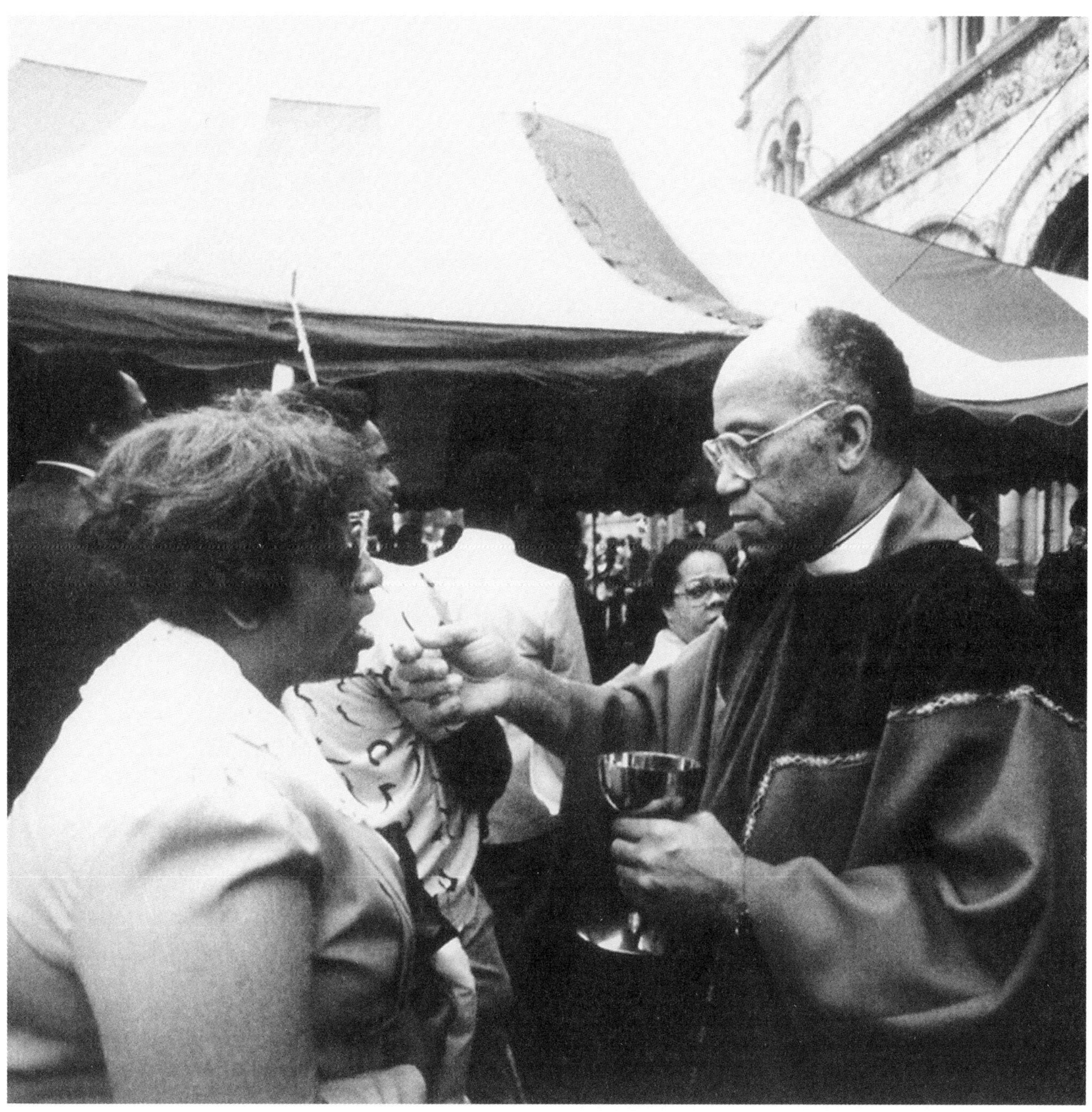

More than 1.5 million African Americans belong to the Roman Catholic Church (AP/Wide World Photos, Inc.).

now identifying herself as a Yoruba priestess, has provided low-key advocacy of these traditions in her bestselling works.

Success and Failure Within African American Churches

The most successful African American ministers nowadays employ as many forms of media as possible in order to find and keep their audiences. T. D. Jakes, for example, might seem at first glance to be just a typical pastor of a megachurch, the Potter's House in Dallas, with 15,000 members. But what sets him above the crowd is his authorship of over one dozen books, many of them bestsellers, a popular program on the Black Entertainment Television (BET) cable network, and an active revival schedule that finds him packing venues such as Atlanta's Georgia Dome in July 1998. His popular Internet web page makes his thought widely available to the computer literate. Johnnie Coleman, pastor of the Christ Universal Temple, runs a seminary for pastors and has a radio ministry. Her fellow Chicagoan,

Minister Louis Farrakhan of the Nation of Islam, also gets his message out through radio broadcasts and an active publishing program, including a weekly newspaper *The Final Call* sold on street corners nationwide. While pastors continue to spread their ideas through sermons on cassette tapes and in print, the most successful find many more ways to reach out.

One prominent African American minister who has encountered some failures is Henry J. Lyons, a St. Petersburg, Florida, Baptist minister who in 1994 became president of the National Baptist Convention of the USA, Inc. On July 9, 1997, Lyons's wife Deborah Lyons was arrested and charged with arson at a Florida home that her husband owned together with Bernice Edwards, director of public relations for his denomination and Henry Lyons's alleged mistress. This eventually led to state and national criminal investigations and indictments against Henry Lyons. Florida authorities charged Lyons with racketeering and grand theft in February 1998. They alleged that he had misappropriated denominational funds and swindled millions of dollars from large corporations by selling bogus membership lists. Five months later, Lyons was indicted by the federal government on 56 counts of extortion, fraud, and tax evasion. Lyons requested forgiveness from his local congregation and his denomination. On February 27, 1999, Lyons was convicted of all three counts brought against him by the state of Florida. On March 16, 1999, he resigned his office as president of the National Baptist Convention, and S. C. Cureton assumed the post until new elections were held. Lyons then pleaded guilty to five charges brought by the federal government on the following day. He was sentenced to five and one half years in a federal penitentiary and had to return $214,500 of donations that he had not distributed.

Increase of Church Burnings in the South

African American churches in the South have been under fire-literally-in the 1990s. These incidents of church arson invoked grievous memories of racist violence during the 1960s, particularly the bombing of Birmingham's Sixth Street Baptist Church in which four small girls were killed on September 15, 1963. In 1996, the peak year, 119 of 297 churches affected by arson nationwide were predominantly African American. In other words, while African American churches constituted about six percent of the nation's churches, more than forty percent of arson cases occurred that year at African American churches.

In response, President Clinton declared the "investigation and prevention of church arsons to be a national priority." In June 1996, President Clinton established the National Church Arson Task Force and proposed a three-pronged strategy that called for prosecution of the arsonists, the rebuilding of church edifices, and the prevention of additional fires. In addition, on July 3, he signed the Church Arson Prevention Act of 1996, which passed both chambers of the Congress unanimously.

Independently, Mac Charles Jones, associate general secretary for racial justice of the National Council of Churches of Christ, met with pastors of more than thirty burned-out churches and heard numerous stories of racist graffiti and threats issued against the pastors. African Americans concerned that the conflagrations are related have taken steps towards fighting the terrorism. To that end, the NAACP urged the Justice Department to investigate; in compliance, a full-scale civil rights investigation was initiated. The Southern Christian Leadership Conference (SCLC) also instituted a fund for the affected congregations.

Despite federal government involvement though, only 34 percent of the cases have been solved as of November 1998. (Those who have been charged with arson of African American churches have included 68 whites, 37 African Americans, and one Hispanic American.) In addition, neither the Federal Bureau of Investigation (FBI) nor the Bureau of Alcohol, Tobacco and Firearms (ATF)—which together have more than two hundred agents on the case—have been able to find a common link among these crimes.

◆ AFRICAN AMERICAN DENOMINATIONS

African-American Catholic Congregation

The Imani Temple, the first African-American Catholic Congregation, was founded in Washington, DC, by George Augustus Stallings, Jr., a former Roman Catholic priest, in July of 1989. The schism occurred when Stallings performed a mass based on an experimental rite currently being used in Zaire, in defiance of the prohibition of his archbishop, James Hickey. This was the first schism from the Roman Catholic Church in the United States since 1904. Stallings also voiced a number of criticisms of the Roman Catholic Church at the time of the schism: "There are not enough black priests, not enough black church members, and some of the relatively few black churches that exist are being closed and consolidated. The black experience and black needs are addressed minimally in church services and life." He also asserted that "we could no longer afford to worship white gods in black houses." Thirteen African American Catholic bishops issued a statement denouncing Stallings and accused him of expressing "personal disappointment [and] individually felt frustration" under the cover of charges of racism.

Reminiscent of the 1960s church bombings, numerous African American churches in the South were destroyed by arson during the 1990s (AP/Wide World Photos, Inc.).

Black Catholic reactions to these developments were mixed. Many expressed sympathy for Stallings's concerns but were unwilling to leave the Roman Catholic Church. Stallings assumed the title of archbishop of Imani Temple in 1991 and, at the same time, ordained a woman to the priesthood of the African American Catholic Congregation. Stallings has also relaxed the Catholic teaching on abortion for his congregation members and has declared the Reverend Dr. Martin Luther King, Jr. to be a saint. In forming his denomination, he has experienced some setbacks. Several formerly close associates split with Stallings in 1991, alleging a lack of fiscal accountability in the church and accusing him of taking his liturgical innovations too far. In 1994, Stallings dedicated a new cathedral for his denomination in Washington, DC. As of the same year, his denomination claimed 4,200 members in seven cities in the United States and in Lagos, Nigeria.

African Methodist Episcopal Church

The African Methodist Episcopal (AME) Church was founded in 1816 at a conference convened in Philadelphia by Richard Allen, who was elected as its first bishop. In the following years, it grew throughout the North and Midwest and, after the Civil War, expanded quickly throughout the South and the West. In 1991, the church claimed about 3.5 million members, about 1 million of whom are found in churches in Africa, South America, and the Caribbean as a result of successful missionary efforts. It oversees about 8,000 churches, and the AME Church sponsors seven colleges and two seminaries in the United States and several colleges and educational centers in Liberia and South Africa. Payne Theological Seminary is located in Wilberforce, Ohio, at the site of the church's oldest school, Wilberforce University, founded in 1856. Turner Theological Seminary is one of six schools that have joined to form the Interdenominational Theological Center in Atlanta. About one-third of local AME congregations sponsor low-income housing, schools, Job Corps programs, or care for senior citizens. The African Methodist Episcopal Church's chief governing bodies are the General Conference, the Council of Bishops, and the General Board. It publishes the following periodicals: the *Christian Recorder;* the *Voice of Missions*, and the *AME Church Review.*

Members actively participate in the service at the First African Methodist Episcopal Church in Los Angeles (AP/Wide World Photos, Inc.).

African Methodist Episcopal Zion Church

Originally known as the African Methodist Episcopal Church, the African Methodist Episcopal Zion Church was founded in 1821 in New York City. James Varick was elected its first "superintendent"; the title of the presiding officer was later changed to bishop. In 1848, the word "Zion" was added to the name of this church in order to avoid confusion with that founded by Richard Allen. It grew slightly prior to 1860, but expanded quickly in such Southern states as North Carolina and Alabama after the Civil War.

As of 1997, the African Methodist Episcopal Zion Church claimed approximately1.3 million members, 100,000 of whom lived in Africa, England, India, South America, or the Caribbean. It possesses nearly 3,100 churches worldwide. The church supports three colleges, two of which are junior colleges, and one seminary. The four-year college and the seminary are Livingstone College and Hood Theological Seminary, both located in Salisbury, North Carolina. The denomination is governed by a general conference, a board of bishops, and a correctional council. Its publications include the weekly *Star of Zion*, the *Quarterly Review*, the monthly *Missionary Seer*, and the quarterly *Church School Herald*.

African Orthodox Church

The African Orthodox Church was founded in 1921 by Archbishop George Alexander McGuire, once a priest in the Protestant Episcopal Church. McGuire was the chaplain for Marcus Garvey's United Negro Improvement Association, but Garvey soon disavowed his chaplain's efforts to found a new denomination. This church is today an autonomous and independent body adhering to an "orthodox" confession of faith. Its nearly 5,100 members worship in some 17 churches.

African Theological Archministry

In 1973 a group of African Americans founded a voodoo kingdom in South Carolina called Oyotunji. This kingdom was run by the leader of the African Theological Archministry, King Efuntola. The king and his followers relocated to South Carolina from Harlem, mov-

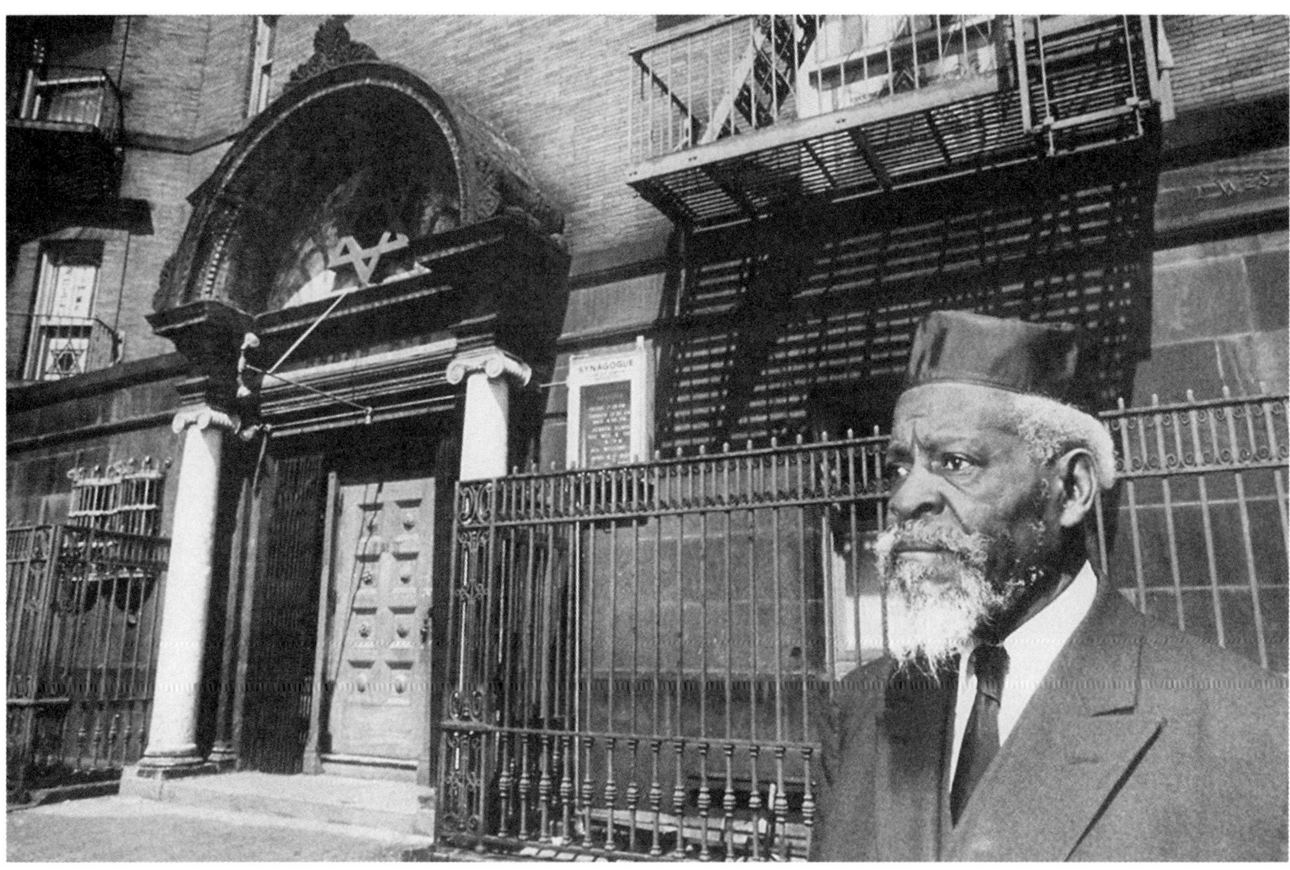

An African American rabbi stands in front of his Bronx, New York synagogue (New York Daily News).

ing their Shango Temple to Beaufort County. The king received his voodoo training in Nigeria, and his followers worship various gods and deities that represent different forces in life. The affiliated membership of the group is estimated at 10,000.

African Union First Colored Methodist Protestant Church, Inc.

This denomination was formed in 1866 by a merger of the African Union Church and the First Colored Methodist Protestant Church. The African Union Church traced its roots to a Union Church of Africans founded in 1813 by Peter Spencer in Wilmington, Delaware. Today, this denomination has a membership of about 8,000.

Apostolic Overcoming Holy Church of God, Inc.

This Pentecostal denomination, originally known as the Ethiopian Overcoming Holy Church, was incorporated in Alabama in 1920. Evangelistic in purpose, it emphasizes sanctification, holiness, and the power of divine healing. As of 1994, it claimed 173 churches and about 12,000 members.

Bible Way Church of Our Lord Jesus Christ World Wide, Inc.

Founded in 1957, this Pentecostal tradition claimed three hundred churches and 250,000 members as of 1994. It publishes *The Bible News Voice* biweekly.

Black Jews

Nearly 100,000 African Americans consider themselves Jewish. Included among these are the Commandment Keepers, founded in Harlem in 1919 by a Nigerian-born man known as "Rabbi Matthew"; the Church of God and Saints in Christ founded in 1896 in Lawrence, Kansas, by William Crowdy; and the Church of God founded in Philadelphia by Prophet F. S. Cherry. In terms of doctrine, these groups share little more than a dislike of Christianity and an affection for the Old Testament. Some black Jews claim descent from the Falasha Jews of Ethiopia, who now reside in Israel. However, few black Jews are recognized as such by orthodox rabbis.

The Church of God and Saints of Christ is probably the largest of these groups, with more than two hundred

President Bill Clinton visits an African American Baptist church congregation (AP/Wide World Photos, Inc.).

churches and a membership of 38,000. The World African Hebrew Israelite Community—a religious sect that believes blacks in the Western Hemisphere are the descendants of the original Hebrews and, as such, are the rightful heirs of the Holy Land of Israel—has 3,000 members throughout the United States and an additional 1,500 living in Israel. Since the late 1960s, they have been led by the spiritual leader Ben Ami Ben-Israel, formerly a Chicago bus driver named Ben Carter.

Christian Methodist Episcopal Church

The Christian Methodist Episcopal (CME) Church, known until 1954 as the Colored Methodist Church, is the third largest African American Methodist body in the United States. It was founded after the Civil War, when some African American Methodist churches desiring to join neither the African Methodist Episcopal or African Methodist Episcopal Zion Churches successfully petitioned the Methodist Episcopal Church, South, for the right to form their own denomination. The first CME General Conference was held at Jackson, Tennessee, in 1870. There the church's first two bishops, William H. Miles and Richard Vanderhorst, were elected.

In 1994, the Christian Methodist Episcopal Church estimates its membership at over 1 million persons, of whom 75,000 were located overseas. It possesses about 3,000 churches and maintains five church-affiliated colleges, as well as the Phillips School of Theology, a seminary that is part of the consortium known as the Interdenominational Theological Center in Atlanta. Its periodicals include the bimonthly *Christian Index* and the monthly *Missionary Messenger*.

Church of Christ (Holiness) U.S.A.

This denomination was organized in 1907 by Bishop Charles Price Jones, a renowned and prolific gospel song and hymn writer. The church traces its roots to an 1894 church established by Jones and C. H. Mason, but Jones and Mason parted company thirteen years later after the two men disagreed about whether speaking in tongues was necessary to prove baptism of the Holy Spirit. (Jones insisted that it was not.) Some 160 churches and 9,300 members belong to this denomination, which upholds the possibility of sanctification and Christian perfection. The church operates Christ Missionary and Industrial College, in Jackson, Mississippi.

Church of God by Faith

This Pentecostal denomination was founded in Florida in 1914. Its membership is concentrated in the Southeast.

Church of God in Christ

The Church of God in Christ (COGIC) was organized in 1897 by two former Baptist preachers, Charles H. Mason and C. P. Jones, and was initially strongest in Alabama, Mississippi, and Tennessee. Mason reorganized COGIC in 1907, when he and Jones parted on the issue of speaking in tongues. At that time, Mason was appointed "general overseer and chief apostle" of the Church, as well as its first bishop. It has subsequently expanded very rapidly throughout the United States, especially in African American neighborhoods in the inner cities.

As of 1991, COGIC claimed about 5.5 million members and 15,300 churches. It possesses bible colleges and a junior college, with plans for a university (All Saints University in Memphis) some time in the future. Its Charles H. Mason Theological Seminary is part of the Interdenominational Theological Center in Atlanta. It is governed by a general assembly, a general council of elders, the board of bishops, and the general board composed of 12 bishops elected by the general assembly to four-year terms. In 1995, Bishop Chandler David Owens was elected presiding bishop over the organization, the fastest-growing Christian group in the United States.

Churches of God, Holiness

This denomination was organized by K. H. Burruss in Georgia in 1914. It split off from the Church of Christ (Holiness) U.S.A. Membership in the group's 40-odd churches totals some 25,000.

Fire Baptized Holiness Church

This church was organized on an interracial basis as the Fire Baptized Holiness Association in Atlanta, Georgia, in 1898; its African American members formed the Fire Baptized Holiness Church in 1908. The church subscribes to standard Pentecostalist doctrines on divine healing, speaking in tongues, and sanctification. As of 1968, it had about fifty churches and a membership of about 9,000.

Nation of Islam

After the death of Elijah Muhammad in 1975, his son Warith D. Muhammad assumed leadership of the movement. Warith Muhammad shifted dramatically away from his father's teachings of black nationalism, stating that whites could become members. He sought to bring his movement in accord with Orthodox Islam, and he eventually succeeded, renaming the Nation of Islam as the World Community of Al-Islam in the West and then as the American Muslim Mission before the merger was accomplished. Three other splinter groups formed, the largest headed by Louis Farrakhan, who split from Muhammad to reestablish the Nation of Islam on the basis of Elijah Muhammad's original black separatist teachings. The remaining two traditions are led by John Farrakhan and Caliph Emmanuel A. Muhammad.

National Baptist Convention of America, Inc.

The National Baptist Convention of America was formed in 1915, as a result of a schism with the National Baptist Convention, USA, Inc. over the issue of control of the denominational publishing house. The supporters of Richard Henry Boyd, chairman of the board of the publishing house, established this convention when Boyd's opponents had attempted unsuccessfully to bring the publishing house more firmly under denominational control. In 1987 it was said to possess 3.5 million members and 2,500 churches. However, more congregations split off in 1988 to form the National Missionary Baptist Association, when the new denomination also tried to assert control over its publishing house. It has missions in Jamaica, Panama, Haiti, the Virgin Islands, and Africa, and supports fifteen colleges.

National Baptist Convention of the USA, Inc.

The National Baptist Convention was formed in 1895, through the union of three smaller church organizations, the oldest of which had been founded only 15 years earlier: the Baptist Foreign Mission Convention of the U.S.A.; the American National Baptist Convention; and the National Baptist Educational Convention of the USA. The National Baptist Convention incorporated itself after a dispute over the publishing house led to a schism in 1915.

The National Baptist Convention, Inc., is governed by a 15-member board of directors and a nine-member executive board. It is a supporter of the American Baptist Theological Seminary in Nashville, Tennessee, and of six other colleges. Its publications include the semimonthly *National Baptist Voice*. The convention dedicated its World Center Headquarters in Nashville, Tennessee, in 1989. In 1994, Rev. Dr. Henry J. Lyons was elected as the sixth president of the National Baptists, the largest African American religious order in the United States. On March 16, 1999, Rev. Lyons resigned his office amidst serious state and federal charges against him. S.C. Careton assumed the post of president until new elections were held.

The National Baptist Convention, Inc., as of 1992, claimed 8.2 million members, 100,000 of whom were in

Elijah Muhammad (Corbis Corporation [Bellevue])

foreign countries. Litigation documents concerning its former president, Rev. Lyons, however, established that the denomination's membership in 1998 could be more accurately estimated at one million persons. It possesses 33,000 local churches.

National Missionary Baptist Convention

Founded in 1988, this group boasted 3.2 million members in 1995 and more than five hundred churches. Rev. W. T. Snead was elected president of the Convention in 1994.

National Primitive Baptist Convention of America

African American and white Primitive Baptists separated after the Civil War. Although having long avowed opposition to church organization above the congregational level, it was not until 1907 that African American Primitive Baptists formed the National Primitive Baptist Convention. Each congregation is independent, and a decision by officials of a local church is final. Belief in "the particular election of a definite number of the human race" is included within its creed. In 1975, they possessed a membership of 250,000 in 606 churches.

Pentecostal Assemblies of the World, Inc.

An estimated one million members belong to the 1,760 churches of an organization founded in 1906. The church holds that speaking in tongues is vital to spiritual rebirth and that believers should be baptized only in the name of Jesus. Since its origins, it has accepted the ordination of women in the ministry.

Progressive National Baptist Convention, Inc.

The Progressive National Baptist Convention, Inc. was formed in 1961, as a result of a schism in the National Baptist Convention of the U.S.A., Inc. The schism resulted from a dispute over leadership occasioned by differences over tactical strategies in the struggle for civil rights. Those, including Martin Luther King, Jr., committed to such tactics as nonviolent civil disobedience left to form the new denomination. The convention's motto is "Unity, Service, Fellowship, and Peace." It is a financial supporter of six colleges. It has active missions in Haiti and Africa. The Convention claims 2.5 million members and more than 2,000 churches and is governed by a sixty-member executive board headed by Rev. Bennett Smith, Sr. Although it has no

African American women waiting to be baptized in the Potomac River (Archive Photos, Inc.).

publishing house of its own, it does publish a quarterly periodical titled the *Baptist Progress*.

Rastafarians

Members of this religion regard the Ethiopian Emperor Haile Selassie, who died in 1975, a supreme being. Marcus Garvey, a Jamaican-born nationalist who advocated a back-to-Africa movement in the United States in the early 1920s, is also a central figure in the faith. Reggae musician Bob Marley, a Rastafarian, helped to increase the religion's popularity in the United States.

Today, Rastas differ on specific dogma, but they basically believe that they are descended from black Hebrews exiled in Babylon and, therefore, are true Israelites. They also believe that Haile Selassie, whose name before ascending the throne was Lij Ras Tafari Makonnen, is the direct descendent of Solomon and Sheba, and that God is black. Most white men, they believe, have been worshipping a dead god and have attempted to teach the blacks to do likewise. They hold that the Bible was distorted by King James, and that the black race sinned and was punished by God with slavery. They view Ethiopia as Zion, the Western world as Babylon, and believe that one day they will return to Zion. They preach love, peace, and reconciliation between races, but warn that Armageddon is imminent.

Rastas do not vote, tend to be vegetarians, abhor alcohol, and wear their hair in long, uncombed plaits called dreadlocks. The hair is never cut, since it is part of the spirit, nor is it ever combed. Estimates of their numbers in the United States and around the world vary widely.

Triumph the Church and Kingdom of God in Christ

Founded in 1902, this denomination is identified by their belief in the Pentecostal forms of baptism, but their rejection of speaking in tongues. The type of baptism ceremony in this church is called "fire-baptism."

United Church of Jesus Christ

The United Church of Jesus Christ split from the Church of God in Christ in 1945 over the issue of the Holy Trinity verses a theory of the "Oneness in Godhead," which it follows. This splinter sect was named the Church of God in Christ (Apostolic) and was founded by Bishop Randolph Carr. In 1965, disputes over the lifestyle of Bishop Carr led Monroe Saunders and most of the church's members to leave and found the present-day United Church of Jesus Christ.

◆ RELIGIOUS LEADERS

(To locate biographical profiles more readily, please consult the index at the back of the book.)

Jaramogi Abebe Agyeman (1911–)

Founder

Jaramogi Abebe Agyeman was born Albert Cleage, Jr., in 1911, in Indianapolis, Indiana. His physician father relocated the family to Detroit a short time later, and Cleage undertook social work as a profession before earning a degree in divinity from Oberlin College in 1943. After his ordination, he headed Congregational churches in Kentucky and Massachusetts; Cleage's work at the latter was notable for the community outreach and economic programs that he enacted. Returning to Detroit, the minister became head of a Presbyterian congregation that split off into its own church in 1953.

This fellowship, known as the Central United Church of Christ (CUCC), soon became a political powerhouse among Detroit's increasingly significant African American community during the 1950s. Cleage's growing interest in the Black Power movement of the 1960s—and especially the teachings of Nation of Islam leader Malcolm X—led the pastor to create a separate denomination from the CUCC in 1967, based on historical surmisings that Jesus was of African descent. The focal point of the church—and the symbolic gesture that attracted many to it—was a powerful 18-foot mural of the Black Madonna. The Black Christian Nationalist movement and its cornerstone congregation, the Shrine of the Black Madonna, soon became an influential religious, social, political, and economic force in the city.

Basing the church's tenets on both teachings of visionaries, such as Malcolm X, Elijah Muhammad, and Marcus Garvey, Cleage preached economic self-sufficiency to his flock and put the words into action by the creation of numerous social service programs, including a community grocery outlet, in answer to the inflated prices then common to white-owned stores in the African American neighborhoods, and a bookstore stocked with the significant African nationalist literature of the day. The Shrine of the Black Madonna expanded into other American cities over the next several years, but the imprint it left on Detroit was perhaps Cleage's most significant achievement. In the late 1960s and early 1970s, after contentious 1967 race riots put aside any hopes of smooth integration between a diminishing white population and an increasingly frustrated African American citizenry, Cleage and the church's active membership were credited with helping elect numerous African American political leaders, judges, and school board members who remained a vital force in Detroit well into the 1990s. Cleage authored two books *The Black Messiah* and *Black Christian Nationalism* before taking the name Jaramogi Abebe Agyeman.

Noble Drew Ali (1886–1929)

Religious Leader

Noble Drew Ali, whose birth name was Timothy Drew, was born in North Carolina in 1886. He is principally important for his role in establishing the first North American religious movement combining black nationalist and Muslim themes with rejection of Christianity as the religion of whites. In 1913, he established the first Moorish Science Temple in Newark, New Jersey. He taught that African Americans were "Asiatics" who had originally lived in Morocco before enslavement. Every people, including African Americans, needed land for themselves, he proclaimed, and North America, which he termed an "extension" of the African continent, was the proper home for African Americans. The holy book for the Moorish Science Temple was a "Holy Koran," which was "divinely prepared by the Noble Prophet Drew Ali." (This book should not be confused with the Q'uran of Islam.) Every member of the Temple carried a card stating that "we honor all the Divine Prophets, Jesus, Mohammed, Buddha and Confucius" and that "I AM A CITIZEN OF THE U.S.A."

In the 1920s, the Moorish Science Temple expanded to Pittsburgh, Detroit, and Chicago. Noble Drew Ali also started several small businesses, which he ran together with his followers. In 1929 Drew Ali was stabbed to death in his Chicago office, in an apparent strife over the leadership of the Temple. The Moorish Science Temple survived Drew Ali's death, but the Nation of Islam was able to attract some of its followers.

Richard Allen (1760–1831)

Civil Rights Activist, Bishop

Born a slave in Philadelphia on February 14, 1760, Allen converted to Christianity in 1777 and, soon thereafter, bought his freedom. He then travelled widely through the Middle Atlantic States as an exporter. Francis Asbury, the first bishop of the Methodist Episcopal Church, asked Allen to join him as a travelling companion, stipulating that Allen would not be allowed to fraternize with slaves and would sometimes have to sleep in his carriage. Allen refused to accept such an offer, instead settling down in Philadelphia, where he helped to found the Free African Society, an African American society for religious fellowship and mutual aid. One day in the early 1790s, Allen was worshipping in Philadelphia's St. George's Methodist Church when he was pulled off his knees during prayer by white deacons who insisted that Allen was sitting outside the area reserved for African Americans. Allen left, establishing his own church for Philadelphia's African Americans in a converted blacksmith shop in 1794. White Methodists tried to exert their control over his church in various ways, which Allen resisted successfully. In 1816, after the Pennsylvania Supreme Court settled a suit over this church in Allen's favor, Allen called for a conference of African American Methodists. The African Methodist Episcopal Church was founded at this conference, and Allen was consecrated as its first bishop. Allen remained both religiously and politically active in his later years, and he was especially active in opposing schemes to colonize free African Americans in Africa.

Carl Bean (1946?–)

Clergyman

Since 1985, Bishop Carl Bean, D.M. has been running two projects: the Minority AIDS Project (MAP) and the Unity Fellowship Church for African American gays and lesbians. Starting as a Bible study group, the church quickly took root, with chapters spreading to New York City, Detroit, Washington, DC, Philadelphia, Dallas, and Seattle by 1996. Meanwhile, MAP has become the largest AIDS agency serving African Americans in the United States.

Born and raised as a Baptist in Baltimore, Bean was an avid churchgoer in his youth. He grew up singing gospel, even participating in a Broadway gospel revue. Openly gay, Bean wanted to help liberate ostracized people of color—gay or straight—because he himself had once felt shunned by the church. Reaching out to the disenfranchised, Bean's followers believe that "Love is for everyone."

In 1991, the fellowship embarked on a campaign to work with gangs. Often getting referrals from social workers, Bean's congregation has earned a reputation for doing whatever is required to get people's lives on track. From distributing cash grants for food and bills to paying for funerals, Unity Fellowship members give back to the community.

Sister Thea Bowman (1938–1990)

Writer, Educator, Religious Leader

Born in Canton, Mississippi, in 1938, Thea Bowman, daughter of a medical doctor, joined the Roman Catholic Church at age twelve because of the Catholic education she had received. Three years later, she joined the Franciscan Sisters of Perpetual Adoration. She was extensively educated, earning a Ph.D. in literature and linguistics and was a distinguished teacher who taught elementary and high schools, as well as at colleges. She helped to found the Institute of Black Catholic Studies at Xavier University and was a distinguished scholar known for her writings on Thomas More. But it is probably for the spiritual inspiration that she provided in numerous lectures, workshops and concerts that she will be best remembered. She said that she brought to her church "myself, my black self, all that I am, all that I have, all that I hope to become, my history, my culture, my experience, my African American song and dance and gesture and movement and teaching and preaching and healing."

Nannie Helen Burroughs (1883–1961)

Baptist Lay Leader, Educator

Born in Orange Springs, Virginia, Nannie Helen Burroughs became one of the most significant Baptist lay leaders of the twentieth century. She addressed the National Baptist Convention in Virginia in 1900 on the subject "How the Sisters are Hindered from Helping" and from that time until her death more than sixty years later, she exercised pivotal leadership. She was elected corresponding secretary for the Woman's Convention, Auxiliary to the National Baptist Convention, U.S.A., Inc., and in 1948 she became president of the Women's Convention. She founded the National Training School for Women and Girls, emphasizing industrial arts and proficiency in African American history, in Washington, DC. She edited such periodicals as the *Christian Banner* and was the author of such books as the *Roll Call of Bible Women*.

Calvin O. Butts III (1949–)

Religious Leader

Calvin Butts spent the first eight years of his life on the Lower East Side of New York City, where he was born in 1949. In 1957, the family moved to Queens, New York. During the summer breaks from school, Butts's parents would send him down South to stay with his grandmothers who lived near another in rural Georgia. It was in these early formative years that Butts first became acquainted with church.

After graduating from Flushing High School, where he was class president his senior year, Butts was accepted to Morehouse College. The year was 1967, an explosive time in the American civil rights struggle. Butts attended lectures, rallies, and speeches at Morehouse by Martin Luther King, Jr. and other African American leaders. Following one of these very emotional events, Butts found himself immersed in a riot and actually assisted in the firebombing of a local store. Shortly thereafter, he renounced his capitulation to violence.

Just before his graduation from college, Butts was approached by two young seminarians trying to recruit students for their school. Later, he would receive his master's degree in divinity from Union Theological Seminary. While attending the Seminary, Butts raised a few eyebrows through his controversial stance on homosexuality. He has since defended the social and civil rights of gays, which he had once denounced.

Butts was recruited as a junior minister in 1972 by William Epps. During this time, his responsibilities included making hospital visits and conducting funeral services. From the very beginning, though, Butts realized the Abyssinian pulpit provided a great foundation from which to preach. For instance, he was quite vocal in his opposition to police brutality, along with any other form of violence.

Since assuming the pastoral role at Harlem's Abyssinian Baptist Church, which boasts more than 5,000 parishioners, Butts has also been involved the community. He has sat on the board of the Harlem Young Men's Christian Association (YMCA). Also, Butts has supported presidential hopefuls such as Ross Perot. He was the co-chair of Perot's New York campaign. The political arena is one in which Calvin Butts will continue to explore. In the 1990s, he showed interest in running for city mayor and for statewide office.

Katie Cannon (1950–)

Presbyterian Minister, Educator, Feminist

Cannon was born January 3, 1950, in Kannopolis, North Carolina. As she approached adulthood, Cannon found that only two roads were available to most African American women in her community—they could work in the local mill or become a school teacher. The teachers that she knew played an important role in the early years of her life; she thrived in the supportive and protective environment of the academic environment, though the bite of racism was still all too real to her. African Americans were prohibited from public places, such as the library and the local pool, and Cannon was determined to escape.

Cannon enrolled in Barber-Scotia College. She graduated with a B.S. in 1971, after rising to the top of her senior class, making the dean's list, and being named Miss Barber-Scotia. The following fall, Cannon went on to study at Johnson C. Smith Seminary of the Interdenominational Theological Center (ITC) in Atlanta, Georgia—one of the two accredited African American seminaries at the time. During her time there Cannon was exposed to every aspect of the ministry. Majoring in Old Testament studies, she was only one of four women in her class. Upon completion of her studies, Cannon received her master's degree in divinity in 1974.

Cannon served as pastor at the Ascension Presbyterian Church in New York City for three years. Her work there was followed by an administrative position at the New York Theological Seminary, then, ready to resume her scholarly endeavors, Cannon decided to attend Union Theological Seminary, where she received her master's degree in philosophy, as well as a Ph.D. As of 1993, Cannon serves as the associate professor of Christian ethics at Philadelphia's Temple University. In 1995, a compilation of previously published essays was released as *Katie's Cannon: Womanism and the Soul of the Black Community.*

Johnnie Coleman

Religious Leader, Educator

Coleman grew up in Mississippi during the 1920s. A graduate of Wiley College in Texas and a school teacher in Mississippi and Chicago, Coleman was diagnosed in 1953 with an incurable disease. However, all of her symptoms disappeared after she moved to Kansas City to study at the Unity School of Christianity. Nonetheless, Coleman suffered from racial discrimination at the Unity School. Only her threat to leave the school just short of graduation won her the ability to live on campus and eat in the campus cafeteria. Her south side Chicago church began as a study group in 1956 with only five members. In 1958, she named her church the Christ Universal Temple, and in 1963 she moved to the Chatham section of South Chicago.

In the early 1970s, she served as the first African American president of the Association of Unity Churches. Nevertheless, she still found racism too prevalent within the predominantly white denomination. Consequently, in 1974, she formed the Universal Foundation for Better Living, Inc., an association of churches devoted to the "positive thinking" derived from the New Thought movement. In the 1970s, she opened the Johnnie Coleman Institute to teach her doctrines derived from New Thought and, in the 1980s, began a broadcast ministry. Teaching her congregation members to discover the power of God within themselves, she has been a long-time advocate of Holy Materialism and Practical Christianity. By 1989, 23 churches belonged to the Universal Foundation, and her own congregation has increased in size to 12,000 members.

James H. Cone (1938–)

Author, Theologian, Educator

Born in Fordyce, Arkansas, in 1938, James Cone received a B.A. from Philander Smith College, a B.D. from Garrett Evangelical Seminary, and an M.A. and Ph.D. from Northwestern University. After teaching at Philander Smith and Adrian Colleges, Cone moved to

Union Theological Seminary in 1969. He is currently the Charles A. Briggs Professor of Systematic Theology. Cone is the author of numerous books including *Black Theology and Black Power* (1969); *The Spirituals and the Blues* (1972); *For My People: Black Theology and the Black Church* (1984); and most recently, *Martin and Malcolm and America: A Dream or a Nightmare* (1991).

Perhaps more than any other African American theologian, Cone has provided a systematic exposition of the argument that since God, according to the Bible, is on the side of the poor and oppressed, that in the American context, God is siding with the black liberation struggle. He has made this argument using a diverse set of sources including the writings of modern European theologians such as Karl Barth and the writings and speeches of Malcolm X and Martin Luther King, Jr. Cone has worked painstakingly in the past two decades to build ties between black, feminist, and third world liberation theologians.

Suzan Johnson Cook
Religious Leader, Author

Raised in the Bronx, New York, Rev. Suzan Johnson Cook was a communications student at Emerson College, when she went to Ghana as an exchange student. There she entertained notions of joining the ministry. She would later enroll at the United Theological Seminary, where she pursued a doctorate. Just as her role model Presbyterian minister Katie Cannon had found earlier, entering into the pastorship was a task rote with difficulty for a woman, but Cook carved a niche and persevered. Eager to assist other women in pursuing the ministry, she later directed Black Women in the Ministry, sponsored by the New York City Mission Society.

In 1983, Cook began 11 years of preaching at Mariner's Temple, the oldest Baptist facility in Manhattan. Her rapport with the small congregation led her to become the first African American woman elected to senior pastor of a Baptist church in the United States. Her preaching skills have won her recognition as one of the "Fifteen Greatest Black Women Preachers" by *Ebony* (Nov., 1997). During her years with the church membership swelled from sixty to more than one thousand members. Cook became the first woman to be appointed chaplain of the New York City Police Department in 1990, when then-Mayor David Dinkins selected her. Three years later, President Bill Clinton chose her for a White House fellowship, the first female minister to be so recognized. She subsequently served on President Clinton's National Advisory Board on Race. Cook has authored several books including *Wise Women Bearing Gifts: Joys and Struggles of Their Faith* and *Preaching in Two Voices: Sermons on the Women in Jesus's Life.*

Wallace D. Fard (?–1992)
Religious Leader

W. D. Fard's background is fiercely contested. According to the Nation of Islam, Fard was born in Mecca in 1877 to a black man named Alfonso and a Caucasian woman. Members of the Nation believed that Fard was highly educated, both in England and at the University of Southern California, and that he had been trained as an Arabian diplomat. The Federal Bureau of Investigation, however, contended that Fard was born in New Zealand or Oregon to either Hawaiian or Polynesian parents (possibly one parent was British), and that he was a convicted bootlegger during Prohibition. In 1926, he received a sentence of six months to six years for drug sales in California. Upon his release in 1929, he immediately headed for Detroit.

As a door-to-door salesman, Fard approached African Americans in Detroit, selling silk fabrics and raincoats. Soon he was advising his customers on their diet and health and teaching them about what he said was their true religion, the religion of black people in Africa and Asia. Here Fard was clearly influenced by the teachings of the Moorish Science Temple and by the Ahmaddiya Muslim movement, a Muslim splinter group that preached the imminent arrival of the Mahdi or Messiah. Fard told his listeners of the one true God, Allah. He presented himself as the intermediary between God and humanity. He claimed that Allah was soon to destroy the wicked white world and establish a heaven on earth for his followers. Fard taught his followers that they were not American, owed no allegiance to the American flag, and that they should discard their "slave names." His mission, however, was to achieve "freedom, justice, and equality" for African Americans. He established a University of Islam to teach African Americans the truth about their past, and a paramilitary organization, the Fruit of Islam. Fard attracted numerous followers, perhaps as many as 8,000, within the African American community in Detroit. His most capable follower was a Georgia-born man named Elijah Poole, who was renamed Elijah Muhammad. In 1931, Fard designated Muhammad as his supreme minister.

The already considerable interest of Detroit police in Fard's activities increased further when one of his followers, in November 1932, killed a white neighbor as a sacrifice to Allah. Fard strongly denied that he had ordered the killing, asserting that his teachings had been misunderstood. Still, the police, fearing the growing strength of Fard's movement, put pressure on him to leave Detroit. Lowering his profile, Fard was able to remain in Detroit some months, transferring control of the movement to Elijah Muhammad during that time. But in May 1933, Fard was arrested for disturbing the peace, and he finally assented to demands from the police that he leave Detroit. Fard's later life is as mysterious as his early years. It is said that Fard moved to Chicago and that Elijah Muhammad kept in contact with him for about one year, but his whereabouts after June 1934, were unknown. Following Elijah Muhammad's guidance, however, most members of the Nation of Islam, continued to regard Fard as Allah appearing in person to African Americans.

Father Divine (1879–1965)

Religious Leader, Organization Executive/Founder

Father Divine was born George Baker in 1879 in Rockville, Maryland. In 1902, he moved to Baltimore. Baker visited California in 1906 and attended the Azusa Street Revival, which marked the beginning of Pentecostalism. The following year, after returning to Baltimore, Baker—under the moniker "The Messenger"—became associated with Sam Morris, a Pennsylvania African American man who called himself Father Jehovia, and John Hickerson, also known as Reverend Bishop St. John the Divine, in a house church. All three men had been influenced by the New Thought movement of the Unity Church and considered themselves inwardly divine. After a series of personal and theological quarrels, the three men parted company in 1912.

In 1914, Baker moved to Valdosta, Georgia. Threatened by local authorities, Father Divine left Georgia the same year. After additional travels in the South, he settled in Brooklyn in 1917, where he worked as an "employment agent" for the few followers still loyal to him. His first marriage was to an African American woman named Peninniah, whom he apparently met while living in Brooklyn. Calling his meeting place "Heaven," he soon attracted a larger following and moved to Sayville, Long Island in 1919. It was at this time that Father Divine began to provide shelter and food to the poor and homeless. Spiritually, Father Divine fostered what amounted to a massive cooperative agency, based on the communal spirit of the Last Supper. His movement practiced complete racial equality. Services included songs and impromptu sermons and were conducted without Scripture readings and the use of clergy. Once he was sentenced to six months in jail as a public nuisance, but the ensuing publicity only enhanced his popularity.

The Divine movement, a non-ritualistic cult whose followers worshiped their leader as God incarnate on earth, grew rapidly in the 1930s and 1940s, with "Father" speaking out across the country and publicizing his views in *New Day*, a weekly magazine published by his organization. He set up "Peace Mission Kingdom" in the United States and throughout the world. After Peninniah's death in 1946, Father Divine married his "Sweet Angel," a 21-year old Canadian stenographer known thereafter as Mother Divine. Father Divine died peacefully at Woodmont, an estate that he had acquired in the Philadelphia suburbs, and his wife pledged to continue the work of the movement.

Father Divine (AP/Wide World Photos, Inc.)

Elijah John Fisher (1858–1915)

Community Activist, Minister

Elijah Fisher exemplifies the great charismatic African American preachers of the nineteenth and early twentieth centuries who, with very little formal education, built large religious institutions, counseled racial pride, and expounded the cause of African Americans as a people.

Born in La Grange, Georgia, in 1858, the youngest of eight boys in a family of seventeen children, Fisher's father was an unordained preacher of a Baptist congregation that met in a white church. Fisher worked in a Baptist parsonage as a boy slave and was taught to read by a former house slave and a white missionary. In his teens, he worked in mines in Alabama and then as a butler, all the while studying theology on his own time. Though he lost a leg in an accident, Fisher became pastor of several small country churches in his early twenties and then, in 1889, of the Mount Olive Baptist

Church in Atlanta. In that year, he enrolled in the Atlanta Baptist Seminary, passed his examinations, and went to preach in Nashville and then Chicago where he led the Olive Baptist Church from 1902 until his death.

Throughout his life, Fisher continued his studies, preached from coast to coast, and involved the churches in youth work, food programs for poor people, and African American businesses. An active member of the Republican party, Fisher strongly criticized African Americans who advised their brethren to rely solely on the good will of whites and publicly criticized Booker T. Washington for not speaking out against lynching.

Floyd Flake (1945–)

Religious Leader, Member of Congress

Born in Los Angeles, Flake came from humble beginnings: he was one of thirteen children, and his father was a janitor. He graduated with a B.A. degree from Wilberforce University in 1967 and an M.A. from Payne Theological Seminary in 1970. He subsequently worked as a social worker, marketing analyst, and the dean of students before being called to pastor Allen A.M.E. Church in Queens, New York, in 1976. The church prospered under his leadership. By 1986, Allen A.M.E. had grown to include 6,000 members. Flake also founded a Christian school at Allen and headed the Allen Home Care Agency for the Elderly. In the latter role, he supervised the construction of a $12 million facility.

In 1986, he ran and won a seat in the U.S. House of Representatives. For eleven years, he served in Congress while remaining pastor of Allen A.M.E. Church. He was particularly interested in small business and affirmative action issues and was influential in securing federal government set-asides for minority-owned small businesses. In November 1997, he resigned his seat in Congress so that he could devote his full-time energies again to his church.

Reverend Floyd H. Flake (AP/Wide World Photos, Inc.)

"Sweet Daddy" Grace (1881–1960)

Religious Leader, Sales Agent

Born in 1881 in the Cape Verde Islands, "Sweet Daddy" Grace probably opened his first church in New Bedford, Massachusetts, in 1921, but his first success occurred five years later when he opened a church in Charlotte. Grace's church, the United House of Prayer for All People, had an ecstatic worship style, where speaking in tongues was encouraged. Grace claimed great powers, including the power of faith healing, and he stated that "Grace has given God a vacation, and since God is on His vacation don't worry Him... If you sin against God, Grace can save you, but if you sin against Grace, God cannot save you." Even the numerous products that he sold, such as "Daddy Grace" coffee, tea, soaps, and hand creams, were reputed to have healing powers. By the time of his death in 1960, the church had 375 branches and about 25,000 members nationwide.

Barbara C. Harris (1930–)

Executive Director, Bishop, Deacon

Born in Philadelphia in 1930, Barbara Harris, a former public relations executive, was ordained a deacon in the Protestant Episcopal Church in 1979 and a priest one year later. She served as the priest-in-charge of an Episcopalian Church in Norristown, Pennsylvania, the interim pastor of a church in Philadelphia, and the executive director of the publishing company associated with the Episcopal Church. In February of 1989, she was consecrated as suffragan or assistant bishop for the diocese of Massachusetts. She thus became the first woman bishop in the history of the Episcopal Church. She received considerable support, despite the concerns of some that her views were too liberal. Her supporters said that, despite the lack of a college degree or seminary training, she would broaden the outreach of her church.

Barbara Harris performing an Anglican Church service in 1989 (AP/Wide World Photos, Inc.).

James Augustine Healy (1830–1900)
Educator, Religious Leader

James Augustine Healy was the first African American Catholic bishop in the United States. (Healy's brother, Patrick Francis Healy, was a Jesuit priest who served as president of Georgetown University from 1873 to 1882.) For twenty-five years he presided over a diocese covering the states of Maine and New Hampshire. A native of Macon, Georgia, Healy received his education in the North, first at Franklin Park Quaker School in Burlington, New York, and later at Holy Cross in Worcester, Massachusetts. Healy graduated from the latter with first honors. Healy continued his studies abroad and was ordained in Paris at Notre Dame Cathedral in 1854. He then returned to the United States.

Pastor of a predominantly Irish congregation that was at first reluctant to accept him, Bishop Healy performed his priestly duties with devotion and eventually won the respect and admiration of his parishioners—particularly after performing in his office during a typhoid epidemic. Thereafter, he was made an assistant to Bishop John Fitzpatrick of Boston, who appointed him chancellor and entrusted him with a wide variety of additional responsibilities. In 1875, he was named bishop of Portland, Maine and, in this capacity, he founded sixty parishes, as well as 18 schools.

Joseph Henry Jackson (1904–1990)
Organization Executive/Founder, Theologian, Civil Rights Activist

From 1953 to 1982, Joseph H. Jackson was the president of the National Baptist Convention, U.S.A., Inc., the third largest Protestant denomination in the United States and the largest of the predominantly African American churches. Born in Rudyard, Mississippi, in 1904, Jackson later held a B.A. from Jackson College, a M.A. from Creighton University, and a B.D. from Rochester Colgate School of Divinity. After pastoring churches in Mississippi, Jackson accepted a call to pastor the historic Olivet Baptist Church in 1941. His role in the civil rights movement was a fairly conservative one. He was supportive of the efforts of Martin Luther King, Jr. during the Montgomery bus boycott of 1955, but criticized the massive nonviolent civil disobedience campaigns of the early 1960s. Jackson's main emphasis was on the need for African Americans to build a viable economic base. His favorite slogan was "From Protest to Production." He was supportive of Baptist missions in Africa and attempted to finance them by developing farmland in Liberia.

T. D. Jakes (1956–)

Religious Leader, Author

T.D. Jakes, a West Virginia native, began his preaching while as a student at West Virginia State University. After the chemical plant that employed him closed, and his father died of kidney disease, Jakes undertook ministry on a full-time basis. Initially, he ministered in Morganton, West Virginia, and then in Dallas, Texas, where his megachurch congregation today has nearly 15,000 members. He travels widely to undertake revival services. His 1998 revival in Atlanta drew 52,000 attendees. His ministry is also featured on Black Entertainment Television (BET). His books are largely aimed at encouraging and uplifting African American women. His two most popular books, which are filled with extensive passages from and interpretation of the Bible, are *Woman, Thou Art Loosed* and *The Lady, Her Lover and Her Lord.*

Absalom Jones (1746–1818)

Religious Leader

Absalom Jones rose from slavery to become the first African American Episcopal priest and principal founder of St. Thomas, the first African American Episcopal church. Jones was born a slave in Sussex, Delaware, on November 6, 1746. In 1762 his mother, five brothers, and sister were sold, and Jones was taken to Philadelphia, where he worked in a store and learned to write. In 1778 he began to ask to purchase his own freedom, but he was not manumitted until 1784.

Jones became a licensed Methodist lay preacher sometime around 1786, focusing on teaching and pastoral work. In May of 1787, Jones joined African American religious leader Richard Allen and others in forming the Free African Society. The African Church of St. Thomas was later dedicated in 1794.

As the unofficial leader of the church, Jones seemed an obvious choice as a lay reader. After becoming lay reader in 1794, he was ordained deacon on August 6, 1795. Jones became the first African American episcopal priest in 1804. He died in 1818.

Absalom Jones (Schomburg Center for Research in Black Culture)

Leontine T.C. Kelly (1920–)

Bishop

Leontine T.C. Kelly, the first African American woman bishop in any large U.S. denomination, was born in Washington, DC, in 1920. She received a M.Div. degree from Union Theological Seminary in Richmond, Virginia, in 1969. She served as a schoolteacher, pastor of Virginia churches, and a staff member of the Virginia Conference of Churches before being elected a bishop in the United Methodist Church in 1984. She presided over the California-Nevada conference, but resigned her office of bishop in 1989. She is married to James David Kelly and has four children.

Isaac Lane (1834–1937)

Educational Administrator, Religious Leader

A great religious leader and educator whose life spanned more than a century, Isaac Lane was born a slave in Jackson, Tennessee, in 1834. Self-educated, in 1856 he was granted a license to exhort, a category assigned to African Americans who were forbidden to preach, in the Methodist Episcopal Church South. Lane was ordained a minister in 1865. In 1873 he was made a bishop of the Colored Methodist Episcopal Church (now known as the Christian Methodist Episcopal Church) at a salary so low that he had to raise cotton to supplement his income and support his wife and 11 children. His missionary work was instrumental in establishing the CME Church in Louisiana and Texas. In the 1880s, he established Lane College in Jackson with $9,000 that he raised. He died in 1937.

Jarena Lee (1783–1849)

Women's Rights Activist, Minister

Born in 1783, in Cape May, New Jersey, Lee worked as a servant for a family that lived near Philadelphia. She had a conversion experience in 1804, but was unable to find a church with which to unite until she heard Richard Allen, founder of the African Methodist Episcopal Church, preach in Philadelphia. She experienced a call to preach in approximately 1808, and she sought permission to do so from Richard Allen on two occasions. On her first attempt in 1809, Allen refused her request. Eight years later, however, he granted it and licensed her as a preacher. Subsequently, she traveled throughout the North and Midwest, and many of her listeners, especially women, were moved by her eloquent preaching. After Allen's death in 1831, male African Methodist Episcopal preachers in Philadelphia attempted to deny her permission to preach from their pulpits, but she continued her ministry, despite such harassment. In 1848, she attempted to form a connection of female African Methodist Episcopal preachers for mutual support, but her organization soon fell apart. Many African American women, especially within the African Methodist Episcopal Church, view Jarena Lee as a courageous foremother and a model for church activism.

George Liele (1750–1820)

Educator, Religious Leader

Born a slave in Virginia around 1750, George Liele was sold to a slaveowner in Georgia. He experienced a Christian conversion after hearing a sermon by Matthew Moore, a white preacher, in 1773. Liele began conducting worship services on nearby plantations and, with Moore's sponsorship, soon became the first ordained African American Baptist preacher in America. Liele's slave master, Henry Sharp, granted him his freedom before Sharp was killed in the American Revolution. Liele preached at the Silver Bluff Baptist Church in Silver Bluff, South Carolina, probably the first independent African American congregation formed in North America, as well as a location outside Savannah. One of his notable converts was Andrew Bryan who founded the First African Baptist Church in Savannah. Some whites attempted to reenslave Liele, but a British officer in Savannah ensured that he would maintain his freedom. Liele emigrated to Jamaica in 1784, and he started a school and preached to a small Baptist congregation in Kingston. Liele was married a woman that he converted in Savannah, and his four American-born children accompanied him to Jamaica.

Eugene A. Marino (1934–)

Archbishop

Born May 29, 1934, in Biloxi, Mississippi, Eugene Marino received his training at Epiphany Apostolic College and St. Joseph Seminary. He was ordained to the priesthood in 1962. The next year Marino was made director of St. Joseph Seminary. He also continued his educational studies at Catholic University, Loyola University, and Fordham University, where he earned a master of arts degree in 1967.

In 1971, Marino was named vicar general of the Josephites and served as an auxiliary bishop in Washington, DC, after his ordination to the episcopate in 1974. Marino became the first African American Roman Catholic archbishop in 1988, when he was appointed to preside over the Atlanta archdiocese. He retired in 1990, in the midst of sex scandal, when an affair he was having with a woman was exposed. In 1993, ex-bishop Marino and Vicki Long, the woman in question, reunited and began a life together.

Charles H. Mason (1866–1961)

Religious Leader

Born in 1866 to former slaves on a farm outside Memphis, Tennessee, Charles Mason was converted at the age of 14 and joined a Missionary Baptist church. Mason obtained a preaching license from the Missionary Baptists in 1893 and, in the same year, he claimed to have the experience of entire sanctification, thus aligning himself with the Holiness movement. He had little formal education beyond a brief period of study at the Arkansas Bible College. In 1895, the Baptists expelled him because of his beliefs on sanctification. Mason then held holiness revivals in Mississippi with the help of Charles Price Jones, a prolific writer of hymns and gospel songs, and others. In Lexington, Mississippi, his meetings were held in an abandoned cotton gin house. Despite an armed attack, probably by hostile African Americans, he achieved much success and many new converts with his revival preaching. In 1897, Mason and Jones founded a new Holiness church and called it the Church of God in Christ; they worked together harmoniously over the next decade.

In 1907, Mason attended the Azusa Street Revival conducted by William Seymour in Los Angeles, and he received the gift of speaking in tongues. He believed that the ability to speak in tongues was a necessary precondition for baptism of the Spirit. He and Jones disagreed

Archbishop Eugene Marino (Corbis Corporation [Bellevue])

Reverend Harold Perry standing in front of the St. Louis Basilica in New Orleans in 1965 (AP/Wide World Photos, Inc.).

on this point and parted company. Mason reformed the Church of God in Christ along the lines of his new spiritual insights. Over the next four decades, Mason, as bishop, general overseer, and "chief apostle," shepherded his denomination through a period of tremendous growth. He traveled extensively, preaching at revivals throughout the United States and the world. He was imprisoned for making pacifist statements during World War I. He died in 1961.

William Henry Miles (1828–1892)
Religious Leader

Born a slave in Kentucky in 1828, Miles was manumitted by his owner in her will. He joined the Methodist Episcopal Church, South, and soon perceived a call to preach. In 1859, he was ordained a deacon. Uncertain about church affiliation after the war, he investigated the possibility of joining the African Methodist Episcopal Zion Church, but soon thought better of it. Thus he remained a preacher in the Methodist Episcopal Church, South, until its African American members, those who had decided not to join the African Methodist Episcopal or African Methodist Episcopal Zion Churches, were allowed to form a separate denomination, the Colored Methodist Episcopal Church. At the initial General Conference of the Colored Methodist Episcopal Church in 1870, Miles was elected one of the denomination's first two bishops. He was an active advocate of African American colleges, especially those affiliated with the CME Church, such as Lane College in Jackson, Tennessee, and Paine Seminary in Atlanta, Georgia. He died in 1892.

Harold Robert Perry (1916–1991)
Educator, Religious Leader

Harold Robert Perry was consecrated a bishop of New Orleans on January 6, 1966—and thus became the first African American Catholic bishop in the United States in the twentieth century. One of six children, Perry was born the son of a rice mill worker and a domestic cook in Lake Charles, Louisiana in 1916. He entered the Divine Word Seminary in Mississippi at the age of 13, was ordained a priest in 1944, and spent the next fourteen years in parish work. In 1958, he was appointed rector of the seminary. Louisiana has the largest concentration of African American Catholics in the South, some 200,000 in all. In 1989, Perry was one of

Reverend Adam Clayton Powell, Sr. speaking before the pulpit (Corbis Corporation [Bellevue]).

thirteen African American bishops serving Catholic parishes around the nation. He died on July 17, 1991.

Adam Clayton Powell, Sr. (1865–1953)
Religious Leader, Community Activist

Adam Clayton Powell, Sr., father of the late U.S. representative from Harlem, was largely responsible for building the Abyssinian Baptist Church into one of the most celebrated African American congregations in the world. Born in Virginia in 1865, Powell attended school locally and, between sessions, worked in the coal mines of West Virginia. After deciding to enter the ministry, he began his studies at Wayland Academy (now Virginia Union University), working his way through as a janitor and waiter. He later attended the Yale University School of Divinity and served as pastor of the Immanuel Baptist Church in New Haven.

Powell became pastor of Abyssinian in 1908, when it had a membership of only 1,600 and was fiscally indebted by over $100,000. By 1921, the church had not been made solvent, but was able to move into a $350,000 Gothic structure. (This is its present location on 138th Street in Harlem.) During the Depression, Powell opened soup kitchens for Harlem residents and served thousands of meals. Later he and his son campaigned vigorously to expand job opportunities and city services in Harlem. Powell retired from Abyssinian in 1937 and died in 1953.

Joseph Charles Price (1854–1893)
Civil Rights Activist, Minister, Prohibitionist

Born in Elizabeth City, North Carolina, in 1854 to a free mother, Price was educated in the school established for freed African Americans, and later at Shaw and Lincoln Universities, graduating from the latter in 1879. At age 21, he was licensed to preach in the African Methodist Episcopal Zion Church, and he received the ordination of elder six years later. Price was renowned for the eloquence of his public addresses. It was Price who was the most responsible for the African Methodist Episcopal Zion Church's success in establishing a church college—Livingstone College in North Carolina—after ministers in that denomination had failed in several previous attempts. As president of Livingstone College, he quickly gave his school a solid grounding, both academically and financially. For example, he raised $10,000 for his school during a lecture tour of England. He was an active participant in politics, campaigned for civil rights and prohibition, and assumed such offices as chairman of the Citizens' Equal Rights Association of Washington, DC. He died from kidney failure in 1893.

William Joseph Seymour (1870–1922)
Civil Rights Activist, Religious Leader

Born in Centerville, Louisiana, in 1870 to parents who had been slaves, Seymour taught himself to read and write. In 1900, Seymour encountered the prominent promoter of Holiness doctrine, Martin Knapp, and studied under him. He then suffered a bout of smallpox that left him blind in one eye. He was ordained as an evangelist by the "Evening Light Saints," a group that eventually became known by the title Church of God (Anderson, Indiana). Moving to Houston, he sat immediately outside the door of white evangelist Charles Parham's segregated classroom, while Parham lectured on Christian doctrine and, especially, on the importance of speaking in tongues.

In 1906, Seymour moved to Los Angeles to pastor a small African American Holiness church, but his congregation, opposed to Seymour's contention that speaking in tongues was a very important part of Christian experience, dismissed him after one week. Seymour continued to hold religious meetings, attracting an interracial audience. A widely publicized outburst of speaking in tongues brought him an even larger audience, so he moved his "Apostolic Faith Gospel Mission" to a former AME Church building on Azusa Street. The extremely successful meetings that he held before ecstatic, interracial throngs of listeners over the next three years have been universally acknowledged as the beginnings of modern Pentecostalism, both in the United States and around the world. Seymour was greatly saddened when the racial unity displayed in the early stages of Pentecostalism began to break apart under the pressures exerted by racial discrimination in the nation at large. He was holding services at the Azusa Street mission until his death in 1922.

Amanda Berry Smith (1837–1915)

Organization Executive/Founder, Evangelist/ Missionary

Born in Long Green, Maryland, in 1837, Smith was manumitted during her childhood after her father paid for her freedom. She had a spiritual conversion experience in 1856 and began attending religious meetings faithfully. She resisted identification with any single denomination, and her religious practice was most strongly influenced by Quakers and Methodists. Attendance at the religious meetings of white evangelists Phoebe Palmer and John Inskip introduced her to Holiness doctrine, and she experienced entire sanctification in 1868. Her husband died the following year, and Smith soon became a full-time travelling evangelist. She never sought to breach the barriers against women's ordination erected by male preachers, stating that the calling she had received directly from God was justification enough for her ministry.

From 1878 to 1890, Smith worked as a missionary in England, Ireland, Scotland, India, and Liberia. A Methodist bishop who heard her preach in India stated that he "had never known anyone who could draw and hold so large an audience as Mrs. Smith." On her return to the United States in 1890, she preached widely and wrote her autobiography in 1893, an extremely detailed work now regarded as a classic. Her last twenty years were devoted to the construction and management of the Amanda Smith Orphan's Home for Colored Children in Illinois. She died in 1915.

Stephen Gill Spottswood (1897–1974)

Organization Executive/Founder, Religious Leader, Civil Rights Activist

Bishop of the African Methodist Episcopal Zion Church from 1952 to 1972 and board chairman of the National Association for the Advancement of Colored People from 1961 until his death in 1974, Bishop Spottswood embodied the religious faith and intellectual incisiveness that has produced so many effective African American religious activists.

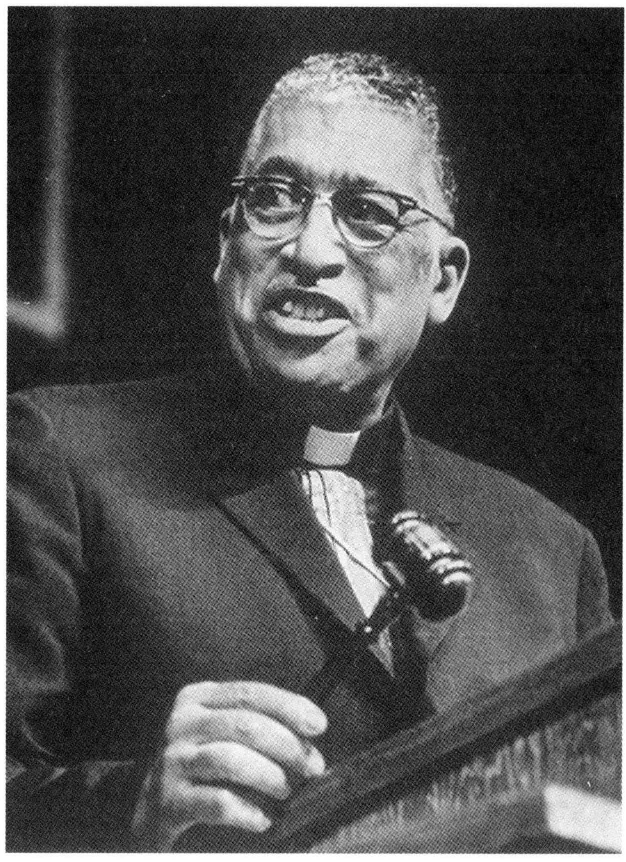

Bishop Stephen Spottswood (AP/Wide World Photos, Inc.)

Spottswood was born in Boston on July 18, 1897, attended Albright College, Gordon Divinity School, and then received a PhD. in divinity from Yale University. As a religious leader, Bishop Spottswood was president of the Ohio Council of Churches and served on the boards of numerous interfaith conferences, as well as heading the African Methodist Episcopal Zion Church. His activity with the NAACP started in 1919, when he joined the organization. He was appointed to the national board in 1955. In 1971, he became the center of a political storm when he chastised the Nixon administration for its policies toward African Americans and refused, under strong pressure from the administration, to retract his comments. He died on December 1, 1974.

George Augustus Stallings, Jr. (1948–)

Theologian

Born in New Bern, North Carolina, in 1948, Stallings received his B.A. from St. Pius X Seminary in 1970. He received his B.S. in theology from the University of St. Thomas Aquinas in 1973 and his M.A. in pastoral theolo-

Reverend George Stallings speaking at a press conference in 1989 (AP/Wide World Photos, Inc.).

gy the following year. In 1975, he was granted a licentiate in sacred theology by the University of St. Thomas Aquinas. In 1974 Stallings was ordained and was named pastor of St. Teresa of Avila in 1976. (St. Teresa of Avila Church is located in one of Washington, DC's poor African American neighborhoods.)

While pastor at St. Teresa, Stallings stressed that the contributions of Africans and African Americans to Christianity should be recognized and that the needs of African Americans must be addressed by the Catholic Church. In an effort to confront what he considered the Catholic Church's racial insensitivity, he made use of what is known as the Rite of Zaire, incorporated jazz and gospel music to the Mass, and added readings by celebrated African American writers to the liturgy. For these actions, Stallings received much criticism. In1988 he was removed from St. Teresa of Avila and named head of evangelism for Washington, DC.

In 1989 Stallings, still convinced that the Catholic Church was not meeting the cultural, spiritual, and social needs of African American Catholics, announced that he would leave the diocese to found a new congregation, the Imani Temple African-American Catholic Congregation. In 1991, Bishop Stallings ordained former Roman Catholic nun Rose Vernell as a priest. The congregation's membership is currently estimated at 3,500 members.

Leon Howard Sullivan (1922–)

Labor Activist, Civil Rights Activist, Vocational/Educational Counselor, Organization Executive/Founder

Sullivan was born October 16, 1922, in Charlestown, West Virginia. After being ordained a Baptist minister at the age of 17, Sullivan earned a B.A. from West Virginia State College (1943) and an M.A. from Columbia University (1947). Sullivan also attended the Union Theological Seminary (1945) and earned a D.D. from Virginia Union University.

From 1950 to 1988, Sullivan was the pastor of the Zion Baptist Church in Philadelphia. Much of his efforts during his ministry were directed toward improving employment prospects of African Americans. During the 1950s, he organized a selective patronage campaign, boycotting Philadelphia businesses that employed too few African American employees. Sullivan's campaign experienced some success, but businesses requested workers with technical skills that few African Americans possessed.

Accordingly in 1964, Sullivan founded the Opportunities Industrialization Center (O.I.C.) in order to impart employment skills to inner city youths. With money from a Ford Foundation grant, the Center offered training in electronics, cooking, power-sewing, and drafting. By 1980, the O.I.C. operated programs in 160 cities. Sullivan was also a major force in many other economic development initiatives, such as the Philadelphia Community Investment Cooperative; Zion Investment Associates, which makes available seed money for new African American business ventures; and Self-Help. His acceptance within the business community is well symbolized by his long-time membership on the boards of General Motors and Philadelphia's Girard Bank, as well as his association with Progress Aerospace Inc. and Mellon Bank.

Sullivan is also renowned for his leadership in addressing international issues as they affect the African American community and, in particular, for his intensive involvement in political and economic reform in South Africa. In the mid-1970s, he devised his "Sullivan Principles," which successfully encouraged American-owned companies in South Africa to hire more black workers and to treat them equitably in relation to promotions and working conditions. Sullivan, however, parted company with President Reagan's "constructive engagement" policy toward South Africa and, in 1987, endorsed a policy of South African divestment. In the same year, Sullivan received the Franklin D. Roosevelt

Four Freedoms Medal. Upon retiring from the Zion Baptist Church in 1988, Sullivan was made pastor emeritus.

Gardner C. Taylor (1918–)
Civil Rights Activist, Religious Leader, Community Activist

Rev. Taylor is widely regarded as the dean of the nation's African American preachers. He received a B.A. degree from Leland College in 1937 and a B.D. degree from the Oberlin Graduate School of Theology in 1940. Taylor has long been a community activist: He demonstrated for civil rights and suffered arrest for civil disobedience with Martin Luther King, Jr. in the 1960s, and he introduced Nelson Mandela to a New York audience in 1990. He is a trusted counselor to former New York mayor David Dinkins. Taylor served on the New York City Board of Education. He is the past president of the New York Council of Churches and the past vice president of the Urban League in New York City. After 42 years as pastor of the Concord Baptist Church in Brooklyn, Taylor resigned his post in 1990.

Howard Thurman (1899–1981)
Author, Theologian, Civil Rights Activist, Educator

Born in Daytona Beach, Florida, on November 18, 1899, Thurman studied at Morehouse College, Rochester Theological Center, and Haverford College. Thurman, named by *Life* magazine as one of the twelve great preachers of the twentieth century, served as a pastor to a Baptist church in Ohio and, from 1944 to 1953, to an interracial and interdenominational Fellowship church that he founded in San Francisco. He also served as dean of the chapel at Howard University from 1932 to 1944, as well as Boston University from 1953 until his retirement. Thurman was one of the leading theologians of his time, writing *The Negro Spiritual Speaks of Life and Death* and about his opposition to segregation and support of the Civil Rights movement in *This Luminous Darkness*. Altogether, he authored nineteen books including an autobiography published in 1979. He died on April 10, 1981.

Iyanla Vanzant (1954–)
Author, Yoruba Priestess, Lawyer

Vanzant is the author of several books on spirituality that have topped *Blackboard* including *Tapping the Power Within*(1992), *Acts of Faith* (1993), *Interiors: A Black Woman's Healing* (1995), *Value in the Valley* (1995), *The Spirit of a Man* (1996), *In the Meantime* (1998), and *One Day My Soul Just Opened Up* (1998). Her own life has served as an inspiration for many of her readers, as it has furnished rich material for her books. Her mother died when she was two years old, and she suffered from rape, spousal abuse, and nervous breakdowns. Yet, she managed to turn her life around. Her years of dependence on welfare ended in 1978, when she matriculated in Medgar Evers College in Brooklyn and subsequently in law school. She served as a public defender in Philadelphia, but left that career behind for public speaking and writing self-help books.

She is currently the director of Inner Visions Life Maintenance Center, headquartered in Silver Springs, Maryland, and dedicated to the spiritual empowerment of African American women and men. Brought up in the Baptist and Pentecostalist faiths, she has since been initiated as a Yoruba priestess. Her writings draw widely from such diverse sources as African spirituality, Christianity, New Thought, and such Eastern religions as Buddhism.

James Varick (1750–1827)
Abolitionist, Bishop, Deacon

Born near Newburgh, New York, around 1750, to a slave mother, Varick was a leader in the movement among African American Methodists in New York to set up a separate congregation. This was accomplished with the formation of the Zion Church in 1796. Ten years later, Varick was ordained a deacon by Bishop Francis Asbury. Varick sought to obtain full ordination as elder for himself and other African American ministers and would have preferred to have received such an ordination within the Methodist Episcopal Church, but this did not prove possible. He did not favor joining Richard Allen's African Methodist Episcopal Church, especially since Allen had been attempting to set up a New York congregation seen by Varick as in competition with the Zion Church. Eventually, Varick participated in setting up the African Methodist Episcopal Zion Church, and he was elected the first superintendent or bishop. He was also deeply involved in issues relating to freedom and human rights, preaching against the slave trade in 1808 and subscribing to the first newspaper in the United States owned by African Americans, *Freedom's Journal*. He died in 1827.

Cornel West (1953–)
Scholar, Educator, Social Critic, Author

The grandson of Rev. Clifton L. West, Sr., pastor of the Tulsa Metropolitan Baptist Church, Cornel West was born on June 2, 1953, in Tulsa, Oklahoma. West developed skills of critical thinking and political action almost from birth. By age 17, he was enrolled as an undergraduate student at Harvard. Taking eight courses per semester during his junior year, he was able to graduate *magna cum laude* one year early. He received an A.B. in Near Eastern languages and literature in 1973.

Immediately afterward, he completed his M.A. (1975) and Ph.D. (1980) at Princeton University.

Professor of religion and director of Afro-American Studies at Princeton University since 1989, Cornel West's analytical speeches and writing on issues of morality, race relations, cultural diversity, and progressive politics have made him a keeper of the prophetic African American religious tradition. West has taught the philosophy of religion at both Union Theological Seminary (1977–1983, 1988) and Yale Divinity School (1984–1987). A complex individual, he juggles his theological concerns with his political convictions. West serves dual roles as prophet and intellectual within and beyond the African American community. His writings combine a castigation for moral failure with an optimism that insists on the possibility—through struggle—of making a world of stricter morality real.

West's first books were published in the early 1980s, but he wrote many of them in the late 1970s. In the early 1980s, he encountered the Democratic Socialists of America (DSA), an organization that shaped the version of democratic socialism that he would subsequently adopt and promote in his works. Those include *Black Theology and Marxist Thought,* (1979) *Prophesy Deliverance! An Afro-American Revolutionary Christianity* (1982), and *The Ethical Dimensions of Marxist Thought* (1991). West's impassioned and insightful writings also make a resounding appeal for cross-cultural tolerance and unity, while urging individuals to recognize the power of diversity within a society. Following those lines are such works as: *Breaking Bread: Insurgent Black Intellectual Life,* which he co-edited with bell hooks in 1991; *Beyond Eurocentrism and Multiculturalism* (1993); *Race Matters* (1993), perhaps his best known book, and *Jews & Blacks: The Hard Hunt for Common Ground,* co-written with Michael Lerner in 1995.

◆ RELIGIOUS STATISTICS

Religious Bodies—Selected Data

[Includes the self-reported membership of religious bodies with 60,000 or more as reported to the *Yearbook of American and Canadian Churches*. Groups may be excluded if they do not supply information. The data are not standardized so comparisons between groups are difficult. The definition of "church member" is determined by the religious body]

RELIGIOUS BODY	Year reported	Churches reported	Membership (1,000)	Pastors serving parishes [1]
African Methodist Episcopal Church [2]	1991	8,000	3,500	(NA)
African Methodist Episcopal Zion Church	1997	3,098	1,252	2,571
American Baptist Churches in the U.S.A.	1996	5,807	1,503	4,323
Armenian Apostolic Church of America	1995	28	180	23
Assemblies of God	1996	11,884	2,468	18,100
Baptist Bible Fellowship International, The	1995	3,600	1,500	(NA)
Baptist General Conference	1996	875	136	(NA)
Baptist Missionary Association of America	1996	1,349	232	1,250
Buddhist [3]	1990	(NA)	401	(NA)
Christian and Missionary Alliance, The	1996	1,850	312	1,578
Christian Brethren (a.k.a. Plymouth Brethren)	1997	1,150	100	(NA)
Christian Church (Disciples of Christ)	1996	3,840	910	3,359
Christian Churches and Churches of Christ	1988	5,579	1,072	5,525
Christian Congregation, Inc., The	1996	1,437	115	1,433
Christian Methodist Episcopal Church	1983	2,340	719	(NA)
Christian Reformed Church in North America	1996	737	202	635
Church of God (Anderson, IN)	1996	2,327	229	2,921
Church of God (Cleveland, TN)	1995	6,060	753	3,121
Church of God in Christ, The	1991	15,300	5,500	28,988
Church of God of Prophecy, The	1996	1,910	70	5,155
Church of Jesus Christ of Latter-day Saints, The	1996	11,000	4,800	(NA)
Church of the Brethren	1996	1,106	142	838
Church of the Nazarene	1996	5,135	608	5,111
Churches of Christ	1996	14,000	2,250	11,000
Community Churches, International Council of	1995	517	250	491
Conservative Baptist Association of America	1992	1,084	200	(NA)
Coptic Orthodox Church	1992	85	180	65
Cumberland Presbyterian Church	1996	774	88	(NA)
Diocese of the Armenian Church of America	1991	72	414	49
Episcopal Church, The	1996	7,415	2,537	8,037
Evangelical Covenant Church, The	1997	615	93	565
Evangelical Free Church of America	1995	1,224	243	1,936
Evangelical Lutheran Church in America	1996	10,936	5,181	9,778
Free Methodist Church of North America	1996	1,050	75	(NA)
Free Will Baptists, National Association of	1996	2,491	210	2,800
Full Gospel Fellowship of Churches & Ministers International	1995	650	195	725
General Association of Regular Baptist Churches	1996	1,440	116	(NA)
General Baptists (General Association of)	1996	830	68	798
General Conference Mennonite Brethren Churches	1996	368	82	590
Grace Gospel Fellowship	1992	128	60	160
Greek Orthodox Archdiocese of North and South America	1997	532	1,950	(NA)
Hindu [3]	1990	(NA)	227	(NA)
Independent Fundamental Churches of America	1995	670	70	(NA)
International Church of the Foursquare Gospel	1996	1,773	230	2,322
International Pentecostal Holiness Church	1996	1,658	164	1,452
Jehovah's Witnesses	1996	10,671	976	(NA)
Jewish [3]	1990	(NA)	3,137	(NA)
Lutheran Church - Missouri Synod, The	1996	6,099	2,601	5,315
Mennonite Church	1996	1,004	91	1,525
Muslim / Islamic [3]	1990	(NA)	527	(NA)
National Association of Congregational Christian Churches	1997	429	69	558
National Baptist Convention of America, Inc.	1987	2,500	3,500	8,000
National Baptist Convention, U.S.A., Inc	1992	33,000	8,200	32,832
National Missionary Baptist Convention of America	1992	(NA)	2,500	(NA)
Old Order Amish Church	1993	898	81	3,592
Orthodox Church in America	1995	600	2,000	650
Pentecostal Assemblies of the World	1994	1,760	1,000	4,262
Pentecostal Church of God, Inc.	1996	1,230	112	(NA)
Presbyterian Church in America	1995	1,299	268	1,522
Presbyterian Church (U.S.A.)	1996	11,328	3,637	9,532
Progressive National Baptist Convention, Inc.	1995	2,000	2,500	(NA)
Reformed Church in America	1996	909	304	915
Religious Society of Friends (Conservative)	1994	1,200	104	(NA)
Reorganized Church of Jesus Christ of Latter-day Saints	1995	1,160	178	16,671
Roman Catholic Church, The	1996	22,728	61,208	(NA)
Romanian Orthodox Episcopate of America	1996	37	65	37
Salvation Army, The	1995	1,264	453	3,645
Serbian Orthodox Church in the U.S.A. and Canada	1986	68	67	60
Seventh-day Adventist Church	1996	4,363	809	2,337
Southern Baptist Convention	1996	40,565	15,692	37,955
Unitarian Universalist [3]	1990	(NA)	502	(NA)
United Church of Christ	1996	6,110	1,453	4,627
United Methodist Church, The	1996	36,361	8,495	36,666
Wesleyan Church (USA), The	1996	1,580	118	1,800
Wisconsin Evangelical Lutheran Synod	1996	1,235	413	1,217

NA Not available. [1] Does not include retired clergy or clergy not working with congregations. [2] Figures obtained from the *Directory of African American Religious Bodies, 1991.* [3] Figures obtained from the National Survey of Religious Identification, a survey conducted by the City University of New York in 1990 and published in *One Nation Under God: Religion in Contemporary American Society,* by Barry Kosmin and Seymour Lachman (1993).

Source: National Council of the Churches of Christ in the USA, New York, NY, *1998 Yearbook of American and Canadian Churches,* annual (copyright).

Literature

◆ African American Writers of Colonial America
◆ African American Literature during the Antebellum Period ◆ The "New Negro" Movement
◆ The Harlem Renaissance ◆ African American Writers in the Mid–Twentieth Century
◆ The Black Arts Movement ◆ African American Literature of the Late Twentieth Century
◆ Novelists, Poets, and Playwrights

by Lean'tin LaVerne Bracks and Jessie Carney Smith

African American literature in the United States reached an artistic pinnacle in the period between World War I and World War II with the Harlem Renaissance. Since then the role of African American writing has maintained a certain level of visibility and embraced themes ranging from the highly-charged and socio-political works to private and introspective themes. The Black Arts movement of the 1960s and 1970s brought acclaim and prominence to many African American writers and fostered the growth of many African American studies departments at universities around the country. In the 1980s and 1990s, African American writers were working in every genre—from scriptwriting to poetry—as their names consistently appeared on bestseller lists.

◆ AFRICAN AMERICAN WRITERS OF COLONIAL AMERICA

The first African American to publish a book was Phillis Wheatley. Published in 1773, *Poems on Various Subjects, Religious and Moral, by Phillis Wheatley, Negro Servant to Mr. John Wheatley, of Boston, in New England* made a tremendous impact on white colonial America, since many felt that African Americans were not capable of the depth of feeling required to write poetry. Soon after its publication, Wheatley gained such international recognition that she was granted her freedom.

Another important early African American writer was Olaudah Equiano, whose literary work *The Interesting Narrative of the Life of Olaudah Equiano, or Gustavus Vassa, the African, Written by Himself* was published in 1789. Considered the first autobiography written by an African American, *The Interesting Narrative* became a bestseller within Equiano's lifetime, with nine English editions and one American edition including translations in Dutch, German, and Russian. In a farther-reaching sense though, it influenced later slave narrative writings, such as Frederick Douglass's *The Life and Times of Frederick Douglass.*

Therefore, Wheatley and Equiano, along with such other early writers as Jupiter Hammon and Lucy Terry, demonstrated that African Americans could command written language through various literary genres, as well as represent themselves effectively through writing.

◆ AFRICAN AMERICAN WRITERS DURING THE ANTEBELLUM PERIOD

Perhaps the greatest satisfaction for African American writers during the period prior to the Civil War was having the freedom to write. Actually, knowing how to read and write was a tremendous accomplishment for many African Americans. This was due to the fact that only sporadic attempts at systematic instruction of Africans in colonial America had been made, and stringent laws were later passed in the nineteenth century that prohibited whites from teaching African Americans to read and write.

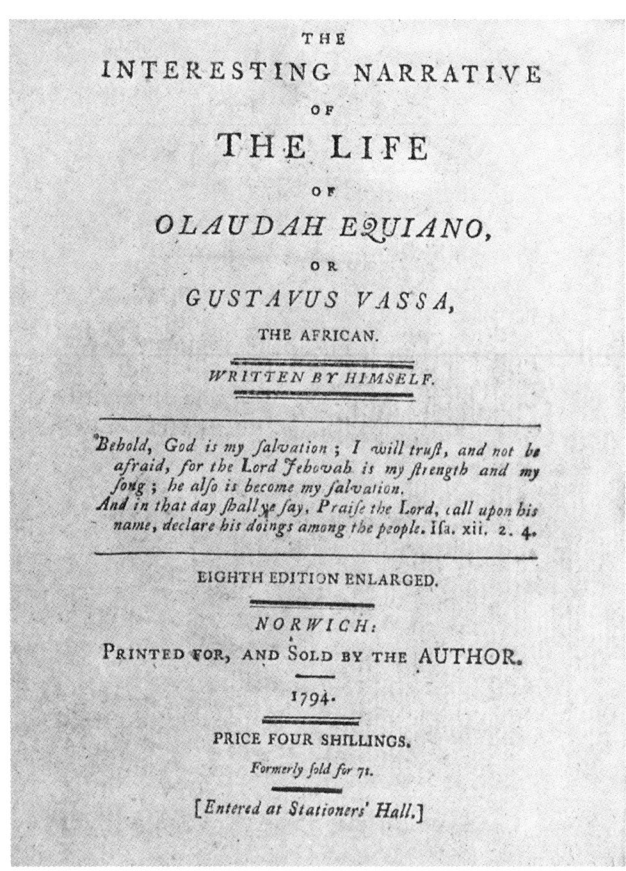

THE

INTERESTING NARRATIVE

OF

THE LIFE

OF

OLAUDAH EQUIANO,

OR

GUSTAVUS VASSA,

THE AFRICAN.

WRITTEN BY HIMSELF.

Behold, God is my salvation; I will trust, and not be afraid, for the Lord Jehovah is my strength and my song; he also is become my salvation.
And in that day shall ye say, Praise the Lord, call upon his name, declare his doings among the people. Isa. xii. 2. 4.

EIGHTH EDITION ENLARGED.

NORWICH:

PRINTED FOR, AND SOLD BY THE AUTHOR.

1794.

PRICE FOUR SHILLINGS.

Formerly sold for 7s.

[*Entered at Stationers' Hall.*]

Olaudah Equiano's autobiography served as the first slave narrative in American literary history (The Library of Congress).

The Slave Narratives

The slave narrative, in particular, is an important part of the African American literary tradition as it utilized the language of slaves's captors as a method of rebellion, and it served as a preface and a foundation for continued expression through fiction, poetry, essays, and other texts. During the early to mid-nineteenth century, slave narratives, as influenced by captivity narratives and religious conversion texts, established themes and structural considerations that had been previously overlooked. Although many readers may consider the narratives by such persons as Frederick Douglass, William Wells Brown, Frances E. W. Harper, or Harriet A. Jacobs more political than artistic, the ability to adapt and utilize language in a manner that showed the glaring inconsistencies and inhumanity of slavery must be recognized as an accomplishment of letters. The full extent of these writers's revolutionary thoughts were channeled through these traditional subjects of the Bible and neoclassicism. However, the restructuring and inclusion of the African American perspective created a viable means of resistance and expression.

◆ THE "NEW NEGRO" MOVEMENT

With the end of the Civil War and the beginning of the era of Reconstruction, African American writers were eager to address subjects of personal and individual freedom. However, continuing attitudes forced African American writers to continue to address issues of "the master mentality" and "plantation politics." Few writers could support themselves by their writing, and many went unknown. Such writers as George Moses Horton received some acclaim for their work, but only briefly.

As the United States moved into the close of the nineteenth century, other African American writers, such as Paul Laurence Dunbar, Pauline Hopkins, and Charles Waddell Chesnutt, found an audience that appreciated their work. White society, however, still controlled much of publishing in America; African American work was often filtered and distorted through this lens. As a result, much of the "New Negro" movement work published by African Americans attempted to prove that African Americans could fit into middle-American society. In fact, much of the literature of this era portrayed African Americans as being happy with their assigned lot. Yet some writers—Dunbar and Chesnutt, for example—tried to break the chains of this imposed expression. They presented a view of African American life as it really was, not as society wanted it to be.

The accomplishments of African American writers during the time prior to the Harlem Renaissance attests to both the use of literary forms and the purpose in finding their own voices. Although themes were often muted and subjected to continuous scrutiny, the use of imagery, language, and a new perspective opened the way for African American writers to focus more on the wealth of their culture and the African American experience in a truthful and honest fashion.

◆ THE HARLEM RENAISSANCE

Resistant to the easy categorization of a timeline, the Harlem Renaissance began around World War I and extended into the early 1930s. It began with the movement of African American artists and writers into Harlem from practically every state in the country. By the 1920s Harlem was the largest community of black individuals in the world, encompassing Africans, people from the West Indies, the Caribbean, and the Americas. This community, similar to many urban communities in the North, saw the collective energies of persons joining together to celebrate the wealth of African American culture. While Harlem served as the hub of artistic activity, Washington, DC, was also a place where many artists congregated to explore the new perspectives and ideas of the time.

Although free expression was essential to artists of the Harlem Renaissance, stereotypes that permeated the American culture made their writings appear rebellious. The conscious agenda of these mostly young, African American artists concerned the definition and celebration of African American art and culture and a desire to change the preconceived and erroneous notions most Americans had of African American life.

As African American journals such as *Crisis* and *Opportunity* began to flourish, it became possible for African American writers to publish in a style that suited their tastes. Jessie Redmon Fauset, who was also a writer and editor of *Crisis* magazine, did much to support the work of women writers. The largest group of women who were participants in the Harlem Renaissance found their literary identities not so much in Harlem, but in Washington, DC, in the company of host poet Georgia Douglas Johnson and other artists. Also, African American writers discovered that some white patrons in the publishing field were, in fact, interested in promoting their work. The new generation of African American artists, referred to as "New Negroes," sought to chisel out a unique, African-centered culture for African Americans.

Important writers of this era include Langston Hughes, Countee Cullen, Claude McKay, Nella Larsen, and Zora Neale Hurston. These younger writers were encouraged by the older, established writers, critics, and editors including W. E. B. Du Bois, with his journal *Crisis*, and Charles S. Johnson, editor of *Opportunity*, a sponsor of many literary contests. In fact, Langston Hughes and others contend that the Renaissance came about because of the nurturing of older writers including Jessie Fauset and Alain Locke.

The Harlem Renaissance shifted away from the moralizing work that had been characteristic of much of post-Reconstruction writing that decried racism. W. E. B. Du Bois and Alain Locke realized, as did many of the emerging young writers, that literary efforts that catered to changing the conscience of the United States was no longer useful nor should it be a primary consideration for the artist. These writers felt communicating the African American experience through every facet of artistic mediums would, in itself, expound upon ills of a racist world. Issues then could be expressed through the lives of working-class and middle-class characters as the text sought to paint a realistic picture.

In this time of discovery for African Americans of the view from within, many also saw the changing relationships between blacks and whites. Literature reintroduced white America to a people who needed, wanted, and would eventually demand full participation in the society for which they had lived, labored, and died. This perspective would end the goal of convincing white America of African American entitlement and, instead, focus on self-education and exploration of the quality of the African American experience. It paved the way for power through art to inspire the masses and the writers of the 1960s.

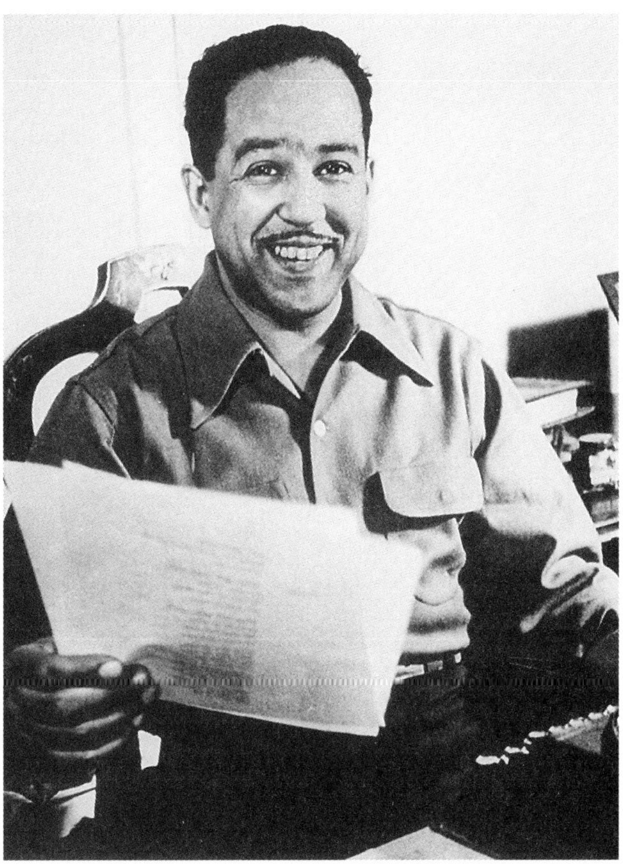

Langston Hughes (Corbis Corporation [Bellevue])

◆ AFRICAN AMERICAN WRITERS IN THE MID-TWENTIETH CENTURY

As the Great Depression of the 1930s deepened, the Harlem Renaissance slowly faded. Richard Wright's publication in 1940 of *Native Son* marked a new era in African American literature. The years from 1940 to 1955 served as a transition period for African American literature; they bridged the richly creative period of the Renaissance with the more intense creativity and sociopolitical activity that was to define the work produced during the Civil Rights movement.

With the publication of his classic novel *Native Son*, Wright maintained that the era of the Harlem Renaissance—with its motto of art for art's sake'—must end

Richard Wright

and be replaced with works directly intended to stop racism. He also believed that African Americans were an essential part of American society. These tenets became the foundation for the ideology of the Civil Rights movement.

During this time, other African American writers, notably poets, were taking a different road in their quest to be heard. Such poets as Gwendolyn Brooks, Melvin B. Tolson, Margaret Walker, and Robert Hayden were using classical and mythical themes in their works. Indeed, Brooks won a Pulitzer Prize in 1950 for her book *Annie Allen.* These poets used a blend of extreme eclecticism with realistic, African American issues. The blend was successful, as their writing was met with acceptance in the university community.

Ralph Ellison's *Invisible Man,* arguably one of the best novels published in the United States during this century, James Baldwin's *Go Tell It on the Mountain,* and Ann Petry's *The Street* were three other books that brought serious African American issues to mainstream culture. In addition, many African American works were gaining acceptance with the mainstream literary establishment and being taught in English classes around the country.

◆ THE BLACK ARTS MOVEMENT

The Black Arts movement, sometimes called the Black Aesthetics movement, was the first major African American artistic movement since the Harlem Renaissance. Beginning in the early 1960s and lasting through the mid-1970s, this movement was fueled by the anger of Richard Wright, Ralph Ellison, Ann Petry, and other notable African American writers.

The artistic movement flourished alongside the civil rights marches and the call for the independence of the African American community. As phrases such as "Black is beautiful" were popularized, African American writers of the Black Arts movement consciously set out to define what it meant to be an African American writer in a white culture. While writers of the Harlem Renaissance seemed to investigate their identity within, writers of the Black Arts movement desired to define themselves and their era before being defined by others.

For the most part, participants in the Black Arts movement were supportive of separatist politics and a black nationalist ideology. Rebelling against the mainstream society by being essentially anti-white, anti-American, and anti-middle class, these artists moved from the Renaissance view of art for art's sake into a philosophy of art for politics's sake.

The Black Arts movement attempted to produce works of art that would be meaningful to the African American masses. Towards this end, popular African American music of the day, including John Coltrane's jazz and James Brown's soul, as well as street talk, were some of the inspirational forces for their art. In fact, much of the language used in these works was aggressive, profane, and shocking—this was often a conscious attempt to show the vitality and power of African American activists. These writers tended to be revolutionaries, supporting both radical and peaceful protests for change as promoted by Malcolm X and Martin Luther King, Jr. In addition, they believed that artists had more of a responsibility than just art: artists also had to be political activists in order to achieve nationalist goals.

Leading writers in this movement included Imamu Amiri Baraka (Leroi Jones), whose poetry was as well known as his political prowess, and Haki R. Madhubuti (Don L. Lee), a poet and essayist who sold more than 100,000 copies of his books without a national distributor. Ishmael Reed, on the other hand—an early organizer of the Black Arts movement—later dissented with some of the movement's doctrines and became inspired more by the black magic and spiritual practices of the West Indies (in what he called the "HooDoo Aesthetic"). Other organizers and essayists include Larry Neal, Ethridge Knight, Addison Gale Jr., and Maulana Karenga.

Nikki Giovanni (Courtesy of Nikki Giovanni)

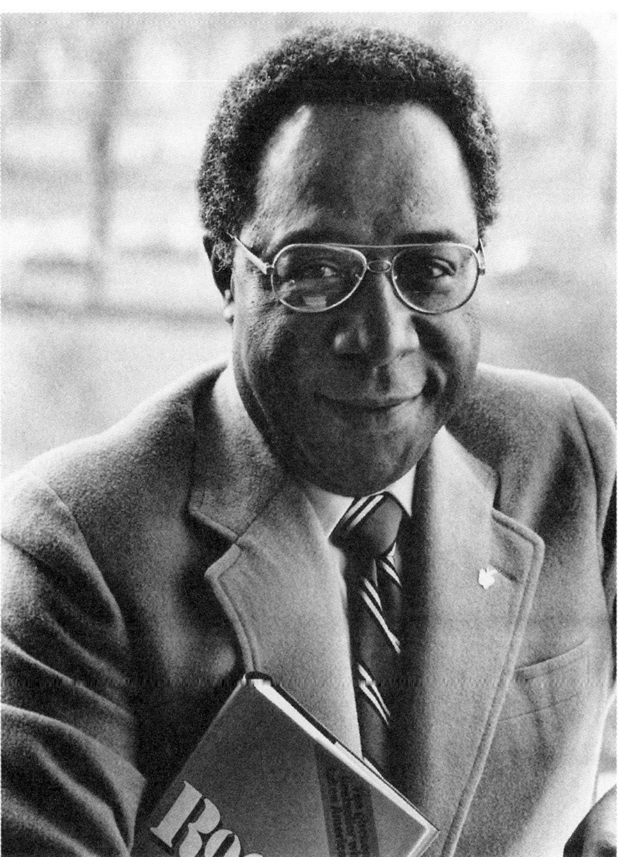

Alex Haley (Corbis Corporation [Bellevue])

Nikki Giovanni was one of the first poets of the Black Arts movement to receive recognition. She advocated in her work militant replies to white oppression and demonstrated through her performances that music is an inextricable part of the African American tradition in all aspects of life. Sonia Sanchez was another leading voice of the movement. She managed to combine feminism with her commitment to nurturing children and men in the fight for black nationalism. She joined up with the Nation of Islam from 1972 to 1975 and, through her association with the Black Arts movement, managed to instill stronger support for the role of women in that religion.

◆ AFRICAN AMERICAN LITERATURE OF THE LATE TWENTIETH CENTURY

Since the Black Arts movement, African American writing has become more legitimized in the United States, and African American studies departments have emerged in many universities around the country. Variety was the key to African American writing, and barriers were dismantled in various genres. For example, Octavia Butler and Samuel Delany in the works of science fiction and Donald Goines in detective fiction rivaled their contemporaries. Novels of both folk history and the urban experience were equally well received, and many artists found that they could straddle more than one genre—Alice Walker and Gayl Jones being good examples.

Alex Haley's *Roots* was perhaps one of the greatest African American writing coups of the late twentieth century. With his book, as well as the highly popular television miniseries that followed, many African Americans were encouraged to discover their own African roots. Books that explored the history of African Americans in other areas, namely the American West, the South, and the North were also published and eagerly received by African Americans.

Many African American women of this period wrote in response to the Black Arts movement, protesting the role that they felt women played in the male-oriented black nationalist movement. Zora Neale Hurston's work was resurrected and used for inspiration and impetus in their work. The women's liberation movement also supported these women by allowing their works to reach a wider audience. In this way, the somewhat female-repressive politics of the Black Arts movement provoked women writers to express their own unique voice. Alice Walker, Gayl Jones, Toni Morrison, Terry McMillan, and Gloria Naylor are examples of successful women authors who have become prominent figures in the publishing world. By the 1980s, African American women writers were, in fact, at the leading edge of the publishing industry—in quality as well as quantity of work.

Many African American writers of this period shifted their attention away from writing about the disparity between blacks and whites in the United States and toward themes of self-reflection and healing. This was evident in many writers's works including Toni Morrison, John Edgar Wideman, and Kristin Hunter. The decade of the 1990s also became the benefactor of a broad spectrum of African American works that explored the breath of life experiences—past and present.

Finally, several writers and their works have been heralded on both the national and international level. Charles R. Johnson received the 1990 National Book Award for *Middle Passage.* In 1993 Maya Angelou wrote and read the poem "On the Pulse of Morning" for the inauguration of President Bill Clinton. Toni Morrison won the Nobel Prize in literature in 1993 for her novel *Beloved.* In that same year, Rita Dove was named U.S. poet laureate, a post in the Library of Congress. As the twenty-first century arrives on the horizon, African American writers continue to look into their own world for answers rather than letting others define their past, present, or future.

Maya Angelou (AP/Wide World Photos, Inc.)

◆ NOVELISTS, POETS, AND PLAYWRIGHTS

(To locate biographical profiles more readily, please consult the index at the back of the book.)

Raymond Andrews (1934–1991)
Novelist

Born in 1934 in Madison, Georgia, Raymond Andrews left his sharecropper home for Atlanta at 15 years of age. Once establishing himself, he attended high school at night and went on to the U.S. Air Force (1952–1956) and attended Michigan State University before moving to New York City. While working in New York in a variety of jobs: airline reservations clerk, hamburger cook, photo librarian, proofreader, inventory taker, mail room clerk, messenger, air courier dispatcher, and bookkeeper. He also perfected his literary skills.

Andrews's first novel *Appalachee Red* (1978), set in the African American neighborhood of a northern Georgia town called Appalachee, was widely acclaimed. In the opinion of the reviewer for the *St. Louis Globe Democrat,* his work marked the literary debut of a significant modern American novelist of the stature of a Richard Wright or James Baldwin. The following year Raymond Andrews was the first recipient of the annual James Baldwin Prize presented by Dial Press at a ceremony attended by Baldwin.

Andrews's second work *Rosiebelle Lee Wildcat Tennessee: A Novel* (1980) chronicled the 40-year reign beginning in 1906, of the spiritual and temporal leader of the African American community of Appalachee. *Baby Sweets* (1983), Andrews's third novel, which is the name given to the brothel operated by the eccentric son of Appalachee's leading citizen that provides African American prostitutes to the white population. It was published by Dial Press and illustrated by Andrew's brother, Benny, which was the case with all of Andrew's novels. This novel examines how the intermingling of the races affects an entire community, both black and white.

Maya Angelou (1928–)
Novelist, Poet, Actress

Maya Angelou, born Marguerite Johnson on April 4, 1928, is a writer, journalist, poet, actress, singer, dancer, playwright, director, and producer. Angelou spent her formative years shuttling between her native St. Louis; a tiny, totally segregated town in Arkansas; and San Francisco, where she realized her ambition of becoming that city's first African American streetcar conductor. But her true mark came later in life as her words became a symbol of hope that touched the soul of the United States. Perhaps the ultimate recognition of her talent came when President-elect Bill Clinton asked the poet to compose and recite an inaugural poem for his swearing-in ceremony in 1993. Before reaching that point, however, Angelou experienced a great variety of life's offerings, as inspired by her mother, grandmother, and other female role models in her life.

During the 1950s, Angelou studied dance with Pearl Primus in New York City, later appearing as a nightclub singer there, as well as in San Francisco and Hawaii. She toured with the U.S. State Department's production of *Porgy and Bess* in the mid-1950s. She began the following decade in the position of northern coordinator of the Southern Christian Leadership Conference. Angelou went abroad working as an editor for *The Arab Observer*, an English-language weekly published in Cairo. While living in Accra, Ghana, under the black nationalist regime of Kwame Nkrumah, she taught music, drama, and wrote for the *Ghanian Times*. Angelou later went to Sweden to study cinematography.

Angelou became a national celebrity in 1970 with the publication of *I Know Why the Caged Bird Sings*, the first volume of her autobiography, which detailed her encounters with Southern racism and a pre-pubescent rape by her mother's lover. The work was nominated for that year's National Book Award. Three additional volumes of Angelou's autobiography were published: *Gather Together in My Name* (1974); *Singin' and Swingin' and Gettin' Merry Like Christmas* (1976); and *The Heart of a Woman* (1981).

Angelou's published works also include: *Just Give Me a Cool Drink of Water 'fore I Die: The Poetry of Maya Angelou* (1971); *Oh Pray My Wings Are Gonna Fit Me Well*(1975); *And Still I Rise* (1978); *Shaker Why Don't You Sing?* (1983); *All God's Children Need Traveling Shoes* (1986); and *Wouldn't Take Nothing for My Journey Now* (1993). In addition, Angelou's works include: *Mrs. Flowers: A Moment of Friendship; Now Sheba Sings the Song;* and *Phenomenal Woman: Four Poems Celebrating Women.*

Not limited to writing, Angelou dabbled both in front of and behind the camera. In 1977, she was nominated for an Emmy award for her portrayal of Nyo Boto in the television adaptation of Alex Haley's best-selling novel *Roots*. She also starred in the 1993 made-for-television movie *There Are No Children Here*, which co-starred Oprah Winfrey. That same year, Angelou wrote poetry for John Singleton's *Poetic Justice* and played a small role in the film. The following year, Angelou appeared in a television commercial, reading a version of her poem "Still I Rise" for the United Negro College Fund's Fiftieth Anniversary. She co-starred with Winona Ryder, Anne Bancroft, and Ellen Burstyn in *How to Make an American Quilt* (1995). Also active behind the scenes, she became the first African American woman to have a movie produced with *Georgia, Georgia* (1972), based on one of her books; and directed the film *All Day Long* in 1974.

The 1990s held many highlights for the sought-after poet, who remained as active as she had been earlier in her career. On January 20, 1993, Angelou read her newly-created "On the Pulse of Morning" during the inauguration of President Bill Clinton. This event occurred just a few days after her play *And Still I Rise* was performed in Washington, DC. In 1994, Angelou narrated a World Choir '94 concert held at the Georgia Dome, where the festival featured 10,000 singers from ten different countries. She also gave a reading at the National Black Arts Festival that year. In 1995, Angelou delivered "A Brave and Startling Truth" at a United Nation's fiftieth anniversary ceremony held in San Francisco, read Sterling Brown's "Strong Men" at the inauguration of Washington, DC, Mayor Marion Barry, and was a keynote speaker, along with First Lady Hillary Rodham Clinton, at the twenty-fifth anniversary of the Joint Center for Political and Economic Studies.

Angelou has been the recipient of many awards including a Golden Eagle Award for the 1977 documentary *Afro-American in the Arts*, a Matrix Award from Women in Communications, Inc. in 1983, a North Carolina award in literature in 1987, a "best-mannered" citation from the National League of Junior Cotillions in 1993, a Medal of Distinction from the University of Hawaii's Board of Regents in 1994, and a Spingarn Medal from the NAACP that year. In 1981, Wake Forest University gave Angelou a lifetime appointment as Reynolds Professor of American Studies.

Houston A. Baker, Jr. (1943–)

Writer, Literary Critic, Scholar, Educator

Houston A. Baker was born in Louisville, Kentucky, on March 22, 1943. In spite of the racist attitudes that permeated his environment, he went on to see himself as more than a victim. He attended Howard University and received a bachelor's degree in English and his master's and doctoral degrees from the University of California at Los Angeles. Out of his youthful experiences he became an advocate for the Black Power movement, which advocated black nationalism in the period of the late 1960s and 1970s.

As a young scholar, Baker shifted his critical perspective toward an African American aesthetic in African American literature. In other words, he considered art an instrument of cultural expression toward the liberation of black people that should be recognized in the study of African American works.

As editor of the book *Black Literature in America* (1971), an anthology of African American writers, he began to produce books that gave voice to artistic and literary experiences found in the study of African American literature. Among others, his books include: *Twentieth-Century Interpretations of Native Son* (1972); *A Many-Colored Coat of Dreams: The Poetry of Countee Cullen* (1974); *No Matter Where You Travel, You Still Be Black* (1979); *The Journey Back: Issues in Black Literature and Criticism* (1980); *Narrative of the Life of Frederick Douglass, An American Slave, Written by Himself* (1982); *Blues, Ideology, and Afro-American Literature: A Vernacular Theory* (1984); *Modernism and the Harlem Renaissance* (1987); *Afro-American Poetics: Revision of Harlem and the Black Aesthetic* (1988); *Black Feminist Criticism and Critical Theory* (1988); *Afro-American Literary Study in the 1990's* (1989); and *Black Studies, Rap and the Academy* (1993).

A prolific contributor to numerous scholarly journals and publications as well as president of the Modern Language Association of America in 1992, Baker is considered one of the leading African American intellectuals of his time. As a professor and director of the Center for the Study of Black Literature and Culture at the University of Pennsylvania, Baker continues to pursue a more active approach to literary studies.

James Baldwin (1924–1987)
Novelist, Essayist, Playwright

Born in New York City on August 2, 1924, James Baldwin turned to writing after an early career as a boy preacher in Harlem's storefront churches. He attended Frederick Douglass Junior High School in Harlem and later graduated from DeWitt Clinton High School, where he was editor of the school magazine. Three years later, he won a Eugene Saxton Fellowship, which enabled him to write full-time. After leaving the United States, Baldwin resided in France as well as in Turkey.

Baldwin's first novel *Go Tell It on the Mountain* was published in 1953 and received critical acclaim. Two years later his first collection of essays *Notes of a Native Son* again won favorable critical acclaim. This was followed in 1956 by the publication of his second novel *Giovanni's Room.* His second collection of essays *Nobody Knows My Name* established him as a major voice in American literature.

In 1962, *Another Country,* Baldwin's third novel, was a critical and commercial success. A year later, he wrote *The Fire Next Time,* an immediate best-seller and regarded as one of the most brilliant essays written in the history of African American protest. Since then, two of Baldwin's plays *Blues for Mister Charlie* and *The Amen Corner* have been produced on the New York stage where they achieved modest success. His novel *Tell Me How Long the Train's Been Gone* was published in 1968. Baldwin himself regarded it as his first "grown-up novel," but it generated little enthusiasm among critics.

After a silence of several years, the question of whether Baldwin had stopped writing was widely debated. He published the 1974 novel *If Beale Street Could Talk.* In this work, the problems besetting a ghetto family are portrayed with great sensitivity and humor. Baldwin's skill as a novelist is evident as he conveyed his own sophisticated analyses through the mind of his protagonist, a young woman. To many critics, however, the novel lacked the undeniable relevance and fiery power of Baldwin's early polemical essays.

Baldwin's other works during this time include: *Going to Meet the Man* (short stories); *No Name in the Street; One Day When I Was Lost,* a scenario based on Alex Haley's *The Autobiography of Malcolm X*; *A Rap on Race* with Margaret Mead; and *A Dialogue* with Nikki Giovanni. He was one of the rare authors who worked well alone or in collaboration. Other books by Baldwin include: *Nothing Personal* (1964) with photographs by Richard Avedon; *The Devil Finds Work* (1976), about the movies; his sixth novel *Just Above My Head* (1979); and *Little Man, Little Man: A Story of Childhood* (1977), a book for children. He wrote 16 books in all.

In 1979, Baldwin's novel *Just Above My Head,* which dealt with the intertwined lives from childhood to adulthood of a gospel singer, his brother, and a young girl who is a child preacher, was published. The next year Baldwin's publisher released *Remember This House,* described as Baldwin's "memoirs, history and biography of the civil rights movement" interwoven with the biographies of three assassinated leaders: Martin Luther King, Jr., Malcolm X, and Medgar Evers. Meanwhile, in his lectures Baldwin remained pessimistic about the future of race relations.

His last three books were *The Evidence of Things Not Seen* (1985) about the killing of 28 African American youths in Atlanta, Georgia, in the early 1980s; *The Price of the Ticket: Collected Non-fiction 1948–1985* (1985); and *Harlem Quartet* (1987). Baldwin spent most of the remainder of his life in France. In 1986, the French government made him a commander of the Legion of Honor, France's highest civilian award. He died at his home in France, on November 30, 1987, at the age of 63.

Toni C. Bambara (1939–)
Writer

Toni Cade Bambara was born Toni Cade in New York City in 1939, and later took on the name of Bambara,

James Baldwin (AP/Wide World Photos, Inc.)

after finding the signature "Bambara" on a sketchbook located among the materials in her great-grandmother's trunk. Bambara's mother, who was profoundly influenced by the Harlem Renaissance, strongly encouraged her daughter to explore her creative side and the influences of culture.

Coming of age in the 1960s and 1970s allowed Bambara to participate in both the nationalist and the women's liberation movements. In 1970, Bambara edited *The Black Woman: An Anthology*, which, being the first of its kind, was recognized as beginning the renaissance of African American women's literature. Throughout her career, much of Bambara's writings have explored the experiences of the African American community and, in particular, experiences of African American women.

While working in community focused positions and pursuing her writing, Bambara received her B.A. from Queens College in New York in 1959 and her M.A. from City College of New York in 1964. Bambara's active career in academia and her numerous awards have exemplified her desire to use art to promote the social and political welfare of the African American community—but not at the expense of the African American woman. Her works include: *Gorilla, My Love* (1972); *The Sea Birds Are Still Alive* (1977); *The Salt Eaters* (1980), which received the American Book Award; and *If Blessing Comes* (1987).

Imamu A. Baraka (Leroi Jones) (1934–)
Poet, Playwright, Essayist

Amiri Baraka was born Leroi Jones in Newark, New Jersey on October 7, 1934. He attended Rutgers University in Newark and Howard University in Washington, DC. In 1958 Baraka founded *Yugen* magazine and Totem Press. From 1961 to 1964, Baraka worked as an instructor at New York's New School for Social Research. In 1964 he founded the Black Arts Repertory Theater. He has since taught at the State University of New York at Stony Brook, University of Buffalo, Columbia University, George Washington University, and San Francisco State University, and has served as director of the community theater, Spirit House, in Newark.

In 1961, Baraka published his first book of poetry *Preface to a Twenty Volume Suicide Note.* His second book *The Dead Lecturer* was published in 1964. Fame eluded him, however, until the publication of his play *Dutchman* in 1964, which received the Obie award for

Imamu Amiri Baraka (Courtesy of Imamu Amiri Baraka)

Arna Bontemps (Corbis Corporation [Bellevue])

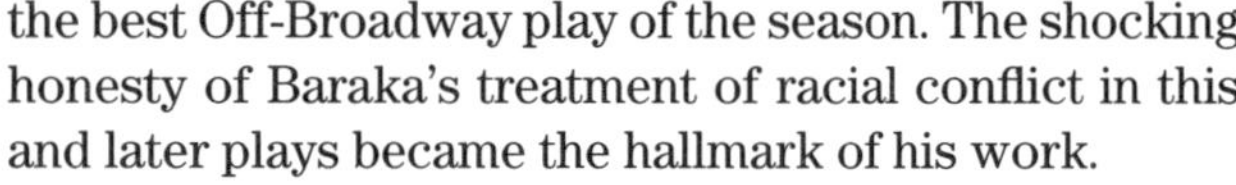

the best Off-Broadway play of the season. The shocking honesty of Baraka's treatment of racial conflict in this and later plays became the hallmark of his work.

During the late 1960s Baraka became a leading black power spokesman in Newark. He became head of the Temple of Kawaida, which Baraka describes as an "African religious institution—to increase black consciousness." The Temple and Baraka soon became a focal point of African American political activism in the racially-polarized city. In 1972 Baraka achieved prominence as an African American leader as chairman of the National Black Political Convention.

In 1966, Baraka's play *The Slave* won second prize in the drama category at the First World Festival of Dramatic Arts in Dakar, Senegal. Baraka's other published plays include: *The Toilet* (1964); *The Baptism* (1966); *The System of Dante's Hell* (1965); *Four Black Revolutionary Plays* (1969); *J-E-L-L-O* (1970); and *The Motion of History and Other Plays* (1978). He has edited with Larry Neal *Black Fire: An Anthology of Afro-American Writing* (1968) and *Afrikan Congress: A Documentary of the First Modern Pan-African Congress* (1972). His works of fiction include *The System of Dante's Hell* (novel, 1965) and *Tales* (short stories, 1967). Baraka has also published the following titles: *Black Music; Blues People: Negro Music in White America; Home: Social Essays; In Our Terribleness: Some Elements and Meanings in Black Style* with Billy Abernathy; *Raise Race Rays Raze: Essays Since 1965;* and *It's Nation Time, Kawaida Studies: The New Nationalism, A Black Value System and Strategy and Tactics of a Pan Afrikan Nationalist Party.*

Arna W. Bontemps (1902– 1973)

Poet, Novelist

Arna Wendell Bontemps was one of the most productive African American writers of the twentieth century. Born in Alexandria, Louisiana, on October 13, 1902, and raised in California, Bontemps received his B.A. degree from Pacific Union College in Angwin, California, in 1923 and his M.A. degree from the University of Chicago in 1943. In 1924, his poetry first appeared in *Crisis* magazine, the NAACP periodical edited by W. E. B. Du Bois. Two years later, *Golgotha Is a Mountain* won the Alexander Pushkin Award and, in 1927, *Nocturne at Bethesda* achieved first honors in the *Crisis* poetry contest. *Personals*, Bontemps's collected poems, was published in 1963.

In the late 1920s, Bontemps decided to try his hand at prose, and over the next decade produced such novels as *God Sends Sunday* (1931), *Black Thunder* (1936), and *Drums at Dusk* (1939). His books for young people include *We Have Tomorrow* (1945) and *Story of the Negro* (1948). Likewise of literary merit are such children's books as *Sad-Faced Boy* (1937) and *Slappy Hooper* (1946). He edited *American Negro Poetry* and two anthologies with Langston Hughes, among others.

In 1968, Bontemps completed the editing of a volume of children's poetry. Other publications included: *One Hundred Years of Negro Freedom* (1961); *Anyplace But Here* (published in 1966 in collaboration with Jack Conroy); *Black Thunder* (1968 reprint); *Great Slave Narratives* (1969); *The Harlem Renaissance Remembered: Essays* (1972, 1984); and *The Old South.* He also edited several anthologies. In 1997 his book *The Pasteboard Bandit* was published posthumously. Bontemps died in Nashville on June 4, 1973, of a heart attack.

Gwendolyn Brooks (1917–)
Poet

Gwendolyn Brooks was the first African American to win a Pulitzer Prize. Brooks received this prestigious award in 1950 for *Annie Allen,* a volume of her poetry that had been published one year earlier. Brooks has been associated with the Black Arts movement of the late 1960s. Long a trailblazer, in 1985 she became the first African American woman to be appointed poetry consultant by the Library of Congress.

Brooks was born on June 7, 1917, in Topeka, Kansas, moved to Chicago at an early age, and graduated from Wilson Junior College in 1936. In 1945, she completed a book of poems *A Street in Bronzeville* and was selected by *Mademoiselle* magazine as one of the year's ten most outstanding American women. She became a fellow of the American Academy of Arts and Letters in 1946, and received Guggenheim Fellowships for 1946 and 1947. In 1949, she won the Eunice Tietjen Prize for Poetry in the annual competition sponsored by *Poetry* magazine for the same work that won her that year's Pulitzer. She was named poet laureate of the state of Illinois in 1968.

Brooks's insights into the potential alienation of African American life have been represented in the body of her work, which includes a collection of children's poems *Bronzeville Boys and Girls* (1956); a novel *Maud Martha* (1953); and two books of poetry *The Bean Eaters* (1960) and *Selected Poems* (1963). She has also written *In the Mecca,* winner of the 1968 Anisfield-Wolf Award; *Riot; The World of Gwendolyn Brooks; Report from Part One: The Autobiography of Gwendolyn Brooks; Family Pictures; Beckonings; Aloneness; Primer for Blacks;* and *To Disembark.* Her poems and stories have also been published in magazines and two anthologies *Soon, One Morning* and *Beyond the Angry Black.* The publication of *Selected Poems* in 1964 earned her the Robert F. Ferguson Memorial Award. She has edited *A Broadside Treasury* and *Jump Bad, A New Chicago Anthology.*

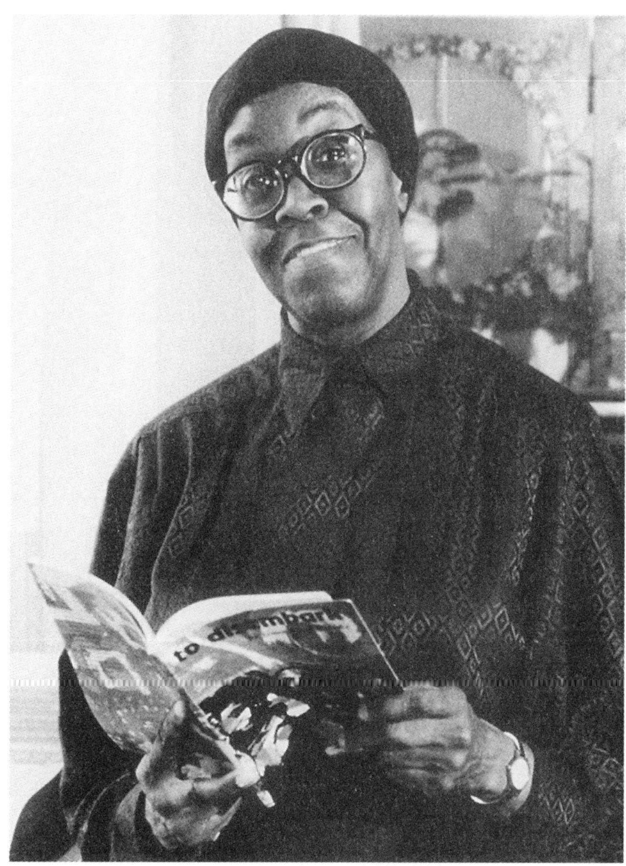

Gwendolyn Brooks (Corbis Corporation [Bellevue])

Among the other honors Brooks has received, Western Illinois University established The Gwendolyn Brooks Center for African American Literature in 1985. In 1988, she was inducted into the National Women's Hall of Fame. She won an *Essence* Award that year and a Frost Medal from the Poetry Society of America In 1990. In 1994, Brooks was named the year's Jefferson lecturer by the National Endowment for the Humanities, the highest honor for intellectual achievement bestowed by the U.S. government. The same year, Chicago's Harold Washington Library Center unveiled a bronze bust of Brooks prominently located in the facility, and the National Book Foundation awarded her the Medal for Distinguished Contribution to American Letters and $10,000 for her lifetime of achievement. In 1995, Brooks received the National Medal of Arts from U.S. President Bill Clinton.

Claude Brown (1937–)
Novelist

Claude Brown was born in 1937 in New York state. His claim to literary fame rests largely on his best-selling autobiography *Manchild in the Promised Land*, which was published in 1965 when he was 28 years of age. The book is the story of Brown's life in Harlem and, in the process, becomes a highly realistic documentary of life in the ghetto. It tells of Brown's escapades with the Harlem Buccaneers, a "bopping gang," and of his later involvement with the Forty Thieves, an elite stealing division of this same gang.

After attending the Wiltwyck School for emotionally disturbed and deprived boys, Brown returned to New York, was later sent to Warwick Reform School three times, and eventually made his way downtown to a small loft apartment near Greenwich Village. Changing his lifestyle, Brown finished high school and went on to graduate from Howard University in 1965.

Brown began work on his autobiography in 1963, submitting a manuscript of some 1,500 pages that was eventually cut and reworked into the finished product over a two-year period. Brown completed law school in the late 1960s and began practicing in California. In 1976, he published *The Children of Ham* about a group of young African Americans living as a family in a condemned Harlem tenement, begging, stealing, and doing whatever is necessary to survive.

William W. Brown (1815–1884)
Novelist, Playwright

William Wells Brown was the first African American to publish a novel, the first to publish a drama, and the first to publish a travel book. Born a slave in Lexington, Kentucky, on March 15, 1815, and taken to St. Louis as a young boy, Brown worked for a time in the offices of the *St. Louis Times* and then took a job on a riverboat on the Mississippi. In 1834, Brown fled to Canada, taking his name from a friendly Quaker whom he met there. While working as a steward on Lake Erie ships, he educated himself and became well known as a public speaker. In 1849, he went to England and Paris to attend the Peace Congress, remaining abroad for five years.

Brown's first published work *The Narrative of William H. Brown* (1847) went into three editions within eight months. A year later, a collection of his poems was published *The Anti-Slavery Harp* and in 1852 his travel book *Three Years in Europe* appeared in London. Brown's *Clotel, or the President's Daughter*, a melodramatic novel about miscegenation, was first published in London in 1853. As the first novel by an African American (it subsequently went through two revisions), its historical importance transcends its aesthetic shortcomings.

Brown's other books include: the first African American drama *The Escape, or a Leap for Freedom* (1858); *The Black Man: His Antecedents, His Genius, and His Achievements* (1863); *The Negro in the American Rebellion: His Heroism and Fidelity* (1867); and *The Rising Son* (1874).

Ed Bullins (1935–)
Playwright, Essayist, Poet

Ed Bullins was born in Philadelphia on July 2, 1935, and grew up in Los Angeles. Bullins is a writer of drama, and one of the founders of Black Arts/West in the Fillmore District of San Francisco. He patterned this experiment after the Black Arts Repertory Theater School in Harlem, which was founded and directed by Imamu Baraka. In 1977, when *Daddy*, the sixth play in his "Twentieth-Century Cycle," opened at the New Federal Theatre in New York's Henry Street Settlement, Bullins in an interview with the *New York Times* foresaw African American theatrical producers taking plays to cities with large African American populations. A leader of the African American theater movement and creator of more than fifty plays, he has yet to have a play produced on Broadway.

Bullins's main themes are the violence and tragedy of drug abuse and the oppressive life style of the ghetto. He presents his material in a realistic and natural style. Between 1965 and 1968, he wrote *The Rally, How Do You Do, Goin' a Buffalo, Clara's Old Man, The Electronic Nigger*, and *In The Wine Time*. He has also produced *The Fabulous Miss Marie*.

He has been a creative member of Black Arts Alliance, working with Baraka in producing films on the West Coast. Bullins has been connected with the New Lafayette Theater in Harlem where he was a resident playwright. His books include: *Five Plays; New Plays from the Black Theatre* (editor); *The Reluctant Rapist; The New Lafayette Theatre Presents; The Theme Is Blackness; Four Dynamite Plays; The Duplex; The Hungered One: Early Writings;* and *How Do You Do: A Nonsense Drama.*

Octavia E. Butler (1947–)
Novelist

Born in Pasadena, California, on June 22, 1947, Octavia Butler is a graduate of Pasadena City College. She has attended science fiction workshops, including the Clarion Science Fiction Writers' Workshop, and is a member

Ed Bullins (AP/Wide World Photos, Inc.)

of Science Fiction Writers of America. Her writing has focused on the impact of race and gender on future society. In 1985, Butler won three of science fiction's highest honors for her novella *Bloodchild: Novellas and Stories*: the Nebula, Hugo, and Locus awards. She also won a Hugo in 1984 for her short story "Speech Sounds." The 1987 novella *The Evening and the Morning and the Night* was nominated for a Nebula Award. In 1995, Butler won a MacArthur Foundation fellowship.

Butler's other works include the Patternmaster series, consisting of the novels *Patternmaster* (1976), *Mind of My Mind* (1977), *Survivor* (1978), *Wild Seed* (1980), and *Clay's Ark* (1984); the historical fantasy *Kindred* (1979); the Xenogenesis Trilogy, *Dawn: Xenogenesis* (1987), *Adulthood Rites* (1988), and *Imago* (1989); and the dystopian *Parable of the Sower* (1993). She has also served as a contributor to such science fiction publications as *Clarion*, *Future Life*, and *Isaac Asimov's Science Fiction Magazine*.

Charles W. Chesnutt (1858–1932)

Novelist

Called the first major African American fiction writer and the first of his race to balance African American and white characters in an African American novel, Charles Waddell Chesnutt holds a prominent place in American literary history. His best fiction dealt with the current issues of his time; he handled satire entertainingly, and he was direct and insightful in his nonfiction works and speeches.

Born in Cleveland, Ohio, on June 20, 1858, Chesnutt moved to North Carolina with his family at the age of eight. Largely self-educated, he was admitted to the Ohio bar in 1887, the same year in which his first story "The Goophered Grapevine" was published in the *Atlantic Monthly.* This was followed in 1899 by two collections of his stories *The Conjure Woman* and *The Wife of His Youth.*

Chesnutt's first novel *The House Behind the Cedars* (1900) dealt with a young girl's attempt to "pass" for white. A year later, *The Marrow of Tradition* examined the violence of the post-Reconstruction period. His final novel *The Colonel's Dream* was published in 1905 and typified Chesnutt's ingratiating approach to his art, one that the writers of the Harlem School were later to reject. Chesnutt also wrote a biography *Frederick Douglass* (1899). He died on November 15, 1932.

Alice Childress (1920–1994)
Playwright, Novelist

Born in Charleston, South Carolina, on October 12, 1920, actress and author Alice Childress studied acting at the American Negro Theatre and attended Radcliffe Institute from 1966 to 1968, through a Harvard University appointment as a scholar-writer. Her plays are *Florence* (one-act play); *Gold Through the Trees; Just a Little Simple* (based on Langston Hughes's *Simple Speaks His Mind*); *Trouble in Mind; Wedding Band; Wine in the Wilderness;* and *When the Rattlesnake Sounds: A Play About Harriet Tubman.*

Childress also edited *Black Scenes* (1971), excerpts from plays in the Zenith series for children. Her other books include: *Like One of the Family: Conversations from a Domestic's Life* (1956); *A Hero Ain't Nothing but a Sandwich* (novel, 1973); *A Short Walk* (1979); *Rainbow Jordan* (1981); and *Many Closets* (1987). Childress's play *Trouble in Mind* won the Obie Award in 1956, as the best original off-Broadway production. In the 1980s she wrote a play based on the life of African American comedienne Jackie (Moms) Mabley. The play was produced in New York City.

Childress's work was noted for its frank treatment of racial issues, its compassionate yet discerning characterizations, and its universal appeal. Her books and plays often dealt with such controversial subjects as miscegenation and teenage drug addiction. Childress died of cancer complications on August 14, 1994.

Countee Cullen (1903–1946)
Poet

Born Countee Porter on May 30, 1903, in Baltimore, he was orphaned at an early age and adopted by Rev. Frederick Cullen, pastor of New York's Salem Methodist Church. At New York University, Cullen won Phi Beta Kappa honors and was awarded the Witter Bynner Poetry Prize. In 1925, while still a student at New York University, Cullen completed *Color*, a volume of poetry which received the Harmon Foundation's first gold medal for literature two years later.

In 1926, Cullie earned his M.A. at Harvard and a year later finished both *The Ballad of the Brown Girl* and *Copper Sun.* This was followed in 1929 by *The Black Christ*, written during a two-year sojourn in France on a Guggenheim Fellowship. In 1927, he edited *Caroling Dusk: An Anthology of Verse by Negro Poets.* The book was reprinted in 1972.

Upon his return to New York City, Cullen began a teaching career in the public school system. During this period, he also produced a novel *One Way to Heaven* (1932), *The Medea and Other Poems* (1935), *The Lost Zoo* (1940), and *My Lives and How I Lost Them* (1942, 1971). In 1947, a year after his death, Cullen's own selections of his best work were collected in a volume published under the title *On These I Stand.* Cullen died of uremic poisoning on January 9, 1946, in New York City.

Samuel R. Delany (1942–)
Novelist

Born in Harlem on April 1, 1942, and a published writer at the age of 19, Samuel Ray Delany has been a prolific writer of science fiction, novelettes and novels. His first book was *The Jewels of Aptor* (1962), followed by *Captives of the Flame* (1963), *The Towers of Toron* (1964), *City of a Thousand Suns* (1965), *The Ballad of Beta-2* (1965), *Babel-17* (1966), *Empire Star* (1966), *The Einstein Intersection* (1967), *Out of the Dead City* (1968), and *Nova* (1968). *Babel-17* and *The Einstein Intersection* both won Nebula awards from the Science Fiction Writers of America, as did his short stories "Aye, and Gomorrah" and "Time Considered as a Helix of Semi-Precious Stones," which also won a Hugo Award at the World Science Fiction Convention in Heidelberg. Delany co-edited the speculative fiction quarterly *Quark, Nos. 1, 2, 3, 4* with his former wife, award-winning poet Marilyn Hacker. He also wrote, directed, and edited the half-hour film *The Orchid.* In 1975, Delany was Visiting Butler Chair professor of English at the State University of New York at Buffalo.

Delany's other books include: *Distant Stars* (1981); *Stars in My Pocket Like Grains of Sand* (1984); *The Splendor and Misery of Bodies of Cities* (1985); *Flight from Neveryon* (1985); *Neveryona* (1986); and *The Bridge of Lost Desire* (1988). His non-fiction works include: *The Jewel-Hinged Jaw; The American Shore; Starboard Wine; The Straits of Messina; The Motion of Light in Water* (autobiography, 1988); *The Mad Man* (1994); *They Fly at Ciron* (1995); and *Atlantis: Three Tales* (1995).

Rita Dove (1952–)
Poet, Educator

Rita Dove was born on August 28, 1952, in Akron, Ohio. She received a B.A. from Miami University in Oxford, Ohio, in 1973, and an M.F.A. degree from the University of Iowa in 1977. Dove also attended the University of Tubingen in Germany in 1974 and 1975.

Dove began her teaching career at Arizona State University in 1981 as an assistant professor. She spent 1982 as a writer-in-residence at Tuskegee Institute (now Tuskegee University). By 1984, she was an associate professor and by 1987, a full professor. Dove, who has served on the editorial boards of the literary journals *Callaloo, Gettysburg Review*, and *TriQuarterly*, joined the University of Virginia's English Department in 1989. She teaches creative writing.

Rita Dove (AP/Wide World Photos, Inc.)

Dove won the 1987 Pulitzer Prize for poetry for a collection titled *Thomas & Beulah.* Her themes are universal, encompassing much of the human condition and occasionally commenting on racial issues. She also published *Yellow House on the Corner* (1980), *Museum* (1983), *Fifth Sunday* (short stories, 1985), *Grace Notes* (1989), *Selected Poems* (1993), *Through the Ivory Gate* (novel, 1993), *Mother Love* (1995), and *The Darker Face of the Earth: A Verse Play in Fourteen Scenes* (1995).

In addition to the Pulitzer Prize, Dove won many honors including Presidential scholar (1970); Fulbright scholar (1974, 1975); a literary grant from the National Endowment for the Humanities (1978, 1989); Guggenheim fellow (1983, 1984); General Electric Foundation Award for Younger Poets (1987); Ohio Governor's Award (1988); Andrew W. Mellon Fellowship (1988, 1989); University of Virginia Center for Advanced Studies fellow (1989–1992); the Walt Whitman Award (1990); and the Kennedy Center Fund for New American Plays Award for *The Darker Face of the Earth* (1995).

Dove was named U.S. poet laureate, a one-year Library of Congress post, in 1993. She was the first African American and the youngest person ever to earn the appointment. On April 22, 1994, PBS aired a piece entitled "Poet Laureate Rita Dove" on *Bill Moyer's Journal.* She hoped to use the position to revive public interest in serious literature.

Paul Laurence Dunbar (1872–1906)
Poet

The first African American poet to gain a national reputation in the United States, Paul Laurence Dunbar was also the first to use African American dialect within the formal structure of his work. Born of former slaves in Dayton, Ohio, on June 27, 1872, Dunbar worked as an elevator operator after graduating from high school. His first book of poetry *Oak and Ivy* was privately printed in 1893 and was followed by *Majors and Minors*, which appeared two years later. Neither book was an immediate sensation, but there were enough favorable reviews in such magazines as *Harper's* to encourage Dunbar in the pursuit of a full-fledged literary career. In 1896, Dunbar completed *Lyrics of a Lowly Life*, the single work upon which his subsequent reputation was irrevocably established.

Before his untimely death in 1906, Dunbar had become the dominant presence in the world of African American poetry. His later works included: *Lyrics of Sunshine and Shadow* (1905); *Li'l Gal* (1904); *Howdy, Honey, Howdy* (1905); *A Plantation Portrait* (1905); *Joggin' erlong* (1906); and *Complete Poems*, published posthumously in 1913. This last work contains not only the dialect poems which were his trademark, but many poems in conventional English as well. The book enjoyed such enormous popularity that it has, to this day, never gone out of print. He also published four novels including *The Sport of Gods*, *The Love of Landry*, and *The Uncalled*, and four volumes of short stories.

Ralph Ellison (1914–1994)
Novelist, Essayist

Ralph Ellison's critical and artistic reputation rests largely on a single masterpiece, his first and only novel *Invisible Man.* An instant classic, the novel was given the National Book Award for fiction in 1952 and the Russwurm Award in 1953. Years in the making, the novel's success heralded the emergence of a major writing talent. Ellison worked at a second novel for more than forty years, but at the time of his death, the untitled work was still incomplete.

Ellison was born in Oklahoma City, Oklahoma, on March 1, 1914, and came to New York City in the late 1930s, after having studied music at Tuskegee Institute (now Tuskegee University) for three years. Initially interested in sculpture, he turned to writing after coming under the influence of T.S. Eliot's poetry and as a direct consequence of his friendship with novelist Richard Wright. He worked for the Federal Writer's Project

Ralph Ellison (Archive Photos, Inc.)

and wrote for a variety of publications during the late 1930s to early 1940s. In 1942, he became the managing editor of the *Negro Quarterly*. He began writing *Invisible Man* in 1945. During World War II, Ellison worked as a cook in the U.S. Merchant Marines.

In addition to the National Book Award, Ellison won a Rockefeller Foundation Award in 1954; was elected to the National Institute of Arts and Letters; received a Medal of Freedom from President Lyndon Johnson in 1969; was named chevalier de l'Ordre des Arts et Lettres by France in 1969; and was given a National Medal of Arts in 1985. Ellison was the recipient of more than one dozen honorary degrees including doctor of letters degrees from Harvard University (1974) and Wesleyan University (1980). Three years after the publication of *Invisible Man*, the American Academy of Arts and Letters awarded Ellison the Prix de Rome, which enabled him to live and write in Italy until 1957.

Back in the United States, Ellison began an academic career. He taught Russian and American literature courses at Bard College in Annandale-on-Hudson, New York, for three years and spent the early 1960s as a visiting professor at University of Chicago, Yale, and Rutgers, where he was a writer-in-residence. From 1970 to 1980, Ellison was the Albert Schweitzer Professor of Humanities at New York University.

Ellison's second work was a book of essays entitled *Shadow and Act*. Published in 1964, excerpts from the book have been printed in several literary journals. Ellison began writing his second novel *Juneteenth* in 1954 and continued to revise it until he died. (A 1967 fire destroyed 350 pages of his unfinished second novel's manuscript.) In 1982, the thirtieth anniversary edition of *Invisible Man* with a new introduction by Ellison was published. In 1986, a second collection of essays and talks was published as *Going to the Territory*. *The Collected Essays of Ralph Ellison*, edited by John F. Callahan, was published posthumously in 1995.

Ellison died of pancreatic cancer in New York City on April 16, 1994. On May 26, 1994, a memorial tribute to him was held at the American Academy of Arts and Letters in New York.

Mari Evans (1923–)
Poet

Born in Toledo, Ohio, in 1923, Evans studied at the University of Toledo. In 1963, her poetry was published in *Phylon*, *Negro Digest*, and *Dialog*. Two years later she was awarded a John Hay Whitney Fellowship. One of her better known works is *The Alarm Clock*, which deals with the rude awakening of the African American to the white "establishment." It captures and summarizes the civil rights scene of the 1960s in the United States.

Evans's books include: *I Am a Black Woman; Where Is All the Music?; Black Women Writers (1950–1980): A Critical Evaluation* (1984), edited by Evans, covering 15 African American women poets, novelists, and playwrights; *Nightstar: Poems from 1973–1978* (1980); *J. D.; I Look at Me; Singing Black; The Day They Made Benani;* and *Jim Flying High.*

Jessie Redmon Fauset (1882–1961)
Writer, Editor, Educator

Jessie Redmon Fauset, born April 27, 1882, was a central figure during the Harlem Renaissance not only for encouraging the careers of many of the major writers of the time, but also through her own literary contributions to the movement. In 1919 Fauset became literary editor of *Crisis* magazine, founded by W. E. B. Du Bois and held that position until 1927. As an editor Fauset excelled, for under her leadership, *Crisis* magazine outsold its rival magazine *Opportunity*, started by Charles S. Johnson. She also realized Du Bois's plan for a periodical focusing on children six to sixteen called *The Brownies Book* and was its functional editor .

Fauset's editorial experiences and travel heightened her own sensibilities about the images of African Americans. Her writings professed an awareness of the racism and sexism that existed during the 1920s and 1930s. She contributed numerous short stories, essays, critiques, poetry, and reviews to the magazine and published her first novel *There is Confusion* in 1924. The book was her response to an unrealistic portrayal of African Americans by white novelist T. S. Stribling. After Fauset's break from *Crisis* in 1927, she established her place as an author and published *Plum Bun: A Novel without a Moral* (1929), *The Chinaberry Tree* (1931), and *Comedy, American Style* (1933).

Fauset, who had received her B.A. from Cornell University in 1905 (Phi Beta Kappa) and her M.A. from the University of Pennsylvania in 1919, taught at both Fisk University in the summer and in high school and college settings. In later years, she returned to teaching, partially because the publishing world was still not ready for an African American, let alone a woman. Fauset died in Philadelphia on April 30, 1961, of hypertensive heart disease. Recently, Fauset's contribution to the dialogue about race, class, and gender have been more fully recognized in her work. She not only challenged the world of publishing with her own work, but by assisting other artists made it possible for unrealistic and negative perceptions of African Americans to be confronted.

Rudolph Fisher (1897–1934)

Writer, Physician, Community Leader

Although he was a radiologist, Rudolph Fisher was best known as a leading writer during the Harlem Renaissance. Fisher wrote short stories and novels that depicted real life in the Harlem community and was also the first African American to write detective fiction.

Fisher was born on May 9, 1897, in Washington, DC. He grew up in a middle-class family who saw that he was rigorously educated at primary and secondary schools in Providence, Rhode Island, and New York City. He graduated Phi Beta Kappa from Brown University with B.A. and M.A. degrees. In 1924, Fisher graduated summa cum laude from Howard University Medical School in Washington. During his medical internship at Freedmen's Hospital in the same city, he published his first short story "The City of Refuge" in the *Atlantic Monthly.*

Continuing his medical education, from 1925 to 1927 Fisher trained at Columbia University's College of Physicians and Surgeons. He entered private practice and continued his writing as well, publishing five short stories in *Atlantic Monthly* and *McClure's*, an essay in *American Mercury*, and an article in the *Journal of Infectious Diseases.*

Fisher published his first novel *The Walls of Jericho* in 1928. In the novel Fisher blends all of Harlem life into one story and bridges the gap between the classes. *The Conjure-Man Dies: A Mystery Tale of Dark Harlem* (1932) was his second novel and the first full-length detective novel with all-African American characters published by an African American author. Fisher published two children's stories in 1932 and 1933, "Ezekiel" and "Ezekiel Learns," and in 1933 he published two short stories "Guardians of the Law" and "Miss Cynthie." The latter work also appeared in *Best Short Stories of 1934.*

In addition to his writing career, Fisher was superintendent of the International Hospital in Manhattan from 1929 to 1932. Between 1930 and 1934, he was a roentgenologist for the New York City Health Department and served in the 369th Infantry. He died of cancer on December 16, 1934, in New York City.

Charles Fuller (1939–)

Playwright

Charles Fuller was born on March 5, 1939, in Philadelphia, Pennsylvania. He became "stagestruck" in his high school days when he went to the Old Walnut Street Theater in his native Philadelphia and saw a Yiddish play starring Molly Picon and Menasha Skulnik. He did not understand a word of it, "but it was live theater, and I felt myself responding to it," he said.

In 1959, Fuller entered the army and served in Japan and South Korea, after which he attended Villanova University and La Salle College. While Fuller was working as a housing inspector in Philadelphia, the McCarter Theater in Princeton, New Jersey produced his first play. The theme concerned interracial marriage, and its creator is quick now to tag it "one of the world's worst interracial plays." However, during this time he met members of The Negro Ensemble Company and, in 1974, he wrote his first play *In the Deepest Part of Sleep* for them. For NEC's tenth anniversary, Fuller wrote *The Brownsville Raid* about the African American soldiers who were dishonorably discharged on President Teddy Roosevelt's orders in 1906 after a shootout in Brownsville, Texas. The play was a hit and Fuller followed it a few seasons later with *Zooman and the Sign*, a melodrama that won two Obie awards.

A Soldier's Play, which won a Pulitzer Prize in 1982, was his fourth play for The Negro Ensemble Company. This drama dealing with a murder set in a backwater New Orleans army camp in 1944, opened NEC's fifteenth anniversary season in 1981 with a long run and was hailed by the *New York Times* as "tough, taut and fully realized." *A Soldier's Play* became *A Soldier's Story* when it was produced as a film in 1984 by Columbia Pictures. Fuller wrote the screenplay and African American actor Howard E. Rollins Jr. was the film's star.

Charles Fuller (AP/Wide World Photos, Inc.)

The recipient of the Guggenheim Foundation Fellowship, the Rockefeller Foundation, and the National Endowment for the Arts and CAPS Fellowships in playwrighting, Fuller describes himself as a playwright who happens to be African American, rather than an African American playwright.

Ernest J. Gaines (1933–)
Novelist, Short Story Writer

Ernest J. Gaines was born on a plantation in Louisiana, on January 15, 1933. He moved to California in 1949, where he did his undergraduate study at San Francisco State College. In 1959, he received the Wallace Stegner Fellowship in creative writing. The following year he was awarded the Joseph Henry Jackson Literary Award.

Gaines's first novel was *Catherine Carmier* (1964). Others followed, including *Of Love and Dust* (1967), *Barren Summer* (completed in 1963 but never published), *The Autobiography of Miss Jane Pittman* (1971), *A Warm Day in November* (for young people), and *In My Father's House* (1978). Ironically, the book *The Autobiography of Jane Pittman* was banned in a Conroe, Texas, seventh-grade racial tolerance course in 1995; the school censored the work, citing the liberal use of racial slurs. The 1974 television production of *The Autobiography of Miss Jane Pittman* starring Cicely Tyson boosted Gaines's reputation. Gaines's *A Gathering of Old Men*, published in 1983, was made into a movie as well. In 1994, Gaines's 1993 work *A Lesson Before Dying* won the National Book Critics Circle award for fiction.

Nikki Giovanni (1943–)
Poet

Nikki Giovanni was born in Knoxville, Tennessee, on June 7, 1943. She studied at the University of Cincinnati from 1961 to 1963 and received her B.A. from Fisk University in 1967. She also attended the University of Pennsylvania School of Social Work for one year and Columbia University School of the Arts for one year in the late 1960s.

In 1969, Giovanni taught at Queens College (CUNY) and Rutgers University before founding a communications and publishing company called NikTom, Ltd. In the mid- to late 1980s, she resumed teaching, spending the year of 1984 as a visiting professor at Ohio State University and the subsequent three years at Mount Joseph on the Ohio as a creative writing professor. Since 1987, Giovanni has taught at Virginia Polytechnic Institute and State University, first as a visiting professor and then as a full professor of English beginning in 1989. That year, she also directed the Warm Hearth Writer's Workshop. From 1990 to 1993, Giovanni served on the board of directors for the Virginia Foundation for the Humanities and Public Policy.

Giovanni's first book of poetry *Black Feeling, Black Talk*, published in the mid–1960s, was followed by *Black Judgment* in 1968. These two works were combined as *Black Feeling, Black Talk, Black Judgment* in 1970. By 1974, Giovanni's poems could be found in many African American literature anthologies, and she also became a media personality through her television appearances, during which she read her poetry. Many of her poems were put to soul or gospel music accompaniment. Such recordings include: *Truth Is on Its Way*, winner of the National Association of Radio and Television Announcers Award in 1972; and *Spirit to Spirit*, a videocassette produced by PBS, winner of the Oakland Museum Film Festival Silver Apple Award in 1988.

A prolific author, Giovanni's books include: *Re: Creation* (poetry); *Spin a Soft Black Song: Poems for Children; Night Comes Softly: Anthology of Black Female Voices* (nonfiction); *My House* (poetry); *Gemini: An Extended Autobiographical Statement* (nonfiction); *Ego Tripping and Other Poems for Young People*; *A Dialogue: James Baldwin and Nikki Giovanni* (nonfiction); and *A Poetic Equation: Conversations Between Nikki Giovanni and Margaret Walker* (nonfiction). Her other works include: *The Women and the Men: Poems* (1975); *Cotton Candy on a Rainy Day* (poetry, 1978); *Vacation Time: Poems for Children* (1980), dedicated to her son, Tommy, and winner of the Children's Reading Roundtable of Chicago Award; *Those Who Ride the Night Winds* (poetry,1984); *Sacred Cows . . . and Other Edibles* (nonfiction, 1988), winner of the Ohioana Library Award in 1988; *Grand Mothers: Poems, Reminiscences, and Short Stories About the Keepers of Our Traditions* (1994); *Racism 101* (nonfiction); *Knoxville, Tennessee* (coauthored with Larry Johnson, 1994); *The Selected Poems of Nikki Giovanni* (1995); *Blues for all the Changes* (collection of poems, 1999); and *Grand Fathers: Reminiscences, Poems, Recipes, and Photos of the Keepers of Our Traditions* (1999).

Giovanni won several awards throughout her career including the Highest Achievement Award in 1971 from *Mademoiselle;* life membership to the National Council of Negro Women in 1973; the Outstanding Woman of Tennessee in 1985; the *Cincinnati Post* Post-Corbett Award in 1986; and a Governor's Award in the Arts from the Tennessee Arts Commission in 1999. In addition, Giovanni received honorary degrees from numerous institutions.

Eloise Greenfield (1929–)

Children's Author

Born Eloise Little on May 17, 1929, in Parmele, North Carolina, Greenfield moved to Washington, DC, as a baby and grew up happily in a close-knit, urban neighborhood. After attending Minor Teachers College, she worked in various clerical and secretarial positions. By 1950, she had begun experimenting with creative writing. After years of studying and persevering, Greenfield met fellow writers and made valuable contacts when she joined the District of Columbia Black Writers Workshop in the early 1970s. Soon thereafter, her picture book *Bubbles* was published.

With that initial success, Greenfield established her own niche within the arena of children's books and has published, on average, one book each year. Having a goal of encouraging children to develop positive attitudes about themselves, Greenfield's stories capture both the unique and universal experiences of growing up as an African American. Much of her fiction, as in the novel *Sister,* is concerned with bonding within African American families. Greenfield's biographies of distinguished African Americans and poetic picture books have appeared on "notable" book lists and have placed the author in demand as a speaker at writers's conferences and in classrooms of her young fans.

Alex Haley (1921–1992)

Journalist, Novelist

The author of the widely acclaimed novel *Roots* was born in Ithaca, New York, on August 11, 1921, and reared in Henning, Tennessee. The oldest of three sons of a college professor father and a mother who taught grade school, Haley graduated from high school at fifteen and attended college for two years before enlisting in the United States Coast Guard as a messboy in 1939.

A voracious reader, Haley began writing short stories while at sea, but it took eight years before small magazines began accepting his stories. By 1952, the Coast Guard had created a new rating for Haley-chief journalist-and he began handling United States Coast Guard public relations. In 1959, after twenty years of military service, he retired from the Coast Guard and launched a new career as a freelance writer. He eventually became an assignment writer for *Reader's Digest* and moved on to *Playboy,* where he initiated the "Playboy Interviews" feature.

One of the personalities Haley interviewed was Malcolm X—an interview that inspired Haley's first book *The Autobiography of Malcolm X* (1965). Translated into eight languages, the book has sold more than six million copies. Pursuing the few slender clues of oral family history told to him by his maternal grandmother in Tennessee, Haley spent the next 12 years traveling three continents tracking his maternal family back to a Mandingo youth named Kunta Kinte, who was kidnaped into slavery from the small village of Juffure in Gambia, West Africa. During this period, he lectured extensively in the United States and in Great Britain on his discoveries about his family in Africa and wrote many magazine articles on his research in the 1960s and the 1970s. He received several honorary doctor of letters degrees for his work.

The book *Roots,* excerpted in *Reader's Digest* in 1974 and heralded for several years, was finally published in the fall of 1976 with very wide publicity and reviews. In January 1977, ABC-TV produced a 12-hour series based on the book, which set records for the number of viewers. With cover stories, book reviews, and interviews with Haley in scores of magazines and many newspaper articles, the book became the number one national best-seller, sold in the millions, and was published as a paperback in 1977. *Roots* truly became a phenomenon. It was serialized in the *New York Post* and the *Long Island Press.* Instructional packages, lesson plans based on *Roots,* and other books about *Roots* for schools were published, along with records and tapes by Haley.

Haley's book stimulated interest in Africa and in African American genealogy. The United States Senate passed a resolution paying tribute to Haley and comparing *Roots* to *Uncle Tom's Cabin* by Harriet Beecher Stowe in the 1850s. The book received many awards including the National Book Award for 1976 special citation of merit in history and a special Pulitzer Prize in 1976 for making an important contribution to the literature of slavery. *Roots* was not without its critics, however. A 1977 lawsuit brought by Margaret Walker charged that *Roots* plagiarized her novel *Jubilee.* Another author, Harold Courlander, also filed a suit charging that *Roots* plagiarized his novel *The African.* Courlander received a settlement after several passages in *Roots* were found to be almost verbatim from *The African.* Haley claimed that researchers helping him had given him this material without citing the source.

Haley received the NAACP's Spingarn Medal in 1977. Four thousand deans and department heads of colleges and universities throughout the country in a survey conducted by *Scholastic Magazine* selected Haley as America's foremost achiever in the literature category. The ABC-TV network presented another series *Roots: The Next Generation* in February, 1979 (also written by Haley). *Roots* had sold almost 5 million copies by December, 1978, and had been reprinted in 23 languages.

In 1988, Haley conducted a promotional tour for a novella titled *A Different Kind of Christmas* about slave escapes in the 1850s. He also promoted a drama *Roots: The Gift*, a two-hour television program shown in December, 1988. This story revolved around two principal characters from *Roots* who are involved in a slave break for freedom on Christmas Eve. Haley's drama *Queen*, which he had begun writing before his death, was aired on television in 1998, starring Halle Berry.

Haley died February 10, 1992, of a heart attack.

Virginia Hamilton (1936–)

Children's and Young Adult Author

Virginia Hamilton was born on March 12, 1936, into a large extended family in rural Yellow Springs, Ohio. Her career as an author was directly influenced by her parents, who were avid storytellers themselves. She attended nearby Antioch College from 1952 to 1955, ultimately graduating from Ohio State University in 1958. Determined to be a writer, Hamilton settled in New York City and studied the craft at the New School for Social Research. She worked at a variety of jobs and moved back to Yellow Springs before publishing her first book *Zeely* in 1967. Issued during an era of racial strife, *Zeely* was one of the first books for young readers in which African American characters were portrayed as people living with average, universal circumstances as opposed to constantly dealing with politically and racially related problems, such as integration.

After her second novel *The House of Dies Dreary* received the 1968 Edgar Allen Poe Award for best juvenile mystery of the year, Hamilton went on to write and edit more than thirty children's and young adult books within various genres. Her canon includes well-researched historical fiction, contemporary urban novels about teenagers, science fiction and supernatural tales, biographies of the historical figures Paul Robeson and W. E. B. Du Bois, and collections of African American folklore and slavery era "liberation" stories.

Hamilton has been repeatedly honored for her work including winning the Hans Christian Andersen Medal, Newbery Honor Book Award, National Book Award, Coretta Scott King Award, and the MacArthur Foundation Prize in 1995. Many of her works have appeared on notable "best books" lists, and she has inspired an Annual Virginia Hamilton Conference. Hamilton stands as one of the predominant creative forces behind multicultural works for young readers.

Jupiter Hammon (1711–?)

Poet, Tract writer

Jupiter Hammon was born October 17, 1711, probably near Oyster Bay on Long Island, New York. He was one of the first African American poet to have his work published in the United States. *An Evening Thought, Salvation by Christ, with Penitential Cries* appeared in 1761, when Hammon was a slave belonging to a Mr. Lloyd of Long Island, New York. Due to his fondness for preaching, the major portion of Hammon's poetry is religious in tone and is usually dismissed by critics as being of little aesthetic value because of its pious platitudes, faulty syntax, and forced rhymes. Hammon's best-known work is a prose piece *An Address to the Negroes of the State of New York* delivered before the African Society of New York City on September 24, 1786. This speech was published the following year and went into three editions. He died between 1790 and 1806.

Lorraine Hansberry (1930–1965)

Playwright

Born in Chicago on May 19, 1930, Hansberry studied art at Chicago's Art Institute, the University of Wisconsin, and, finally, in Guadalajara, Mexico. Hansberry wrote the award-winning play *A Raisin in the Sun* while living in New York's Greenwich Village, having conceived the play after reacting negatively to what she called "a whole body of material about Negroes. Cardboard characters. Cute dialect bits. Or hip-swinging musicals from exotic scores." The play opened on Broadway on March 11, 1959, at a time when it was generally held that all plays dealing with African Americans were "death" at the box office. Produced, directed, and performed by African Americans, it was later made into a successful movie starring Sidney Poitier. It was then adapted into *Raisin*, a musical that won a Tony Award in 1974.

Hansberry's second Broadway play *The Sign in Sidney Brustein's Window* dealt with "the western intellectual poised in hesitation before the flames of involvement." Shortly after its Broadway opening, Hansberry succumbed to cancer on January 12, 1965, in New York City.

Hansberry's books, in addition to the two published plays, include: *To Be Young, Gifted and Black; The Movement: Documentary of a Struggle for Equality;* and *Les Blancs: The Collected Last Plays of Lorraine Hansberry.*

Frances E. W. Harper (1825–1911)
Writer, Poet, Activist

Frances Ellen Watkins Harper, the first African American woman to publish a short story, was one of the most prolific African American women writers of the nineteenth century. She was known also for essays, poetry, and for her single novel *Iola Leroy.* Beyond her writings, Harper was an effective traveling lecturer and a supporter of emancipation, the temperance movement, and of the African American women's movement.

Harper was born to free parents in 1825 in Baltimore, Maryland, on September 24, 1825. She was never able to reconcile the death of her mother, a traumatic experience that occurred when Harper was only three years old. She was raised by relatives and attended William Watkins Academy for Negro Youth—a prestigious school in Baltimore that her uncle founded. Uncomfortable in the slave city of Baltimore, Harper moved to Ohio in 1850 and became the first woman teacher at the newly-founded Union Seminary, later a part of Wilberforce University. In 1854, she became a permanent lecturer for the Maine Anti-Slavery Society and spoke throughout New England, Ohio, New York, and elsewhere. "The bronze muse," as she became known, gave fiery speeches and often incorporated her poetry into her lectures. So successful and stirring were her presentations that the Pennsylvania Anti-Slavery Society hired her as a lecturer as well. She held her audiences spellbound and spoke with dignity and composure. Although she wrote and lectured on other topics, her attention to antislavery caused scholars to refer to her as an abolitionist poet.

Harper's first volume of poems and prose was published in 1851 as *Forest Leaves*, also printed as *Autumn Leaves.* Her literary career was actually launched in 1854 when she published *Poems on Miscellaneous Subjects;* the work was printed in Boston and Philadelphia and reissued in 1857, 1858, 1864, and 1871. Included in the work were several anti-slavery poems such as "The Slave Mother" and "The Slave Auction," yet most of the poems dealt with women's rights, temperance, religion, and other current issues.

Her writings in the *Christian Recorder* promoted her work as a journalist. Harper's writings in the journal included the serialized novel *Minnie's Sacrifice*, the dramatic poem "Moses: A Story of the Nile," a series of poems by "Aunt Chloe," and the fictionalized essays "Fancy Etchings." She wrote other serials, but it was not until 1892 that she published in book form her first and best-known work *Iola Leroy, Or, Shadows Uplifted.* The novel aims to present a true picture of slavery and the Reconstruction, to promote humanity, and to foster a sense of racial pride in African Americans. Her collections of poems that followed included works previously issued but supplemented with other examples of her writings: *The Sparrow's Fall and Other Poems* (c.1894); *Light Beyond Darkness, The Martyr of Alabama* (c.1895); and *Atlanta Offering: Poems* (1895). In 1900 she published *Poems* and, the following year, *Idylls of the Bible.*

Harper's activities also included work with the YMCA, for which she helped develop Sunday schools; the Colored Section of the Philadelphia and Pennsylvania Women's Christian Temperance Union; and the American Women's Suffrage Association. She helped organize the National Association of Colored Women. Harper died in Philadelphia on February 20, 1911.

Robert E. Hayden (1913–1980)
Poet

Robert E. Hayden was born on August 4, 1913, in Detroit, Michigan. A graduate of Detroit City College, now Wayne State University, Hayden was chief researcher on African American history and folklore for the Federal Writers Project in 1936. He went on to do advanced work in English, play production, and creative writing at the University of Michigan. While there, he twice won the Jule and Avery Hopwood Prize for poetry. Hayden also completed radio scripts and a finished version of a play about the Underground Railroad, *Go Down Moses.*

Hayden's first book of poems *Heart-Shape in the Dust* was published in 1940 shortly before he assumed the music and drama critic function for the *Michigan Chronicle.* He taught at Fisk University from 1946 to the early 1970s and later at the University of Michigan. His works include: *The Lion and the Archer* (with Myron O'Higgins); *A Ballad of Remembrance; Selected Poems;*

Words in the Mourning Time; and *The Night-Blooming Cereus.* He edited *Kaleidoscope: Poems by American Negro Poets* and *Afro American Literature: An Introduction* (with David J. Burrows and Frederick R. Lapsides). His other books include: *Figure of Time; Angle of Ascent: New and Selected Poems;* and *American Journal* (poems). In 1975, the Academy of American Poets elected him its fellow of the year, and in 1976, he was awarded the Grand Prize for Poetry at the First World Festival of Negro Arts in Dakar, Senegal. From 1976 to 1978, he served as consultant in poetry at the Library of Congress. He was a professor of English at the University of Michigan at the time of his death on February 25, 1980.

Essex Hemphill (1957–1995)

Poet, Essayist, Editor, Gay Rights Activist

Hemphill was born in 1957 in Chicago, but spent parts of his childhood in Indiana, South Carolina, and Washington, DC. After attending the University of Maryland and the University of the District of Columbia, Hemphill began to explore the inner conflicts he experienced as a gay African American male by writing poetry.

For several years Hemphill was a contributor of verse to such journals as *Essence*, *Black Scholar*, and *Obsidian.* In the late 1980s, he became involved with a project begun by Joseph Beam, an anthology of gay African American poetry called *In the Life.* Hemphill was a contributor to the 1986 volume and took the editorship of its sequel after Beam died of AIDS-related illnesses in 1988. The work was published as *Brother to Brother: New Writings by Black Gay Men* in 1991.

Hemphill became involved in several film projects around this time as well, nearly all of them controversial in some way, which coincided with his aim to make the two communities, the African American and the gay American, enter into a new, more contemporary dialogue with one another. He wrote verse for *Looking for Langston,* a British film that addressed the sexuality of Harlem Renaissance poet Langston Hughes and brought down the ire of the executor of the Hughes estate, and also contributed to and appeared in *Tongues Untied.* This last project, Marlon Riggs's celebratory look at gay African American male culture, was deemed too spicy even for public television at one point.

In 1992, Hemphill saw another book of his own verse published, *Ceremonies: Prose and Poetry.* During the early part of the decade, he became involved in a project interviewing elderly members of the African American gay community in order to provide a glimpse into a period before either gay or civil rights were mentioned. He also contributed to the book *Life Sentences: Writers, Artists, and AIDS.* Hemphill died on November 4, 1995 at the age of 38.

Chester Himes (1909–1984)

Novelist

Born in Jefferson City, Missouri, on June 29, 1909, Chester Himes was educated at Ohio State University and later lived in France and Spain. In 1945, he completed his first novel *If He Hollers Let Him Go*, the story of an African American working in a defense plant. His second book *The Lonely Crusade* (1947) was set in similar surroundings. His other books included: *The Third Generation; Cotton Comes to Harlem; Pinktoes; The Quality of Hurt: The Autobiography of Chester Himes;* and *Black on Black: Baby Sister and Selected Writings.*

Following a stroke that confined him to a wheelchair, Himes and his wife lived in Alicante, Spain. In 1977, they returned to New York City for the publication of the concluding volume of his autobiography *My Life of Absurdity.* Himes died in Spain on November 12, 1984, at the age of 75. A prolific author of almost twenty books, several of his popular novels are being reprinted posthumously in hardcover and paperback editions.

Pauline E. Hopkins (1859–1930)

Writer, Editor, Playwright, Singer, Actress

Although her contemporaries gave her less recognition than modern scholars, Pauline Elizabeth Hopkins became known for promoting racial issues in her short stories, novels, and in her work as editor of the journal *The Colored American.*

Born in Portland, Maine, in 1859, Hopkins moved to Boston when she was still a child and graduated from Girls High School. At age 15 years of age, she entered a writing contest supported by writer William Wells Brown and sponsored by the Congregational Publishing Society in Boston and won a ten-dollar prize for her essay "The Evils of Intemperance and Their Remedies."

Hopkins established the Colored Troubadours and performed with the group for twelve years. On July 5, 1880, in Boston, the Troubadours performed her first play *Slaves' Escape: or the Underground Railroad,* also known as *Peculiar Sam,* which Hopkins had completed a year earlier. During her tenure with the group, she also wrote the play *One Scene from the Drama of Early Days.*

Hopkins helped to establish *The Colored American;* its first issue in May, 1900, published her short story "The Mystery Within Us." Later, the magazine published Hopkins's series of biographical sketches "Famous Women of the Negro Race" and "Famous Men of the Negro

Chester Himes (AP/Wide World Photos, Inc.)

Race." About this time the magazine published serialized versions of three of her novels *Hagar's Daughter: A Story of Southern Caste Prejudice* (1901–1902), *Winona: A Tale of Negro Life in the South and Southwest* (1902), and *Of One Blood: or The Hidden Self* (1902–1903). Her first novel, however, *Contending Forces: A Romance Illustrative of Negro Life North and South*, was published by a Boston firm in 1900. She resigned from *The Colored American* in 1904.

In 1905, Hopkins wrote briefly for *Voice of the Negro;* after that her literary career began to decline. She founded her own publishing company, the P. E. Hopkins and Company, and in February and March, 1916, contributed two articles to *New Era Magazine*. She lived in obscurity after 1916 and died on August 13, 1930, as a result of severe burns.

George Moses Horton (1797?–1883?)
Poet

George Moses Horton was the first African American professional man of letters in the United States and one of the first professional writers of any race in the South. He was the first African American southerner to have a volume of poetry published.

Horton was born into slavery in North Carolina around 1797. While growing up on a farm he cultivated a love of learning. With the aid of his mother and her Wesley hymnal, Horton learned to read, although he did not learn to write until years later. While working as a janitor at the University of North Carolina, Horton wrote light verse for some students in exchange for spending money.

Some of Horton's early poems were printed in the newspapers of Raleigh and Boston. When Horton published his first book of poems in 1829, he entitled it *The Hope of Liberty*, in the belief that profits from its sales would be sufficient to pay for his freedom. His hopes did not materialize, however, and he remained a slave until the Emancipation Proclamation. (This book was reprinted in 1837 under the title *Poems by a Slave.*) In 1865, he published "Naked Genius," a poem containing many bitter lines about his former condition that were in sharp contrast to the conformist verse of earlier African American poets. Although he lived in Philadelphia for a while, it appears that he returned to the South where he died around 1883. Richard Walser's *The Black Poet* was written about Horton and published in 1967.

Langston Hughes (1902–1967)
Poet, Novelist, Playwright

Born in Joplin, Missouri, on February 1, 1902, James Langston Hughes moved to Cleveland at the age of fourteen, graduated from Central High School, and spent a year in Mexico before studying at Columbia University. After roaming the world as a seaman and writing some poetry as well, Hughes returned to the United States. While attending Lincoln University in Pennsylvania, he won the Witter Bynner Prize for undergraduate poetry. In 1930, he received the Harmon Award, and in 1935, with the help of a Guggenheim Fellowship, traveled to Russia and Spain.

The long and distinguished list of Hughes's prose works includes: *Not Without Laughter* (1930); *The Big Sea* (1940); and *I Wonder as I Wander* (1956), his autobiography. To this must be added such collections of poetry as *The Weary Blues* (1926); *The Dream Keeper* (1932); *Shakespeare in Harlem* (1942); *Fields of Wonder* (1947); *One Way Ticket* (1949); *Selected Poems* (1959); and the posthumously published *The Panther and the Lash: Poems of Our Times* (1969).

Hughes was also an accomplished song lyricist, librettist, and newspaper columnist. Through his newspaper columns he created Jesse B. Semple, a Harlem character known as Simple. Simple is the quintessential "wise fool" whose experiences and insights capture the frustrations felt by African Americans. Hughes's Simple sketches have been collected in several volumes and were adapted for the musical stage in *Simply Heavenly*.

Through much of the 1960s, Hughes edited several anthologies in an attempt to popularize African American authors and their works. Some of these works are *An African Treasury* (1960), *Poems from Black Africa* (1963), *New Negro Poets: U.S.A.* (1964), and *The Best Short Stories by Negro Writers* (1967). Published posthumously was *Good Morning Revolution: Uncollected Writings of Social Protest.* Hughes wrote many plays including *Emperor of Haiti* and *Mulatto,* which was produced on Broadway in the 1930s. He also wrote gospel music plays, such as *Tambourines to Glory Black Nativity* and *Jericho—Jim Crow.* He died on May 22, 1967.

Zora Neale Hurston (1903–1960)
Novelist, Folklorist

Zora Neale Hurston was born on January 7, 1903, in Eatonville, Florida. After traveling north as a maid with a Gilbert and Sullivan company, Hurston acquired her education at Morgan State College, Howard University, and Columbia University. While at Howard under Alain Locke's influence, she became a figure in the Harlem Renaissance, publishing short stories in *Opportunity* and serving with Langston Hughes and Wallace Thurman on the editorial board of the magazine *Fire!*

Zora Neale Hurston (AP/Wide World Photos, Inc.)

In 1934, *Jonah's Gourd Vine* was published after her return to Florida. Her most important novel *Their Eyes Were Watching God* appeared three years later. *Moses, Man of the Mountain* (1939) was followed in 1948 by *Seraph on the Suwanee.* Her other three works are two books of folklore, *Mules and Men* (1935) and *Tell My Horse* (1938), and *Dust Tracks on a Road* (1942). Her autobiography was reprinted in 1985 with a new introduction and with several altered chapters restored.

Toward the end of her life, Hurston was a drama instructor at the North Carolina College for Negroes in Durham (now North Carolina Central University). She died in obscurity and poverty on January 28, 1960. Since then, six of her works have been reprinted with new introductions. Hurston is celebrated each year in Eatonville, Florida, where the Zora Neale Hurston Festival is held.

Charles R. Johnson (1948–)
Novelist, Essayist, Cartoonist

Charles Johnson, only the second African American man to win the National Book Award (Ralph Ellison was the first), was born on April 23, 1948, in Evanston, Illinois. He began his career as a political cartoonist in the early 1970s. During the same time period, he was heavily involved in organizations that supported the formation of African American studies as a discipline. Johnson's development as a novelist took shape while receiving his B.A. in 1971 from Southern Illinois University at Carbondale and subsequently his M.A. in philosophy in 1973. Out of these experiences Johnson developed situations in his books that dealt with philosophical discussions about race, identity, and culture.

Johnson's literary works include both novels and short stories, beginning with *Faith and the Good Thing* (1974), *Oxherding Tale* (1982), *The Sorcerer's Apprentice* (short stories 1986), and *Middle Passage* (1990), which received the National Book Award that year.

Georgia Douglas Johnson (1886–1966)
Poet

As one of the first modern African American women poets to gain recognition, Georgia Douglas Johnson, whose collections of verse were published between 1918 and 1930, is an important link in the chain of African American women lyric poets. Johnson's life spanned most of the literary movements of this century, and her Washington, DC, home was the popular gathering place of early Harlem Renaissance writers.

Johnson was born in Atlanta, Georgia, on September 10, 1886. She was educated in the public schools of the city and at Atlanta University, and she went on to attend Howard University in Washington, DC, and Oberlin Conservatory of Music in Ohio.

Initially, she was interested in musical composition, but gradually Johnson turned to lyric poetry. After teaching school in Alabama, she moved to Washington, DC, with her husband, who had been appointed as recorder of deeds by President William Howard Taft. While in the nation's capital, she too engaged in government work while completing such books as *The Heart of a Woman* (1918), *Bronze* (1922), *An Autumn Love Cycle* (1928), and *Share My World*, published in 1962.

Johnson was a prolific writer; over two hundred of her poems were published in her four literary works; other poems and several dramas have appeared in journals and books, primarily edited by African Americans. She died of a stroke on May 14, 1966.

James Weldon Johnson (1871–1938)

Poet, Lyricist, Civil Rights Leader

Similar to W. E. B. Du Bois, African American intellectual James Weldon Johnson played a vital role in the Civil Rights movement of the twentieth century as poet, teacher, critic, diplomat, and NAACP official. Johnson is perhaps most often remembered as the lyricist for "Lift Every Voice and Sing," the song that is often referred to as the African American national anthem.

Born on June 17, 1871, in Jacksonville, Florida, Johnson was educated at Atlanta and Columbia Universities. His career included service as a school principal, a lawyer, and a diplomat (U.S. consul at Puerto Cabello, Venezuela, and later in Nicaragua). From 1916 to 1930, he was a key policymaker of the NAACP, eventually serving as the organization's executive secretary. From 1932 until his death, he was professor of creative writing at Fisk University in Nashville, Tennessee.

In his early days, Johnson's fame rested largely on his lyrics for popular songs, but in 1917 he completed his first book of poetry *Fifty Years and Other Poems*. Five years later, he followed this work with *The Book of American Negro Poetry*, and in 1927, he established his literary reputation with *God's Trombones*, a collection of seven folk sermons in verse. Over the years, this work has been performed countless times on stage and television.

In 1930, Johnson finished *St. Peter Relates an Incident of the Resurrection*, and three years later, his lengthy autobiography *Along This Way* appeared. Johnson died on June 26, 1938, following an automobile accident in Maine.

Gayl Jones (1949–)

Novelist, Poet, Short Story Writer, Educator

Born in Lexington, Kentucky, in 1949, Gayl Jones received a bachelor's degree in English from Connecticut College in 1971 and a master's degree in creative writing from Brown University in 1973. From 1975 to 1981, she was professor of English at the University of Michigan. Jones's work includes two novels *Corregidora* (1975) and *Eva's Man* (1976), short stories, and several collections of poetry including *Song for Anninho* (1981), *The Hermit Woman* (1983), *Xarque and Other Poems* (1985), and *Liberating Voices* (1991).

June Jordan (1936–)

Poet, Novelist

Born in Harlem, New York, on July 9, 1936, poet, novelist, essayist, educator, and activist June Jordan attended Barnard College and the University of Chicago. Throughout the 1960s and 1970s, she taught Afro-American literature, English, and writing at several colleges and universities including CUNY, Connecticut College, Sarah Lawrence College, Yale University, and State University of New York at Stoney Brook, where she spent most of her career as director of the poetry center and creative writing program. She left State University in 1989 to teach Afro-American studies and women's studies at the University of California at Berkley. Jordan co-founded and co-directed The Voice of the Children, Inc., a creative workshop.

A prolific writer, Jordan's poems have been published in many magazines, newspapers, and anthologies, and she received a Rockefeller Grant in creative writing in 1969. Her poetry includes: *Who Look at Me* (1969); *Some Changes* (1971); *New Days: Poems of Exile and Return* (1974); *Passion: New Poems, 1977–1980* (1980); *Living Room: New Poems* (1985); *Lyrical Campaigns: Selected Poems* (1989); and *Naming Our Destiny: New and Selected Poems* (1989). Jordan's books for children and young people include: *His Own Where* (1971), nominated for the National Book Award; *Fannie Lou Hamer* (1972); *Dry Victories* (1972); and *Kimako's Story* (1981).

Author of two plays, Jordan has also published essays including: *Civil Wars* (1981); *On Call: Political Essays* (1985); *Moving Towards Home: Political Essays* (1989); and *Technical Difficulties: African American Notes on the State of the Union* (1992). In addition, she has edited several anthologies, such as *Soulscript: Afro-American Poetry* (1970).

Adrienne Kennedy (1931–)

Writer, Playwright

Born in Pittsburgh, Pennsylvania, on September 13, 1931, Adrienne Lita Hawkins grew up in Cleveland, Ohio. She received a B.A. in education from Ohio State in 1953, and married Joseph C. Kennedy one month later. In 1955, she and her husband moved to New York, and Kennedy studied writing at the American Theatre Wing and at Columbia University, completing her first play *Pale Blue Flowers* which was never produced or published.

In 1960, Kennedy and her husband traveled to Europe and then Ghana on a grant from the Africa Research Foundation. Her writing became more focused, and she published a story in *Black Orpheus* magazine. At the age of 29, Kennedy wrote *Funnyhouse of a Negro*, a one-act play. Edward Albee selected and co-directed the play for production in New York's Circle in the Square. It ran from January 14 to February 9, 1964 at the East End Theatre in New York.

Kennedy's next play *The Owl Answers* produced in 1965, won her a second Stanley Award from Wagner College of Staten Island, New York. Since the mid-1960s, she has written many full-length and one-act plays including *Sun: A Poem for Malcolm X Inspired by His Murder* (1968), *A Movie Star Has to Star in Black and White* (1976), *Black Children's Day* (1980), and *Diary of Lights* (1987). Later, the University of Minnesota Press published collections of her work including *The Alexander Plays* (1992). In 1996, her latest plays *Sleep Deprivation Chamber* and *June and Jean in Concert* were produced at the Joseph Papp Public Theater and the Susan Stein Shiva Theater, respectively. Kennedy wrote an autobiography that was published in 1987 and titled *People Who Led to My Plays.*

Kennedy's plays are hallmarks of the American experimental theater, avant-garde and non-traditional in the extreme. She has won many awards for her bold and clear vision including an Obie Award in 1964 and a Pierre Lecomte du Novy Award from the Lincoln Center in 1994. In addition to winning many fellowships and grants, Kennedy has been a lecturer at several universities including Yale, Princeton, Brown, Harvard, and at Berkeley of California. She also served as an International Theatre Institute representative in Budapest in 1978.

Jamaica Kincaid (1949–)

Writer

Jamaica Kincaid was born Elaine Potter Kincaid on May 25, 1949, in St. Johns, Antigua. After leaving Antigua at 16 years of age and moving to New York, Kincaid held several positions, while seeking her niche in the United States. Her writing career began as a contributor to the *New Yorker* magazine. Once becoming a staff member, Kincaid had her collection of stories and other short pieces, which mainly ran in the magazine from 1974 to 1976, published under the title *At the Bottom of the River* (1983). It was four years before Kincaid published her first work of fiction *Annie John* (1985). This work was later followed by *A Small Place* (1988), *Annie Gwenn Lilly Pam & Tulip* (1989), and *Lucy*(1990).

With her lyrical style and semi-autobiographical focus, Kincaid addresses themes about lasting scars from childhood experiences, ambivalence toward parents, the mother-daughter relationship and the search for identity.

Yusef Komunyakaa (James Willie Brown, Jr.) (1941–)

Poet, Educator

Yusef Komunyakaa was born James Willie Brown, Jr. in 1941, in the segregated, culturally-desolate mill town of Bogalusa, Louisiana. He came to love reading and poetry as a child and at age 16 years of age began pursuing his own talents. After high school graduation, Komunyakaa joined the U.S. Army and was sent to Vietnam to act as a reporter and editor for a military newspaper in 1969. Although he felt estranged from American society upon his return from Vietnam, Komunyakaa enrolled at the University of Colorado and later graduate school at Colorado State University. He received a second master's degree from the University of California at Irvine. A creative writing workshop proved inspirational and his first book of poetry *Dedication and Other Darkhorses* was published in 1977. With the release of his second volume two years later, Komunyakaa accepted a series of fellowships and teaching positions, enabling him to pursue a career as a poet.

While working in New Orleans in 1983, Komunyakaa began to come to terms with his experiences in Vietnam through his writing. This challenge resulted in several sophisticated books filled with cultural influences that portray basic elements of humanity. In 1985, the poet left New Orleans to accept a position as a visiting professor at Indiana University in Bloomington. By 1987, having published two more books of poetry, Komunyakaa became an associate professor in the Afro-American and English studies departments at the university. For personal and religious reasons, the poet changed his name from James Willie Brown, Jr. to Yusef Komunyakaa. With the publication of *Neon Vernacular*, he was awarded the 1994 Pulitzer Prize in poetry along with the $50,000 Kingsley Tufts Poetry Award given by the Claremont Graduate School. Komunyakaa's themes of memory and self-definition—as an African American man and a veteran of Vietnam—lend his works a sense of strength and spiritual tenacity.

Nella Larsen (1891–1964)
Novelist, Librarian, Nurse

Nella Larsen was born in 1891 in Chicago, Illinois, of a Danish mother and a West Indian father. She attended Fisk University's Normal (High) School in Nashville, Tennessee, and from 1909 to 1912, the University of Copenhagen in Denmark. Three years later, she graduated from the Lincoln School for Nurses in New York City. In addition to her writing, she worked alternately as a nurse and librarian, having attended the New York Public Library training school from 1921 to 1923. After one year as head nurse at Tuskegee Institute (now Tuskegee University), she became supervising nurse at the Lincoln Hospital in New York City until 1918, when she joined the city's department of health. During the next forty years, she worked as a children's librarian at the New York Public Library (1924–1926), Gouverneur Hospital (1944–1961), and the Metropolitan Hospital (1961–1964), all in New York City. Writing, however, is what made her famous.

In the 1920s, Larsen began contributing to children's magazines. At the same time, she found herself immersed in the literary and political activities of the ongoing Harlem Renaissance. Larsen's first novel *Quicksand* (1928) received a bronze medal from the Harmon Foundation. The groundbreaking novel developed themes around African American women's sexuality and about mixed racial identity. Her second major work *Passing* (1929) led to her becoming the first African American woman to be awarded a Guggenheim Fellowship in creative writing (1930). More than thirty years after her death on March 20, 1964, Larsen's novels were reissued, and she finally achieved recognition as one of the most important writers of the Harlem Renaissance.

Julius Lester (1939–)
Writer, Educator

Julius Lester was born in St. Louis, Missouri, in 1939. He grew up in Kansas City, Kansas, and Nashville, Tennessee, where his father led congregations as a Methodist minister. Lester spent the summers of his youth in rural Arkansas, experiencing racism and segregation firsthand. A gifted student, he was an avid musician and aspired to become a writer.

Lester obtained a B.A. in English from Fisk University. He became politically active in the civil rights struggle as a folksinger and photographer of Southern rallies. As a member of the Student Non-Violent Coordinating Committee (SNCC) in the mid-1960s, Lester became head of its photo department and visited North Vietnam to document the effects of U.S. bombing missions. He began publishing ideological books that defended African American militancy including *The Angry Children of Malcolm X* and *Revolutionary Notes.* From 1966 to 1968 Lester served as director of the prestigious Newport Folk Festival and released two record albums himself.

Having achieved fame for his artistic pursuits, Lester was hired to host live radio shows at the public broadcasting station WBAI-FM in New York City. Around the same time, he published two books for children that saw immediate success. *Black Folktales* compiled African legends and slave narratives and *To Be a Slave*, a collection of stories based on oral history accounts, received a Newbery Honor Book citation. In 1971, Lester began hosting the New York public television program "Free Time." His career as an award-winning academician began that same year, when he was hired as professor of Afro-American Studies at the University of Massachusetts-Amherst. He settled there in 1975 and became a full-time professor and author.

Lester flourished as an author by releasing novels and storybooks (with illustrator Jerry Pinkney) that reflected his interests in African American history, folklore, and politics. *Long Journey Home*, a finalist for the National Book Award, explores the everyday lives of African Americans during the Reconstruction period. Lester's *Tales of Uncle Remus: The Adventures of Brer Rabbit*, traditional stories retold in a contemporary southern African American voice, were well-received by teachers and librarians who granted it the Coretta Scott King Award. His 1994 adult novel *And All Our Wounds Forgiven* tracks dramatic events in the 1960s. Lester's individualism and resistance to racial and religious categorization is evident in two autobiographies *All Is Well* and *Lovesong: Becoming a Jew.*

When he converted to Judaism in mid-life, Lester was ousted from Amherst's renamed African American Studies Department in 1988. Persevering through yet another career change, he moved to the University's Near Eastern and Judaic Studies Department. Since that time he has also taught in the history and English departments. Lester's latest publication for young adults was his 1995 racially repositioned novelization of *Othello.*

Audre Lorde (1934–1993)
Poet

Audre Lorde was born in New York City; graduated with a masters in library science from Columbia University; was poet-in-residence at Tougaloo College; taught at Lehman College, Bronx; and taught at John Jay College and CCNY. She received a National Endowment for the Arts grant and a Cultural Council Foundation grant for poetry.

Her books of poetry included: *Cables to Rage* (1970); *The First Cities* (1968); *From a Land Where Other People Live* (1973); *Coal* (1968); *The New York Head Shop and Museum* (1974); *Between Ourselves* (1976); *The Black Unicorn* (1978); *Chosen Poems–Old and New* (1982); *Zami: A New Spelling of My Name* (1982); *Sister/Outsider: Essays and Speeches* (1984); *Lesbian Poetry: An Anthology* (1982); and *Woman Poet–The East* (1984). Lorde's poetry has been published in many anthologies, magazines, and lesbian books and periodicals. Lorde died of cancer on November 17, 1992.

Claude McKay (1890–1948)
Poet

Born the son of a farmer in Jamaica (then British West Indies) on September 15, 1890, Claude McKay began writing early in life. Two books of his poems *Songs of Jamaica* and *Constab Ballads* were published just after he turned twenty years of age. In both, he made extensive use of Jamaican dialect.

In 1913, McKay came to the United States to study agriculture at Tuskegee Institute (now Tuskegee University) and at Kansas State University, but his interest in poetry induced him to move to New York City, where he published his work in small literary magazines. McKay then made a trip to England. While there, he completed a collection of lyrics entitled *Spring in New Hampshire.* When he returned to the United States, he became associate editor of *The Liberator* under Max Eastman. In 1922, he completed *Harlem Shadows*, a landmark work of the Harlem Renaissance period.

McKay then turned to the writing of such novels as *Home to Harlem* (1928), *Banjo* (1929), and four other books including an autobiography and a study of Harlem. *The Passion of Claude McKay: Selected Prose and Poetry 1912–1948*, edited by Wayne Cooper, was published in 1973. McKay traveled abroad before returning to the United States, where he died on May 22, 1948. His final work *Selected Poems* was published posthumously in 1953.

During World War II, when Winston Churchill addressed a joint session of the United States Congress in an effort to enlist American aid in the battle against Nazism, the climax of his oration was his reading of the famous poem "If We Must Die," originally written by McKay to assail lynchings and mob violence in the South. McKay's *Trial by Lynching* (1967), edited and translated stories, and his *The Negroes in America* (1979 or 1980), edited and translated from the Russian language, have also been published. Many of his works have been reprinted since his death including: *Home to Harlem; Banana Bottom; Banjo* (1970); *A Long Way From Home* (1970); *Harlem: Negro Metropolis* (1972); and *Selected Poems of Claude McKay* (1971). *Songs of Jamaica* and *Constab Ballads* have been bound together as *The Dialect Poems of Claude McKay.* Wayne F. Cooper's *Claude McKay: Rebel Sojourner in the Harlem Renaissance* (1987) is an important book detailing McKay's life and work.

Terry McMillan (1951–)
Novelist

Terry McMillan was born on October 18, 1951, and raised in Port Huron, Michigan. She attended Los Angeles City College, but later transferred to Berkeley and then to Columbia University to study film. She later enrolled in a writing workshop at the Harlem Writers Guild and was accepted at the MacDowell Colony in 1983. She has taught at the University of Wyoming and the University of Arizona.

McMillan published her first short story when she was 25 years old. Her subsequent novels include *Mama* (1987), *Disappearing Acts* (1989), and *Waiting to Exhale* (1992). She also edited the anthology of contemporary African American fiction entitled *Breaking Ice: An Anthology of Contemporary African-American Fiction* (1992). In 1997 she published *How Stella Got Her Groove Back.*

Waiting to Exhale hit the *New York Times'* bestseller list within one week of being in print and remained there for several months. Hardcover publisher Viking printed 700,000 copies and Pocket Books, which published the paperback version, paid $2.64 million for the rights to the work. In 1995, the novel was adapted into one of the most highly-touted films of the year. Directed by Forest Whitaker, the film version starred Angela Bassett, Whitney Houston, Lela Rochon, and Loretta Devine. Wesley Snipes and Gregory Hines had smaller roles. *How Stella Got Her Groove Back* was also made into a popular film.

In 1993, New York Women in Communication gave McMillan a Matrix Award. In 1994, the NAACP Legal Defense and Educational Fund honored McMillan at a luncheon.

James Alan McPherson (1943–)
Short Story Writer

James McPherson, born in Savannah, Georgia, on October 16, 1943, received his B.A. degree in 1965 from Morris Brown College in Atlanta, a law degree from Harvard University in 1968, and an M.F.A. degree from the University of Iowa in 1969. He has taught writing at several universities including the University of Virginia in Charlottesville, where he taught fiction writing. At the present time, he teaches writing at the University of Iowa and is a contributing editor of *Atlantic Monthly.*

Terry McMillan

His short stories have appeared in several magazines. *Hue and Cry*, a collection of short stories published in 1969, was highly praised by Ralph Ellison. Named a Guggenheim fellow in 1972 and 1973, McPherson's second book of short stories *Elbow Room* was published in 1977 and received the Pulitzer Prize for fiction in the following year. McPherson was one of the three African American writers who were awarded five-year grants by the McArthur Foundation of Chicago for exceptional talent in 1981.

Haki Madhubuti (Don L. Lee) (1942–)
Poet, Essayist, Publisher

Haki Madhubuti exemplifies the attempt of a person to create a unified self and live a holistic life—not one that is fragmented by the poet, educator, and journalist that Madhubuti has become.

Born Don L. Lee on February 23, 1942, in Little Rock, Arkansas, Madhubuti and his family moved to Detroit a year later. After his father left home and his mother died, he moved to Chicago at age 16 to live with an aunt. He graduated from Chicago City College with an A.A. degree and later received an M.F.A. degree from the University of Iowa.

From 1961 to 1966, Madhubuti prepared to become a writer: he read a book daily and wrote a two-hundred word review of each book. He published his first volume of poetry *Think Black* in 1966. In 1967, he joined Johari Amini (Jewel Latimore) and Carolyn Rogers in launching the Third World Press; it became the longest continuously-operated African American press in the United States. His other works of poetry published in the 1960s were *Black Pride* (1968) and *Don't Cry, Scream* (1969). Later he taught and served as a writer-in-residence at numerous universities including Chicago State, Cornell, Howard, Morgan State, and the University of Illinois.

In the 1970s he published *Directionscore: Selected and New Poems* and *To Gwen with Love*. His *Dynamic Voices: Black Poets of the 1960s*, published in 1971 by Broadside Press, provided a critical context for writers of the Black Arts movement from one who participated in it. Here the writer defined the role of the African American literary critic and set standards for the critic to follow. The next year he founded *Black Books Bulletin*.

In 1973, Madhubuti changed his name from Don L. Lee to Haki Madhubuti, which, in Swahili, means "justice," "awakening," and "strong." He moved to Howard University that year where he was poet-in-residence. During the 1980s, he began teaching at Chicago State, where he remains as professor of English. His works from the 1970s into the 1990s include: *The Clash of Faces* (1978); *Say That the River Turns: The Impact of Gwendolyn Brooks* (1987); *Killing Memory, Seeking Ancestors* (1987); and *Black Men: Obsolete, Single, Dangerous?;* and *African American Families in Transition: Essays in Discovery, Solution, and Hope* (1990). He also edited *Why L.A. Happened: Implications of the '92 Los Angeles Rebellion* (1993) and *Claiming Earth: Race, Rage, Rape, Redemption: Blacks Seeking a Cultural Enlightened Empowerment* (1994). Although still a poet, in the 1990s he strengthened his skills as an essayist.

Among his honors, Madhubuti has received the DuSable Museum Award for Excellence in Poetry, National Council of Teachers of English Award, the Sidney R. Yates Advocate Award, and the African Heritage Studies Association citation. Later, he was also honored with the Distinguished Writers Award from the Middle Atlantic Writers Association in 1984 and the American Book Award in 1991. In 1984, he was the only poet selected to represent the United States at the International Valmiki World Poetry Festival held in New Delhi, India.

In addition to his teaching duties, Madhubuti is a director of the National Black Holistic Retreat, which he co-founded in 1984. He also remains as publisher and editor of Third World Press.

Paule Marshall (1929–)
Writer

Paule Marshall was born Valenza Pauline Burk on April 9, 1929, in Brooklyn, New York. Marshall's parents were emigrants from Barbados, and she grew up in a community with strong West Indian influences. Although Marshall did some writing in her childhood years, her serious devotion to writing began in 1954 as exercise at the end of her work day. The result was her first short story "The Valley Between."

Marshall's work, which centers on people of African descent, sets out to create images that celebrate the human spirit and put asunder all forms of political and social oppression. Marshall has received numerous awards and fellowships and her novels include: *Brown Girl, Brownstones* (1959); *Soul Clap Hands and Sing* (1961); *The Chose Place, the Timeless People* (1969); *Praisesong for the Widow* (1983); and *Daughters* (1991). Short stories and essays are also a part of Marshall's contributions to an African-centered literary experience.

Loften Mitchell (1919–)
Playwright

Born on April 15, 1919, in Columbus, North Carolina, and raised in Harlem in the 1920s, Loften Mitchell began to write as a child, creating scripts for backyard shows that he and his brother performed. After completing junior high school, he decided to enroll at New York Textile High because he had been promised a job on the school newspaper. But Mitchell soon realized that he needed the training of an academic high school and, with the help of one of his teachers, transferred to DeWitt Clinton.

Graduating with honors, Mitchell found a job as an elevator operator and a delivery boy to support himself while he studied playwriting at night at the City College of New York. However, he met a professor from Talladega College in Alabama who helped him win a scholarship to study there. He graduated with honors in 1943, having won an award for the best play written by a student.

After two years of service in the U. S. Navy, Mitchell enrolled as a graduate student at Columbia University in New York. A year later, he accepted a job with the city's department of welfare as a social investigator and continued to attend school at night. During this time, he wrote one of his first successful plays, *Blood in the Night*, and in 1957 he wrote *A Land Beyond the River*, which had a long run at an off-Broadway theater and was also published as a book.

The following year Mitchell won a Guggenheim award, which enabled him to return to Columbia University and write for a year. Since then, he has written a new play *Star of the Morning*, the story of Bert Williams, famous African American entertainer.

In 1967 Mitchell published a study of African American theater entitled *Black Drama*. His other books include: *Tell Pharaoh*, a play; *The Stubborn Old Lady Who Resisted Change* (1973), a novel; and *Voices of the Black Theatre* (1976). Mitchell also wrote the books for various Broadway musicals including *Ballads for Bimshire* (1963), *Bubbling Brown Sugar* (1975), *Cartoons for a Lunch Hour* (1978), *A Gypsy Girl* (1982), and *Miss Ethel Waters* (1983).

Toni Morrison (1931–)
Novelist, Editor

Born Chloe Anthony Wofford in Lorain, Ohio, on February 18, 1931, Toni Morrison received a B.A. degree from Howard University in 1953, and an M.A. from Cornell in 1955. After working as an instructor in English and the humanities at Texas Southern University and Howard University, Morrison eventually became a senior editor at Random House in New York City, where, for more than twenty years, she was responsible for the publication of many books by African Americans including Middleton Harris's *The Black Book* (edited by Toni Morrison) and books by Toni Cade Bambara, among others. From 1971 to 1972, Morrison was also an associate professor at the State University of New York at Purchase. Throughout the 1970s and 1980s, she wrote and published her novels, in addition to holding visiting professorships at Yale University and Bard College. From 1984 to 1989, she served as Albert Schweitzer Professor of the Humanities at the State University of New York at Albany. In 1989, Morrison became the Robert F. Goheen Professor of the Humanities at Princeton University.

Morrison's first novel *The Bluest Eye* was published in 1969, followed by *Sula*, which won the 1975 Ohioana Book Award. Morrison's third novel *Song of Solomon* (1977) received the 1977 National Book Critics Circle Award and the 1978 American Academy and Institute of Arts and Letters Award. *Tar Baby* was published in 1981, followed by the play *Dreaming Emmett* first produced in Albany, New York, in 1986. *Beloved*, published in 1987, is regarded by some as her most significant work. The historical novel won both the Pulitzer Prize for fiction and the Robert F. Kennedy Award. *Beloved* was also a finalist for the 1988 National Book Critics Circle Award and was one of the three contenders for the Ritz Hemingway Prize in Paris, from which no winner emerged. In addition, *Beloved* was a National Book Award finalist. In the 1990s, Morrison has written a collection of essays and two novels—*Jazz* (1992) and *Paradise* (1997).

Toni Morrison (AP/Wide World Photos, Inc.)

Morrison was elected to the American Institute of Arts and Letters in 1981 and gave the keynote address at the American Writers' Congress in New York City in the fall of that year. She won the New York State Governor's Art Award in 1986. In 1993, the American Literature Association's Coalition of Author Societies founded The Toni Morrison Society, an education group, in Atlanta. Later in the year, Morrison received her highest honor and made history when she became the first African American recipient of the Nobel Prize in Literature, an award that included an $825,000 prize. In 1995, her alma mater, Howard University, bestowed her with an honorary doctorate.

Walter Mosley (1952–)
Novelist

Walter Mosley achieved national publicity when, during the 1992 U.S. presidential campaign, Bill Clinton credited him as his favorite mystery writer. Born on January 12, 1952, and raised in the Watts and Pico-Fairfax districts of Los Angeles, Mosely's unique heritage is attributed to an African American father from the deep South and a white, Jewish mother whose family emigrated from Eastern Europe. After drifting among a variety of jobs, including potter, caterer, and computer programmer, he settled in New York City and attended the writing program at City College. By 1987 he had become a full-time writer. Although Mosley's first book, a short psychological novel entitled *Gone Fishin'*(later released in 1997) was turned down by numerous agents, he achieved rapid success in 1990 with *Devil in a Blue Dress*. In the next several years, *A Red Death, White Butterfly*, and *Black Betty* were also greeted with critical acclaim.

Mosley incorporates social and racial issues into gripping novels that authentically portray inner city life in the African American neighborhoods of post-World War II Los Angeles. His creation of the recurring multidimensional character, private investigator Ezekiel ("Easy") Rawlins, was heavily influenced by the experiences of Mosley's own father as an African American soldier in World War II and later a southern immigrant in California. With his African American viewpoint and confrontation of shifting societal and moral issues, Mosley has been praised for breaking new ground within the mystery and detective genre and inspiring a new brand of African American fiction. Mosley's success is destined to continue as he is planning nine or ten novels in all for the Rawlins series, eventually bringing the protagonist into the early 1980s.

Mosley received several honors including the John Creasey Memorial Award and Shamus Award for outstanding mystery writing. In 1990, the Mystery Writers of America nominated *Devil in a Blue Dress* for an Edgar Award. The film version of *Devil in a Blue Dress*, with a screenplay penned by the author, was released in 1996. Directed by Carl Franklin, the film starred Denzel Washington as Rawlins. In 1995, Mosely published *R. L.'s Dream*, a fictional meditation on the blues. In the following year, he released *A Little Yellow Dog*. In 1997, he published the book *Always Outnumbered, Always Outgunned*, introducing his most compelling new character since the debut of Easy Rawlins: Socrates Fortlow, a tough, brooding ex-convict determined to challenge and understand the violence and anarchy in his world—and in himself.

Walter Dean Myers (1937–)
Young Adult Writer

Walter Milton Myers was born in Martinsburg, West Virginia, in 1937. Upon the death of his mother at age three, he was raised by a foster couple, Herbert and Florence Dean, in Harlem. Myers began writing as a child and was praised in grade school for his academic achievements. Determined to further his education, he joined the U.S. Army at 17 years of age, enabling him to pay part of his college tuition with money from the G.I. Bill. In 1969, upon the publication of his first picture book for children, Myers was determined to become a professional writer. *Where Does the Day Go?* was honored by the Council on Interracial Books for Children and established Myers as an author who addressed the needs of minority children.

Myers worked as a senior editor for the Bobbs-Merrill publishing house, released more picture books, and began writing young adult stories in the 1970s. Since then he has published more than two dozen novels in which he tackles urban social issues, such as teen pregnancy, crime, drug abuse, and gang violence. Myers's authentic dialogue and ability to capture the universal ties and strengthening powers of family and friendship within African American communities prompted great response from teenage readers. Committed to producing quality literature for African American children, he branched into fairy tales, ghost stories, science fiction, adventure sagas, and a popular biography entitled *Malcolm X: By Any Means Necessary.* Myers has won a variety of awards including the Coretta Scott King Award and the Newbery "honor book" citation for *Scorpions.* Myers's novels, particularly *Hoops*, *Fallen Angels*, and *Motown and Didi: A Love Story*, are an enduring presence on both high school and young adult recommended reading lists.

Gloria Naylor

Gloria Naylor (1950–)
Novelist

Gloria Naylor was born in New York City on January 25, 1950, and still lives there. She received a B.A. in English from Brooklyn College in 1981 and an M.A. in Afro-American Studies from Yale University in 1983. She has taught writing and literature at George Washington University, New York University, Brandeis University, Cornell University, and Boston University. In 1983, she won the American Book Award for first fiction for her novel *The Women of Brewster Place*, which was produced for television in 1988. Her second novel was *Linden Hills* published in 1985. Her third novel *Mama Day* (1988) was written with the aid of a grant from the National Endowment for the Arts. In 1988, Naylor was awarded a Guggenheim Fellowship. In 1993, Naylor published a new novel *Bailey's Café.*

Ann Lane Petry (1912–1997)
Novelist, Short Story Writer

Ann Petry was born in Old Saybrook, Connecticut, on October 12, 1912, where her father was a druggist. After graduating from the College of Pharmacy at the University of Connecticut, she went to New York where she found employment as a social worker and newspaper reporter, studying creative writing at night.

Her early short stories appeared in *Crisis* and *Phylon.* In 1946, after having received a Houghton Mifflin Fellowship, she completed and published her first novel *The Street. The Street* focuses on the lives of African American women in a crowded tenement. Through her exploration of this subject, Petry became the first African American woman writer to address the problems African American women face as they live in the slums. Petry also wrote *Country Place* (1947), *The Narrows* (1953), and *Miss Muriel and Other Stories* (1971). Her works for children and young people include *The Drugstore Cat*, *Harriet Tubman*, *Tituba of Salem Village*, *Legends of Saints*, and a fourth book for children and young people. Many of her earlier novels are being reprinted. Petry died on February 28, 1997.

Ishmael Reed (1938–)
Novelist, Poet

Born in Chattanooga, Tennessee, on February 22, 1938, Ishmael Reed grew up in Buffalo, New York. He attended State University of New York at Buffalo from

Ishmael Reed (AP/Wide World Photos, Inc.)

1956 to 1960. He worked as a reporter and later as an editor for the *Newark Advance* in New Jersey before co-founding the *East Village Other* in 1965. Reed spent the next few years teaching prose and guest lecturing at different institutions including the University of California at Berkeley. In 1971, he co-founded Yardbird Publishing Co., Inc. After four years as the editorial director, he co-founded Reed, Cannon & Johnson Communications Co., a publisher and producer of videos, and in 1976, the Before Columbus Foundation, which produced and distributed works by unestablished ethnic writers.

A controversial man, Reed has published poetry, novels, plays, and prose. Considered by some to be misogynistic and cynical, others find his work innovative. He is committed to creating an alternative African American aesthetic, which he calls Neo-HooDooism. One hallmark of the movement is the reliance on satire and social criticism.

Reed's works of poetry include: *catechism of d neoamerican hoodoo church* (1971); *Conjure* (1972), which was nominated for the National Book Award; *Chattanooga* (1973); *A Secretary to the Spirits* (1978); and *New and Collected Poetry* (1988). His poetry has also appeared in numerous anthologies and magazines including *The Poetry of the Negro*, *The New Black Poetry*, *The Norton Anthology*, *Cricket*, and *Scholastic* magazine.

Reed's novels include: *The Free-lance Pallbearers* (1967); *Yellow Back Radio Broke Down* (1969); *Mumbo Jumbo*, which also received a National Book Award nomination; *The Last Days of Louisiana Red* (1974); *Flight to Canada* (1976); *The Terrible Twos* (1982); *Reckless Eyeballing; The Terrible Threes* (1989); and *Japanese by Spring*. He also wrote three plays: *The Lost State of Franklin* (1976); *Savage Wilds;* and its sequel *Savage Wilds II*.

Prose works by Reed include: *Shrovetide in Old New Orleans* (1978); *God Made Alaska for the Indians: Selected Essays* (1982); and *Writin' Is Fightin': Thirty-seven Years of Boxing on Paper* (1988).

Reed's career has been rich in recognition. In 1974, he won the John Simon Guggenheim Memorial Foundation Award for fiction. The next year he received a Rosenthal Foundation Award and an honor from the National Institute of Arts and Letters. In 1978, Reed earned the Lewis Michaux and American Civil Liberties awards. The following year he was given the Pushcart Prize. He has received fellowships from the Wisconsin Board and Yale University's Calhoun College in 1982; grants have come from New York State, the National Endowment for the Arts, and the California Arts Council.

Sonia Sanchez (1934–)

Poet, Playwright

Sonia Sanchez was born on September 9, 1934, in Birmingham, Alabama. She studied at New York University and Hunter College in New York City. She is married to Etheridge Knight, an African American writer of poetry and fiction. She has taught at San Francisco State College and is now teaching in the Black Studies Department of Temple University in Philadelphia. Her plays were published in *The Drama Review* (Summer 1968) and in *New Plays from the Black Theatre* (1969), edited by Ed Bullins. Her poems also have been published in many other magazines and anthologies. Books written or edited by her include six volumes of poetry: *Homecoming* (1969); *We a Bad People* (1970); *It's a New Day* (1971); *A Blues Book for Blue Black Magical Women* (1973); *Love Poems* (1975); and *I've Been a Woman* (1978). Sanchez has edited two anthologies: *Three Hundred and Sixty Degrees of Blackness Comin at You, An Anthology of the Sonia Sanchez Writers Workshop at Countee Cullen Library in Harlem* (1971); and *We Be Word Sorcerers: Twenty-five Stories by Black Americans* (1973). She has also written *A Sound Investment* (1979), a collection of short stories; and *homegirls and handgrenades* (1984).

Ntozake Shange (AP/Wide World Photos, Inc.)

Ntozake Shange (1948–)
Playwright, Poet, Novelist

A playwright and poet, Paulette Linda Williams was born in Trenton, New Jersey, on October 18, 1948; she changed her name to Ntozake Shange in 1971. She graduated from Barnard College and received her master's degree from the University of Southern California, where she did other graduate work. She studied Afro-American dance in California and actually performed with the Third World Collective, Raymond Sawyer's Afro-American Dance Company, Sounds in Motion, and West Coast Dance Works.

Shange taught at Sonoma Mills College in California from 1972 to 1975. She went on to teach at CUNY and Douglas College to finish out the 1970s, before becoming the Mellon Distinguished Professor of Literature at Rice University in 1983. For three years she worked as an associate professor of drama at the University of Houston.

Shange's play *For Colored Girls Who Have Considered Suicide When the Rainbow is Enuf*, a choreopoem (poetry and dance), was first produced in California, after her dance-drama *Sassafrass* was presented in 1976. Later *For Colored Girls* was produced in New York City, where it had a long run before going on to other cities. It earned Tony, Grammy, and Emmy award nominations in 1977. Among the other works by Shange that have been produced on the stage are *Spell #7, A Photograph: Lovers in Motion* (1979), and *Boogie Woogie Landscapes* (1979). *For Colored Girls* has been published as a book, and Shange's collection *Three Pieces* (1981) contains *Spell #7, A Photograph: Lovers in Motion*, and *Boogie Woogie Landscapes.*

Other books by Shange include: *Nappy Edges* (poetry, 1978); *Sassafrass, Cypress & Indigo* (novel, 1982); *A Daughter's Geography* (poetry, 1983); *From Okra to Greens* (a play, 1984); *See No Evil: Prefaces & Accounts, 1976–1983* (1984); *Betsey Brown* (novel, 1985); and *Liliane: Resurrection of the Daughter* (novel, 1994).

A version of *Betsey Brown* for the stage, with music by the jazz trumpeter and composer Baikida Carroll, opened the American Music Theater Festival in Philadelphia, March 25, 1989. Shange directed Ina Cesaire's *Fire's Daughters* in 1993. The Broadway version of *For Colored Girls/When the Rainbow Is Enuf* was revived in 1995.

Shange received an Obie Award in 1981 for *Mother Courage and Her Children* and a *Los Angeles Times* Book Prize for poetry that year for *Three Pieces.* A Guggenheim fellow, Shange has been given awards by the Outer Critics Circle and the National Black Theater Festival (1993). She also won the Pushcart Prize.

Lucy Terry (1730–1821)
Poet

Lucy Terry is generally considered one of the first African American poet in the United States. In a ballad that she called "Bars Fight," she recreated an Indian massacre that occurred in Deerfield, Massachusetts, in 1746 during King George's War. "Bars Fight" has been hailed by some historians as the most authentic account of the massacre.

A semi-literate slave in the household of Ensign Ebenezer Wells, she won her freedom and was married to a freed man named Prince. The Prince house served as a center for young people who gathered to listen to their hostess's storytelling. Lucy Terry was a strong woman who argued eloquently for her family's rights in several cases.

Wallace H. Thurman (1902–1934)
Novelist, Playwright, Ghostwriter, Journalist

A caustic critic of African American writing, Wallace Thurman was a member of the New Negro movement known as the Harlem Renaissance. Wallace Henry Thurman, called "Wally" by his friends, was born on August 16, 1902, in Salt Lake City. He graduated from the

University of Utah in 1922, having studied pre-medicine. He did post-graduate work in 1923 at the University of Southern California. He read widely and knew about the Harlem Renaissance then taking place in New York. He attempted a West Coast counterpart of the Harlem Renaissance and established his own short-lived literary magazine *The Outlet*. He moved to New York City the following year.

Thurman was managing editor of the *Messenger* from spring to fall 1926, then moved to *The World Tomorrow*, a white-owned monthly. By now Thurman and Langston Hughes had become good friends. They were a part of a new school known as Harlem Renaissance writers. The group included Arna Bontemps (whom he had known in Los Angeles), Nella Larsen, Dorothy West, Countee Cullen, Jessie Fauset, Aaron Douglas, Zora Neale Hurston, and Gwendolyn Bennett. In the summer of 1926, Thurman and the group established *Fire!*, a short-lived literary magazine that was both obscene and revolutionary. The magazine was to provide another outlet beyond *Crisis* and *Opportunity* magazines for young African American writers to have their works published. He had financed the magazine himself and spent four years paying its debt.

In 1927, many of Thurman's articles were published in prestigious magazines, such as *New Republic* and *Dance Magazine*, further helping to establish him as a critic. The next year, McFadden Publications added Thurman to its editorial staff, and he continued to write. In 1929 he published *The Blacker the Berry the Sweeter the Juice*, an autobiographical novel that embraced intra-race color prejudice and self-hatred. Thurman was also the ghostwriter for several magazines and books. He wrote several plays as well; one of them, *Cordelia the Crude*, premiered on Broadway where it received mixed reviews. It went on to Chicago and Los Angeles .

In 1932, Thurman published two other novels: *Infants of the Spring* and *The Interne*. An alcoholic homosexual, Thurman was often depressed and suicidal. He became ill with tuberculosis and died in New York on December 22, 1934.

Jean Toomer (1894–1967)

Novelist, Poet

Jean Toomer's *Cane*, published in 1923, has been called one of the three best novels ever written by an African American—the others being Richard Wright's *Native Son* and Ralph Ellison's *Invisible Man*. According to Columbia University critic Robert Bone, "Cane is by far the most impressive product of the Negro Renaissance."

A mixture of poems and sketches, *Cane* was written during that period in which most African American writers were reacting against earlier "polite" forms by creating works marked by literary realism. Toomer even went beyond this realm to the threshold of symbol and myth, using a "mystical" approach which is much more akin to the contemporary mood than it was to the prevailing spirit of his own day. *Cane* sold only 500 copies on publication, and it was still little known until reprinted recently with new introductions. Much has been written about Toomer and *Cane* in recent years, including a *Cane* casebook.

Jean Toomer (The Beinecke Rare Book and Manuscript Library)

Born in Washington, DC, in December of 1894, Toomer was educated in law at the University of Wisconsin and City College of New York before he turned to writing. The transcendental nature of his writings is said to have stemmed in part from his early study under Gurdjieff, the Russian mystic.

Toomer also published quite a bit of poetry. Darwin T. Turner edited *The Wayward and The Seeking: A Collection of Writings by Jean Toomer* (1980), a book of his poetry, short stories, dramas, and autobiography. Other books about Toomer and his writings include: Therman O'Daniel's *Jean Toomer: A Critical Evaluation* (1985); over forty essays of the most thorough, up-to-date scholarship on Toomer; Robert B. Jones and Margery Toomer Latimer's *The Collected Poems of Jean Toomer* (1988); 55 poems; and Nellie Y. McKay's *Jean Toomer, Artist: A Study of His Literary Life and Work, 1894–1936* (1984, 1987). Toomer died on March 10, 1967.

Alice Walker (1944–)

Poet, Novelist

Alice Walker was born in Eatonton, Georgia, on February 9, 1944. She was educated at Spelman College (1961–1963) and Sarah Lawrence College, from which she received her B.A. in 1965. That year, she worked as a voter registrator in Georgia and worked for the welfare department in New York City. In 1967, she moved to Mississippi, where she was an African American literature consultant for Friends of the Children of Mississippi. From 1968 to 1971, she was a writer-in-residence at Jackson State and Tougaloo Colleges. Moving to Boston, she then lectured at Wellesley and the University of Massachussetts until 1973. While teaching in the early 1970s, she was a Radcliffe Institute fellow.

Walker's work began to be published in the late 1960s, starting with *Once: Poems* in 1968. Two years later she published the novel *The Third Life Grange Copeland.* These two works were quickly followed by a succession of works. Among them were: *Revolutionary Peturnias and Other Poems* (1973), which earned a National Book Award nomination and the Lillian Smith Award; *In Love and Trouble: Stories of Black Women*, recipient of a Richard and Hinda Rosenthal Foundation Award from the American Academy and Institute of Arts and Letters; and *Langston Hughes: American Biography* (for children).

The novel *Meridian* (1976) was followed in 1979 by a book of poetry entitled *Goodnight, Willie Lee, I'll See You in the Morning* and an edited work by Walker titled *I Love Myself When I'm Laughing . . . and Then Again When I Am Looking Mean and Impressive: A Zora Neale Hurston Reader.* The reader was particularly important because it brought about a resurgence of interest in a Harlem Renaissance writer who had been overshadowed by other, better known authors.

In the 1980s, Walker more formally resumed her teaching career, spending the year of 1982 as the Fannie Hurst Professor of Literature at Brandeis University, while also serving as a distinguished writer as the University of California at Berkeley. In 1984, she co-founded Wild Trees Press. That decade's works include: the short story collection *You Can't Keep a Good Woman Down* (1981); two collections of essays and journal entries *In Search of Our Mothers' Gardens: Womanist Prose* (1983) and *Living by the Word: Selected Writings, (1973–1987);* a book of poetry entitled *Horses Make a Landscape Look More Beautiful* (1984); *To Hell With Dying* (juvenile story, 1988); and the novel *The Temple of My Familiar* (1989). In 1986, she received the O. Henry Award for her short story "Kindred Spirits."

Alice Walker (AP/Wide World Photos, Inc.)

Walker's most well-received work, however, was the 1983 novel *The Color Purple.* Written in the form of a series of letters, the novel was nominated for the National Book Critics Circle Award and won the 1983 Pulitzer Prize as well as an American Book Award. The best-selling book was adapted into an award-winning film featuring Whoopi Goldberg, Danny Glover, Oprah Winfrey, and Margaret Avery.

In the 1990s, Walker has continued writing. *Possessing the Secret of Joy,* loosely a sequel to *The Color Purple,* was released in 1992. *The Same River Twice: Honoring the Difficult* came out four years later. Her latest novel *By the Light of My Father's Smile* was published in 1998.

Holder of numerous honorary degrees, Walker has received a Merrill Fellowship for writing, a National Endowment for the Arts grant, a Radcliffe Institute Fellowship, and other honors.

Margaret Walker (AP/Wide World Photos, Inc.)

Margaret A. Walker (Margaret Walker Alexander) (1915–1998)
Poet, Novelist

Margaret Walker was born on July 7, 1915, in Birmingham, Alabama, and received her early education in Alabama, Louisiana, and Mississippi. She earned her B.A. from Northwestern University and her M.A. (1940) and Ph.D. (1966), both from the University of Iowa.

In 1942, Walker published *For My People* and, two years later, was awarded a Rosenwald Fellowship for creative writing. She has taught English and literature at Livingston College in North Carolina, West Virginia State College, and Jackson State College in Mississippi. Her novel *Jubilee* appeared in 1965. *For My People* was reprinted in 1969. Her other works are *Prophets for a New Day, How I Wrote Jubilee, October Journey*, and *A Poetic Equation: Conversations Between Nikki Giovanni and Margaret Walker.* The date of June 17, 1976, was proclaimed Margaret Walker Alexander Day by the mayor of her native Birmingham.

Walker's other works include *Richard Wright: Daemonic Genius* (1988). A second edition of *A Poetic Equation: Conversations between Nikki Giovanni and Margaret Walker* was published in 1983. She died on November 30, 1998, in Chicago.

Dorothy West (1907–1998)
Writer

Dorothy West was the last surviving member of the Harlem Renaissance, the period of the late 1920s and early 1930s when an outpouring of writing and poetry exuded from the pens and typewriters of African American writers based in Harlem. West was known as "the Kid" by such luminaries as Countee Cullen, Langston Hughes, Richard Wright, and Zora Neale Hurston. West wrote short stories for the *New York Daily News* in the 1930s, and twice, during the Great Depression, founded African American literary journals, most notably the *New Challenge.*

West was born on June 2, 1907, in Boston. She later moved to New York City, but eventually returned home, moving into her family's summer home in Oak Bluffs on Martha's Vineyard in 1943. Five years later she wrote her first novel *The Living Is Easy* based on the affluent world of African American achievers. West continued to write short stories for the *Daily News* from her Oak Bluffs home for the next 25 years.

Dorothy West (AP/Wide World Photos, Inc.)

In the 1950s, West began a second novel *The Wedding*, but could not find a publisher interested in handling it. With its theme on interracial marriage, it may have been too hot a topic for the times and was put aside by West in an unfinished state. Instead, West started contributing short pieces to the Vineyard's daily newspaper in the 1970s.

West once again enjoyed fame in the 1990s. In 1992, West's stories caught the eye of former First Lady Jacqueline Onassis, an editor at Doubleday and a summer resident of Martha's Vineyard. Onassis encouraged West to finish *The Wedding*, and the two of them began meeting weekly. With Onassis acting as West's editor, the novel finally was published in 1995. West dedicated the novel to Onassis. The story was made into a television movie, produced by Oprah Winfrey, and aired in 1998. West died on August 16, 1998.

Phillis Wheatley (1753–1784)
Poet

Born in Senegal in 1753, Phillis Wheatley was brought to the United States as a slave and received her name from Susannah Wheatley, the wife of the Boston tailor who had bought Phillis. Wheatley received her early education in the household of her master. Her interest in writing stemmed from her reading of the Bible and the classics under the guidance of the Wheatley's daughter, Mary.

In 1770, her first poem was printed under the title "A Poem by Phillis, A Negro Girl on the Death of Reverend George Whitefield." Her book *Poems on Various Subjects: Religious and Moral* was published in London in 1773, the first book of poetry published by an African American. She took a trip to England for health reasons, but later returned to the United States and was married. She published the poem "Liberty and Peace" in 1784, shortly before her death. Most of the old books of her poems, letters, and memories about her life were reprinted in the late 1960s and early 1970s. Two books about Wheatley are Julian D. Mason, Jr.'s *The Poems of Phillis Wheatley* (1966) and William H. Robinson's *Phillis Wheatley, A Biography* (1981). Robinson also compiled and published *Phillis Wheatley: A Bio-Bibliography* (1981).

Although George Washington was among her admirers (she had once sent him a tributary poem, which he graciously acknowledged), her poetry is considered important today largely because of its historical role in the growth of African American literature. Wheatley's poetry reflects Anglo-Saxon models, rather than her African heritage. It is, nevertheless, a typical example of the verse manufactured in a territory—the British colonies—not yet divorced from its maternal origins. Wheatley died on December 5, 1784.

John Edgar Wideman (1941–)
Writer, Educator

Wideman has been one of the leading chroniclers of life in urban black America, depicting the widening chasm between the urban poor and the white power structure in the United States. He is known for intertwining ghetto experiences with experimental fiction techniques, personal history, and social events to highlight deep cultural conflicts. A prolific writer, Wideman is the only two-time winner of the prestigious PEN/Faulkner Award for literature, one for *Sent for You Yesterday* (1983), and one for *Philadelphia Fire* (1990). In addition to novels, he has written short stories and nonfiction including *Brothers and Keepers* (1984), a juxtaposition of his life and that of his younger brother, incarcerated for taking part in a larceny/murder. The examination of the two brothers's different lives was nominated for the National Book Critics Circle Award.

Born on June 14, 1941, in Washington, DC, Wideman was the first of five children. Growing up in Pittsburgh, where the family moved, Wideman attended highly-regarded Peabody High School. A top student, he was also class president and captain of the basketball team.

Enrolling at the University of Pittsburgh on a scholarship, he earned a B.A. in 1963. During his undergraduate career, Wideman made the Big Five Basketball Hall of Fame, won the university's creative writing prize, and was elected to Phi Beta Kappa. He received a Rhodes Scholarship to England's Oxford University, becoming the first African American to receive such recognition in more than fifty years. With a B.A. in philosophy obtained from Oxford's New College in 1966, Wideman began writing and teaching at such institutions as the Universities of Pennsylvania, Wyoming, and, since 1986, Massachusetts at Amherst.

August Wilson (1945–)
Playwright

One of the most important voices in the American theater, playwright August Wilson has become a spokesperson for the black experience in America today. Since his first stage success *Ma Rainey's Black Bottom* in 1984, he has celebrated people of color in several plays, all set in a different decade in the twentieth century. In 1997, he elicited a public debate involving many prominent theater critics on the use of theater as a vehicle for cultural nationalism.

Wilson was born in Pittsburgh, Pennsylvania, in 1945 and the oldest of six children. His mother was a house cleaner, his absent father, a baker. He left school at 15 due to the racist abuse he endured there. But he continued his education in the local library, reading all the literature by African American writers, such as Ralph Ellison, Langston Hughes, Richard Wright, and others. He published a few poems in *Black World* and *Black Lines* in the early 1970s after absorbing the works of Robert Frost, Dylan Thomas, and Amiri Baraka.

It was when Wilson discovered the writings of Malcolm X that he decided to use cultural nationalism, African American people working toward cultural self-determination, as a basis for playwriting. In 1969, he helped found the African American activist theater company Black Horizons on the Hill which focused on politicizing the community and raising African American consciousness. He staged some early plays through this association, but moved to St. Paul, Minnesota, in 1978 where he says he gained some clarity and became less radicalized. He immediately wrote *Jitney* for the Minneapolis Playwrights Center and won a fellowship prize.

Wilson moved the location of *Jitney* and his next work *Fullerton Street* back to Pittsburgh and produced them at the Allegheny Repertory Theater. After two years of work at the National Playwright Conference, his first major work *Ma Rainey's Black Bottom* caught the eye of Yale Repertory Theater's artistic director Lloyd Richards. Together, they have staged almost all of Wilson's works, Richards directing them himself.

Each of Wilson's plays tells the story of a different segment of the African American experience. *Ma Rainey's Black Bottom* tells how African American entertainers were exploited by whites in the 1920s. His next play *Joe Turner's Come and Gone* discusses the migration of African Americans from rural Southern areas to the industrial cities of the North. *Fences* became an immediate hit when it opened on Broadway in 1987. Actor James Earl Jones played the main character, Troy Maxson, who dreams of playing professional baseball in the 1950s, only to be victimized by white racism. This play won the Pulitzer Prize and other awards for Wilson.

In 1990, August Wilson won his second Pulitzer Prize for *The Piano Lesson*, a play that focuses on a family conflict over selling an heirloom piano once traded for slave ancestors whose portraits are carved into it. Then he produced *Two Trains Running* in 1992, a play about the late 1900s when racial strife and the Vietnam War divided the nation.

Wilson moved to Seattle in the early 1990s. His next play *Seven Guitars* opened in 1996. Set in Pittsburgh in 1948, the unseen main character's death is being mourned at a wake. The seven characters reminisce with music and dream the future. This is another successful production by Wilson and director Lloyd Richards.

The 1997 debate began when Wilson gave a keynote speech to the Theater Communications Group Conference. Entitled "The Ground on Which I Stand," it celebrated the achievements of African American theater and insisted that African American theater was understood and appreciated only by those living the African American experience. He castigated the New York mainstream theater and its critics for lack of support for African American theater. In turn, many New York critics, including Robert Brustein, Frank Rich, and John Simon, published editorial columns analyzing Wilson's speech. Ultimately, a face-to-face debate was held by Wilson and Brustein in January 1998 to discuss the cultural intentions of theater: Wilson/politicization vs. Brustein/universal truth. At the end of the evening the issue remained alive and well. Wilson had revisited his earlier black nationalist beliefs and continues to evoke questions about the African American experience.

Richard Wright (1908–1960)
Novelist

Born on September 4, 1908, on a plantation near Natchez, Mississippi, Wright drew on his personal experience to dramatize racial injustice and its brutalizing effects. In 1938, under the auspices of the Works Progress Administration Illinois Writers Project, Wright published *Uncle Tom's Children*, a collection of four novellas based on his Mississippi boyhood memories. The book won an award for the best work of fiction by a WPA writer, and Wright received a Guggenheim Fellowship.

Two years later, *Native Son*, a novel of Chicago's African American ghetto, further enhanced Wright's reputation. A Book-of-the-Month Club choice, it was later a successful Broadway production under Orson Welles's direction and was filmed in South America with Wright himself in the role of Bigger Thomas. He published *Twelve Million Black Voices* in 1941.

In 1945, Wright's largely autobiographical *Black Boy* was selected by the Book-of-the-Month Club and went on to become his second best-seller. Wright later moved to Paris where he continued to write fiction and nonfiction including: *The Outsider* (1953); *Black Power* (1954); *Savage Holiday* (1954, 1965); *The Color Curtain* (1956); *White Man Listen* (1957); *The Long Dream* (1958); *Lawd Today* (1963); *Eight Men* (1961); and *American Hunger* (1977), a continuation of Wright's autobiographical work *Black Boy*.

Wright died of a heart attack on November 28, 1960. There are over a dozen books written about him, two casebooks on *Native Son*, a children's book, and a critical pamphlet in a writer's series.

Appendix

◆African American Recipients of Selected Awards
◆African American Federal Judges
◆African American Olympic Medalists

◆ AFRICAN AMERICAN RECIPIENTS OF SELECTED AWARDS

ACADEMY AWARD OF MERIT (OSCAR)—ACADEMY OF MOTION PICTURE ARTS AND SCIENCES

Best Performance by an Actor in a Leading Role

1963 Sidney Poitier, in *Lilies of the Field*

Best Performance by an Actor in a Supporting Role

1982 Louis Gossett, Jr., in *An Officer and a Gentleman*

1989 Denzel Washington, in *Glory*

1996 Cuba Gooding, Jr., in *Jerry Maquire*

Best Performance by an Actress in a Supporting Role

1939 Hattie McDaniel, in *Gone with the Wind*

1990 Whoopi Goldberg, in *Ghost*

Best Original Score

1984 Prince, for *Purple Rain*

1986 Herbie Hancock, for *'Round Midnight*

AMERICAN ACADEMY AND INSTITUTE OF ARTS AND LETTERS AWARD

Art

1946 Richmond Barthé

1966 Romare Bearden

1971 Norman Lewis

Literature

1946 Gwendolyn Brooks; Langston Hughes

1956 James Baldwin

1961 John A. Williams

1970 James A. McPherson

1971 Charles Gordone

1972 Michael S. Harper

1974 Henry Van Dyke

1978 Lerone Bennett, Jr.; Toni Morrison

1985 John Williams

1987 Ernest J. Gaines

1992 August Wilson

Music

1974 Olly Wilson

1981 George Walker

1988 Hale Smith

1991 Tania J. Leon

AUSTRALIAN OPEN

Men's Singles

1970 Arthur Ashe

Men's Doubles

1977 Arthur Ashe

Women's Doubles

1957 Althea Gibson, with Darlene Hard

CONGRESSIONAL GOLD MEDAL

1978 Marian Anderson

1990 Jesse Owens

1994 Colin L. Powell, Jr.

1998 Little Rock Nine: Jean Brown Trickey, Carlotta Walls LaNier, Melba Patillo Beals, Terrence Roberts, Gloria Ray Karlmark, Thelma Mothershed Wair, Ernest Green, Elizabeth Eckford, and Jefferson Thomas

1999 Rosa Louise McCauley Parks

EMMY AWARD—ACADEMY OF TELEVISION ARTS AND SCIENCES

Primetime Awards

Outstanding Lead Actor in a Drama Series

1966 Bill Cosby, in "I Spy" (NBC)

1967 Bill Cosby, in "I Spy" (NBC)

1968 Bill Cosby, in "I Spy" (NBC)

1991 James Earl Jones, in "Gabriel's Fire" (ABC)

1998 Andre Braugher, in "Homicide: Life on the Street" (NBC)

Outstanding Lead Actor in a Comedy, Variety, or Music Series

1959 Harry Belafonte, in "Tonight with Belafonte"

1985 Robert Guillaume, in "Benson" (ABC)

Outstanding Lead Actress in a Comedy, Variety, or Music Series

1981 Isabel Sanford, in "The Jeffersons" (CBS)

Outstanding Lead Actress in a Comedy or Drama Special

1974 Cicely Tyson, in "The Autobiography of Miss Jane Pittman" (CBS)

Outstanding Lead Actress in a Miniseries or Special

1991 Lynn Whitfield, in "The Josephine Baker Story" (HBO)

1997 Alfre Woodard, in "Miss Evers' Boys" (HBO)

Outstanding Supporting Actor in a Comedy, Variety, or Music Series

1979 Robert Guillaume, in "Soap" (ABC)

Outstanding Supporting Actor in a Miniseries or Special

1991 James Earl Jones, in "Heatwave" (TNT)

Outstanding Supporting Actress in a Drama Series

1984 Alfre Woodard, in "Doris in Wonderland" episode of "Hill Street Blues" (NBC)

1991 Madge Sinclair, in "Gabriel's Fire" (ABC)

1992 Mary Alice, in "I'll Fly Away" (NBC)

Outstanding Supporting Actress in a Comedy, Variety, or Music Series

1987 Jackee Harry, in "227"

Outstanding Supporting Actress in a Miniseries or Special

1991 Ruby Dee, in "Decoration Day," *Hallmark Hall of Fame* (NBC)

Outstanding Directing in a Drama Series

1986 Georg Stanford Brown, in "Parting Shots" episode of "Cagney & Lacey" (ABC)

1990 Thomas Carter, in "Promises to Keep" episode of "Equal Justice" (ABC)

1991 Thomas Carter, in "In Confidence" episode of "Equal Justice" (ABC)

1992 Eric Laneuville, in "All God's Children" episode of "I'll Fly Away" (NBC)

Outstanding Producing in a Miniseries or Special

1989 Suzanne de Passe, in "Lonesome Dove"

Outstanding Producing in a Variety, Music, or Comedy Special

1984 Suzanne de Passe, in "Motown 25: Yesterday, Today and Forever"

1985 Suzanne de Passe, in "Motown at the Apollo"

Outstanding Variety, Music, or Comedy Special

1997 "Chris Rock: Bring on the Pain" (HBO)

Outstanding Achievement in Music Composition

1971 Ray Charles, in "The First Nine Months Are the Hardest" (NBC)

1972 Ray Charles, in "The Funny Side of Marriage" (NBC)

Outstanding Achievement in Music Composition for a Series

1977 Quincy Jones and Gerald Fried, in "Roots" (ABC)

Outstanding Choreography

1981 Debbie Allen, for "Come One, Come All" episode of "Fame"

1982 Debbie Allen, for "Class Act" episode of "Fame"

1989 Debbie Allen, for "Motown 30: What's Goin' On!"

Daytime Awards

Outstanding Talk Show

1987 "The Oprah Winfrey Show"

1988 "The Oprah Winfrey Show"

1989 "The Oprah Winfrey Show"

1991 "The Oprah Winfrey Show"

1992 "The Oprah Winfrey Show"

1994 "The Oprah Winfrey Show"

1995 "The Oprah Winfrey Show"

1996 "The Oprah Winfrey Show"

1997 "The Oprah Winfrey Show"

Outstanding Talk Show Host

1987 Oprah Winfrey, "The Oprah Winfrey Show"

1991 Oprah Winfrey, "The Oprah Winfrey Show"

1992 Oprah Winfrey, "The Oprah Winfrey Show"

1993 Oprah Winfrey, "The Oprah Winfrey Show"

1994 Oprah Winfrey, "The Oprah Winfrey Show"

1995 Oprah Winfrey, "The Oprah Winfrey Show"

1996 Montel Williams, "The Montel Williams Show"

Sports Awards

Outstanding Sports Personality/Studio Host

1998 James Brown (Fox Sports Network)

Outstanding Sports Event Analyst

1997 Joe Morgan (ESPN/NBC)

Outstanding Sports Journalism

1995 "Broken Promises" and "Pros and Cons" episodes of "Real Sports with Bryant Gumbel"

1998 "Diamond Buck$" and "Winning at All Costs" episodes of "Real Sports with Bryant Gumbel"

Hall of Fame Award

1992 Bill Cosby

1994 Oprah Winfrey

FRENCH OPEN

Men's Doubles

1971 Arthur Ashe

Women's Singles

1956 Althea Gibson

Women's Doubles

1956 Althea Gibson

1999 Venus and Serena Williams

GRAMMY AWARDS—NATIONAL ACADEMY OF RECORDING ARTS AND SCIENCES

Record of the Year

1963 *I Can't Stop Loving You*, by Count Basie

1967 *Up, Up and Away*, by 5th Dimension

1969 *Aquarius/Let the Sun Shine In*, by 5th Dimension

1972 *The First Time Ever I Saw Your Face*, by Roberta Flack

1973 *Killing Me Softly with His Song*, by Roberta Flack

1976 *This Masquerade*, by George Benson

1983 *Beat It*, by Michael Jackson

1984 *What's Love Got To Do with It?*, by Tina Turner

1985 *We Are the World*, by USA For Africa; produced by Quincy Jones

1988 *Don't Worry, Be Happy*, by Bobby McFerrin

1991 *Unforgettable*, by Natalie Cole with Nat "King" Cole

1993 *I Will Always Love You*, by Whitney Houston

1995 *Kiss From a Rose* by Seal

Album of the Year

1973 *Innervisions*, by Stevie Wonder; produced by Stevie Wonder

1974 *Fulfillingness' First Finale*, by Stevie Wonder; produced by Stevie Wonder

1976 *Songs in the Key of Life*, by Stevie Wonder; produced by Stevie Wonder

1983 *Thriller*, by Michael Jackson; produced by Quincy Jones

1984 *Can't Slow Down*, by Lionel Richie; produced by Lionel Richie and James Anthony Carmichael

1990 *Back on the Block*, by Quincy Jones; produced by Quincy Jones

1991 *Unforgettable*, by Natalie Cole

1999 *The Miseducation of Lauryn Hill*, by Lauryn Hill; produced by Lauryn Hill

HEISMAN MEMORIAL TROPHY—DOWNTOWN ATHLETIC CLUB OF NEW YORK CITY, INC.

1961 Ernie Davis, Syracuse University, TB

1965 Michael Garrett, University of Southern California, TB

1968 O. J. Simpson, University of Southern California, TB

1972 Johnny Rodgers, University of Nebraska, FL

1974 Archie Griffin, University of Ohio State, HB

1975 Archie Griffin, University of Ohio State, HB

1976 Anthony (Tony) Dorsett, University of Pittsburgh, HB

1977 Earl Campbell, University of Texas, FB

1978 Billy Sims, University of Oklahoma, HB

1979 Charles White, University of Southern California, TB

1980 George Rogers, University of South Carolina, HB

1981 Marcus Allen, University of Southern California, TB

1982 Herschel Walker, University of Georgia, HB

1983 Mike Rozier, University of Nebraska, TB

1985 Bo Jackson, Auburn University, TB

1987 Tim Brown, University of Notre Dame, FL

1988 Barry Sanders, Oklahoma State University, HB

1989 Andre Ware, University of Houston, QB

1991 Desmond Howard, University of Michigan, WR

1993 Charlie Ward, Florida State University, QB

1994 Rashaan Salaam, Colorado, RB

1995 Eddie George, Ohio State, RB

1997 Charles Woodson, University of Michigan, DB/R

1998 Ricky Williams, University of Texas at Austin, TB

CLARENCE L. HOLTE LITERARY PRIZE (BIANNUAL)—CO-SPONSORED BY THE PHELPS-STOKES FUND AND THE SCHOMBURG CENTER FOR RESEARCH IN BLACK CULTURE OF THE NEW YORK PUBLIC LIBRARY

1979 Chancellor Williams, for *The Destruction of Black Civilization: Great Issues of a Race from 4500 B.C. to 2000 A.D.*

1981 Ivan Van Sertima, for *They Came Before Columbus*

1983 Vincent Harding, for *There Is a River: The Black Struggle for Freedom in America*

1985 No award

1986 John Hope Franklin, for *George Washington Williams: A Biography*

1988 Arnold Rampersad, for *The Life of Langston Hughes, Volume 1 (1902-1941): I, Too, Sing America*

KENNEDY CENTER HONORS—JOHN F. KENNEDY CENTER FOR THE PERFORMING ARTS

1978 Marian Anderson

1979 Ella Fitzgerald

1980 Leontyne Price

1981 William "Count" Basie

1983 Katherine Dunham

1984 Lena Horne

1986 Ray Charles

1987 Sammy Davis, Jr.

1988 Alvin Ailey

1989 Harry Belafonte

1990 Dizzy Gillespie

1991 Fayard and Harold Nicholas

1992 Lionel Hampton

1993 Arthur Mitchell; Marion Williams

1994 Aretha Franklin

1995 B. B. King; Sidney Poitier

1996 Benny Carter

1997 Jessye Norman

1998 Bill Cosby

MARTIN LUTHER KING, JR. NONVIOLENT PEACE PRIZE—MARTIN LUTHER KING, JR. CENTER FOR NONVIOLENT SOCIAL CHANGE, INC.

1973 Andrew Young

1974 Cesar Chavez

1975 John Lewis

1976 Randolph Blackwell

1977 Benjamin E. Mays

1978 Kenneth D. Kaunda; Stanley Levison

1979 Jimmy Carter

1980 Rosa Parks

1981 Ivan Allen, Jr.

1982 Harry Belafonte

1983 Sir Richard Attenborough; Martin Luther King, Sr.

1984 No award

1985 No award

1986 Bishop Desmond Tutu

1987 Corazon Aquino

1988 No award

1989 No award

1990 Mikhail Gorbachev

1991 No award

1992 No award

1993 Jesse Jackson

MISS AMERICA—MISS AMERICA ORGANIZATION

1984 Vanessa Williams (New York); Suzette Charles (New Jersey)

1990 Debbye Turner (Missouri)

MISS BLACK AMERICA—J. MORRIS ANDERSON PRODUCTION COMPANY

1968 Sandy Willliams (Pennsylvania)

1969 G. O. Smith (New York)

1970 Stephanie Clark (District of Columbia)

1971 Joyce Warner (Florida)

1972 Linda Barney (New Jersey)

1973 Arnice Russell (New York)

1974 Von Gretchen Sheppard (California)

1975 Helen Ford (Mississippi)

1976 Twanna Kilgore (District of Columbia)

1977 Claire Ford (Tennessee)

1978 Lydia Jackson (New Jersey)

1979 Veretta Shankle (Mississippi)

1980 Sharon Wright (Illinois)

1981 Pamela Jenks (Massachusetts)

1982 Phyllis Tucker (Florida)

1983 Sonia Robinson (Wisconsin)

1984 Lydia Garrett (South Carolina)

1985 Amina Fakir (Michigan)

1986 Rachel Oliver (Massachusetts)

1987 Leila McBride (Colorado)

1989 Paula Swynn (District of Columbia)

1990 Rosie Jones (Connecticut)

1991 Sharmelle Sullivan (Indiana)

1992 Marilyn DeShields

1993 Pilar Ginger Fort

1994 Karen Wallace

1995 Asheera Ahmad

MISS USA—MADISON SQUARE GARDEN TELEVISION PRODUCTIONS

1990 Carole Gist (Michigan)

1992 Shannon Marketic

1993 Kenya Moore (Michigan)

1994 Frances Louise "Lu" Parker

1995 Chelsi Smith (Texas)

1996 Ali Landry

MS. OLYMPIA WINNERS—INTERNATIONAL FEDERATION OF BODYBUILDERS, WOMEN'S BODYBUILDING CHAMPIONS

1983 Carla Dunlap

1990 Lenda Murray

1991 Lenda Murray

1992 Lenda Murray

1993 Lenda Murray

1994 Lenda Murray

1995 Lenda Murray

MR. OLYMPIA WINNERS—INTERNATIONAL FEDERATION OF BODYBUILDERS, MEN'S BODYBUILDING CHAMPIONS

1967 Sergio Oliva

1968 Sergio Oliva

1982 Chris Dickerson

1984 Lee Haney

1985 Lee Haney

1986 Lee Haney

1987 Lee Haney

1988 Lee Haney

1989 Lee Haney

1990 Lee Haney

1991 Lee Haney

1998 Ronnie Coleman

NATIONAL BASEBALL HALL OF FAME

1962 Jackie Robinson

1969 Roy Campanella

1971 Leroy R. "Satchel" Paige

1972 Josh Gibson; Walter "Buck" Leonard

1973 Roberto W. Clemente; Monte Irvin

1974 James T. "Cool Papa" Bell

1975 William "Judy" Johnson

1976 Oscar M. Charleston

1977 Ernest Banks; Martin Dihigo; John H. Lloyd

1979 Willie Mays

1981 Andrew "Rube" Foster; Robert T. Gibson

1982 Hank Aaron; Frank Robinson

1983 Juan A. Marichal

1985 Lou Brock

1986 Willie L. "Stretch" McCovey

1987 Ray Dandridge; Billy Williams

1988 Willie Stargell

1990 Joe Morgan

1991 Rod Carew; Ferguson Jenkins

1993 Reggie Jackson

1995 Leon Day

1996 Bill Foster

1997 Willie Wells

1998 Larry Doby

1999 Orlando Cepeda; Joe Williams

NATIONAL BASKETBALL HALL OF FAME

1972 Robert Douglass

1974 Bill Russell

1976 Elgin "The Big E" Baylor; Charles Cooper

1978 Wilt Chamberlain

1979 Oscar Robertson

1981 Clarence Gaines; Willis Reed

1983 Sam Jones

1984 Nate Thurmond

1986 Walt "Clyde" Frazier

1987 Wes Unseld

1988 William "Pop" Gates; K.C. Jones; Lenny Wilkins (player)

1989 Dave Bing; Elvin Hayes; Earl "The Pearl" Monroe

1990 Nate "Tiny" Archibald

1991 Lusia Harris-Stewart; Connie Hawkins; Bob Lanier

1992 Walt Bellamy; Julius "Dr. J" Erving; Calvin Murphy

1994 Kareem Abdul-Jabbar; Cheryl Miller

1995 George Gervin; David Thompson

1996 Alex English

1998 Marques Haynes, Lenny Wilkins (coach)

1999 Wayne Embry, John Thompson

NATIONAL BOOK AWARD—NATIONAL BOOK FOUNDATION

1953 Ralph Ellison, for *Invisible Man*, Fiction

1969 Winthrop D. Jordan, for *White over Black: American Attitudes toward the Negro, 1550-1812*, History and Biography

1983 Gloria Naylor, for *The Women of Brewster Place*, First Novel; Joyce Carol Thomas, for *Marked By Fire*, Children's Literature; Alice Walker, for *The Color Purple*, Fiction

1990 Charles Johnson, for *Middle Passage*, Fiction

1991 Melissa Fay Green, for *Praying for Sheetrock*, Nonfiction

1992 Edward P. Jones, for *Lost in the City*, Fiction

NATIONAL MEDAL OF ARTS—NATIONAL ENDOWMENT FOR THE ARTS

1985 Ralph Ellison (writer); Leontyne Price (singer)

1986 Marian Anderson (singer)

1987 Romare Bearden (artist); Ella Fitzgerald (singer)

1988 Gordon Parks (photographer and film director)

1989 Katherine Dunham (choreographer); Dizzy Gillespie (musician)

1990 Riley "B. B." King (musician)

1991 James Earl Jones (actor); Billy Taylor (musician)

1994 Harry Belafonte (singer)

1995 Gwendolyn Brooks (poet); Ossie Davis (actor); Ruby Dee (actress)

1996 The Harlem Boys Choir (chorale); Lionel Hampton (musician)

1997 Betty Carter (singer)

1998 Fats Domino (singer)

NATIONAL SOCIETY OF ARTS AND LETTERS GOLD MEDAL OF MERIT AWARD

1982 Andre Watts (music)

NATIONAL TRACK AND FIELD HALL OF FAME—THE ATHLETICS CONGRESS OF THE USA

1974 Ralph Boston; Lee Calhoun; Harrison Dillard; Rafer Johnson; Jesse Owens; Wilma Rudolph; Malvin Whitfield

1975 Ralph Metcalfe

1976 Robert Hayes; Hayes Jones

1977 Robert Beamon; Andrew W. Stanfield

1978 Tommie Smith; John Woodruff

1979 Jim Hines; William DeHart Hubbard

1980 Wyomia Tyus

1981 Willye White

1982 Willie Davenport; Eddie Tolan

1983 Lee Evans

1984 Madeline Manning Mims

1986 Henry Barney Ewell

1988 Gregory Bell

1989 Milt Campbell; Edward Temple

1990 Charles Dumas

1994 Cornelius Johnson; Edwin Moses

1995 Valerie Brisco; Florence Griffith Joyner

1997 Evelyn Ashford; Henry Carr; Renaldo Nehemiah

NEW YORK DRAMA CRITICS' CIRCLE AWARD

Best American Play

1959 *A Raisin in the Sun*, by Lorraine Hansberry

1975 *The Taking of Miss Janie*, by Ed Bullins

1982 *A Soldier's Play*, by Charles Fuller

1996 *Seven Guitars*, by August Wilson

Best New Play

1985 *Ma Rainey's Black Bottom*, by August Wilson

1987 *Fences*, by August Wilson

1988 *Joe Turner's Come and Gone*, by August Wilson

1990 *The Piano Lesson*, by August Wilson

NOBEL PEACE PRIZE—NOBEL FOUNDATION

1950 Ralph J. Bunche

1964 Martin Luther King, Jr.

NOBEL PRIZE IN LITERATURE—NOBEL FOUNDATION

1993 Toni Morrison

PRESIDENTIAL MEDAL OF FREEDOM—UNITED STATES EXECUTIVE OFFICE OF THE PRESIDENT

1963 Marian Anderson; Ralph J. Bunche

1964 John L. Lewis; Leontyne Price; A. Philip Randolph

1969 Edward Kennedy "Duke" Ellington; Ralph Ellison; Roy Wilkins; Whitney M. Young, Jr.

1976 Jesse Owens

1977 Martin Luther King, Jr. (posthumously)

1980 Clarence Mitchell

1981 James H. "Eubie" Blake; Andrew Young

1983 James Cheek; Mabel Mercer

1984 Jack Roosevelt "Jackie" Robinson (posthumously)

1985 William "Count" Basie (posthumously); Jerome "Brud" Holland (posthumously)

1987 Frederick Douglass Patterson

1988 Pearl Bailey

1991 Colin L. Powell

1992 Ella Fitzgerald

1993 Arthur Ashe, Jr. (posthumously); Thurgood Marshall (posthumously); Colin L. Powell

1994 Dorothy Height; Barbara Jordan

1995 William Thaddeus Coleman, Jr.; John Hope Franklin; A. Leon Higginbotham, Jr.

1996 John H. Johnson; Rosa Parks

1998 James Farmer

PROFESSIONAL FOOTBALL HALL OF FAME

1967 Emlen Tunnell

1968 Marion Motley

1969 Fletcher "Joe" Perry

1971 Jim Brown

1972 Ollie Matson

1973 Jim Parker

1974 Richard "Night Train" Lane

1975 Roosevelt Brown; Leonard "Lenny" Moore

1976 Leonard "Len" Ford

1977 Gale Sayers; Bill Willis

1980 Herb Adderley; David "Deacon" Jones

1981 Willie Davis

1983 Bobby Bell; Bobby Mitchell; Paul Warfield

1984 Willie Brown; Charley Taylor

1985 O. J. Simpson

1986 Ken Houston; Willie Lanier

1987 Joe Greene; John Henry Johnson; Gene Upshaw

1988 Alan Page

1989 Mel Blount; Art Shell; Willie Wood

1990 Junious "Buck" Buchanan; Franco Harris

1991 Earl Campbell

1992 Lem Barney; John Mackey

1993 Larry Little; Walter Payton

1994 Tony Dorsett; Leroy Kelly

1995 Lee Roy Selmon

1996 Charlie Joiner; Mel Renfro

1997 Mike Haynes

1998 Mike Singletary; Dwight Stephenson

1999 Eric Dickerson; Lawrence Taylor

PULITZER PRIZE—COLUMBIA UNIVERSITY GRADUATE SCHOOL OF JOURNALISM

Biography or Autobiography

1994 *W. E. B. Du Bois: Biography of a Race, 1968–1919*, by David Levering Lewis

Journalism: Commentary

1996 E. R. Shipp

Journalism: Feature Writing

1999 Angelo B. Henderson

Letters: Drama

1970 *No Place To Be Somebody*, by Charles Gordone

1982 *A Soldier's Play*, by Charles Fuller

1987 *Fences*, by August Wilson

1990 *The Piano Lesson*, by August Wilson

Letters: Fiction

1978 *Elbow Room*, by James Alan McPherson

1983 *The Color Purple*, by Alice Walker

1988 *Beloved*, by Toni Morrison

Letters: Poetry

1950 *Annie Allen*, by Gwendolyn Brooks

1987 *Thomas and Beulah*, by Rita Dove

Letters: Special Awards and Citations

1977 Alexander Palmer Haley, for *Roots*

Music: Special Awards and Citations

1976 Scott Joplin

1996 George Walker

1997 Wynton Marsalis

1999 Edward Kennedy "Duke" Ellington (posthmously)

ROCK AND ROLL HALL OF FAME

1986 Chuck Berry; James Brown; Ray Charles; Sam Cooks; Fats Domino; Little Richard; Robert Johnson; Jimmy Yancey

1987 The Coasters; Bo Diddley; Aretha Franklin; Marvin Gaye; Louis Jordan; B.B. King; Clyde McPhalter; Smokey Robinson; Big Joe Turner; T-Bone Walker; Muddy Waters; Jackie Wilson

1988 The Drifters; Barry Gordy, Jr.; The Supremes

1989 The Ink Spots; Otis Redding; Bessie Smith; The Soul Stirrers; The Temptations; Stevie Wonder

1990 Louis Armstrong; Hank Ballard; Charlie Christian; The Four Tops; Holland, Dozier, and Holland; The Platters; Ma Rainey

1991 La Vern Baker; John Lee Hooker; Howlin' Wolf; The Impressions; Wilson Pickett; Jimmy Reed; Ike and Tina Turner

1992 Blue Brand, Booker T. and the M.G.'s; Jimi Hendrix; Isley Brothers; Elmore James; Doc Pomus; Professor Longhair; Sam and Dave

1993 Ruth Brown; Etta James; Frankie Lymon and the Teenagers; Sly and the Family Stone; Dinah Washington

1994 Willie Dixon; Bob Marley; Johnny Otis

1995 Al Green; Martha and the Vandellas; The Orioles

1996 Little Willie John; Gladys Knight and the Pips; The Shirelles

1997 Mahalia Jackson; The Jackson Five; Parliament

1998 Jelly Roll Morton; Lloyd Price

1999 Charles Brown; Curtis Mayfield; The Staple Singers

SPRINGARN MEDAL—NATIONAL ASSOCIATION FOR THE ADVANCEMENT OF COLORED PEOPLE

1915 Ernest E. Just—head of the department of physiology at Howard University Medical School.

1916 Charles Young—major in the United States Army.

1917 Harry T. Burleigh—composer, pianist, singer.

1918 William Stanley Braithwaite—poet, literary critic, editor.

1919 Archibald H. Grimké—former U.S. Consul in Santo Domingo, president of the American Negro Academy, author, president of the District of Columbia branch of the NAACP.

1920 William Edward Burghardt DuBois—author, editor, organizer of the first Pan-African Congress.

1921 Charles S. Gilpin—actor.

1922 Mary B. Talbert—former president of the National Association of Colored Women.

1923 George Washington Carver—head of research and director of the experiment station at Tuskegee Institute.

1924 Roland Hayes—singer.

1925 James Weldon Johnson—former United States Consul in Venezuela and Nicaragua, author, editor, poet; secretary of the NAACP.

1926 Carter G. Woodson—editor, historian; founder of the Association for the Study of Negro Life and History.

1927 Anthony Overton—businessman; president of the Victory Life Insurance Company (the first African American organization permitted to do business under the rigid requirements of the State of New York).

1928 Charles W. Chesnutt—author.

1929 Mordecai Wyatt Johnson—the first African American president of Howard University.

1930 Henry A. Hunt—principal of Fort Valley High and Industrial School, Fort Valley, Georgia.

1931 Richard Berry Harrison—actor.

1932 Robert Russa Moton—principal of Tuskegee Institute.

1933 Max Yergan—secretary of the YMCA in South Africa.

1934 William Taylor Burwell Williams—dean of Tuskegee Institute.

1935 Mary McLeod Bethune—founder and president of Bethune Cookman College.

1936 John Hope—president of Atlanta University.

1937 Walter White—executive secretary of the NAACP.

1939 Marian Anderson—singer.

1940 Louis T. Wright—surgeon.

1941 Richard Wright—author.

1942 A. Philip Randolph—labor leader, international president of the Brotherhood of Sleeping Car Porters.

1943 William H. Hastie—jurist, educator.

1944 Charles Drew—scientist.

1945 Paul Robeson—singer, actor.

1946 Thurgood Marshall—special counsel of the NAACP

1947 Percy Julian—research chemist.

1948 Channing H. Tobias—minister, educator.

1949 Ralph J. Bunche—international civil servant, acting United Nations mediator in Palestine.

1950 Charles Hamilton Houston—chairman of the NAACP Legal Committee.

1951 Mabel Keaton Staupers—leader of the National Association of Colored Graduate Nurses.

1952 Harry T. Moore—state leader of the Florida NAACP.

1953 Paul R. Williams—architect.

1954 Theodore K. Lawless—physician, educator, philanthropist.

1955 Carl Murphy—editor, publisher, civic leader.

1956 Jack Roosevelt Robinson—athlete.

1957 Martin Luther King, Jr.—minister, civil rights leader.

1958 Daisy Bates and the Little Rock Nine—for their pioneer role in upholding the basic ideals of American democracy in the face of continuing harassment and constant threats of bodily injury.

1959 Edward Kennedy "Duke" Ellington—composer, musician, orchestra leader.

1960 Langston Hughes—poet, author, playwright.

1961 Kenneth B. Clark—professor of psychology at the City College of the City University of New York, founder and director of the Northside Center for Child Development, prime mobilizer of the resources of modern psychology in the attack upon racial segregation.

1962 Robert C. Weaver—administrator of the Housing and Home Finance Agency.

1963 Medgar Wiley Evers—NAACP field secretary for Mississippi, World War II veteran.

1964 Roy Wilkins—executive director of the NAACP.

1965 Leontyne Price—singer.

1966 John H. Johnson—founder and president of the Johnson Publishing Company.

1967 Edward W. Brooke III—the first African American to win popular election to the United States Senate.

1968 Sammy Davis, Jr.—performer, civil rights activist.

1969 Clarence M. Mitchell, Jr.—director of the Washington Bureau of the NAACP, civil rights activist.

1970 Jacob Lawrence—artist, teacher, humanitarian.

1971 Leon H. Sullivan—minister.

1972 Gordon Alexander Buchanan Parks—writer, photographer, filmmaker.

1973 Wilson C. Riles—educator.

1974 Damon Keith—jurist.

1975 Hank Aaron—athlete.

1976 Alvin Ailey—dancer, choreographer, artistic director.

1977 Alexander Palmer Haley—author, biographer, lecturer.

1978 Andrew Young—United States Ambassador to the United Nations, diplomat, cabinet member, civil rights activist, minister.

1979 Rosa Parks—community activist.

1980 Rayford W. Logan—educator, historian, author.

1981 Coleman A. Young—mayor of the City of Detroit, public servant, labor leader, civil rights activist.

1982 Benjamin E. Mays—educator, theologian, humanitarian).

1983 Lena Horne—performer, humanitarian.

1984 Tom Bradley—government executive, public servant, humanitarian.

1985 William H. "Bill" Cosby—comedian, actor, educator, humanitarian.

1986 Benjamin Lawson Hooks—executive director of the NAACP.

1987 Percy Ellis Sutton—public servant, businessman, community leader.

1988 Frederick Douglass Patterson—doctor of veterinary medicine, educator, humanitarian, founder of the United Negro College Fund.

1989 Jesse Jackson—minister, political leader, civil rights activist.

1990 L. Douglas Wilder—governor of Virginia.

1991 Colin L. Powell—general in the United States Army, chairman of the Joint Chiefs of Staff.

1992 Barbara C. Jordan—educator, former congresswoman.

1993 Dorothy L. Height—president of the National Council of Negro Women.

1994 Maya Angelou—poet, author, performing artist.

1995 John Hope Franklin—historian.

1996 A. Leon Higginbotham, Jr.—jurist, judge

1997 Carl T. Rowan—journalist.

1998 Myrlie Evers-Williams—former chair, board of directors, NAACP

1999 Earl G. Graves, publisher and media executive

SULLIVAN AWARD—AMATEUR ATHLETIC UNION

1961 Wilma Rudolph

1981 Carl Lewis

1983 Edwin Moses

1986 Jackie Joyner-Kersee

1988 Florence Griffith-Joyner

1991 Mike Powell

1993 Charlie Ward

1996 Michael Johnson

1998 Chamique Holdsclaw

TONY (ANTOINETTE PERRY) AWARD—LEAGUE OF AMERICAN THEATERS AND PRODUCERS

Actor (Dramatic)

1969 James Earl Jones, for *The Great White Hope*

1975 John Kani, for *Sizwe Banzi*; Winston Ntshona, for *The Island*

1987 James Earl Jones, for *Fences*

Supporting or Featured Actor (Dramatic)

1982 Zakes Mokae, for *Master Harold. . . and the Boys*

1992 Larry Fishburne, for *Two Trains Running*

1994 Jeffrey Wright, for *Angels in America*

1996 Ruben Santiago-Hudson, for *Seven Guitars*

Actor (Musical)

1970 Cleavon Little, for *Purlie*

1973 Ben Vereen, for *Pippin*

1982 Ben Harvey, for *Dreamgirls*

1992 Gregory Hines, for *Jelly's Last Jam*

Supporting or Featured Actor (Musical)

1954 Harry Belafonte, for *John Murray Anderson's Almanac*

1975 Ted Rose, for *The Wiz*

1981 Hinton Battle, for *Sophisticated Ladies*

1982 Cleavant Derricks, for *Dreamgirls*

1983 Charles "Honi" Coles, for *My One and Only*

1984 Hinton Battle, for *The Tap Dance Kid*

1991 Hinton Battle, for *Miss Saigon*

1997 Chuck Cooper, for *The Life*

Supporting or Featured Actress (Dramatic)

1977 Trazana Beverley, for *For Colored Girls Who Have Considered Suicide/When the Rainbow Is Enuf*

1987 Mary Alice, for *Fences*

1988 L. Scott Caldwell, for *Joe Turner's Come and Gone*

1997 Lynne Thigpen, for *An American Daughter*

Actress (Musical)

1962 Diahann Carroll, for *No Strings*

1968 Leslie Uggams, for *Hallelujah, Baby*

1974 Virginia Capers, for *Raisin*

1982 Jennifer Holliday, for *Dreamgirls*

1989 Ruth Brown, for *Black and Blue*

1996 Audra McDonald, for *Master Class*

Supporting or Featured Actress (Musical)

1950 Juanita Hall, for *South Pacific*

1968 Lillian Hayman, for *Halleluja, Baby*

1970 Melba Moore, for *Purlie*

1975 Dee Dee Bridgewater, for *The Wiz*

1977 Delores Hall, for *Your Arms's Too Short To Box with God*

1978 Nell Carter, for *Ain't Misbehavin*

1992 Tonya Pinkins, for *Jelly's Last Jam*

1994 Audra McDonald, for *Carousel*

1996 Ann Duquesnay, for *Bring in 'Da Noise, Bring in 'Da Funk*

1997 Lillias White, for *The Life*

Play

1974 *The River Niger*, by Joseph A. Walker

1987 *Fences*, by August Wilson

UNITED STATES MEDAL OF HONOR

Civil War

Army

William H. Barnes, Private, Company C, 38th United States Colored Troops.

Powhatan Beaty, First Sergeant, Company G, 5th United States Colored Troops.

James H. Bronson, First Sergeant, Company D, 5th United States Colored Troops.

William H. Carney, Sergeant, Company C, 54th Massachusetts Infantry, United States Colored Troops.

Decatur Dorsey, Sergeant, Company B, 39th United States Colored Troops.

Christian A. Fleetwood, Sergeant Major, 4th United States Colored Troops.

James Gardiner, Private, Company 1, 36th United States Colored Troops.

James H. Harris, Sergeant, Company B, 38th United States Colored Troops.

Thomas R. Hawkins, Sergeant Major, 6th United States Colored Troops.

Alfred B. Hilton, Sergeant, Company H, 4th United States Colored Troops.

Milton M. Holland, Sergeant, 5th United States Colored Troops.

Alexander Kelly, First Sergeant, Company F, 6th United States Colored Troops.

Robert Pinn, First Sergeant, Company I, 5th United States Colored Troops.

Edward Radcliff, First Sergeant, Company C, 38th United States Colored Troops.

Charles Veal, Private, Company D, 4th United States Colored Troops.

Navy

Aaron Anderson, Landsman, *USS Wyandank.*

Robert Blake, Powder Boy, *USS Marblehead.*

William H. Brown, Landsman, *USS Brooklyn.*

Wilson Brown, *USS Hartford.*

John Lawson, Landsman, *USS Hartford.*

James Mifflin, Engineer's Cook, *USS Brooklyn.*

Joachim Pease, Seaman, *USS Kearsarge.*

Interim Period

Navy

Daniel Atkins, Ship's Cook, First Class, *USS Cushing.*

John Davis, Seaman, *USS Trenton.*

Alphonse Girandy, Seaman, *USS Tetrel.*

John Johnson, Seaman, *USS Kansas.*

William Johnson, Cooper, *USS Adams.*

Joseph B. Noil, Seaman, *USS Powhatan.*

John Smith, Seaman, *USS Shenandoah.*

Robert Sweeney, Seaman, *USS Kearsage, USS Jamestown.*

Western Campaigns

Army

Thomas Boyne, Sergeant, Troop C, 9th United States Cavalry.

Benjamin Brown, Sergeant, Company C, 24th United States Infantry.

John Denny, Sergeant, Troop C, 9th United States Cavalry.

Pompey Factor, Seminole Negro Indian Scouts.

Clinton Greaves, Corporal, Troop C, 9th United States Cavalry.

Henry Johnson, Sergeant, Troop D, 9th United States Cavalry.

George Jordan, Sergeant, Troop K, 9th United States Cavalry.

William McBreyar, Sergeant, Troop K, 10th United States Cavalry.

Isaiah Mays, Corporal, Company B, 24th United States Infantry.

Issac Payne, Private (Trumpeteer) Seminole Negro Indian Scouts.

Thomas Shaw, Sergeant, Troop K, 9th United States Cavalry.

Emanuel Stance, Sergeant, Troop F, 9th United States Cavalry.

Augustus Walley, Private, Troop 1, 9th United States Cavalry.

John Ward, Sergeant, Seminole Negro Indian Scouts.

Moses Williams, First Sergeant, Troop 1, 9th United States Cavalry.

William O. Wilson, Corporal, Troop 1, 9th United States Cavalry.

Brent Woods, Sergeant, Troop B, 9th United States Cavalry.

Spanish-American War

Army

Edward L. Baker, Jr., Sergeant Major, 10th United States Cavalry.

Dennis Bell, Private, Troop H, 10th United States Cavalry.

Fitz Lee, Private, Troop M, 10th United States Cavalry.

William H. Thompkins, Private, Troop G, 10th United States Cavalry.

George H. Wanton, Sergeant, Troop M, 10th United States Cavalry.

Navy

Joseph B. Noil, Non-combatant Service, *USS Powhatan*.

Robert Penn, Fireman, First Class, *USS Iowa*.

World War I

Army

Freddie Stowers, Corporal, Company C, 371st Infantry Regiment, 93rd Infantry Division.

World War II

Army

Vernon Baker, First Lieutenant.

Edward A. Carter, Jr., Staff Sergeant.

John R. Fox, First Lieutenant.

Willy F. James, Jr., Private First Class.

Ruben Rivers, Staff Sergeant.

Charles L. Thomas, First Lieutenant.

George Watson, Private.

Korean War

Army

Cornelius H. Charlton, Sergeant, 24th Infantry Regiment, 25th Division.

William Thompson, Private, 24th Infantry Regiment, 25th Division.

Vietnam War

Army

Webster Anderson, Sergeant, Battery A, 2nd Battalion, 320th Artillery, 101st Airborne Division.

Eugene Ashley, Jr., Sergeant, Company C, 5th Special Forces Group (Airborne), 1st Special Forces.

William M. Bryant, Sergeant First Class, Company A, 5th Special Forces Group, 1st Special Forces.

Lawrence Joel, Specialist Sixth Class, Headquarters and Headquarters Company, 1st Battalion, 173d Airborne Brigade.

Dwight H. Johnson, Specialist Fifth Class, Company B, 1st Battalion, 69th Armor, 4th Infantry Division.

Garfield M. Langhorn, Private First Class, Troop C, 7th Squadron, 17th Cavalry, 1st Aviation Brigade.

Matthew Leonard, Platoon Sergeant, Company B, 1st Battalion, 16th Infantry, 1st Infantry Division.

Donald R. Long, Sergeant, Troop C, 1st Squadron, 4th Cavalry, 1st Infantry Division.

Milton L. Olive III, Private First Class, Company B, 2nd Battalion 503d Infantry, 173d Airborne Brigade.

Riley L. Pitts, Captain, Company C, 2nd Battalion, 27th Infantry, 25th Infantry Division.

Charles C. Rogers, Lieutenant Colonel, 1st Battalion, 5th Infantry, 1st Infantry Division.

Rupert L. Sargent, First Lieutenant, Company B, 4th Battalion, 9th Infantry, 25th Infantry Division.

Clarence E. Sasser, Specialist 5th Class, Headquarters Company, 3rd Battalion, 60th Infantry, 90th Infantry Division.

Clifford C. Sims, Staff Sergeant, Company D, 2nd Battalion, 501st Infantry, 101st Airborne Division.

John E. Warren, Jr., First Lieutenant, Company C, 2nd Battalion, 22d Infantry, 25th Infantry Division.

Marines

James A. Anderson, Jr. Private First Class, 2nd Platoon, Company F, 2nd Battalion, 3rd Marine Division.

Oscar P. Austin, Private First Class, Company E, 7th Marines, 1st Marine Division.

Rodney M. Davis, Company B, First Battalion, 5th Marines, 1st Marine Division.

Robert H. Jenkins, Jr., Private First Class, 3rd Reconnaissance Battalion, 3rd Marine Division.

Ralph H. Johnson, Private First Class, Company A, 1st Reconnaissance Battalion, 1st Marine Division.

UNITED STATES OPEN

Men's Singles

1968 Arthur Ashe

Women's Singles

1957 Althea Gibson

1958 Althea Gibson

Mixed Doubles

1957 Althea Gibson

UNITED STATES POET LAUREATE

1993 Rita Dove (served until 1995)

UNITED STATES POSTAL SERVICE STAMPS ON AFRICAN AMERICAN HISTORY

Louis Armstrong

Benjamin Banneker

William "Count" Basie

James Pierson Beckwourth

Mary McLeod Bethune

James Hubert "Eubie" Blake

Ralph Johnson Bunche

George Washington Carver

Nat "King" Cole

Bessie Coleman

John Coltrane

Allison Davis

Benjamin O. Davis, Sr.

Frederick Douglass

Charles Richard Drew

(W)illiam (E)dward (B)urghardt Du Bois

Jean Baptiste Pointe Du Sable

Paul Laurence Dunbar

Edward Kennedy "Duke" Ellington

Erroll Garner

(W)illiam (C)hristopher Handy

Coleman Hawkins

Matthew Alexander Henson

Billie Holiday

Mahalia Jackson

James Price Johnson

James Weldon Johnson

Robert Johnson

Scott Joplin

Percy Lavon Julian

Ernest Everett Just

Martin Luther King, Jr.

Joe Louis

Hudson William Ledbetter, "Leadbelly"

Roberta Martin

Jan E. Matzeliger

Clyde McPhatter

Charles Mingus

Thelonious Sphere Monk

Ferdinand "Jelly Roll" Morton

James Cleveland "Jesse" Owens

Charlie "Bird" Parker

Bill Pickett

Salem Poor

Gertrude "Ma" Rainey

(A)sa Philip Randolph

Otis Redding

John Roosevelt "Jackie" Robinson

James Andrew "Jimmy" Rushing

Bessie Smith

Henry Ossawa Tanner

Sonny Terry
Sister Rosetta Tharpe
Sojourner Truth
Harriet Tubman
Madame C. J. Walker
Clara Ward
Booker Taliaferro Washington
Dinah Washington
Ethel Waters
Muddy Waters
Ida Bell Wells-Barnett
Josh White
Howlin' Wolf
Carter Godwin Woodson
Whitney Moore Young

WIMBLEDON—ALL ENGLAND LAWN TENNIS AND CROQUET CLUB

Men's Singles

1975 Arthur Ashe

Ladies' Singles

1957 Althea Gibson

1958 Althea Gibson

Ladies' Doubles

1957 Althea Gibson, with Darlene Hard

1958 Althea Gibson, with Maria Bueno

◆ AFRICAN AMERICAN FEDERAL JUDGES

PRESIDENT FRANKLIN D. ROOSEVELT

1937	William H. Hastie*	District Court, Virgin Islands
1939	Harnian E. Moore*	District Court, Virgin Islands

PRESIDENT HARRY S TRUMAN

1945	Irvin C. Mollison*	United States Customs Court
1949	William H. Hastie*	Court of Appeals, Third Circuit
1949	Harnian E. Moore (a)*	District Court, Virgin Islands

PRESIDENT DWIGHT D. EISENHOWER

1957	Scovel Richardson*	United States Customs Court
1958	Walter Gordon*	District Court, Virgin Islands

PRESIDENT JOHN F. KENNEDY

1961	James B. Parsons**	Senior Judge, District Court, Illinois
1961	Wade M. McCree**	District Court, Michigan
1961	Thurgood Marshall**	Court of Appeals, Second Circuit

PRESIDENT LYNDON B. JOHNSON

1964	Spottswood Robinson**	District Court, District of Columbia
1964	A. Leon Higginbotham**	District Court, Pennsylvania
1965	William B. Bryant	Senior Judge, District Court, District of Columbia
1966	Wade H. McCree*	Court of Appeals, Sixth Court
1966	James L. Watson	United States Customs Court
1966	Constance B. Motley	Senior Judge, District Court, New York
1966	Spottswood Robinson	Senior Judge, Court of Appeals for the Federal Circuit
1966	Aubrey E. Robinson	Chief Judge, District Court, District of Columbia
1967	Damon Keith**	District Court, Michigan
1967	Thurgood Marshall*	Associate Justice, Supreme Court
1967	Joseph C. Waddy**	District Court, District of Columbia

PRESIDENT RICHARD M. NIXON

1969	Almeric Christian**	District Court, Virgin Islands
1969	David W. Williams	Senior Judge, District Court, California
1969	Barrington D. Parker	Senior Judge, District Court, District of Columbia
1971	Lawrence W. Pierce**	District Court, New York
1971	Clifford Scott Green	District Court, Pennsylvania
1972	Robert L. Carter	Senior Judge, District Court, New York
1972	Robert M. Duncan**	Military Court of Appeals
1974	Robert M. Duncan**	District Court, Ohio

PRESIDENT GERALD R. FORD

1974	Henry Bramwell**	Senior Judge, District Court, New York
1976	George N. Leighton**	Senior Judge, District Court, Illinois
1976	Matthew Perry**	Military Court of Appeals
1976	Cecil F. Poole**	District Court, California

PRESIDENT JIMMY CARTER

1978	Almeric Christian (a)**	Chief Judge, District Court, Virgin Islands
1978	U.W. Clemon	District Court, Alabama
1978	Robert F. Collins**	District Court, Louisiana

1978	Julian A. Cook, Jr.	District Court, Michigan
1978	Damon J. Keith	Court of Appeals, Sixth Circuit
1978	A. Leon Higginbotham*	Court of Appeals, Third Circuit
1978	Mary Johnson Lowe	District Court, New York
1978	Theodore McMillian	Court of Appeals, Eighth Circuit
1978	David S. Nelson	District Court, Massachusetts
1978	Paul A. Simmons**	District Court, Pennsylvania
1978	Jack E. Tanner	District Court, Washington
1979	Harry T. Edwards	Court of Appeals for the Federal Circuit
1979	J. Jerome Farris	Court of Appeals, Ninth Circuit
1979	Joseph W. Hatchett	Court of Appeals, Eleventh Circuit
1979	Terry J. Hatter	District Court, California
1979	Joseph C. Howard	District Court, Maryland
1979	Benjamin T. Gibson	District Court, Michigan
1979	James T. Giles	District Court, Pennsylvania
1979	Nathaniel R. Jones	Court of Appeals, Sixth Circuit
1979	Amalya L. Kearse	Court of Appeals, Second Circuit
1979	Gabrielle Kirk McDonald**	District Court, Texas
1979	John Garrett Penn**	District Court, District of Columbia
1979	Cecil F. Poole	Court of Appeals, Ninth Circuit
1979	Matthew J. Perry	District Court, South Carolina
1979	Myron H. Thompson	District Court, Alabama
1979	Anne E. Thompson	District Court, New Jersey
1979	Odell Horton	District Court, Tennessee
1979	Anna Diggs Taylor	District Court, Michigan
1979	Horace T. Ward	District Court, Georgia
1979	Alcee L. Hastings***	District Court, Florida
1980	Clyde S. Cahill, Jr.**	District Court, Missouri
1980	Richard C. Erwin	District Court, North Carolina
1980	Thelton E. Henderson	District Court, California
1980	George Howard, Jr.	District Court, Arkansas
1980	Earl B. Gilliam	District Court, California
1980	Norma Holloway Johnson	District Court, District of Columbia
1980	Consuela B. Marshall	District Court, California
1980	George White	District Court, Ohio

PRESIDENT RONALD REAGAN

1981	Lawrence W. Pierce	Court of Appeals, Second Circuit
1982	Reginald Gibson	United States Court of Claims
1984	John R. Hargrove	District Court, Maryland
1984	Henry Wingate	District Court, Mississippi
1985	Ann Williams	District Court, Illinois
1986	James Spencer	District Court, Virginia
1987	Kenneth Hoyt	District Court, Texas
1988	Herbert Hutton	District Court, Pennsylvania

PRESIDENT GEORGE BUSH

1990	Clarence Thomas**	Court of Appeals for the Federal Circuit
1990	James Ware	District Court, California
1991	Saundra Brown Armstrong	District Court, California
1991	Fernando J. Giatan	District Court, Missouri
1991	Donald L. Graham	District Court, Florida
1991	Sterling Johnson	District Court, New York
1991	J. Curtis Joyner	District Court, Pennsylvania
1991	Timothy K. Lewis	District Court, Pennsylvania

1991	Joe B. McDade	District Court, Illinois
1991	Clarence Thomas	Associate Justice, Supreme Court
1992	Garland E. Burrell, Jr.	District Court, California
1992	Carol Jackson	District Court, Missouri
1992	Timothy K. Lewis	Court of Appeals, Third Circuit

PRESIDENT BILL CLINTON

1993	Henry Lee Adams	District Court, Florida
1993	Wilkie Ferguson	District Court, Florida
1993	Raymond Jackson	District Court, Virginia
1993	Gary Lancaster	District Court, Pennsylvania
1993	Reginald Lindsay	District Court, Massachusetts
1993	Charles Shaw	District Court, Missouri
1994	Deborah Batts	District Court, New York
1994	Franklin Burgess	District Court, Washington
1994	James Beaty, Jr.	District Court, North Carolina
1994	David Coar	District Court, Illinois
1994	Audrey Collins	District Court, California
1994	Clarence Cooper	District Court, Georgia
1994	Michael Davis	District Court, Minnesota
1994	Raymond Finch	District Court, Virgin Islands
1994	Vanessa Gilmore	District Court, Texas
1994	A. Haggerty	District Court, Oregon
1994	Denise Page Hood	District Court, Michigan
1994	Napoleon Jones	District Court, California
1994	Blance Manning	District Court, Illinois
1994	Theodore McKee	Circuit Court, Third Circuit
1994	Vicki Miles‐LaGrange	District Court, Oklahoma
1994	Solomon Oliver, Jr.	District Court, Ohio
1994	Barrington Parker, Jr.	District Court, New York
1994	Judith Rogers	Circuit Court, District of Columbia
1994	W. Louis Sands	District Court, Georgia
1994	Carl Stewart	Circuit Court, Fifth Circuit
1994	Emmet Sullivan	Circuit Court, District of Columbia
1994	William Walls	District Court, New Jersey
1994	Alexander Williams	District Court, Maryland
1995	R. Guy Cole	Circuit Court, Sixth Circuit
1995	Curtis Collier	District Court, Tennessee
1995	Wiley Daniel	District Court, Colorado
1995	Andre Davis	District Court, Maryland
1995	Bernice B. Donald	District Court, Tennessee
1996	Charles N. Clevert, Jr.	District Court, Wisconsin
1996	Joseph A. Greenaway, Jr.	District Court, New Jersey
1997	Eric L. Clay	Circuit Court, Sixth Circuit
1997	Algenon L. Marbley	District Court, Ohio
1997	Martin J. Jenkins	District Court, California
1997	Henry H. Kennedy, Jr.	District Court, District of Columbia
1998	Gregory Sleet	District Court, Delaware
1998	Ivan L.R. Lemelle	District Court, Louisiana
1998	Sam A. Lindsay	District Court, Texas
1998	Johnnie B. Rawlinson	District Court, Nevada
1998	Margaret Seymour	District Court, South Carolina
1998	Richard Roberts	District Court, District of Columbia
1998	Gerald Bruce Lee	District Court, Virginia
1998	Lynn Bush	Court of Federal Claims

1998	Stephan P. Mickle	District Court, Florida
1998	Victoria Roberts	District Court, Michigan
1998	Raner Collins	District Court, Arizona
1998	Ralph Tyson	District Court, Louisiana
1999	William Hibbler	District Court, Illinois

(a) Reappointment

* Deceased

** No longer serving

*** Impeached and removed from the court

◆ AFRICAN AMERICAN OLYMPIC MEDALISTS

Place/Year	Athlete	Event	Place	Time/Distance
St. Louis, 1904	George C. Poag	200 M Hurdles	3rd	
	George C. Poag	400 M Hurdles	3rd	
London, 1908	J.B. Taylor	1600 M Relay	1st	3:29.4
Paris, 1924	Dehart Hubbard	Long Jump	1st	24′ 5.125″
	Edward Gourdin	Long Jump	2nd	23′ 10″
Los Angeles, 1932	Eddie Tolan	100 M Dash	1st	10.3
	Ralph Metcalfe	100 M Dash	2nd	10.3
	Eddie Tolan	200 M Dash	1st	21.2
	Ralph Metcalfe	200 M Dash	3rd	21.5
	Edward Gordon	Long Jump	1st	25′ .75″
Berlin, 1936	Jesse Owens	100 M Dash	1st	10.3
	Ralph Metcalfe	100 M Dash	2nd	10.4
	Jesse Owens	200 M Dash	1st	20.7
	Matthew Robinson	200 M Dash	2nd	21.1
	Archie Williams	400 M Run	1st	46.5
	James DuValle	400 M Run	2nd	46.8
	John Woodruff	800 M Run	1st	1:52.9
	Fritz Pollard, Jr.	110 M Hurdles	3rd	14.4
	Cornelius Johnson	High Jump	1st	6′8″
	Jesse Owens	Long Jump	1st	26′ 5.75″
	Jesse Owens	400 M Relay	1st	39.8
	Ralph Metcalfe	400 M Relay	1st	39.8
London, 1948	Harrison Dillard	100 M Dash	1st	10.3
	Norwood Ewell	100 M Dash	2nd	10.4
	Norwood Ewell	200 M Dash	1st	21.1
	Mal Whitfield	400 M Run	3rd	46.9
	Willie Steele	Long Jump	1st	25′ 8″
	Herbert Douglass	Long Jump	3rd	25′ 3″
	Lorenzo Wright	400 M Relay	1st	40.6
	Harrison Dillard	1600 M Relay	1st	3:10.4
	Norwood Ewell	1600 M Relay	1st	3:10.4
	Mal Whitfield	1600 M Relay	1st	3:10.4
	Audrey Patterson	200 M Dash	3rd	25.2
	Alice Coachman	High Jump	1st	5′ 6.125″
Helsinki, 1952	Andrew Stanfield	200 M Dash	1st	20.7
	Ollie Matson	400 M Run	3rd	46.8
	Mal Whitfield	800 M Run	1st	1:49.2
	Harrison Dillard	110 M Hurdles	1st	13.7
	Jerome Biffle	Long Jump	1st	24′ 10″
	Meredith Gourdine	Long Jump	2nd	24′ 8.125″
	Harrison Dillard	400 M Relay	1st	40.1
	Andrew Stanfield	400 M Relay	1st	40.1
	Ollie Matson	400 M Relay	1st	40.1
	Bill Miller	Javelin	2nd	237
	Milton Campbell	Decathlon	2nd	6,975 pts.
	Floyd Patterson	Boxing: Middleweight	1st	
	Norvel Lee	Boxing: Light Heavyweight	1st	
	Nathan Brooks	Boxing: Flyweight	1st	
	Charles Adkins	Boxing: Light Welterweight	1st	
	Barbara Jones	400 M Relay	1st	45.9
Melbourne, 1956	Andrew Stanfield	200 M Dash	2nd	20.7
	Charles Jenkins	400 M Run	1st	46.7
	Lee Calhoun	110 M Hurdles	1st	13.5
	Charles Dumas	High Jump	1st	6′ 11.25″
	Gregory Bell	Long Jump	1st	25′ 8.25″
	Willye White	Long Jump	2nd	19′ 11.75″
	Ira Murchison	400 M Relay	1st	39.5
	Leamon King	400 M Relay	1st	39.5
	Charles Jenkins	400 M Relay	1st	39.5
	Lou Jones	1600 M Relay	1st	3:04.8

Place/Year	Athlete	Event	Place	Time/Distance
	Milton Campbell	Decathlon	1st	7,937 pts.
	Rafer Johnson	Decathlon	2nd	7,587 pts.
	K.C. Jones	Men's Basketball	1st	
	Bill Russell	Men's Basketball	1st	
	James Boyd	Boxing: Light Heavyweight	1st	
	Mildred McDaniel	High Jump	1st	5′ 9.25″
	Margaret Matthews	400 M Relay	3rd	44.9
	Isabelle Daniels	400 M Relay	3rd	44.9
	Mae Faggs	400 M Relay	3rd	44.9
	Wilma Rudolph	400 M Relay	3rd	44.9
Rome, 1960	Les Carney	200 M Dash	2nd	20.6
	Lee Calhoun	110 M Hurdles	1st	13.8
	Willie May	110 M Hurdles	2nd	13.8
	Hayes Jones	110 M Hurdles	3rd	14
	Otis Davis	400 M Run	1st	44.9
	John Thomas	High Jump	3rd	7′ .25″
	Ralph Boston	Long Jump	1st	26′ 7.75″
	Irvin Robertson	Long Jump	2nd	26′ 7.25″
	Otis Davis	1600 M Relay	1st	3:02.2
	Rafer Johnson	Decathlon	1st	8,392 pts.
	Oscar Robertson	Men's Basketball	1st	
	Walt Bellamy	Men's Basketball	1st	
	Bob Boozer	Men's Basketball	1st	
	Wilbert McClure	Boxing: Light Middleweight	1st	
	Cassius Clay	Boxing: Light Heavyweight	1st	
	Edward Crook	Boxing: Middleweight	1st	
	Quincelon Daniels	Boxing: Light Welterweight	3rd	
	Earlene Brown	Shot Put	3rd	53′ 10.25″
	Wilma Rudolph	100 M Dash	1st	11
	Wilma Rudolph	200 M Dash	1st	24
	Martha Judson	400 M Relay	3rd	44.5
	Lucinda Williams	400 M Relay	3rd	44.5
	Barbara Jones	400 M Relay	3rd	44.5
	Wilma Rudolph	400 M Relay	3rd	44.5
Tokyo, 1964	Robert Hayes	100 M Dash	1st	9.9
	Henry Carr	200 M Dash	1st	20.3
	Paul Drayton	200 M Dash	2nd	20.5
	Hayes Jones	110 M Hurdles	1st	13.6
	Robert Hayes	400 M Relay	1st	39
	Paul Drayton	400 M Relay	1st	39
	Richard Stebbins	400 M Relay	1st	39
	John Thomas	High Jump	2nd	7′ 1.75″
	John Rambo	High Jump	3rd	7′ 1″
	Ralph Boston	Long Jump	2nd	26′ 4″
	Walt Hazzard	Men's Basketball	1st	
	Lucius Jackson	Men's Basketball	1st	
	Charles Brown	Boxing: Featherweight	3rd	
	Ronald Harris	Boxing: Lightweight	3rd	
	Joe Frazier	Boxing: Heavyweight	1st	
	Robert Carmody	Boxing: Flyweight	3rd	
	Wyomia Tyus	100 M Dash	1st	11.4
	Edith McGuire	100 M Dash	2nd	11.6
	Edith McGuire	200 M Dash	1st	23
	Wyomia Tyus	400 M Relay	2nd	43.9
	Edith McGuire	400 M Relay	2nd	43.9
	Willye White	400 M Relay	2nd	43.9
	Marilyn White	400 M Relay	2nd	43.9
Mexico City, 1968	Jim Hines	100 M Dash	1st	9.9
	Charles Greene	100 M Dash	3rd	10
	Tommie Smith	200 M Dash	1st	19.8
	John Carlos	200 M Dash	3rd	20
	Lee Evans	400 M Run	1st	43.8

Place/Year	Athlete	Event	Place	Time/Distance
	Larry James	400 M Run	2nd	43.9
	Ron Freeman	400 M Run	3rd	44.4
	Willie Davenport	110 M Hurdles	1st	13.3
	Ervin Hall	110 M Hurdles	2nd	13.4
	Jim Hines	400 M Relay	1st	38.2
	Charles Greene	400 M Relay	1st	38.2
	Mel Pender	400 M Relay	1st	38.2
	Ronnie Ray Smith	400 M Relay	1st	38.2
	Wyomia Tyus	400 M Relay	1st	42.8
	Barbara Ferrell	400 M Relay	1st	42.8
	Margaret Bailes	400 M Relay	1st	42.8
	Mildrette Netter	400 M Relay	1st	42.8
	Lee Evans	1600 M Relay	1st	2:56.1
	Vince Matthews	1600 M Relay	1st	2:56.1
	Ron Freeman	1600 M Relay	1st	2:56.1
	Larry James	1600 M Relay	1st	2:56.1
	Edward Caruthers	High Jump	2nd	7′ 3.5″
	Bob Beamon	Long Jump	1st	29′ 2.5″
	Ralph Boston	Long Jump	3rd	26′ 9.25″
	Spencer Haywood	Men's Basketball	1st	
	Charlie Scott	Men's Basketball	1st	
	Michael Barrett	Men's Basketball	1st	
	James King	Men's Basketball	1st	
	Calvin Fowler	Men's Basketball	1st	
	John Baldwin	Boxing: Light Middleweight	3rd	
	Alfred Jones	Boxing: Middleweight	3rd	
	Albert Robinson	Boxing: Featherweight	2nd	
	Ronald Harris	Boxing: Lightweight	1st	
	James Wallington	Boxing: Light Welterweight	3rd	
	George Foreman	Boxing: Heavyweight	1st	
	Wyomia Tyus	100 M Dash	1st	11
	Barbara Ferrell	100 M Dash	2nd	11.1
	Madeline Manning	800 M Run	1st	2:00.9
Munich, 1972	Robert Taylor	100 M Dash	2nd	10.24
	Larry Black	200 M Dash	2nd	20.19
	Vince Matthews	400 M Run	1st	44.66
	Wayne Collett	400 M Run	2nd	44.80
	Rod Milburn	110 M Hurdles	1st	13.24
	Eddie Hart	400 M Relay	1st	38.19
	Robert Taylor	400 M Relay	1st	38.19
	Larry Black	400 M Relay	1st	38.19
	Gerald Tinker	400 M Relay	1st	38.19
	Randy Williams	Long Jump	1st	27′ .25″
	Arnie Robinson	Long Jump	3rd	26′ 4″
	Jeff Bennet	Decathlon	3rd	7,974 pts.
	Wayne Collett	400 M Dash	2nd	44.80
	Marvin Johnson	Boxing: Middleweight	3rd	
	Ray Seales	Boxing: Light Welterweight	1st	
	Cheryl Toussain	1600 M Relay	2nd	3:25.2
	Mable Fergerson	1600 M Relay	2nd	3:25.2
	Madeline Manning	1600 M Relay	2nd	3:25.2
Montreal, 1976	Millard Hampton	200 M Dash	2nd	20.29
	Dwayne Evans	200 M Dash	3rd	20.43
	Fred Newhouse	400 M Run	2nd	44.40
	Herman Frazier	400 M Run	3rd	44.95
	Willie Davenport	110 M Hurdles	3rd	13.38
	Edwin Moses	400 M Hurdles	1st	47.64
	Millard Hampton	400 M Relay	1st	38.83
	Steve Riddick	400 M Relay	1st	38.83
	Harvey Glance	400 M Relay	1st	38.83
	John Jones	400 M Relay	1st	38.83
	Herman Frazier	1600 M Relay	1st	2:58.7

Place/Year	Athlete	Event	Place	Time/Distance
	Benny Brown	1600 M Relay	1st	2:58.7
	Maxie Parks	1600 M Relay	1st	2:58.7
	Fred Newhouse	1600 M Relay	1st	2:58.7
	Arnie Robinson	Long Jump	1st	27′ 4.75″
	Randy Williams	Long Jump	2nd	26′ 7.25″
	James Butts	Triple Jump	2nd	56 8.5″
	Phil Ford	Men's Basketball	1st	
	Adrian Dantley	Men's Basketball	1st	
	Walter Davis	Men's Basketball	1st	
	Quinn Buckner	Men's Basketball	1st	
	Kenneth Carr	Men's Basketball	1st	
	Scott May	Men's Basketball	1st	
	Philip Hubbard	Men's Basketball	1st	
	Johnny Tate	Boxing: Heavyweight	3rd	
	Leo Randolph	Boxing: Flyweight	1st	
	Howard David	Boxing: Lightweight	1st	
	Sugar Ray Leonard	Boxing: Light Welterweight	1st	
	Michael Spinks	Boxing: Middleweight	1st	
	Leon Spinks	Boxing: Light Heavyweight	1st	
	Rosalyn Bryant	1600 M Relay	2nd	3:22.8
	Shelia Ingram	1600 M Relay	2nd	3:22.8
	Pamela Jiles	1600 M Relay	2nd	3:22.8
	Debra Sapenter	1600 M Relay	2nd	3:22.8
	Lusia Harris	Women's Basketball	2nd	
	Charlotte Lewis	Women's Basketball	2nd	
Los Angeles, 1984	Carl Lewis	100 M Dash	1st	9.9
	Sam Graddy	100 M Dash	2nd	10.19
	Carl Lewis	200 M Dash	1st	19.80
	Kirk Baptiste	200 M Dash	2nd	19.96
	Alonzo Babers	400 M Run	1st	44.27
	Antonio McKay	400 M Run	3rd	44.71
	Earl Jones	800 M Run	3rd	1:43.83
	Roger Kingdom	110 M Hurdles	1st	13.20
	Greg Foster	110 M Hurdles	2nd	13.23
	Edwin Moses	400 M Hurdles	1st	47.75
	Danny Harris	400 M Hurdles	2nd	48.13
	Sam Graddy	400 M Relay	1st	37.83
	Ron Brown	400 M Relay	1st	37.83
	Calvin Smith	400 M Relay	1st	37.83
	Carl Lewis	400 M Relay	1st	37.83
	Sunder Nix	1600 M Relay	1st	2:57.91
	Roy Armstead	1600 M Relay	1st	2:57.91
	Alonzo Babers	1600 M Relay	1st	2:57.91
	Antonio McKay	1600 M Relay	1st	2:57.91
	Michael Carter	Shot Put	1st	21.09 m
	Carl Lewis	Long Jump	1st	8.54 m
	Al Joyner	Triple Jump	1st	17.26 m
	Mike Conley	Triple Jump	2nd	17.18 m
	Evelyn Ashford	100 M Dash	1st	10.97
	Alice Brown	100 M Dash	2nd	11.13
	Valerie Brisco-Hooks	200 M Dash	1st	21.81
	Florence Griffith	200 M Dash	2nd	22.04
	Valerie Brisco-Hooks	400 M Run	1st	48.83
	Chandra Cheeseborough	400 M Run	2nd	49.05
	Kim Gallagher	800 M Run	2nd	1:58.63
	Benita Fitzgerald-Brown	100 M Hurdles	1st	12.84
	Kim Turner	100 M Hurdles	2nd	12.88
	Judi Brown	400 M Hurdles	2nd	55.20
	Valerie Brisco-Hooks	1600 M Relay	1st	3:18.29
	Chandra Cheeseborough	1600 M Relay	1st	3:18.29
	Lillie Leatherwood	1600 M Relay	1st	3:18.29
	Sherri Howard	1600 M Relay	1st	3:18.29

Place/Year	Athlete	Event	Place	Time/Distance
	Jackie Joyner	Heptathlon	2nd	6,386 pts.
	Tyrell Biggs	Boxing: Super Heavyweight	1st	
	Henry Tillman	Boxing: Heavyweight	1st	
	Frank Tate	Boxing: Light Middleweight	1st	
	Virgil Hill	Boxing: Middleweight	2nd	
	Evander Holyfield	Boxing: Light Heavyweight	3rd	
	Steven McCrory	Boxing: Flyweight	1st	
	Meldrick Taylor	Boxing: Featherweight	1st	
	Pernell Whitaker	Boxing: Lightweight	1st	
	Jerry Page	Boxing: Light Welterweight	1st	
	Mark Breland	Boxing: Welterweight	1st	
	Patrick Ewing	Men's Basketball	1st	
	Vern Fleming	Men's Basketball	1st	
	Michael Jordan	Men's Basketball	1st	
	Sam Perkins	Men's Basketball	1st	
	Alvin Robertson	Men's Basketball	1st	
	Wayman Tisdale	Men's Basketball	1st	
	Leon Wood	Men's Basketball	1st	
	Cathy Boswell	Women's Basketball	1st	
	Teresa Edwards	Women's Basketball	1st	
	Janice Lawrence	Women's Basketball	1st	
	Pamela McGee	Women's Basketball	1st	
	Cheryl Miller	Women's Basketball	1st	
	Lynette Woodard	Women's Basketball	1st	
Seoul, 1988	Carl Lewis	100 M Dash	1st	9.92
	Calvin Smith	100 M Dash	2nd	9.99
	Joe DeLoach	200 M Dash	1st	19.75
	Carl Lewis	200 M Dash	2nd	19.79
	Steve Lewis	400 M Run	1st	43.87
	Butch Reynolds	400 M Run	2nd	43.93
	Danny Everett	400 M Run	3rd	44.09
	Roger Kingdom	110 M Hurdles	1st	12.98
	Tonie Campbell	110 M Hurdles	3rd	13.38
	Andre Phillips	400 M Hurdles	1st	47.19
	Edwin Moses	400 M Hurdles	3rd	47.56
	Butch Reynolds	1600 M Relay	1st	2:56.16
	Steve Lewis	1600 M Relay	1st	2:56.16
	Antonio McKay	1600 M Relay	1st	2:56.16
	Danny Everett	1600 M Relay	1st	2:56.16
	Carl Lewis	Long Jump	1st	8.72 m
	Mike Powell	Long Jump	2nd	8.49 m
	Larry Myricks	Long Jump	3rd	8.27 m
	Florence Griffith-Joyner	100 M Dash	1st	10.54
	Evelyn Ashford	100 M Dash	2nd	10.83
	Florence Griffith-Joyner	200 M Dash	1st	21.34
	Shelia Echols	400 M Relay	1st	41.98
	Florence Griffith-Joyner	400 M Relay	1st	41.98
	Evelyn Ashford	400 M Relay	1st	41.98
	Alice Brown	400 M Relay	1st	41.98
	Jackie Joyner-Kersee	Long Jump	1st	24′ 3.5″
	Jackie Joyner-Kersee	Heptathlon	1st	7,291 pts.
	Denean Howard-Hill	1600 M Relay	2nd	3:15.51
	Valerie Brisco	1600 M Relay	2nd	3:15.51
	Diane Dixon	1600 M Relay	2nd	3:15.51
	Florence Griffith-Joyner	1600 M Relay	2nd	3:15.51
	Kim Gallagher	800 M Run	3rd	1:56.91
	Andrew Maynard	Boxing: Light Heavyweight	1st	
	Ray Mercer	Boxing: Heavyweight	1st	
	Kennedy McKinney	Boxing: Bantamweight	1st	
	Riddick Bowe	Boxing: Super Heavyweight	2nd	
	Roy Jones	Boxing: Middleweight	2nd	
	Kenny Monday	Wrestling: Freestyle	1st	

Place/Year	Athlete	Event	Place	Time/Distance
	Nate Carr	Wrestling: Freestyle	3rd	
	Zina Garrison	Tennis: Doubles	1st	
	Zina Garrison	Tennis: Singles	3rd	
	Tom Goodwin	Baseball	1st	
	Ty Griffin	Baseball	1st	
	Cindy Brown	Women's Basketball	1st	
	Vicky Bullett	Women's Basketball	1st	
	Cynthia Cooper	Women's Basketball	1st	
	Teresa Edwards	Women's Basketball	1st	
	Jennifer Gillom	Women's Basketball	1st	
	Bridgette Gordon	Women's Basketball	1st	
	Katrina McClain	Women's Basketball	1st	
	Teresa Weatherspoon	Women's Basketball	1st	
	Willie Anderson	Men's Basketball	3rd	
	Stacey Augmon	Men's Basketball	3rd	
	Bimbo Coles	Men's Basketball	3rd	
	Jeff Grayer	Men's Basketball	3rd	
	Hersey Hawkins	Men's Basketball	3rd	
	Danny Manning	Men's Basketball	3rd	
	J.R. Reid	Men's Basketball	3rd	
	Mitch Richmond	Men's Basketball	3rd	
	David Robinson	Men's Basketball	3rd	
	Charles D. Smith	Men's Basketball	3rd	
	Charles E. Smith	Men's Basketball	3rd	
Barcelona, 1992	Dennis Mitchell	100 M Dash	3rd	10.04
	Gail Devers	100 M Dash	1st	10.82
	Mike Marsh	200 M Dash	1st	20.01
	Michael Bates	200 M Dash	3rd	20.38
	Gwen Torrence	200 M Dash	1st	21.81
	Quincy Watts	400 M Run	1st	43.50
	Steve Lewis	400 M Run	2nd	44.21
	Johnny Gray	800 M Run	3rd	1:43.97
	Mike Marsh	400 M Relay	1st	37.40
	Leroy Burrell	400 M Relay	1st	37.40
	Dennis Mitchell	400 M Relay	1st	37.40
	Carl Lewis	400 M Relay	1st	37.40
	Evelyn Ashford	400 M Relay	1st	42.11
	Esther Jones	400 M Relay	1st	42.11
	Carlette Guidry-White	400 M Relay	1st	42.11
	Gwen Torrence	400 M Relay	1st	42.11
	Tony Dees	110 M Hurdles	2nd	13.24
	Kevin Young	400 M Hurdles	1st	46.78
	Sandra Farmer	400 M Hurdles	2nd	53.69
	Janeene Vickers	400 M Hurdles	3rd	54.31
	Andrew Valmon	800 M Relay	1st	2:55.74
	Quincy Watts	800 M Relay	1st	2:55.74
	Michael Johnson	800 M Relay	1st	2:55.74
	Steve Lewis	800 M Relay	1st	2:55.74
	Natasha Kaiser	800 M Relay	2nd	3:20.92
	Gwen Torrence	800 M Relay	2nd	3:20.92
	Jearl Miles	800 M Relay	2nd	3:20.92
	Rochelle Stevens	800 M Relay	2nd	3:20.92
	Hollis Conway	High Jump	3rd	7′ 8″
	Carl Lewis	Long Jump	1st	28′ 5.5″
	Mike Powell	Long Jump	2nd	28′ 4.25″
	Joe Greene	Long Jump	3rd	27′ 4.5″
	Jackie Joyner-Kersee	Long Jump	3rd	23′ 2.5″
	Mike Conley	Triple Jump	1st	59′ 7.5″
	Charlie Simpkins	Triple Jump	2nd	57′ 9″
	Jackie Joyner-Kersee	Heptathlon	1st	7,044 pts.
	Tim Austin	Boxing: Flyweight	3rd	
	Chris Byrd	Boxing: Middleweight	2nd	

Place/Year	Athlete	Event	Place	Time/Distance
	Kevin Jackson	Wrestling: Middleweight	1st	
	Charles Barkley	Men's Basketball	1st	
	Clyde Drexler	Men's Basketball	1st	
	Patrick Ewing	Men's Basketball	1st	
	Magic Johnson	Men's Basketball	1st	
	Michael Jordan	Men's Basketball	1st	
	Karl Malone	Men's Basketball	1st	
	Scottie Pippen	Men's Basketball	1st	
	David Robinson	Men's Basketball	1st	
	Vicky Bullett	Women's Basketball	3rd	
	Daedra Charles	Women's Basketball	3rd	
	Cynthia Cooper	Women's Basketball	3rd	
	Teresa Edwards	Women's Basketball	3rd	
	Carolyn Jones	Women's Basketball	3rd	
	Katrina McClain	Women's Basketball	3rd	
	Vickie Orr	Women's Basketball	3rd	
	Teresa Weatherspoon	Women's Basketball	3rd	
Atlanta, 1996	Dominique Dawes	Gymnastics: Floor Exercise	3rd	
	Dominique Dawes	Gymnastics: Team	1st	
	Michael Johnson	200 M Dash	1st	19.32
	Michael Johnson	400 M Run	1st	43.49
	Allen Johnson	110 M Hurdles	1st	12.95
	Mark Crear	110 M Hurdles	2nd	13.09
	Derrick Adkins	400 M Hurdles	1st	47.54
	Calvin Davis	400 M Hurdles	3rd	47.96
	Tim Harden	400 M Relay	2nd	38.05
	Jon Drummond	400 M Relay	2nd	38.05
	Michael Marsh	400 M Relay	2nd	38.05
	Dennis Mitchell	400 M Relay	2nd	38.05
	LaMont Smith	1600 M Relay	1st	2:55.99
	Alvin Harrison	1600 M Relay	1st	2:55.99
	Derek Mills	1600 M Relay	1st	2:55.99
	Anthuan Maybank	1600 M Relay	1st	2:55.99
	Dan O'Brien	Decathlon	1st	8,824 pts.
	Charles Austin	High Jump	1st	7′ 10″
	Carl Lewis	Long Jump	1st	27′ 10.75″
	Joe Greene	Long Jump	3rd	27′ .50″
	Kenny Harrison	Triple Jump	1st	59′ 4″
	Gail Devers	100 M Dash	1st	10.94
	Gwen Torrence	100 M Dash	3rd	10.96
	Kim Batten	400 M Hurdles	2nd	53.08
	Tonja Buford-Bailey	400 M Hurdles	3rd	53.22
	Gail Devers	400 M Relay	1st	41.95
	Chryste Gaines	400 M Relay	1st	41.95
	Gwen Torrence	400 M Relay	1st	41.95
	Inger Miller	400 M Relay	1st	41.95
	Rochelle Stevens	1600 M Relay	1st	3:20.91
	Maicel Malone	1600 M Relay	1st	3:20.91
	Kim Graham	1600 M Relay	1st	3:20.91
	Jearl Miles	1600 M Relay	1st	3:20.91
	Jackie Joyner-Kersee	Long Jump	3rd	22′ 11″
	Floyd Mayweather	Boxing: Featherweight	3rd	
	Terrance Cauthen	Boxing: Lightweight	3rd	
	Rhoshii Wells	Boxing: Middleweight	3rd	
	Antonio Tarver	Boxing: Light Heavyweight	3rd	
	Nate Jones	Boxing: Heavyweight	3rd	
	David Reid	Boxing: Light Middleweight	1st	
	Teresa Edwards	Women's Basketball	1st	
	Ruth Bolton	Women's Basketball	1st	
	Lisa Leslie	Women's Basketball	1st	
	Katrina McClain	Women's Basketball	1st	
	Sheryl Swoopes	Women's Basketball	1st	

Place/Year	Athlete	Event	Place	Time/Distance
	Nikki McCray	Women's Basketball	1st	
	Dawn Staley	Women's Basketball	1st	
	Venus Lacey	Women's Basketball	1st	
	Carla McGhee	Women's Basketball	1st	
	Mitch Richmond	Men's Basketball	1st	
	Scottie Pippin	Men's Basketball	1st	
	Gary Payton	Men's Basketball	1st	
	Charles Barkley	Men's Basketball	1st	
	Hakeem Olajuwon	Men's Basketball	1st	
	David Robinson	Men's Basketball	1st	
	Penny Hardaway	Men's Basketball	1st	
	Grant Hill	Men's Basketball	1st	
	Karl Malone	Men's Basketball	1st	
	Reggie Miller	Men's Basketball	1st	
	Jacque Jones	Baseball	3rd	

Index

Personal names, place names, events, organizations, and various subject areas or keywords contained in the *Reference Library of Black America* are listed in this index with corresponding volume and page numbers indicating text references. Page numbers appearing in boldface indicate major treatments of topics, such as biographical profiles and organizational entries. Page numbers appearing in italics refer to photographs, illustrations, and maps found throughout the reference work.

A

B

C

D

E

G

H

I

J

K

M

N

O

P

Q

R

T

U

W

X

Y

Z